SEVENTH EDITION

Writing in the Disciplines

A Reader and Rhetoric for Academic Writers

Mary Lynch Kennedy
SUNY Cortland

William J. Kennedy
Cornell University

PEARSON

Boston   Columbus   Indianapolis   New York   San Francisco   Upper Saddle River
Amsterdam   Cape Town   Dubai   London   Madrid   Milan   Munich   Paris   Montréal   Toronto
Delhi   Mexico City   São Paulo   Sydney   Hong Kong   Seoul   Singapore   Taipei   Tokyo

Senior Acquisitions Editor: Brad Potthoff
Senior Marketing Manager: Sandra McGuire
Project Coordination, Text Design, and Electronic Page Makeup: Integra
Senior Cover Design Manager/Cover Designer: Nancy Danahy
Cover Photo: © rob casey/Alamy. Seattle Central Public Library,
   designed by Dutch architect, Rem Koolhaas
Photo Researcher: PreMediaGlobal/Michelle McKenna
Image Permissions: Lee Scher
Text Permissions: Glenview/Wesley Hall
Senior Manufacturing Buyer: Mary Ann Gloriande
Printer and Binder: STP Courier Corporation
Cover Printer: STP Courier Corporation

Library of Congress Cataloging-in-Publication Data

Kennedy, Mary Lynch
   Writing in the disciplines : a reader and rhetoric for academic writers / Mary Lynch Kennedy,
William J. Kennedy. — 7th ed.
      p. cm.
   Includes index.
   ISBN-13: 978-0-205-72662-2
   ISBN-10: 0-205-72662-3
   1. College readers.   2. Interdisciplinary approach in education—Problems, exercises, etc.   3. English
language—Rhetoric—Problems, exercises etc.   4. Academic writing—Problems, exercises, etc.
   I. Kennedy, William J. (William John)   II. Title.
   PE1417.K45 2011
   808'.0427—dc22
                                                                        2011002704

1 2 3 4 5 6 7 8 9 10—CRW—14 13 12 11

www.pearsonhighered.com

Student Edition ISBN-13: 978-0-205-72662-2
Student Edition ISBN-10:   0-205-72662-3

Brief Contents

Contents

3   Critical Analysis   69

8 Writing Research Papers   235

■ PART II

An Anthology of Readings   283

Natural Sciences and Technology   **285**

9 Who Owns Your Body?   289

WHO OWNS YOUR BODY PARTS? • Kerry Howley   290
Examines differences between human organ donations and human tissue donations and explores the moral, social, and legal consequences that follow from them.

10   Human/Robot Interaction   321

13   Social Class and Inequality   449

Humanities   490

16 Three Visual Portfolios 576

Preface

TO OUR READERS IN APPRECIATION

In this seventh edition of *Writing in the Disciplines: A Reader and Rhetoric for Academic Writers*, we incorporate the suggestions of students and instructors who have used the sixth edition as well as the recommendations of other reviewers. We continue to emphasize scholarly, source-based academic writing, and in this edition we provide a solid body of academic readings that serve as touchstone texts for the essays we teach our students to write. We hold as a foundational premise the idea that students in undergraduate composition courses should develop critical reading and writing skills for inquiry, learning, and communication. Unlike most other textbooks on the market, this one emphasizes readings documented with academic sources, exemplifying academic genres and modeling academic conventions that students are expected to learn as they move toward various disciplinary majors and concentrations.

We retain nearly half of the reading selections from the sixth and earlier editions and add twenty-three new selections, for a total of forty-one readings. We have updated chapters on reading and writing in the sciences to include topics on trafficking in body parts and tissue ("Who Owns Your Body?"), robotics ("Human/Robot Interaction"), and high-tech surveillance ("Privacy and Technology"). We have likewise updated chapters on reading and writing in the social sciences and humanities with new reading selections on the topics of the changing American family, social class and inequality, and rock music and cultural values. We are immensely grateful to our reviewers for suggesting which reading selections from earlier editions have worn thin, which have held their appeal, and which have now profited from renovation.

ORGANIZATION AND APPROACH

Writing in the Disciplines: A Reader and Rhetoric for Academic Writers teaches students how to use reading sources as idea banks for college papers. Part I offers extensive coverage of critical reading and the fundamental writing strategies of planning, organizing, drafting, revising, and editing. In addition to covering paraphrasing and quoting, it offers guidelines for writing a wide range of classroom genres. We cover genres that play a major role in writing courses and are frequently assigned in courses in various disciplines: response to a text, summary, abstract, précis, critical analysis, rhetorical analysis, comparative analysis, literary analysis, visual analysis, causal analysis, exploratory synthesis, literature review, thesis-driven synthesis, argument-synthesis, and research paper. Knowledge of these genres is indispensable for students to become skilled critical readers and proficient academic writers.

Part II of *Writing in the Disciplines* provides an anthology of readings in the humanities, the natural sciences and technology, and the social sciences, with articles representing various rhetorical approaches across academic disciplines. These articles, along with the accompanying instructional apparatus, help develop students' abilities to think critically and reason cogently as they read, compose, and revise. The activities and questions that accompany each reading encourage students to approach academic writing as a process: to preview the source, set reading goals, and ponder the general topic before reading; to annotate the text and think critically while reading; and to reflect on the source and identify content, genre, organization, stylistic features, and rhetorical context after reading. We also show students how to draw on annotations, notes, and preliminary writing to produce first drafts of academic essays and how to revise essays at the drafting stage as well as later in the writing process. Additional activities help students to use ideas from different sources to produce synthesis essays and research papers.

The first chapter of Part I focuses upon active critical reading strategies that entail exercises in prereading, close reading, and annotation. Chapter 2 focuses on formal and informal responses to texts as registered in paraphrases; summaries, including the abstract and the précis; and the use of quotations. Throughout the book, we refer to these activities as initiating an "academic conversation" with the sources. Chapter 3 focuses on critical analysis. It provides a detailed demonstration of the reading-writing process, from prereading to editing. It also examines essay structures, from the introduction and thesis statement through the body of the essay to its conclusion, and teaches students how to revise for content, organization, style, grammar, and mechanics. Chapter 4 deals with particular kinds of analytical writing that address readings of specific texts. The kinds of analysis include literary, comparative, rhetorical, process, and causal. Chapter 5 explains how to analyze visual images and guides students through the process of writing an essay based on visual material. Chapter 6 guides students through the process of writing three forms of synthesis essays: exploratory synthesis, review of the literature, and thesis-driven synthesis. Chapter 7 provides detailed explanations of how to write source-based argument-synthesis essays, and Chapter 8 covers library and Web-based electronic research strategies directed toward writing a research paper.

Part II, Chapters 9 through 16, provides an anthology of forty-one reading selections. These selections offer fully documented scholarly articles as well as articles written by specialists for nonspecialized readers. We believe that selections derived from popular as well as scholarly sources represent the types of readings professors assign in introductory and lower-level courses. Psychology professors, for instance, know that first-year students cannot interpret most psychological research reports until they have acquired a basic knowledge of the discipline and learn its principles of experimental methodology and statistical analysis. However, first-year students can read summaries and analyses of psychological research written for nonspecialists. Many of the selections in *Writing in the Disciplines* are readings that might appear on a reserve list as supplements to an introductory-level textbook. We make no assumptions about students' prior knowledge. Our intent is to model first-year-level reading assignments, not to exemplify professional standards within the disciplines.

We have organized the anthology by dividing the academic curriculum into three major fields: the natural sciences and technology, the social sciences, and the humanities. Each chapter of readings deals with a topic that is widely studied in the field but can be understood regardless of the reader's expertise in that field. For example, the natural sciences section presents chapters on human organ trafficking, robotics, and surveillance technology, without requiring the reader to have advanced skills in biology, physics, or computer science for comprehension. Throughout the anthology, we have tried to interrelate disciplinary topics. For example, the social sciences section offers chapters on redefining the American family and on social class and inequality. Chapters in the humanities section complement them with short stories and visual portfolios on themes of family, inequality, and ethnic diversity. Reading assignments in these chapters help students view these topics from a range of perspectives, and the readings provide diverse commentary from experts in different disciplines as well as from generalists, specialists in other academic fields, and popular journalism.

In the introduction to each section of the anthology, we characterize the field of study with a discussion of its subdisciplines, methodology, logic, and vocabulary. We then describe writing within the field by examining authors' perspectives, goals, organizational patterns, literary devices, and rhetorical styles. We recognize that there is no absolute standard for categorizing intellectual activities. For example, although we have classified technology as a discipline within the natural sciences, we could as well have placed it within the social sciences, depending on the methodology the researchers use. Throughout the book, we point out overlaps among disciplines and also capitalize on them in synthesis assignments at the end of each chapter. Despite the imprecision of these categories, we believe that important differences in approaches to scholarship and writing do exist among the three main academic areas. Students who understand these differences will read more critically and write more persuasively.

■ IMPROVEMENTS IN THE SEVENTH EDITION

▨ Part I: Reading and Writing in the Academic Disciplines

The language that is privileged and rewarded by the academic community is vastly different from our students' ways of talking and writing. It is wishful thinking to assume that students will learn this language through assimilation and gradual socialization. Even engaged, committed students find the standards and conventions of scholarly writing abstract. We are increasingly convinced that we need to make explicit the role students play as participants in academic conversations and make transparent the language they are expected to write and speak. For that reason, the seventh edition explicitly addresses the conventions of a wide range of genres of academic writing, analyzes published texts that represent these genres, and guides students through the process of mastering the genres and reproducing them in academic papers.

We differentiate between journalistic styles of writing that draw on other texts but do not involve parenthetical citation, lists of references, or footnotes and scholarly academic writing that employs these conventions. A sizable number of our anthology selections are written in the scholarly style of academic writing that we are asking students to practice in the essays they write for this book's assignments. Ironically, many composition anthologies rely solely on selections from popular discourse but expect students to write about the readings using the language and conventions of academic discourse.

In this seventh edition, we strongly emphasize the habits of mind that favor academic reading and writing, especially the habit of asking questions. Throughout the book we stress the importance of developing a questioning frame of mind. Every chapter contains guidelines for posing and answering questions about texts. For example, in Chapter 1 alone we have Questions for Analyzing Literal Content of Texts, Questions for Analyzing the Genre of Texts, Questions for Analyzing Stylistic Features of Texts, Questions for Analyzing the Rhetorical Context of Texts, and Questions for Analyzing Writing Assignments.

Also in Chapter 1, we introduce the concept of "intertextuality," and across the book we carry the motif of academic writing as inscribing an "academic conversation" among the voices in a text. In subsequent chapters we provide concrete examples of such a conversation. Chapters 3 through 8 present examples of student-written essays of critical analysis, literary analysis, comparative analysis, visual analysis, exploratory synthesis, literature review, thesis-driven synthesis, argument-synthesis, and research paper, all of which draw upon various sources. In each case we have presented a constellation of excerpts from those sources to show how student writers adapted them, analyzed them, assimilated them, and argued for or against the positions they represent. Students whose exposure to public debate is restricted to *Good Morning America* or afternoon talk shows have a very limited view of criticism, argument, and debate, and think of them as shallow and angry. The readings in our chapters illustrate the give-and-take of current debates that are being waged in both public and academic settings. Above all, they show students the various ways participants in academic conversations view and write about debatable issues, using them as touchstone texts for various genre conventions and principles of academic writing.

Other changes to Part I include, for example, an expanded, in-depth coverage of

- Analysis and evaluation (six forms of analysis)
- Synthesis (three forms of synthesis)
- Source-based argument, including discussion of using different types of arguments for different purposes
- Research paper (three forms) and updated advice for using online databases, subject directories, search engines, and other electronic tools.

Before asking students to write papers in a particular genre, we introduce them to the genre by having them read and analyze a representative touchstone text. Then we guide them through the reading-writing process by tracing the path of a student writer. We found this approach to be very successful in our earlier editions, and in this edition we continue to expand upon it.

An especially important goal of our presentation has been to implement the "Outcomes Statement" of the Council of Writing Program Administrators (WPA) as a basis for teaching reading and writing skills in undergraduate composition courses. This statement (April 2002, amended July 2008), which can be found at <http://wpacouncil.org/positions/outcomes.html>, outlines for instructors the now widely held objectives in the areas of rhetorical knowledge, critical thinking, reading and writing processes, and usage of conventions. Its precepts include responding to the needs of different audiences and different kinds of rhetorical situations; writing in several genres; understanding a writing assignment as a series of tasks that involve inquiry, learning, thinking, and communicating; emphasizing the process of writing multiple drafts with control of the features of standard usage; and engaging with a variety of technologies to produce effective outcomes. As relatively experienced readers, writers, and instructors, we are aware that no single course or sequence of courses in any composition program can attain all these goals. We believe, however, that this "Outcomes Statement" articulates a set of principles worthy of striving toward.

Part II: An Anthology of Readings

In Part II of *Writing in the Disciplines*, we have retained our readers' favorite selections, and, at their request, have reinstated some selections from earlier editions. The three anthology chapters on natural sciences and technology present fifteen entirely new readings that focus on recent developments in repurposing body tissue, robotics, and surveillance technology. These supplement three other readings in the sciences used as examples in Part I. The two social sciences chapters in Part II present four new readings. In the humanities section, at the request of our reviewers, we have retained the chapter on rock music and cultural values and included two readings from the sixth edition as well as three new selections. In Chapter 15 are the retained short fiction selections on stories of ethnic difference. In this seventh edition, we again present a chapter on three visual portfolios, which contains sets of images on three of the topics covered elsewhere in the book: families, inequality, and ethnic diversity.

Finally, we have refined the guide to documentation and the comparison of the MLA (Modern Language Association) and APA (American Psychological Association) styles in the Appendix. As we are aware that the language of the academic community differs from our students' ways of speaking and writing, so are we aware that academic documentation differs from styles of documentation (or the lack of them) in the popular press. The fact is that—even in scholarly publication—many journals, university presses, commercial presses, and specialized professional publications have their own "house styles" for documentation that differ markedly from the MLA and APA styles. The articles that we have reprinted throughout this book appear with a wide range of documentation styles, and we have made no effort to "normalize" them. Students who pursue library and Web-based research will quickly confront a bewildering array of such styles. Part of our mission is to acculturate students to this reality. While we believe that the MLA and APA styles of documentation should be taught to and used by academic writers, we also think that students must recognize them for what they are: classroom conventions, many of their details honored more in the breach than in the observance within the world at large. Notwithstanding this sentiment, we have tried our best to make the MLA and APA formats comprehensible and useful to students and instructors alike.

ACKNOWLEDGMENTS

Once again, in the seventh edition we have relied on the work of many researchers and scholars in composition and reading. We are particularly grateful to Ann Brown, Kenneth Bruffee, Linda Flower, Christina Haas, John Hayes, and Bonnie Meyer. We used pilot versions of *Writing in the Disciplines* in first-year-level writing courses at Cornell University and SUNY at Cortland, and we are indebted to our students for their comments and suggestions. We appreciate the generous assistance we received from Brad Potthoff, Senior Acquisitions Editor, who supervised our project with consummate skill and professionalism. We also appreciate the assistance we received from Editorial Assistant Nancy C. Lee, as well as from Senior Marketing Manager Sandra McGuire and the other members of the production team: Nancy Danahy, Michelle McKennea, Lee Scher, Wesley Hall, and Mary Ann Gloriande. We give special thanks to our infinitely resourceful project manager, Amanda Zagnoli, at Integra.

We are also indebted to our reviewers for their helpful ideas and suggestions: Cynthia Anderson, University of Central Arkansas; Lisa Beckelhimer, University of Cincinnati; Christina Riley Brown, Mercyhurst College; Richard Carr, University of Alaska Fairbanks; Michael R. Catanzaro, The University of Toledo; Mary A. Cooksey, Indiana University East; Ana Douglass, Truckee Meadows Community College; Robert S. Imbur, The University of Toledo; Ginny Pompei Jones, UNC-Pembroke; Jeannette E. Riley, UMass Dartmouth; and Lisa M. Ruch, Bay Path College.

Finally, we are grateful to Hadley M. Smith, Ithaca College, for his constant generosity, support, good humor, and sound advice. He joined us in editing the first five editions of this book and his collaboration is still evident on every page of this edition, except where we have floundered in the absence of his counsel.

Mary Lynch Kennedy
William J. Kennedy

Reading and Writing in the Academic Disciplines

Active Critical Reading

Prereading and Close Reading

■ ACADEMIC READING-WRITING PROCESS

In college, you will encounter English that is more formal and specialized than the spoken and written language you know. We refer to this language as *academic* reading and writing. Eventually, you will become comfortable with it, but first you must learn its conventions and practice using them to communicate with your professors and fellow students. This textbook will help you to do so.

Most of the writing assignments you receive in college will require you to write about material you have read in books, articles, or other sources. Reading and writing go hand in hand. For that reason, you should familiarize yourself with a process that combines the two activities. We describe that process in the box below. It begins with critical reading and progresses to writing as you plan, draft, and revise your work.

✶ OVERVIEW OF THE ACADEMIC READING-WRITING PROCESS

Active Critical Reading

Prereading. Preview the text, set your goals, and freewrite.

Close reading. Mark, annotate, elaborate on, and pose questions about the text. Questions address three areas: (1) content; (2) genre, organization, and stylistic features; and (3) rhetorical context.

Postreading. Write a personal response; compose paraphrases and summaries; and record quotations.

Planning

Formulating a thesis. Arrive at a preliminary understanding of the point you wish to make in your paper.

(continued)

3

Organizing.   Decide how you will use the textual sources in your paper and how you will develop your argument.

Drafting

Drafting.   Weave the source material (usually in the form of quotations, paraphrases, and summaries) with your own ideas to create paragraphs and, ultimately, a complete paper, typically with an introduction, a body, and a conclusion.

Reworking

Revising.   Lengthen, shorten, or reorder your paper; change your prose to make it more understandable to your reader; make sentence-level, phrase-level, and word-level stylistic changes; or, in some cases, make major conceptual or organizational alterations to incorporate what you learned during the process of drafting.

Editing.   Proofread your paper for errors in sentence structure, usage, punctuation, spelling, and mechanics, and check for proper manuscript form.

You don't have to follow the stages of this process in lockstep fashion, beginning with prereading and ending with editing. Your movement may be **recursive** and the phases may be intermixed. You may find yourself revising *as* you are drafting as well as after you have completed a draft of your paper. You will read the texts before you write, but you will probably reread portions of them during and after the drafting phase. Writing occurs at any point in the process. You will jot down ideas before you read the texts, annotate the texts as you read, or rewrite parts of the initial draft of your paper.

■ CONVERSATION WITH THE TEXTS

You will be having a **conversation with your texts** throughout the entire process of reading and writing. Both reading and writing constitute forms of conversation. When you read, you converse with an author. When you write, you converse with your readers. The more you think of the reading-writing process as an extended form of conversation, the easier it will be for you to develop your academic skills in both reading and writing.

> Recursive: a conversation as you go back and forth from reading to writing to rereading to rewriting.

We devote the first two chapters of this book to describing and illustrating the academic reading-writing process as a form of conversation. For convenience, we begin with reading and proceed through the phases in the order outlined in the preceding overview. Keep in mind that academic writers may not apply the process sequentially.

■ ACTIVE CRITICAL READING

Effective reading is essential because academic writing is frequently based on reading sources. College writers rarely have the luxury of composing essays based entirely on their own ideas and personal experiences. Typically, professors specify a topic and expect students to formulate a thesis or position and support it by drawing on published sources—textbooks, scholarly books, journal articles, Web sites, newspapers, and magazines—along with lecture notes, interviews, and other forms of information. When you use sources in your papers, you need to practice effective paraphrasing, summarizing, and quoting. The key to becoming an accomplished academic writer is to become a skilled reader.

> Academic writing depends on paraphrasing, summarizing, and quoting from sources.

Critical readers are ***active readers***. They relate the text to texts they have read before, they tap into prior knowledge, and they engage personal experiences. These activities enable them to self-regulate their reading comprehension. Usually when we have difficulty understanding texts, it is because we lack the appropriate background and cannot make connections.

To become an active reader, try out the strategies listed in the box below.

ACTIVE CRITICAL READING STRATEGIES

Prereading

- Preview the text and derive questions that will help you set goals for close reading.
- Recall your prior knowledge and express your feelings about the reading topic. Freewrite and brainstorm.

Close Reading

- Mark, annotate, and elaborate on the text.
- Take notes.
- Pose and answer questions about three aspects of the text: (1) content; (2) genre, organization, and stylistic features; and (3) rhetorical context.

Postreading

- Review the text and your notes.
- Write a personal response.
- Record paraphrases, summaries, and quotations for future reference.

■ Keeping a Writer's Notebook

As you can see from the strategies listed in the box above, critical reading is accompanied by various types of writing: freewriting and brainstorming, taking notes, posing and answering questions, responding from personal experience, paraphrasing, summarizing, and quoting. Readers need a place to record all this writing. We suggest that you use a writer's notebook. You can purchase a notebook or create one online.

You will fill your writer's notebook with informal writing, some of which will emerge in the formal writing you do at a later date. Writer's notebooks are places to collect material for future writing. They are different from journals in this respect. Journal writing can be an end in itself. You can keep a journal to record and reflect on what happens each day or you can use a journal for more specific purposes, for example, to respond to teachers' questions. A writer's notebook is not an end in itself. The entries are recorded with an eye toward later writing. They may become the basis for an essay, provide evidence for an argument, or serve as repositories of apt quotations. Consider your writer's notebook a record of your conversations with texts, as well as a storehouse for collecting material you can draw on when writing.

> Active reading requires active, responsive writing.

◼️ PREREADING

Prereading lays the groundwork for comprehension. Just as you wouldn't plunge into an athletic activity "cold," you wouldn't set out to read a difficult text without preparation. The more challenging the reading, the more important the prereading activities become. The prereading strategies you select depend on the text's character and level of difficulty. Two useful techniques are (1) **previewing** and asking questions that will help you set goals for close reading, and (2) **freewriting** or **brainstorming** to recall your prior knowledge or feelings about the topic.

◼️ Preview the Text and Ask Questions That Will Help You Set Goals for Close Reading

Before you do a close reading, give the text a quick inspection. This overview will give you a general idea of the content and organization. You will improve your comprehension if you ask yourself the questions in the box below.

PREREADING QUESTIONS

- What does the title indicate the text will be about?
- How do the subtitles and headings function? Do they reveal the organizational format (for example, introduction, body, conclusion)?
- Is there biographical information about the author? What does it tell me about the text?
- Do any topic sentences of paragraphs seem especially important?
- Are there other salient features of the text, such as enumeration, italics, boldface print, indention, diagrams, visual aids, or footnotes? What do these features reveal about the text?

- Does the text end with a summary? What does the summary reveal about the text?
- What type of background knowledge do I need to make sense of this text?
- Why am I reading this text?

An especially useful previewing technique mentioned above is to turn the title, sub-title, and subheadings into questions and try to answer them before reading. Consider how one of our students used this technique to preview Kerry Howley's article "Who Owns Your Body Parts?" (Chapter 9). Converting the title into a question, she asked, "*Why would any-one ask, 'Who Owns Your Body Parts?' Don't we own the parts of our own bodies?*" Then she converted the subtitle, "Everyone's Making Money in the Market for Body Tissue—Except the Donors," into a question: "*Is there actually a market in which people profit from buying and selling body tissue that is donated to science?*" Finally, she transforms the subheadings—"Resting in Pieces," "The Invisible Hand," "Selling the Gift of Life," "The Disassembly Line," "Scandal and Reform," and "Exploitation and Repugnance"—into questions.

STUDENT'S CONVERSION OF SUBHEADINGS INTO QUESTIONS

Subheading: "Resting in Pieces"
Student's question: Is Howley suggesting that when we die, we won't be "resting in peace" because our bodies will be cut up in pieces?

Subheading: "The Invisible Hand"
Student's question: Could this refer to the people who are profiting from the sales of tissue without the knowledge of the donators of the tissue?

Subheading: "Selling the Gift of Life"
Student's question: I know that people donate their human remains, but do some people actually sell organs and body parts?

Student's Answer to Questions: We are probably going to get some type of an exposé about how body parts are bought and sold without the knowledge and consent of the donors.

EXERCISE 1.1

Continue where our student left off. Turn to pages 298–301 and convert the subheadings into questions. Answer them as best you can.

Your response to the previous Prereading Questions will give you a sense of what the text is about. Based on that information, you will respond to "Why am I reading this text?" by setting an appropriate **purpose** for your close reading. You may be used to your high-school teachers setting a purpose for reading assignments. For example, "Read this chapter to find three factors that influence global warming" or "When you have finished the story, write your reaction to Sammy's decision to quit his job at the A&P."

Prereading: Ask questions about

Title
Subtitle and headings
Author's biography
Topic sentences
Printed format
Summary

In college, you will often set your own purpose for reading, and the purpose you select will depend on your overall goal. This textbook focuses on the overall **goal of reading** for the purpose of writing. If your immediate goal is to search for a fact or relevant bit of information to put in your essay, you may scan looking for key words. Or you may read for other reasons: to locate an opposing position, to obtain background information, to determine how other writers have approached your topic. What is important to remember is that after you have sized up the text, you need to decide why you are reading it.

Goals for reading:

- information
- opposing position
- additional background

■ Use Freewriting and Brainstorming to Recall Your Prior Knowledge and Express Your Feelings About the Reading Topic

The background knowledge, experiences, and biases you bring to bear on a text affect your understanding. As you read, you construct new knowledge by relating the text to what you already know. Prior knowledge paves the way for understanding. For example, before reading about alternatives to the traditional nuclear family in Pauline Irit Erera's "What Is a Family?" (pp. 416–28), think about the kinds of families you already know: two-parent families, single-parent families, families including stepparents, families with stepsiblings, and so forth. Your prior knowledge will help you to process Erera's argument. Or, before reading Simon Frith's "Toward an Aesthetic of Popular Music" (see pp. 497–510), reflect on your tastes in music.

Two ways to trigger prior knowledge and experiences are freewriting and brainstorming. By **freewriting,** we mean *jotting down anything that comes to mind about a topic.* Write nonstop for five or ten minutes without worrying about usage or spelling. Put down whatever you want. **Brainstorming** uses a *process of free association.* Start the process by skimming the reading source and listing key words or phrases. Then run down the list and record associations that come to mind when you think about these target concepts. Don't bother to write complete sentences; just write down words and phrases. Give your imagination free rein.

Freewriting triggers prior knowledge.

Brainstorming builds upon a preview of key words.

For an example, look at the freewriting and brainstorming of our student as she continues to read Kerry Howley's "Who Owns Your Body Parts?" (pp. 290–301).

EXCERPT FROM STUDENT'S FREEWRITING:

I plan to donate my organs when I die. I haven't thought about donating other body parts like tissue, but I suppose I should. I've always thought that the dead person's organs are given to people who are awaiting transplants. I don't think body parts should be bought and sold.

EXCERPT FROM STUDENT'S BRAINSTORMING LIST:

1. Demand for human tissue: I'm aware of the growing demand for human organs, but I never thought about the need for skin, bones, and other parts of the body.
2. AlloDerm: This appears to be a commercial product derived from dead people's skin. Is it legal to sell the skin of cadavers?
3. Donor recruitment and compensation: I think people will be reluctant to donate organs and tissue that end up being sold for profit.

When you use freewriting or brainstorming to tap into what you already know about a topic, you will better understand the text and read more objectively. You will be more conscious of your opinions and biases and less likely to confuse them inadvertently with those of the author. You may also find that freewriting and brainstorming help break ground for the paper that you will eventually write. They enable you to generate ideas for comparison, contrast, reinforcement, or contestation in your paper. As an argumentative "other" voice that helps to test the claims of your reading, freewriting can show the direction that your further reading and rewriting might take.

■ CLOSE READING

When you read, you actively construct meaning. You are not a passive decoder who transfers graphic symbols from the written page to your mind. Think of the process **as a two-way conversation between the reader and the text**. Articulate what you are thinking, and ask questions when you need more information or have difficulty understanding. To keep the interaction between the reader and the text dynamic, read with pencil in hand, annotating and marking the text, taking separate notes, and posing and answering questions.

> Close reading is a two-way conversation between reader and text.

■ Mark, Annotate, and Elaborate on the Text

Mark the text by underlining, highlighting, circling, drawing arrows, boxing, and bracketing important ideas. **Annotate** by making marginal notes and recording brief responses. **Elaborate** by amplifying or supplementing the text by adding comments. Draw on your knowledge and experiences to extend, illustrate, or evaluate. You can apply the text to situations the author does not envision, or you can provide analogies, examples, or counterexamples.

Mark texts.
Make notes.
Supplement text.

We provide a complete set of strategies for elaborating on texts in the box below.

STRATEGIES FOR ELABORATING ON TEXTS

Expand Text.

- Agree or disagree with a statement in the text, giving reasons for your agreement or disagreement.
- Compare or contrast your reactions to the topic (for example, "At first I thought ..., but now I think ...").
- Extend one of the points. Think of an example and see how far you can take it.
- Discover an idea implied by the text, but not stated.
- Provide additional details by fleshing out a point in the text.
- Illustrate the text with an example, an incident, a scenario, or an anecdote. *short story*
- Embellish the text with a vivid image, a metaphor, or an example.
- Draw comparisons between the text and books, articles, films, or other media.
- Validate one of the points with an example.
- Make a judgment about the relevance of one of the statements in the text.
- Impose a condition on a statement in the text. (For example, "If ..., then....")
- Qualify an idea in the text. Take a single paragraph and speculate on extensions of or exceptions to its claims.
- Extend an idea with a personal recollection or reflection. Personalize one of the statements. Try to imagine how you would behave in the same situation.
- Speculate about one of the points by:
  Asking questions about the direct consequences of an idea
  Predicting consequences
  Drawing implications from an idea
  Applying the idea to a hypothetical situation
  Giving a concrete instance of a point made in the text

Question Text.

- Draw attention to what the text has neglected to say about the topic.
- Test one of the claims. Ask whether the claim really holds up.

- Assess one of the points in light of your own prior knowledge of the topic or with your own or others' experiences.
- Question one of the points.
- Criticize a point in the text. Take a single paragraph and question every claim in it.
- Assess the usefulness and applicability of an idea.

Diagram Text.

- Classify items in the text under a superordinate category.
- Look for unstated text relations. Skim through the text once more to see whether statements at the end connect with those at the beginning and middle. Draw arrows to display the connections.
- Outline hierarchies of importance among ideas in the text.

Here is how one of our students marked, annotated, and elaborated on a passage from Kerry Howley's "Who Owns Your Body Parts?" (pp. 290–301).

Passage from Howley	Student Annotations
About 30,000 Americans donated tissue in 2005, and the number rises every year. Anecdotal evidence suggests that most of their families have no idea their tissue will be bought and sold. "There is a disincentive in alerting the families as to what might happen," says Goodwin, the DePaul University law professor, "because the families might—I think would—oppose their family members' ending up in the stream of commerce."	I wonder how many donated tissue this year. I'll have to Google it. Might? I'm sure most people would definitely object to this.
A 2001 report from the Department of Health and Human Services found that "tissue banking and processing practices have gradually diverged from donor families' expectations." Tissue banks have argued that grieving families are too fragile for hard-nosed talk about the marketplace, and no federal law requires tissue procurement organizations to tell donors that their loved ones may end up in a phalloplasty. The United Anatomical Gift Act includes stringent informed consent standards for organs but is silent on the matter of tissue.	Fragile or not, they are still entitled to know where their loved one's body ends up. What is a phalloplasty? Are there no policies or legislation governing the tissue industry?

Notice how the student marks the text. She does little underlining and highlighting. Do not overuse highlighting markers. It is hard to decide what is important when you read through a text for the first time. Every sentence may seem significant. But if you highlight a large percentage of the text, you will have a lot to reread when you study for an exam or look for material to put in a paper. Highlighting is a mechanical process that does not actively engage you with the text. It merely gives the illusion that you are reading effectively. **Instead of highlighting, write out summary statements and reactions**. Writing will help you to process the information.

In addition to her judicious underlining, our student circles unfamiliar vocabulary ("phalloplasty") and boxes key transitions ("and," "but"). You might prefer stars or asterisks to circles and boxes. **Feel free to develop your own symbol system for marking texts,** but be sure to use it consistently.

> Instead of highlighting, write summaries and mark text with symbols.

After marking and annotating the passage, our student adds her own ideas.

ELABORATION OF HOWLEY'S TEXT

I think it is unethical to accept donated tissue without informing the family of how it will be used. If I gave consent to have a family member's tissue used for research purposes, I would be incensed if that tissue was sold commercially to a wealthy person who wanted elective plastic surgery. We need legislation that will govern tissue donation. The United Anatomical Gift Act should be amended to prohibit companies from freely profiteering in donated tissue.

The student's response is an example of assertive reading. Instead of accepting the tissue banks' position on informing donors' families, she challenges it. As she continues to question and rebut the text, she will begin to formulate her own position on the controversy.

Record your elaborations in your writer's notebook. This record will be useful if you intend to write a paper that gives your view on the ideas in the text. It will certainly help your critical analysis of the reading material by pointing to passages that raised questions, offered insights, and provoked your responses the first time you read them. The ultimate goal of marking, annotating, and elaborating is to involve you intellectually with the text and to give you access to it without rereading. Writing out marginal or separate notes is the best way to accomplish this.

> Record in writer's notebook.

EXERCISE 1.2

Read Sherry Turkle's "Alone Together: The Robotic Moment" (pp. 322–31). Use the critical reading strategies we have described so far and practice the process approach to reading. First, preview the text and derive questions. Then recall your prior knowledge and express your feelings by freewriting and brainstorming. Finally, mark, annotate, and elaborate on the text.

■ Take Effective Notes

When you encounter difficult texts, you may want to take more extensive notes to supplement your annotations and elaborations. These supplementary notes can be in the form of outlines, summaries, or paraphrases of key passages; lists of significant pages or paragraphs; or any combination of these elements. Regard them as a record of your conversation with the texts. When you take notes, pay special attention to thesis statements and topic sentences. The **thesis** is the focal point of the entire piece: the major point, position, or objective the author demonstrates or proves. A **topic sentence** is the main idea of a paragraph or another subdivision of the text.

Thesis statements express major idea of essay.

Both the thesis and the topic statement may require more than one sentence, so do not assume that you should always search for a single sentence. Nor should you make assumptions about their location. The thesis statement is typically in the introductory paragraph, but it can also appear elsewhere. Topic sentences are often at the beginnings of paragraphs, but not always; they can appear in the middle or at the end as well. Some paragraphs do not contain explicit topic sentences; the main idea is implied through an accumulation of details, facts, or examples.

Topic sentences express major idea of each paragraph or subdivision.

If the text is easy to read and has straightforward content, you can streamline note-taking and annotating procedures to capture only the most basic ideas. But remember that it is natural to forget much of what you have read; even relatively simple ideas can slip from your memory unless you record them in notes or annotations. And, of course, when you are working with library sources, note-taking is indispensable.

■ Pose and Answer Questions About the Text

A useful method for note-taking is to pose questions about the text and answer them as you read. If you are reading a textbook chapter, first look at the reader aids: the preview outline at the beginning, the introductory or concluding sections, and the review questions at the end. Also check out chapter or section headings for the concepts or issues that the chapter covers. Using these reader aids, generate questions about what the chapter will be about and answer them as you read. Formulate questions based on section headings and visual layout. This strategy works best if you record your answers as you locate the relevant material. Write your answers in your writer's notebook so that you can return to them later and find the important ideas you took away from the reading. Too often, students spend hours reading only to find several days later that they remember virtually nothing and must reread all the material. Although it takes extra time to pose and answer questions, it can reduce time spent rereading texts.

A powerful strategy that will increase your reading comprehension is to ask questions about three specific aspects of the text: (1) content; (2) genre, organization, and stylistic features; and (3) rhetorical context. When you ask these questions, you will be reading in three different but not necessarily separate ways. Critical readers use all three strategies simultaneously and harmoniously, but for convenience sake we will discuss them one by one.

Determine:

- content
- genre, organization, and stylistic features
- rhetorical context

Reading for Content

When you read for content, you read to determine the literal meaning of the text. Begin with the big picture—the overall topic—and then delve deeper to determine the main idea and the support for the main point. Ask yourself the questions in the box below:

QUESTIONS FOR ANALYZING THE LITERAL CONTENT OF TEXTS

- What is the topic or focal point of the text?
- What is the main idea, major point, or central claim?
- What other ideas are important?
- How does the text support, qualify, and develop the claim or position?
- What inferences, judgments, or conclusions are drawn?

Let's ask these questions as we read a passage from Arthur Caplan's "The Trouble with Organ Trafficking" (pp. 307–09).

PASSAGE FROM CAPLAN*

Proponents of markets in body parts argue that the only way to counter the shortage of organs and tissues available for transplant is to legitimize the international trade that is already occurring sub rosa in people, organs, and tissues. Given the gap between supply and demand, those in need will do whatever they can to obtain organs and tissues for themselves. Rather than try to battle an underground market, we should simply legalize it and regulate it as necessary.

There are four major problems with the conclusion that the way to combat organ trafficking is to make it legal. First, there is no reason to think that most nations have the resources to regulate a market in organs effectively. After all, even the United States, Britain, and Germany proved unable to regulate their banking, housing, and securities sectors.

Second, there are other ways to expand the availability of organs and tissue that do not involve treating human beings as commercial body-parts factories. Nations could institute presumed-consent policies, asking those who do not want to be donors to carry cards or register their objection in computer registries. When supplemented with appropriate training and resources, these systems have proven very effective in Spain, Belgium, Austria, and other nations.

Third—and perhaps the greatest problem with legalizing organ and body-part markets—is that such markets prey on the grim circumstances of the poor. Fourth, they clearly violate the medical ethics of physicians and health-care workers.

- What is the topic or focal point of the text? The topic is legalizing the market for organs and body parts.
- What is the main idea, major point, or central claim? Caplan claims that there are problems with arguing that we can control black market trafficking of organs and body parts by making

---

*From Caplan, Arthur. "The Trouble with Organ Trafficking." *Free Inquiry* 29.6 (October/November 2009). Web. 15 Aug. 2010. Reprinted by permission of the author.

it legal. In the first paragraph, he presents the position of those who favor legalization. In the next three paragraphs, he defends his position against legalizing the markets.

- **What other ideas are important?** Toward the beginning of the passage, Caplan explains that there is an underground market in body parts because demand exceeds supply.

- **How does the text support, qualify, and develop the claim or position?** Caplan offers four reasons why the marketing of body parts should not be legalized: (1) nations will not be able to regulate the markets, (2) organs and tissue can be made available in other ways, (3) legalization will exploit the poor, and (4) legalization violates medical ethics.

- **What inferences, judgments, or conclusions are drawn?** We can conclude that Caplan is vehemently opposed to unregulated trade in body parts and any attempts to legalize it.

Asking pointed questions about content enables you to read with an active purpose rather than merely trying to get through all the words on the page. In addition to being able to restate and interpret the meaning of the text, it is important to be able to describe its characteristics and structure.

Reading for Genre, Organization, and Stylistic Features
Genre
You may recall your English teacher using the word *genre* to characterize different types of literature, for example, novel, short story, poem. *Genre* is a French word meaning "kind," "sort," or "style." Traditionally, in English class, the word is used to refer to different categories of writing that are marked by distinctive content, form, and style. Recently, *genre* has acquired a broader meaning. This new perspective views genres in terms of their social situation and purpose. For example, letters enable us to communicate with others in writing.

Genre, a specific kind of writing ⟶ social situation and purpose

Particular genres of letter writing allow us to express amorous feelings (love letter), seek a job (letter of application), sympathize with a loved one (letter of condolence), or criticize the manufacturer of our new microwave (letter of complaint). These letters share attributes, yet they differ according to the writer's purpose. You would not open your business letter with the salutation "My Dear Personnel Director." Nor would you add the postscript "P.S. I forgot to mention that I am an expert typist." In order to achieve the goal of presenting yourself as an intelligent job applicant, you would be much more formal and concise.

At the end of her watershed essay "Genre as Social Action," Carolyn Miller writes, "For the student, genres serve as keys to understanding how to participate in the actions of a community" (165). By the time you arrive at college, you know how letter writing and other genres in the public realm function in the wider community, and you are probably very knowledgeable about more specialized genres in areas that interest you. Those who enjoy rock music will know the characteristics of heavy metal, punk rock, glam rock, and grunge, and enthusiasts of electronic music will be able to differentiate among techno, trance, industrial music, house music, and electro hip-hop.

EXERCISE 1.3

As a class, come up with a list of television genres. Then break into small groups. Each group will select a genre, explain its purpose, describe its features and conventions, and answer the following questions:

- What purpose does the genre serve?
- To what audience is it directed?
- How are the features and conventions adapted to the purpose and audience?

A representative from each group will report to the class.

Some of you may know more about genres of the music you listen to and the genres of the shows you watch on television than genres you see in print. To test your knowledge of written genres, complete the exercise presented below.

EXERCISE 1.4

Break into small groups. Assign each of the numbered passages to a different group. Read the passage and answer the following questions:

- What purpose does the text serve?
- Who is the audience for the text?
- Are assumptions made about class, age, gender, and ethnicity?
- What knowledge is the reader assumed to have?
- Would you characterize the style as literary or scientific?
- Can you describe other characteristics and textual properties?
- What is the genre?

Passage 1

"TOM!"

No answer.

"TOM!"

No answer.

"What's gone with that boy, I wonder? You TOM!"

No answer.

The old lady pulled her spectacles down and looked over them about the room; then she put them up and looked out under them. She seldom or never looked THROUGH them for so small a thing as a boy; they were her state pair, the pride of her heart, and were built for "style," not service—she could have seen through a pair of stove-lids just as well. She looked perplexed for a moment, and then said, not fiercely, but still loud enough for the furniture to hear:

"Well, I lay if I get hold of you I'll—."

Passage 2

Two roads diverged in a yellow wood,
And sorry I could not travel both
And be one traveler, long I stood
And looked down one as far as I could
To where it bent in the undergrowth.

Passage 3

More recently, a study of 8000 male Harvard graduates showed that chocaholics lived longer than abstainers. Their longevity may be explained by the high polyphenol levels in chocolate. Polyphenols reduce the oxidation of low-density lipoproteins and thereby protect against heart disease. Such theories are still speculative.

   Coincidentally or otherwise, many of the world's oldest supercentenarians, e.g. Jeanne Calment (1875–1997) and Sarah Knauss (1880–1999), were passionately fond of chocolate. Jeanne Calment habitually ate two pounds of chocolate per week until her physician induced her to give up sweets at the age of 119—three years before her death aged 122. Life-extensionists are best advised to eat dark chocolate rather than the kinds of calorie-rich confectionery popular in America.

Passage 4

[Enter the Ghost, and Prince Hamlet following]
Hamlet: Whither wilt thou lead me? Speak. I'll go no further.
Ghost: Mark me.
Hamlet: I will.
Ghost: My hour is almost come
When I to sulph'rous and tormenting flames
Must render up myself.
Hamlet: Alas, poor ghost! (1.5.1-4)

Passage 5

HOUSE THINKING
A Room-By-Room Look at How We Live
By Winifred Gallagher
329 pp. HarperCollins Publishers $24.95

I spend my days examining, room by room, how we live—"house thinking," as Winifred Gallagher would have it. Mine is a job that some intellectuals might disdain. No matter: most people (including some of the smartest) spend a great deal of time thinking about houses, whether professionally or out of sheer love. So I welcome any book that takes seriously a subject as old as recorded history and as deeply felt as anything else in our lives.

Passage 6

Respondents were administered the *Celebrity Attitude Scale* (CAS: McCutcheon et al., 2002). Originally termed the Celebrity Worship Scale, this instrument is a 34-item scale in which respondents are asked to indicate their attitude towards a favourite celebrity (that they themselves have named) using a number of items that use a response format of "strongly agree" equal to 5 and "strongly disagree" equal to 1. Please refer to Table 1 for all the items of this scale.

Most likely, the above exercise demonstrated that you are already familiar with literary genres such as novels, plays, and poems, and nonliterary genres such as book reviews and scientific articles. If knowledge of genre is a key "to understanding how to participate in the actions of a community" (Miller 165), in order to succeed in college, you need to learn additional genres of academic writing.

Genres in Academic Writing and in Writing Classes   As you become more familiar with academic writing, you will be able to identify specialized genres such as scientific research articles, engineering reports, case histories, and legal briefs. In this book, we concentrate on the classroom genres that play a major role in writing courses and are frequently assigned in courses in various disciplines: response to a text, summary, abstract, précis, critical analysis, comparative analysis, critique of visual argument, exploratory synthesis, literature review, thesis-driven synthesis, argument-synthesis, and research paper. Knowledge of these genres is indispensable if you want to become a skilled critical reader and a proficient academic writer. See Table 1–1 for an overview of various academic genres.

Role of Genre in Reading and Writing   Knowledge of the genre of a text aids reading comprehension because it prepares you to approach the text with a set of expectations and make intelligent predictions. When reading a newspaper article, you look for a headline and a byline, and you expect answers to five questions—who? what? where? when? and how?—to be placed early in the article. If you are familiar with the genre of the scientific research article, you anticipate four major subdivisions: Introduction, Methods, Results, and Discussion.

Genre sets up expectations about content.

When reading an argument essay, you expect the writer to lay out both sides of the controversy, make concessions to parties holding opposing views, and then refute their claims by marshalling evidence to support his or her thesis. Genre knowledge is a shorthand for making sense of the text.

You should be aware that the form of writing called "argument" is found in many genres besides the classic academic essay. The major forms of writing—argument, exposition, description, and narration—are sometimes referred to as genres. They are really the building blocks with which various genres are written, and they can play important roles in many genres. For example, narration can be used in fictional genres, such as novels and short stories, as well as in nonfictional genres such as travel writing and historical accounts. A genre such as source-based synthesis may incorporate narration, description, exposition, and argument.

TABLE 1–1   Classroom Genres of Academic Writing

Genre	Characteristics	Writer's Rhetorical Purpose
Response to a text	An essay in which the writer relates his or her own ideas to those in the text and, in so doing, presents an *informed* outlook. The essay balances personal expression and textual content.	Share reaction to the text with other readers.
Summary	A condensed version of an original text that shortens the original without changing its meaning.	Give readers a condensed version of the original text.
Abstract	A brief summary, usually only a paragraph or two. It usually appears after the title of a paper and before the longer text itself, though sometimes it is presented on a separate page.	Give readers descriptive summary information that will help them decide if it is worth their time to read the entire article.
Précis	A summary that strictly follows the order of the original text. It is usually no longer than one-quarter of the original.	Give readers a miniature version of the original text.
Critical analysis	An analysis that examines the text's argument by looking closely at the author's line of reasoning.	Share interpretation with readers, and, ideally, convince them of an enlightened reading of the text that warrants their attention and should be taken seriously. A more focused purpose is to evaluate the author's argument in terms of its strengths and weaknesses.
Comparative analysis	An analysis of texts that shows what the similarities and differences represent, reveal, or demonstrate.	Analyze texts to show how one text corroborates or debates the other and to develop and articulate a critical view toward what you are comparing.
Rhetorical analysis	An examination of *how a text is written*. It pays attention to what the text talks about, but its main focus is the strategies and devices the author uses to convey the meaning.	Share interpretation with readers, and, ideally, convince them of an enlightened reading of the text that warrants their attention and should be taken seriously. A more *focused purpose* is to evaluate the author's rhetorical context and strategies.
Process analysis	An outline and explanation of the steps in an operation.	Explain and comment on the sequence of particular steps in a process, emphasize important points, provide supplementary information, and include caveats about what can go wrong.
Causal analysis	An identification and explanation of the reasons why something happens.	Examine why a phenomenon or event is occurring, investigate possible causes of a problem, or examine effects.
Critique of visual argument	An analysis of a photograph, film, video, or other visual text to interpret and evaluate its meaning and cultural significance.	Prompt viewers to find similar layers of meaning and significance when they view visuals.

(*continued*)

TABLE 1–1   continued

Genre	Characteristics	Writer's Rhetorical Purpose
Exploratory synthesis essay	An analysis of two or more texts that share a topic or interest. It identifies grounds for grouping the textual components and organizes this textual material under a controlling theme. The writer presents informative results in a straightforward manner. Such a synthesis often tries to define a topic or issue in an expository style that emphasizes the coverage of data rather than any further questioning or interpretation of the data.	Unfold or unravel a topic or question to make it clearer to readers. The synthesis might crack open a concept, place an issue in historical context, or clarify sides in a controversy. The synthesis is objective and nonjudgmental.
Literature review	An analysis of two or more texts that share a topic or interest. It identifies grounds for grouping the textual components, and organizes the textual material under a controlling theme.	Provide background and explain a topic, problem, or issue to readers by examining a wide array of published research studies.
Thesis-driven synthesis	A synthesis of two or more texts that share a topic or interest. It identifies grounds for grouping the textual components and organizes the textual material under a controlling theme.	Communicate thesis and point of view. The writer takes a position on the topic or issue. The writer's position is explicit in a direct statement of judgment or opinion on the matter at hand. The thesis is supported by reasons that are based on evidence.
Argument synthesis	A synthesis of two or more texts that share a topic or interest. It identifies grounds for grouping the textual components and organizes the textual material under a controlling theme.	Persuade readers that a particular position is reasonable and worthy of support. The synthesis focuses on an issue or question that is debatable. The writer anticipates, acknowledges, and addresses alternative views.
Research paper	A paper that starts with a question or problem that requires collecting facts, opinions, and perspectives from books, journal articles, Web sites, newspapers, and other sources. The writer analyzes the texts, identifies grounds for grouping the textual components, and organizes this textual material under a controlling theme. A research paper may include the genres listed above.	Unfold or unravel a topic or question to make it clearer to the readers or take a position on the topic or issue or persuade readers that the writer's position is reasonable and worthy of support.

As you move from one genre to another, you will soon learn each genre's conventions and stylistic techniques. You will recognize that genres written in a literary style have personal pronouns and active verbs, and genres written in a scientific style contain passive voice, a large amount of information packed into sentences, lengthy subjects composed of many words, restricted use of "I," heavy nominalization, and abstraction. You will learn that writing related to technology (for example, Web documents) has relatively short paragraphs, topic sentences for each paragraph, conciseness, summaries, inverted pyramid style, and use of hypertext links.

Just as genres provide frameworks for readers, they act as structuring devices for writers as well. A knowledgeable writer knows that her book review will differ from her book report. For both genres, she will begin by giving her readers general information about the text (title, author, publisher, copyright date, number of pages, genre). She will discuss setting, characters, plot; and she will offer a personal opinion.

Awareness of genre helps readers and writers.

However, the knowledgeable writer knows that the two genres differ in purpose. The purpose of the book report is to summarize the main characteristics of the book and to offer a brief personal opinion. The object of the book review is to evaluate the book. The writer does this by assessing whether or not the author has accomplished his or her purpose and by comparing the text to other books in the genre or to other books written by the same author. The writer knows her readers will expect her to devote a good portion of the review to evaluation.

Readers of book reviews assume that they will receive a synopsis of the book, but more important, they expect to read the writer's evaluation. Their purpose for reading the review is to see whether the book is worth reading. If the writer breaches the contract by offering too much summary and too little evaluation, readers will be dissatisfied. As you familiarize yourself with the genres of academic writing, you will acquire clear expectations about the purpose of texts, their conventions and organization, and their stylistic features.

To identify the genre, ask questions about how the text functions. The questions are presented in the box below.

QUESTIONS FOR IDENTIFYING THE GENRE OF TEXTS

- Does the text demonstrate an identifiable genre?
- Can I describe the form or components of this genre?
- How is the text organized?
- How do the different parts function in relation to the whole?
- Can I identify distinctive conventions of the genre?

Organization

As you know, texts have recognizable parts, such as introductions, conclusions, theses or main-idea statements, topic sentences, and paragraphs. As you read, ask yourself such questions as:

- Where does this introduction end?
- What point is the author making in this paragraph?
- How does this paragraph relate to the one that comes before and after it?
- How does the paragraph contribute to the main idea?

TABLE 1–2   Patterns for Developing and Organizing Texts

Pattern	Writer's Purpose
Time order, narration, process	To present ideas or events in a chronological sequence, to tell what happened (narration), or to describe a sequence of actions (process)
Antecedent and consequence	To present causes (antecedents) or examine effects or cause-and-effect outcomes (consequences); to reveal the causes of a particular outcome or phenomenon or to explain its consequences, usually by explaining the relationship between the causes and effects
Description	To present the physical attributes, parts, or setting of the topic, often in order to give a personal impression of the person, place, or thing being described
Statement and response	To present a statement and give a reaction, often in a question-and-answer, problem-and-solution, or remark-and-reply format
Comparison and contrast	To present the similarities or differences between objects, approaches, or viewpoints
Example	To present illustrations or instances that support an idea
Analysis and classification	To divide the topic into parts (analyze) or to group parts or facets of the topic according to some principle or characteristic (classify)
Definition	To explain a word, concept, or principle
Analogy	To show the similarity between things that otherwise bear little or no resemblance, to explain something by comparing it point by point with something similar

Texts are also arranged in identifiable patterns. In your own essays, you have used organizational patterns such as cause and effect and comparison and contrast. Table 1–2 identifies the most common patterns and gives a brief description of each.

Occasionally, writers tell readers how they are organizing the text. In the introductory paragraph to "Academic Dishonesty: What Is It and Why Do Students Engage in It?", Bernard E. Whitley, Jr. and Patricia Keith-Spiegel inform their readers that they will explore four features of the topic:

> In this chapter we discuss the nature of academic dishonesty and its definitions, reasons students give for cheating, institutional and student characteristics associated with cheating, and the extent to which cheating actually leads to higher grades. (16)

When writers explain what they are doing and direct you to read in a certain way, you know what to expect. When they don't supply this information, you have to determine the pattern of development yourself.

A key to unlocking the meaning of a text is to identify the pattern of organization. **Texts may display a single organizational pattern, but more likely they have overlapping patterns**. An initial, quick read will give you a sense of the text's major organizational pattern. Keep this pattern in mind during your close reading. At that time, annotate the passages that display other patterns of development. Consider how our student annotated the following passages from Joshua Foer's article "The Kiss of Life."

JOSHUA FOER, "THE KISS OF LIFE"*

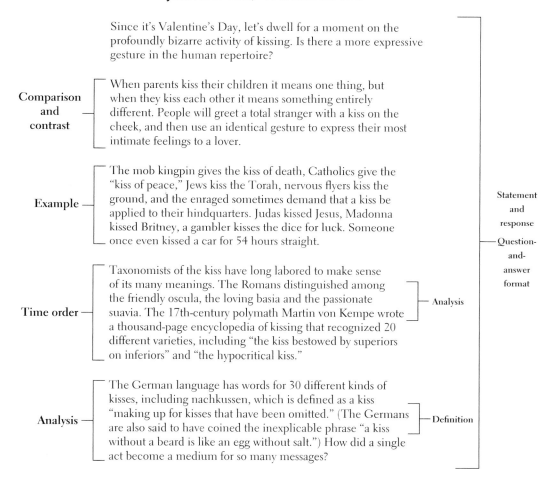

Since it's Valentine's Day, let's dwell for a moment on the profoundly bizarre activity of kissing. Is there a more expressive gesture in the human repertoire?

Comparison and contrast

When parents kiss their children it means one thing, but when they kiss each other it means something entirely different. People will greet a total stranger with a kiss on the cheek, and then use an identical gesture to express their most intimate feelings to a lover.

Example

The mob kingpin gives the kiss of death, Catholics give the "kiss of peace," Jews kiss the Torah, nervous flyers kiss the ground, and the enraged sometimes demand that a kiss be applied to their hindquarters. Judas kissed Jesus, Madonna kissed Britney, a gambler kisses the dice for luck. Someone once even kissed a car for 54 hours straight.

Time order

Taxonomists of the kiss have long labored to make sense of its many meanings. The Romans distinguished among the friendly oscula, the loving basia and the passionate suavia. The 17th-century polymath Martin von Kempe wrote a thousand-page encyclopedia of kissing that recognized 20 different varieties, including "the kiss bestowed by superiors on inferiors" and "the hypocritical kiss."

Analysis

Analysis

The German language has words for 30 different kinds of kisses, including nachkussen, which is defined as a kiss "making up for kisses that have been omitted." (The Germans are also said to have coined the inexplicable phrase "a kiss without a beard is like an egg without salt.") How did a single act become a medium for so many messages?

Definition

Statement and response

Question-and-answer format

*Joshua Foer, "The Kiss of Life." *The New York Times*, February 14, 2006, section 1, Op Ed page. Copyright 2006 *The New York Times* Company.

The general plan for this article is **Statement and Response**. The opening paragraph asks about kissing, "Is there a more expressive gesture in the human repertoire?" and the article answers this question. Within this overall pattern of question and answer, we see paragraphs organized to present comparisons and contrast (see paragraph 2, "When …, but when …"), examples (paragraph 3), and time order (paragraph 4). And in a paragraph organized with time order, we see sentences that display analysis.

EXERCISE 1.5

Choose from among the nine patterns of organization in Table 1–2 to identify the patterns in the following passages:

- Pages 369–70, paragraphs 9–10, Jonathan Franzen, "'I Just Called to Say I Love You'"
- Pages 433–34, paragraphs 1–2, Andrew Cherlin, "The Origins of the Ambivalent Acceptance of Divorce"
- Pages 410–11, paragraph 5, Robert L. Barret and Bryan E. Robinson, "Children of Gay Fathers"

Remember that in some instances, patterns of development will overlap.

Stylistic Features

In addition to identifying genre and organizational patterns, critical readers pay attention to stylistic features of texts. They examine sentence structure and vocabulary. They observe that scholarly writers often draw extensively on evidence from published sources or original research that they carefully document. They expect academic texts to be written in a formal voice, in sentences with a number of coordinated and parallel elements. They notice when academic texts adopt a more conversational tone and informal style and deviate from accepted conventions.

As you become familiar with a range of academic texts, you will anticipate certain textual features. For example, when you read texts dealing with science and technology, the subject of the first three chapters in our anthology, you will take note of specialized terminology. You will do this because you recognize that technical vocabulary changes constantly, so that mastering the current buzzwords is crucial. Like other critical readers of technical literature, you will seek out experimental verification of any new, startling conclusions or look for references to other work in the field.

> Style: sentence structure, choice of diction and specialized terminology, formal or informal voice, coordinated and parallel elements

To give you a clearer understanding of stylistic features, we will examine two texts. Read the following passages by Barbara Ehrenreich and Pauline Irit Erera before you read our comparison of the two texts. In the first passage, drawn from "Serving in Florida" (p. 471), Ehrenreich is describing Jerry's, a restaurant where she has taken a job as a server.

Ehrenreich (paragraph 11):   Picture a fat person's hell, and I don't mean a place with no food. In there is everything you might eat if eating had no bodily consequences—the cheese fries, the chicken-fried steaks, the fudge-laden desserts—only here every bite must be paid for, one way or another, in human discomfort. The kitchen is a cavern, a stomach leading to the lower intestine that is the garbage and dishwashing area, from which issue bizarre smells combining the edible and the offal: creamy carrion, pizza barf, and that unique and enigmatic Jerry's scent, citrus fart. The floor is slick with spills, forcing us to walk through the kitchen with tiny steps, like Susan McDougal in leg irons. Sinks everywhere are clogged with scraps of lettuce, decomposing lemon wedges, water-logged toast crusts. Put your hand down on any counter and you risk being stuck to it by the film of ancient syrup spills, and this is unfortunate because hands are utensils here, used for scooping up lettuce onto the salad plates, lifting out pie slices, and even moving hash browns from one plate to another.

In the second passage, drawn from "What Is a Family?" (p. 417), Erera distinguishes among institutional, ideological, and actual-practice definitions of "family":

> ***Erera (paragraph 4):*** The family is not simply a social institution. It is an ideological construct laden with symbolism and with a history and politics of its own. As Jagger and Wright (1999) put it, "The groupings that are called families are socially constructed rather than naturally or biologically given" (p. 3). In studying families, we need to keep clear the distinctions between the institutionalized family, the ideology of the family, and the lives of actual families. Although social and economic forces shape family life, our understanding of family is shaped by the evolving patterns of the actual families around us. Furthermore, conceptions of what constitutes a family are necessarily rooted in time and place. White, Western, two-parent families have generally been regarded, explicitly or implicitly, as the model or template against which we compare all families, regardless of culture, ethnicity, race, or class. This parochial view distorts our understanding of diverse families by considering them deviations from the norm (Smith, 1995; Thorne, 1982).

Comparison of the Stylistic Features of the Texts

	Ehrenreich
Point of view	Addresses readers directly, prompting them to action: "Picture a fat person's hell …"; "Put your hand down on any counter …"; and uses informal, second-person, "you," as well as first-person, "I," point of view.
Voice	Uses active voice and assertive is/are verbs that register the writer's personal observation: "this is unfortunate"; "The kitchen is a cavern"; "The floor is slick."
Language and tone	Uses informal language, including contractions—"don't"—and colorful, colloquial language—"pizza barf," "citrus fart"—and creates an informal tone. Also uses figurative language: compares the kitchen to a stomach and the garbage and dishwashing areas to the lower intestine; makes a humorous simile comparing the servers, walking in small steps, to "Susan McDougal in leg irons." Susan McDougal, a former business partner of President Clinton, was convicted of fraud and of refusing to testify against the president. Newspaper photos pictured her being led off to jail, shackled in ankle chains and handcuffs.
Sentence structure	Uses complex sentence structure, but lengthy phrases and clauses seem clear to readers because their movement is sequential.
Textual sources	Does not include parenthetical citations, a list of references, or endnotes.

	Erera
Point of view	Uses more formal, third-person point of view.
Voice	Employs passive voice: "our understanding of family is shaped"; "two-parent families have generally been regarded."
Language and tone	Uses formal language and tone: "we need to keep clear the distinctions"; "regarded, explicitly or implicitly, as the model or template."
Sentence structure	Uses complex sentence structure, and lengthy phrases and clauses require readers to connect their parts to larger wholes in order to understand their meaning.
Textual sources	Includes parenthetical citations in the text and a list of references at the end of the article. The parenthetical citations indicate where Erera found the information she has quoted, summarized, or paraphrased; for example: "(Smith, 1995; Thorne, 1982)."

Our analysis is based on point of view, voice, language, tone, choice of sentence structures, and reliance on other textual sources. **Point of view** establishes *whether a text is written in the first-person (I, we), second-person (you), or third-person (it, they) form* and **voice** refers to *whether the verb is cast in an active mode (e.g., "I made a mistake") or a passive mode (e.g., "A mistake was made").* Both are important stylistic features of academic writing. Use of the first-person form is frowned upon in many fields of academic writing. If writers use it at all, they use it sparingly. First-person is appropriate for Ehrenreich, however, because she is writing about her own experiences doing investigative fieldwork. Ehrenreich's use of the first-person "I" and her direct references to the reader, "you," lend force and vigor to her prose and enable her to write in a strong active voice. Erera on the other hand uses the third-person point of view and the passive voice, exemplifying a typical fashion of academic writing. For example, "Although social and economic forces shape family life, our understanding of family is shaped by the evolving patterns of the actual families around us."

As our analysis shows, Ehrenreich's word choice and tone are less scholarly and more down-to-earth than Erera's. Ehrenreich uses witty, everyday language; humor; and vivid detail. Erera's vocabulary is straightforward. She doesn't use specialized terminology or jargon, but her language is much more formal than Ehrenreich's. Both writers use complex sentences, some of which are packed with a good deal of information.

The stylistic feature that clearly distinguishes Erera's style from Ehrenreich's and marks Erera as a classic academic writer is her citing of textual sources. Ehrenreich draws on published sources elsewhere in *Nickel and Dimed*, the book from which we excerpted the passage, but not to the extent we see in the Erera text. The practice of relating one's own text to other published texts by citing, quoting, paraphrasing, and summarizing them is called **intertextuality**. We will discuss this hallmark of academic writing below.

Our analysis of the two passages leads us to conclude that Erera writes in a formal style characteristic of many genres of academic writing. She uses a certain amount of passive voice, scholarly tone, and references to prior publications. In contrast, Ehrenreich has a relaxed, conversational style that we associate with informal writing. We have provided a detailed analysis of the two passages in order to show you the roles stylistic features play in writing. We don't expect you to perform an exhaustive stylistic analysis each time you read a text. However, knowledge of stylistic features such as point of view, voice, language, tone, choice of sentence structures, and reliance on other textual sources will better enable you to read critically and appreciate how the writer's style contributes to the text. On the occasions when you wish to delve deeper to analyze style, ask yourself the questions in the box below.

In your own writing, you will learn to master styles that are appropriate to particular fields. The lab reports you write for science courses will be formal, with concise sentences describing procedural matters. The personal essays you compose for English courses will be less formal, with free-flowing sentences rich in descriptive detail. The stylistic feature that will be most important to master is the practice of drawing on other texts.

QUESTIONS FOR ANALYZING THE STYLISTIC FEATURES OF TEXTS

- Is the text written in first-person (I, we), second-person (you), or third-person (it, they)? What does the point of view contribute to the style?
- Are the verbs in active voice or passive voice?

- Does the text contain straightforward language or is the vocabulary specialized?
- What can I say about sentence length and complexity? Are the sentences simple and unpretentious or complex, remote, and scholarly?
- How do the point of view, language, and sentence structure contribute to the tone?
- How extensive are the references to other texts? Are there parenthetical citations, lists of references, footnotes, or endnotes?
- What do my answers to the preceding questions indicate about the stylistic features of the text?

Intertextuality   **Intertextuality** is *a conversation that a text records with other texts.* It refers to the way writers relate the findings of other texts to their own texts, often by incorporating them in the form of direct quotations, paraphrases, summaries, or other types of references such as footnotes or endnotes, and always citing the source of the information. Footnotes and parenthetical references provide classic examples of intertextuality. Look back to the passage by Pauline Erera on page 25. Erera quotes from G. Jager and C. Wright's book *Changing Family Values*, and she summarizes information from two scholarly articles, one by T. E. Smith and the other by B. Thorne. She fully identifies these sources in the list of references at the end of her article.

The convention of drawing on other texts is not confined to academic writing. Newspapers and magazines contain articles that incorporate information from other texts. But the journalistic style of writing usually does not involve parenthetical citation, lists of references, footnotes, or endnotes. On page 23, we provided excerpts from Joshua Foer's *New York Times* article "The Kiss of Life." Consider an additional paragraph from the same article, which draws upon Charles Darwin's *The Expression of the Emotions in Man and Animals.*

> Even though all of this might suggest that kissing is in our genes, not all human cultures do it. Charles Darwin was one of the first to point this out. In his book "The Expression of the Emotions in Man and Animals," he noted that kissing "is replaced in various parts of the world by the rubbing of noses." Early explorers of the Arctic dubbed this the Eskimo kiss. (Actually, it turns out the Inuit were not merely rubbing noses, they were smelling each other's cheeks.)

Foer directly quotes from Darwin's book, but nowhere does he provide citations to pages or give bibliographical information about publisher and date of publication. Nor does he represent the title of Darwin's book in italics, as the standard format of academic bibliographies requires. Instead Foer places both the title and the quotation within separate quotation marks. The convention of meticulously citing and documenting sources is not always followed outside of the academic community. Sometimes magazine writers likewise cite facts without explaining where they came from, and depending on their editorial policies, some newspapers publish reports based on statements of unnamed sources. In academic writing, however, there is a strict protocol of convention for citing sources, both to document the writer's use of sources and to enable readers to refer to these same sources for further information and clarification. In Chapter 8 and in the Appendix, we explain these conventions so that you, as an academic writer, can follow them when you cite sources.

EXERCISE 1.6

For this exercise, use the Questions for Analyzing the Stylistic Features of Texts (p. 26–27) to analyze the stylistic features of passages from three reading selections:

- Noel Sharkey, "The Ethical Frontiers of Robotics," paragraph 11, page 359
- Lynn Olcott, "The Ballad of a Single Mother," paragraphs 1–4, page 446
- Brink Lindsey, "Culture of Success," paragraph 11, page 455

Reading for Rhetorical Context

Critical readers have a keen interest in the rhetorical context of the text. When we speak of *rhetoric*, we mean the author's use of language for an intended effect. An important word here is *intended*. Both writing and reading are intentional. They are deliberate actions, guided by a purpose.

> Rhetorical context: author's purpose, author's intended audience, circumstances of production, author's position toward other texts, the larger conversation

When you do a close reading of the text focusing on its content, genre, organization, and stylistic features, you perform a **textual analysis**. Another type of analysis is also important: **rhetorical analysis**. Rhetorical analysis examines *the author's purpose and motivation for writing the text, the intended audience, the circumstances surrounding the text's production, the author's position toward other writers and other texts,* and *the larger conversation of which the text is a part.* It also explores *how the author's choice of genre, organizational structure, and stylistic features advances his or her purpose.* To perform a rhetorical analysis, ask yourself the questions in the box below.

QUESTIONS FOR ANALYZING THE RHETORICAL CONTEXT OF TEXTS

- What is the author's purpose? What do I perceive as the effect the author intends to have on the audience? What role does the author assume in relation to the audience?
- What do I know about the author's background and credibility?
- How does the choice of genre, organizational structure, and stylistic features advance the author's purpose?
- For whom is the author writing? In what type of publication—scholarly journal, popular magazine, local or national newspaper—was the text first published? Who reads this publication?
- In what year was the text published? What was on people's minds? Is the text current or dated?
- What feeling, event, phenomenon, circumstance, or social practice prompted the author to write the text?
- How is the author drawing on other writers and other texts? How does he or she view what others have said about the topic?

You can answer some of these questions by drawing inferences from the text itself. Other questions require you to undertake research.

Equally important as the environment in which the author writes the text is the environment in which the reader receives it. You also need to consider the rhetorical context of the **act of reading**—*the reader's purpose and the circumstances surrounding the reading.* In this section, we explain how to analyze both contexts as a means of improving comprehension.

Rhetorical Context of the Text

We have depicted the rhetorical context of the text in the diagram in Figure 1–1.

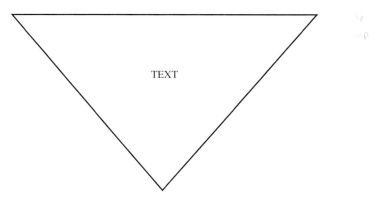

RHETORICAL CONTEXT OF A TEXT

AUTHOR/WRITER

- What is the author's purpose?
- What do I perceive as the effect the author intends to have on the audience?
- What do I know about the author's background and credibility?
- How does the author's choice of genre, organizational structure, and stylistic features advance his or her purpose?

AUDIENCE/READER

- For whom is the author writing?
- Where was the text first published?
- Who reads this publication?

TEXT

CIRCUMSTANCES SURROUNDING TEXT'S PRODUCTION/ LARGER CONVERSATION OF WHICH THE TEXT IS A PART

- In what year was the text published? What was on people's minds?
- What prompted the author to write the text? Can I identify a circumstance, event, or social practice?
- How is the author drawing on other writers and other texts? How does he or she view what others have said about the topic?

Figure 1–1

Our diagram is based on the classic communication triangle. There are three points of the triangle: the writer, the reader, and the circumstances surrounding the text's production. Each point influences the others; and all directly inform how the reader responds to the text. To illustrate the process of analyzing the rhetorical context of a text, we will use Andrew J. Cherlin's "The Origins of the Ambivalent Acceptance of Divorce," pages 433–39, as an example. Study the diagram, read Cherlin's article, and then read the sections devoted to the various questions.

- *What is the author's purpose? What do I perceive as the effect the author intends to have on the audience? What role does the author assume in relation to the audience?* From the article's title, "The Origins of the Ambivalent Acceptance of Divorce," we can infer that Cherlin will explain the origins of Americans' ambivalent acceptance of divorce. He hopes to convince his readers that historically, Americans have lamented divorce and divorce-based single-parenthood but believed that sometimes divorce is inevitable and acceptable. On the other hand, historically there has been no acceptance of nonmarital childbearing. The writer's purpose may not be obvious, but if you ask the right questions, you will discover the imperative—the feeling, view, incident, or phenomenon—that inspired the author to write. You'll be entering the author's conversation in a meaningful way.

- *What do I know about the author's background and credibility?* Cherlin is a distinguished professor of public policy and sociology at a major university, and he has recently published two books on American families. It seems reasonable to conclude that he is a respected authority in the field of family studies.

- *How does the choice of genre, organizational structure, and stylistic features advance the author's purpose?* In order to answer this question, you need to step back to ask how the author uses various rhetorical strategies to achieve a particular effect. As we discovered earlier, Cherlin wants to convince his readers that Americans have had a long-standing ambivalence toward divorce and divorce-based single-parenthood, but that historically they have rejected single women who bear children outside of marriage. In the opening paragraph, Cherlin explains that he is responding to a claim made by Margaret Usdansky, a sociologist who studied depictions of single-parent families in samples of popular magazines. Usdansky argues that over time, divorce-based single-parenthood became prevalent and as a result, today it is readily accepted, whereas nonmarital childbearing is still stigmatized. In the second paragraph, Cherlin questions Usdansky's suggestion that prevalence results in acceptance. He notes that nonmarital childbearing has also become much more common, yet it is not accepted. In the remainder of the article, Cherlin builds his case by providing an historical analysis of Americans' attitudes toward divorce and nonmarital childbearing from colonial times to the present.

    A closer look at the stylistic features of the article reveals that Cherlin uses straightforward language that will appeal to his readers. And he draws extensively from scholarly sources to demonstrate his command of the material.

- *For whom is the author writing? In what type of publication—scholarly journal, popular magazine, local or national newspaper—was the text first published? Who reads this publication?* Proficient writers tailor their texts to their readers. If you can identify the audience, you're well on your way to determining what the author is trying to accomplish. An important factor is where the text was published. Academic writers address the university community, whereas staff writers for magazines such as *Newsweek* or *Time* write for general audiences. Writers may address readers of a particular political persuasion. For example, writers for the *National Review* anticipate a readership that is conservative whereas writers for *The Nation* expect their readers to be liberal. Cherlin's article originally appeared in the *Journal of Marriage and Family*. For the past seventy years, the *Journal of Marriage and Family* has been the leading research journal in the field of family studies. The journal is read by scholars, teachers, and students interested in various aspects of family life.

- *In what year was the text published? What was on people's minds? Is the text current or dated?* The article originally appeared in the May 2009 issue of the *Journal of Marriage and Family*. In the United States, sixty percent of marriages currently end in divorce, and the number of nonmarital births continues to increase steeply.

- *What feeling, event, phenomenon, circumstance, or social practice prompted the author to write the text?* The first two paragraphs of the article identify the phenomenon that impelled Cherlin to write: Usdansky's research on the content of magazine and journal articles. She found a gradual acceptance of divorce-based single-parenthood but a continued rejection of nonmarital childbearing. Usdansky suggests that divorce-based single parents are accepted because they are so prevalent. Cherlin maintains that this is an incomplete explanation, and he goes on to argue that Americans have been ambivalent toward divorce since the colonial era.

- *How is the author drawing on other writers and other texts? How does he or she view what others have said about the topic?* Many academic texts are multivocal because they represent the voices of many different writers. As we noted earlier, academic writers often draw on the words and utterances of other writers. Sometimes the author simply mentions another writer or text. Other times, the author quotes, paraphrases, or summarizes other writers or texts. Authors draw on different texts to acknowledge what various individuals have written about the topic, to provide the reader with background information, to support their position, and to develop their argument.

We can categorize the ways authors use sources to build arguments according to the following scheme. A writer constructs a one-dimensional argument by presenting a thesis and supporting it with texts that argue a similar viewpoint. A writer creates a two-dimensional argument by drawing on sources for direct support and also for counter-arguments. Such a two-dimensional argument anticipates and deals with views that are contrary to those of the writer. Cherlin relies heavily on secondary sources. His four-page article contains seventeen footnotes. His argument is two-dimensional. It refutes a claim made by another researcher. In making his case, Cherlin draws on other texts to "place Usdansky's late-20th-century findings in context" (434).

EXERCISE 1.7

As a homework assignment, your professor will assign one of the selections in the anthology section of this book. In class, form collaborative learning groups and assign one of the Questions for Analyzing the Rhetorical Context of Texts, page 28, to each group.

Reconvene the entire class. On the chalkboard, construct a triangle similar to the diagram we presented on page 29. As each group representative reads the group's answers to the rhetorical reading question, have someone record the answers on the diagram. After all have been heard from, the entire class can discuss any points on which students disagree.

Rhetorical Context of Your Own Reading

As a critical reader, you should be just as aware of the circumstances surrounding your own reading and writing process as you are of the circumstances surrounding the production of text(s) you are reading. Take the book you are reading right now. We wrote Part I with you in mind. We address the text directly to students in a college writing class. We selected the readings in Part II with you in mind, but the authors of these selections wrote them for other audiences in response to other rhetorical situations. All were originally published elsewhere. For example, Herbert J. Gans addresses readers of *Dissent* in "The War Against the Poor Instead of Programs to End Poverty." *Dissent* is a quarterly magazine of politics and culture, and its readership consists of people from all walks of life in the general public. It is important to acknowledge that the audience a writer has in mind is not the only audience that ends up reading the text.

When you read texts, enunciate clear-cut rhetorical goals. In college writing courses, you will be expected to write about reading sources. If your assignment is to summarize the text, read with the goal of extracting and rewording main ideas. If your assignment is to write a critical analysis of a text, read to examine its various elements and judge them according to a set of established criteria.

> Assignments:
>
> - detailed and directive
> - loosely structured and open-ended

Analyze Writing Assignments

The first step is to be sure you understand the writing assignment. In college, you will receive writing assignments that include detailed directions and explicit criteria and writing assignments that are more loosely structured and open-ended. Read the assignment two or three times, underline key words that are crucial to your aim and purpose, and ask yourself the questions in the box below.

These questions will help you develop a mind-set for the assignment and define a rhetorical purpose that will direct your work. If you are unable to answer them, ask your professor for additional information.

QUESTIONS FOR ANALYZING WRITING ASSIGNMENTS

- What is the topic or issue I will be writing about? Has the professor specified the topic and supplied all the readings? Do I have to select the readings and define and limit the topic myself?
- What task do I have to perform? What words serve as clues to the nature of this task? The list that follows includes typical directives for assignments. As you read each directive, speculate about what you would have to do.

Directives for Academic Assignments

abstract, agree (or disagree), analyze, appraise, argue, assess, classify, compare/contrast, convince, criticize, critique, defend, define, delineate, demonstrate, describe, differentiate, discuss, distinguish, establish cause-effect, estimate, evaluate, exemplify, explain, explore, expound on, furnish evidence, give examples, identify, illustrate, judge, list, make a case for or against, paraphrase, picture, predict, present, prove, recount, refute, relate, report, respond to, restate, review, show, solve, state, suggest, summarize, support, survey, trace

- Does the assignment require me to adopt a particular perspective on the issue, a recognizable genre, or a particular plan of development?
- Do I already hold a position on the issue that I intend to develop or defend?
- For whom am I writing—for the professor, classmates, or some other audience? What are the audience's expectations? How much knowledge does my audience have about the topic? Is the audience familiar with the reading source? Will I have to supply background information?
- What reading sources will I use? Will the professor allow me to include personal reactions, experiences, and subjective interpretations? Does the professor expect me to demonstrate knowledge I have acquired from lectures, discussions, or experiments as well as from readings? Am I limited in the number and kind of reference materials I can use?
- How shall I document and list my sources? Which style sheet shall I use?
- What is the approximate length of the paper?
- Does the professor expect me to submit preliminary drafts as well as the final copy?

EXERCISE 1.8

Examine the assignments presented below by writing out answers to the Questions for Analyzing Writing Assignments. Make note of the questions you are unable to answer. When you have finished, exchange your work with a peer and discuss any of your answers that differ.

Assignments

- When you were growing up, were you ever involved in class wars? When did you first become conscious of social class, social stratification, and economic inequality? Write a narrative essay recounting your experiences.

- Write a critical analysis of Benazir Bhutto's argument about the difference between reactionary Islam and progressive Islam, with particular attention to her interpretation of Islamic teaching about women's equality with men and their mutual capacity for public action and political leadership. Address your essay to a student who might have a different assessment of Islamic teaching.

- Drawing on Isabel Allende's "The Proper Respect" and Bharati Mukherjee's "Jasmine," write a five- to six-page essay in which you evaluate the two authors' narrative representations of outsiders' efforts to succeed as insiders in multicultural societies. Address your essay to members of the academic community at large as a critical review in your college newspaper.

WORKS CITED

Browning, Dominique. "House Thinking." *New York Times Book Review* 26 Mar. 2006. Print.

"Chocolate." *Chocolate: Directory of Chocolatiers*, n.d. Web. 18 Mar. 2006.

Frost, Robert. "The Road Not Taken." *Complete Poems.* New York: Henry Holt, 1949. Print.

Maltby, John, Liza Day, Lynn E. McCutcheon, James Houran, and Diane Ashe. "Extreme Celebrity Worship, Fantasy Proneness and Dissociation: Developing the Measurement and Understanding of Celebrity Worship within a Clinical Personality Context." *Personality and Individual Differences* 40.2 (2006): 273–83. Web. 18 Mar. 2006.

Miller, Carolyn. "Genre as Social Action." *Quarterly Journal of Speech* 70 (1984): 151–67. Web. 18 Mar. 2006.

Shakespeare, William. *Hamlet.* Ed. Robert S. Miola. New York: Norton, 2010. Print.

Twain, Mark. *Tom Sawyer.* Ed. Robert H. Hirst et al. *The Mark Twain Library.* Berkeley, CA: U of California P, 2010. 3. Print.

Whitley, Bernard E., Jr., and Patricia Keith-Spiegel. *Academic Dishonesty, An Educator's Guide.* Mahwah, NJ: Erlbaum, 2002. Print.

Responses, Paraphrases, Summaries, and Quotations

In Chapter 1, you learned the importance of *prereading*—previewing the text, freewriting, and setting your goals—and *close reading*—marking, annotating, elaborating on, and posing questions about (1) content; (2) genre, organization, and stylistic features; and (3) rhetorical context. After your close reading of the text, you enter a phase we call *postreading*. **Postreading** is *the period in which you revisit, reread, and reexamine the text*. It is also the time for transforming yourself from a reader to a writer.

We recommend that before you make the transition from reader to writer, you take time to reflect on the text you have just comprehended. Focus on your experience of reading the text for your own enjoyment. Express your personal thoughts about it, and connect it to your real-life experiences. This mode of response will make you more aware of what you bring to the text as a reader. Your personal experiences may cause you to react in certain ways, and they may draw you to certain compelling words, phrases, and sentences that record your conversation with the text.

In the postreading phase of the reading-writing process, you will revisit, reread, and reexamine the text in other ways. Whenever you intend to draw on reading sources in your future writing, take some time immediately after reading to paraphrase, summarize, or quote passages that may be particularly useful as a record of your conversation with the text. You will continue to paraphrase, summarize, and quote as you compose and revise your essay, but you are best prepared to do this while the reading is still fresh in your mind. Remember that one of the chief goals of active reading is to eliminate the need for rereading the source when you sit down to draft your essay.

■ WRITE AN INFORMAL RESPONSE

Open your writer's notebook and draft a page or two, writing freely in response to self-directed prompts or respond to the questions in the box below. The purpose of this exercise is to write from a personal point of view. Bring emotion, personal association, and narrative to bear on the text, and react from your own interpretive framework.

PROMPTS FOR PERSONAL RESPONSE TO THE TEXT

- How do the ideas in the text connect with my own life? What associations can I make?
- What experiences do I recall?
- What images does the text create in my mind?
- Am I drawn to particular words, phrases, or sentences?
- Is there anything in the text that I agree with, reject, or wonder about?
- Does the text contain ideas that lead me to speculate, reflect, or make predictions?
- What else in the text do I relate to?

EXERCISE 2.1

Read the article by Ronna Vanderslice, "When I Was Young, an A Was an A: Grade Inflation in Higher Education," printed below. The author is a professor of education at Southwestern Oklahoma State University, and her article was published in 2004 in *Phi Kappa Phi Forum*. This publication is the quarterly magazine of Phi Kappa Phi, an honor society for faculty and students in colleges and universities.

After you've read the article, analyze it by using the critical reading strategies you learned in Chapter 1. Ask and answer questions about its content (p. 14); genre, organization, and stylistic features (p. 21, pp. 26–27); and rhetorical context (p. 28).

RONNA VANDERSLICE

WHEN I WAS YOUNG, AN A WAS AN A: GRADE INFLATION IN HIGHER EDUCATION*

People often criticize elementary and secondary schools for their low standards and elevated grades. Political candidates use higher standards in education as a platform for their campaigns; yet institutions of higher education cannot deny the statistics: only 10 to 20 percent of all college students receive grades lower than a B–. This figure means that between 80 and 90 percent of all college students receive grades of either A or B (Farley, cited in Sonner). In 1969, 7 percent of all students received grades of A– or higher. By 1993, this proportion had risen to 26 percent. In contrast, grades of C or less moved from 25 percent in 1969 to 9 percent in 1993. The pattern, which continues today, reveals an issue that concerns academicians and the general public alike.

One may wonder why this is a problem. For one, employers seem very concerned that good grades on transcripts have very little meaning. It is extremely difficult to differentiate between competent students and incompetent ones by viewing a transcript from most institutions of higher education today. Also, students may be left with an incorrect picture of their own competence. Most importantly, how grades relate to student learning and understanding is not clear. Variety in grading practices across disciplines and between institutions further complicates the question of what exactly an A means.

Universities must initiate reforms that increase standards instead of decreasing them. Even though some educators clearly see the wrong in grade inflation, for others it has become such a routine that universities must be explicit in their plan of remedy for this situation. A head-on approach that has been used lately is to include on student transcripts not only the grade for the class, but also the average grade for all students enrolled in the class. Indiana University, Eastern Kentucky University, and Dartmouth College are institutions that have used some type of indexing system. Harvey Mansfield, a longtime critic of grade inflation, uses a similar approach within his own classroom at Harvard University, giving each student two grades: one for the registrar and the public record, and the other in private. The private grades give students a realistic, useful assessment of how well they did and where they stand in relation to others.

Indiana University also proposed a three-year moratorium on the use of student evaluations in personnel decisions as a method to curb the problem of too many high grades. The university believes that removing concerns over student complaints about receiving lower grades might motivate all instructors to reset their standards, free from the pressures to give A's in exchange for high evaluations (McSpirit). Felton recommends that universities rethink the validity of student-opinion surveys as a measure of teaching effectiveness.

Other institutional practices include requiring schools and departments to review grading practices with the goal of bringing rigor to their programs. An emphasis in student recruitment on what is expected of students in terms of academic preparation also may be worthwhile (Wilson). In addition, faculty should take an active approach in insisting that academic standards are an essential part of the academic ethic and that by rewarding mediocrity, we discourage excellence (Wilson). Simply recognizing that grade inflation devalues your content to students is a necessary step in the right direction. Wilson points out that grade inflation reveals a loss of faculty morale. It signifies that professors care less about their teaching. Anyone who cares a lot about something is very critical in making judgments about it. Far from the opposite of caring, being critical is the very consequence of caring.

REFERENCES

Felton, J. et al. "Web-based Student Evaluations of Professors: The Relations between Perceived Quality, Easiness, and Sexiness." *Assessment and Evaluation in Higher Education*, 29.1 (2004): 91–109.

Mansfield, H. C. "Grade Inflation: It's Time to Face the Facts." *Chronicle of Higher Education*, 47.30 (2001): B24.

McSpirit, S. "Faculty Opinion on Grade Inflation: College and University." *The Journal of the American Association of Collegiate Registrars*, 75.3 (2000): 19–26.

Sonner, B. A. "A Is for 'Adjunct': Examining Grade Inflation in Higher Education." *Journal of Education for Business*, 76.1 (2000): 5–9.

Wilson, B. P. "The Phenomenon of Grade Inflation in Higher Education." *National Forum*, 79.4 (1999): 38–41.

EXERCISE 2.2

When you have completed your close reading of the text, use the prompts we have provided to write a personal response of at least 100 words.

After you have written your response, break into groups of three. Each student will read his or her response to the rest of the group. Then, as a group, read the sample student response below. Compare it to the responses you shared in your groups.

STUDENT'S PERSONAL RESPONSE

I question whether grade inflation is as widespread as Vanderslice claims. My writing teacher told the class not to expect high grades because the average grade for all sixty sections of the composition courses is between a B– and a C+. At my college 80 and 90 percent of students aren't getting As and Bs.

The solutions aren't very appealing to students. I'm already hyper about grades. I don't need two grades instead of one. I don't care if my B– in English is below the class average of B+. I do my best. I'm not trying to be better than everyone else. I feel the same about public grades and private grades. They focus on competition. Ever since kindergarten, I've been compared to my peers. I want to reduce the emphasis on grades. If we must have them, one is enough. I think the proposal to get rid of student evaluations is self-serving on the teachers' part. If they're going to do that, they should also get rid of professors' evaluations of students.

■ CONVERT INFORMAL RESPONSE TO RESPONSE ESSAY

Occasionally, professors ask students to write formal essays in response to designated texts. Your informal postreading response can serve as the basis for this type of formal response essay. Consider the following assignment:

Write a brief essay in response to one of the reserve readings on grade inflation.

The assignment does not ask you to draw exclusively on personal experience. Nor does it require you to draw exclusively on the reading source. It asks you to relate your own ideas to those in the text—and in so doing to present an *informed* outlook. Using the student response to Ronna Vanderslice's "When I Was Young, an A Was an A: Grade Inflation in Higher Education," we will show you how to write an essay that balances personal expression and textual content.

■ Compose a Thesis

Your first move is to compose a thesis. A **thesis** is *the central idea you intend to develop in your essay.* In a response essay, the thesis expresses the writer's overall reaction to the text; for example, agreement and disagreement, criticism and speculation, qualifications and extensions.

Thesis: the central idea in the essay, the motor of the essay.

Reread the student response on page 38 and characterize the student's reaction to the text. In her opening sentence, the student says she thinks Vanderslice is exaggerating the problem of grade inflation. Later she questions Vanderslice's solutions for dealing with the problem. Thus, her overall response is to question and disagree with the text. This goal is central to her response essay. For the present, her preliminary or working thesis is "Vanderslice has exaggerated the problem of grade inflation and offered unsatisfactory solutions."

■ Move from Writer-Based Prose to Reader-Based Prose

As you transfrom your informal personal response into a formal response essay, you should be aware of two important concepts: writer-based prose and reader-based prose. **Writer-based prose** is *writing for self* whereas **reader-based prose** is *writing for others*. Writer-based prose is egocentric. The ideas make sense to the writer, but the writer makes minimal if any effort to communicate the ideas to someone else. You can compare writer-based prose to a set of personal notes in which the writer puts down information that is meaningful personally but may not make sense to a larger audience. In contrast, reader-based prose clearly conveys ideas to other people. The writer does not assume that the reader will understand automatically but, rather, provides information that will facilitate the reader's comprehension. It is easy to forget about the audience amid all the complications in producing the first draft of an academic essay. That's why first drafts are quite often writer-based. An important function of revising is to convert this writer-based prose to something the reader can readily understand.

> Writer-based prose: writing for yourself
> Reader-based prose: writing for others to read

To convert an informal, writer-based personal response to a formal, reader-based response essay, follow the procedure in the box below.

CONVERTING AN INFORMAL PERSONAL RESPONSE TO A FORMAL RESPONSE ESSAY

- Reread your personal response and formulate a thesis.
- Convert writer-based prose to reader-based prose by:

  identifying the text and author

  summarizing the text

  making explicit connections between your personal reactions and the target text

  changing casual language to more formal prose

  adding a title

  citing and documenting the source

EXERCISE 2.3

This exercise is divided into two parts: a homework assignment and an in-class collaborative writing assignment.

Homework assignment: Reread Ronna Vanderslice's "When I Was Young, an A Was an A: Grade Inflation in Higher Education" on pages 36–37 and the student personal response on page 38. Use the procedure in the box above to convert the personal response to a response essay. Make two copies of your essay and bring it to the next class.

In-class assignment: Divide the class into groups of three. Each student should distribute the copies of his or her essay to the other students in the group and then read his or her essay to the group. When everyone has had a turn, compose a group essay by drawing on the positive features of each student's essay. Then read the sample response essay printed below. Compare your group essay to the sample and make revisions as necessary.

SAMPLE RESPONSE ESSAY

CENTER TITLE   AUTHOR'S LAST NAME   PAGE NUMBER

1/2"
Sarver 1

Julian Sarver

English 12

Professor Stearns

September 23, 2006

Perspectives on Grade Inflation

Is grade inflation so serious a problem that professors should change the way they grade their students? Ronna Vanderslice, a professor of education at Southwestern Oklahoma State University, thinks grade inflation is a major issue that colleges and universities need to address. According to Vanderslice, forty years ago very few students received high grades. Now most receive As and Bs. In "When I Was Young, an A Was an A: Grade Inflation in Higher Education," Vanderslice suggests a number of reforms that will curb grade inflation and raise standards. I question whether grade inflation is as widespread as Vanderslice claims, and I have grave reservations about the solutions she proposes.

Vanderslice writes that "grades of C or less moved from 25 percent in 1969 to 9 percent in 1993," and today they continue to spiral upward. My writing teacher told our class not to expect high grades because the average grade for all sixty sections of the composition courses is between a B- and a C+. This leads me to question Vanderslice's claim that "between 80 and 90 percent of all college students receive grades of A or B" (24). That is not happening at my college.

Even if grade inflation is getting out of hand, the solutions Vanderslice proposes are not very appealing to students. One suggestion

USE 8½" BY 11" PAPER FOR EACH PAGE. USE DOUBLE SPACES BETWEEN ALL LINES. LEFT-JUSTIFY ALL LINES IN THE TEXT OF THE PAPER. DO NOT RIGHT-JUSTIFY, EVEN IF YOUR WORD PROCESSOR PROVIDES THIS FEATURE.

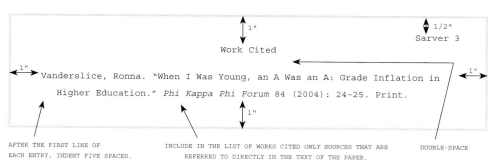

INDENT
FIVE SPACES

AUTHOR'S LAST NAME   PAGE NUMBER

1"
1/2"
Sarver 2

is "to include on student transcripts not only the grade for the class, but also the average grade for all students enrolled in the class" (24). I am already overly anxious about grades. I do not need two grades instead of one. I have no desire to know that my B- in English is below the class average of B+. I do my best. I am not trying to be better than everyone else.

A second suggestion is to give students public grades and private grades. Vanderslice explains, "The private grades give students a realistic, useful assessment of how well they did and where they stand in relation to others" (24). Again, the focus is on competition. Ever since kindergarten, I have been compared to my peers. I propose that we reduce the emphasis on grades. If we must have them, one is enough.

1"   1"

A third recommendation is to abolish students' evaluation of courses so that professors would be "free from the pressures to give A's in exchange for high evaluations" (24). I think this proposal is self-serving on the teachers' part. Colleges should eliminate professors' evaluations of students as well as students' evaluations of professors. This would lead to a healthier, less competitive atmosphere.

1"

1"
1/2"
Sarver 3

Work Cited

1"
Vanderslice, Ronna. "When I Was Young, an A Was an A: Grade Inflation in
    Higher Education." *Phi Kappa Phi Forum* 84 (2004): 24-25. Print.
1"

1"

AFTER THE FIRST LINE OF   INCLUDE IN THE LIST OF WORKS CITED *ONLY* SOURCES THAT ARE   DOUBLE-SPACE
EACH ENTRY, INDENT FIVE SPACES.   REFERRED TO DIRECTLY IN THE TEXT OF THE PAPER.

EXERCISE 2.4

Compare the student personal response on page 38 and the sample response essay on pages 40–41. On the response essay, mark and annotate the following elements:

Thesis

Identification of text and author

Summary of text

Explicit connections between the personal reactions and the target text

Places where casual language has been changed to more formal prose

Title

Citation and documentation of the text

Share your work with a peer and discuss any differences in your markings and annotations.

■ PARAPHRASE

When you **paraphrase** a sentence, paragraph, or other segment of a text, you *translate it into your own words.* Paraphrasing is a powerful operation for academic writing. Too often, beginning academic writers use direct quotations instead of paraphrases. Quotations are necessary only when you need the precise wording of the original. We will discuss reasons for quoting later in this chapter. Because paraphrasing is an active process that forces you to grapple with the text, it promotes comprehension. It is no wonder that professors ask students to paraphrase rather than quote. They know that if students can paraphrase a text, then they understand it.

> Paraphrase: an active effort to grasp all the meaning in a passage.

A paraphrase differs from a summary. *A paraphrase includes all the information in the original, whereas a summary contains only the most important ideas.* When you want to record the fully detailed meaning of a passage, paraphrase it. If you are interested only in the gist, write a summary. In general, relatively small sections of the original—often a sentence or two—are paraphrased, and larger chunks of text are summarized.

Paraphrasing requires you to make substantial changes to the vocabulary and sentence structure of the text. It is not enough to substitute a few synonyms and keep the same sentence structure and order of ideas. The following examples, based on an excerpt from Michael Heim's "From Interface to Cyberspace" (see Works Cited, p. 68), show adequate and inadequate paraphrases.

Original sentence: Virtual-reality systems can use cyberspace to represent physical space, even to the point that we feel telepresent in a transmitted scene, whether Mars or the deep ocean.

Inadequate paraphrase: Virtual-reality systems can represent physical space by using cyberspace, even to the extent that people feel telepresent in a scene that is transmitted, perhaps Mars or the deep ocean (Heim 80).

Adequate paraphrase: We can achieve the illusion of being present in remote locations, for example, the planet Mars or deep parts of the ocean, by using virtual-reality equipment that creates a cyberspace representation of real-world space (Heim 80).

The writer of the inadequate paraphrase shuffled the words in the original sentence but retained the vocabulary, sentence structure, and order of ideas. If you do not intend to make major changes to the passage, then quote it word for word.

■ Simplified Paraphrasing Procedures

You can sometimes paraphrase by using simple paraphrasing procedures. We will describe two of them: (1) look away from the text and restate the ideas, and (2) rewrite the original passage for a new audience.

Look Away from the Text and Restate the Ideas

We will illustrate this strategy with a passage from John J. Conley's "Narcissus Cloned" (see Works Cited, p. 67). Read the passage twice. Then ask yourself, "What is the main idea, and what are the details that support this idea?" Look away from the text and restate the main idea and details in your own words. Then look back at the text to check the accuracy of your paraphrase.

> *Text:* The task of developing a moral response to the advent of human cloning is rendered all the more problematic by the superficial debate our society is currently conducting on the issue. Whether on the editorial page of the *New York Times* or on Phil and Oprah's television screen, the discussion tends to obscure the key moral problems raised by this practice. (Conley 16)

The text asserts that it is difficult to formulate a moral response to the practice of human cloning because the public debate about it is so shallow. The text supports this assertion by pointing out that neither newspaper editorials nor talk shows give in-depth treatment of the topic. Looking away from the text, we come up with the following paraphrase:

> *Paraphrase:* Public debates about human cloning, especially what we read in newspaper editorials and see on talk shows, gloss over serious issues and are so shallow and superficial that it is difficult to develop a serious moral response to this new practice (Conley 16).

Next, we reread the original to check the accuracy of our paraphrase, and then we weave the paraphrase into our essay. We have summarized the procedure in the box below.

SIMPLIFIED PARAPHRASING PROCEDURE

- Read the passage two or three times.
- Ask yourself, "What is the main idea, and what are the details that support that idea?"
- Look away from the text and restate the main idea and details in your own words.
- Reread the original to check the accuracy of your paraphrase.
- Weave the paraphrase into your essay.
- Provide documentation.

Rewrite the Original Passage for a New Audience

Another simple procedure for paraphrasing is to rewrite the text for a new audience. To illustrate, look at the following sentence from "Being and Believing: Ethics of Virtual Reality," an editorial from a medical journal (see Works Cited, p. 67). The sentence describes a computer-based system (virtual reality) designed to simulate a real-world situation:

> The overall effect was that the observer experienced a computer-generated artificial or virtual reality (VR) whose credibility depended largely on the agreement between the simulated imagery and the familiar sensible world. (283)

Let's say your objective is to paraphrase the sentence for an audience of high-school students. You don't want to talk over the students' heads, so you put the sentence into simpler language:

> The effectiveness of a virtual reality system depends upon the extent to which it can create an environment of computer images that appear lifelike ("Being and Believing" 283).

Notice that the parenthetical documentation gives an abbreviated article title rather than an author's name. That is because the article was written by the medical journal's editorial staff and was not attributed to a specific author. To learn more about documentation conventions, see the Appendix.

EXERCISE 2.5

Break into pairs. Both students in the pair will use simplified procedures to paraphrase the same passage from Arthur Caplan's "The Trouble with Organ Trafficking" (p. 309). One student will look away from the text and restate the ideas and the other will rewrite the text for a new audience. When you have finished, compare your paraphrases and decide which is more accurate.

> Selling organs, even in a tightly regulated market, violates the existing bioethical framework of respect for persons since the sale is clearly being driven by profit. In the case of living persons it also violates the ethics of the health-care professions. (Caplan 309)

■ Systematic Paraphrasing Procedure

Paraphrasing often requires you to express abstract ideas in a more concrete form. When a passage includes difficult concepts and complex language, it may be hard to reword it and still preserve the original meaning. You will need a systematic paraphrasing procedure, such as the one in the following box.

SYSTEMATIC PARAPHRASING PROCEDURE

- Read the passage two or three times.
- Identify the major ideas.
- Change the order of major ideas, maintaining the logical connections among them.

- Substitute synonyms for words in the original, making sure the language in your paraphrase is appropriate for your audience.
- Combine or divide sentences as necessary.
- Compare the paraphrase with the original to make sure that the rewording is sufficient and the meaning has been preserved.
- Weave the paraphrase into your essay in accordance with your rhetorical purpose.
- Document the paraphrase.

Paraphrasing is not a lockstep process that always follows the same sequence. You may use fewer than all eight strategies or vary the order in which you apply them. For illustration, follow along as we paraphrase a sentence from Carl Sagan's *Broca's Brain* (see Works Cited, p. 68), using all the strategies in approximately the order listed. We are addressing an audience of first-year college students.

> There is nothing inhuman about an intelligent machine; it is indeed an expression of those superb intellectual capabilities that only human beings, of all the creatures on our planet, now possess. (Sagan 292)

Identify the Major Ideas

First, read the text two or three times to determine the major ideas.

Major ideas

There are two central points: (1) an assertion about intelligent machines: they are not inhuman, and (2) an argument to back up the assertion: that these machines demonstrate humans' unique intelligence.

1. There is nothing inhuman about an intelligent machine;
2. It is indeed an expression of those superb intellectual capabilities that only human beings, of all the creatures on our planet, now possess.

Change the Order of Ideas, Maintaining the Logical Connections Among Them

Next, change the order of the sentence, placing the second point before the first. To accommodate this switch, substitute the noun phrase *An intelligent machine* for *It* so that the subject is clear at the outset of the sentence. Then add *which demonstrates that* to indicate the logical relationship between the two units.

1. An intelligent machine is indeed an expression of those superb intellectual capabilities that only human beings, of all the creatures on our planet, now possess;
2. which demonstrates that there is nothing inhuman about an intelligent machine.

Reorder and connect.

Substitute Synonyms for Words in the Original

At this juncture, it is important to think about your audience. Sagan's language is easy to understand. If the words in the original text are too formal or sophisticated, choose vocabulary more accessible to your readers. Begin your search for synonyms *without* consulting a dictionary or a thesaurus. Many students rush to reference books and copy synonyms without considering how they fit into the general sense of the sentence. Paraphrases filled with synonyms taken indiscriminately from a dictionary or a thesaurus can be awkward and confusing.

> Search for synonyms.

As a rule of thumb, try not to repeat more than three consecutive words from the original. Occasionally, you may need to repeat a phrase, but whenever possible, substitute synonyms. You don't have to substitute a synonym for every word in the text. Repeat words that are central to the meaning or have no appropriate synonyms, such as the word "inhuman" in our example.

Returning to the example, by substituting synonyms, doing a little more rearranging, and providing context where necessary, you will arrive at the following paraphrase:

> Since artificial intelligence results from humans beings' unique intellectual talents, the technology should not be regarded as inhuman (Sagan 292).

Combine or Divide Sentences as Necessary

There is no particular need to divide the paraphrase, but for illustration we split it into two short sentences:

> Artificial intelligence results from humans beings' unique intellectual talents. Thus, the technology should not be regarded as inhuman (Sagan 292).

> Tighten or break down: combine or divide sentences.

Compare the Paraphrase with the Original

Compare the paraphrase with the original sentence to see if you have reworded sufficiently yet have retained the meaning of the original.

> Size up the texts.

Original: There is nothing inhuman about an intelligent machine; it is indeed an expression of those superb intellectual capabilities that only human beings, of all the creatures on our planet, now possess.

Paraphrase: Since artificial intelligence results from humans beings' unique intellectual talents, the technology should not be regarded as inhuman (Sagan 292).

In this case, the paraphrase seems adequate. In other cases, you might need to revise the paraphrase, possibly by reapplying one of the strategies we have already discussed.

Weave the Paraphrase into Your Essay

Weave the paraphrase into your essay in a way that helps further your rhetorical purpose.

> Blend into your own text.

Consider the following example:

Excerpt from essay: Even though we live in a technologically advanced society, many Americans still feel uncomfortable with the idea of machine intelligence. Science fiction abounds with stories of computers whose "inhuman" logic poses a threat to human values. But as Sagan points out, since artificial intelligence results from humans beings' unique intellectual talents, the technology should not be regarded as inhuman (292). These thinking machines are an extension of our own abilities rather than a challenge to our humanity.

Notice that we did not plop the paraphrase into the paragraph. Instead, we tried to show the role it plays in our conversation with the original text. Since Sagan's view contrasts with the point expressed in the preceding sentence, we began with the word "But." Then, we attributed the material to Sagan by writing "as Sagan points out." At the end of the sentence, we provided the page number in parentheses. A paraphrase is successful only to the extent that it fits smoothly into the essay for which it was intended.

Document Your Paraphrase

Failing to document a paraphrase is considered plagiarism, an offense that can have serious consequences. Always cite the author of the text, enclose the page numbers in parentheses, and provide an entry on the Works Cited page. Notice how we documented the paraphrase in the preceding example.

> - Cite your source.
> - Document your citation.

EXERCISE 2.6

Apply the steps in the Systematic Paraphrasing Procedure (pp. 44–45) to the following passage taken from Caroline Rubin's "The Gendered Language of Gamete 'Donation'" (pp. 313–19). Work through the steps in the process one by one and record the results of each step, just as we did on pages 45–47 with the sentence from Carl Sagan's book. Write your paraphrase for an audience of first-year college students who have not read the article.

> Egg donors are recruited with images of babies and families and appeals to altruism, while sperm donors are recruited with cartoon sperm and promises of high earnings potential and other personal benefits. Egg donors must profess a desire to help infertile couples start a family (even if in reality they are financially motivated) if they are to be accepted into a donation program, whereas sperm donors must simply have their medical history check out. (Rubin 318)

Revise your paraphrase. Submit with the final paraphrase all the preliminary work you produce at each stage of the paraphrasing process.

EXERCISE 2.7

Form collaborative learning groups of three students each. Have each group member take responsibility for one of the following passages from Pauline Irit Erera's "What Is a Family?" (pp. 416–28).

a. The decline in the number of babies placed for adoption precipitated an increased interest in international adoptions as an alternative. Because these adoptions often involved children who were racially and/or ethnically different from their adoptive parents, the adoption could not be kept secret as had been the practice in the past. The growing acceptance of adoptive families, in turn, facilitated a greater acceptance of stepfamilies and other families not related by blood. (420)

b. With the increasing numbers and visibility of single-parent, step-, and adoptive families, the gay liberation movement opened the way for the emergence of gay and lesbian families. Some gay men and lesbians were divorced and had custody of the children, becoming in the process single-parent families. Others chose to give birth to a child within the lesbian/gay relationship. (420)

c. Another factor contributing to family diversity since the 1970s, and especially to foster families and grandmother-headed families, has been a dramatic increase in the imprisonment of women and mothers, a legacy of the war on drugs with its harsh sentencing policies. Most of the women in prison are there for drug-related offenses, often because of the activities of a male partner. (420)

- Use the Systematic Paraphrasing Procedure (pp. 44–45) to paraphrase your passage. Write your paraphrase for an audience of first-year college students who have not read Erera's article.
- When all group members have finished their paraphrases, pass the sheet with your paraphrase to the person on your left and receive the paraphrase of the person on your right. On a new sheet of paper, paraphrase the passage you received from the person on your right. Do not refer to the original text.
- When all group members have finished their paraphrases, pass sheets once more to the left and again paraphrase the passage you receive.
- Your group should now have serial paraphrases that have gone through three versions for each of the passages from Erera. Working together, compare the original of each passage with the final version of the paraphrase. Does the paraphrase preserve the meaning of the original? If not, where did the meaning get lost? Which steps in the paraphrasing process worked well, and which were problematic? Make sure your group recorder notes the conclusions the group comes to.
- When the class reconvenes, have the recorders explain the conclusions groups reached about the paraphrasing process.

■ SUMMARIZE

Whether you are writing a standard summary, a brief abstract of a journal article, or a formal précis of an extended argument, your fundamental task is to capture the overall gist of the text, to shorten the original without changing its meaning.

> Summarize in broad strokes.

The following strategies will serve you well.

SUMMARIZING STRATEGIES

- Preview the text and recall your prior knowledge of the topic.
- Read the text using critical reading strategies (marking, annotating, elaborating, taking content notes, and posing and answering questions).
- Identify the most important ideas and the significant connections among those ideas.
- Delete unimportant detail, irrelevant examples, and redundancy.
- Identify and imitate the organizational pattern of the text.
- Construct a graphic overview.
- Identify and incorporate the rhetorical context and purpose.
- Combine ideas in sentences and paragraphs.
- Document your summary.

You need not apply these strategies in order. Nor do you have to use all nine of them. Choose ones that are appropriate for the source with which you are working. You can write a standard summary simply by explaining the rhetorical context and purpose. Lengthy, complex summaries may require the full range of strategies.

■ Standard Summary

You can construct a standard summary by using strategies that you will find useful for all summaries.

Apply Summarizing Strategies
Strategies for summarizing include:

Preview the Text, Recall Your Prior Knowledge of the Topic, and Use Critical Reading Strategies
The first two summarizing strategies recap the active reading techniques that we covered earlier. Assertive reading is imperative for summarizing. Marking and annotating main ideas, taking notes, and identifying the organization plan and rhetorical purpose and context are helpful preparation.

> Preview.

Identify the Most Important Ideas and the Significant Connections Among These Ideas
Your annotations and notes should direct you to the most important ideas in the text. Write out the main ideas and explain how they are related to each other. A summary is more than a retelling of main ideas; it should indicate relationships among the ideas and tie them together in coherent paragraphs.

Identify main ideas.

Delete Unimportant Detail, Irrelevant Examples, and Redundancy

Cross out or label as nonessential any material that is repetitive, excessively detailed, or unrelated to the main idea. Academic sources are often highly redundant because authors repeat or illustrate complex concepts in order to give the reader more than one chance to understand them.

Eliminate details.

Identify and Imitate the Organizational Pattern of the Source

On page 22, we identified nine organizational plans for academic writing: (1) time order, narration, process; (2) antecedent-consequent, cause-effect; (3) description; (4) statement-response; (5) comparison/contrast; (6) example; (7) analysis/classification; (8) definition; (9) analogy. Rarely do authors restrict themselves to a single plan; they usually use these plans in combination. When you identify the organizational pattern, you can follow it as the skeleton for your summary. Organization conveys meaning, so you will be helping your reader to follow the train of thought.

Determine organizational pattern.

Construct a Graphic Overview

A useful technique for identifying the principal ideas and determining how they tie together is to create a visual display. You may choose from among many different types of displays, including flow charts, spider maps, Venn diagrams, cluster diagrams, fishbone diagrams, sequence charts, column charts, and ladders. We will focus on the graphic overview. A **graphic overview** is *a diagram that represents the central ideas in a reading source, shows how they are related, and indicates the author's overall purpose.* It is a blueprint charting the text's main ideas.

Visual display: graphic overview

We will walk through the process of constructing a graphic overview. First, review your underlining, notes, and annotations, and select key words and concepts. Determine the overall organizational structure of the text and identify subsidiary organizational patterns. Then, depict the relationships among the ideas by drawing boxes or circles connected by lines or arrows. Label the boxes to show how the various points are interrelated. Be creative!

The graphic overview shown in Figure 2–1 was constructed by one of our students to represent the principal content of Ronna Vanderslice's "When I Was Young, an A Was an A: Grade Inflation in Higher Education," which appears on pages 36–37. Reread the article before you study the student's graphic overview. Keep in mind that creating a graphic overview is a highly individual process. A single, definitive graphic overview does not exist for each text. Countless variations are possible.

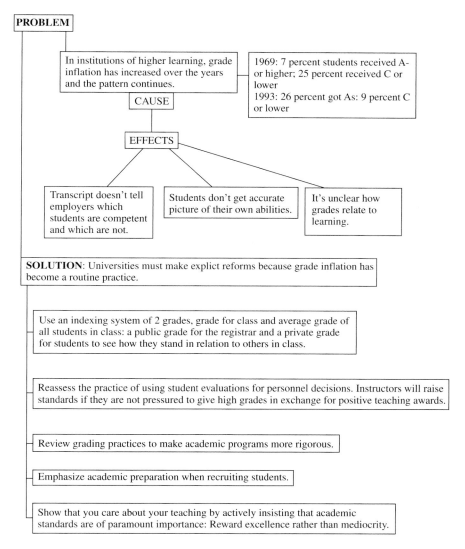

Figure 2–1   Sample Graphic Overview

The graphic overview forces you to think about the big picture. You have to manipulate chunks of information like pieces in a puzzle and determine how they best fit together. The graphic overview allows you to visualize relationships among main ideas and perceive the text's web of meaning. Notice that the overview of Vanderslice's article highlights the central organizational pattern of problem-solution as well as the secondary pattern of cause-effect. You should find it easy to summarize this source after you have seen its main ideas diagrammed on a single page.

You can make a graphic overview of a text of any length—a single paragraph, sequence of paragraphs, or complete article—but the strategy works best if you fit the diagram on a single page so that you can see it all at once. This limits the amount of detail in the graphic overview, but if you cram in lots of details, you will soon lose sight of the big picture. The graphic overview works best for recording the general outlines of an argument. When you are working with lengthy texts and want more than a broad outline, you may find the one-page format too restrictive.

You may wish to work with computer-generated graphic overviews. We provide directions for creating a simple graphic overview with Microsoft Word 97–2004. If you are working with other word-processing software, consult the software's Help directory and search for "diagrams."

DIRECTIONS FOR CREATING A GRAPHIC OVERVIEW WITH MICROSOFT WORD

1. Open a blank Word document.
2. Go up to the main menu bar and click **Insert**.
3. Select **Text Box** from the Insert menu. A box will be displayed. Select the box by clicking on it.
4. Click on the corner of the box and drag your mouse to make the box the size you want it. Then click outside the box to deselect it.
5. Click inside the box and type in words and sentences.
6. Create additional boxes by repeating Steps 3, 4, and 5.
7. Move boxes around by selecting them (click on the edge). With your cursor on the edge, drag the box around the page.
8. Connect the boxes with the following procedure:
   - Go up to the Main menu and click on **View**. Scroll down to Toolbars.
   - From the Toolbar menu, select **Drawing**. The Drawing toolbar contains a button with a line on it. Click on this button to highlight it.
   - Bring your cursor to the edge of one box and drag it to the edge of a second box. A line will appear. Each time you wish to draw a line, go back to the line button and highlight it.
   - To delete boxes and lines, click on the edge of the box or on the line to highlight it. Then press **Delete**.

Before we show you how to convert a graphic overview to a written summary, we need to remind you about the importance of the rhetorical context of the text.

Identify and Incorporate the Rhetorical Context and Purpose

Your summary needs to include information about the rhetorical context of the text. This is particularly true if it is a stand-alone summary rather than one that will become part of a longer essay.

Rhetorical context and rhetorical purpose

To determine the rhetorical context, ask yourself the Questions for Analyzing the Rhetorical Context of Texts on page 28. Rhetorical purpose refers to how the author tries to affect or influence the audience. Sometimes the purpose is easily identified because it emerges as a controlling feature of the piece, such as in an argumentative text or a highly opinionated editorial. At other times the purpose may not be self-evident.

As the following summary of Ronna Vanderslice's "When I Was Young, an A Was an A: Grade Inflation in Higher Education" (see pp. 36–37) illustrates, once you have identified the rhetorical context and purpose, you have launched a concise summary.

SAMPLE BRIEF SUMMARY OF RONNA VANDERSLICE'S "WHEN I WAS YOUNG, AN A WAS AN A: GRADE INFLATION IN HIGHER EDUCATION"

In her article "When I Was Young, an A Was an A: Grade Inflation in Higher Education," Ronna Vanderslice, a professor of education at Southwestern Oklahoma State University, asserts that grade inflation is an increasingly serious problem that universities must counteract. She develops her position by pointing out that college transcripts no longer give accurate information to students or to their potential employers. Writing in Phi Kappa Phi Forum, she urges university faculty to reform their grading practices and offers various suggestions for doing so.

Combine Ideas in Sentences and Paragraphs

For your summary to flow clearly, you need to take the key ideas you have depicted in your graphic overview, make elements parallel, or add logical connectors. You may also compress several words or phrases into fewer words and reduce items in the same class to a single category.

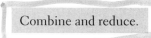

Combine and reduce.

Document Your Summary

Even when you have summarized a text in your own words, you must acknowledge the title and the author. As with paraphrasing, summarizing a source without proper documentation is considered plagiarism. Always cite the text at the point where you use it in your writing and include a complete reference in the works cited list at the end of your paper. We explain how to set up a works cited list in the Appendix.

Document your citation.
Cite your sources.

Now we will draw on several of the strategies described above to illustrate the process of writing a summary. Let's assume that you are preparing to write an essay on grade inflation. You locate the Vanderslice article on pages 36–37. You read the article using the active strategies we described earlier—carefully previewing, annotating, taking notes, and posing and answering questions as you read. After identifying the main ideas and significant connections among them, you delete unimportant details and examples. Then, using the text's organizational pattern as your cue, you construct a graphic overview. (See Figure 2–1, p. 51.) You identify the rhetorical context of Vanderslice's article. Lastly, using the graphic overview as your guide, you combine ideas in sentences and paragraphs and compose the summary.

SAMPLE SUMMARY

Summary of Ronna Vanderslice's "When I Was Young, an A was an A: Grade Inflation in Higher Education"

In her article "When I Was Young, an A Was an A: Grade Inflation in Higher Education," Ronna Vanderslice, a professor of education at Southwestern Oklahoma State University, asserts that we should be concerned about increasing incidents of grade inflation in colleges and universities. As a result of this lowering of standards, college transcripts do not tell employers which students are competent and which are not. Students themselves are not getting accurate pictures of their abilities. Most important, there is no clear standard of how grades relate to learning.

Vanderslice asserts that universities must make explicit reforms to halt this routine practice. She offers a number of concrete suggestions for raising standards. One recommendation is to use an indexing system of two grades, the grade for the class and the average grade of all the students in the class: a public grade for the registrar and a private grade for students to see how they stand in relation to their peers.

Another suggestion is to reassess the practice of using student evaluations for personnel decisions. Instructors will raise their standards if they are not pressed to give high grades in exchange for positive teaching evaluations. Other recommendations are for professors to review their grading practices to make academic programs more rigorous, for college recruiters to make students aware of the academic preparation they will need, and for professors to show they care about their teaching by actively insisting that academic standards are of paramount importance and by rewarding excellence instead of mediocrity.

Work Cited

Vanderslice, Ronna. "When I Was Young, an A Was an A: Grade Inflation in Higher Education." Phi Kappa Phi Forum 84 (2004): 24–25. Print.

EXERCISE 2.8

Read a selection from Part II of this book. Use the summarizing strategies we have discussed to produce a 250-word summary of the text. Write for an audience of first-year college students who have not read the article. Submit your graphic overview as well as the final summary.

EXERCISE 2.9

First-Day Activities:

- Form collaborative learning groups of five students each.
- Assign to each group one of the reading selections from Part II of this book. Each group should work with a different text. Group members should read their articles outside class.

Second-Day Activities:

- Divide into collaborative groups.

- Working as a group and following the steps outlined in this chapter, produce a graphic overview and a 250-word summary of your article. You may want to work through each step in the process together, with the recorder noting the results of your discussion. Write for an audience of first-year college students who have not read the article.

- Reconvene the entire class. Each group recorder should read the group's summary and describe any problems the group encountered.

◾ The Abstract

An **abstract** is *a brief summary*, often only a paragraph or two. It usually appears after the title of a paper and before the longer text itself, though sometimes it is presented on a separate page. Abstracts often accompany lab reports, journal articles, grant proposals, and conference presentations. They can also be published as stand-alone documents. When you conduct research, you will use databases of abstracts, for example, *Periodical Abstracts*, *Social Science Abstracts*, or *Education Abstracts*.

> The abstract: a very brief, descriptive key tool.

The purpose of an abstract is to give readers a descriptive summary of information that will help them decide if it is worth their time to read the entire article. Chapter 12 in Part II of this book contains articles on the changing American family. Let's say you have read these articles and are conducting further research on children in single-parent families. In the database *Social Science Abstracts*, you locate a reference to "Family Structure Effects on Parenting Stress and Practices in the African American Family," an article by Daphne S. Cain and Terri Combs-Orme published in June 2005 in the *Journal of Sociology and Social Welfare*:

FAMILY STRUCTURE EFFECTS ON PARENTING STRESS AND PRACTICES IN THE AFRICAN AMERICAN FAMILY*

CAIN, DAPHNE S.; COMBS-ORME, TERRI

Journal of Sociology and Social Welfare v. 32 no. 2 (June 2005) pp. 19–40

Abstract: The predominant approach to African-American parenting research focuses on disadvantages associated with single parenthood to the exclusion of other issues. The current research suggests that this does not represent the diversity in family structure configurations among African-American families, nor does it give voice to the parenting resilience of single mothers. We argue that rather than marital status or family configuration, more attention needs to be given to the inadequacy of resources for this population. In the current study, we examined the parenting of infants by African-American mothers and found that mothers' marital status and family configuration did not affect parenting stress or practices. This suggests, then, that single mothers parent as well as their married, partnered, and multigenerational

*Reprinted by permission of School of Social Work, Western Michigan University.

counterparts. It seems that the economic status and parenting perceptions of mothers contributed more to parenting stress than did marital status or family structure. Our study, then, challenges the accepted wisdom in our political and popular culture that has insisted upon the centrality of the nuclear family to all aspects of familial and even national health. Instead, we have shown that a true commitment to strong families and healthy children begins with a focus on the debilitating effects of poverty in the African-American community.

After reading the abstract, you decide whether it will be worth your while to read the twenty-one-page article.

Components of an Abstract

An examination of the sample abstract reveals the following components:

- Title and Author Information

    "Family Structure Effects on Parenting Stress and Practices in the African American Family"

    Cain, Daphne S.; Combs-Orme, Terri

    Journal of Sociology and Social Welfare v. 32 no. 2 (June 2005) pp. 19–40

- Objective, purpose, question, or problem—what the author is researching or demonstrating

    "We argue that rather than marital status or family configuration, more attention needs to be given to the inadequacy of resources for this population."

- Why the research is important

    "The predominant approach to African-American parenting research focuses on disadvantages associated with single parenthood to the exclusion of other issues. The current research suggests that this does not represent the diversity in family structure configurations among African-American families, nor does it give voice to the parenting resilience of single mothers."

- Methods or design—how the topic was studied or how the study was implemented

    "In the current study, we examined the parenting of infants by African-American mothers."

- Results or outcomes—what the researcher discovered

    "… and found that mothers' marital status and family configuration did not affect parenting stress or practices. This suggests, then, that single mothers parent as well as their married, partnered, and multigenerational counterparts. It seems that the economic status and parenting perceptions of mothers contributed more to parenting stress than did marital status or family structure."

- Conclusions, implications, or further questions

    "Our study, then, challenges the accepted wisdom in our political and popular culture that has insisted upon the centrality of the nuclear family to all aspects of familial and even national health. Instead, we have shown that a true commitment to strong families and healthy children begins with a focus on the debilitating effects of poverty in the African-American community."

The abstract follows the sequence of the original text, and it is written in a style that is clear, concise, and direct.

Writing an Abstract of Your Own Work

If you receive an assignment to write an abstract of a published journal article or of an essay, project, or study you have undertaken, keep in mind that your goal is to give readers a mini version of the text so that they can decide if it is worthwhile to read the entire document. Include the essential components.

COMPONENTS OF AN ABSTRACT

- Title and author information
- Objective, purpose, question, or problem—what researcher has researched or demonstrated
- Why the research is important
- Methods or design—how the study was implemented. In certain fields—for example, the sciences and social sciences—you need to explain the particular research method, the setting, the population, and the instruments used.
- Results or outcomes—what was discovered
- Conclusions, implications, or further questions

When writing an abstract of a published article, pay special attention to the introduction and summary, for they will contain key points, and make note of the headings and subheadings.

EXERCISE 2.10

Read the following abstract and write a paragraph explaining the extent to which the abstract contains the components listed above.

JAMA, The Journal of the American Medical Association, Sept 22, 1989 v262 n12 p1659(5) Adolescents and their music: insights into the health of adolescents. *Elizabeth F. Brown; William R. Hendee.*

Abstract: During adolescence teenagers are expected to progress toward more adult-like behavior despite the fact that these years are normally marked by rebellious and alienating expressions toward adults and authority figures. The music that adolescents choose to listen to is an important element in their lives, considering that they usually listen to over 10,000 hours of music between the seventh and twelfth grades. The sexual and violent lyrics of rock music and a considerable body of existing research on the interplay between adolescent development and music is examined. Selection of music may reflect the teenager's inner struggles and serve as a medium for socialization. Several studies indicated that students with poor academic performance were more involved in rock music than their successful peers; a researcher suggested that this immersion may reflect their alienation from school. Adolescents often incorrectly interpreted the explicit messages of current rock music; they may respond more to general themes of rebellion than to specific lyrics. Immediately after watching violent and sexual videos teenagers indicated a change in their opinions about acceptable sexual behaviors. Whether their behavior changed and whether some teens are more vulnerable than others is unknown. Physicians are advised to be familiar with the music preferences of adolescents in attending to their general mood, health and well-being.

EXERCISE 2.11

Your college is holding an undergraduate conference and you have decided to submit a paper. Select an essay you have written for this or another college class and write an abstract of no more than 100 words. Give your abstract to a peer and ask the student to explain what your paper is about. If your classmate is unable to describe your paper, you need to revise the abstract and resubmit it.

■ The Précis

Another type of summary is called the **précis** (pronounced *pray-see*). The word *précis* is sometimes used interchangeably with *summary*, but a précis is different from a summary in that it does not include the title, author, or information about the rhetorical context and rhetorical purpose of the text. It also omits references to the author, such as "Vanderslice asserts." *A précis strictly follows the order of the original text, and it is usually no longer than one-quarter of the original.*

> Précis: a neutral summary that parallels the order of the original.

Reread the summary of Ronna Vanderslice's article "When I Was Young, an A Was an A: Grade Inflation in Higher Education" on page 54 and compare it to the following précis.

SAMPLE PRÉCIS

PRÉCIS OF RONNA VANDERSLICE'S "WHEN I WAS YOUNG, AN A WAS AN A: GRADE INFLATION IN HIGHER EDUCATION"

Statistics show that grade inflation continues to be a problem in higher education. College transcripts do not tell employers which students are competent and which are not. Students do not get accurate pictures of their abilities, and there is no clear relationship between grades and student learning. Universities must raise standards. One reform is to use an indexing system of two grades, a public grade for the record and a private grade for students to see how they stand in relation to their peers. Colleges should also reassess the practice of using student evaluations for personnel decisions because instructors will raise standards if they are not pressed to give high grades in exchange for positive teaching evaluations. Professors should review grading practices and make academic programs more rigorous, and college recruiters should stress the importance of academic preparation. Professors should actively insist on high academic standards and reward excellence instead of mediocrity. (Vanderslice 24–25)

Notice that the précis eliminates attribution to the author; for example, "Vanderslice asserts" and "she offers," and it pares down the 252-word summary to 149 words, which is one-fourth of the original text.

Procedure for Writing a Précis

We have outlined the procedure for writing a précis in the box below.

PROCEDURE FOR WRITING A PRÉCIS

- Read the text using critical reading strategies (marking, annotating, elaborating, taking content notes, and posing and answering questions).
- Identify the most important ideas and the significant connections among these ideas.
- Delete unimportant detail, irrelevant examples, and redundancy.
- Combine ideas in sentences and paragraphs, following the same sequence as the original text.
- Continue to pare down the précis until it is roughly one-fourth of the original.
- Document your précis.

EXERCISE 2.12

Divide the class into groups of three. Your professor will assign a reading selection to each group, or you may choose a selection from Part II of this book. One student will write a summary of the article, another an abstract, and the third a précis. When you have finished, exchange papers and critique each other's work.

■ QUOTE

When you compose essays based on sources, make an effort to use summaries or paraphrases rather than quotations. As a general rule, repeat passages word for word only if they are exceptionally well expressed or contain special forms of writing, such as definitions, key concepts, clever sayings, testimonials, or poetic language. When you take notes, paraphrase the original text instead of quoting it, unless its wording is particularly striking.

For convenience, in this section we will explain how to incorporate quotations in drafts of your essay, as well as how to select quotations for inclusion in your postreading notes.

■ Reasons for Quoting

When is it advisable to use a direct quotation instead of a paraphrase? We have provided tips in the box below.

WHEN TO USE DIRECT QUOTATIONS

- To retain the meaning and authenticity of the original text
- To lend support to an analysis or evaluation
- To capture exactly language that supports your point
- To employ a stylistic device
- To capture language that is unusual, well crafted, striking, or memorable

---

A typical reason for quoting is *to retain the meaning or authenticity of the original text.* Assume you have read the selections on privacy and technology in Chapter 11, and have received an assignment to write an essay on civil liberties and individuals' constitutional rights. You decide to quote directly from relevant parts of the U.S. Constitution. It would not be wise to paraphrase the Constitution, since the exact wording is crucial to its interpretation. When precise wording affects your argument, you need to quote.

Another purpose for quoting is *to lend support to an analysis or evaluation.* When you analyze and evaluate texts, you need to identify specific passages that support your interpretation. We discuss analysis and evaluation of essays in Chapter 4. For now, we illustrate with a passage from an essay by Valerie Babb, "'The Joyous Circle': The Vernacular Presence in Frederick Douglass's Narratives" (see Works Cited, p. 67).

> In the *Narrative* Douglass recalls slavery's intent to foster fragmentation:
>> My mother and I were separated when I was but an infant—before I knew her as my mother. It is a common custom, in the part of Maryland from which I ran away, to part children from their mothers at a very early age.... For what this separation is done, I do not know, unless it be to hinder the development of the child's affection toward its mother, and to blunt and destroy the natural affection of the mother for the child. This is the inevitable result. (48)
>
> Douglass's detailing of lost domesticity is especially moving, designed to elicit empathy from all but the most resistant reader. (368)

A third purpose for quoting is *to capture exactly language that supports your point.* In "Redeeming the Rap Music Experience" (pp. 516–31), Venise Berry quotes high-school students' responses about growing up black:

> When Upward Bound students were asked to respond to the work-sheet question, "How has growing up black, in your opinion, made a difference in your life?" a theme ran through the responses: the need to struggle or fight. Carlos, for instance, said being black causes him to struggle more for what he wants. He said, "At school, on TV, everywhere, other people get the things they want, but not me." Titus and Karon felt they had to fight a lot because of the color of their skin. "Fighting," according to Titus, "not only with people of other races." Damon explained, "Color really doesn't matter, but just because I'm black people expect me to be able to play sports and fight." When Damon went on to

list the things which he felt might hinder him in his future success, his list included skin color, money, and friends. (526)

These quotations lend a sense of reality to Berry's discussion. The exact language tells the reader much more than a paraphrase would reveal.

Another reason to use a direct quotation is *to employ it as a stylistic device*—for example, to open or close an essay. Peter Elbow opens his essay "Closing My Eyes as I Speak, An Argument for Ignoring Audience" (see Works Cited, p. 67) with an apt quotation:

Very often people don't listen when you speak to them. It's only when you talk to yourself that they prick up their ears. When I am talking to a person or a group and struggling to find words or thoughts, I often find myself involuntarily closing my eyes as I speak. (50)

John Ashberry

A final reason for quoting is *to capture language that is unusual, well crafted, striking, or memorable*. Notice how our student Karla Allen employs Charles Dickens's memorable lines:

In Charles Dickens's words, "It was the best of times, it was the worst of times" (3). While big corporations were reaping larger profits than ever before, many smaller companies and individuals found themselves out of work.

■ Altering Quotations

It is permissible to alter direct quotations, either by deleting some of the author's words or by inserting your own words, as long as you follow conventions that alert your audience to what you are doing. The sentence below, taken from an editorial in *The Lancet* entitled "Being and Believing: Ethics of Virtual Reality" (see Works Cited, p. 67), was quoted in a student paper. The student used an *ellipsis*, a set of three spaced periods, to show where words were left out.

ORIGINAL

Although the motives behind clinical VR experimentation may be praiseworthy—e.g., it may replace the prescription of harmful psychotropics—the fact that experimentation may be well intended does not preclude early examination of ethical issues.

STUDENT'S QUOTATION

Using virtual reality to help disabled people extend their physical capabilities seems attractive, but it is not without pitfalls. As the editors of the medical journal The Lancet state, "Although the motives behind clinical VR experimentation may be praiseworthy … the fact that experimentation may be well intended does not preclude early examination of ethical issues" (283).

Notice that the student has used three periods with a space before each one and a space after the last one (. . .).

To show an omission in quoted material that occurs at the end of your sentence, use a normal period followed by three spaced periods. Do not use an ellipsis to indicate that words have been omitted from the beginning of a quotation.

When you insert your own words into a quotation, signal your insertion by placing the words within brackets. Notice how our student uses this convention, as well as ellipses, when she quotes from Mary Ann Rishel's short story "Steel Fires" (see Works Cited, p. 68):

ORIGINAL

They had a hand in it. Helped make the steel. Forged. Pressed. Rolled. Cast. Hammered steel. But they didn't invent steel. They didn't design a bridge. They didn't think up new uses for steel. They weren't idea men.

STUDENT'S QUOTATION

Rishel explains, "They [laborers] had a hand in it…. But they didn't invent steel…. They weren't idea men" (13).

By inserting the bracketed word *laborers*, the student clarifies the meaning of the pronoun *They*.

■ Documenting Quotations

If the quotation occupies no more than four typed lines on a page, enclose it in double quotation marks. If it is longer, set the entire quotation apart from your text by indenting it ten spaces (see Figure 2–2).

Notice that in the long, set-off quotation in Figure 2–2, the parenthetical citation goes outside the final punctuation. For short quotations, place the parenthetical citation between the final quotation marks and the closing punctuation. The following example draws on Warren Robinett's article "Electronic Expansion of Human Perception," published in *Whole Earth Review* (see Works Cited, p. 68).

Robinett observes, "Though it [virtual reality] sounds like science fiction today, tomorrow it will seem as common as talking on the telephone" (21).

The phrase "Robinett observes" leads into the quotation and acknowledges the author. It is important to introduce quotations rather than dropping them into your paper without providing a context. Later in this chapter, we provide tips for weaving quotations into your essay.

At the end of his article Stephens reminds us of both the promise and threat of high-tech crime fighting.

Once privacy is gone it will be difficult to restore. Once mind control is accomplished it will be difficult to reestablish free thought. But with proper safeguards the superior investigative techniques and more effective treatment of offenders that the new technology offers promise a safer saner society for us all. (25)

Unfortunately, Stephens overlooks important advantages of crime fighting technology and the….

Figure 2–2

◼ Quoting a Direct Quotation

When you quote a quotation, you must acknowledge the author of the quotation as well as the author of the text in which the quotation appears. Consider the following example from Melissa Ianetta's article (see Works Cited, p. 68) about the Scottish scholar Hugh Blair:

> In order to make his ideas available both for schoolroom study and for the private learner, Blair revised and expanded the lectures he gave at Edinburgh University between 1762 and 1782. Evidently, his pedagogical purpose answered a widely felt need: the Rhetoric was, as William Charvat observes, a book "which half the educated English-speaking world studied" (qtd. in Schmitz 96). As Stephen Carr has recently calculated, from the time of its publication to 1911, there were "283 versions of Lectures on Rhetoric and Belles Lettres [...] including 112 complete Lectures, 110 abridgements, and 61 translations" (78). As this range of publication might indicate then, Blair's text was widely popular, if such an appellation should be applied to a work commonly used as a textbook. (406)

Ianetta includes a quotation from William Charvat that she found in a book by Schmitz. She informs the reader of this by placing "(qtd. in Schmitz 96)" immediately after the quotation. On her works cited page, she gives an entry for Schmitz's book; she does not list William Charvat. "Qtd. in" is the standard MLA abbreviation for "quoted in." Whenever you present a quotation, you must link both the original author's name (in this case, Charvat) and the quoting author's name (in this case, Schmitz) to the quotation in order for the documentation to be complete.

◼ Weaving Quotations into Your Essay

You can weave a quotation into your writing in several ways. You can refer to the author by citing the name before the quotation, within the quotation, or after it. Another option is to acknowledge the author in a complete sentence followed by a colon, as in option d in the box below. Option e is permissible, but it should be used sparingly. Whenever possible, use an **attributive verb or phrase** to integrate quotations into your essays. These verbs signal your conversation with the text that you are quoting. Consider examples from a student paper; the page numbers refer to the journal in which the article originally appeared. We have italicized and boldfaced the attributive verbs or phrases.

WEAVING QUOTATIONS INTO YOUR ESSAY

Here are five options:

Option a—Acknowledgment of author before the quotation:

Robinett writes, "Virtual reality, as its name suggests, is an unreal, alternate reality in which anything could happen" (17).

capitalize

(continued)

Option b—Acknowledgment of author within a quotation:

"Virtual reality, as its name suggests," **states Robinett**, "is an unreal, alternate reality in which anything could happen" (17).

Option c—Acknowledgment of author after a quotation:

"Virtual reality, as its name suggests, is an unreal, alternate reality in which anything could happen," **observes Robinett** (17).

Option d—Acknowledgment of author in complete sentence followed by a colon:

Robinett provides us with a concise definition of this new technology: "Virtual reality, as its name suggests, is an unreal, alternate reality in which anything could happen" (17).

Option e—Quotation followed by author's name: *avoid This.*

"Virtual reality, as its name suggests, is an unreal, alternate reality in which anything could happen" (**Robinett** 17).

Note that all five options require you to cite the page number in parentheses. If you are using Modern Language Association (MLA) style, the foregoing method of documentation will suffice. The style of the American Psychological Association (APA) is slightly different in that the publication date follows the author's name, and the abbreviation for "page" is always included. For options a, b, c, and d, you would write (1991, p. 17). For option e, you would write (Robinett, 1991, p. 17). When you use option e, don't forget to provide transitions between your own ideas and those of the text. Inexperienced writers sprinkle their papers with direct quotations that have little connection with the rest of the text. You can avoid this problem by leading into quotations with the verbs listed in the following box.

VERBS AND PHRASES FOR INTRODUCING QUOTATIONS

Verbs

accuses	acknowledges	admits
adds	advocates	agrees
ascertains	asks	analyzes
assents	assesses	argues
agrees (disagrees)	addresses	answers
begins	believes	categorizes
challenges	claims	comments
compares	complains	concedes
contends	contrasts	critiques

considers	concurs	concludes
continues	cites	declares
defines	delineates	describes
determines	demonstrates	differentiates
discovers	distinguishes	emphasizes
envisions	evaluates	examines
explores	expounds on	finds
furnishes	grants	implies
investigates	inquires	identifies
interjects	lists	maintains
makes the case	measures	notes
objects	observes	offers
points out	posits	postulates
presents	proposes	proves
questions	rationalizes	reasserts
remarks	replies	refers to
reports	reviews	says
shows	states	stipulates
stresses	suggests	summarizes
surveys	synthesizes	traces
views	warns	winds up
writes		

Phrases

According to X	In her recent essay, X notes
As X argues	In his article, X claims
As X explains it	Scholars such as X argue
As X has shown	To cite X
As X puts it	X calls attention to the problem that
As X reminds us	X provides the evidence that
As X sees it	X pursues the claim that
In X's view	X puts the point well that
In X's words	X seems to suggest that

You can use these verbs and phrases as lead-ins to summaries and paraphrases as well as to quotations.

■ Practices to Avoid

Two practices to avoid are **floating quotations** and **quotations strung together** without adequate connecting sentences. A floating quotation is plopped into the paper without any connecting ideas or transitional phrases.

> *Floating quotation:* Today single-parent families, especially those headed by mothers, are subjected to increasingly demanding schedules and levels of stress. "Despite the number of women who take on both parental and economic roles, not all women can do so; few can parent totally alone" (Goldschneider and Waite 202). The viability of single-parent families became a major issue in the presidential campaign.

> *Revision:* Today single-parent families, especially those headed by mothers, are subjected to increasingly demanding schedules and levels of stress. Sociologists Frances K. Goldschneider and Linda Waite explain, "Despite the number of women who take on both parental and economic roles, not all women can do so; few can parent totally alone" (202). Goldschneider and Waite emphasize that women today need more help than ever when raising families.

The revised paragraph provides a framework for the quotation. The quoted text is introduced ("Sociologists Frances K. Goldschneider and Linda Waite explain") and then commented upon ("Goldschneider and Waite emphasize that women today need more help than ever when raising families"). Valerie Babb uses a similar sequence in the example on page 60. She leads the reader into the quotation with the author, title, and an introduction, and she follows it with a comment.

A good rule of thumb, especially if you are writing for an English or other humanities course that requires MLA documentation, is to use the following convention in your writing:

- Introduce the quotation with an attributive verb or phrase.
- Give the quotation.
- Follow it with a comment or explanation.

The other practice to avoid is stringing quotations together without connections. Never string a sequence of quotations together without communicating the significance of the quoted material to your reader. If you use nothing more than transitions to link the quotations, your text will resemble a patchwork quilt. Always introduce the quotations and integrate them with your own thoughts on the topic.

> *Quotations strung together:* On the subject of crime in the inner cities, Magnet does not think that "society has so oppressed people as to bend them out of their true nature" (48). "Examine the contents of their minds and hearts and what you will find is free-floating aggression, weak consciences, anarchic beliefs, detachment from the community and its highest values," he states (48). This condition is a "predictable result of unimaginably weak families, headed by immature irresponsible girls, who are at the margin of the community, pathological in their own behavior ..." (Magnet 48).

> *Revision:* On the subject of crime in the inner cities, Magnet does not think that "society has so oppressed people as to bend them out of their true nature" (48). Magnet maintains that criminals lack conscience and internal inhibitions. He exhorts us: "Examine the contents of their minds and hearts and what you will find is free-floating

aggression, weak consciences, anarchic beliefs, detachment from the community and its highest values" (48). Magnet attributes this condition to inadequate socialization. He argues that it is the "predictable result of unimaginably weak families, headed by immature irresponsible girls, who are at the margin of the community, pathological in their own behavior …" (48). To put it another way, lawlessness is a consequence of inadequate parenting.

EXERCISE 2.13

Scan Pauline Irit Erera's "What Is a Family?" (pp. 416–28) for places where the author has quoted directly. Can you make any generalizations about how Erera uses direct quotations to build her argument?

EXERCISE 2.14

- Form collaborative learning groups of five students each, as described in the Preface, or fashion groups according to your own method. Assume that your group is preparing to write a collaborative essay about rock music. (You will not actually write the essay.)

- Choose one group member to read aloud the first five paragraphs of Venise Berry's "Redeeming the Rap Experience" (pp. 516–31). After each paragraph, decide which sentences, if any, contain information that you might use in your essay. Which of these sentences would you paraphrase, and which would you quote? Explain your decisions.

- At the end of the small-group session, the recorder should have a list of sentences and, for each sentence, an indication of whether it would be quoted or paraphrased and why. Reconvene the entire class. Have each group recorder read the list of sentences and explanations. Discuss points of agreement and difference.

WORKS CITED

Babb, Valerie. "'The Joyous Circle': The Vernacular Presence in Frederick Douglass's Narratives." *College English* 67 (2005): 365–77. Web. 21 Oct. 2010.

"Being and Believing: Ethics of Virtual Reality." *The Lancet* 338.8762 (1991): 283–84. *Academic Search Premier.* Web. 20 Oct. 2010.

Brown, Elizabeth F., and William R. Hendee. "Adolescents and Their Music: Insights into the Health of Adolescents." *Journal of the American Medical Association* 262 (1989): 1659. *InfoTrac OneFile Plus.* Web. 28 Mar. 2006.

Cain, Daphne S., and Terri Combs-Orme. "Family Structure Effects on Parenting Stress and Practices in the African American Family." *Journal of Sociology and Social Welfare* 32 (2005): 19. *H. W. Wilson.* Web. 28 Mar. 2006.

Conley, John J. "Narcissus Cloned." *America* 170.5 (1994): 15–17. *InfoTrac Academic OneFile.* Web. 20 Oct. 2010.

Dickens, Charles. *A Tale of Two Cities.* New York: Pocket Library, 1957. Print.

Elbow, Peter. "Closing My Eyes as I Speak, An Argument for Ignoring Audience." *College English* 49.1 (1987): 50–69. Print.

Goldschneider, Frances K., and Linda J. Waite. *New Families, No Families? Demographic Change and the Transformation of the American Home.* Berkeley, CA: U of California P, 1991. Print.

Heim, Michael. "From Interface to Cyberspace." *The Metaphysics of Virtual Reality.* New York: Oxford UP, 1993. 72–81. Print.

Ianetta, Melissa. "'To Elevate I Must First Soften': Rhetoric, Aesthetic, and the Sublime Traditions." *College English* 67 (2005): 400–20. Print.

Magnet, Myron. *The Dream and the Nightmare: The Sixties' Legacy to the Underclass.* New York: William Morrow, 1993. Print.

Rishel, Mary Ann. "Steel Fires." Unpublished short story, 1985. Print.

Robinett, Warren. "Electronic Expansion of Human Perception." *Whole Earth Review* 72 (Fall 1991): 17–21. *InfoTrac Academic OneFile.* Web. 20 Oct. 2010.

Sagan, Carl. "In Defense of Robots." *Broca's Brain.* New York: Ballantine, 1980. Print.

Stephens, Gene. "High-Tech Crime Fighting: The Threat to Civil Liberties. *The Futurist* 24.4 (1990): 2–25. *InfoTrac Academic OneFile.* Web. 20 Oct. 2010.

Three

Critical Analysis

■ **PART I: CRITICAL ANALYSIS**

Critical analysis appears in many guises in academic writing. Professors and college researchers exemplify it in their scholarly publications. Students exemplify it in their written reports, short essays, and term papers. Topics for critical analyses cover scientific issues, behavioral issues, literary or psychological questions, practical or procedural methodologies, and disciplinary and interdisciplinary concerns. For example:

- Donald French, a professor in the Department of Zoology at Oklahoma State University, writes a *policy analysis* of his university's proposal to add "rank in class" to grades on student transcripts.

- A student in American History 101 writes an *historical analysis* of the campaign for women's suffrage.

- A student in an art appreciation course writes a *critical analysis* of Renoir's *Luncheon of the Boating Party.*

- Stephen J. Ceci, a professor of child development at Cornell, writes a *scientific analysis* of children's testimony in criminal child abuse trials.

- George Kuh, a professor of education at Indiana University, writes a *comparative analysis* of the impact colleges and universities have on students' character development as compared to their intellectual development.

- James Phelan, a professor of English at Ohio State University, writes a *literary analysis* of John Edgar Wideman's short story "Doc's Story."

- An economics major writes a *critical review* of Jeffrey Sachs's 2005 book *The End of Poverty.*

Analysis abounds in all fields of academia. As the preceding examples illustrate, academic writers analyze a wide range of topics, issues, and texts. Analysis is a habit of mind required for critical reading and academic writing. In Chapter 1, our chapter devoted to critical reading, the word *analysis* appears twenty-five times, and it figures predominantly throughout the rest of this book.

Yet, *analysis* is one of those ambiguous terms that often mystify students. Whether the assignment is to analyze a literary text, a process, a trend, a policy, or two contrasting events, students are not sure how to proceed. Quite simply, **analysis** is *a process of breaking down something complex into simpler elements that will make it more understandable.* Analysis underpins a wide range of academic genres. Prior to writing a summary, a synthesis, an argument, or a research paper, one must engage in analysis. Analysis functions as a self-contained genre in forms of writing like the ones we've listed at the beginning of this chapter.

Analysis is frequently incorporated into other genres. A scientific lab report may contain a process analysis, and a sociolological/economic position paper may include a causal analysis explaining the relationships between antecedents and results.

Focus of the Chapter

The focus of this chapter is analytic reading and analytic writing. We cover a range of writing with emphasis on **critical analysis**, meaning *analysis with an argumentative and evaluative edge.* In keeping with the theme of this book, our focus is on the analysis of written texts and, in Chapter 16, of visual texts. From the outset, it is important to understand the differences between straightforward analysis and critical analysis or evaluation. Figure 3–1 makes the distinctions clear.

The directives in your assignment will indicate whether your purpose is to analyze or to evaluate. The diagram in Figure 3–1 lists the verbs typically associated with each activity. The operations for analysis and evaluation are comparable, but critical analysis requires you to judge the effectiveness and worth of the text after you have dissected and interpreted it.

The reason to put an analysis in writing is to communicate your interpretation of data in hopes that it will heighten your readers' understanding and appreciation. Your analysis should enlighten your audience by revealing something that is not immediately obvious.

Writers of critical analysis have a sharpened purpose: to accompany their interpretation with an evaluation of the text's strengths and weaknesses. Figure 3–1 also displays some of the genres typically associated with analysis.

Adopting a Questioning Frame of Mind

To become a successful academic writer, you have to adopt a way of thinking that favors analysis. You need to cultivate the frame of mind of a questioner. If you are not already someone who views texts with a critical eye, prepare yourself to assume this new disposition.

Analysis is stimulated by questions. Look back at Chapter 1 and you will find questions for analyzing the literal content of texts, questions for analyzing the stylistic features of texts, questions for analyzing rhetorical context, and questions for analyzing writing assignments. Questions promote analysis, as long as you know which questions to ask. Three basic questions apply to all texts: What is said? Why is it viewed that way? How is it said?

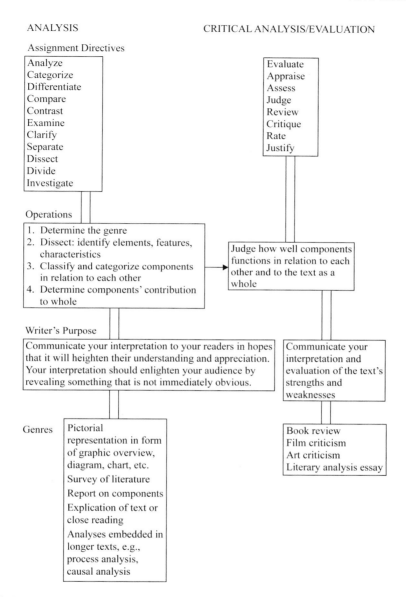

Figure 3–1   Comparison of Analysis and Critical Analysis

BROAD QUESTIONS FOR ANALYSIS

- What is said?
- Why is it viewed this way?
- How is it said?

The amount of emphasis you place on each of these questions will determine the type of analysis you will produce. Questions 1 and 2 focus on the text's argument and line of reasoning and lead to a **critical analysis**. Question 3 will examine the text's stylistic features and rhetorical context and result in a **literary analysis** or a **rhetorical analysis**.

In Chapter 1, you learned three sets of critical reading questions, the first for analyzing the literal content of a text; the second for analyzing the genre, organization, and stylistic features; and the third for analyzing the rhetorical context. These questions are the foundation for all types of analysis. In this chapter, you will learn how to build on these questions to probe further toward a more intellectually rigorous analysis and evaluation. In the three boxes below, we elaborate the original sets of questions by asking whether or not the text has accomplished its purpose.

QUESTIONS FOR CRITICAL ANALYSIS OF CONTENT OF TEXTS

- What is the topic or focal point of the text?
- What is the main idea, major point, or central claim? Is it plausible, defensible, and illuminating? Is it a reasonable position, or does the author come across as someone with an axe to grind?
- What other ideas are important? Do they follow logically from the thesis?
- What aspects of the topic or issue are emphasized? Are these aspects appropriate and sufficient, or does the text fail to consider important aspects of the topic? Where are the gaps; what is not said? If the text were to address the issue in all its complexity, what would have to be added?
- How does the text support, qualify, and develop the claim or position? Is the evidence relevant, accurate, and substantial enough to support the thesis, or does it fall short and only partially support the thesis? Which points need more support and explanation?
- What inferences, judgments, or conclusions can be drawn? Do they follow logically from the evidence? Are they sound, valid, and justifiable? Are alternative inferences, judgments, and conclusions just as reasonable?
- What assumptions underlie the thesis and are explicitly stated or taken for granted? Will readers question these assumptions?
- Does the text position the reader as someone of a particular theoretical, political, or ideological persuasion? Is this a fair and accurate perception of the reader?
- Does the text anticipate and acknowledge other points of view, or does it fail to recognize that there are different ways of viewing the issue?
- What are the implications or consequences of the argument and reasoning presented in the text? Are the implications and consequences reasonable, accurate, and probable, or should we explore other possibilities?

QUESTIONS FOR CRITICAL ANALYSIS OF GENRE, ORGANIZATION, AND STYLISTIC FEATURES OF TEXTS

- Does the text demonstrate an identifiable genre? Can you describe the special characteristics of that genre?
- Is the genre appropriate? Does it contribute to the argument? Would the writer have been better able to convey the message in a different form?
- How do the different components of the genre function in relation to the text as a whole? Are certain components stressed at the expense of others?
- How does the organization contribute to the meaning of the text? Would the meaning be better represented if the parts were arranged differently—for example, if the thesis were disclosed in the introduction instead of the conclusion; if the narrative had progressed from past to present instead of from present to past; if reasons were ordered from most important to least important instead of vice versa?
- Does the language serve to heighten and illuminate the topic? Is it merely adequate? Does it detract?
- Does the writer use figurative language (for example, similes, metaphors, personification) to explore the subject? Is the figurative language appropriate or confusing, inexact, or misleading? Is the vocabulary unnecessarily formal or pompous? Does the writer use strange, unusual, or overly technical words where common ones would do? Does the writer clarify ideas when necessary?
- Are you struck by rhythmic, balanced, symmetrical, or graceful sentences, or are the sentences disorganized and awkward? Is the writer concise, or does he or she try to pack too many ideas into long, sprawling sentences?
- Do the writer's references or allusions illuminate or add significantly to the subject matter? Take account of the writer's formal references to other written sources as well as to other types of references and allusions. (An allusion, not to be mistaken for "illusion," is a reference to some literary, cultural, or historical piece of information, whether through direct or indirect citation, that taps the reader's knowledge or memory.)
- Are the references to other written sources welcome additions to the text, or do they appear to be superfluous?

QUESTIONS FOR CRITICAL ANALYSIS OF RHETORICAL CONTEXT OF TEXTS

- What effect does the author intend the text to have on the audience?
- For whom is the author writing? Where was the text first published? Who reads this publication?
- In what year was the text published? What was on people's minds? What prompted the author to write the text? Can you identify a circumstance, event, or social practice?
- Does the author supply the reader with sufficient background information, or does he or she make erroneous assumptions about the reader's previous knowledge?
- What is the writer's persona or stance (attitude or rhetorical posture), and how does it contribute to his or her point? Is it suitable, or does it detract from the piece?

(continued)

- How does the writer's voice contribute to the text's effectiveness? Are the voice and tone appropriate or unnecessarily pompous or formal?
- What do we know about the author's background and credibility? Does the author come across as authoritative, creditable, and reliable, or are you left with questions about his or her background, prestige, political or religious orientation, or overall reputation?

 How is the author drawing on other writers and other texts? How does he or she view what others have said about the topic?

Whenever you read texts, especially sources that will inform your writing, systematically ask as many of the above questions as possible. In time, you will internalize the questions and cultivate a questioning frame of mind. When you receive an assignment that calls for written analysis, you will gravitate toward the questions that best serve your purpose. You will draw from a subset of the questions, and you may even focus your analysis on a small number of core questions.

Types of Analyses You Will Be Asked to Write

College students analyze myriad topics and texts. Sometimes your analyses will take the form of **self-contained** essays, and other times they will be **embedded** in larger projects. Sometimes your goal is to give a close reading of a text simply to show your readers your interpretation. Other times your goal is to advance a particular interpretation: for example, a gender-based analysis of Ibsen's *A Doll's House*.

Critical analysis is both a self-contained genre and a pattern of development that is embedded in many other genres. It plays a dominant role in such professional genres as book reviews, movie reviews, art criticism, policy analyses, and comparative analyses, and in such academic genres as the literary analysis essay and the rhetorical analysis essay.

In this chapter, we will focus upon the genre of a self-contained critical analysis essay, though we will also discuss embedded analyses in other genres. You will learn how to write a critical analysis as we walk you through the academic reading-writing process of constructing such an essay, beginning with prereading and ending with editing. Chapter 4 covers literary analysis and comparative analysis. In Chapter 5 we discuss analysis of visual texts and in Chapter 7 we delve deeper into analysis of formal arguments.

Importance of Genre Knowledge

When you set out to analyze a text, if you don't know what you are looking for, you will be stymied from the start. Before you dissect the text, you need to identify the attributes, characteristics, or features most frequently associated with it. In English classes you'll have difficulty writing an analysis of a poem if you are unfamiliar with literary features such as narrative voice, imagery, figurative language, sound, and rhythm. In history classes you'll have difficulty analyzing an historical event if you lack information about the chronological context or background of the event, the primary decisions made, the key decision-makers, the secondary players, the advocates, and the dissenters.

The best way to discover the attributes, characteristics, or features most frequently associated with the text is to identify its genre. Genre knowledge is a topic we introduced in Chapter 1. We pointed out that the key to successful critical reading is identifying the genre, organization, and stylistic features of the text. Genre knowledge is also a key to intelligent analysis. Identify the genre, and you will unlock information about the text's organizing principle and constituent parts.

For illustration, let's say you are enrolled in an elective course in children's literature. One unit of the course concerns fairy tales, and you have decided to write your critical analysis paper on *Snow White*. You've been exposed to fairy tales since childhood, so you have ready knowledge of the genre. You know that because a fairy tale is a story, its organizing principle is narration. (To review organizing principles, see p. 22.) Thinking back to dozens of fairy tales you've read, you can easily identify characteristics of the genre: conflict between good and evil; heroes, heroines, and villains; magical elements; settings involving royalty (kings, queens, princes, princesses, and castles), peasants, fantastic characters (witches, monsters, dwarfs, giants), and nature (forests, mountains, streams); a dilemma; a happy ending; and typical phrases such as "once upon a time" and "they lived happily ever after." With knowledge of these elements, you are well on your way to analyzing the story of Snow White and her wicked stepmother.

Similar sorts of knowledge are required for other kinds of analyses. In order to analyze a piece of music, you need to know about melody, rhythm, harmony, dynamics, timbre, and form. In order to analyze an art work, you need to know about style, surfaces, colors, textures, shape, sizes, and volumes.

On the other hand, suppose you are enrolled in a course in American government and you have been asked to analyze *Washington v. Glucksberg* (96–110) 521 U.S. 702 (1997) on the topic of physician-assisted suicide. You have not yet read the chapter of your textbook devoted to legal briefs, so you know nothing about the genre. You are flummoxed and you don't know where to begin. Before you can write an intelligent analysis, you will have to read a number of legal briefs in order to ascertain the organizing principle and determine the characteristics of the genre.

For any analysis assignment, early in the process you need to ask yourself the following questions:

- Can I identify the genre?
- What is the organizing principle or pattern for this genre?
- What are the constituent parts: the attributes, characteristics, or features most frequently associated with this genre?

EXERCISE 3.1

Break into groups of three. Each group will read one of the selections in the anthology section of this book. As a homework assignment, one student will answer the questions for Critical Analysis of Content; the second will answer the questions for Critical Analysis of Genre, Organization, and Stylistic Features; and the third will answer the questions for Critical Analysis of Rhetorical Context. When the group reconvenes, each student should summarize and share his or her responses. One student from each group will report to the class.

■ Approaches to Analysis

Another problem students encounter when they are assigned an analysis is that they don't know what to do after they've dissected the text. After you've broken down the text, the next step is to examine the nature and function of the key components. Ask yourself:

- What is the nature of each component and what is its relationship to the other components?
- How does each component affect or function in the work as a whole?

This examination will result in a more sophisticated understanding and intelligent interpretation of the text.

If you wish, when you write an analysis essay, you can give equal weight to all of the components of the text you are examining. You might select this approach if you are writing an explication of the text or close reading of a piece of literature in an English class. It is more likely that you will zero in on a few key components, view the text through a critical lens, or compare the text to a source that is similar. You can use each of these approaches independently or in combination.

APPROACHES TO ANALYSIS

- Zero in on key elements.
- View the text through a critical lens.
- Compare the text to a source that is similar.

Zero in on Key Elements

After you examine the various components of the text, you may discover one or more features that have a special function or play a significant role in the way the work achieves its purpose. You can make these features the focal point of your analysis. You will still give consideration to other features, but you will focus on one feature or a small subset of features.

Returning to our earlier examples, instead of giving equal weight to all of the literary elements in a poem, you might focus on the role of imagery; instead of evaluating all aspects of an historical event, you might investigate the role of the advocates and the dissenters; instead of evaluating all of the characteristics of *Snow White*, you might analyze maternal conflict in the fairy tale.

Sometimes the focal point of your analysis is predetermined because your professors stipulate what they want you to do.

View the Text Through a Critical Lens

Another approach is to use a **critical lens** to frame your analysis. The critical lens *focuses the analysis on certain aspects of the subject and enables you to discuss it from a particular perspective and point of view.* For example, instead of writing a broad-based analysis of the phrase *American dream*, you might analyze the concept of the American dream in terms of migrant workers' recent experiences in California. Examining the concept through migrant workers' eyes, you will focus the analysis on a certain group of immigrants at a particular point in time. The critical lens may be a person, theory, principle, concept, quotation, or any other controlling idea that frames the subject or text.

If you were to examine analysis assignments given by college professors, you would find that a large number of them provide students with a critical lens. Rarely are students asked "to analyze Barbie™." The assignment would be "Write a feminist analysis of Barbie as a female stereotype." Critical lens essays are sometimes taught in high school. One of the tasks on the New York State Regents Examination in English is called the Critical Lens Essay. In such a critical lens essay, high-school students are given a quotation and asked to interpret two works of literature through the perspective of the quotation. Given the quotation "Love has no age, no limit; and no death" (John Galsworthy, *The Forsyte Saga*), a student might analyze *King Lear* and *Romeo and Juliet*.

Keep in mind that you must have in-depth knowledge of the critical frame you are applying to the text. In order to write an economic analysis of school tracking, you must have adequate knowledge of economic scholarship. Toward the beginning of the analysis, you would tell your readers what an economic analysis entails. Then, as you develop and support your thesis in the body paragraphs of the paper, you would use the principles of economic analysis to show how tracking reproduces class inequities.

Compare the Text to a Source That Is Similar

Another way to analyze a text is through the lens of a source that is comparable. For example, you could analyze the representation of Dracula in the Bram Stoker novel *Dracula* and in the Francis Ford Coppola film by the same name. In this type of analysis, your purpose would be more pointed than to show the similarities and differences between the novel and the film. You would make a claim, perhaps arguing that Coppola portrays Dracula by faithfully adapting the character in the novel.

For an example of comparative analysis, read how the drama critic Terry Teachout opens his review of *Well* and *Pen*, two plays that opened in spring 2006 (see Works Cited, p. 118):

> No theatrical season can call itself complete without a new play about a weird mother. This week there are two and, not surprisingly, they bear certain family resemblances. Both have monosyllabic titles, both contain elements of fantasy, both are graced by splendid performances by the actresses who play the ladies in question—and neither is any good, though one is a good deal more ambitious than the other. (W9)

In the review, Teachout uses *Well*, the "more ambitious" play, as a lens for evaluating *Pen*, which he considers to be less successful.

> Except for Jayne Houdyshell's performance, I didn't like anything about *Well*. (I didn't laugh once.) Still, I freely admit that, as awful as it is, it's more interesting than David Marshall Grant's *Pen*, the latest in Playwrights Horizons' fast-growing string of excessively similar plays about family life. (W9)

Notice that Teachout begins the review by identifying three elements the two plays have in common: titles, fantasy, leading actor performances. The fourth commonality is that neither play is good. A difference between the two plays is that one is "more ambitious," and, as we discover later in the review, "more interesting" than the other.

The practice of using comparison to show the relative weight of one text as compared to another may be new to you. You are probably more familiar with the classic comparison and contrast essay in which you take two texts of seemingly equal value, make a list of their similarities and differences, and compose an essay comparing them along the lines of stated criteria. Comparative analysis is different in that one text becomes the lens for evaluating the other. In Chapter 4, we discuss comparative analysis in more detail.

EXERCISE 3.2

Select one of the texts in the anthology section of this book and explain how you would analyze it with varying degrees of specificity. Identify the focus of analysis:

- Zero in on key elements.
- View the text through a critical lens.
- Compare the text to a source that is similar.

Example: Suppose that the text is *To Kill a Mockingbird.*

Zero in on key elements. I would focus on characterization and analyze how the character of Scout evolves in the novel.

View the topic or text through a critical lens. I would use the principle of "social justice" as a lens for analyzing the novel.

Compare the text to something similar. I would analyze the courtroom scenes in John Grisham's *A Time to Kill* and Harper Lee's *To Kill a Mockingbird.*

For most analyses, you will not be using the three approaches discretely. You will be using them in combination. For example, in order to analyze the courtroom scenes in John Grisham's *A Time to Kill* and Harper Lee's *To Kill a Mockingbird*, you have to zero in on a key element such as setting. You also have to use your knowledge of courtroom procedures as a lens for analyzing the criminal trials.

EXERCISE 3.3

Here is a list of typical analysis and evaluation assignments. Divide the class into groups and give a subset of the assignments to each group. Students will examine the extent to which each assignment affects the writer's scope. Does the topic restrict the writer to one or more of the three approaches?

- Zero in on key elements.
- View the text through a critical lens.
- Compare the text to a source that is similar.

Or does it allow the writer freedom to use any approach or combination of approaches? A representative from each group will report to the class.

Assignments

- Write a critique of Vincent van Gogh's "Starry Night."
- Give your assessment of two arguments on stem-cell research.
- Write a book review of Philip Roth's historical novel *The Plot Against America.*
- Relate one of Dickens's novels to the state of the class struggle in Victorian England.
- Write a critique of Martin Scorsese's film *The Age of Innocence.*

- Write a critical analysis in which you focus on characterization in *Pride and Prejudice*.
- Select three poems and analyze e.e. cummings's use of space.
- Analyze two political candidates' positions on universal health care insurance.
- Write an economic analysis of how school tracking reproduces social class inequities.
- Write a rhetorical analysis of Martin Luther King's "I Have a Dream" speech.
- Evaluate nature imagery in two of the Seamus Heaney poems we have read.
- Analyze the role and quality of light in three paintings by Rembrandt.
- Write a comparative analysis of the architecture of Filippo Brunelleschi and Michelozzo di Bartolommeo in the Italian Renaissance.
- Analyze and evaluate Andreas Ronan's editorial on changes in U.S. immigration policies.
- Write a psychological analysis of Islamist extremism.
- Analyze the presence of fate in *Romeo and Juliet*.

▓ Purpose of Critical Analysis

A critical analysis of a text examines its argument by looking closely at the author's line of reasoning. When you receive an assignment that calls for critical analysis, think in terms of textual elements such as *thesis or major claim, evidence, point of view, assumptions, inferences, judgments, conclusions,* and *implications.* Examine what the text says and also what the text doesn't say: its *gaps, omissions,* and *oversights.*

The overall purpose of writing a critical analysis is to share your interpretation with your readers, and, ideally, to convince them that your enlightened reading of the text warrants their attention and should be taken seriously. A more focused purpose is to evaluate the author's argument in terms of its strengths and weaknesses.

▓ Critical Analysis and the Academic Conversation

Critical analyses play a major role in intellectual debates and conversations waged in the public realm as well as in academia. These conversations focus on hot-button issues such as global warming, the troubled economy, abortion, gay marriage, immigration, U.S. foreign policy, the wars in Iraq and Afghanistan, health care reform, and a host of other controversial topics, some of which appear in Part II of this book. In Chapter 10 we offer a group of texts dealing with humans' growing dependence on robots and the ensuing debate about whether robots are capable of interacting with humans and ultimately replacing us. A special area of concern is the role of robots as caretakers of the young and the elderly. We will illustrate critical analysis with a text on the topic of childcare robots. This text will supplement the readings in Chapter 10. Before presenting it, we will give you background and introduce you to some of the participants in the academic conversation about childcare robots.

Robots are ubiquitous. They play a role in manufacturing, the military, ocean and space exploration, hospital operating rooms, and increasingly in the home. For example, millions of robotic vacuum cleaners are in use, and experts predict that most households will own a robot within the next forty or fifty years. Domestic robots that perform chores are accepted as useful additions to the household. Household robots that take care of children, however, are highly controversial. Two of the key players in the debate are Noel Sharkey and Amanda Sharkey, professors at the University of Sheffield in England. In 2010 the Sharkeys published "The Crying Shame of Robot Nannies: An Ethical Appraisal" in the journal *Interaction Studies: Social Behaviour and Communication in Biological and Artificial Systems.* Sharkey and Sharkey decry the use of childcare robots and argue that they pose grave dangers for children and society. In the introductory section of their article, they provide anecdotes of parents who sing the praises of the Hello Kitty Robot, a childcare robot with a hefty price tag of $5,000. According to the product description, this robo kitty "can chat with you in 3 different situations: 1 As a close friend; 2 With the family; 3 Guessing game. This is a perfect robot for whoever does not have a lot of time to stay with child." Sharkey and Sharkey's introduction further reveals how the authors develop the article*:

> What follows is an examination of the present day and near-future childcare robots and a discussion of potential ethical dangers that arise from their extended use in caring for babies and young children. Our biggest concern is about what will happen if children are left in the regular or near-exclusive care of robots. First we briefly examine how near-future robots will be able to keep children safe from harm and what ethical issues this may raise. Then we make the case, from the results of research on child-robot interaction, that children can and will form pseudo-relationships with robots and attribute mental states and sociality to them. Children's natural anthropomorphism could be amplified and exploited by the addition of a number of methods being developed through research on human-robot interaction, for example, in the areas of conversation, speech, touch, face and emotion recognition. We draw upon evidence from the psychological literature on attachment and neglect to look at the possible emotional harm that could result from children spending too much time exclusively in the company of mechanical minders.
>
> In the final section, we turn to current legislation and international ethical guidelines on the care and rights of children to find out what protections they have from sustained or exclusive robot care. Our aim is not to offer answers or solutions to the ethical dangers but to inform and raise the issues for discussion. It is up to society, the legislature and the professional bodies to provide codes of conduct to deal with future robot childcare. (3)

"The Crying Shame of Robot Nannies" sparked a robust debate. In fact, an entire issue of *Interaction Studies* (vol. 11, issue 2) was devoted to the controversy. Among the experts and scholars who joined the academic conversation and wrote analyses and critiques of the Sharkey and Sharkey article are David Feil-Seifer and Maja J. Matarić. Their critical analysis "Dry Your Eyes: Examining the Roles of Robots for Childcare Applications" was also published in *Interaction Studies* in 2010. Feil-Seifer is a computer scientist and Matarić is a professor of computer science and neuroscience and director of the Center for Robotics and Embedded Systems at the University of Southern California. Before continuing, please take the time to read the analysis in its entirety. Note that at the end of this article, the style for documenting its sources differs from the MLA or APA styles that most college instructors expect undergraduate students to use. The reason is that some publishing houses have developed their own "house styles" for work that they publish. Such is the case here. We will discuss the MLA and APA styles in the Appendix.

*From Sharkey, Noel, and Amanda Sharkey. "The Crying Shame of Robot Nannies: An Ethical Appraisal." *Interaction Studies: Social Behaviour and Communication in Biological and Artificial Systems* 11.2 (2010): 161–90. With kind permission by John Benjamins Publishing Company, Amsterdam/Philadelphia. www.benjamins.com.

Dry Your Eyes:
Examining the Roles of Robots for Childcare Applications

David Feil-Seifer and Maja J. Matarić

1. Introduction

In their article, Sharkey & Sharkey (2010) present an ethical appraisal which argues that using robots as replacement for childcare applications could lead to neglect on the part of the parents and attachment disorders on the part of the children. They combine current commercial robot marketing trends with educated extrapolation to describe how childcare robots of the present and future could lead to misunderstanding and thus misuse of technology. Specifically, parents could believe that robots are capable caregivers, and therefore abdicate too much parenting responsibility to machines. In addition, children could believe that robots are reliable social role models and therefore abdicate judgment and emulate incorrect/inappropriate behavior. This scenario, while frightening, is based on some incorrect assumptions regarding both human perception of social robots and the intended role of socially assistive robot technology (Feil-Seifer & Matarić, 2005).

This critique will not attempt to argue for or against using robots in childcare, but rather present an alternative appraisal grounded in the current state of socially assistive robotics research. In this way, we will refute the Sharkey & Sharkey argument and present a counter-argument that demonstrates that current research in socially assistive robotics is leading away from scenarios where a robot is the sole caregiver of a child.

We believe that raising ethical concerns about technology is important and valuable. However, such concerns must be based on realistic trends and probabilities, so that their outcomes lead to important and relevant issues in childcare, and do not instead distract from those very issues.

2. Sharkey argument

The crux of the Sharkey & Sharkey argument is that the use of robots in childcare could lead to social neglect of the child. This neglect can come in several forms: the parents could be convinced that the child is receiving adequate care when the robot is not able to provide that care; the child could be led to think that the robot is providing normal social interaction when it is not; and manufacturers of a robot could exaggerate the robot's capabilities so that the users believe that it is able to adequately care for the child. We aim to clarify the low likelihood of these scenarios.

Feil-Seifer, David, and Maja J. Matarić. "Dry Your Eyes: Examining the Roles of Robots for Childcare Applications." *Interaction Studies: Social Behaviour and Communication in Biological and Artificial Systems* 11.2 (2010): 208–13. With kind permission by John Benjamins Publishing Company, Amsterdam/Philadelphia. www.benjamins.com.

2.1. Delusion of social competence

The authors assert that the expressive capabilities of current robots, and therefore   5
those of robots in the foreseeable future, give the appearance of social competence.
With regards to childcare applications, this includes the abilities to recognize speech,
make eye contact, and make purposeful movements, and that these expressive capabilities can deceive users into thinking that the robot is more capable than it is, because
robots do and will continue to lack critical elements of understanding social behavior,
such as natural language processing (NLP), activity recognition, etc.

The argument made by the authors is partially correct. However, while there   6
are specialized areas of human–machine interaction where strides have been made
in NLP, activity recognition, etc., these are currently narrow and repetitive. For unrestricted childcare domains and applications, such abilities are not within reach in the
foreseeable future.

The authors also present evidence that current robot manufacturers are advertising   7
robots as childcare solutions. These robots, as alluded to above, are probably not well
suited to being the only supervision of a child. This presents the probability that robot
vendors could/are exaggerating the capabilities of a robot in potentially irresponsible ways.

These points, while troubling if true, are not well supported by the state-of-the-art   8
in relevant research. Our work and that of others that is exploring using social robots
as therapeutic tools for children with autism spectrum disorders (ASD) found that the
best robots of today are not capable of interacting convincingly with young children
in unconstrained, free-play scenarios (Feil-Seifer et al., 2009). We used a humanoid
robot that could turn its head and body to face a child, follow it around the room,
and make social gestures in response to the actions and vocalizations of the child,
most of the criteria named by Sharkey & Sharkey as what would be convincing to
young children. However, we found that the children in the study (aged 5–10) quickly
determined that the robot was not as socially intelligent as a human being. One even
remarked, matter-of-factly, that he thought that the robot was learning disabled. This
suggests that children, both those with social disorders and typically developing ones,
are able to discern a robot's real social capabilities, and are not easily fooled or fooled
for very long. These findings are also supported by other works (Robins et al., 2005;
Plaisant et al., 2000; Kanda et al., 2004).

The delusion of social competence relies on the user observing social behavior   9
appropriate for the current social situation in order for the delusion to be sustained.
While some robots can briefly carry on an appropriate and engaging social interaction,
no robots as yet can carry on a meaningful and unrestricted social interaction convincingly enough for a human (adult or child) to be deceived into thinking that the robot
is socially competent. For such a misconception to occur, the robot would need to be
much more capable than the authors suggest or that the state-of-the-art makes possible.

2.2. Lack of attention and attachment disorders

Sharkey & Sharkey further assert that the lack of proper attention on the part of the robot   10
(or, more accurately, by the parents) could lead to attachment disorders. They present a
review of psychological literature that shows how the lack of certain nurturing social attention can lead to various relationship issues, and how such damage can occur any time
during the development process. We are not psychologists and cannot comment on the

likelihood of attachment disorders, but we agree that a lack of nurturing social interaction can lead to developmental issues. However, we do not feel that the current state of childcare robots will lead to such conditions where they would not exist otherwise.

Attachment disorders directly resulting from robot involvement in childcare 11 could be caused by two scenarios:

1. The child is placed in the care of a robot for too long because the parents, through inattention toward the robot's care of the child, are unaware of the robot's inability to care for the child; or
2. The child is placed in the care of a robot for too long because the parents have been incorrectly led to believe that the robot is able to care for the child.

In the first scenario, the parent believes that the robot can care for the child 12 when in fact it cannot. This would lead to neglect of the child when the child is placed in the robot's care. As discussed above, parents and even children are able to quickly determine the social ability of the robot after a few minutes observing the robot interacting with a user (more importantly any lack thereof). If the parent does not notice this, or if the parent ignores this fact and leaves the child in the robot's care anyway, then that would constitute neglect as much as if the parent left the child under the supervision of other insufficient surrogate care, such as a television, video game, or an unqualified human caretaker. This is not a neglect situation that is specific to a robot.

In the second scenario, the robot's manufacturer misleads the parent to believe 13 that the robot can care for the child when in fact it cannot. The potential for neglect is the same as above, but the responsibility for that neglect would be shared between the manufacturer and the parent. Assuming that the social delusion created by the robot can be dispelled quickly by observing the robot in social situations, a parent need only give a childcare robot the same evaluation that one would give a new caregiver or babysitter in order to correctly determine what the robot is capable of. Again, this is not a situation that is unique to robot caregivers.

Thus, it is important to note that the conditions that could cause neglect based on 14 inadequate supervision are the result of factors not directly linked to childcare robots, but rather by the neglect of the parents, or by negligent advertisement of childcare services. The use of any technology, including television, video games, and computers, with children is a decision that each family makes for itself, after careful consideration and deliberation, and only when accompanied by vigilant monitoring for any misuse.

3. Counter-argument

We contend that socially assistive robots (Feil-Seifer & Matarić, 2005), namely robots 15 that provide assistance through social interaction, are not being studied or designed to be replacements for human beings in caregiving roles, but as an augmentation of care that is already in place (Feil-Seifer & Matarić, 2005).

The field of assistive robotics in general, and socially assistive robotics in particular, 16 is very young and as such is subject to rapid evolution. The goal of the field has been to develop intelligent systems capable of providing assistance by enhancing existing care. For example, Paro, a robotic seal studied in eldercare situations (Wada et al., 2003) was used in the common areas of nursing homes. The robot was designed to be an interesting social entity. Researchers observed that the residents spent more time in the common areas when the robot was present, increasing the amount of time spent interacting with other people compared to time spent in their rooms. Similar examples include robots used in common areas of elementary schools (Kanda et al., 2003) and those used for children with ASD (Kozima et al., 2007).

The key element of all of these studies was that the robot was used not to replace human care and social interaction, but rather to supplement and enhance such care and interaction. As the field of socially assistive robotics develops, benchmarks and performance metrics for evaluating the robot system are being proposed that would take into account how any human–robot interaction affects the human–human interaction that was occurring naturally (Feil-Seifer et al., 2007; Tsui et al., 2008).   17

In summary, active research into human–robot interaction for assistive applications is aimed at using robots to encourage, not stifle, human–human interaction. It is important for ethical appraisals to be conducted frequently to verify that this philosophy, which now dominates the field, is not replaced by a less healthy scenario, such as that presented by Sharkey & Sharkey.   18

4. Conclusions

There are many valid reasons to be concerned about how childcare robotics could lead to neglect on the part of parents. However, we believe that the ethical dilemma posed by Sharkey & Sharkey is not well grounded in the majority of socially assistive robotics research, and that the concerns raised by the authors regarding the potential for neglect caused by childcare robots are not particular to robots, but apply to any technological or other childcare surrogate. In summary, as childcare robots move closer to becoming a reality, parents, roboticists, and legislators should remain vigilant about ethical issues, but take care to separate what undesirable human (including parent, marketers, etc.) behavior may be facilitated by robotics technology from what may be caused by robotics, and for that matter any other technology in our daily lives.   19

References

Feil-Seifer, D., & Matarić, M. (2005, July). Defining socially assistive robotics. In *Proceedings of the international conference on rehabilitation robotics* (p. 465–468). Chicago, IL.

Feil-Seifer, D. J., Black, M. P., Flores, E., Clair, A. B. S., Mower, E. K., Lee, C.-C., et al. (2009, October). *Development of socially assistive robots for children with autism spectrum disorders* (Tech. Rep.). Los Angeles, CA: USC Interaction Lab Technical Report CRES-09-001.

Feil-Seifer, D. J., Skinner, K. M., & Matarić, M. J. (2007). Benchmarks for evaluating socially assistive robotics. *Interaction Studies: Psychological Benchmarks of Human–Robot Interaction*, 8 (3), 423–439.

Kanda, T., Hirano, T., Eaton, D., & Ishiguro, H. (2003, October). Person identification and interaction of social robots by using wireless tags. In *Ieee/rsj international conference on intelligent robots and systems (iros2003)* (p. 1657–1664). Las Vegas, NV.

Kanda, T., Ishiguro, H., Imai, M., & Ono, T. (2004, November). Development and evaluation of interactive humanoid robots. In *Proceedings of ieee (special issue on human interactive robot for psychological enrichment)* (Vol. 92, p. 1839–1850).

Kozima, H., Yasuda, Y., & Nakagawa, C. (2007, August). Social interaction facilitated by a minimally-designed robot: Finding from longitudinal therapeutic practices for autistic children. In *Proceedings of the international conference on robot and human interactive communication* (p. 599–604).

Plaisant, C., Druin, A., Lathan, C., Dakhane, K., Edwards, K., Vice, J., et al. (2000). A story-telling robot for pediatric rehabilitation. In *Proceedings of the fourth international acm conference on assistive technologies* (p. 50–55). Arlington, VA.

Robins, B., Dautenhahn, K., Boekhorst, R. te, & Billard, A. (2005, July). Robotic assistants in therapy and education of children with autism: Can a small humanoid robot help encourage social interaction skills? *Special issue "Design for a more inclusive world" of the international journal Universal Access in the Information Society (UAIS)*, 4 (2), 105–120.

Sharkey, N., & Sharkey, A. (2010). The crying shame of robot nannies: an ethical appraisal. *Interaction Studies: Social Behaviour and Communication in Biological and Artificial Systems*, 11.

Tsui, K., Yanco, H., Feil-Seifer, D. J., & Matarić, M. J. (2008, August). Survey of domain-specific performance measures in assistive robotic technology. In *National institute for standards and technology (nist) performance metrics for intelligent systems workshop*. Washington, D.C.

Wada, K., Shibata, T., Saito, T., Sakamoto, K., & Tanie, K. (2003, September). Psychological and Social Effects of One Year Robot Assisted Activity on Elderly People at a Health Service Facility for the Aged. In *Proceedings of the ieee international conference on robotics and automation (icra)* (pp. 2785–2790). Taipei, Taiwan.

▨ Examination of "Dry Your Eyes: Examining the Roles of Robots for Childcare Applications," David Feil-Seifer and Maja J. Matarić's Critical Analysis of Noel Sharkey and Amanda Sharkey's "The Crying Shame of Robot Nannies: An Ethical Appraisal"

Feil-Seifer and Matarić divide their critical analysis into four sections: "Introduction," "Sharkey argument," "Counter-argument," and "Conclusions." In the introduction, the authors give the gist of the Sharkeys' argument and their main objection to it. They argue that the frightening scenarios Sharkey and Sharkey describe are unrealistic and improbable because the scenarios are based on incorrect assumptions. Feil-Seifer and Matarić claim that according to current research, parents will not likely leave their parenting responsibilities to machines, and children will not likely develop attachment disorders as a result of having robots as social role models.

Feil-Seifer and Matarić open the section entitled "Sharkey argument" by summarizing the argument—"The use of robots in childcare could lead to social neglect of the child" (81)—and listing various scenarios that portray the neglect. They then subdivide this section into "Delusion of social competence" and "Lack of attention and attachment disorders." In the first subsection, they address Sharkey and Sharkey's claims that personal robots deceive people into thinking that the robots are more socially competent than they are. While Feil-Seifer and Matarić concede that the authors are "partially correct" (82), they affirm that the extreme consequences are not supported by current research on the capabilities of social robots. As evidence, they summarize their own studies on the use of social robots with autistic children. In the second subsection, "Lack of attention and attachment disorders," Feil-Seifer and Matarić take up Sharkey and Sharkey's claim that children who are monitored by robots will develop attachment disorders. They admit that inadequate nurturing and unsatisfactory social interaction can have negative effects on child development, but they point out that these effects should be attributed to parents' misuse of childcare robots or to faulty advertisements that mislead parents to expect more from these robots than is realistic. In paragraphs 12–14, they develop their argument.

In the third section of the critical analysis, Feil-Seifer and Matarić present a counterargument: Social robots "are not being studied or designed to be replacements for human beings in caregiving roles, but as an augmentation of care that is already in place" (83). In paragraphs 16 and 17, they support their claim by describing the research. In the final section of the analysis, Feil-Seifer and Matarić reiterate their position and caution parents, roboticists, and legislators to "separate what undesirable human (including parent, marketers, etc.) behavior may be facilitated by robotics technology from what may be caused by robotics, and for that matter any other technology in our daily lives" (84).

Feil-Seifer and Matarić interrogate the Sharkey and Sharkey text with questions comparable to the "Questions for Critical Analysis of Content of Texts" on page 72. These questions provide writers of critical analyses with the criteria they need to evaluate arguments, such as the reasonableness of an author's position, the anticipation of alternative views, a consideration of the issue in all its complexity, and the reliability of available evidence. The table below depicts the meat of Feil-Seifer and Matarić's critique.

Sharkey & Sharkey's claims	Feil-Seifer and Matarić's evaluative criteria	Feil-Seifer and Matarić's evidence
"Expressive capabilities of current robots . . . give the appearance of social competence."	S & S's assertion "is partially correct . . . [but] not well supported by the state-of-the-art in relevant research."	Feil-Seifer and Matarić's research found that "the best robots of today are not capable of interacting convincingly with young children. . . . These findings are also supported by other works (Robins et al., 2005; Plaisant et al., 2000; Kanda et al., 2004)."
Children cared for by robots could be neglected, and they could develop attachment disorders.	S & S's predictions are highly unlikely. S & S do not explore other possiblilities. "We do not feel that the current state of childcare robots will lead to such conditions where they would not exist otherwise."	"Conditions that could cause neglect based on inadequate supervision are the result of factors not directly linked to childcare robots, but rather by the neglect of the parents, or by negligent advertisement of childcare services."
Robots will replace parents and human caregivers.	S & S's assumption is incorrect. They fail to consider an important aspect of the topic. "Robots that provide assistance through social interaction . . . are not being studied or designed to be replacements for human beings in caregiving roles, but as an augmentation of care that is already in place."	Feil-Seifer and Matarić cite a number of research studies as support.

When you write your own critical analysis, you might decide to follow the logic of Feil-Seifer and Matarić's text.

ORGANIZATION OF CRITICAL ANALYSIS

Bring your readers into the conversation:

explain issue, text, and author of text, and state your position/thesis.

↓

Summarize the text.

↓

Discuss major claims.

↓

Acknowledge points of agreement, discuss weaknesses of the text, provide evidence.

Give counterargument, if appropriate.

↓

Conclude with point about the larger conversation.

Now that you have read an example of a critical analysis and have witnessed how authors adapt the conventions of critical analysis to fit their purposes, we will guide you through the process of writing a critical analysis essay. First, we will review the defining characteristics of a critical analysis.

REVIEW OF THE DEFINING CHARACTERISTICS OF A CRITICAL ANALYSIS

- Writer's purpose: Share your interpretation of a text with readers to convince them that your enlightened analysis and evaluation should be taken seriously.
- Elements of the text:

  Writer's thesis/appraisal of the text

  Thesis developed by focusing on evaluative criteria such as thesis/major claim of focal text, evidence, point of view, assumptions, inferences, judgments, conclusions, implications

  Emphasis on gaps, omissions, oversights in text

  Summary of major points in the text

  Use of paraphrase, quotation, and summary to support the critique

---

■ PART II: WRITING A CRITICAL ANALYSIS: A DETAILED DEMONSTRATION OF THE READING-WRITING PROCESS

The remainder of this chapter will illustrate the various stages of critical reading, textual analysis, pre-paper planning, rough-draft writing, comprehensive revision, and final editing that are involved in an academic paper.

Let us suppose that you received the following assignment:

Select an educational issue we have discussed this semester. The issue can be related to primary, secondary, or higher education. Choose an article dealing with the issue and critique its argument and line of reasoning.

For our purposes in this example, suppose you have chosen Ronna Vanderslice's article on grade inflation, "When I Was Young, an A Was an A: Grade Inflation in Higher Education," which we worked on in Chapter 2. You will find the article on pages 36–37.

■ Critical Reading

Your first steps are to clarify the assignment, set your rhetorical goal, and consider your audience.

> *Clarify assignment.* The assignment is straightforward. It asks you to select a text and evaluate the argument and line of reasoning. As you already know from Figure 3–1 and our previous discussion, analysis goes hand in hand with evaluation.
>
> *Set rhetorical goal.* The purpose of your critical analysis is to judge the effectiveness and worth of the text, after you have dissected and interpreted it, and to convey that judgment to your readers.
>
> *Consider audience.* The assignment does not stipulate an audience, so you can assume your readers will be the professor and interested classmates.

Prereading

You will recall from Chapter 1 that the next operation is prereading. Preview the text and derive questions that will help you set goals for close reading. Then recall your prior knowledge and express your feelings about the reading topic. Freewrite and brainstorm in your writer's notebook.

Preview the Text and Ask Questions About It

Review the eight Prereading Questions on pages 6–7 and respond to the questions that are relevant. For our purposes, these questions are the following:

- What does the title indicate the text will be about? The title indicates that the author believes that when she was in college, there was no grade inflation.
- Is there biographical information about the author? What does it tell me about the text? The documentation reveals that the author is a professor of education at Southwestern Oklahoma State University. The article was published in Phi Kappa Phi Forum. A Google search revealed that readers of this journal are faculty and student members of the national honor society Phi Kappa Phi.
- Do any topic sentences of paragraphs seem especially important? The first sentence of the second paragraph mentions a problem, and the first sentence of the third paragraph says, "Universities must reform." The setup of the article is probably problem-solution.
- What type of background knowledge do I need to make sense of this text? I need to know more about the history, causes, and effects of grade inflation.

Recall Your Prior Knowledge and Express Your Feelings About the Reading Topic
If you need some prompts to trigger your personal experiences, review the Prompts for Personal Response to the Text on page 36.

I question whether grade inflation is a problem. My writing teacher told the class not to expect high grades because the average grade for all sixty sections of the composition courses is between a B— and a C+.

The Prereading operations will improve your comprehension and enable you to read more objectively. You will also be more conscious of your opinions and biases and less likely to confuse them inadvertently with those of the author.

Close Reading
Turn back to page 36 and reread the Vanderslice article with pencil in hand, **annotating**, **marking**, and **elaborating on the text**. *Mark* the text by underlining, highlighting, circling, drawing arrows, boxing, and bracketing important ideas. *Annotate* by making marginal notes and recording brief responses. *Elaborate* by amplifying or supplementing the text with comments. We provide a complete set of strategies for elaborating on texts on pages 10–11.

The next operation, *pose and answer questions about the text*, lays the foundation for your critical analysis. Earlier in this chapter, we pointed out that the key to writing an effective analysis is acquiring a questioning frame of mind. Begin with the broad, preliminary questions we discussed earlier:

- What is said? *Grade inflation is getting worse and more widespread. Universities must institute reforms to combat this routine practice.*
- Why is it viewed this way? *Since the author is a professor, she thinks grade inflation is a serious problem.*
- How is it said? *With great urgency—she says universities must reform.*
- Is the text comparable to another work with which the reader is familiar? *In our textbook, we have other articles on grade inflation.*
- Does the text demonstrate an identifiable genre? *It seems to be a proposal. She states a problem and offers solutions.*
- What is the form or special characteristics of that genre, and how do the different components function in relation to each other and to the text as a whole? *There are data on why grade inflation is a growing problem and an explanation of the effects of grade inflation. Then Vanderslice urges universities to reform and she proposes a number of ways they can deal with the problem.*
- How is the text organized? *Problem-solution*

Your next step is to reread the text and ask any of the Questions for Critical Analysis (pp. 72–74) that you have not yet answered.

- What is the main idea, major point, or central claim? Is it plausible, defensible, and illuminating? Is it a reasonable position, or does the author come across as someone with an axe to grind? *Because grade inflation has increased and become a routine practice, universities must make explicit reforms that will raise standards. If, indeed, grade inflation is a serious, widespread problem, Vanderslice's position is reasonable.*

- What aspects of the topic or issue are emphasized? The effects of grade inflation and ways to curtail it.
- Are these aspects appropriate and sufficient, or does the text fail to consider important aspects of the topic? More attention could be paid to the phenomenon of grade inflation itself. What is it? What are possible causes of grade inflation? Does everyone agree?
- Where are the gaps; what is not said? If the text were to address the issue in all its complexity, what would have to be added? I don't think all professors equate elevated grades with lower standards. Nor do they believe that they are rewarding mediocrity rather than excellence. I also question whether grade inflation is as widespread as the author claims.
- How does the text support, qualify, and develop the claim or position? Is the evidence relevant, accurate, and substantial enough to support the thesis, or does it fall short and only partially support the thesis? Which points need more support and explanation? The data in support of the rise in grade inflation are dated and limited. Haven't any surveys been published since 1993?
- What inferences, judgments, or conclusions can be drawn? Do they follow logically from the evidence? Are they sound, valid, and justifiable? Are alternative inferences, judgments, and conclusions just as reasonable? I could infer that higher grades are due to better teaching, easier exams, or brighter, better-prepared students. Grade inflation might not be occurring everywhere.
- What assumptions underlie the thesis and are explicitly stated or taken for granted? Will readers question these assumptions? There are many assumptions. First, since V. doesn't mention alternative views, I assume that she thinks all her readers will concur with her assessment of the problem.
- Does the text anticipate and acknowledge other points of view, or does it fail to recognize that there are different ways of viewing the issue? Other views are not represented. I think students would view V's solutions differently. They wouldn't be in favor of the two-grade system, and they'd feel disempowered if their evaluations of professors weren't taken seriously.
- What are the implications or consequences of the argument or reasoning presented in the text? Are the implications and consequences reasonable, accurate, and probable, or should we explore other possibilities? I think we have to explore other possibilities. Why would the two-grade system raise standards and curtail grade inflation? How does ignoring student evaluations improve the quality of teaching?

Notice that we did not respond to all of the Questions for Critical Analysis. In this book, we supply you with dozens of ways of questioning a text. You need not use all of them; select only the ones that best serve your purpose.

Postreading

Now it is time to transform yourself from a reader to a writer. Before you make this transition, we recommend that you express your personal thoughts about the text. By relating your real-life experiences to the text, you will become more aware of what you can add to the argument.

PERSONAL RESPONSE

The solutions aren't very appealing. I'm already hyper about grades. I don't need two grades instead of one. I don't care if my B— in English is below the class average of B+. I do my best. I'm not trying to be better than everyone else. I feel the same about public grades and private grades. They focus on competition. Ever since kindergarten,

I've been compared to my peers. I want to reduce the emphasis on grades. If we must have them, one is enough. I think the proposal to get rid of student evaluations is self-serving on the teachers' part. If they're going to do that, they should also get rid of professors' evaluations of students.

Planning

The operations you have performed for critical reading—questioning the text, taking notes, annotating, elaborating on the text, and writing a personal response—will provide you with raw materials for your essay. Your next challenge is to give form to the raw materials. Find common threads among them, organize them, delete extraneous or inappropriate items, and, if necessary, return to the text to extract more information. This is the work of planning, the stage when you impose your own rhetorical goal and begin to exercise control over the material you have collected and generated.

Formulate a Working Thesis and Decide on Your Approach

In a critical analysis essay, the writer's goal is to dissect and evaluate the text's argument and line of reasoning. The thesis will express this interpretation and evaluation of the text. Your first move is to arrive at a *working thesis* or preliminary understanding of the point you wish to make in your paper. Throughout the writing process, your thesis will evolve. It will be the product of a good deal of exploratory reading and prewriting. Eventually, you will arrive at the version of the thesis you will develop in your paper. Your thesis should reflect your rhetorical purpose—the effect you wish to have on your readers—and it may also reflect your organizational plan.

To form a working thesis, review the prewriting you have produced to date and ask yourself:

- Have I focused my responses on one feature of the text or on a small subset of features? Which critical analysis questions produced lengthy and substantive responses?
- Am I able to group responses that pertain to similar features of the text? Does a theme or pattern emerge?

Your answers to these questions will determine your approach; that is, whether you will zero in on key elements, view the text through a critical lens, or compare the text to a source that is similar.

When you sort through the writing you've produced so far, you find that your responses focus on weaknesses in the text: insufficient evidence, questionable assumptions, and lack of consideration of alternative ways of viewing the issue. You decide your approach will be to focus on this subset of features.

You jot down the following working thesis:

"When I Was Young, an A Was an A: Grade Inflation in Higher Education" is problematic in that it has insufficient evidence, questionable assumptions, and lack of consideration of alternative ways of viewing the issue.

Verify That You Have Support for Your Thesis

Return to the relevant parts of the text to check for supporting material. Each time you make a point about a textual feature, your essay should provide textual evidence in the form of a quotation, a paraphrase, or a summary. At this juncture, go back to the text and mark passages you will use to support your points. If you cannot find enough textual evidence, consider changing your focus.

Decide on an Organizational Plan

After you come up with a working thesis and select an approach, your next step is to identify the organizational format you will use. Reexamine your prewriting. Categorize and try out several grouping schemes to find what works best. Review the organizational plans on page 22 to see which is most appropriate for critical analysis essays.

Time order, narration, process   Example

Antecedent-consequent/cause-effect   Analysis/classification

Description   Definition

Statement-response   Analogy

Comparison/contrast

For example, if your purpose is to show the negative implications and consequences of the text's argument, you might develop your essay in a cause-and-effect format. If you wish to weigh the text's strengths against its weaknesses, you could use the comparison and contrast format.

- State your thesis and the criteria you are using to evaluate the text.
- Allocate one or more body paragraphs to each criterion, developing each point with specific evidence from the text.

The various patterns of organization may be used individually, or they may overlap.

After studying your prewriting, you decide that the argument format best suits your purpose. You sketch out the following loose plan:

"When I Was Young, an A Was an A: Grade Inflation in Higher Education" is problematic in that it has questionable assumptions, insufficient evidence, and lack of consideration of alternative ways of viewing the issue.

    Write introduction. Summarize the article.

    Make point about insufficient evidence: data only go up to 1993.

    Make point about questionable assumptions:

      • elevated grades = lowered standards

      • two-grade system will raise standards; students use criteria of grades to evaluate professors.

Make point about lack of consideration of alternative ways of viewing the issue: no regard for students' point of view.

    Write conclusion.

This loose plan suggests that the body of the essay will contain three paragraphs, each focusing on an evaluative criterion and each claiming a weakness in the text and supplying evidence to substantiate that claim.

If you prefer, display your plan as a *graphic overview* (see p. 50) or as a formal outline. The graphic overview will depict major ideas and show how they are related. Some students are more comfortable with a *formal outline* than with loose plans or a graphic overview. Traditional outlines are based on the following structure:

I.
    A.
        1.
            a.
                i.
                ii.
            b.
        2.
    B.
II.

The formal outline provides a clear hierarchical structure useful for imposing order on a topic that is complicated and has a number of discrete subtopics. The following is a segment of a formal outline for the critical analysis:

    A. a basic assumption is that elevated grades indicate lower standards, but it could be that
        1. professors are doing a better job teaching
        2. students are better prepared
        3. teachers are using more suitable tests and exams
    B. assumption that changing grading system will raise standards
        How will two-grade device raise standards?

■ Drafting

When you sit down to write a draft of your essay, you will find that you've already generated a fair amount of material. Now comes the challenge of weaving together (1) the points you are making about the text and (2) the supportive textual evidence. You may find it necessary to change, rearrange, or eliminate some of the material you have assembled. This process will be less daunting if you observe the guidelines listed in the following box.

ROUGH-DRAFT GUIDELINES

- You need not include all your preliminary work in your draft.
- You don't have to follow your outline religiously or incorporate it completely.
- You don't have to—and probably shouldn't—begin at the beginning. Many writers start with the body paragraphs and write the introduction and conclusion later. After all, you can't introduce a person until he or she is present, so you shouldn't expect to introduce a paper until you've finished writing the body paragraphs.
- As you revise, you should focus on higher-order concerns, such as ideas and organization, and not get bogged down with spelling, punctuation, and word choice. You can return to these lower-level concerns when you have completed the draft.

Keep these guidelines in mind as you consider the six strategies for drafting shown in the following box. Apply these strategies liberally and flexibly; drafting does not necessarily follow a set procedure or a fixed sequence.

DRAFTING STRATEGIES

- Select and use organizational plans for individual paragraphs.
- Weave direct quotations, paraphrases, and summaries in with your own ideas, and supply proper documentation.
- Decide on an introductory paragraph.
- Construct a conclusion.
- Develop a list of references or works cited.
- Title your essay.

For convenience, we describe the strategies in the order in which they appear in the Drafting Strategies box above. You need not apply them in that order. For instance, you may find it easier to begin with the introduction and then to compose the body of the essay. Whatever you do, don't get stymied by a particular sequence. Try another approach if you find yourself staring at a blank page or waiting for sentences to come to you. Move on to sections you can write readily. Later you can return to the parts that caused difficulty.

Plan Individual Paragraphs

As you draft the body of your essay, follow the organizational plan you chose at the prewriting stage. For our illustration, it is the plan for an argument. Develop each paragraph in accordance with this top-level structure. Needless to say, as you compose individual paragraphs, other organizational patterns will come into play. Most writers use multiple patterns to organize their prose. Again, we should point out that if your prewriting plan proves unworkable, or if you discover a new direction for the paper in the process of drafting, don't hesitate to rethink the organizational format.

Your paragraphs should be unified and coherent. Each one should develop a central idea, and all the sentences should contribute to that idea in some way. You may need more than one topic sentence to express the paragraph's dominant ideas. You can achieve coherence by repeating words and ideas, rewording, and using transitional expressions ("also," "for example," "thus," "similarly," "consequently," and so on). All these devices show readers the logical links between sentences.

Here are the body paragraphs for the first draft of the critique of Ronna Vanderslice's "When I Was Young, an A Was an A: Grade Inflation in Higher Education":

Vanderslice writes that "grades of C or less moved from 25 percent in 1969 to 9 percent in 1993" and today they continue to spiral upward (24). On what evidence is she basing this claim? And where are the statistics for the years between 1993 and 2004, when the article was written? My writing teacher told our class not to expect high grades because the average grade for all sixty sections of the composition courses is between a B− and a C+. This leads me to question Vanderslice's claim that "between 80 and 90 percent of all college students receive grades of A or B" (24). Is grade inflation occurring across the board, or are some colleges more guilty than others?

The text's most basic problematic assumption is that elevated grades are indicative of lowered standards. But there are other reasonable explanations for higher grades. It could be that professors are doing a better job of teaching. Perhaps today's college students are better prepared and smarter than they were in previous decades. Maybe professors are using improved, more authentic, and more valid measures of assessment.

A questionable assumption underlies Vanderslice's recommendation that professors change their grading practices by giving students two grades instead of one. The author assumes that this system will help to solve the problem of grade inflation, but she fails to explain how this practice will raise standards. The number of As and Cs will remain the same. The two-grade system also assumes that students are interested in how they stack up against their peers. This may not be the case at all. They may be less interested in competition than in mastery of subject matter.

Another solution for curbing grade inflation is to reassess the practice of using student evaluations for personnel decisions involving faculty. This proposal assumes that students give high evaluations to professors that give high grades and low evaluations to professors that have rigorous standards. It also assumes that professors are so insecure that they cave in to student pressure. The implications of this proposal are dangerous: A professor who performs poorly in the classroom will be rewarded. If the personnel committee does not look at student evaluations, no one will ever know. One could argue that this proposal is also self-serving. Colleges should eliminate professors' evaluations of students as well as students' evaluations of professors? This would lead to a healthier, less competitive atmosphere.

These are decent first-draft paragraphs, with one major exception: the last three fail to include direct references to the text. Each point that is made about the text needs to be backed up by a quotation, paraphrase, or summary.

Use Quotations, Paraphrases, and Summaries

Quotations, paraphrases, and summaries are the principal ways to integrate material from sources into an essay. In Chapter 2, we covered in detail how to compose paraphrases and summaries and how to extract quotations as you take notes. If you need to supplement your notes with additional paraphrases, summaries, and quotations, return to those procedures. Remember that the reading-writing process is recursive. It is not uncommon for writers to read the source texts at the drafting stage.

When you employ quotations, paraphrases, or summaries in academic essays, be sure to differentiate them from your own words and document the text as we described in Chapter 2. Always provide your readers with some identification of the source, usually the author and the page number (for printed sources) and, if necessary, the title. The reason for including this information is to allow interested readers to locate the complete reference in the list of sources at the end of the paper. Be sure you know which documentation style your professor requires.

Take note of how we incorporated quotations and paraphrases into the three paragraphs:

The text's most basic problematic assumption is that elevated grades are indicative of lowered standards. The opening sentence places "low standards" side by side with "elevated grades," and the third paragraph states that the objective of the proposed reforms is to "increase standards instead of decreasing them." But there are other reasonable explanations for higher grades. It could be that professors are doing a better job of teaching. Perhaps today's college students are better prepared and smarter than they were in previous decades. Maybe professors are using improved, more authentic, and more valid measures of assessment.

A questionable assumption underlies Vanderslice's recommendation that professors change their grading practices. She recommends Harvard professor Harvey Mansfield's method of assigning two grades, a public grade for the registrar and a private grade for the student. Vanderslice explains, "the private grades give students a realistic, useful assessment of how well they did and where they stand in relation to others" (24). The author assumes that this system will help to solve the problem of grade inflation, but she fails to explain how this practice will raise standards. The number of As and Cs will remain the same. The two-grade system also assumes that students are interested in how they stack up against their peers. This may not be the case at all. They may be less interested in competition than in mastery of subject matter.

Another solution for curbing grade inflation is to reassess the practice of using student evaluations for personnel decisions involving faculty. Citing a moratorium at Indiana University, Vanderslice writes, "The university believes that removing concerns about student complaints about receiving lower grades might motivate all instructors to reset their standards, free from the pressures to give A's in exchange for high evaluations" (24). This proposal assumes that students give high evaluations to professors that give high grades and low evaluations to professors that have rigorous standards. It also assumes that professors are so insecure that they cave in to student pressure. The implications of this proposal are dangerous: A professor who performs poorly in the classroom will be rewarded. If the personnel committee does not look at student evaluations, no one will ever know. One could argue that this proposal is also self-serving. Colleges should eliminate professors' evaluations of students as well as students' evaluations of professors? This would lead to a healthier, less competitive atmosphere.

Whether or Not to Include a Summary of the Text

When writing a critical analysis, you have to decide whether you will include a summary of the text or simply mention the main points you are critiquing. If you include a summary, its length depends on your purpose. You may want to provide your readers with a comprehensive summary that covers all the major aspects of the source, or you may want to focus on the aspects that concern you most. Refer to the summarizing strategies on page 49. You will find them very helpful.

Remember that your objective is to integrate the summary of the text with your own ideas on the topic. Once you order and classify your ideas and establish your direction, adapt the summary to your purpose. You need not summarize the entire text, only the sections that relate to your purpose. The summary should highlight the passages that prompted your evaluation and refer only incidentally to other portions of the text.

Write Introductory Paragraphs

A strong introduction ought to interest readers, announce the text and topic, disclose your thesis or an attitude, and establish your voice. It may also, when appropriate, present background information essential to understanding the topic and indicate the organizational plan.

Here is the introductory paragraph for the draft of the critical analysis of "When I Was Young, an A Was an A: Grade Inflation in Higher Education."

Is grade inflation a serious problem of college professors? Ronna Vanderslice, a professor of education at Southwestern Oklahoma State University, in her article "When I Was Young, an A Was an A: Grade Inflation in Higher Education," asserts that grade inflation is an increasingly serious problem that universities must counteract. Writing in <u>Phi Kappa Phi Forum,</u> the journal of a national honor society, she urges university faculty to reform their grading practices and offers various suggestions for doing so. Her argument is problematic in that it rests on insufficient evidence and questionable assumptions, and it neglects to consider alternative ways of viewing the issue.

The introduction presents the following components: *use of question as paper opener, identification of author and her major claim, title of the text, thesis of the critical analysis.*

The opening sentences of an essay are crucial. They should engage readers and encourage them to read on. These initial sentences also establish the writer's voice as formal or informal, academic or conversational. Some forms of academic writing require you to write in a very professional voice and open your paper in a designated way. For instance, research studies often begin with a one-paragraph abstract or summary of the study's principal findings. As we noted in Chapter 2, abstracts are written in formal, objective language. Other types of essays give you more freedom and allow you to use an informal opening that speaks directly to the reader.

There are several openers you could use. For example, if you were writing an essay on cloning human beings, you could open it with a *quotation from the reading source*:

> Social critic Barbara Ehrenreich warns, "Human embryos are life-forms, and there is nothing to stop anyone from marketing them now, on the same shelves with Cabbage Patch dolls" (86). Perhaps we are headed for a future where, as Ehrenreich suggests, we will purchase rather than bear our children.

You could start out with *an anecdote, a brief story*, or *a scenario*:

> Imagine that you are a clone, an exact copy, of either your mother or your father rather than a combination of genetic material from both of them.

Or you could open with a *question*:

> Is there any justification for reproductive cloning?

Alternatively, you can begin by *providing background information*:

> Cloning, a genetic process that makes it possible to produce an exact, living replica of an organism, has been applied to simple organisms for years. Now it is possible to clone complex animals, even human beings.

Other opening strategies are to begin with a fact or a statistic, a generalization, a contradiction, or a thesis statement. *Avoid opening with clichés or platitudes* ("As we contemplate cloning, we should remember that fools rush in where angels fear to tread"), *dictionary definitions* ("According to *Webster's International Dictionary*, 'cloning' is . . ."), or *obvious statements* ("Cloning is a very controversial topic").

Components of Introductory Paragraphs

Paper opener
>   Question
>   Quotation
>   Anecdote, brief story, or scenario
>   Background information
>   Fact or statistic
>   Generalization
>   Contradiction
>   Thesis

Identification of author and major claim
Title of text
Thesis of critical analysis

EXERCISE 3.4

Read the opening paragraphs of each of the selections in Chapter 10. For each selection, identify the components of the introductory paragraph and the type of paper opener the author uses.

Recast the Thesis

As you write the introduction, leave open the possibility of revising the working thesis that you derived earlier in the process (see p. 91). Make sure that the thesis still expresses your main idea. You don't have to situate the thesis in any particular place. Thesis statements often occur toward the end of the introduction, after the opening explanation of the general topic and identification of the source; however, they can occur elsewhere, even at the beginning of the introductory paragraph. For example, the thesis of Vanderslice's text, "Universities must initiate reforms that increase standards instead of decreasing them," appears in the third paragraph of the article.

Wherever you place the thesis, be sure that you express it adequately and provide your reader with enough context to understand it fully. In academic writing, a thesis statement may occupy several sentences. The complex issues that academic essays deal with cannot always be formulated adequately in a single sentence.

Just as the thesis statement can consist of more than one sentence, the introduction can comprise more than one paragraph. Notice how our student Maura Grady opens her essay on immigration with two introductory paragraphs. The first stresses the significance of her personal experience; the second identifies the key topic the paper will address and presents Maura's thesis statement.

I am a second-generation American. My grandparents emigrated to the United States from the west of Ireland in the 1920s to pursue the American Dream and make a better life for their children. Like most immigrants, they came to this country to labor in low-paying jobs, the Kellys as cab driver and domestic worker, the Gradys as longshoreman and laundress. I never read about "little people" like them in my history textbooks. Textbook writers must think along the same lines as the Irish maid in Ronald Takaki's "A Different Mirror": " 'I don't know why anybody wants to hear my history. . . . Nothing ever happened to me worth the tellin' " (541).

Historically, women fortunate enough to gain entry into the United States, women like my grandmothers—Irish maids, Chicana cleaners, and Japanese " 'wives [who did] much work in the fields' " (546)—have been even more silenced than their male counterparts. The women whom male immigrants left behind—wives and lovers barred from entering the country—have never had the opportunity to tell their tales. As revisionist historians Takaki and others relate the stories of the "little people," I hope they remember to give women a strong voice. I want my daughters to be able to look into the " 'mirror' of history" and through the lens of the present to see "who [women] have been and hence are" (541) and what they have the potential to become.

Lengthy articles in scholarly journals often have a multiparagraph subsection labeled "Introduction" that includes information needed to understand the thesis statement. Sometimes a complex paper opener requires a separate paragraph. For instance, an essay that evaluates the social consequences of cloning human beings might begin with a dramatized scenario, perhaps a description of a family in which the children were clones of their parents, to provide a test case for the author's argument. The details of this scenario might require one or more paragraphs. These opening paragraphs would be followed by a paragraph that zeroes in on the topic and presents the thesis.

Write Conclusions

The concluding paragraph should do more than recapitulate the high points of the discussion that precedes it. A summary of the main points is justified, but you should also consider the techniques in the following box:

TIPS FOR WRITING CONCLUSIONS

- Stress the significance of your thesis rather than simply repeating it.
- Predict the consequences of your ideas.
- Call your readers to action.
- End with a question, an anecdote, or a quotation.
- Summarize your main points.

Consider the conclusion of the critical analysis essay that we've been discussing:

"When I Was Young, an A Was an A: Grade Inflation in Higher Education" tackles an important issue, but it is based on too many questionable assumptions. If Vanderslice had provided more data, addressed the issue of grade inflation in all its complexity, and given more consideration to the implications of her proposals, her readers would be better served and they would take her article more seriously.

EXERCISE 3.5

Reread the concluding paragraphs of each of the reading selections in Chapter 11. Identify the concluding technique each author uses. If it is not one of the four techniques listed above, do your best to describe the way the author ends the text.

Prepare Lists of References or Works Cited

At the end of source-based papers, you need to construct a list of the texts you quote, paraphrase, summarize, or cite in your essay. The list should contain an entry for every source you use, and it should be alphabetized according to the authors' last names. The Appendix of this textbook provides guidelines for setting up the list of Works Cited for the MLA documentation style and the list of References for the APA style.

The Work Cited list for the critical analysis, constructed according to MLA guidelines, contains only one source:

WORK CITED

Vanderslice, Ronna. "When I Was Young, an A Was an A: Grade Inflation in Higher Education." *Phi Kappa Phi Forum* 84 (2004): 24–25. Print.

Title the Essay

Your title should indicate your perspective and, if possible, capture the spirit of the issue you are addressing. A title such as "A Critique of 'When I Was Young, an A Was an A: Grade Inflation in Higher Education'" identifies the genre and text, nothing more. Another direct title, "Vanderslice's Problematic Solutions," is formed by *lifting key words* from the critical analysis. If you prefer a title that is less straightforward, you can choose from a number of options for deriving titles. One alternative is to *let the title reflect your organizational plan*. An essay that develops according to the comparison/contrast pattern might be titled "A Professor's View of Grade Inflation vs. the Perspective of the Silenced Student." Another alternative is to *use a hook* that will interest your reader, for example, "As Grades Go Up, Do Standards Go Down?" Still another option is a title that expresses a *generalization, followed by a specific point*, for example, "Grade Inflation: A Practice That Has Become Routine"; or a *specific point followed by a generalization*, for example, the title Vanderslice uses for her essay. You could also title your paper with an *apt phrase* from the reading source or from your essay itself. A *catchy saying* or a *relevant quotation* from some other text could also be used.

The possibilities for titles are limited only by your creativity. Here is a title for the critical analysis essay: "Grade Inflation: Which Is More Questionable, the Problem or the Solutions?"

TIPS FOR TITLING ESSAYS

- Identify the genre and text.
- Extract key words from your essay.
- Reflect your organizational plan.
- Use a hook to interest your readers.
- Express a generalization, followed by a colon, followed by a specific point.
- Express a specific point, followed by a colon, followed by a generalization.
- Use an apt phrase from a reading source.
- Use a catchy phrase.
- Use a relevant quotation.

EXERCISE 3.6

Review the titles of the reading selections in Chapter 12. Explain the relevance of each title and describe the strategy the author uses.

At this point, you will have finished a complete draft of your paper. Congratulations! You are now entitled to take a break from your assignment. But remember that a paper presented only in first-draft form is unlikely to earn you a high grade. A conscientiously revised paper will display your writing to its best advantage. So, you must now turn to a full-scale revision of your paper before you hand it in. This last phase includes both reworking your ideas and your presentation and copyediting your paper for errors in standard form or usage. It can be the most rewarding phase of the writing process because you will see your ideas take stronger, clearer shape and hear your voice emerge with confidence and authority. You will also find that cleaning up your grammar, spelling, punctuation, and other mechanics will reassure you about having written a good paper. It is wise to set your first draft aside for some time before you revise it. Experience shows that you will come back to it with freshness and alertness, keen to spot weak arguments, poor evidence, awkward transitions, and stylistic mistakes that you did not realize you had made.

▓ Revise the Preliminary Draft

To varying degrees, writers revise while they are drafting as well as after they have produced fully formed papers. Those who do a great deal of revision as they are composing their drafts may come up with polished products that require minimal changes. Those who prefer to scratch out rough first drafts may make substantial changes as they rewrite in multiple versions. Whether you are an in-process reviser or a post-process reviser, you should keep in mind certain effective principles of revision.

PRINCIPLES OF REVISION

- Do not allow your in-process revision to interfere with your draft.
- Restrict in-process revising to important elements, such as ideas and organization.
- Check that you have a clear thesis and convincing support, and as you move from one part of the paper to another, be sure you are progressing logically, maintaining your focus, and supplying appropriate transitions.
- Be sensitive to your readers' needs. But leave concerns like word choice, sentence structure, punctuation, spelling, and manuscript format until after you have finished a full draft of the paper.

The best revisions do more than correct errors in usage, punctuation, and spelling. Here is the revision of the first draft of the critical analysis essay.

Student's Critical Analysis Essay: Revision of Preliminary Draft

GRADE INFLATION: WHICH IS MORE QUESTIONABLE, THE PROBLEM OR THE SOLUTIONS?

Is grade inflation ^such a serious ~~problem of~~ ^concern that college professors? [should change the way they grade their students?] Ronna

Vanderslice, a professor of education at Southwestern Oklahoma State

University, [The argument she presents in] ~~in her article~~, "When I was Young, an A Was an A: Grade

Inflation in Higher Education," ~~asserts~~ ^claims that grade inflation is an

increasingly serious problem. ~~that universities must counteract.~~

[According to Vanderslice, forty years ago very few students received high grades. Now most receive As and Bs. As a result, transcripts no longer give accurate information to students or to their potential employers.]

Writing in *Phi Kappa Phi Forum*, the journal of a national honor society, ^Vanderslice
~~she~~ urges university faculty to reform their grading practices

and ^she offers various suggestions for doing so. ~~Her argument~~ is problematic

in that it rests on insufficient evidence and questionable assumptions,

and it neglects to consider alternative ways of viewing the issue.

Vanderslice writes that "grades of C or less moved from 25 percent

in 1969 to 9 percent in 1993" (24), and today they continue to spiral

upward. On what evidence is she basing this claim? And where are the

statistics for the years 1993 to 2004, when the article was written?

My writing teacher told our class not to expect high grades because

the average grade for all sixty sections of the composition courses

is between a B— and a C+. This leads me to question Vanderslice's

claim that "between 80 and 90 percent of all college students receive

grades of A or B" (24). Is grade inflation occurring across the board,

or are some colleges more guilty than others?

The text's most basic ~~problematic~~ assumption is that elevated

grades are indicative of lowered standards. The opening sentence places

"low standards" side by side with "elevated grades," and the objective

^Vanderslice's
of ~~the proposed~~ reforms is to "increase standards instead of decreasing

them." ^(24) ^But there are other reasonable explanations for higher grades.

It could be that professors are doing a better job of teaching. Perhaps

today's college students are better prepared and smarter than they were in
previous decades. ^Or m^ Maybe professors are using ~~improved,~~ more authentic and
more valid measures of assessment.

A ~~questionable~~ ^puzzling^ assumption underlies Vanderslice's recommendation
that professors ^should^ change their grading practices. ~~She recommends~~ ^Vanderslice proposes^ Harvard
professor Harvey Mansfield's method of assigning two grades, a public
grade for the registrar and a private grade for the student. Vanderslice
explains, "~~t~~^T^he private grades give students a realistic, useful assessment
of how well they did and where they stand in relation to others" (24).
The author assumes that this system will help to solve the problem of
grade inflation, but she fails to explain how ~~this practice~~ ^it^ will raise

Granted, students will learn how they rank in class, but

standards. ^t^ ~~T~~he number of ^"public"^ ^As and Cs~~ will~~ ^could very well^ remain the same. The two-grade

the ones that count on the transcript,

system also assumes that students ~~are interested in~~ ^want to know^ how they stack up
against their peers. This may not be the case at all. They may be less
interested in competition than in mastery of subject matter.

Another ^of Vanderslice's^ solution ^s^ for curbing grade inflation is to reassess the
practice of using student evaluations for personnel decisions involving
faculty. Citing a moratorium at Indiana University, Vanderslice writes,
"The university believes that removing concerns about student complaints
about receiving lower grades might motivate all instructors to reset
their standards, free from the pressures to give A's in exchange for high

are two assumptions. One is

evaluations" (24). ^Underlying^ This proposal ~~assumes~~ that students give high evaluations to professors ^who^ ~~that~~ give high grades and low evaluations to professors

who give low grades and maintain

~~that have~~ rigorous standards. It also assumes that professors are so

Is there any research that demonstrates that either of these assumptions is valid?   Another concern is

insecure that they cave in to student pressure. ^t^ ~~The~~ ^dangerous^ ^The^ implications of this
proposal ~~are dangerous:~~ a professor who performs poorly in the classroom
could very likely receive promotion or tenure.
~~will be rewarded.~~ If the personnel committee does not look at ~~student~~ ^course^

the effect the professor has on students.

evaluations, no one will ever know. One could ^also^ argue that this proposal is

~~also~~ self-serving. _{Why shouldn't} ~~Colleges~~ _C~~should~~ eliminate professors' evaluations of students as well as students' evaluations of professors? This would lead to a healthier, less competitive atmosphere.

> The issue of grade inflation is not new. If grades are increasing and if universities have lowered their standards, reforms are necessary.

"When I Was Young, an A Was an A: Grade Inflation in Higher Education" tackles an important issue^{Too bad} ~~but~~ it is based on ~~too~~ ^{so} many questionable assumptions. If Vanderslice had provided more data, addressed the issue of grade inflation in all its complexity, and given more consideration to the implications of her proposals, her readers would be better served and they would take her article more seriously.

Work Cited

Vanderslice, Ronna. "When I Was Young, an A Was an A: Grade Inflation in Higher Education." *Phi Kappa Phi Forum* 84 (2004): 24-25. Print.

We revised the first paragraph by sharpening the opening sentence and fleshing out our points with paraphrases from the text. We left paragraph 2 as is, and made a few editorial changes to paragraph 3. In paragraph 4, we made additional editorial changes, revising awkward or imprecise word choices, and we added a concession. We reworded parts of paragraph 5, added clarifications, inserted a question about Vanderslice's evidence, and provided smoother transitions. Finally, in the conclusion we added an acknowledgment of the seriousness of the issue we discussed. Notice that throughout the draft, we adhere to special conventions that academic writers follow when writing about texts, shown in the box below.

SPECIAL CONVENTIONS FOR WRITING ABOUT TEXTS

- Use the present tense when explaining how the author uses particular procedures and writing techniques.
- Identify the author of the source by first and last name initially and thereafter only by the last name.
- Keep these conventions in mind at the beginning of the process and, if necessary, make the necessary changes at the time of revision.

Revise Ideas

When you revise your draft, your first priority should be to make changes in meaning by reworking your ideas. You might *add information, introduce a new line of reasoning, delete extraneous information or details,* or *rearrange the order of your argument.* Revision should always serve to sharpen or clarify meaning for your readers. Ask yourself the questions in the following box.

REVISING IDEAS

- Is my paper an adequate response to the assignment?
- Is my rhetorical purpose clear? How am I attempting to influence or affect my readers?
- Does everything in the draft lead to or follow from one central thesis? If not, which ideas appear to be out of place? Should I remove any material?
- Do individual passages of my paper probe the issues and problems implied by the thesis in sufficient detail? What do I need to add?
- Will the reader understand my central point?

The process of drafting stimulates your thinking and often brings you to new perspectives. You may see links among pieces of information and come to conclusions that had not occurred to you at the planning stage. As a result, first drafts are often inconsistent; they may start with one central idea but then depart from it and head in new directions.

Allow yourself to be creative at the drafting stage but when you revise, make sure that you express a consistent idea throughout your entire essay. Check to see if you have drifted away from your thesis in the subsequent paragraphs or changed your mind and ended up with another position. If you have drifted away from your original goal, examine each sentence to determine how the shift took place. You may need to eliminate whole chunks of irrelevant material, add more content, or reorder some of the parts. After you make these changes, read over your work to be sure that the new version makes sense, conforms to your organizational plan, and shows improvement.

Revise Organization

When you are satisfied that your draft expresses the meaning you want to get across to your readers, check that your ideas connect smoothly with each other. Your readers should be able to follow your train of thought by referring back to preceding sentences, looking ahead to subsequent sentences, and paying attention to transitions and other connective devices. Ask yourself the questions in the following box.

REVISING ORGANIZATION

- Is my organizational plan or form appropriate for the kind of paper I've been assigned? If not, can I derive another format?
- Do I provide transitions and connecting ideas? If not, where are they needed?
- Do I differentiate my own ideas from those of the text?
- What should I add so that my audience can better follow my train of thought?

(continued)

- What can I eliminate that does not contribute to my central focus?
- What should I move that is out of place or needs to be grouped with material elsewhere in the paper?
- Do I use a paper opener that catches the reader's attention?
- Does each paragraph include a topic sentence(s) and does all the material in this paragraph support it?
- Does my conclusion simply restate the main idea or does it offer new insights?
- Does my essay have an appropriate title?

EXERCISE 3.7

Obtain a copy (photocopy or extra computer-generated copy) of at least two pages of a paper you have written. Select a paper written for any course, either a final draft or a rough draft. (Your instructor may elect to distribute a single essay to the entire class.)

Apply the questions listed in the boxes on Revising Ideas (p. 105) and Revising Organization (pp. 105–06) to the piece of writing. Ask yourself each question and handwrite on the essay any revisions that seem necessary.

Submit the original essay along with your revised version.

EXERCISE 3.8

In preparation for this exercise, the instructor needs to copy a short student essay (not more than two pages) for each class member. A preliminary draft will work best. Form collaborative learning groups of five students each.

Select one student to read the essay aloud. Other group members should follow along, noting on their own copies passages that would profit from revision according to the principles of Revising Ideas and Organization discussed above.

Select another student to read aloud the questions from the Revising Ideas (p. 105) and Revising Organization (pp. 105–06) boxes. After each question is read, discuss whether it suggests any revisions that might improve the essay, and have the recorder write out the changes on which the group agrees.

Reconvene the entire class. Each group recorder should report the revisions the group made and explain why they are necessary. Try to account for differences in revisions.

Revise Style

You may associate the term *style* with works of high literary art—the style, say, of a poem by John Keats or a novel by Emily Brontë. In actuality, however, every piece of writing displays a style of its own, whether it be a business report by a professional analyst or a note of reminders by a roommate or a family member. A style, a tone, a sense of voice and attitude, and above all a sense of liveliness and energy (or their absence) emerge from the writer's choice and use of words; the length and complexity of the writer's sentences; and the writer's focus on sharp, meaningful, reader-based expression. When you revise for style, you consider the effect your language choices have on your audience. We will discuss five ways to improve writing style.

STRATEGIES FOR IMPROVING STYLE

- Move from writer-based prose to reader-based prose.
- Add your own voice.
- Stress verbs rather than nouns.
- Eliminate ineffective expressions.
- Eliminate sexist language.

Move from Writer-Based Prose to Reader-Based Prose

Throughout this book, we continually stress the importance of audience. It is imperative to keep your readers in mind throughout the entire reading-writing process, and especially at the revising stage. Making a distinction between *writer-based prose* and *reader-based prose* will help you attend to audience needs as you revise. We already introduced you to these two concepts on page 39. Writer-based prose is egocentric because the writer records ideas that make sense to him or her, but the writer makes minimal if any effort to communicate those ideas to someone else. In contrast, reader-based prose clearly conveys ideas to other people. The writer does not assume anything; she provides information that will facilitate the reader's comprehension.

It is easy to forget about your readers amid all the complications in producing the first draft of an academic essay. That's why first drafts are quite often writer-based. An important function of revising is to convert this writer-based prose to something the reader can readily understand.

To illustrate writer-based prose, we have reproduced a student's reaction to two articles on computer intelligence. As you read the student essay, place checks next to the sentences that are writer-based.

Both of these articles deal with the present and future status of computers. Carl Sagan tends to agree with Ulrich Neisser except that Sagan thinks computers are changing rapidly, whereas Neisser believes they will remain the same for quite some time.

Both articles discuss differences between computer intelligence and human intelligence. To prove that human intelligence is different, Sagan uses the example with a U.S. Senator. Neisser agrees with Sagan by stating that a computer has no emotions, no motivation, and does not grow. Neisser feels that this is where humans have the advantage over computers. As stated in the introductory paragraph, the authors differ in one major way: Sagan thinks that the computer's ability will change soon, while Neisser thinks that it will be some time before that happens.

The other issue the articles discuss concerns social decisions. Both writers feel that computers should not be allowed to make social decisions. Sagan believes a computer shouldn't make social decisions if it can't even pass the test in the example. Neisser also goes back to this example. He also states that the computer only deals with the problems that it is given. It has no room for thought, since it is confined just to finding the answer. Once again, the only place Sagan and Neisser seem to contrast is about the length of time it will take for the computer to be able to make social decisions.

I agree more with Sagan than with Neisser. The rapid growth of computers will continue, and the issues will constantly change.

Notice that our writer assumes the audience is familiar with both the assignment and the articles on which it is based. For example, the introduction begins "Both of these articles…" as if the reader knows in advance which articles will be discussed (see Works Cited, p. 118). The first sentence tells us only that the articles discuss the computer's "status," a term that conveys little to anyone who has not read the texts. The second sentence states that Neisser and Sagan agree on something, but it does not indicate what ideas they supposedly share. The writer has simply failed to take into account that the reader may or may not be able to follow the train of thought. Similar failures to consider the audience occur throughout the essay. Below, we have transformed its introduction from writer-based prose to reader-based prose.

The articles "In Defense of Robots" by Carl Sagan and "The Imitation of Man by Machine" by Ulrich Neisser both deal with the computer's potential to match the intellectual accomplishments of humans. Sagan and Neisser agree that there is currently a wide gap between machine and human intelligence. However, Sagan argues that the gap will quickly narrow, whereas Neisser maintains that computer and human intelligence will always be significantly different.

As you revise your first drafts, make sure that you have provided the necessary context or background for material taken from sources. Unless the assignment indicates that the audience has read the sources, do not assume that your readers will share your prior knowledge and experience.

Add Your Own Voice

After you've written your paper, read it aloud. Better still, ask a friend to read it aloud to you. Does your writing sound like it's really yours? Or does it sound stiff, wooden, impersonal, colorless? Would your paper be better if it resonated with some of your spoken personality?

Richard Lanham devotes his book *Revising Prose* to helping writers project their own voices and breathe life into their writing. Among his suggestions are the following:

- If too many of the sentences wind endlessly around themselves without stopping for air, try dividing them into units of varying length.
- Give a rhythm to your prose by alternating short sentences with longer ones, simple sentences with complex ones, statements or assertions with questions or exclamations.
- Bring your readers into the essay by addressing them with questions and commands, expressions of paradox and wonderment, challenge and suspense.

Try these strategies. They can bring the sound of your own voice into otherwise silent writing and liven it considerably. Be careful, though. Some professors prefer a relentlessly neutral style devoid of any subjective personality. Proceed cautiously.

Stress Verbs Rather Than Nouns

Pack the meaning in your sentences into strong verbs rather than nouns or weak verbs. See how the following example uses verbs and nouns. We have underlined the nouns and italicized the verbs.

> *Original:* The creation of multiple copies of an individual through the process of cloning *is* now an actual feasibility.
>
> *Revision:* Scientists can now *clone* multiple copies of a human.

The first version uses nouns to get the message across, but the revised version uses a verb. Notice that the first version contains only a single verb, *is*. *Is* and other forms of the verb *be* (*are, was, were, be, being, been*) are weak and lifeless because they draw their meaning from the nouns preceding and following them. Sentences that are structured around *be* verbs depend heavily on nouns to convey their central ideas. These "noun-style" sentences are characterized by forms of the verb *be* (*is, are*, and so on) and by nominalization. **Nominalization** is *the practice of making nouns from verbs or adjectives by adding suffixes (-ance, -ence, -tion, -ment, -ness, -sion, -ity, -ing)*. For example, *preserve* becomes *preservation* and *careless* becomes *carelessness*.

An additional sign of nominalization is frequent use of prepositions and prepositional phrases. In the following example, we have underlined the *be* forms, the instances of nominalization, and the prepositions in the sentence we considered earlier. Notice that the revision does not rely on *be* verbs or nominalizations.

> *Original:* The creation of multiple copies of an individual through the process of cloning is now an actual feasibility.
>
> *Revision:* Scientists can now clone multiple copies of a human.

Of course, there are occasions when *be* verbs or nominalizations are appropriate. Problems arise only when these forms are overused. Although there is no absolute rule, you should look closely when you find more than one *be* verb or nominalization per sentence. You need not analyze the nouns and verbs in every paper you write, but periodically you should check the direction in which your style is developing. Over time, you will find that less analysis is necessary because you will be using more active verbs and fewer prepositions and nominalizations.

Eliminate Ineffective Expressions

Avoid ineffective expressions and words that do not contribute directly to the meaning of your paper. Notice how the underlined words and phrases in the following passage do not advance the writer's goals.

> Basically, those in support of surrogate motherhood claim that this particular method of reproduction has brought happiness to countless infertile couples. It allows a couple to have a child of their own despite the fact that the woman cannot bear children. In addition, it is definitely preferable to waiting for months and sometimes years on really long adoption lists. In my opinion, however, surrogate motherhood exploits the woman and can be especially damaging to the child. Obviously, poor women are affected most. In the event that a poor couple cannot have a child, it is rather unlikely that they will be able to afford the services of a surrogate mother. Actually, it is fertile, poor women who will

become "breeders" for the infertile rich. In any case, the child is <u>especially</u> vulnerable. The <u>given</u> baby may become involved in a custody battle between the surrogate mother and the adopting mother. If the <u>individual</u> child is born handicapped, he or she may be <u>utterly</u> rejected by both mothers. <u>Surely</u>, the child's welfare should be <u>first and foremost</u> in everyone's mind.

The underlined elements are either overused, hackneyed words and phrases or unnecessary qualifiers, intensifiers, or modifiers. None of these words further the writer's intentions. They are inherently vague. Check to see if ineffective expressions occur frequently in your writing.

Eliminate Sexist Language

Always reread your drafts to be sure that you have avoided sexist language. Use the masculine pronouns "he" and "his" and nouns with -*man* and -*men* (*mailman, policemen,* and so on) only when they refer to a male or a group composed entirely of males. Don't use these forms to refer to women. Instead, use the techniques listed in the following box.

TECHNIQUES FOR AVOIDING SEXIST LANGUAGE

- Use pronouns that recognize both sexes ("his or her" or "her or his").
- Use the plural rather than the singular. Plural pronouns by their very nature do not specify gender ("they" and "their").
- Use nouns that are not gender-specific ("mail carrier" and "police officer").

Observe how we use these techniques to revise sexist language in the following example:

Original: A physician must consider the broader social consequences of supplying new reproductive technologies to his patients. Likewise, each scientist working on genetic engineering must be aware of the potential social impact of his research.

Revision: Physicians must consider the broader social consequences of supplying new reproductive technologies to their patients. Likewise, scientists working on genetic engineering must be aware of the potential social impact of their research.

EXERCISE 3.9

Obtain a copy (photocopy or extra computer-generated copy) of at least two pages of a paper you have written. Select a paper written for any course, either a final draft or a rough draft. (Your instructor may elect to distribute a single essay to the entire class.)

Revise the draft according to the advice in this chapter, keeping in mind the following guidelines:

- Move from writer-based to reader-based prose.
- Vary sentence length.

- Stress verbs rather than nouns.
- Use words effectively.
- Detect sexist language.
- Add your own voice.

>   Handwrite on the essay any revisions that seem necessary.
>   Submit the original version of the essay along with your revised version.

EXERCISE 3.10

In preparation for this exercise, the instructor will need to copy a short student essay (not more than two pages) for each class member. A preliminary draft will work best. Form collaborative learning groups of five students each.

Select one student to read the essay aloud. Other group members should follow along, noting on their own copies words, phrases, sentences, and whole passages that would profit from revision and editing according to the principles of revising and editing signaled above.

Select another student to read aloud the following list of revising and editing concerns:

- Moving from writer-based to reader-based prose
- Varying sentence length
- Stressing verbs rather than nouns
- Using words effectively
- Detecting sexist language
- Adding your own voice

After each concern is read, discuss whether it suggests any revisions that might improve the essay, and have the recorder write out the changes on which the group agrees.

Reconvene the entire class. Each group recorder should report the revisions the group made and explain why they are necessary. Try to account for differences in revisions.

Conferences and Peer Review

When you are satisfied with your preliminary draft, make arrangements to share it with your teacher or a classmate. Before you proceed any further, you need to get some feedback on what you have written so far.

Instructor Conferences

If your instructor invites students to schedule conferences, be sure to take advantage of this opportunity. The conference will be beneficial to you if you approach it with the correct mind-set and adequate preparation. Don't expect your instructor to correct your work or tell you what to do. You should assume a proactive role: Set the agenda and do most of the talking. After the teacher reads your draft—preferably, you should read it to the teacher—inquire about what worked well and what fell flat. Be prepared to explain what you are trying to achieve and point out the parts of the paper you feel good about and the parts you think need work. Most important, be ready to answer the teacher's questions.

Peer Reviews

If your teacher agrees, make arrangements to have a classmate or a friend review your preliminary draft and give you feedback. If that is not possible, set the paper aside for a few days and then review it yourself. Respond to the questions listed in the box that follows.

QUESTIONS FOR HELPING A WRITER REVISE A CRITICAL ANALYSIS ESSAY

- What is the rhetorical purpose? Has the writer provided an insightful interpretation of the text and in so doing explained how certain characteristics contribute to its meaning?
- Does the writer move beyond interpretation to the strengths and weaknesses of the text?
- Does everything in the draft lead to or follow from the writer's thesis? If not, which ideas seem to be out of place?
- Is the writer sensitive to your concerns?
    a. Are you given sufficient background information, summary, title, and the author? If not, what is missing?
    b. Does the writer provide clear transitions and connecting ideas that differentiate his or her own ideas from those of the source text?
    c. Does the writer display an awareness of the author of the text by referring to the author by name or personal pronoun ("Smith states," "she explains")? Or does the writer personify the source ("the article states," "it explains")?
- Which organizational format does the writer use: cause and effect, comparison and contrast, or argument? If another pattern is used, is it appropriate for an analysis essay?
- Has the writer made you aware of the criteria for the evaluation? On which characteristics of the text is the analysis focused? If the bases for the analysis are unclear, explain your confusion.
- Does the writer support each of his or her points with direct evidence (quotations, paraphrases, summaries) from the source? If not, where are they needed?
- Does the writer provide smooth transitions and connecting ideas as he or she moves from one point of analysis to another? If not, where is evidence needed?
- Do you hear the writer's voice throughout the essay? Describe it.
- What type of paper opener does the writer use? Is it effective? Why or why not?
- Does the paper have an appropriate conclusion? Can you suggest an alternative way of ending the essay?
- Is the title suitable for the piece? Can you suggest an alternative title?
- Has the writer followed academic writing conventions, such as:
    a. Writing in present tense when explaining how the author of the source uses particular procedures and techniques?
    b. Identifying the author initially by first name and last name and thereafter only by last name?
    c. Indenting long quotations in block format?

■ **Editing**

When you have finished your revision, read your paper aloud once again to catch any glaring errors. Then reread the essay line by line and sentence by sentence. Check for correct usage, punctuation, spelling, mechanics, manuscript form, and typos. If you are especially weak in editing skills, and if it is all right with your instructor, go to your campus writing center or get a friend to read over your work.

This stage of revision encompasses the rules for usage, punctuation, spelling, and mechanics. We cannot begin to review all these rules in this textbook. You should think seriously about purchasing a few solid reference books, such as a good dictionary; a guide to correct usage, punctuation, and mechanics; and a documentation manual like the *MLA Handbook for Writers of Research Papers* or the *Publication Manual of the American Psychological Association.* Your campus bookstore and your college library will have self-help books for improving spelling, vocabulary, and usage. Browse through them and select the ones that best serve your needs.

Here are questions to ask yourself as you edit your paper. Remember that you need to abide by all the rules of standard written English.

QUESTIONS FOR EDITING

- Are all my sentences complete?

  Original: Certain feminists claim that the new reproductive technologies exploit women. While other feminists argue that these same technologies help liberate women from traditional, oppressive roles.

  Revision: Certain feminists claim that the new reproductive technologies exploit women, while other feminists argue that these same technologies help liberate women from traditional, oppressive roles.

- Have I avoided run-on sentences, both fused sentences and comma splices?

  Original: Science fiction writers have long been fascinated with the prospect of cloning, their novels and short stories have sparked the public's interest in this technology.

  Revision: Science fiction writers have long been fascinated with the prospect of cloning, and their novels and short stories have sparked the public's interest in this technology.

- Do pronouns have clear referents, and do they agree in number, gender, and case with the words for which they stand?

  Original: A scientist who works on new reproductive technologies should always consider the social consequences of their work.

  Revision: A scientist who works on new reproductive technologies should always consider the social consequences of his or her work.

- Do all subjects and verbs agree in person and number?

  Original: Not one of the new reproductive technologies designed to increase couples' fertility have failed to incite controversy.

(continued)

Revision: Not one of the new reproductive technologies designed to increase couples' fertility has failed to incite controversy.

- Is the verb tense consistent and correct?

  Original: Some futurists claim that eugenics will provide the answers needed to ensure the survival of the human race. They predicted that by the year 2050, human reproduction will be controlled by law.

  Revision: Some futurists claim that eugenics will provide the answers needed to ensure the survival of the human race. They predict that by the year 2050, human reproduction will be controlled by law.

- Have I used modifiers (words, phrases, subordinate clauses) correctly and placed them where they belong?

  Original: Currently, scientists across the nation work to clone various species with enthusiasm.

  Revision: Currently, scientists across the nation work enthusiastically to clone various species.

- Have I used matching elements within parallel construction?

  Original: Proposed reproductive technology projects include creating ways for sterile individuals to procreate, developing cures for genetic disease, and eugenic programs designed to improve the human species.

  Revision: Proposed reproductive technology projects include creating ways for sterile individuals to procreate, developing cures for genetic disease, and designing eugenic programs to improve the human species.

- Are punctuation marks used correctly?

  Original: The potentially dire social consequences of genetic engineering, must be examined carefully, before we embrace this powerful new frightening technology.

  Revision: The potentially dire social consequences of genetic engineering must be examined carefully before we embrace this powerful, new, frightening technology.

- Are spelling, capitalization, and other mechanics (abbreviations, numbers, italics) correct?

  Original: Research on Reproductive Technology is not often funded by The Government, since these innovations are so controversial.

  Revision: Research on reproductive technology is not often funded by the government, since these innovations are so controversial.

Manuscript Format

For this stage of revision, you need a great deal of patience and a good pair of eyes. Ask yourself the questions in the box below. They are based on the format recommended by the *MLA Handbook for Writers of Research Papers.* The format recommended by the APA is slightly different (see pp. 602–08).

MANUSCRIPT CHECKLIST

- Have I typed my last name and the page number in the upper right-hand corner of each page?
- Have I provided my full name, the course, the professor's name, and the date?
- Have I centered my title and typed it without underlining it?
- Have I indented the first line of each paragraph five spaces?
- Have I double-spaced and left one-inch margins on all sides throughout the paper?
- Are all typed words and corrections legible?
- Will my audience be able to tell which thoughts are mine and which are derived from sources?
- Are all quotations enclosed in quotation marks and properly punctuated?
- Have I properly documented all quotations, paraphrases, and summaries?
- Do I include all sources in a Works Cited list?

In Figure 3–2 on pages 115–17, we annotate the final draft of the critical analysis essay to show the important features of MLA manuscript format.

STUDENT'S CRITICAL ANALYSIS ESSAY: FINAL DRAFT

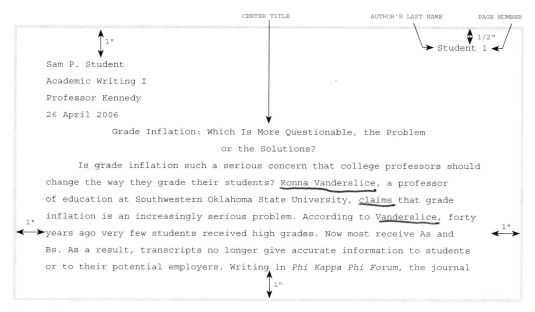

CENTER TITLE   AUTHOR'S LAST NAME   PAGE NUMBER

1/2"
Student 1

1"

Sam P. Student
Academic Writing I
Professor Kennedy
26 April 2006

Grade Inflation: Which Is More Questionable, the Problem
or the Solutions?

Is grade inflation such a serious concern that college professors should change the way they grade their students? Ronna Vanderslice, a professor of education at Southwestern Oklahoma State University, claims that grade inflation is an increasingly serious problem. According to Vanderslice, forty years ago very few students received high grades. Now most receive As and Bs. As a result, transcripts no longer give accurate information to students or to their potential employers. Writing in *Phi Kappa Phi Forum*, the journal

1"   1"

1"

Figure 3–2

1"

of a national honor society, Vanderslice urges university faculty to reform their grading practices and she offers various suggestions for doing so. The argument she presents in "When I Was Young, an A Was an A: Grade Inflation in Higher Education" is problematic in that it rests on insufficient evidence and questionable assumptions, and it neglects to consider alternative ways of viewing the issue.

Vanderslice writes that "grades of C or less moved from 25 percent in 1969 to 9 percent in 1993" (24) and today they continue to spiral upward. On what evidence is she basing this claim? And where are the statistics for the years 1993 to 2004, when the article was written? My writing teacher told our class not to expect high grades because the average grade for all sixty sections of the composition courses is between a B− and a C+. This leads me to question Vanderslice's claim that "between 80 and 90 percent of all college students receive grades of A or B" (24). Is grade inflation occurring across the board, or are some colleges more guilty than others?

The text's most basic assumption is that elevated grades are indicative of lowered standards. The opening sentence places "low standards" side by side with "elevated grades," and the objective of Vanderslice's reforms is to "increase standards instead of decreasing them" (24). But there are other reasonable explanations for higher grades. It could be that professors are doing a better job of teaching. Perhaps today's college students are better prepared and smarter than they were in previous decades. Or maybe professors are using more authentic and more valid measures of assessment.

1"

1"

A puzzling assumption underlies Vanderslice's recommendation that professors should change their grading practices. Vanderslice proposes Harvard professor Harvey Mansfield's method of assigning two grades, a public grade for the registrar and a private grade for the student. Vanderslice explains, "The private grades give students a realistic, useful assessment of how well they did and where they stand in relation to others" (24). The author assumes that this system will help to solve the problem of grade inflation, but she fails to explain how it will raise standards. Granted, students will learn how they rank in class, but the number of "public" As and Cs, the ones that count on the transcript, could very well remain the same. The two-grade system also assumes that students want to know how they stack up against their peers. This may not be the case at all. They may be less interested in competition than in mastery of subject matter.

Another of Vanderslice's solutions for curbing grade inflation is to reassess the practice of using student evaluations for personnel decisions

1"

Student 3

involving faculty. Citing a moratorium at Indiana University, Vanderslice writes, "The university believes that removing concerns about student complaints about receiving lower grades might motivate all instructors to reset their standards, free from the pressures to give A's in exchange for high evaluations" (24). Underlying this proposal are two assumptions. One is that students give high evaluations to professors who give high grades and low evaluations to professors who give low grades and maintain rigorous standards. It also assumes that professors are so insecure that they cave in to student pressure. Is there any research that demonstrates that either of these assumptions is valid? Another concern is the dangerous implications of this proposal: a professor who performs poorly in the classroom could very likely receive promotion or tenure. If the personnel committee does not look at course evaluations, no one will ever know the effect the professor has on students. One could also argue that this proposal is self-serving. Why shouldn't colleges eliminate professors' evaluations of students as well as students' evaluations of professors? This would lead to a healthier, less competitive atmosphere.

The issue of grade inflation is not new. If grades are increasing unjustifiably and if universities have lowered their standards, reforms are necessary. "When I Was Young, an A Was an A: Grade Inflation in Higher Education" tackles an important issue. Too bad it is based on so many questionable assumptions. If Vanderslice had provided more data, addressed the issue of grade inflation in all its complexity, and given more consideration to the implications of her proposals, her readers would be better served and they would take her article more seriously.

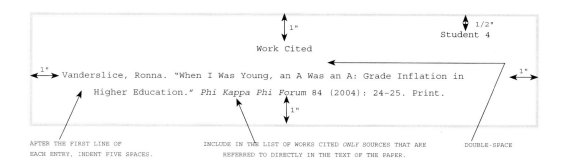

1"

1/2"
Student 4

Work Cited

1"
Vanderslice, Ronna. "When I Was Young, an A Was an A: Grade Inflation in
    Higher Education." *Phi Kappa Phi Forum* 84 (2004): 24–25. Print.

1"

1"

AFTER THE FIRST LINE OF
EACH ENTRY, INDENT FIVE SPACES.

INCLUDE IN THE LIST OF WORKS CITED *ONLY* SOURCES THAT ARE
REFERRED TO DIRECTLY IN THE TEXT OF THE PAPER.

DOUBLE-SPACE

WORKS CITED

Ehrenreich, Barbara. "The Economics of Cloning." *Time.* Time, 22 Nov. 1993: 86. Web. 1 Apr. 2006.

"Hello-Kitty-Robot." *Amazon.com*, n.d. Web. 21 Oct. 2010.

Lanham, Richard. *Revising Prose.* 2nd ed. New York: Macmillan, 1987. Print.

Neisser, Ulrich. "The Imitation of Man by Machine." *Science* 139 (1963): 193–97. Web. 19 Oct. 2010.

Sagan, Carl. "In Defense of Robots." *Broca's Brain.* New York: Ballantine, 1980. 280–92. Print.

Teachout, Terry. "Mother Knows Worst." *Wall Street Journal.* The Wall Street Journal, 7 Apr. 2006: W9. Web. 16 Oct. 2010.

Four

Literary Analysis and Comparative Analysis

This chapter focuses on two forms of analytical writing: essays that address the reading of literary texts and essays that address similarities and differences. The chapter also offers tips for writing other types of analytical essays.

■ LITERARY ANALYSIS

We will focus our **literary analysis** upon a brief discussion of poetry. Poetry is the most concentrated of literary genres, and its major characteristics exemplify those of all the other genres. For this reason, the questions we might ask about reading poetry, the topics we might pursue in analyzing it, and the strategies we might adopt for writing about it bear much in common with those we might direct toward other literary forms such as the short story, drama, and novel.

Like fiction, poetry presents the voice of an imagined character as it offers a particularized expression of some thought, idea, emotion, or lived sensation. In poetry, we identify this character as "**the poem's speaker**," a speaker who may or may not necessarily overlap with the individual poet who composed the poem.

Like drama, poetry presents the voice of this speaker in an imagined dialogue or conversation with another person or persons. It differs from drama in that it usually does not present the other person's voice as well—it allows us to hear only one side of the conversation and to imagine what the other side might say. In poetry, we identify this other person as the speaker's "**addressee**" (that is, the person whom the speaker addresses) or "**implied audience**," and we are prompted to flesh out a concrete impression of this person's special characteristics.

Like fiction and drama, poetry also presents a rhetorical context, a moment in which its speaker interacts with the addressee or with some other individual who has brought the speaker to a crisis and has prompted him or her to suspend business as usual and perhaps to consider making a change.

■ Process of Writing a Literary Analysis Essay

Viewed in this way, poetry is not so different from other literary genres, nor is it really more difficult to read, enjoy, or comprehend. It presents us with the **voice** of a speaker, with some prompts to imagine other characters with whom the speaker interacts, with the suggestion of a **dramatic situation** that brings them together, and with the possibility of a crisis that will necessitate some change in the speaker's environment. Such features prevail, whether in a twelve-line poem, a twelve-page short story, a twelve-scene drama, or a twelve-chapter novel. Consequently, the tools that you use to analyze poetry will be the same tools that you use to analyze short fiction, plays, or long fiction.

The reading strategies and exercises that follow will focus on poetry, but their principles will pertain to other literary forms as well. To reinforce these principles, we present them with a set of collaborative discussion assignments based on analyzing the words of a popular song of your choosing. A song is a poem accompanied by music, and in analyzing the text of a song, we bring to it the same kinds of questions about content, genre, organization, style, and rhetorical context that we bring to analyzing a literary text.

The following pages present a writing assignment based on a poem that a student named Ipek Kadife will analyze in a critical paper. We will examine Ipek's written responses to prompts for Prereading; Reading for Content; Reading for Genre, Organization, and Stylistic Features; and Reading for Rhetorical Context, and we will conclude with her finished and revised literary analysis.

The writing assignment asked Ipek to do the following:

> Select one of the poems in your online course packet and analyze it as a dialogue between the poet and an interlocutor. What kind of "voice" characterizes the poem's speaker? What kind of interlocutor does it address? What kind of conversation does it suggest between them? How do the formal elements of meter, rhyme, "poetic license," and figurative diction project a specific tone that haunts this conversation?

Ipek has selected a well-known poem by the American poet Emily Dickinson (1830–1886):

Me from Myself—to Banish*

Me from Myself—to Banish—
Had I Art—
Impregnable my fortress
Unto All Heart—

But since Myself—assault Me—
How have I peace
Except by subjugating
Consciousness?

---

*Poem 642, (1862): Reprinted by permission of the publishers and the Trustees of Amherst College from *The Poems of Emily Dickinson*, Thomas H. Johnson, ed., Cambridge, Mass.: The Belknap Press of Harvard University Press, Copyright © 1951, 1955, 1979, 1983 by the President and Fellows of Harvard College.

And since We're mutual Monarch

How this be

Except by Abdication —

Me — of Me?

Here are general prompts for Prereading; Reading for Content; Reading for Genre, Organization, and Stylistic Features; and Reading for Rhetorical Context. Ipek's paper on literary analysis is based on them. So too is the set of exercises on the words of a popular song that you can find on the Internet.

Prereading Questions

As you would with any other kind of writing, skim through the poem before you concentrate your attention on reading it word for word. What does its title suggest? What does its visual arrangement on the page — especially if it appears divided into sections or subsections — imply about its organization? From its first few lines, what can you deduce about the character of its speaker? What, if anything, can you provisionally assume about the character of the addressee? What hints does it provide about some dramatic situation that might have brought the speaker and the addressee into conversation?

IPEK KADIFE'S RESPONSE TO PREREADING EMILY DICKINSON'S "ME FROM MYSELF—TO BANISH"

The speaker seems to be in conflict with herself. She would like to banish herself from herself. The addressee must be someone included within the pronoun "we" in line 9. The speaker and the addressee evidently share something important in common. This "we" might represent just some other aspect of the speaker's self. The poem is dated in 1862 and was written during the American Civil War. Might the "we" represent Dickinson's contemporaries?

EXERCISE 4.1

Form collaborative groups of five students each that will search the Internet for the words of a contemporary song that the group agrees upon.

Useful Hint: To find the song's text on the Internet, use a search engine such as Google. Type in the name of the song and, for good measure, the name of the major performer with whom it is associated. The Web site for the group U2, for example, found at U2.com, offers the lyrics of every song the group has created. As with every sort of intellectual property, however, the site cautions that these lyrics are available only for personal research or limited educational use and are to be credited with the usual documentary information when they are quoted.

After locating the text, individuals in the group should report to one another how their impressions of the song might have changed after reading the lyrics. Each group should then examine and discuss the lyrics to ask what kind of person emerges from the song. Here are questions to consider:

- What kind of character does the song attribute to its singer or speaker?
- What kind of character does it attribute to the person whom the singer or speaker is addressing?
- What situation has brought them together, and what dimensions of this situation lend a dramatic depth to the song?

The recorder should take notes and present them to the class at the end of the exercise.

Reading for Content

Since poems present the voice of a speaker who is engaged in some sort of dramatic situation that might unfold in a story, play, or novel, the questions that we ask of a particular poem's content should focus on the components of this situation:

- What kind of drama does the poem suggest?
- What is happening to the speaker?
- How does what is happening implicate the addressee or some presumed other person?
- How does the speaker react to what is happening?
- Does the speaker convey a consistent attitude toward the event? Or does the speaker's attitude evolve in some changing fashion?

IPEK KADIFE'S RESPONSE TO READING FOR CONTENT IN EMILY DICKINSON'S "ME FROM MYSELF—TO BANISH"

If the speaker is experiencing some conflict with herself, she feels uneasy about it. The other person implied in "we" seems part of the conflict. If this "we" represents some other aspect of the speaker's self, she has to learn to adapt to the situation. Her attitude seems to evolve from feeling puzzled about being unable to resolve the conflict to accepting that she must surrender part of herself to resolve it. If the conflict concerns something that happened in or around Amherst in 1862, what might it be?

EXERCISE 4.2

Collaborative groups of five students each should continue to examine the lyrics of a popular song that they have located on the Internet. Here are some questions to consider:

- What is happening to the singer as he or she addresses the listener?
- How does the song express or imply some particular situation that has involved the singer in an emotional conflict?
- What is the singer's attitude toward this conflict?
- How does the singer's attitude change or develop during the course of the song?

The recorder should take notes and present them to the class at the end of the exercise.

Reading for Genre, Organization, and Stylistic Features
Genre

The specific markers of poetry as a genre are **meter**, or recurrent numbers of syllables and sound stresses on individual lines, and **rhyme**, or recurrent echoes of sound at the ends of lines. Both meter and rhyme may fall into patterns that repeat themselves throughout the poem. Or they may not. Many poems in "free verse" appear to have no pattern of meter or rhyme at all.

Questions to ask include: How many syllables appear on each line? Do they gather into rhythmic clusters of two, three, or four syllables on individual lines? Do they display a pattern of regular sound stresses? Do groups of lines display a pattern of repetition and/or variation? How many rhyme words punctuate the lines? Do these rhyme words gather into clusters? Do they display a regular pattern?

IPEK KADIFE'S RESPONSE TO READING FOR GENRE IN EMILY DICKINSON'S "ME FROM MYSELF—TO BANISH"

As I count the syllables on each line, I find that every odd-numbered line regularly has seven syllables. The even-numbered lines alternate between three and four syllables. These lines also rhyme in each stanza, though the rhyme in the middle stanza (peace/consciousness) is not exact.

EXERCISE 4.3

Collaborative groups of five students each should continue to examine the lyrics of a popular song that they have located on the Internet. Here are questions to consider:

- How many syllables appear on each line? Do they gather into any rhythmic clusters? Do they sustain any pattern?
- What about rhyme words in this song? Is there a distinct rhyming pattern?

The recorder should take notes and present them to the class at the end of the exercise.

Organization

Poems with a strict metrical form repeat the same **rhythmic pattern** in each stanza. Poems with a strict **rhyme scheme** likewise repeat the same rhyming pattern in each **stanza**. Many poems vary these patterns with great subtlety. Others display no rhythmic or rhyming patterns at all. Questions to ask include:

- What metrical patterns emerge? How are they repeated or varied?
- What rhyming patterns emerge? How are they repeated or varied?
- Do these patterns appear in other poems by other authors, where they might be identified with such particular forms as sonnets, couplets, limericks, nursery rhymes, hymns, odes, and the like?

IPEK KADIFE'S RESPONSE TO READING FOR ORGANIZATION IN EMILY DICKINSON'S "ME FROM MYSELF—TO BANISH"

The poem has three stanzas that approximate each other, with the variations of three- and seven-syllable lines mentioned above. Such a regular pattern lends itself to musical accompaniment—the lyrics for many songs are written in stanzas so that the musical rhythm and tempo can be repeated with the same number of beats in each stanza. The short stanzas of Dickinson's poem remind me of the way hymns look when they are printed for churchgoers. That might seem right for the churchgoing population of Amherst in 1862.

> **EXERCISE 4.4**
>
> Collaborative groups of five students each should continue to examine the lyrics of a popular song that they have located on the Internet. Questions to ask include:
>
> - Is the song divided into stanzas with notable repetitions and variations of form?
> - Are there any "openers" or recurring refrains? Or is the song instead "through-composed" in a single forward movement?
> - What other songs does it resemble?
>
> The recorder should take notes and present them to the class at the end of the exercise.

Stylistic Features

The language and sentence structures of many poems take **poetic license** with diction and syntax as they deploy unusual words or unusual grammar for striking effects. Rare usage, compressed expression, and inverted word order exemplify this license. **Figures of speech** such as metaphor, simile, personification, synecdoche (or part-for-the-whole), and metonymy (or sign-for-the-thing meant) likewise galvanize poetic styles. Questions to ask include:

- What is strange or exceptional about the heightened use of language in this poem?
- What is strange or exceptional about its syntax?
- How does this strangeness complicate or qualify the poem's meaning? How does it multiply the possibilities of interpreting the poem's characters or dramatic action?

IPEK KADIFE'S RESPONSE TO READING FOR STYLISTIC FEATURES IN EMILY DICKINSON'S "ME FROM MYSELF—TO BANISH"

The first sentence is hard to understand as it is written because it is so compact. If I try to paraphrase it, I have to expand the sentence to get something like this: "If only I had the art to banish myself from myself; but my fortress of self-defense is so strong that it resists my own efforts to break it down." As for figures of speech, the words "fortress" and "peace" suggest that there's a war going on somewhere in the background. 1862 was the second year of the American Civil War, no? Do the military metaphors refer to this war?

> **EXERCISE 4.5**
>
> Collaborative groups of five students each should continue to examine the lyrics of a popular song that they have located on the Internet. Here are questions to consider:
>
> - Does its use of diction and grammar suggest ordinary language? Or do its selection of words and its combination of sentence structures transmit a special kind of expression?
> - Do you find its lyrics "catchy" and unique? Why?
>
> The recorder should take notes and present them to the class at the end of the exercise.

Reading for Rhetorical Context

Since a poem usually records only a single speaker's discourse, it leaves his or her **conversation with other speakers** in the shadows. Reading such poetry invites you to fill in the gaps with your own imagination about what is left unsaid. In this way, as a reader of poetry you become part of the conversation. Questions to ask include:

- If this poem were recast in the form of a short story or drama, what would the rest of the dialogue record?
- What aspects of time, place, or situation would the context convey?
- Would we necessarily identify the poem's speaker with its historical author, or might we instead understand the poem as a fiction in its own right?
- What allusions does the poem make to other poems?

IPEK KADIFE'S RESPONSE TO READING FOR RHETORICAL CONTEXT IN EMILY DICKINSON'S "ME FROM MYSELF—TO BANISH"

After reading several poems by Emily Dickinson, I have no idea who she really was. As our professor told us, her contemporaries thought she was eccentric and they called her "the Myth of Amherst." She responded to their exaggerations about her by calling herself "a supposed person." This "supposed person" certainly wrote poems that portray quite a character. Her eccentricity stands out in the context of the Civil War.

EXERCISE 4.6

Collaborative groups of five students each should continue to examine the lyrics of a popular song that they have located on the Internet. Here are questions to consider:

- What story or drama is the song working to portray?
- If the singer is a well-known entertainer, do we really think that the lyrics communicate a bare-all confession? Or do we instead participate in the conversation with the tacit understanding that the performance is instead a fiction?

The recorder should take notes and present them to the class at the end of the exercise.

Here is Ipek Kadife's completed and revised paper of literary analysis on Emily Dickinson's "Me from Myself—to Banish."

STUDENT'S LITERARY ANALYSIS ESSAY

Ipek Kadife

English 11

Prof. Orhan Mitchell

October 12, 2006

Emily Dickinson and America's Civil War

Emily Dickinson is one of the most enigmatic poets we've read in our course packet. As we discussed in class, her neighbors in Amherst, Massachusetts, regarded her as a reclusive eccentric and called her "the Myth of Amherst" (Mitchell). She responded to their stories about her by

referring to herself as a "supposed person" (Mitchell). As reclusive as she
seemed to be, she still pursued a literary career with ferocity and determination. This strange blend of passivity and aggression characterizes her
poetry. We may never know what "real person" lurks behind the many voices
that speak in her poetry. And we may never know which real persons (if any)
her poems address. But we can listen to her poetry as it speaks in dialogue
with the shared issues of her time. "Me from Myself—to Banish" was written
in 1862 during the earliest months of the Civil War. I am going to argue
that the divided voice banishing "Me from Myself" addresses a nation suddenly at war with itself.

    The poem begins with one wishful statement in a convoluted syntax—"Me from
Myself—to Banish— / Had I Art"—and follows it with two questions. The opening
statement amounts to a poetic license from ordinary language, and its strained
effect conveys the painful self-division that the speaker senses within herself. Straightened out, the stanza means: "If only I had the art to banish myself from myself; but my fortress of self-defense is so strong that it resists
my own efforts to break it down." Its dominant metaphor depicts banishment from
a fortress. This figure of a military coup dominates the questions posed in the
next stanza. Here the speaker refers to an "assault" on herself and she asks how
she might have "peace" without "subjugating" herself. In the final stanza, the
use of force results in the "Abdication" of an authoritarian "Monarch" who has
absorbed the speaker and her partner as a "We" into some "mutual" conflict.

    The poem's rhyme scheme and its rhythms express a similar sense of strain.
At first their patterns seem simple: each short line of seven syllables is followed by a shorter line of three or four syllables. Likewise, the rhyme scheme
verges on free verse, as only the second and fourth lines in each stanza seem
to rhyme. On the printed page, the poem looks like a hymn in some denominational
song book. But if so, it's a cracked hymn. The rhyme in the middle stanza is
definitely off-key: "peace / fortress" rhyme only if we make "peace" sound like
"pess" or "fortress" sound like "fortrice." Did the townspeople of Amherst pro-
nounce these words like that in 1862? I doubt it. Likewise the poem's rhythms
wage war against each other. Instead of the expected three syllables, the fourth
and sixth lines offer four syllables. When in the sixth line the speaker asks,
"How have I peace," its disruption signals her inner confusion. The third stanza
does, I'll admit, convey a rhythmic regularity. But its coordination appears
elusive as its content refers to political unrest and a monarch's abdication.
Significantly, the total number of syllables in the poem is 62, the cardi-
nal numbers of the year in which Dickinson composed the poem at the start of
America's war against itself.

How, then, might the poem address the specter of this national war and the conscience of its participants? Does its cracked hymn point to discord in a confederated state? Does its "supposed person" offer her own psychological self-division as an emblem of the social self-division north and south of the newly created borders? I find it symptomatic that the poem's pronouns move from "Me," "Myself," and "I" in the first two stanzas to "We" at the beginning of the third stanza. Here the speaker refers to the duality that she feels because of her internal conflict. But the plural pronoun encompasses her readers and broader audience as well. Nowhere does the poem effectuate itself as a dialogue. And yet its passionate urgency everywhere suggests that it converses not just with itself but with a nation against itself. The final metaphor of a "Monarch" in "Abdication" reminds us that this nation believed it had already thrown off the chains of an earlier monarchy, only to find itself now enthralled to a greater threat. Was the poet who wrote these lines a mad recluse or a mere eccentric? Come again?

Works Cited

Dickinson, Emily. *The Poems of Emily Dickinson.* Ed. Thomas S. Johnson. 3 vols.
    Cambridge: Harvard UP, 1955. Print
Mitchell, Orhan. "Emily Dickinson." Cornell University, Ithaca, NY. 1 Oct.
    2006. Lecture.

◾ COMPARATIVE ANALYSIS

In high school you probably wrote essays in which you examined two issues, figures, or texts and discussed their points of similarity and difference. It's possible that the object of the comparison was simply to weigh things equally and report similarities and differences as an end in itself. In college, the object of comparison and contrast assignments is usually more complex. Your college professors will expect you to undertake a deeper analysis of the issues and texts by constructing a context or frame of reference and articulating an insightful thesis. The task, then, is not simply to compare and contrast one issue, figure, or text with another. It is instead to develop and articulate a critical view toward what you are comparing. As you evaluate the different positions, you will be moving toward an argument about their relative strengths and weaknesses. You will soon arrive at a position of your own. At this point, you can then formulate a thesis about the issues at stake.

In your college classes you will incorporate comparisons into longer writing projects, and you will also compose stand-alone comparative analysis essays. We will illustrate comparative analyses of both types. To illustrate the first type, we will examine a section of "Looking Forward to Sociable Robots" by Glenda Shaw-Garlock. You will find the entire article in Chapter 10. The subject of this article is "humanoid social robots," robots that are built to resemble humans and interact and communicate with them in a meaningful way. Shaw-Garlock focuses on Kismet, a robot developed at the Massachusetts Institute of Technology (MIT), and Repliée, a robot developed at Osaka University in Japan. As she examines the specific characteristics of the two robots, she investigates the underlying societal conditions that contributed to each robot's development and reception. Her thesis is that more research needs to be done on human-robot interaction and that in order to do that research, scientists need "a set of conceptual tools that are capable of engaging with the boundary contradictions that robot-human relations evoke" (352). Before you read the excerpt that follows, you might like to take a look at Kismet and Repliée-Q2. Kismet has its own Web site at <http://www.ai.mit.edu/projects/humanoid-robotics-group/kismet/kismet.html>. For a view of Repliée-Q2, visit Professor Hiroshi Ishiguro's laboratory at Osaka Univeristy: <http://www.is.sys.es.osaka-u.ac.jp/development/0006/index.en.html>.

EXCERPT FROM "LOOKING FORWARD TO SOCIABLE ROBOTS"

UTILITARIAN VERSUS AFFECTIVE ROBOTS

Generally speaking, there are two classes of social robots: the *utilitarian* humanoid social robot and the *affective* humanoid social robot [11, 77]. Utilitarian social robots are sometimes referred to as domestic robots or service robots and are designed to interact with humans mainly for instrumental or functional purposes. Examples familiar to North Americans include: ATMs, vending machines, and automated telephone and answering systems. Less familiar examples include: help desk receptionists, salespersons, private tutors, travel agents, hospital food servers, and museum tour guides. This category of social robot typically involves regarding robots as "very sophisticated appliances that people use to perform tasks" [11].   1

Affective humanoid social robots on the other hand, are robots that are designed to interact with humans on an emotional level through play, sometimes therapeutic play, and perhaps even companionship. Contemporary examples include, Tiger Electronic's hamsters-like *Furby* and Sony's puppy-like robot *AIBO*. Japan's National Institute of Advanced Industrial Science and Technology created Paro, a harp seal robot, to serve as companions for Japan's expanding number of senior citizens [40] and therapeutic playmates for children with Autism [19]. Turkle refers to this class of robot as *relational artifacts*, defining them as "artifacts that present themselves as having 'states of mind' for which an understanding of those states enriches human encounters with them" [67]. Unlike the utilitarian robot, this category of robot demands a more social form of human-robot interaction, meaning this class of robot requires a level of functionality and usability that will allow it to interact with human agents within the context of natural social exchange.   2

Kismet and Repliée, the robots under consideration in this paper, fall into the category of affective social robot in that they are capable of interacting with humans using   3 facial expression, gaze direction, and vocalization and thereby engage in the affective dynamics of human relationships. Upon reviewing the literature it seems clear that in the future social robots will increasingly fall into the hybrid category (yet unnamed) between strictly utilitarian and affective. For example, Heerink et al. [35] consider therapeutic social robots, such as Paro, as a hybrid category that it is utilitarian because it functions as an assistive technology and affective or "hedonic" in that it serves an affective or emotional function. As such, the tasks that social robots will be expected to perform will become more complex and in turn so shall the robots themselves. (250)

Shaw-Garlock, Glenda. "Looking Forward to Sociable Robots." *International Journal of Social Robotics* 1.3 (2009): 249–60. Print.

In paragraphs 1 and 2, Shaw-Garlock has a simple and straightforward rhetorical goal: to enable her readers to distinguish between two classes of social robots: utilitarian humanoid robots and affective humanoid robots. After reading these paragraphs, the reader understands that the two types of robots have different functions and require different degrees of robot-human interaction. In these paragraphs, Shaw-Garlock defines each type of robot, describes its function, gives examples, and explains the degree of human interaction the robot requires. She uses an arrangement called a "block," "text-by-text," "consecutive," "one-side-at-a-time," or "summary" approach.

▦ Block Arrangement

When writers use this type of arrangement, they first present information about one subject and then present corresponding information about the second subject. Usually, a transition informs the reader as to whether the two subjects are being contrasted or compared. In the above passage, the transitional phrase "on the other hand" prepares the reader for an explanation of differences.

> **Block Arrangement**
> **Utilitarian social robots**
> > Purpose of the design
> > Examples
> > Required degree of human interaction
> **Affective humanoid social robots**
> > Purpose of the design
> > Examples
> > Required degree of human interaction

▦ Point-by-Point Arrangement

Another way to organize a comparison is in a "point-by-point," "alternating," or "back-and-forth" pattern. Using this arrangement, the writer discusses one feature or point as it relates to both of the items that are being compared. Had Shaw-Garlock arranged the section in this way, she would have devoted the first paragraph to robot design and the second paragraph to human interaction, and then developed each paragraph by showing how utilitarian and affective robots compare with respect to each feature.

> **Point-by-Point Arrangement**
>
> Purpose of the design and examples
>> Utilitarian social robots
>>
>> Affective humanoid social robots
>
> Required degree of human interaction
>> Utilitarian social robots
>>
>> Affective humanoid social robots

Before you compare two subjects or texts, you must decide on the bases or grounds for the comparison. In other words, the two subjects need to have something in common. In the above passage, Shaw-Garlock's grounds for comparing the two types of social robots are that both robots are designed to assist humans and both correspondingly require a certain amount of human-robot interaction.

Paragraph 3 reveals the author's deeper goal: to show where Kismet and Repliée fit into the scheme of things (they are affective humanoid social robots) and to propose a thesis about the nature of social robots in the future. Shaw-Garlock believes "in the future social robots will increasingly fall into the hybrid category (yet unnamed) between strictly utilitarian and affective" (250).

■ Reflect Upon What Comparisons and Contrasts Reveal

Inexperienced writers often think that the sole object of a comparison and contrast essay is to identify similarities and differences without further commentary. They write paragraphs comparable to paragraphs 1 and 2 above and simply tack on an introduction with a predictable thesis along the lines of "Social robots differ in significant ways." Then they conclude by saying, "Thus, utilitarian social robots and affective social robots have notable differences." In a more complex comparative analysis essay, you need to take the process a step further. Examine the competing arguments, step back, and then reflect on what their similarities and differences represent, reveal, or demonstrate. Let us look at how Shaw-Garlock does this in another section of the article.

Section 4.1 of "Looking Forward to Sociable Robots" focuses on the relationship between the Kismet and Repliée physical bodies and their general and social intelligence. The argument that Shaw-Garlock advances is that societal assumptions or preconditions have played a role in determining whether behavior or appearance was the most important consideration in the robot's creation.

EXCERPT FROM "LOOKING FORWARD TO SOCIABLE ROBOTS"

4.1 EMBODIED AND SOCIAL INTELLIGENCE

From the early stage of Kismet's development, there was the explicit assumption that   1
embodiment is connected to intelligence and learning. "The point was, if you really
wanted to understand human intelligence, it was important to have a human-like

body, to have human-like interactions with the world…[and] that in order to learn from experience, you have to have something to get experience through, and that of course is this body situated in this environment" [8, 60]. Similarly, a distinguishing feature within Japanese robotics is the idea of embodied intelligence, consistent with the behavior-based approach which guides the research project Kismet. The central idea here is a shift from AI projects that 'think' intelligently to projects that 'act' intelligently. Under this view, intelligence may not be abstracted to some algorithmic equation but requires physical grounding or a material foundation (body). In this way, "embodied intelligence blurs the conceptual distinction between life and cognition, and between living and intelligent behavior" [57]. Ishiguro's project takes the principles underlying Kismet's project a step beyond being embodied (a material basis in the world) and being situated (sensory input effecting behavior) and to it adds an extremely sophisticated level of human like verisimilitude [36].

We can also distinguish between Kismet and Repliée in terms of *social intelligence*   2 or the degree to which each may be considered "a full-fledged social participant" [10].

> If the robot's observable behaviour adheres to a person's social model for it during unconstrained interactions in the full complexity of the human environment, then we argue that the robot is socially intelligent in a genuine sense. Basically, the person can engage the robot as one would another socially responsive creature, and the robot does the same. At the pinnacle of performance, this would rival human–human interaction. [10]

Comparing the social intelligence realized by the two robots under consideration, it may be concluded that Kismet is a highly convincing socially intelligent creature but less compelling aesthetically as a humanoid agent. Breazeal describes the rich interaction between test subjects and Kismet as taking "place on a physical, social, and affective level. In so many ways, they treat Kismet as if it were a socially aware, living creature" [8].

Repliée on the other hand, is highly believable in terms of her aesthetic appear-   3 ance, indeed she passes as a human 70% of time in short interval (2 second) recognition tests [37, 38, 45]. However, in terms of her ability to engage with humans as a genuine social agent Repliée is quite limited relative to Kismet. Utilizing Breazeal's [10] matrix of humanoid social robots, Repliée falls into the 'social interface' category.

> This subclass of robots uses human-like social cues and communication modalities in order to facilitate interactions with people (i.e., to make the interactions more natural and familiar)…commonly, an interface model is used, such as robot museum tour guides, where information is communicated to people using speech and sometimes with reflexive facial expressions. Because this class of robot tends to value social behaviour only at the interface, the social model that the robot has for the person tends to be shallow (if any) and the social behavior is often pre-canned or reflexive. [10]

Conversely, Kismet is a fully "sociable creature" in that it possesses its "own internal goals and motivations…proactively engage[s] people in a social manner not only to benefit the person (e.g., to help perform a task, to facilitate interaction with the robot, etc.), but also to benefit itself" [10]. In conclusion, we can say that the degree of social intelligence achieved in each project highlights the artificial intelligence bias (associated with the view that behavior is of primary importance in human-robot interaction) in Kismet and the aesthetic bias (associated with the view that appearance is at least as important as behavior in human-robot interaction) in Repliée. (251–252)

Shaw-Garlock, Glenda. "Looking Forward to Sociable Robots." *International Journal of Social Robotics* 1.3 (2009): 249–60. Print.

Here the author is reflecting upon differences between the robots' humanlike appearance and their humanlike behavior. She represents Repliée as more successful in appearance and Kismet as more responsive in behavior. As she compares and contrasts them, she concludes that social and cultural factors determine the robots' respective value. Because of Japan's historical appreciation of aesthetic artifice, the developers of Repliée value appearance more than behavior. Because of America's historic interest in pragmatic results, the reverse is true for the developers of Kismet. We might outline the author's reflections as follows.

OUTLINE OF AUTHOR'S REFLECTIONS

Paragraph 1

Embodied intelligence

In the creation of both Kismet and Repliée, an underlying principle was that their "artificial intelligence" would be contained in a material body.

Both Kismet and Repliée have embodied intelligence, but Repliée's body is more lifelike than Kismet's.

Paragraph 2

Social intelligence

Social intelligence is the extent to which the robot is socially responsive to the human with whom it interacts.

Kismet is sociable and engages people very well, but it is "less compelling aesthetically as a humanoid agent."

Repliée passes for a human but is quite limited in genuine social interaction with humans.

Conclusion

Thesis: Different societal assumptions or preconditions are at work here. For Kismet, behavior is more important than appearance, and for Repliée appearance is as important or more important than behavior.

Here the author's expanded analytical goal has been to situate the comparison in a socio-cultural context. Here the competing claims of aesthetics versus practicality determine the respective outcomes. The author does not explicitly state her own preference for one over the other. She does, however, challenge our usual expectations by pointing out that aesthetic appearance rather than practical behavior is an important consideration for many scientists in robotic development.

COMPARATIVE ANALYSIS OF TEXTS

A **comparative analysis** of texts *analyzes a focal text through the lens of another text that is comparable.* The purpose is twofold: to show how one text corroborates or debates the other, and to develop and articulate a critical view toward what you are comparing. An important factor is the basis for the comparison. When you write a comparative analysis, your readers need to know why you chose Text A and Text B rather than Text A and Text C. Keep in mind that you may use the comparative analysis approach in combination with other approaches such as zeroing in on key elements and viewing each text through a particular critical lens.

Don't fall into the trap of doing too much summarizing—giving a synopsis of each text—and then simply explaining how the authors' views are similar and different. You need to take the process a step further.

Ask yourself the questions in the following box. Answers to these questions will shape or expand on your goal.

QUESTIONS TO ASK ABOUT SIMILARITIES AND DIFFERENCES

- How do the views in these two texts relate to one another—as though they were part of a conversation or as a give-and-take of interdependent ideas?
- What happens when they qualify, contradict, or otherwise complicate one another?
- What angle or point of view emerges with regard to the material?

Illustration of Comparison and Contrast of Texts

To illustrate how a published writer expresses an expanded goal, consider the opening paragraphs of "Two Views of Motherhood," a review essay in which sociologist Carol A. Brown compares and contrasts two books: *Engendering Motherhood: Identity and Self-Transformations in Women's Lives* by Martha McMahon and *Bearing Meaning: The Language of Birth* by Robbie Pfeufer Kahn. McMahon's book is pointedly academic whereas Kahn's includes personal experience.

> These books give opposing answers to a question: How do we study and how do we teach about any social relation, in this case motherhood, while taking into account both the personal experiences of the individuals involved and the macrosocial factors that create and vary the institution?
>
> Both books take a feminist perspective, understanding the historical significance of patriarchy and the extent to which gender and male domination affect current concepts and practices. Both recognize the conflicted meaning of childbirth and motherhood as a cause for women's devaluation in a masculist society and as a feminine domain that connects, empowers, and activates women's self-confidence and social presence.
>
> The difference is that between a monograph and a monologue. (355)

Brown frames the book review with a question ("How do we study and how do we teach…?") and she uses the body paragraphs of the comparison and contrast essay to answer this question. ("Both books take a feminist perspective.... Both recognize....) She ends the essay with the following paragraphs:

> I find it ironic that when I sit back and think about what I have taken away from both books, I realize that Kahn, impassioned and personal, spoke to me as a sociologist, while McMahon, cool and academic, spoke to me as a mother.
>
> So the answer to my original question is that there are a variety of ways of teaching about a social relation while taking into account both the personal experiences of the individuals involved and the macrosocial factors that create and vary the institution. Both books are strong on data and analysis; both give us an individual perspective as well as sociological analysis. McMahon's sociology is easier to see because it is in the classic format, but Kahn's sociology is just as suitable to her topic as McMahon's is for hers. (358)

Once you have analyzed the two texts with which you are working, step back to see if there is anything significant about the comparable and contrastive elements you have identified. As the passages from Brown's essay illustrate, she finds it interesting that despite the two books' different approaches, they are equally effective as studies of the sociology of motherhood.

■ Identifying Similarities and Differences

As you read the texts that you intend to compare and contrast, you should annotate them to highlight major correspondences between them. Then do a second reading for the purpose of identifying as many less obvious similarities and differences as you can. In the box below, we provide strategies that will help you discover how two reading sources can be similar and different.

ELABORATING TO UNCOVER COMPARISONS AND CONTRASTS

- Identify points where one text
  agrees or disagrees with the other text
  says something relevant about the topic that the other text has neglected
  qualifies ideas stated by the other text
  extends a proposition made by the other text
- Validate one author's assertion with information provided by the other author.
- Subsume similarities and differences between the texts under subordinate categories.
- Create hierarchies of importance among ideas that are similar or different.
- Make judgments about the relevance of one author's view in relation to the other's view.

Many writers find it useful to design a pictorial representation of the similarities and differences. One useful technique for creating a visual display of similarity and difference is webbing. The web in Figure 4–1 depicts points of difference in Arthur Caplan's "The Trouble with Organ Trafficking" (pp. 307–09) and Sally Satel's "Why We Need a Market for Human Organs" (pp. 310–12).

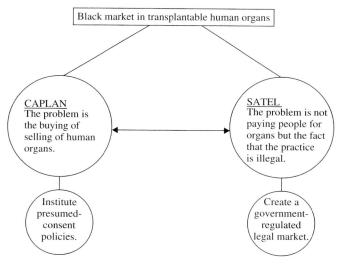

Figure 4–1   Webbing

Once you have identified a point of similarity or difference, summarize it in a short phrase and place it in a box at the center of a sheet of paper. Spin out the web by writing each author's ideas around this key idea node. Circle each of these ideas and connect them with lines to the key idea and, where appropriate, to each other. When you are finished webbing, you will have a visual display of the points of similarity and difference.

■ Process of Writing a Comparative Analysis of Texts

To illustrate the process of composing a comparative analysis of two texts, we will accompany our student Esmé Donnelly as she works through an assignment based on "The Trouble with Organ Trafficking" by Arthur Caplan and "Why We Need a Market for Human Organs" by Sally Satel.

Assignment

Analyze Arthur Caplan's and Sally Satel's views on the topic of organ trafficking. Write for an audience of college students. Your essay should be three to four pages, and you should address it to your classmates.

Both articles are included in Chapter 9 of this book. "The Trouble with Organ Trafficking" was originally published in *Free Inquiry*, the magazine of the Council for Secular Humanism. According to the Web site of the Council, "The mission of the Council for Secular Humanism is to advocate and defend a nonreligious lifestance rooted in science, naturalistic philosophy, and humanist ethics and to serve and support adherents of that lifestance." Satel's article was published in *The Wall Street Journal*, a newspaper that focuses on U.S. and international business and financial news.

On her first reading, Esmé underlines and annotates the texts, jots down her reactions, and marks passages where one text relates to the other. On the second reading, she examines the texts for additional points of similarity and difference, and she takes notes. (See Figure 4–2.)

Satel, Paragraphs 10 and 12
His goal is a regulated, transparent regime backed by the rule of law and devoted to donor protection. (10).... By providing in-kind rewards financed by the government—such as a down payment on a house (one of Dr. Carney's suggestions), a contribution to a retirement fund, or lifetime health insurance....

Esmé's Notes
Caplan counters that a government-regulated market in organs won't work because most nations don't have the resources, and, besides, most can't even regulate their banking, housing, and securities. I think the global recession resulting from the recent financial crisis is evidence of that.

Caplan, Paragraph 9
Third—and perhaps the greatest problem with legalizing organ and body-part markets—is that such markets prey on the grim circumstances of the poor.

Esmé's Notes
Satel says poor people who need instant cash will be deterred by the long waiting period, screening, education, and types of rewards. I think they may be disappointed by these obstacles, but they won't prevent them from selling their organs. Caplan makes a stronger case here.

Caplan, Paragraph 13
In a market—even a regulated one—doctors and nurses still would be using their skills to help living people harm themselves solely for money.

Esmé's Notes
To me, this ethical argument is stronger than Satel's economic argument.

Figure 4–2   Text and Student's Notes

Planning Comparison and Contrast Essays

Next, Esmé selects and orders her ideas and sketches out a blueprint for the essay. She creates two lists: one list for similarities between the sources and the other for differences. An alternative way you might do this is to mark the text wherever you've discovered similarities or differences (use symbols: = for similarities and ≠ for differences). Here are Esmé's two lists:

Similarities:

- Both Caplan and Satel observe that the demand for transplantable organs far outweighs the supply of organs, and, as a result, there is a flourishing, worldwide black market in human organs.
- Both writers agree that illegal organ trafficking is indefensible and has negative consequences for sellers as well as buyers.

Differences:

- Whereas Caplan opposes the selling of organs and tissue for money, Satel supports a legalized market in human organs.
- Caplan proposes to increase the supply through "presumed-consent policies." Satel argues that the only way to increase supply is through financial incentives.
- Caplan argues that legal markets will prey on poor people who will sell their organs because of their desperate circumstances. Satel believes it is possible to create regulated systems of legal exchange that will not exploit desperate poor people.

- Whereas Satel thinks a regulated system of exchange with rewards financed by the government is workable, Caplan says, "There is no reason to think that most nations have the resources to regulate a market in organs effectively."
- Caplan raises a number of ethical objections to the selling of body parts whereas Satel does not.

As Esmé analyzes the similarities and differences, she asks herself three questions: (1) What do the similarities and differences demonstrate? (2) What do they tell me about each of the two texts? (3) How does one text corroborate, debate, reinforce, prove, or disprove the other text? In response to the questions, Esmé forms a generalization about the similarities and differences.

When academic writers compare and contrast texts, their goal is to make a claim or propose a thesis. As we said earlier, sometimes student writers simply describe the similarities and differences. This is a limited rhetorical goal. A more powerful purpose requires the writer to compare and contrast the texts for a specific reason: for example, to describe, explain, or argue a point, or to communicate what the comparison reveals or demonstrates about the subject.

Limited Goal	More Powerful Goal
Bring out similarities and differences in the subject matter.	1. Use the comparison to describe, explain, or argue a position.
	2. Show what the comparison reveals or demonstrates about the subject.

When you read Esmé's essay on pages 140–41, you will see that as she lays out the similarities and differences between the two readings, she aligns herself more with Caplan than with Satel, leading up to the final paragraph, where she concludes that Caplan's argument against the legalization of organ trafficking is more constructive and persuasive than Satel's.

Organizing the Comparison and Contrast Essay

Comparison and contrast essays are organized in a point-by-point format, a block arrangement, or a combination of the two.

ORGANIZATIONAL PATTERNS

Point-by-Point

Introductory Paragraph(s)

1. Paper Opener. See techniques on page 97.
2. Identify the issue(s) and the authors and/or texts.
3. Explain your rhetorical goal (your purpose for comparing the sources).

Body Paragraphs

1. Compare the texts with respect to a single position or argument.
2. Repeat Step 1 for each position or argument you intend to treat.

(continued)

Concluding Paragraph(s)

Block

Introductory Paragraph(s)

1. Paper Opener. See techniques on page 97.
2. Identify the issue(s) and the authors and/or texts.
3. Explain your rhetorical goal (your purpose for comparing the sources).

Body Paragraphs

1. Identify and discuss the positions and arguments expressed in the first text.
2. Compare the positions and arguments expressed in the first text with those expressed in the second text.

Concluding Paragraph(s)

Esmé Donnelly organizes her essay by using a combination of both patterns. Paragraph 2 presents the two authors' positions in point-by-point fashion. The remaining paragraphs present the authors' positions in block fashion, with paragraph 3 devoted to Satel and paragraphs 4, 5, and 6 devoted to Caplan. In the final paragraph Esmé again compares both writers in point-by-point fashion.

Consider how Esmé would have outlined an essay written exclusively in the point-by-point pattern.

OUTLINE FOR COMPARISON ESSAY WRITTEN IN POINT-BY-POINT ARRANGEMENT

Introductory Paragraph(s)

Body Paragraphs

Point 1: how to increase the supply of organs

Satel supports a legalized market in human organs. She argues that the only way to increase supply is through financial incentives.

Caplan opposes the selling of organs and tissue for money. He offers an alternative way to increase the supply: "presumed-consent policies."

Point 2: the effect of legal markets on poor people

Satel believes it is possible to create regulated systems of legal exchange that will not appeal to desperate poor people.

Caplan argues that legal markets will prey on poor people who will sell their organs because of their desperate circumstances

Point 3: medical ethics

Satel does not address the question of medical ethics.

Caplan raises a number of ethical objections to the selling of body parts.

Concluding Paragraph(s)

If Esmé had chosen to write an essay organized solely on the block pattern instead of alternating between Caplan and Satel with each point of comparison, she would have contrasted the texts in blocks, dealing with one text in the first block and switching to the other in the second segment. Her essay would have conformed to the following outline:

OUTLINE FOR COMPARISON ESSAY WRITTEN IN BLOCK ARRANGEMENT

Introductory Paragraph(s)

Body Paragraphs

First Block: Satel

Paragraph: Satel's support of a legalized market in human organs as the only way to increase supply is through financial incentives

Paragraph: Satel's argument that it is possible to create regulated systems of legal exchange that will not appeal to desperate poor people

Paragraph: Satel's argument that a regulated system of exchange with rewards financed by the government is workable

Second Block: Caplan

Paragraph: Caplan opposes the legalization of organ sales and offers instead an alternative way to increase the supply: "presumed-consent policies."

Paragraph: Caplan presents ethical objections to the legalization of organ trafficking.

Concluding Paragraph(s)

Drafting Comparison and Contrast Essays

After Esmé selects an organizational plan, she writes a draft of her essay. This first draft is preliminary. She will have an opportunity to change direction, sharpen her focus, and revise at a later date.

The box that follows lists conventions for comparison essays. As you read Esmé's essay, notice the extent to which she uses them.

CONVENTIONS FOR COMPARISON AND CONTRAST ESSAYS

- Give your readers background about the topic.
- Identify the texts by title and author.
- Indicate the grounds for comparison; that is, the points you are using to compare and contrast the texts.
- Clearly state your thesis.
- Develop each point of comparison by paraphrasing, summarizing, or quoting relevant points in the readings and bringing your prior topic knowledge and experience to bear on the text.
- Clearly differentiate your own ideas from those in the texts.
- Correctly document material you have paraphrased, summarized, or quoted.

SAMPLE COMPARATIVE ANALYSIS ESSAY

Esmé Donnelly

English 131

Professor Kennedy

12 October 2010

The Controversy Over the Selling of Human Organs

Does the end justify the means? Is an action that is physically dangerous and morally questionable excusable if it results in a positive end? Would it be pardonable for a Filipino teenager to undergo risky surgery and then sell his kidney for $5,000 if this transaction saved the life of an American businessman with end-stage renal disease? The answer to this question depends on one's ethical and economic views about the action. Some would say it is wrong to put a price on the human body whereas others would argue that paying people for body parts is the only way to save lives because of the dearth of donated organs.

Key figures in the debate over the proposal to legalize cash payments for organs are Sally Satel, a psychiatrist and scholar at the American Enterprise Institute who received a kidney from a friend in 2006, and Arthur Caplan, Professor of Bioethics at the University of Pennsylvania. Both Satel and Caplan condemn illegal organ trafficking and the corrupt practices of the worldwide black market, and both acknowledge that we must increase the supply of human organs. Satel argues that the best way to stop illegal organ trafficking is to legalize it. Caplan finds this proposal untenable, unethical, and immoral, and he mounts a persuasive argument against it.

Satel's proposal, "Why We Need a Market for Human Organs," appeared in the *Wall Street Journal*. Satel argues that the only way to increase the supply of transplantable organs and end people's dependence on the black market is "by a cash payment to potential donors or through some other form of compensation" (A11). She says critics of legalized markets have mistaken ideas. She corrects the misconception that legalized markets "will inevitably replicate the sins of unauthorized markets" by pointing out that a regulated system will offer ample protection for donors and recipients (A11). In addressing the complaint that a legalized market will exploit poor, desperate people, she proposes a model system that will not appeal to people who need ready cash. It will have "a months-long period of medical screening and education," and the compensation for organs will be government-backed rewards, for example, "a down payment on a house," "a contribution to a retirement fund," or "lifetime health insurance" (A11).

As appealing as Satel's model of a government-controlled market might be, any system of cash payments for human organs raises serious ethical questions. Arthur Caplan discusses these ethical issues, as well as other concerns, in "The Trouble with Organ Trafficking," an article published in the magazine *Free Inquiry*. Caplan is totally against the selling of body parts and body tissue

of living people and cadavers. He believes nations can increase the supply of
organs by instituting "presumed-consent policies, asking those who do not want
to be donors to carry cards or register their objection in computer registries."
He points out, "When supplemented with appropriate training and resources, these
systems have proven very effective in Spain, Belgium, Austria, and other nations."
In contrast, government-regulated markets in organs will not be effective, he
says, because most nations do not have the resources to make them work.

Regardless of whether legalized organ sales would be feasible or not, for
Caplan they are impermissible because they are unethical. The biggest problem
is that even a tightly regulated market will exploit poor people because they
will sell spare body parts to improve their dismal conditions if they have no
other choice. Caplan writes:

> Faced with fiscal ruin or grinding poverty, it may be a "rational"
> decision to sell your body parts (or for that matter your baby or
> your body into prostitution or slavery), but that does not make it a
> matter of free, voluntary choice.

Caplan argues, "All markets do is put a polite façade on exploitation."

Caplan also objects to organ selling because it "violates the ethics of
the health-care professions." Organ removal puts a patient at risk. If surgery
is driven primarily by the donor's desire for financial gain, the physician is
putting the patient at risk for the sake of money. In cases where organs are
procured from cadavers, it is possible that depending on the worth of the potential organ, physicians and families will be tempted to treat the dying patient
less aggressively. According to Caplan, in such situations, "the resulting
distrust and loss of professional standards is a high price to pay to gamble on
the hope that a market may secure more organs and tissues for those in need."

The benefits of paying people for body parts do not outweigh the costs.
Despite Satel's assurances, we cannot dismiss the possibility that a regulated
market in human organs may have negative consequences for both donors and
recipients as well as for health professionals. As Caplan persuasively argues,
the motive for organ donation should continue to be altruism, not money.

Works Cited

Caplan, Arthur. "The Trouble with Organ Trafficking." *Free Inquiry*. Council for
    Secular Humanism. n.d. Web. 4 Oct. 2010.
Satel, Sally. "Why We Need a Market for Human Organs." *Wall Street Journal*.
    Wall Street Journal. 16 May 2008: A11. Web. 20 Sept. 2010.

Notice that Esmé Donnelly's essay follows many but not all of the guidelines we've suggested for comparison and contrast papers. No essay can ever be expected to observe all the guidelines for a particular form of writing, because each topic or issue introduces matters that require their own distinctive treatment. Nevertheless, you will note in Esmé's essay a consistent attention to detail that takes account of her readers' knowledge of the two texts and a careful assessment of the authors' argument, organization, and rhetorical context. The essay reveals that Esmé annotated the reading materials point by point, and it demonstrates that Esmé's argument is clear and systematic from her opening paragraphs about the major differences between Caplan and Satel, through individual paragraphs that focus on each text, to her concluding paragraph about the texts' divergence.

We have presented Esmé's polished essay. Bear in mind that she produced this version after several preliminary drafts, a conference with her instructor, and a peer review. If your professor agrees, ask a classmate to review your essay. If this is not possible, review the essay yourself. We provide questions in the following box.

QUESTIONS FOR HELPING A WRITER REVISE THE FIRST DRAFT OF A COMPARATIVE ANALYSIS ESSAY

- Is the writer's rhetorical purpose clear? Explain how he or she is attempting to influence or affect readers.
- Does the writer explain what the similarities and contrasts reveal or demonstrate, or is the writer's purpose simply to show that similarities and differences exist? If the writer's goal is limited, suggest a more powerful goal.
- Does everything in the essay lead to or follow from one central meaning? If not, which ideas appear to be out of place?
- Will the reader understand the essay, and is the writer sensitive to the reader's concerns?

    Does the writer provide necessary background information about the subject matter, the sources, and their titles and authors? If not, what is missing?

    Throughout the essay, when the writer refers to the source text, does he or she supply the reader with necessary documentation?

    Does the writer provide clear transitions or connecting ideas that differentiate his or her own ideas from those expressed in the texts?

    Does the writer display an awareness of the authors by referring to them by name and personal pronoun ("Smith states," "she explains") rather than personifying the source ("the article states," "it explains")?

- Is the organizational format appropriate for a comparison and contrast essay? Is the writer using point-by-point or block arrangement?
- Has the writer revealed the points of comparison to the reader? Are these criteria or bases for comparison clear or confusing? Explain.
- Does the writer provide transitions and connecting ideas as he or she moves from one source to another or from one point of comparison to the next? If not, where are they needed?
- Do you hear the writer's voice throughout the entire essay? Describe it.

- Does the writer use an opener that catches the reader's attention?
- Does the conclusion simply restate the main idea, or does it offer new insights?
- Does the essay have an appropriate title?
- What other suggestions can you give the writer for improving this draft?

EXERCISE 4.7

Reread Esmé Donnelly's essay. She does not summarize, paraphrase, or quote from all sections of the two texts; instead, she focuses on points where Satel's argument relates specifically to Caplan's. Evaluate her selection. Can you make any generalizations about her selective use of paraphrase and quotation?

■ A BRIEF WORD ABOUT OTHER TYPES OF ANALYSIS ESSAYS

In this last section of the chapter, we will explain three other forms of analysis that are regularly assigned in college courses: rhetorical analysis, process analysis, and causal analysis. We explain the purpose of each type of analysis and suggest questions that will guide your writing process.

■ Rhetorical Analysis

A **rhetorical analysis** examines *how a text is written*. It pays attention to what the text talks about, but its main focus is the strategies and devices the author uses to convey the meaning. As Chapter 1 demonstrated, rhetorical analysis is an important operation of critical reading. If you look back to pages 24–27, you can reread our rhetorical analysis of the stylistic features of Pauline Irit Erera and Barbara Ehrenreich's texts. When you receive an assignment that calls for rhetorical analysis, think in terms of the rhetorical strategies that we presented in Chapter 1. Ask questions about *genre, organization, stylistic features*, and *rhetorical context*. In Chapter 3, we discussed three approaches to analysis: zero in on key elements, view the text through a particular critical lens, and compare the text to a source that is similar. A rhetorical analysis zeroes in on the rhetorical features of the target text.

Similar to the purpose of a critical analysis, the *overall purpose* of a rhetorical analysis is to share your interpretation with your readers, and, ideally, to convince them that your enlightened reading of the text warrants their attention and should be taken seriously. A more *focused purpose* is to evaluate the author's rhetorical context and strategies.

■ Process Analysis

A **process analysis** *outlines the steps in an operation*. In so doing, it often explains and comments on the formation of these steps, emphasizes important relationships among them, provides supplementary information, and includes caveats about what can go wrong. Unlike a summary, a process analysis explains the amount of time the process will take, defines unfamiliar terms, comments on the importance of selected steps, mentions the problems that might be encountered, and gives advice on how the problems could be overcome. In academic writing, you might occasionally be asked to write a self-contained, stand-alone process analysis essay, but more often you'll be called upon to embed a process analysis within other genres of writing.

Process of Writing a Process Analysis

Your first step in writing a process analysis is to identify your purpose. Ronna Vanderslice's "When I Was Young, an A Was an A" reprinted in Chapter 2, pages 36–37, begins with a paragraph narrating the steady inflation of college grades from 1969 to 2004. The author recounts this process in order to launch her thesis that higher education must increase standards that will restore the credibility of a college degree.

Another purpose of a process analysis is to provide readers with directions for completing the task described in the process. You may have written this type of essay in the earlier grades when you were asked to explain processes such as how to make a peanut butter sandwich or how to give your dog a bath. You may be called upon to write a self-contained process analysis essay in one of your college classes. If so, a second consideration, aside from determining your purpose, is deciding how much background information to give your readers. If you are embedding the analysis in a larger project, the context is a given. If you are writing a self-contained analysis, you need to give your audience a reason for reading your analysis.

Here are questions that will prove helpful.

QUESTIONS FOR WRITING A PROCESS ANALYSIS

- Why am I analyzing the process? Do I want my readers to understand the process (supply information) or do I want them to perform the procedure (give directions)?
- Will I provide background information and motivate my readers to read my analysis, or will I be embedding the analysis in a larger piece of writing?
- If I am offering directions, have I made correct assumptions about my readers' level of expertise?
- Have I explained the amount of time the process will take, sequenced the steps, and provided an appropriate level of specificity (enough concrete, detailed explanation)?
- Have I provided supplementary information by:

  defining unfamiliar terms?

  commenting on the importance of selected steps?

  including precautions and warnings about what might go wrong and how to overcome the problems?

  giving follow-up or trouble-shooting advice?
- Have I used an adequate number of chronological transitions?

◼ Causal Analysis

A **causal analysis**, also called cause-and-effect analysis, seeks *to identify the reasons why something happens.* It is used to examine why a phenomenon or event is occurring, to investigate possible causes of a problem, or to examine effects. Often the goal of a causal analysis is to interpret history by studying multiple causes for historical events. A causal analysis may be a self-contained essay or it may be embedded in a longer piece of writing. Chapter 12 contains an historical causal analysis, "The Origins of the Ambivalent Acceptance of Divorce" (pp. 433–39) by Andrew J. Cherlin. Cherlin analyzes the history of American attitudes toward divorce in order to explain contemporary views on single parenting.

Process of Writing a Causal Analysis

You already know a good deal about analyzing causes and effects. The analysis questions you have been using throughout this chapter emphasize the importance of examining reasons as well as implications, conclusions, and consequences. Investigating causes and effects is an operation of critical thinking as well as a format for writing.

QUESTIONS FOR WRITING A CAUSAL ANALYSIS

- Why am I writing this causal analysis—to heighten my readers' awareness or also to argue that some causes or effects are more plausible and explanatory than others?
- Have I sufficiently narrowed the focus of the cause-effect investigation to focus on the most compelling aspects of the issue?
- Have I supplied my readers with sufficient background information about the issue I am analyzing?
- Have I supported my points with textual evidence?
- Have I been able to differentiate among different types of causes?
- Are the causes and effects spelled out, or will my readers have to make inferences?
- Have I used adequate cause-effect transitions (e.g., *accordingly, as a result, because, since, therefore, consequently, for this purpose, hence*)?

EXERCISE 4.8

Read "The Origins of the Ambivalent Acceptance of Divorce" (pp. 433–39) by Andrew J. Cherlin and draw a diagram that depicts how the history of American attitudes toward divorce explains contemporary views on single parenting.

WORKS CITED

Brown, Carol A. "Two Views of Motherhood." *Qualitative Sociology* 23.3 (2000): 355–58. *Academic Search Premier.* Web. 29 Sept. 2010.

Council for Secular Humanism. N.d. Web. 12 Oct. 2010. <http://www.secularhumanism.org/index.php?section=main&page=about>

Five

Visual Analysis

Cultural critics point out that ours is an age increasingly reliant upon **visual imagery** for communication, commentary, documentation, information, instruction, entertainment, and persuasion. Certainly the technology of visual representation over the past century-and-a-half has developed at an exponential rate from the earliest daguerreotype prints through motion pictures and television to digital photography, computer imaging, and multimedia presentation. Developments and improvements in technology are likely to reinforce the importance of visual representation in the workplace, marketplace, scientific sphere, recreational venues, and domestic environment. For these reasons, it is worth-while to develop some analytical skills in viewing visual representations and in writing about them with expression and conviction.

■ PRINCIPLES OF VISUAL ANALYSIS

The major **principles of visual analysis** hold much in common with other forms of anal-ysis. Though this type of analysis will focus on **images** rather than words, it still requires us to concentrate on details and on the connections among them. It will ask us to look for **content** and meaning; to determine what **genre** the image belongs to, what sorts of **organization** give structure to the image, and what **stylistic features** characterize it; and finally to question **rhetorical contexts** concerning who created the image, for whom it was created, and what purpose it served.

As images can be dramatically manipulated through decisions based on **selection, arrangement, inclusion, omission, focus, differentiation,** and the like, we can assume that what we perceive in a picture is not the same as the reality that the picture represents. This assumption holds true whether the picture is a drawing, painting, etching, or cartoon produced by an artist's hand through memory, imagination, direct observation, or some com-bination of them; or whether it is a photograph, video image, computer-generated collage, or the like produced through the eye of a camera set up and controlled by a human being.

This chapter will concentrate on photographs or camera-generated images rather than on hand-crafted or computer-generated images. Not only are photographs amenable to **reproduction** in hard-copy textbooks such as the one in your hands, but they also pose a particularly forceful demonstration of the axiom that all pictures manipulate the **viewer's perception** in dramatic ways. We usually believe that a simple snapshot faithfully records what passed through the **camera's lens**. But we might challenge this belief by analyzing such factors as **distance**, **perspective**, **placement**, **lighting**, **contrast**, and the like.

After such an analysis, we might well develop a healthy skepticism about the alleged "realism" of photographs in newspapers, magazines, and history books that purport to show what actually happened; of photographs in training manuals, cookbooks, and do-it-yourself brochures that lead us to believe we can achieve the same results that are pictured; and of photographs in magazine ads, travel brochures, and supplier catalogues that entice us to buy what is presented for sale. In each case, we will be examining the **hidden persuasion** of photographs, even and especially when such photographs seem far from trying to manipulate their viewers.

▮ PORTFOLIO OF PHOTOGRAPHS

Here is a brief portfolio of four photographs that we will use to study visual analysis in this chapter. Each of the pictures depicts a parent, usually a mother, with a small child in a setting that suggests some components of a workplace environment. Each picture introduces an element of tension or strain associated with the presence of young children in the

Photo 5–1   Young woman using a laptop.
Courtesy of Stockbyte/Getty Images.

Photo 5–2   Mother talking on a telephone holding her baby girl. Courtesy of Purestock/SuperFusion/SuperStock.

Photo 5–3   Mother holding her daughter and using a computer. Courtesy of Stockbyte/Getty Images.

Photo 5–4   A father wearing a business suit and holding his baby. Courtesy of FOTOSEARCH.com.

workplace. With these tensions and strains, the portfolio relates to a debate, often called the "Mommy Wars," that concerns the conflicts that women feel when they evaluate choices available (or not available) to them as working mothers or stay-at-home mothers. It is a topic that will affect most of you directly, whether men or women, as prospective—or perhaps current—life partners and parents, and that affects all of you indirectly—now and in the future—as members of a family, a community, a workplace, a marketplace, and an ever-changing society. As we analyze these four photographs, you might think of the pictures as illustrating arguments in the debate.

◼ OVERVIEW OF VISUAL ANALYSIS

At the beginning of this chapter, we used the words "dramatically" and "in dramatic ways." That's because visual analysis—to a significant extent—resembles literary analysis that focuses upon a **narrative or dramatic situation**, a story or poem with characters who conduct a **conversation** with one another. The genre that visual analysis most resembles is the **detective story**. In Edgar Allan Poe's tale "The Purloined Letter," the detective-hero named Dupin prides himself upon his "lynx eye" that can ferret out details that appear "simple and odd," even "a little *too* plain" and "a little *too* self-evident" (Poe 250). Whereas other characters in the tale see only different parts of a puzzle, Dupin observes "the *radicalness* of these differences" and consequently unlocks their hidden logic (Poe 262).

    Like Poe's hero, the viewer who analyzes a photograph is asked to imagine the story motivating the picture, the template that allows it to make sense, the features that make it distinctive, and the context that has set it in motion. This viewer will bring to the picture the kinds of questions about content, genre, organization, stylistic features, and rhetorical context that a reader who analyzes a literary text brings to a story, play, or poem.

Think of the picture as a text. Photo 5–1, for example, shows two women and a baby. What situation has brought them together? Is the woman in the background the baby's mother? Why does she concentrate upon the woman in the foreground while the other woman concentrates upon her laptop? What attitude does the woman in the background project toward what is going on? The tools that you use to analyze and write about this picture will be the same that you've used to analyze and write about other texts in this book.

◼▉ PROCESS OF WRITING A VISUAL ANALYSIS ESSAY

On pages 161–64 below, our student Lionel Essrog has written a visual analysis of these photographs. In what follows here, we will trace the steps he took in preparing to write this paper. Once again we will review these steps through our general prompts for Previewing; Viewing for Content; Viewing for Genre, Organization, and Stylistic Features; and Viewing for Rhetorical Context. Lionel's paper is based on these prompts. So too is the accompanying set of collaborative exercises on photographs that you and members of your group might gather from newspapers, magazines, or books; on the Web; or in your own family snapshot collections.

▉ Previewing

We begin with previewing the visual material selected for analysis. We might survey the broad **field** of the picture to isolate its major components, its dominant topic, and the positive or negative feelings that it evokes. We should look for a **title**, **caption**, or other verbal clue to define its context. We could ask ourselves whether we have encountered **other pictures like** it, such as those in mass publications, instructional manuals, advertising supplements, school textbooks, private photo albums, coffee table art books, and so forth. We might speculate about the **picture's purpose**—whether to document an event, illustrate a point, teach a lesson, summon the viewer to action, or some other purpose. If we can identify the topic of the picture, we might question whether its presentation corresponds to **what we know or have experienced** of the situation on which it focuses.

At this point, we will still be dealing with generalities, with broadly available issues or meanings. If we can, however, locate some appeal (or perhaps revulsion) that the picture has for us because of some still unknown, unexpected, as yet unarticulated reason, we should take note of this response, too. In Photo 5–1, for example, what relationship might the woman in the foreground bear to the woman and baby in the background? Is she a friend or relative of the woman and baby? Does the woman in the background envy or resent the other woman's freedom to use the laptop? Or is the woman in the foreground actually the baby's mother, and she has entrusted the child to the care of someone else while she attends to work or to some emergency?

Lionel Essrog has been instructed to write an essay of 1,000 words analyzing one or more of the pictures in our visual portfolio on pages 147–48. Here is his specific assignment:

> In an essay of 1,000 words, analyze the form and content of one or more photographs from our visual portfolio on "Moms, Dads, and Babies." Discuss the relationships among the persons or objects pictured and offer a plausible argument about the rhetorical context of the picture or pictures you've selected.

Here is Lionel's first effort to address this topic by freewriting his response to pre-viewing the visual portfolio:

The cliché states, "A picture is worth a thousand words." But I think the opposite can be true. At least words can tell us exactly what is going on. In these pictures, we can only guess at what is happening. In "Young woman using a laptop," what are the other woman and the baby doing in the background? In "Mother talking on a telephone holding her baby girl" is it good or bad that the baby is playing with the computer keyboard while the mother speaks on the telephone? Why is the father so well-dressed in "A father wearing a business suit and holding his baby"? Maybe it's the captions that are failing to tell us what is happening. If they were more informative, at least they could tell us what is going on. At first glance, the pictures are a mystery.

EXERCISE 5.1

- Form collaborative groups of five students each. Have some members of the group search for eye-catching photographs in newspapers, magazines, and illustrated books. Have other members of the group search for pictures on such Web sites as Fotosearch, <http://fotosearch.com>; the Commons on Flickr, <http://www.flickr.com/commons/>; or the Associated Press's AccuNet/ AP, <http://ap.accuweather.com>. Have still other members search through family snapshot collections or, if they are able, produce some on-the-spot pictures with their own cameras.

- When the group has assembled a couple of dozen photographs, sort them out into major categories. Which photographs document an event, illustrate a point, teach a lesson, entertain the viewer with a pleasant or odd perspective, or summon the viewer to specific and deliberate action? Which categories dominate among pictures in the public domain? Which categories dominate among pictures in private collections.

- Discuss as a group how accurately or faithfully each of these pictures corresponds to what we know about the situation or have experienced in our own lives.

- The group's recorder should take notes on this discussion and present a summary when the entire class reconvenes.

■ Viewing for Content

The content of a picture differs from that of a written text because its information appears all at once, enabling viewers to survey its **visual field** in different stages of perception, rather than sequentially in the prescribed order that would appear in a verbal text. It beguiles the viewer into assuming that its visible materials convey obvious, generally transparent, shared meanings. A careful viewer will nonetheless begin to question the picture's

details and its **overall presentation** of meaning. Like Poe's Dupin, such a viewer will come to discover meanings and responses undetected by more casual viewers.

The careful viewer may regard the picture's details as a site where contested **meanings are produced** and the overall presentation as a site where these **meanings are argued**. He or she will then attend to the picture as though it were registering a silent **conversation** with us and other viewers, as perhaps an **argument** between competing claims, or a **drama** with sudden reversals of behavior and response, or a **story** with shifting patterns of action and meaning.

Like a conversation, a picture will project ideas, some dominant and **attention-getting**, others quiet and **subdued**. Like an argument, a picture will incorporate a **focus** that concentrates on some ideas while relegating others to supporting roles. Like a drama, it will show someone or something in a process of change, caught by the camera's shutter in a moment of **arrested time**. Like a story, it will suggest that the player or players in this moment of action have various **connections** to the scene of action, to one another, to what has preceded the picture, and to what will follow.

In Photo 5–2, for example, why is the mother holding her baby as she talks on the phone? Do her half-closed eyes suggest tiredness or concentration on the phone call? Is she fully aware that the baby is fingering the keyboard and perhaps deleting important data that the mother has just fed into her computer? What does the picture tell us about the stresses and strains of childraising and attending to other affairs at the same time?

When you think of a picture as reporting a conversation or delivering a narrative, you will then have a framework for posing questions about its content. Here are some examples of questions you might ask.

QUESTIONS FOR VIEWING CONTENT IN VISUAL ANALYSIS

- What is happening in this picture?
- What has preceded the particular action that is now frozen in time?
- What will follow this action?
- How probable is the scenario that a viewer might construct?
- Who or what are the participants in this action?
- Which participants does the picture include?
- Which participants does it omit? Is the omission casual, or is it an important part of the story?
- Does the particular selection of details result from careful planning (as in a studied pose)?
- Does the selection result from catching a spontaneous action in unplanned movement?
- Does the selection result from cropping or removing content from an already processed photo?
- Why does the picture make some participants seem natural, familiar, realistic, or understandable?
- Why does it make other participants seem unnatural, intensified, exaggerated, or ambiguous?

(continued)

- Why does it situate some participants close to one another? Why does it situate others at a distance?
- Does it include elements that mirror or repeat one another in any significant way?
- Where does it position the action?
- Does it locate the participants in a likely or an unlikely setting?
- Does it depict a familiar or an unfamiliar cultural environment?
- Does it convey an action in the recent past or one in a remote past?

Here is Lionel Essrog's freewritten response to Questionings for Viewing the Content in Visual Analysis. Notice especially how he makes a spontaneous connection between the pictures' collective content and a topic of reading assigned earlier in the course. This topic dealt with "Stay-at-Home Moms vs. Working Moms," which the class referred to in shorthand as the "Mommy Wars." Notice too how he questions whether he might be able to use arguments about the "Mommy Wars" to document his essay on the visual portfolio.

The more I look at them, the more the puzzles in these pictures seem deliberate. In "Young woman using a laptop," the mother in the background seems annoyed at the woman using the computer. Does she want to attract her friend's attention? Does she resent being stuck with baby-care chores? Do we know whether she's really a friend, or even that she's the baby's mother? Is the picture trying to tell us something about the differences between the job of caring for children and the job of working at a computer? Do the well-dressed parents in "Mother holding her daughter and using a computer" and "A father wearing a business suit and holding his baby" try to suggest that it's possible and even easy to have a career and raise children at the same time? These pictures might take part in the conversation about the debate over mothers staying at home or working that we've been reading about in class. What I know about these "Mommy Wars" will help me with the visual analysis.

EXERCISE 5.2

- Ask a friend or classmate to provide you with a snapshot of a family member whom you do not know. Study its details and the overall presentation and ask the questions suggested above. Construct a list of possible answers that point toward a specific scenario.
- Then, ask your friend to tell you the real story that explains the picture. Say, for example, that the picture represents a bride in her wedding gown sitting alone and crying or weeping. What has happened? Is she expressing nervous jitters? Where is the groom? Is he drowning jitters of his own with his pals at the reception bar? Is he eloping with a bridesmaid? Has a jealous rival just shot him? How do you respond when your friend tells you, "Oh, that's my mom's cousin when she got married in 1967. She just caught a piece of dust in her contact lens. Things like that happened in those days."
- What precautions might you take to correct your initial understanding of the picture?

EXERCISE 5.3

- Form collaborative groups of five students each. Review the photographs that members have already culled from newspapers, magazines, books, Web sites such as Corbis.com, family snapshot collections, or on-the-spot pictures taken with personal cameras.

- Choose three or four pictures that typify diverse sorts of content, such as a news photo presenting an action shot of protest marchers, a magazine photo of last season's sportswear, a textbook photo of elected leaders shaking hands, and a family snapshot of Dad doing the dishes.

- Examine and discuss the stories implied in these pictures: what has been selected and emphasized in them, what has been omitted, how the participants appear to relate to one another, what is likely or unlikely about the picture, and what is familiar or unfamiliar.

- If a written source has accompanied the picture, appoint a member of the group to read the source and evaluate how accurate the collaborative understanding of the picture proved to be.

- The group's recorder should take notes on this discussion and present a summary when the entire class reconvenes.

■ Viewing for Genre, Organization, and Stylistic Features

As we have seen in previous chapters of this book, genre, organization, and stylistic features largely reflect **conventions** that have been adopted by the **discourse community** that uses them. Like written texts, photographs have their own categories of genre, forms of organization, and range of stylistic features, all of which rely upon conventions that communities of photographers have established by imitation and example.

These conventions are not immutable—they do change over time. A century ago, for example, wedding portraits were stiffly posed compositions set indoors against artificial studio backdrops. At a later date, they became more relaxed in format and were often set outdoors against natural backgrounds in state parks or public gardens. In recent decades they have emulated "candid" shots sometimes arranged in highly informal situations. In any case, viewers recognize the photos as wedding portraits because they bear conventional characteristics associated with the form. Our recognition of these characteristics depends upon repeated encounters with their conventions. Like Poe's Dupin, we know what we see when we see it.

Recognizing conventions enables us better to assess the meanings and values at stake in the picture that embodies them. Misinterpreting a wedding portrait as a graduation photo, for example, would mean confusing the conventions of wedding gowns with those of academic gowns, of coupled pairings at weddings with those of individuals or mixed groups at graduations, of more or less formality at weddings with spontaneity and bustle at graduations.

The usefulness of applying conventions to both photographs and written texts is that conventions provide shortcuts that help communicate what is going on. We don't need to reinvent or reinterpret each element of the composition anew each time.

Genre

The preceding paragraphs have already indicated some types of genre commonly encountered in photography, such as **documentary action photographs** in newspapers, magazines, and history books that purport to show what truly happened; **instructional photographs** in training manuals, cookbooks, and do-it-yourself brochures that prompt us to try to achieve the same results depicted in them; **advertising photographs** in magazine ads, travel brochures, and supplier catalogues that encourage us to buy what's being sold; **recreational photographs** that entertain or amuse by depicting celebrities, unusual events, or far-off places; or **formal portraits** or **personal snapshots** that commemorate an event or help us recall a memory.

Photo 5–4, for example, presents an impeccably dressed and well-groomed young man in business attire improbably supporting a diapered baby; perhaps the photo marks a promotion that he has just received at work, or perhaps alternatively it reflects an advertising campaign to illustrate his company's friendly policies toward family values.

QUESTIONS FOR VIEWING GENRE IN VISUAL ANALYSIS

- What principles of selection and omission govern the details?
- Which details are emphasized? Which ones are intensified? Which ones are exaggerated?
- What helps us to differentiate important from unimportant details?
- How do the images allow us to decipher hierarchies among the persons or actions represented?
- Which cultural values heighten the composition?
- Which historical values determine the details?
- Which positive and negative emotions are evoked by the picture?
- Which emotions are clearly legible? Which emotions seem ambiguous?
- How manipulated does the final result seem? Has the presenter manipulated the picture from the start by staging or posing it? Has the presenter manipulated it later by evidently adding to it, deleting from it, or rearranging what was there?

EXERCISE 5.4

- Form collaborative groups of five students each. Review the photographs that members have already culled or taken with their own cameras. Choose three or four pictures that typify diverse sorts of content, such as a news photo depicting a person or event of current interest; a magazine photo illustrating a do-it-yourself project; a textbook photo depicting features of the accompanying lesson; or a family portrait commemorating an event such as a graduation, an occasional reunion, or a milestone anniversary.

- Examine and discuss what purposes the pictures serve:
    - To document what happened?
    - To aid in instruction or installation?
    - To inform, advise, or warn?
    - To entertain?
    - To preserve personal or communal memories?

- The discussion should take account of what has been selected and emphasized in these pictures, what has been omitted, what is likely or unlikely about the details, and what is familiar or unfamiliar about them.

- If a written source has accompanied the picture, appoint a member of the group to read the source and evaluate how accurate the collaborative understanding of the picture proved to be.

- The group's recorder should take notes on this discussion and present a summary when the entire class reconvenes.

Organization

Particular genres usually display specially marked features of organization appropriate for their content. News photos of current events, for example, may seem cluttered, haphazard, or occasionally awkward or distasteful, all in the interest of conveying the spontaneity of the moment and the surprise of being there when something unexpected happened. Photographs taken for instructional purposes may seem stripped down, focused on specific details, magnified in close-ups, and devoid of background distractions. Family snapshots taken on special occasions may favor poses and grouping found in professional images of the same sort: the recent graduate flanked by parents, the grandparents on their wedding anniversary surrounded by their grandchildren, the newborn held by one parent and supported by the other.

The conventions for such sorts of organization are so compelling that any variation in them—say, a too-stylized picture of an unruffled sports figure supposedly shown in the throes of performance, or of a bride surrounded by a dozen unrelated men in firefighting gear—would likely provoke comment. Poe's Dupin would certainly spin into action upon noting them. In Photo 5–3, for example, the baby appears unusually contented and the mother unusually engrossed in her computer; the lack of distraction in this picture focuses our attention on a moment of concentration in which the mother succeeds in double-tasking child-raising responsibilities with some other important activity.

QUESTIONS FOR VIEWING ORGANIZATION IN VISUAL ANALYSIS

- Which images are most legible in the picture?
- Which images receive the sharpest focus? Which ones appear blurred?
- Do commanding images appear in the center of the frame, or are they off to one side?
- What shapes or forms appear in the background?
- What shapes or forms appear in the foreground?
- What dominates the top of the picture?
- What dominates its bottom?
- What public images does this photograph evoke, such as well-known historical representations, celebrity shots, cultural landmarks, or advertising icons?

(continued)

- Are there any parallels, duplications, or analogues within the picture, such as different people grouped in identical poses or small children in the foreground imitating actions of adults in the background?
- Are there any contrasts, oppositions, or inversions within the picture, such as impoverished people mingling with wealthy people or well-armed military men confronting ordinary women and children?
- What hierarchical relationships might we decipher in the picture?
- What parts present in the picture might suggest whole images that are not represented in it?

EXERCISE 5.5

- Form collaborative groups of five students each. Review the photographs that members have already culled or taken with their own cameras. Choose three or four pictures that typify different kinds of organization, such as a news photo presenting a candid shot of some current event, a magazine photo depicting a new line of seasonal clothing, an instructional photo illustrating some manual-operational process, or an entertainment photo parodying some promotional scheme or advertising gimmick.

- Examine and discuss what has been selected and emphasized in these pictures, what has been omitted, what appears focused or unfocused, what appears centered or uncentered, what familiar icons or representations seem implied in the particular arrangement, and what relationships of hierarchy or domination emerge among the various images.

- The discussion might also include some speculation about how the photographer may have manipulated the organization before taking the picture or while editing and printing it afterward.

- The group's recorder should take notes on this discussion and present a summary when the entire class reconvenes.

Stylistic Features

Particular genres also display specially marked stylistic features appropriate for their content. Instructional photos aim toward low-contrast, blandly textured images in order to emphasize the major topic of instruction rather than idiosyncratic elements unrelated to it. Publicity photos incorporate high-contrast, strongly textured images in order to project a glamorous, attention-getting, one-of-a-kind ambience. These features usually make use of specific lighting techniques, high- or low-angle shots, elongated or foreshortened perspective, limited or exaggerated scale, and deliberately heightened or subdued color schemes.

Photo 5–1, for example, implies a strong tension between its foreground with the young woman concentrating on her work and its background with another woman and a baby looking at her. What is the picture telling us? As with principles of organization, certain features of style come to be associated with distinct genres, such as wide-angle shots for sports photography, medium close-ups for entertainment photography, and telescopic close-ups for scientific photography.

QUESTIONS FOR VIEWING STYLISTIC FEATURES IN VISUAL ANALYSIS

- Does the picture appear posed, or is it spontaneous?
- How far away is the camera from the object photographed? Does the distance appear to be blown up or exaggerated through the use of a special lens or other special equipment?
- Is the camera placed above or below the object photographed? Is it tilted at an unusual angle?
- Does the lighting appear natural or artificial?
- Is the source of lighting in front of the object, behind it, or to one side of it?
- How do shadows emphasize (or perhaps deemphasize) the contours of the object?
- Were special filters used to heighten or soften the usual contrasts of texture and tone?
- Were some of these stylistic features achieved by using special printing, processing, or editing techniques after the picture was taken?
- What emotional effects do these stylistic choices evoke? Does the picture make us feel happy? sad? alienated? engaged?

EXERCISE 5.6

- Form collaborative groups of five students each. Review the photographs that members have already culled or taken with their own cameras.
- Choose three or four pictures that typify different kinds of stylistic features, such as a news photo presenting an out-of-focus candid shot of some current event, a magazine photo depicting a resplendent new line of seasonal clothing, an instructional photo illustrating some intricate manual operation, or an entertainment photo parodying some already familiar advertising gimmick or promotional scheme.
- Examine and discuss how far the camera appears from the object photographed; whether it is placed above or below the object photographed; if it is tilted at an odd angle; whether the lighting appears natural or artificial; whether its source appears in front of the object, behind it, or to one side of it; and how shadows emphasize (or perhaps deemphasize) the contours of the object.
- The discussion might also include some speculation about how the photographer might have manipulated the organization before taking the picture or while editing and printing it afterward.
- The group's recorder should take notes on this discussion and present a summary when the entire class reconvenes.

Here are Lionel Essrog's freewritten responses to Questions for Viewing Genre, Organization, and Stylistic Features in preparing for his paper on visual analysis. Notice especially how he begins to move from a negative mode of questioning the pictures to a positive mode of speculating about answers. In earlier freewritten responses, he expressed a great deal of bafflement about the photographs. Here he is actively searching for a way to formulate some positive argument about their meaning.

The style of these pictures doesn't allow for too much information to define what's going on. The backgrounds in all of them are pretty bare and they tell us nothing in particular about where the actions are taking place. Their organization makes us concentrate on just the appearance of the people and a few objects (e.g., laptops, computers, telephones) that they are using. I wonder whether the genre of these pictures has something to do with advertising these objects? Or maybe advertising the clothes they are wearing? Perhaps that's true in Photos 3 and 4. But in Photos 1 and 2 the computer equipment and the clothes are not especially well defined. There the emphasis is on the people's faces. So perhaps the story about childraising and careers is what's most important after all. If only the outlines of this story might be clearer! Perhaps I could shuffle some of the possibilities so that, instead of trying to find the single master key, I could allow elements from each of them to shed light on the others.

■ Viewing for Rhetorical Context

Visual images have rhetorical contexts just as written texts do, and they also present arguments. First, they originate with the **people who produced them** and who, like those who produce written texts, have ideas, emotions, and values that they want to communicate. Second, they aim at **viewers** whom they seek to inform, persuade, and perhaps motivate to action, just as written texts aim at readers for the same purposes. Third, like written texts, pictures themselves are embedded in social and cultural situations to which producers and viewers may react in agreement or in opposition—or in many ways in between.

The range of in-between reactions may be astonishingly broad. Some pictures purport to **gratify** viewers with soothing representations of pleasant and familiar situations: think of pictures in a church bulletin celebrating the community's achievements, or pictures in an alumni magazine recalling old friends in a festive mood. Flip ahead to Photo 16–1 in Chapter 16, with its image of a family representing three generations of children, parents, and grandparents. This example presents a highly idealized version of an attractive, intact, seemingly happy family unit.

Other images can **disturb** viewers with representations of violent or repulsive behavior: think of pictures in a sensationalist tabloid displaying the ravages of freak accidents or irresponsible conduct. For an example of disturbing social commentary, flip ahead to Photo 16–17 in Chapter 16, which depicts the harsh treatment accorded by U.S. Border Control to illegal immigrants. Still other photographs may **attract** viewers in subtle and intriguing ways, persuading them to look closer and perhaps change their minds about a certain issue: think of pictures in commercial advertising that urge you to switch your brands of shampoo or footwear.

In each case, such pictures deploy **conventional or unconventional** images in a rhetorical context. Photo 16–10, for example, depicts a homeless man pushing a shopping cart filled with his belongings. The expected response to such an image would be sorrow for his plight. In the background, however, the photograph depicts the gleaming skyscrapers of downtown Denver, inviting a response of awe at their magnificence. Juxtaposed, the responses demand our reconsideration. What links homelessness to corporate America?

Pictures have an extraordinarily persuasive power that may supplement, complement, or go far beyond the power of words **to compel action or assent**. The most familiar genres of photography have a cogent **normalizing effect**. A group photo of schoolmates in a classroom, for example, will show each child in presentable dress at his or her best behavior; the purpose is not just to offer parents a sweet picture of their offspring, or to afford children some memory of a classroom that in fact never appeared that way on a day-to-day basis, but rather to project an **idealized image** of what presentable dress and good behavior should be and of what each student could strive toward.

Photo 16–1, for example, might have appeared in a parenting magazine photo spread on how to unite three generations of a family. Families whose composition, temperament, and financial means differ from those in the photo might question what habits they need to change or cultivate so as to enjoy the same togetherness. Poe's Dupin would point out that few families match the "normal" description pictured in the article even though the magazine is promoting the belief that everyone can aspire to this image.

Images that convey a normalizing effect contrast with those that convey an **alienating effect**. Such an effect serves to warn, admonish, or advise its viewers, as in photojournalism that documents the ramifications of alcohol or drug addiction. It can also serve to stigmatize persons or groups by evoking deformity, oddity, or even malevolence, as in tabloid depictions of obesity or political terrorism. Photo 16–16 shows that in some communities, drivers are warned of illegal border crossings as though immigrants were stupified wild animals. Sometimes the effect can be used for sheer entertainment, as in photo collages that celebrate nonconformity or stubborn eccentricity.

Normalizing and alienating effects converge in **advertising** photographs, which aim to convince viewers that it's normal to prefer one brand over another (especially when it identifies the customer as belonging to an admired group) yet attract the viewer's attention with incongruous, unconventional images. If normalizing effects persuade us to imitate certain behaviors and alienating effects persuade us to avoid others, advertising effects persuade us to buy a product (such as a particular dish detergent) or buy into a movement (such as to vote for a particular political candidate).

Photo 5–3, for example, might serve as an illustration to advertise the desktop computer or the mother's clothing: The baby appears placid and the mother comfortable, as though her access to the computer and her semi-business attire make it possible for her to double-task while caring for her child. All three forms of photographic persuasion show how pictures can move viewers with a rhetoric of imagery instead of words, and how images conduct arguments by manipulating evidence, heightening emotions, changing attitudes, and summoning responses.

When you think of images as doing these things, you will then have a framework for posing questions about their rhetorical context. Imagine that such pictures are entering a conversation about an issue that prompts competing claims. The evidence for these claims is visual, and it can be interpreted from several perspectives. Try to determine what perspective the picture adopts on the information that it presents and how it invites viewers to accept such a perspective as reasonable and advantageous or to reject it as incongruous, invalid, or harmful. Construe the picture in the framework of an argument that challenges you to respond with your own argument about the information it presents.

QUESTIONS FOR VIEWING RHETORICAL CONTEXT IN VISUAL ANALYSIS

- Who is the producer of the image and for whom does he or she work?
- Who are the intended viewers, and what experiences, expectations, preferences, and attitudes do they have?
- Does the picture seek to attract these viewers? Gratify them? Challenge their assumptions? Motivate them to some specific action?
- What might be controversial about the photo's means of attraction, gratification, confrontation, or motivation?
- What normalizing effects does the picture suggest? Do its images invite acceptance and imitation? Do they invite rejection or attack?
- What alienating effects does the picture suggest? Do its images invite consideration and appraisal? Do they invite resistance and criticism?
- Do its images suggest the drawbacks and limitations of standardized thinking?
- What advertising or promotional effects does the picture evoke? Do its images move us to buy a product or buy into ideas represented in the product?
- Do the images convey options or alternatives to the outcomes suggested by what the images represent?

Here are Lionel Essrog's freewritten responses to Viewing for Rhetorical Context in preparing for his essay on the visual portfolio. Notice how he comes close to expressing the thesis that he will eventually state in his essay on pages 161–64.

I don't know who the photographers of these pictures were, or where the photographs originally appeared. But their organization and stylistic features lead me to wonder whether they belong to the genre of advertising. Since I can't specify what kind of product they could be pushing, I wonder whether it's some more general normalizing effect that they're promoting. Despite all the chaos that could be going on with the babies, the parents seem pretty cool and collected. Their attitude seems pretty close to being ideal. In the context of the "Mommy Wars," these pictures could be poster-children (no pun intended) for a marriage of childraising and the workplace. Still, the details are not exactly tidy. I could argue that they talk back to an idealizing attitude and even challenge the ideals imaged on the surface.

EXERCISE 5.7

- Form collaborative groups of five students each. Review the photographs that members have already culled or taken with their own cameras. Choose three or four pictures that typify different kinds of persuasion, such as a photo from a school or social club depicting members pursuing a common activity; a photo from a health magazine depicting the effects of a high-cholesterol, low-exercise diet; or a news photo depicting a candidate for political election chatting up voters during his or her leisure time.

• Examine and discuss how the photographs represent desirable activities, undesirable activities, or activities that may be assessed either positively or negatively according to the particular context at the time. The discussion might also include some speculation about how the photographer might have manipulated the organization before taking the picture or while editing and printing it afterward.

• The group's recorder should take notes on the discussion, and when the entire class reconvenes, he or she should summarize these notes for the class.

Now turn back to the visual portfolio on pages 147–48 above and review these pictures again. Use your review to evaluate the following essay by Lionel Essrog based upon them. The assignment, as you remember, was as follows:

In an essay of 1,000 words, analyze the form and content of one or more photographs from our visual portfolio on "Moms, Dads, and Babies." Discuss the relationships among the persons or objects pictured and offer a plausible argument about the rhetorical context of the picture or pictures you've selected.

You've already read Lionel's freewritten responses to the questions for Previewing; for Viewing for Content; for Viewing for Genre, Organization, and Stylistic Features; and for Viewing for Rhetorical Context. Here is Lionel's completed essay, represented as a finished product after initial drafting, revisions, copyediting, and a final revision for presentation in this anthology.

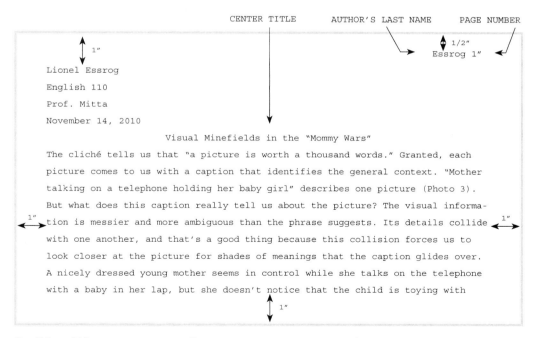

CENTER TITLE   AUTHOR'S LAST NAME   PAGE NUMBER

1/2"
Essrog 1"

1"

Lionel Essrog

English 110

Prof. Mitta

November 14, 2010

Visual Minefields in the "Mommy Wars"

The cliché tells us that "a picture is worth a thousand words." Granted, each
picture comes to us with a caption that identifies the general context. "Mother
talking on a telephone holding her baby girl" describes one picture (Photo 3).
But what does this caption really tell us about the picture? The visual information is messier and more ambiguous than the phrase suggests. Its details collide
with one another, and that's a good thing because this collision forces us to
look closer at the picture for shades of meanings that the caption glides over.
A nicely dressed young mother seems in control while she talks on the telephone
with a baby in her lap, but she doesn't notice that the child is toying with

1"

1"   1"

USE 8½″ BY 11″ PAPER FOR EACH PAGE. USE DOUBLE SPACES BETWEEN ALL LINES. LEFT-JUSTIFY ALL LINES IN THE TEXT OF
THE PAPER. DO NOT RIGHT-JUSTIFY, EVEN IF YOUR WORD PROCESSOR PROVIDES THIS FEATURE.

INDENT FIVE SPACES   AUTHOR'S LAST NAME   PAGE NUMBER

1/2"
1"   Essrog 2

her computer and may be deleting important documents that the mother has stored
on it. While the caption might suggest what is going on, the photo is doing
much more. On the one hand, it wants to idealize the mother's efficiency and
smart-looking appearance and to present the situation as something normal and
expected. On the other, it leaves the barn door open for chaos to break loose.
I am going to argue that details in these pictures talk back to their idealizing
functions and pose a challenge to the otherwise straightforward visual images on
the surface.

The picture captioned "Mother holding her daughter and using a computer"
(Photo 3) provides a clear contrast. Here the mother is well-dressed, confident, and composed while she fingers the keyboard of her computer. The baby is
equally calm and composed, and even mimics her mother's attention to the computer equipment. While the mother focuses on the keyboard and the data that she
is feeding into the computer, the baby looks at the screen in amusement. Still,
the picture is highly abstract. Except for the mother, child, and computer, it
offers no other details to cement its narrative. The background is a flat white
wall, and the table on which the computer rests allows no clutter or confusion

1"   1"

to divert anyone's attention. Real life does not look like this. I wonder how
or whether the picture represents life as we or others know it. The picture's
idealizing function rules its organization. It seems to be saying that any
young mother can take charge and attend to her baby's needs (and note that it
is only one baby and not two or three or more) while also managing to catch up
on a bit of her professional work as she stands in front of her computer.

The same can be said for "A father wearing a business suit and holding his
baby" (Photo 4). Whoever saw a businessman posing for a picture with a child
in diapers, unless someone wanted to use it as some photo-op for a political
campaign or for a better-business family-values blurb? This picture's genre
resembles a formal portrait, except for the baby's diapers. Perhaps this young
father wanted a household snapshot before running off to the office one morning
or upon returning from it one evening. As with "Mother holding her daughter,"
the ambiance is idealized. The picture almost screams at us that the good life
is possible for everyone. And yet, when push comes to shove, it's more likely
than not that this father's wife is a rather privileged stay-at-home mom. Since
this option to be a full-time mom is available to only a small minority of
families, the picture has already passed beyond the attainability of mainstream
North America.

The fallout from the "Mommy Wars," the debate over whether women should
work or be full-time mothers, dominates yet another picture in our portfolio,

1"

"Young woman using a laptop." Here the caption only increases the near-total ambiguity of the picture. The photograph depicts two women and a baby. One woman is seated at a laptop. The other stands behind her in soft focus holding the baby. Which woman is the baby's mother? In one scenario, the seated woman might be the mother, and she has handed her baby to a friend or relative while she catches up on some work at her computer. The agitated look on the other woman's face suggests that she may be uncomfortable taking care of the baby and is hoping that the computer session will soon come to an end. The conflict in the picture pits a nicely dressed, fairly self-assured young woman in the foreground against a vaguely defined, semianxious counterpart with a baby in the background. Its narrative suggests a tension between them, but no single detail or set of details in the picture unlocks the exact source of this tension.

In another scenario, the standing woman could be the baby's mother, and from the perspective of her child-care responsibilities she is looking at her friend with some envy or regret at the relative freedom of her friend's computer work. In yet another scenario, the face of the standing woman may betray neither discomfort nor envy or regret; instead, perhaps the baby has developed a fever or a rash, and her friend is searching the Internet for first-aid advice. In a fourth, but totally fictional, scenario, the young woman at the laptop may be day-dreaming about her friend with the baby in the soft-focus background.

Which scenario is the most probable one? I'd shuffle them together to see how one explanation might illuminate another one. Identifying the standing woman as the baby's mother, I'd say that the picture presents a series of conflicts that challenge her composure. It exposes her anxieties about caring for her child while it also arouses her wish for the security that her friend in the foreground seems to enjoy. At the same time it suggests that the woman in the foreground inhabits her own private world, at least for the time being, immune from the push and pull of emotions that accompany motherhood in all its complex forms. The picture captures the complexity of these feelings as it juxtaposes the two spheres of motherhood and working careerwoman.

One feature prominent in all four photographs is absolutely certain. Taken together, this group of pictures illustrates the contradictions of the "Mommy Wars." The women with babies on the telephone in Photo 2 and at the computer in Photo 3 project competence, success, and career-oriented drive, even if the baby provides a realistic distraction in the first instance and an idealized accompaniment in the second. The father with the baby in Photo 4 stands in a clearly idealized portrait pose. All three pictures imply a normalizing

Essrog 4

effect as they depict working mothers and fathers taking care of young babies without too many of the stresses and strains that we know exist in the real world. Photo 1 by contrast sheds light upon a less tidy aspect of the contrast between the ideal and the real. It consequently draws the accompanying photos into a contemporary dialogue about parenthood, working adults, and stay-at-home moms. It seems to say that the simple assumptions about family life in a world that never really was are always subject to debate.

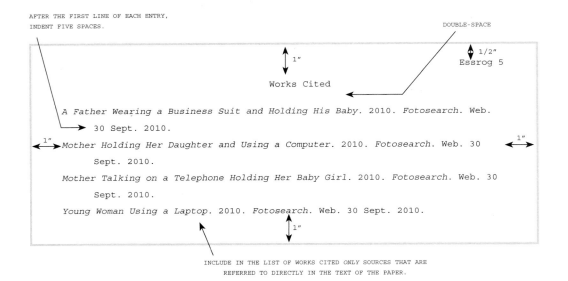

AFTER THE FIRST LINE OF EACH ENTRY,
INDENT FIVE SPACES.

DOUBLE-SPACE

1"

1/2"
Essrog 5

Works Cited

A Father Wearing a Business Suit and Holding His Baby. 2010. *Fotosearch.* Web.
30 Sept. 2010.

1" *Mother Holding Her Daughter and Using a Computer.* 2010. *Fotosearch.* Web. 30
Sept. 2010.

1"

Mother Talking on a Telephone Holding Her Baby Girl. 2010. *Fotosearch.* Web. 30
Sept. 2010.

Young Woman Using a Laptop. 2010. *Fotosearch.* Web. 30 Sept. 2010.

1"

INCLUDE IN THE LIST OF WORKS CITED *ONLY* SOURCES THAT ARE
REFERRED TO DIRECTLY IN THE TEXT OF THE PAPER.

EXERCISE 5.8

- Form collaborative groups of five students each. Members should review the notes the recorder has taken on the preceding exercises in this chapter. Each group should then summarize for itself which principles for Previewing; for Viewing for Content; for Viewing for Genre, Organization, and Stylistic Features; and for Viewing for Rhetorical Context are the most useful ones for writing a paper of visual analysis on the portfolio in this chapter. The group's recorder should organize this summary.

- One student in the group should read Lionel Essrog's paper aloud while the group's other members follow the paper in their textbooks. As the paper is read, each student should take note of features that he or she thinks could still profit from revision.

- After the paper has been read, the group's reporter should then repeat the principles that the group has emphasized for Previewing and Viewing, pausing after each one so that members can comment on how the principles might apply to features that Lionel Essrog might revise in his paper.

- The group's recorder should take notes on which features Lionel should revise, and when the entire class reconvenes, he or she should convey them to the class. The class should them compare recommendations for revision that the groups have formulated.

WORKS CITED

A Father Wearing a Business Suit and Holding His Baby. 2010. *Fotosearch.* Web. 30 Sept. 2010.
Mother Holding Her Daughter and Using a Computer. 2010. *Fotosearch.* Web. 30 Sept. 2010.
Mother Talking on a Telephone Holding Her Baby Girl. 2010. *Fotosearch.* Web. 30 Sept. 2010.
Poe, Edgar Allan. *Selected Titles.* New York: Oxford, 1998. Print.
Young Woman Using a Laptop. 2010. *Fotosearch.* Web. 30 Sept. 2010.

CHAPTER
■ ■ ■ ■ ■ ■

Six

Synthesis

■ ANALYSIS AND SYNTHESIS

Analysis, the topic of Chapters 3, 4, and 5, is the precursor of synthesis. Without it, the broad overview that sustains a synthesis cannot take place. Analysis requires you to perform two operations: (1) Break up the text into its component parts, and (2) Examine the relationship of the parts to each other and to the text as a whole. Synthesis asks you to (1) perform these analysis operations on two or more texts, (2) identify and group textual components that share common attributes, and (3) repackage these components in a new composition.

Let's say your professor asks you to synthesize the arguments presented in three reading selections in this book. First, you must unravel each author's line of reasoning. This analysis will enable you to extract threads—thematic elements, comparable features, similar ideas—that you can weave into the fabric of your synthesis essay.

SYNTHESIS

To synthesize is to:

- Analyze two or more texts that share a topic or interest
- Identify grounds for grouping the textual components
- Organize this textual material under a controlling theme

A synthesis requires you to read and analyze an array of texts—for example, two articles from academic journals, a chapter from a book, and a column from a newspaper. As you read, you try to identify a controlling idea. Then you extract various bits of text and relate them to each other on the basis of thematic consistency. Your reason for performing these operations depends on your rhetorical purpose.

Suppose the purpose of your writing is to define poverty. You would read various texts on the topic, discover commonalities among the texts, select pertinent ideas from each text, mesh them together, and form a definition.

Let's take another purpose. Your politics professor asks you to chart the development of the Arab-Israeli controversy. You would read various texts dealing with the controversy, identify common elements among the texts, combine the historical perspectives, and construct a coherent narrative account.

The preceding examples reveal a distinction between synthesis assignments and comparison and contrast assignments. When you write a comparison-contrast essay, you will work with texts that converge on the same topic and share similarities and differences. For example, you might read two journal articles on the topic of health care reform and compare and contrast the authors' views. The texts already converge on the same topic, however different their premises and conclusions may be. When you write a synthesis essay, you may be working with texts that focus on separate, discrete topics or issues. Your first task is to analyze the texts in order to identify constituent elements of the interlocking materials that you will be able to combine into a single, unified piece of writing.

■ PROCESS OF WRITING SYNTHESIS ESSAYS

■ Examine the Assignment

As with any assignment, when you receive a directive to write a synthesis essay, you need to ask yourself the Questions for Analyzing Writing Assignments (p. 33). If the professor specifies the topic and supplies the readings, you will have much less work to do than if you have to do library-based research, select the readings, and limit the scope of the topic yourself. Assignment A is much less demanding than the open-ended Assignment B.

ASSIGNMENT A

Are the "Mommy Wars" real, or do they represent a fictitious debate promoted by the media? Write a five-page essay in which you synthesize the arguments in Judith Stadtman Tucker's "The Least Worst Choice: Why Mothers 'Opt' Out of the Workforce," Katha Pollitt's "Dangerous Housewives of the Ivy League," and Linda Hirshman's "Homeward Bound."

ASSIGNMENT B

Recently the topic of the "Mommy Wars" has received considerable attention in the press. Write a five-page essay in which you synthesize key arguments in this controversy.

Both assignments ask the student to synthesize. However, sometimes students do not receive such explicit clues as "synthesize the arguments." Many of the directives we list on page 33 might entail synthesis. The determining factor would be the number of sources the writer is expected to use. An important question to ask your professor is "Which sources am I to use?" If your professor expects you to draw upon multiple sources for your paper, then you know you will be writing a synthesis.

One of the biggest mistakes students make when they write synthesis essays is that instead of taking the time to adequately analyze the readings and puzzle out the commonalities among the texts, they rush into the assignment and end up producing a pastiche of summaries instead of a tightly woven synthesis. The result is that sources determine the purpose and direction of the paper instead of the writer determining the purpose. For example, in response to Assignment A, a student writes, "Recently, prominent journalists and scholars have written incisive arguments about the clash between stay-at-home mothers and career mothers." Working with assigned reading selections, the writer develops this anemic thesis by summarizing Stadtman Tucker's, Pollitt's, and Hirshman's arguments, devoting two to three body paragraphs to each author. Then she concludes her essay with the comment, "Stadtman Tucker, Pollitt, and Hirshman agree that the Mommy Wars are real and continue to be controversial."

What the student should have done was examine the assignment to determine a firm rhetorical purpose, analyze the three texts to discover subtopics they share in common, establish grounds for the synthesis, formulate a thesis, and pluck from the sources only the sentences and passages that directly relate to the thesis. The student needed to go beyond a simplistic presentation of information in the reading sources. A synthesis is not a compilation of summaries.

■ Determine Your Rhetorical Purpose: Purposes for Synthesizing Sources

Writers produce syntheses for clear-cut reasons. One purpose is to *provide background and explain a topic, problem, or issue to readers*. We see this purpose realized in reports; for example, "Climate Change 2001: Synthesis Report," edited by Robert T. Watson of the Core Writing Team of the Cambridge Earth, Environment, and Atmospheric Sciences. In college writing classes, this genre of synthesis is called exploratory synthesis. An **exploratory synthesis** *offers a thorough but relatively nonjudgmental analysis of the texts in order to present informative results in a straightforward manner.* Such a synthesis often tries to define a topic or issue in an expository style that emphasizes the coverage of data rather than any further questioning or interpretation of data. The writer makes a point—for example, "Here is some important information you should be aware of"—but does not advance a firm thesis. The writer says to the reader: "You decide how you would like to interpret this information."

A related purpose for synthesizing sources is to *provide background and explain a topic, problem, or issue by examining a wide array of published research studies.* This genre of synthesis is called a **literature review**. In some cases, the writer's goal is simply to communicate the research findings to an interested audience. For example, Greg Druian and Jocelyn A. Butler, researchers at the Northwest Regional Educational Laboratory, published "Schooling Practices and At-Risk Youth: What the Research Shows" in order to inform teachers about educational research. In other cases, the writer's objective is to *demonstrate her grasp of a research field by reviewing a wide range of published research.* Occasionally, literature reviews written for this purpose are self-contained, stand-alone essays, but more often they are part of a larger project. They precede a report describing a research study the writer has carried out.

A third purpose for synthesizing is *to extract from the sources textual evidence and material that will support your thesis.* The thesis is the chief point you are making in your essay. Some refer to a thesis as a claim. We use "claim" to discuss the theses of the argument essays in this chapter. A thesis advances the writer's interpretation or position. It is not a neutral statement. In university classes, you will be writing about complex issues and in so doing entering conversations that are already underway. The best way to join these conversations is to read what others have written about the issues. After you have learned about the issues and thought enough about them to be able to formulate a thesis, you will then decide how you will synthesize these expert voices in you own text. We call this a **thesis-driven synthesis**.

A fourth purpose for synthesizing is *to extract from the sources textual evidence for an argument essay*. In this chapter, we discuss the exploratory synthesis, the literature review, and the thesis-driven synthesis. Chapter 7 is devoted to argument synthesis.

■ Ask Questions to Identify Relationships Among the Sources

Baseline Questions

In Chapter 3, we emphasized the importance of questions. Questioning, the frame of mind that favors analysis, is also the attitude of mind you need for synthesis. Whether your professor has presented you with a set of readings or you have conducted library research and discovered your own texts, at the time of your initial reading ask yourself the five baseline questions in the following box.

BASELINE QUESTIONS FOR INITIAL READING

- What is the major topic that is treated by all the texts?
- What subtopics run across some or all of the texts?
- Do the texts discuss a controversy or debate?
- How do the texts talk to each other with respect to the topic, subtopics, and/or controversy?
- How will my answers to Questions 1 through 4 help me fulfill my rhetorical purpose?

Responses to Questions 1, 2, and 3 in the box above will inform an explanatory synthesis or a review of the literature, and responses to Questions 1 through 4 will inform both a thesis-driven synthesis and an argument synthesis.

EXERCISE 6.1

- Divide the class into groups of three.
- Each group will choose three reading selections from one of the anthology chapters. Each member of the group will read the selection and respond to the five Baseline Questions for Initial Reading.
- Group members will compare their responses and reach consensus.
- Then a representative from each group will report to the class. The professor will use a graphic overview to map the various group findings.

In-Depth Questions

After you have conducted an initial reading of the texts, reread each text and search for ways in which it relates to the other sources. Ask yourself the questions in the following box.

IN-DEPTH QUESTIONS FOR IDENTIFYING RELATIONSHIPS AMONG TEXTS

- Are there other common threads running through this text and the other texts?
- Do the texts contain similar key words or phrases?
- Does the text provide background or additional information about points that are presented in other sources? Additional details about points made in other sources? Evidence for points made in another text?
- Are there places where this text contradicts or disagrees with other texts I have read?
- Are there places where the text supports or agrees with other sources?
- Are there cause-and-effect relationships between this text and the other sources?
- Are there time relationships among the texts?
- Does this text contain elements that can be compared or contrasted with those in other sources?
- Are there any other ways I can categorize the ideas in the reading sources?

EXERCISE 6.2

- Reconvene the groups from the previous exercise.
- Each group should respond to the same set of readings using In-Depth Questions for Identifying Relationships Among Texts.
- Appoint a representative from each group to report to the class.

■ Formulate a Thesis and Review the Texts

After you have responded to the questions and discovered the common elements in the sources, decide on the points you wish to communicate to your readers, and formulate a working thesis. Next, review the texts for the evidence and support you will need to develop each of your points. As you reread the texts, mark or copy into your writer's notebook the bits of information that relate to your argument. When you have located a sufficient amount of relevant information, draft your essay. As you write, you will return to the texts to decide whether to paraphrase, quote, or summarize the supporting material. In the remaining sections of this chapter, we will discuss the exploratory synthesis, the review of the literature, and the thesis-driven synthesis.

■ PROCESS OF WRITING AN EXPLORATORY SYNTHESIS

The purpose of an exploratory synthesis is to unfold or unravel a topic to make it clearer to readers. An exploratory synthesis might crack open a concept, place an issue in an historical context, or clarify the sides in a controversy. The synthesis is objective: The writer is reporting on the sources rather than interpreting or evaluating them. It is important to remember that the "reporting" is selective. The writer identifies a subtopic running across the texts and then selects from the texts bits of information related to the subtopic. The writer does not summarize each text in its totality. Such an operation would result in a string of summaries rather than a synthesis.

To illustrate, let's turn to the topic of "Privacy and Technology," which governs the selection of articles for Chapter 11 in our anthology section. We will follow our student Megan Farr as she writes an exploratory synthesis based on five reading selections from that chapter.

■ Decide on Rhetorical Purpose

Megan decides that her purpose is to place the "Privacy and Technology" controversy in an historical context. In response to the Baseline Questions for Initial Reading (p. 169), Megan has:

- Identified the major issue: whether new technology interferes with privacy or whether it can help to preserve and enhance privacy
- Selected *"historical context" as a subtopic running across the texts* and decided that there are five reading selections in Chapter 11 that will be useful:

  Thomas D. Colbridge, "Kyllo v. United States: Technology v. Individual Privacy"

  Wendy Kaminer, "Trading Liberty for Illusions"

  Catherine Price, "The Anonymity Experiment"

  Jonathan Franzen, "'I Just Called to Say I Love You'"

  The Economist, "If Looks Could Kill"

- Begun to analyze what each text contributes to the historical context and how the texts talk to each other with respect to the subtopic

Turning her attention to the In-Depth Questions for Identifying Relationships Among Texts (p. 170), Megan focuses on time relationships and references to historical context. Then, as she reexamines each text, she looks to see if one text:

- Provides background or additional information and details about the points in other texts
- Provides evidence for points made in another text
- Contradicts, disagrees, or supports another text

Megan marks the texts and copies passages into her writer's notebook. Then she studies the bits of text she has selected to see if she can impose some type of order on them. Since the purpose of her exploratory synthesis is to provide her readers with historical background, Megan decides to order the bits of text chronologically. She does this by constructing a timeline. (See Figure 6–1.)

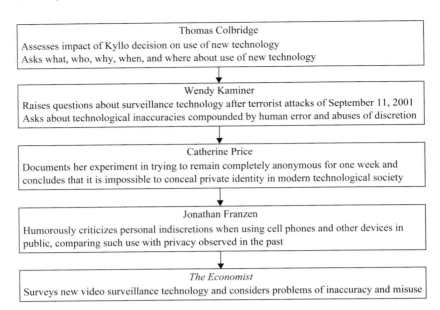

Figure 6–1   Timeline of Background on "Privacy Versus Technology"

◾ Formulate Working Thesis

Megan's next step is to formulate a working thesis. Remember that an exploratory synthesis is a straightforward, objective reporting of the sources. Her thesis will be descriptive, not persuasive. As a preliminary thesis, she writes:

Whether new technology interferes with privacy or whether it can help to preserve and enhance privacy is a long-standing debate that continues to stir controversy.

After she writes a draft of her essay, she may decide to sharpen this thesis. Consider another version of a possible thesis for an exploratory synthesis. If her subtopic was to clarify the sides in the controversy, she might have written:

On the issue of "Privacy Versus Technology," Thomas D. Colbridge and The Economist advocate strict limitations on using technology for police surveillance, while Wendy Kaminer, Jonathan Franzen, and Catherine Price concede that in modern society, it is very difficult to maintain complete privacy amid continuous technological development.

Suppose her subtopic was legal implications in the controversies over privacy and technology. Her thesis might be:

Court decisions on the infringement of privacy through technological surveillance have often reversed themselves, so that further considerations of the issue must take into account the legal ramifications of these reversals.

As Megan develops each of these theses, she would describe with as much neutrality as possible the views of the various authors. She would not state her own position or make a claim.

We present Megan's exploratory synthesis in an annotated and highlighted version in order to illustrate how she draws together summaries, quotations, and paraphrases from a wide range of sources.

Megan Farr

Academic Writing II

Professor Kennedy

20 October 2010

Privacy Versus Technology

The long-standing debate over whether new technology interferes with privacy or whether it can help to preserve and enhance privacy continues to stir controversy. The public might
have thought that this controversy played itself out long before
now, because it has a history that goes back to the invention of
audio and video technology before the middle of the last century.
Even then citizens were clamoring for protection against third-
party wiretapping and photographic surveillance of individuals in private situations. Instead of disappearing, the debate
has been smoldering. In the past decade it has been rekindled
by events associated with protection against terrorism as well
as by the increasing use of personal electronic devices such as
cell phones, digital photography, and the BlackBerry. Luckily for
those of us who belong to a new generation of high-tech involvement, many writers who debate this issue have contextualized it
with useful background.

Summary ———
An FBI agent and legal instructor at the FBI Academy,
Thomas D. Colbridge, closely examines the issue in his article
"*Kyllo v. United States*: Technology v. Individual Privacy."
The Kyllo case involved Danny Kyllo, a man suspected of grow-
ing marijuana in his Oregon home. Without Kyllo's consent, the
police used a thermal imager to scan Kyllo's house. In *Kyllo v.
United States,* the Supreme Court ruled that it was unconstitu-
tional for law enforcement officers to use a thermal imager to
search a private home without first obtaining a search warrant.

Even though Colbridge published his article in October
2001, when anxiety about terrorism had reached a high point
a month after the attacks on the World Trade Center and the
Pentagon, he strictly supports the larger implications of
the Kyllo case against infringement on personal privacy.

Paraphrase and partial quotation

He writes that law enforcement guidelines compel officers to "comply with the constitutional requirements" (30). These requirements protect all "'intimate details'" occurring "within the confines of a home" (30). They limit "devices not generally available to the public" (30). They approve using these devices only "for the broader purpose of public safety" (31). And they stipulate their use only "where people are aware of [their] presence" and "can make a choice to enter the screening area or not" (31). The law obliges officers to assess all these situations.

Colbridge draws from Supreme Court decision.

Paraphrase and partial quotation

An assessment may not be easy, however. Wendy Kaminer in her article "Trading Liberty for Illusions" warns about the misuse of surveillance technology in times of public panic. She has sympathy for the public's acceptance of surveillance at such times when, she writes, "frightened people tend to assume that restrictions on liberty make them safe" (2). She nonetheless questions whether restrictions are effective. Above all, she worries that with such measures, "[t]echnological inaccuracies" can occur and that they can be made worse when "coupled with human errors and abuses of discretion" (3). It is a sober warning that we can appreciate only long after the harm has been done.

Kaminer questions people's confidence about the reliability of technology.

Some observers worry that maybe too much harm has already been done. Is it really possible, they ask, for innocent people to avoid the eye of technology and the effects of electronic surveillance? Many recent commentators on this controversy answer that it may already be too late for anybody to slip beneath the radar. Catherine Price, a writer in *Popular Science*, describes in her article "The Anonymity Experiment" how she tried to shed her private identity for a week in October 2007. She turned off her cell phone and e-mail accounts, retired her credit card, withdrew cash from her bank account, and attempted to assume a new identity that would escape electronic detection.

Summary

The result? After a "week of paranoia," she feels she did a "pretty good job," but nonetheless came to agree with a friend that "'[t]here are all sorts of trails you leave that you'll never even know about'" (53). In modern society, it is probably impossible to conceal your private identity. This doesn't mean, however, that potentially threatening people will always be caught. Such people can be very skillful about concealing their dangerous plots. Technology may enable us to see them without understanding what they are actually doing.

Paraphrase and partial quotation

Price agrees with Kaminer.

Farr 3

On the other side of the ledger, there will always be people who don't mind whether others know about the private details of their lives and who even go out of their way to publicize these details. I am thinking about people who divulge details about themselves on Facebook and other Internet sites in the hope of attracting friends and Internet pals with the same interests.

Summary and partial quotation — As Jonathan Franzen reminds us in his humorous essay "'I Just Called to Say I Love You,'" many people use cell phones in public without regard to eavesdroppers who consciously or unconsciously listen to private conversations conducted in public. For Franzen, these cellular conversations are "insults that keep on insulting" (89) because they disrupt his own personal privacy. He quips, "It's about sparing me from the intrusion of other people's personal lives" (89), and he goes on to recall his parents' sense of privacy in an earlier era.

Franzen describes people who don't mind public exposure.

His father, in particular, had a very reserved personality, which Franzen equates with showing respect for "the public sphere" as a larger entity. *Quotation* — Franzen writes that his father observed "restraint and protocol and reason, because without them, he believed, it was impossible for a society to debate and make decisions in its best interest" (94). Society's best interest remains just as important today.

Respect for the public sphere is nonetheless a two-way street. Just as individuals should show consideration for other people's privacy, so society should show consideration for an individual's privacy. This becomes increasingly difficult to regulate as technology becomes more and more sophisticated. *Summary and partial quotation* — An important article in *The Economist* notes that even the most sophisticated technology is subject to error, and that behavior-recognition systems can easily misinterpret "micro-expressions" that flash for fractions of a second (2). We should be alarmed that many "innocents" may be apprehended while many guilty parties may go free.

The Economist agrees with Kaminer.

The article compares their inaccuracy with the controversial history of lie-detector tests and warns that human beings should "always remain the final arbiters" (3). Are we able to devote resources to hiring and training human beings for the job?

The five articles I have discussed put the issue of "privacy Versus technology" in an interesting perspective. In recent years, and especially since September 11, 2001, the issue of high-tech surveillance has attracted much attention in the public press. The question of privacy nonetheless has a long history of

Farr 4

discussion and debate. As my research has shown, the same question has been asked about every new technology that may expose private information about individuals, whether through wiretapping or thermal imaging systems. As the use of cell phones also demonstrates, the question has two sides: it not only means invading other people's private lives, it also means allowing other people's private lives to disturb someone's own right to privacy. It is worth exploring this history as well as each side of the continuing question.

Farr 5

Works Cited

Colbridge, Thomas D. "*Kyllo v. United States*: Technology v. Individual Privacy." *FBI Law Enforcement Bulletin* 70.10 (2001): 25-31. *Academic Search Premier*. Web. 30 Sept. 2010.

Franzen, Jonathan. "'I Just Called to Say I Love You.'" *Technology Review* 111.5 (2008): 88-95. *WilsonWeb*. Web. 29 Sept. 2010.

"If Looks Could Kill." *The Economist* 389.8603 (2008). *ProQuest*.Web. 20 Sept. 2010.

Kaminer, Wendy. "Trading Liberty for Illusions." *Free Inquiry* 22.2 (2002): 13-14. *InfoTrac Academic OneFile*. Web. 1 Oct. 2010.

Price, Catherine. "The Anonymity Experiment." *Popular Science* 272.3 (2008): 60-66, 90-91. *ProQuest*.Web. 20 Sept. 2010.

As you can see, Megan's introduction and conclusion are the only paragraphs of the essay that do not contain material from source texts. The body of the essay is a mosaic of summaries, quotations, paraphrases, and textual associations. Make note of Megan's use of attribution words and the extent to which she provides background information about the authors. She follows the advice we give in Chapter 2, varying the ways she leads the reader into the textual material, for example:

Colbridge *closely examines*

He *strictly supports*

Kaminer *warns about*

She *questions whether*

Commentators *answer that*

Price *describes how*

As Franzen *reminds us*

He *goes on to recall*

[The] article *notes that*

EXERCISE 6.3

Review Megan's essay and make a list of additional attribution words. Also identify the spots where she offers background about a particular author.

In Chapter 2, we discussed *intertexuality*, which refers to the way writers relate other texts to their own text, often by weaving the other texts into their writing. In the left-hand margin of Megan's essay, we have identified Megan's use of direct quotations, paraphrases, and summaries, and in the right-hand margin we have indicated how the source texts talk to each other. An exploratory synthesis is a quintessential example of in-tertextuality. We recap the strategies for writing an exploratory synthesis in the box below.

RECAP OF STRATEGIES FOR WRITING AN EXPLORATORY SYNTHESIS

- Examine the assignment and decide on your rhetorical purpose.
- Ask Baseline Questions (p. 169) in order to identify the major issue treated by the various texts.
- Locate a theme or subtopic running across the sources.
- Analyze how the texts talk to each other with respect to the subtopic.
- Respond to In-Depth Questions for Identifying Relationships Among Texts (p. 170) to determine the points each text makes about the subtopic.
- Mark the texts and copy passages related to the subtopic into your writer's notebook. Study the bits of text you have selected and impose some type of order on them.
- Formulate a working thesis. Remember that an exploratory synthesis is a straightforward, objective reporting of the sources.
- Write a draft of your essay, returning to source texts for paraphrases, quotations, and summaries.
- Ask a peer to review your paper. (Use Questions for Helping a Writer Revise a Critical Analysis Essay on p. 112.)
- Revise and edit.

■ PROCESS OF WRITING A LITERATURE REVIEW

The purpose of a literature review is to provide background and explain a topic, problem, or issue to readers by examining a wide array of published research studies. As we mentioned earlier, occasionally the writer's goal is simply to communicate the research findings to an interested audience. More typically, the writer seeks to demonstrate her knowledge of a research field in order to lay the foundation for her own research study. More so than with any other type of synthesis, a literature review requires the writer to engage in a sizable amount of library-based research and to sort and re-sort the textual material into manageable, workable categories.

■ Examination of "Adolescents' Expressed Meanings of Music in and out of School": Patricia Shehan Campbell, Claire Connell, and Amy Beegle's Literature Review of the Importance of Music to Adolescents

To illustrate a literature review, we would like you to read a section from Patricia Shehan Campbell, Claire Connell, and Amy Beegle's article "Adolescents' Expressed Meanings of Music in and out of School." The section offers their literature review of research on the importance of music in the lives of adolescents. The objective of their study is to examine the meaning that adolescents attach to music. The authors focus upon the role that music plays in filling emotional needs and forming personal and group identities. In order to contextualize the issue and set the stage for their study, they give their readers background information and point out which facets of the topic have been studied and what approaches have been brought to bear on them. As with the sample article by Feil-Seifer and Matarić (pp. 81–85), note that the style for documenting its sources is its publisher's "house style" and that it differs from the standard MLA or APA styles. For the latter, see the Appendix.

Read the literature review, paying special attention to the various ways Campbell, Connell, and Beegle organize the synthesis and report on and cite the sources. Make note of the similarities and differences between this type of synthesis and the exploratory synthesis we described above. The comparison will reveal the following features of a literature review.

FEATURES OF A LITERATURE REVIEW

- Gives readers workable theories as well as a thorough understanding of the issue.
- Moves one step beyond description and reporting to come to some conclusions about the research. That is, the writer explains the research questions that still have to be answered.
- Analyzes the sources along the lines of key subtopics or themes.
- Organizes the synthesis to focus on ideas rather than sources.
- Uses parenthetical citation to list studies with similar findings; for example, "The literature tends to show that adolescent girls are more invested in music on an emotional level than are their male counterparts (Frith, 1981; North, Hargreaves, & O'Neill, 2000; Wells & Hakanen, 1991)."
- Uses minimal quotation.

Adolescents' Expressed Meanings of Music in and out of School

Patricia Shehan Campbell, Claire Connell, and Amy Beegle

From a developmental perspective, music appears at every stage and age of human   1
growth. In adolescence as in infancy, childhood, and adulthood, music plays a valuable
and valued role in the individual's social-emotional and intellectual-artistic domains.
From age 12 through the high school years, adolescents have been known to embrace
music through their active musical engagement in it and often as passionate consumers
of it (Fine, Mortimer, & Roberts, 1990). In the United States, adolescent consumption
of popular music, for example, is a multi-billion-dollar industry (Geter & Streisand,
1995). Seventy percent of all pop recordings are bought by people ages 12–20 (Brake,
1985), indicating an investment by teenagers of both personal (or family) resources and
time spent in music listening. In fact, Leming (1987) found that American adolescents
listen to music for approximately 4.5 hours per day, while North, Hargreaves, and
O'Neill (2000) reported that British adolescents listen to almost 2.5 hours of music per
day. Likewise, engagement in musical performance by middle and high school students
is not uncommon. In a study of 2,465 British students 13 and 14 years of age, just over
half reported that they either play or at one time played an instrument (North,
Hargreaves, & O'Neill, 2000).

A number of investigators have examined why music is important to adolescents   2
(Arnett, 1995; Gantz, Gartenberg, Pearson, & Shiller, 1978; Larson, 1995; Larson, Kubey,
& Coletti, 1989; North, Hargreaves, & O'Neill, 2000; Roe, 1985; Sun & Lull, 1986;
Tarrant, North, & Hargreaves, 2002; Wells & Hakanen, 1991). Although the results vary
from study to study, common motivations for adolescent involvement with music include
(a) the fulfillment of emotional needs (North, Hargreaves, & O'Neill, 2000; Roe, 1985);
(b) distractions from boredom (Gantz, Gartenberg, Pearson, & Shiller, 1978; Sun & Lull
1986); and (c) the relief of tension and stress (Gantz, Gartenberg, Pearson, & Shiller,
1978). Music may be an element that supports the transformation from child to adult.

Music was also found to provide adolescents with a medium through which to   3
construct, negotiate, and modify aspects of their personal and group identities, offering
them a range of strategies for knowing themselves and connecting with others (Arnett,
1995; Larson, 1995; Tarrant, North, & Hargreaves, 2002). Simon Frith acknowledges
identity formation as one of the main social functions of music (1987, p. 140), and
elsewhere suggests that adolescents wear music as a "badge"—a vehicle for projecting
their inner selves to the world (1981, p. 217). In the different stages of human
development, including the continuous flux of childhood and adolescence, identities
shift and change to adapt to new situations and experiences. Particularly in the adolescent

From pages 221–222 of Campbell, Patricia Shehan, Claire Connell, and Amy Beegle. "Adolescents'
Expressed Meanings of Music in and out of School." *Journal of Research in Music Education* 55.3
(2007). 220–236. Web. 15 Oct. 2010. Copyright © 2007 by MENC: The National Association for
Music Education. Reprinted by permission of SAGE Publications.

years, the individual begins to emerge from the cocoon of familial identity (Larson, 1995; Larson, Kubey, & Coletti, 1989), transforming into a being who has a deeper sense of self, a desire for greater independence, and an increased awareness of public image.

It is also possible that adolescents' assigned identities, especially to their age and gender, might influence divergent trends in their perceptions of the value of music. Larson, Kubey, and Coletti (1989) found that as children make the transition into adolescence, they become less likely to watch television, an activity associated with family, and more likely to spend that leisure time listening to popular music, an activity associated with friends. This desire for independence and personal identity formation is linked to their maturational development. As for gender distinctions, the literature tends to show that adolescent girls are more invested in music on an emotional level than are their male counterparts (Frith, 1981; North, Hargreaves, & O'Neill, 2000; Wells & Hakanen, 1991). While girls have been found to listen to popular music for its emotional benefits, boys tend to be concerned with creating and maintaining an external image for their peers through music (North, Hargreaves, & O'Neill, 2000). Frith (1981) suggested that teenage girls prefer softer music than boys and are more likely to engage with the lyrics of popular songs, particularly those dealing with romantic relationships.

References

Arnett, J. (1995). Adolescents' uses of media for self-socialization. *Journal of Youth and Adolescence*, 24 (5), 519–533.

Brake, M. (1985). *Comparative youth culture: The sociology of youth cultures and youth subcultures in America, Britain and Canada*. London: Routledge and Kegan Paul.

Fine, G. J. A., Mortimer, T., & Roberts, D. F. (1990). Leisure, work, and the mass media. In S. S. Feldman & G. R. Elliott (Eds.), *At the threshold: The developing adolescent* (pp. 225–252). Cambridge, MA: Harvard University Press.

Frith, S. (1981). *Sound effects: Youth, leisure and the politics of rock*. London: Constable Press.

Frith, S. (1987). Towards an aesthetic of popular music. In R. Leppert & S. McClary (Eds.), *Music and society: The politics of composition, performance and reception* (pp. 133–150). Cambridge, UK: Cambridge University Press.

Gantz, W., Gartenberg, H., Pearson, M., & Shiller, S. (1978). Gratifications and expectations associated with pop music among adolescents. *Popular Music and Society*, 6, 81–89.

Geter, T. & Streisand, B. (1995). Recording sound sales: The music industry rocks and rolls to the newest financial rhythms. *U.S. News and World Report*, 25 September, 67–68, 70, 72.

Larson, R. (1995). Secrets in the bedroom: Adolescents' private use of media. *Journal of Youth and Adolescence*, 24 (5), 535–550.

Larson, R., Kubey, R., & Coletti, J. (1989). Changing channels: Early adolescent media choices and shifting investments in family and friends. *Journal of Youth and Adolescence*, 18 (6), 583–599.

Leming, J. S. (1987). Rock music and the socialization of moral values in early adolescence. *Youth and Society*, 18 (4), 363–383.

North, A. C., Hargreaves, D. J., & O'Neill, S. A. (2000). The importance of music for adolescents. *British Journal of Educational Psychology*, 70, 255–272.

Roe, K. (1985). Swedish youth and music: Listening patterns and motivations. *Communication Research*, 12 (3), 353–362.

Sun, S-W., & Lull, J. (1986). The adolescent audience for music videos and why they watch. *Journal of Communication*, 36 (1), 115–125.

Tarrant, M., North, A., & Hargreaves, D. (2002). Youth identity and music. In R. MacDonald, D. J. Hargreaves, & D. Miell (Eds.), *Musical identities* (pp. 134–150). Oxford, UK: Oxford University Press.

Wells, A., & Hakanen, E. (1991). The emotional use of popular music by adolescents. *Journalism Quarterly*, 68 (3), 445–454.

▨ Organize the Literature Review to Focus on Ideas Rather Than Sources

Earlier in this chapter, we pointed out that when students write syntheses, one of their biggest pitfalls is to allow the sources to drive the paper instead of letting their own ideas take the lead. The temptation to let the sources take the lead is especially great when you are writing a review of the literature. It is easy to fall into the pattern of beginning each paragraph with "Such and such a reseacher said." Turn to paragraphs 2, 3, and 4 of Campbell, Connell, and Beegle's "Adolescents' Expressed Meanings of Music in and out of School" to see how the authors avoid this difficulty. Notice how each of the three paragraphs begins with a topic sentence that states an idea before it goes on to cite the researchers' names.

> "A number of investigators have examined why music is important to adolescents."
> "Music was also found to provide adolescents with a medium through which to construct, negotiate, and modify aspects of their personal and group identities."
> "It is also possible that adolescents' assigned identities, especially to their age and gender, might influence divergent trends in their perceptions of the value of music."

Concentrate on the first paragraph and you will see that it is organized carefully according to ideas. Study the graphic representation of this paragraph in Figure 6–2. Note how the sources are used in the service of the ideas, not the other way around.

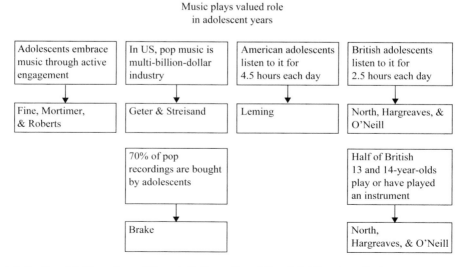

Figure 6–2   Graphic Overview of Campbell, Connell, and Beegle's Literature Review

When you are assigned a literature review, use the strategies in the following box.

RECAP OF STRATEGIES FOR WRITING A LITERATURE REVIEW

- Conduct a wide range of library-based research.
- Identify the subtopics addressed by the various sources.
- Analyze how the texts talk to each other with respect to the subtopics.
- Respond to In-Depth Questions for Identifying Relationships Among Texts (p. 170) to determine the points each text makes about the various subtopics.
- Mark the texts and copy passages into your writer's notebook. Study the bits of text you have selected and impose some type of order on them.
- Create a visual display of the subtopics and the sources related to each subtopic.
- Formulate a working thesis. In your introductory paragraphs, give your readers context and background for your topic and its various subdivisions.
- Organize the review with subdivisions devoted to subthemes.
- In the body paragraphs, review the sources, being careful to subsume the research sources under the subtopic ideas, not the other way around.
- End the review by telling your readers what we know, what we don't know, what's been researched well, what is still up for speculation, and what needs to be done by future researchers.
- Add a page of references.
- Ask a peer to review your paper (use Questions for Helping a Writer Revise a Critical Analysis Essay on p. 112).
- Revise and edit.

◼ PROCESS OF WRITING A THESIS-DRIVEN SYNTHESIS

We have been examining various genres of academic writing with the tacit understanding that all forms of academic writing present arguments of one sort or another. By argument, we do not mean bickering, altercation, or verbal face-off. Instead, we mean a reasoned consideration that the writer has analyzed and explained by responding to earlier writing on the same topic. Such an analysis and explanation amounts to a conversation between one writer and another, and as such it inevitably registers the writer's point of view. This point of view is explicit in the writer's direct statement of judgment or opinion on the matter at hand. The writer is capable of making the direct statement or thesis because she has familiarized herself with the issue by becoming an active participant in the intellectual conversation.

◼ Support Thesis with Evidence

Next, the writer has to decide how to support the thesis. This is where synthesis comes into play. She will return to the reading selections, combing them for sentences and passages that relate directly to her thesis. She will look for support of two types:

- Background information that will enable her to contextualize the issue for her readers and inform them of the conversation
- Evidence that will support her thesis and major points

The most common types of evidence are facts, statistics, and other numerical information; observations based on data (e.g., surveys, polls, studies); examples and analogies; personal experience and anecdotal information; and viewpoints of competent authorities (e.g., testimonies, conclusions drawn from research).

■ Examination of Student's Thesis-Driven Synthesis

To illustrate the process of writing a thesis-driven synthesis, consider the following assignment based upon reading selections in Chapter 12.

> Drawing on Pauline Irit Erera's "What Is a Family?," Robert L. Barret and Bryan E. Robinson's "Children of Gay Fathers," Andrew J. Cherlin's "The Origins of the Ambivalent Acceptance of Divorce," and Lynn Olcott's "The Ballad of a Single Mother," write a four- to five-page essay explaining what American families are like today. Address your essay to an audience of peers.

What follows is an essay by a student, Siryal Benim, written in response to the above assignment.

SAMPLE THESIS-DRIVEN SYNTHESIS ESSAY

Benim 1

Siryal Benim

Academic Writing I

Professor Smith

23 October 2010

New Conceptions of the Traditional Family

Our families today neither resemble nor function like those of just a few decades ago. In the past, American cultural norms suggested that a heterosexual, two-parent, nuclear family was the norm. Pauline Irit Erera in "What Is a Family?" points out that this model can no longer be taken for granted. She writes that the statistic for that type of family was forty-five percent forty years ago but only twenty-six percent in 1998 (463).

[margin note: Paraphase of Erera *]*

She moreover writes that only fifty percent of American children live with their biological parents (463). Other writers such as Andrew J. Cherlin in "The Origins of the Ambivalent Acceptance of Divorce" point out that there has been a long, slow evolution toward accepting divorce and childrearing outside of marriage as individual rights, leading to "a more individualistic view of family life" (227). The past few decades have consequently seen three social upheavals, each popularly termed as sexual-, gender-, and divorce-related. As a direct result of

[margin note: Summary and partial quotation from Cherlin *]*

these changes, our families and lifestyles differ substantially from what they were thirty years ago. The new family structures and lifestyles are occurring by default as often as by choice. It may be that the "alternative" has become the norm.

As the traditional nuclear family is diminishing and different family systems are becoming more common, traditional roles for men and women are changing as well. Men are no longer the sole breadwinners for the family, and in some cases, they may not even be the principal wage earners. The ascension of women in the workforce brings its own set of problems and solutions to family life. The empowerment of some women in the workplace has brought career options, personal fulfillment, and extra income to many women and their families, but it also forces many women—and men—to devise makeshift arrangements for childcare with neighbors, daycare services, and longer school days. In "The Ballad of a Single Mother," Lynn Olcott describes how she often found herself "feeling overwhelmed and exhausted" as she juggled competing responsibilities of family and work (22). The arrangements that she devised brought her children into contact with a wider range of people and experiences and expanded their sense of family network. They were nonetheless the sad result of living "in a society that routinely underpays women, undervalues child care, and ties family health-care access to employment level" (22). In the end, after a full day of work at the office, women are just as exhausted as men. They look to their husbands to assist them with household chores and children.

Paraphrase and quotations from Olcott

But will husbands and fathers willingly adopt this new role? According to Pauline Irit Erera, a wave of backlash and regression swept across American society in the 1990s using the code words "family values" to idealize conventional gender roles in a nuclear family (467). For political conservatives, these roles mean above all the task of full-time motherhood for women. As Erera points out, however, other conservative tenets such as family self-sufficiency and the self-supporting work ethic contradict "family values." In particular, the conservative goal of family self-sufficiency requires women to enter the workforce, yet doing so is "in direct conflict with conservatives' traditional preference for full-time mothers" (467). The burden consequently falls upon families to adjust to the new situation, reapportion male and female gender roles, and introduce

Paraphrase and quotations from Erera

Benim 3

new systems of support to replace older systems that required a fixed dependence of family members on one another.

The dramatic change in men's roles over the past two decades may indicate the rapid deterioration of the old-fashioned nuclear family as a cultural mainstay. Over the past two decades, we have seen a high rate of divorce and the rise of new "traditional" families: family units still headed by adults, but these parents or guardians are not necessarily biologically related to each other's children. Often such units are the result of divorced parents remarrying and bringing step-children into the household. Previously married individuals remarry to create new, sometimes complex family units with various "adoptive" relatives. Erera classifies these families as belonging to a "variant family stereotype" (471). Even this new "merged" family experiences problems and frustrations as "the stereotypes exert pressures on families to try to function in the same mold as the traditional family" (472). Cherlin finds that although divorce "might still be seen as unfortunate," Americans are no longer "likely to criticize someone for wanting one" (228). Consequently, the practice of remarriage after divorce is likely to create new family patterns that will challenge those of the "traditional" family.

Perhaps the most dramatic new family patterns at the beginning of the twenty-first century are those that characterize the families of homosexual couples who either adopt children or procreate through artificial insemination. In "Children of Gay Fathers," Robert L. Barret and Bryan E. Robinson write about men who fathered children in heterosexual marriages before divorcing and "coming out" as gay men. The authors cite studies that find "The parenting styles of gay fathers are not markedly different from those of other single fathers, but gay fathers try to create a more stable home environment and more positive relationships with their children than traditional heterosexual parents" (456). One reason for the extra effort that these men make may be that gay fathers "know their homosexuality causes others to examine their parenting styles more closely" (456). Barret and Robinson acknowledge the risks inherent in relationships between gay parents and their children, especially during volatile teenage years when children become conscious about their own sexuality. But they also cite the preponderance of evidence that concludes that

Summary and partial quotations from Erera

Quotation from Cherlin

Quotations from Barret and Robinson

Benim 4

"a parent's homosexuality has little bearing on the child's sexual orientation" (459).

On an even more general level, Barret and Robinson point out, "Most researchers have concluded that being homosexual is compatible with effective parenting" (457). One result is society's current endorsement of adoptions made by gay men and lesbian women, whether as single parents or as partners in a stable homosexual relationship. Certainly, such families are very different from those of our ancestors. While it remains to be determined in individual cases whether these changes are for better or for worse, it appears that when Cherlin argues, "The principle of individual rights is ascendant" (229), it is inevitable that new concepts of acceptable family life will multiply.

Quotations from Cherlin

Today couples and families have many more options to choose from when making decisions. This freedom comes with its own set of pros and cons. To debate the issue of today's fractured family using sound-bite-styled catch phrases such as "family values" misses the point: values are widely held precepts based on accepted cultural norms that are usually grounded in history or tradition. Quite simply, it is precisely because of the absence of any consensus, morally, spiritually, or otherwise, that an understanding of what constitutes appropriate family behavior cannot be attained. Perhaps we are now creating a new concept of the "traditional" family that will be passed on to subsequent generations.

Benim 5

Works Cited

Barret, Robert L., and Bryan E. Robinson. "Children of Gay Fathers." *Redefining Families: Implications for Children's Development.* Ed. Adele Eskeles Gottfried and Allen W. Gottfried. New York: Plenum Press, 1994. 142-67. Print.

Cherlin, Andrew J. "The Origins of the Ambivalent Acceptance of Divorce." *Journal of Marriage and the Family* 71.2 (May 2009): 226-29. Web. 15 Oct. 2010.

Erera, Pauline Irit. *Family Diversity: Continuity and Change in the Contemporary Family.* Thousand Oaks: Sage, 2002. Print.

Olcott, Lynn. "The Ballad of a Single Mother." *Newsweek.* Newsweek, 30 Oct. 2006: 22. Web. 15 Oct. 2010.

Siryal Benim successfully incorporates material from four reading sources, each of which addresses a different view of the topic. Drawing upon the four texts' perspectives on alternative family patterns, the role of fatherhood, and various moral points associated with these issues, Siryal discusses changes in contemporary family life, arguing that currently available options are very different from traditional family structures; however, these alternative structures may actually be the norm.

We have annotated Siryal's essay for the quotations and paraphrases from the three sources. We have also highlighted Siryal's verbs and phrases of attribution. Notice that he uses a variety of attribution verbs and avoids the monotonous mantra "he said-she said." A distinguishing characteristic of a thesis-driven synthesis essay is that it uses selective summary, paraphrase, and quotation. Place Siryal's essay next to Megan's (pp. 173–76) and you will see a major difference between a thesis-driven synthesis essay and an exploratory synthesis. Siryal uses fragments of the source texts but only insofar as they support his own thesis. The sources serve the thesis. Megan presents a mosaic of texts. She does not state her own position. Her goal is to tell her readers everything the texts say about the background and history of the current controversy over "Privacy Versus Technology."

RECAP OF STRATEGIES FOR WRITING A THESIS-DRIVEN SYNTHESIS

- Firm up your rhetorical purpose: You are reading the texts with the goal of stating your position on the issue.
- Read all the texts to get a general impression of their treatment of the topic and respond to the five Baseline Questions for Initial Reading (p. 169).
- Reread each text to determine the elements it has in common with the other sources and respond to In-Depth Questions for Identifying Relationships Among Texts (p. 170).
- Decide what points you wish to get across to your readers and formulate a working thesis in which you state a position or make a claim.
- Review the texts to discover material you can use to develop each of your points.
- Draft your essay by quoting, paraphrasing, or summarizing relevant supporting information from the texts and by drawing on your knowledge of the basic features of writing: titles, introductions, sentences, paragraphs, transitions, and so on.

◼ REVISING SYNTHESIS ESSAYS

When you have completed a preliminary draft of your essay, schedule a conference with your professor, and if your professor agrees, ask a classmate or a friend to give you suggestions for revision. Use the questions in the box below. Then revise and edit your work.

QUESTIONS FOR REVISING A SYNTHESIS ESSAY

- Is the title appropriate—objective for an exploratory synthesis and a literature review, and reflective of the writer's attitude for a thesis-driven synthesis? If not, can you suggest a more appropriate title?
- Is there an interesting lead that attracts the reader's attention? If not, can you suggest a more appropriate lead?
- Does the writer give you sufficient background information? If not, what else do you need to know?
- Does the writer make his or her overall purpose clear to the reader? If not, what remains fuzzy?
- What is the writer's thesis?
- As you read each paragraph, are you aware of the purpose that the writer is trying to accomplish? If not, where does your mind wander?
- Does the writer identify relationships among texts?
- In each paragraph, does the writer provide sufficient support from the texts? Is there too much summary?
- Does the writer include his or her own commentary when it is appropriate? Is there too much commentary?
- Does the conclusion do more than simply summarize the main points of the paper?
- Does the writer include parenthetical documentation where it is necessary and clearly differentiate among sources?
- Is there a Works Cited page?

EXERCISE 6.4

- Reread Siryal Benim's paper.
- Note the structure of its presentation. After an introductory statement about changes in family patterns, Siryal discusses single mothers, working mothers, conservative values, divorce, step-families, and gay fathers, and then draws on information variously from four sources.
- Read the titles of these sources in the list of Works Cited. What separate topic does each appear to address? Can you make any generalization about Siryal's alternating and selective use of these sources?

EXERCISE 6.5

- Form collaborative learning groups of four students each.
- Assign each member a single source to trace through Siryal's paper. Ask each to comment on the focus that Siryal puts on the material from that particular source.
- When the class reconvenes, have each group recorder explain the conclusions that individual members reached about Siryal's use of particular sources.

WORKS CITED

Barret, Robert L., and Bryan E. Robinson. "Children of Gay Fathers." *Redefining Families: Implications for Children's Development.* Ed. Adele Eskeles Gottfried and Allen W. Gottfried. New York: Plenum Press, 1994. 142–67. Print.

Cherlin, Andrew J. "The Origins of the Ambivalent Acceptance of Divorce." *Journal of Marriage and the Family* 71.2 (May 2009): 226–29. Web. 15 Oct. 2010.

Druian, Greg, and Jocelyn A. Butler. "Schooling Practices and At-Risk Youth: What the Research Shows." *Northwest Regional Educational Laboratory.* Web. 23 Apr. 2006. <http://www.nwrel.org/scpd/sirs/1/topsyn1.html>.

Erera, Pauline Irit. *Family Diversity: Continuity and Change in the Contemporary Family.* Thousand Oaks: Sage, 2002. Print.

Olcott, Lynn. "The Ballad of a Single Mother." *Newsweek.* Newsweek, 30 Oct. 2006: 22. Web. 15 Oct. 2010.

Watson, Robert, and the Core Writing Team of the Cambridge Earth, Environment, and Atmospheric Sciences, eds. "Climate Change 2001: Synthesis Report." 7 Mar. 2002. Web. 15 Mar. 2006. <http://www.cambridge.org/uk/earthsciences/climatechange/reports.htm>.

Seven

Argument

Arguing is an everyday activity. It is a practice that permeates many aspects of our lives. In a conversation among friends, a simple argument might range from whether one brand of shampoo is more effective in controlling bad-hair days than another to whether Saturday or Sunday is a better day to collaborate on a homework assignment. A more consequential argument among family members might concern whether excessive TV viewing interferes with family life. Depending on whose argument prevails, members may find themselves watching more or less TV. A serious argument for an entire community or an entire nation is whether one political candidate rather than another is better prepared to serve the public needs.

Those who argue well have learned how to examine the complexity of issues while maintaining respect for other people's positions. Those who do it poorly resort to simplistic thinking, tunnel vision, and verbal warfare. Argumentative skill is acquired. It is not innate. However, it is worth developing because it will increase your understanding of important issues that you encounter every day. As British scholar Aram Eisenschitz puts it:

> Argument gives students freedom—not the freedom of modularized choices—but the confidence and intellectual autonomy to interrogate academic fragmentation and thereby to reinterpret familiar landscapes and make abstract ideas real. Above all, it makes them aware of the wider implications of ideas that are in daily use and unafraid to challenge the conventions of wisdom. (25)

Learning to argue well in writing, as in speech, is a central concern of the university.

■▟ NATURE OF ACADEMIC ARGUMENT

Academic argument is less a dispute and more a polite exchange of ideas among interested parties. Imagine it as a conversation that you engage in with a group of acquaintances and friends, some of whom hold values and beliefs similar to your own and some of whom see things differently from the way you do. You put your ideas on the table. Some people nod in agreement. Others frown and purse their lips. When you have had your say, the Lip Pursers speak up. They proceed to poke holes in your argument and offer alternative ways of looking at the issue. You listen carefully. Then you respond to the Lip Pursers' objections tactfully, not in a belligerent manner. To be conciliatory, you use expressions such as

Some of what you say is true but...

Your recommendations have some merit, but...

You make a valid point about _____, but the more important issue is _____.

You make a good case about _____, but it overlooks _____.

Your argument addresses part of the problem, but it ought to consider _____.

Granted, _____ is important, but _____ is even more urgent to consider.

And you continue to make your case, bolstering it with evidence and using it to call upon your audience to take decisive action. When you commit an argument to paper, you need to imagine the same conversation and the same give-and-take between you and your readers.

For many students, writing an argument is a challenging task because they have not yet cultivated a disposition for arguing in this noncombative way. Like analyzing and synthesizing, arguing is a habit of mind. And, as with the other two operations, the way you develop a disposition for arguing is by learning to ask the right questions. Later in this chapter we will discuss this rhetorical strategy in more detail.

■ Argument in a Broad Sense and Argument in a Specialized Sense

In the broad sense, every college paper that expresses a thesis is an "argument" because the writer is motivating the reader to accept his or her perspective, position, or point of view. Even if a substantial portion of the essay is devoted to summarizing, paraphrasing, comparing, or contrasting sources, the essay can still form an argument that promotes a distinctive point of view. The choice of materials with their emphasis and arrangement will imply a perspective and demonstrate a position. All of the essays we have discussed up to this point in the book present an argument in the broad sense of the word. All of them set out or explain a particular idea, attitude, or speculative point of view.

A more specialized sense of the word *argument* evokes the goal of moving audiences to a particular action or persuasion. The difference between a written argument in the broad sense of getting your readers to see your point of view and an argument in the narrower sense of persuading your readers to adopt your position is illustrated in the two thesis statements that follow. Both concern the scientific development of robotic machines to reduce human casualties in modern warfare. For some people, the use of these machines is a contested concept. Many writers are embroiled in the controversy over whether the disadvantages of using them outweigh their advantages. Some scientific experts, political leaders, and moral philosophers worry that a proliferation of such devices might escalate the threat of war, increase the chances for their reckless deployment, and consequently result in the loss of human life. (The award-winning film *The Hurt Locker* dramatizes some of these issues.)

THESIS A: ARGUMENT IN THE BROAD SENSE

The development of robotic technology for military purposes promotes false confidence in those who use it, leading to reckless deployment and potential loss of life.

THESIS B: ARGUMENT IN THE SPECIALIZED SENSE

Although the development of robotic technology for military purposes helps to keep combat soldiers out of harm's way, it also promotes false confidence in those who use it, leading to reckless deployment and potential loss of life.

The difference between Thesis A and Thesis B is that the latter is trying to argue about a specific problem associated with alternative uses of sophisticated weaponry: It helps combat soldiers to perform their mission, but it also promotes false confidence. Writer B knows that some of her readers will not agree with her. She expects them to argue that robotic technology always confers great advantages upon our military. When she writes, "Although the development of robotic technology for military purposes helps to keep combat soldiers out of harm's way," she anticipates her readers' opposing response. Later in the body of her essay, she will give reasons why her view, expressed according to "the logic of scientific development," carries more weight than the view of her opponents. Writer A holds the same position as writer B, but she too readily assumes that her readers will agree with her position.

ARGUMENT IN THE BROAD SENSE

- Your thesis states your position, but it is not necessarily arguable and debatable.
- You don't acknowledge and weigh alternative views.
- Your purpose is to present your position. You are not intent on persuading your readers that your position is superior to other positions.

ARGUMENT IN THE SPECIALIZED SENSE

- Your thesis is arguable and debatable.
- You anticipate alternative views, acknowledge them, and address them.
- You are intent on persuading your readers that your position is superior to other positions.

In order to anticipate a reader's opposing response, it is helpful to imagine a range of possible responses based upon a pro versus con list of claims and oppositions to them. In some respects, this is what high-school or college debaters do when they prepare for a public debate. A written argument is certainly not a public debate, but in assembling your materials for such an argument, you could arrange them into pro versus con categories. A good place to start might be *Debatepedia*, a Web site designed by the International Debate Education Association for academic debaters: <http://debatepedia.idebate.org/en/index.php/Welcome_to_Debatepedia!>. Acknowledging its mission to "clarify public debates and improve decision-making globally," the Web site posts pro and con positions along with links to primary readings on thousands of topics related to contemporary social, cultural, scientific, and ethical issues. When you go to the site, type a topic in the "Search" box and explore the listing of pro and con arguments that will appear on your screen. The listing will enable you to position your own claims against those of others when you develop an argument in the specialized sense defined above.

■ Specialized Argument Expressed as Statement Versus Specialized Argument Synthesized with Sources

Clearly it is possible to write an argument that expresses alternative views, acknowledges them, and addresses them in logical terms without referring to specific sources, documentary materials, or quoted support. Op-ed columns in daily newspapers and feature articles in popular magazines routinely offer such arguments as statements of opinion based upon widely known facts and commonly accepted information. Midway through this chapter we will examine such an argument. Written by Michael Crichton on the problem of holding patents for particular gene cells in scientific research, it argues against any third-party ownership of gene cells for research and medical treatment (see below, pp. 217–19). The author wrote his argument based upon his broad knowledge about specialized research and patent law. In this part of the chapter, however, we will discuss arguments that writers have brought into a synthesis with their specialized knowledge of particular sources and quoted materials. This specialized knowledge informs a kind of argument that you will be called upon to write in your college career. Based upon research, the argument shows that you have fully explored your topic in relevant publications, have grasped the pros and cons articulated in the experts' conversations among one another, and have developed a viewpoint that you are willing to argue.

■ DEVELOPING SUPPORT FOR ARGUMENTS

To develop a strong argument, you must impart a breadth and depth to its focus. Try to make the argument two-dimensional. An argument that hammers away at one central idea until it has exhausted all available evidence and concludes by restating the original proposition, as in the following example, is not the kind of argument you want to write.

> The development of robotic technology for military purposes promotes false confidence in those who use it, leading to reckless deployment and potential loss of life.... As a result, we conclude that the development of robotic technology for military purposes promotes false confidence in those who use it, leading to reckless deployment and potential loss of life.

Instead, pursue a rounder, perhaps more oblique path by allowing the argument to recognize its own limitations. Multidimensional argument explicitly acknowledges competing hypotheses, alternative explanations, and even outright contradictions. Consider the following thesis, which takes into account the positive as well as the negative effects of using robotic weaponry:

> The development of robotic technology for military purposes promotes false confidence in those who use it, leading to reckless deployment and potential loss of life even though it also helps to keep combat soldiers out of harm's way.

The value of this approach is that it widens the tunnel vision that repeats only one proposition. It implies that you have explored competing hypotheses and have weighed the evidence for and against each of them. Your readers may or may not agree with your conclusion, but they will certainly respect your effort to set it in a broader context.

■ JOINING THE ACADEMIC CONVERSATION

After reading the preceding section, you may well ask yourself, "How can I possibly explore and weigh the evidence against competing hypotheses if I have limited knowledge of the topic I am writing about?" Your question brings up an important point that student writers often overlook. You can't plunge into an argument and rush to take one side over the other. Before you put pen to paper, you must study the complexities of the issue. The issues you will write about in your college courses, even if they are current topics, are already being debated. Before you write a sentence of your argument essay, you have to become part of this debate. You need to enter into the conversation.

Kenneth Burke, a major philosopher and scholar of rhetoric, gives an apt, frequently quoted description of the situation in which you find yourself:

> Imagine that you enter a parlor. You come late. When you arrive, others have long preceded you, and they are engaged in a heated discussion, a discussion too heated for them to pause and tell you exactly what it is about. In fact, the discussion had already begun long before any of them got there, so that no one present is qualified to retrace for you all the steps that had gone before. You listen for a while, until you decide that you have caught the tenor of the argument; then you put in your oar. Someone answers; you answer him; another comes to your defense; another aligns himself against you, to either the embarrassment or gratification of your opponent, depending upon the quality of your ally's assistance. However, the discussion is interminable. The hour grows late, you must depart. And you do depart, with the discussion still vigorously in progress. (110–11)

We will concretize Burke's parlor discussion by looking at a debate about the military use of robotic technology, the topic of a reading selection that we analyze in the next section of this chapter. Let's say you've been assigned to write an argument-synthesis essay on this topic and that you're looking for a model to galvanize your involvement with the issues. You find this model in the parlor discussion that your research leads you to. The guests who preceded you began discussing the issue over appetizers before dinner, and they continued to converse throughout the dinner. By the time you arrive, they've moved from the dining room to the parlor for desert and coffee. They're scattered around the room chatting in small groups.

As you enter the parlor, you overhear scientific experts talking about the trend among combat military to use robotic technology in dangerous missions so as to prevent casualties in the course of war. Some say that this technology protects soldiers' lives, while others argue that it exposes civilians to real danger. You make your way to the couch in front of the fireplace, where you find a group of politicians arguing about the costs of such technology, both in terms of economic expenditure and in terms of its popularity or unpopularity with the electorate. Later you move to the dessert table, where you listen in on a heated debate among military leaders on the strategic usefulness of this technology. Though it can aid our troops, it also multiplies the chances of computer error and it ramps up competition with the enemy to keep on top of further development. You listen carefully to what all these people are saying and then, as Burke observes, "You put in your oar." You articulate what you think is a reasonable position, but someone immediately challenges your claim. Another guest "comes to your defense; another aligns himself against you." You have become part of the academic conversation.

To extend Burke's metaphor to writing, you dip your oar into the water when you sit down to draft your paper. Before you arrive at this point, you have to

- Read what experts have already written about the issue.
- Examine the various dimensions of the issue by analyzing and evaluating the experts' arguments to determine which are the most convincing, which are reasonable but not terribly persuasive, and which are flawed.
- Articulate a thesis expressing your own position.
- Discover solid reasons to support your thesis.
- Return to the sources to extract evidence you will use to back up each of your reasons.
- Summarize alternative views and reasonable objections to your argument.
- Respond tactfully to these alternative views.
- Decide how you will structure your essay.

In an academic conversation, context means a great deal—and often it provides the best entry for your understanding of the stakes. (Imagine joining an Internet chat group without knowing the players or the causes they champion or whether they're intent on destroying one another, or are instead joking with and perhaps trying to help one another to reach some common goal.) Much depends upon the who, why, what, when, and where that determined the conversation, as the questions in the following box will show.

QUESTIONS TO ASK ABOUT ACADEMIC CONVERSATIONS IN PRINT

The Writing Participants

- Who are the participants and where do they come from?
- Are these participants observers-at-large or contributors with particular skills and appropriate experiences?
- Have these participants just joined the debate or do they have a record of engaging in it?

(continued)

- Have these participants held consistent views on the topic or have they changed their positions over time?
- Who are on which side? Who switch sides? Who belong to no side?

The Reading Audience

- What might we assume about the readers whom the participants specifically address?
- What might we assume about other readers who confront these writings?
- Have the dynamics of the original situation changed since these articles were published?
- Have recent circumstances modified, challenged, rejected, or upheld the participants' claims?
- Has our thinking advanced beyond their positions, or is it still worthwhile to return to them to deepen and extend their claims?

Rhetorical Context

- Why do the participants engage in this conversation? What interests are they furthering or protecting?
- When did these writings appear in print?
- Where did these writings appear in print? Do they derive from largely popular newspaper or magazine articles? Or from predominantly specialized publications for experts in a particular field? Or from some hybrid of the two? Or from some free-wheeling Internet blogosphere?

It's not always easy for newcomers to answer these questions. But with some exposure to the sources of dialogue, the venues of exchange, and the backgrounds of the engaged parties, anyone can begin to map out the investments. (Think of how you first began to make sense of baseball stats or the styles of rap stars or rock artists.) In academic conversations, it pays to know the perceived reputation of the source's appearance:

- Scholarly sources such as academic or professional journals, university press publications, and academic textbooks
- Substantial news or general interest sources, such as national newspapers, documented periodicals, and specialized journals
- Popular press sources, such as local newspapers, general-circulation magazines, and mass-market publications
- Sensationalized sources such as tabloid newspapers and magazines

It also pays to know where the authors have been and what they have previously published:

- Have they had professional experience in the field?
- Is it their primary field of expertise?
- Have they received funding for their work, and from where has it come?
- What else have they written, and who refereed it in reviews and public airings?
- What criticism, approval, or disapproval has their work received, and from whom?

Some of these identifications can be or become pretty esoteric. (One wag declared that professors are people who talk or write in someone else's sleep.) But with a few clues and a little practice, any student in an academic community can draw some picture of the various camps. We aim to provide some clues.

■ EXAMINATION OF "PREDATORS OR PLOWSHARES? ARMS CONTROL OF ROBOTIC WEAPONS": ROBERT SPARROW'S ARGUMENT-SYNTHESIS

As has been our practice, we will discuss a sample published essay before we walk you through the process of writing your own essay. The sample argument-synthesis is Robert Sparrow's "Predators or Plowshares? Arms Control of Robotic Weapons," an article that appeared in the Spring 2009 issue of *IEEP Technology and Society Magazine*, published by Fordham University Press. "IEEP" refers to the Institute for Ethics and Economics Policy at Fordham University.

The author is a Senior Lecturer in the School of Philosophy and Bioethics at Monash University in Victoria, Australia. He specializes in applied ethics and political philosophy and has published extensively on the ethics of robotics, artificial intelligence, military technology, nanotechnology, reproductive technology, and organ transplants. The topic of his article concerns the military use of robotic technology and the dangers of escalating its use in high-tech warfare. It is a topic of widespread "academic conversation" among robotic scientists, political scientists, military strategists, moral philosophers, and the general public.

With his background in technology and applied ethics, Robert Sparrow is well positioned to write an argument-synthesis on this topic. His title "Predators or Plowshares?" refers to the biblical passage "They shall beat their swords into plowshares" (Isaiah 2.4), and it substitutes the idea of robotic weapons as "predators" for the original term "swords." We have slightly abridged Sparrow's article for reasons of space.

■ ■ ■ ■ ■ ■ ■ ■ ■ ■ ■

Predators or Plowshares? Arms Control of Robotic Weapons

Robert Sparrow

With the development of the General Atomics MQ-1 Predator, robotic weapons came   1
of age. The operations of this Unmanned Aerial Vehicle (UAV) in Iraq, Afghanistan, Pakistan, and northern Africa in the last few years have given us a glimpse of the future of high-tech war [6], [14], [24]. It is a future in which thousands of miles separate those firing weapons from those whom they kill, in which joystick jockeys have replaced pilots and soldiers, and in which the psychological barriers to killing are greatly reduced by the

Sparrow, Robert. "Predators or Plowshares? Arms Control of Robotic Weapons." Portions reprinted with permission from *IEEE Technology and Society Magazine*. Fordham University, Spring 2009: 25–29. © 2009 IEEE. Web. 10 Oct. 2010.

distance between weapon operators and their targets. Perhaps more importantly, it is a future in which wars are more likely, in which decisions about when weapons are fired and who they are fired at are increasingly in the hands of machines, and in which the public has little knowledge of—or control over—what is being done in its name. Finally, it is a future that is likely to come about not because it represents a better, less destructive, way of fighting war but because the dynamics driving the development of unmanned weapon systems (UMS) are likely to dictate that they be used more and more often.

Now that we have had a glimpse of this future, it is time to begin thinking about whether—and how—we might avoid it by adopting an arms control regime designed to limit the development and deployment of robotic weapons. 2

Out of Harm's Way

Arguments for arms control are most important when there is a real temptation to develop the weapons they concern. From a military perspective at least, the advantages of UMS are myriad. Remotely piloted systems may help keep some human beings "out of harm's way" by distancing weapons operators from the theater of conflict [31]. They also greatly reduce the "fog of war" by making possible real-time surveillance of the battlespace, which in turn allows lethal force to be used in a more discriminating fashion. 3

In suggesting that there may be reasons to consider arms control of UMS, I am in no way denying the military utility of these systems nor even that they offer some prospect of rendering some aspects of armed conflict "more ethical." However, the danger I wish to highlight here is that each nation's unrestrained pursuit of these advantages may result in a situation in which every nation is worse off than they would have been if none had set off on this path. 4

Psychological Distance

The first and in some ways the most obvious reason for concern about the development of unmanned systems is the possibility that they will undercut warfighters' respect for human life by facilitating "killing at a distance" [41]. It is now possible for the operators of the Predator to fly an entire combat tour in Iraq or Afghanistan without ever leaving Nevada and to kill people they have only ever encountered as pixels on a computer screen. The geographic and psychological distance between the operators and those they target may make it signifycantly easier for them to make the decision to kill [39]. However, the force of this objection to the development of robotic weapons is greatly mitigated when we consider the nature of what the use of such weapons might replace. Shelling from a battleship miles offshore or conducting area bombing from a B-52 hardly involves much contact with, or respect for, the individuals one is killing. Our willingness to tolerate these forms of warfare suggests that concerns about "remote control killing" are not, in themselves, sufficient justification for arms control. 5

Increased Risk of War

A more powerful reason for considering arms control is the danger that the development of unmanned systems will dramatically reduce the threshold of conflict and will increase the risk of accidental war. At the strategic level, the development of robotic 6 weapons may lower the political costs of going to war by promoting the illusion that war can be fought without casualties [6], [16], [19]. It is clear that the possibility of removing American warfighters from the front line of combat is one of the main factors driving interest in UMS in the United States [7], [12], [16], [17], [18, p. 14], [23], [26], [31], [32], [34], [37].

In part, this goal reflects the morally admirable desire to save the lives of U.S.   7 warfighters. However, it is difficult to avoid the suspicion that the desire to minimize the risks to U.S. personnel also stems in part from a perception that the American public has a low tolerance for casualties, which negatively impacts on the ability of the United States to project force abroad [5], [15], [20, p. 79], [26, p. 77]. If it becomes possible to project military power and engage an enemy in combat using a force consisting mainly of UMS, governments may be much more willing to go to war [5, p. 26], [27], [28]. UMS will also lower the threshold of conflict at the strategic level by decreasing the amount of time available to nations to determine whether an attack is imminent, or even under way, and also how to respond if it is.

Part of the U.S. military's interest in UMS, and especially UAVs and Unmanned   8 Undersea Vehicles (UUVs), stems from the belief that it will eventually become possible to deploy unmanned systems for much longer periods and at a greater tempo of operations than manned systems [31]. By taking the human being out of the system, unmanned systems partially decouple the limits of the system from the limits of its operators. UAVs can be smaller, faster, fly higher (or lower), and conduct longer and more dangerous missions than manned systems [40]. For instance, because the operators of Predator and Global Hawk UAVs work in shifts, these systems are capable of near continuous operation and are limited only by the need to refuel and maintain the aircraft [10].

Researchers in the United States are currently working on providing UAVs   9 with the capacity to undergo in-flight refueling [9], [21] in order to further increase the range and extend the period of operations of these systems. Similarly, it is hoped that UUVs will eventually be capable of missions in shallower waters than manned submersibles [13].

The development of long-range UMS capable of extended operations may make   10 it possible for some states to maintain a permanent armed presence just outside the airspace and territorial waters of their potential enemies, in the form of "loitering" UMS. These forces might be capable of carrying out a devastating attack in a fashion that would allow their target very little time to respond. If an attack is suspected or seems imminent, there is a brief window of opportunity between possible contact and destruction available to determine whether one is under attack by UMS. This places states under significant pressure to mobilize their own forces, and increases the chance that war will occur in error.

The widespread use of UMS may also increase the amount of contact between   11 opposing forces during peacetime and so further multiply the opportunities for an accident or incident to escalate to conflict. Thus one can envision that, in the future, not only will strategic rivals patrol the limits of each other's territories with squadrons of UAVs, Unmanned Surface Vehicles (USVs), and UUVs ready to attack at a moment's notice. But these systems may, in turn, be shadowed by further groups of systems poised to destroy them. In these circumstances, accidents or even mere uncertainty about the intentions of an enemy may trigger a full-scale conflict. Placing robots in

space is likely to greatly exacerbate these diffculties [1]. The risk of accidental war triggered by the activities of UMS is only likely to increase in the future because the logic
of the development of unmanned systems clearly points to their eventual deployment
in "fully autonomous" mode.

Despite the insistence of military spokespeople that autonomous robots will 12
never be allowed to kill human beings [16], there are significant reasons to doubt that
this promise will be kept. The satellite links and other communications infrastructure
necessary to operate UAVs remotely are an obvious weak point in the operations of
these systems and are consequently a predictable target for the enemy's countermea-
sures. Those systems that can continue to operate in the absence of these links have
obvious military advantages. Indeed, systems that do not involve a human operator
may possess advantages even where the robustness of communications is not at issue. The limits of the human nervous system serve as a constraint on the capacities
of manned systems. In a limited range of domains at least, computers are capable of
assessing a situation and making a decision faster and more accurately than human
beings [2, pp. 6–7].

As the technology involved in robotic weapons improves, eventually we will 13
reach a point where whenever a manned and an unmanned weapon system go into
combat against each other, the odds will strongly favor the unmanned system [1], [5].
Once this point is reached, warring nations will have to field autonomous weapons
systems or accept a severe military disadvantage. This prospect also establishes a significant incentive for advanced industrial powers to work towards the development of
systems capable of reliable combat operations in the absence of a human operator.

Once autonomous weapons systems come into use then the decision about 14
whether or not to open fire in a particular situation will be in the hands of machines.
The risk will then exist of an accidental war being triggered by the decisions of one or
more autonomous weapon systems....

Motivation for Controls

In one important regard, it is probably too early to expect these arguments for arms 15
control to have much impact. The U.S. currently enjoys such an overwhelming superiority in arms and military technology—including robotic weapons—compared to
any of its potential enemies that it has little incentive to enter into negotiations about
the capacities of its weapon systems. However, this superiority may well be challenged
over the next two or three decades, especially in the area of unmanned systems, which
may be easier to develop and manufacture using commercial off-the-shelf components
than other weapon systems. China, for instance, has a vigorous UAV development
program. Russia also has a significant capacity to design, manufacture, and operate
UAVs. It is also possible that the technology and experience required to manufacture
and field UMS will disperse as a result of the flourishing arms trade in systems manufactured by Britain, Israel, Europe, and other states. It would therefore be unwise to
conclude that the U.S. will always maintain the commanding lead in the area of
unmanned systems technology that it currently possesses. If another nation should
become capable of flying a Predator-type UAV around the skies of North America or
loitering a UUV in the waters offshore of the continental U.S., then the issues I have

raised here will suddenly become as urgent for U.S. policy makers as they are likely to be for other nations well before that time. There is now a growing literature on the ethics of unmanned weapon systems.

Much of this literature is critical, highlighting the many difficult issues these 16 systems—and especially autonomous weapon systems—raise. However, most of these discussions settle for calling for more ethical debate rather than arms control. I hope that by explicitly making the case for arms control in this context I can encourage other participants in the debate to clarify whether they have the courage of their convictions. Without arms control of robotic weapons, the future I outlined at the outset of this piece seems inevitable. With a concerted effort to achieve arms control, there is perhaps a small chance that we will be able to overcome the military logic that would hand over the fighting of war to robots in favor of the human need for peace and security.

References

[1] T. K. Adams, "Future warfare and the decline of human decision-making," *Parameters: U.S. Army War College Quart.*, pp. 57–71, Wint. 2001–2002.

[2] R. C. Arkin, *Governing Lethal Behavior: Embedding Ethics in a Hybrid Deliberative/ Reactive Robot Architecture*, Mobile Robot Laboratory, College of Computing, Georgia Institute of Technology, Atlanta, GA, 2007.

[5] C. Beal, "Briefing: Autonomous weapons systems—Brave new world," *Jane's Defence Weekly*, vol. 33, no. 6, pp. 22–26, 2000.

[6] B. Bender, "Attacking Iraq, from a Nev. Computer," *Boston Globe*, p. A6, Apr. 3, 2005.

[7] R. Boland, "Developing reasoning robots for today and tomorrow," *Signal*, vol. 61, no. 6, pp. 43–46, 2007.

[9] R. Braybrook, "Drones: Complete guide, *Armada Int.*, vol. 31, no. 3, pp. 1–36, 2007.

[10] A. Butler, "Global Hawk UAV supports border ops in Iraq," *Aviation Week & Space Technology*, vol. 166, no. 11, p. 56, 2007.

[12] R. E. (Col.) Chapman, "Unmanned combat aerial vehicles: Dawn of a new age?," *Aerospace Power J.*, vol. 16, no. 2, pp. 60–73, 2002.

[13] Department of the Navy, *The Navy Unmanned Undersea Vehicle (UUV) Master Plan*, 2004; <http://www.navy.mil/navydata/technology/uuvmp.pdf>.

[14] S. B. Donnelly, "Long-distance warriors," *Time*, Dec. 4, 2005.

[15] C. J. Dunlap, Jr., "Technology: Recomplicating moral life for the nation's defenders," *Parameters: U.S. Army War College Quart.*, pp. 24–53, Autm. 1999.

[16] S. Featherstone, "The coming robot army," *Harper's*, pp. 43–52, Feb. 2007.

[17] M. Fielding, "Robotics in future land warfare," *Australian Army J.*, vol. 3, no. 2, pp. 1–10, 2006.

[18] S. Graham, "America's robot army", *New Statesman*, vol. 135, no. 4796, pp. 12–15, 2006.

[19] H. Gulam, and S.W. Lee, "Uninhabited combat aerial vehicles and the law of armed conflict," *Australian Army J.*, vol. 3, no. 2, pp. 1–14, 2006.

[20] J. A. Harley, "Information, technology, and center of gravity," *Naval War College Rev.*, vol. 50, no. 1, pp. 66–87, 1997.

[21] H. Hutchinson, "Advances in self-control," *Mechanical Engineering*, vol. 128, no. 12, pp. 20, 2006.

[22] Jane's Intelligence Digest, "U.S. ties with Pakistan under strain," *Jane's Intelligence Dig.*, June 23, 2006.

[23] S. Kainikara, "UCAVs probable lynchpins of future air warfare," *Asia-Pacific Defence Reporter*, vol. 28, no. 6, pp. 42–45, 2002.

[24] R.D. Kaplan, "Hunting the Taliban in Las Vegas," *Atlantic Monthly*, Aug. 4, 2006.

[25] A. J. Lazarski, "Legal implications of the uninhabited combat aerial vehicle," *Air and Space Power J.*, vol. 16, no. 2, pp. 74–83, 2002.

[26] W. Legien, C-J. Andersson, and G. Hansen, "UUV and USV: Which 'unmanned' for what task?" *Naval Forces*, vol. 27, no. 3, pp. 44–51, 2006.

[27] P. Marks, "Robot infantry get ready for the battlefield", *New Scientist*, vol. 191, no. 2570, p. 28, 2006.

[28] P. Marks, "Armchair warfare," *New Scientist*, vol. 192, no. 2575, p. 24, 2006.

[29] T. Moss, "Airshow China: Chinese companies unveil latest UAV designs," *Jane's Defence Weekly*, Nov. 7, 2008.

[30] J. Mustin, "Future employment of unmanned aerial vehicles," *Air and Space Power J.*, vol. 16, no. 2, pp. 86–97, 2002.

[31] Office of the Under Secretary of Defense, *Joint Robotics Program Master Plan FY2005: Out front in harm's way*. Washington DC: Office of the Undersecretary of Defense (AT&L), Defense Systems/Land Warfare and Munitions, 2005.

[32] G. I. Peterson, "Unmanned vehicles: Changing the way to look at the battlespace," *Naval Forces*, vol. 26, no. 4, pp. 29–38, 2005.

[33] D. Richardson, "U.S. increasing armed UAV use in Southwest Asia, reports suggest," *Jane's Missiles and Rockets*, Nov. 3, 2008.

[34] R. Scarborough, "Special report: Unmanned warfare," *Washington Times*, May 8, 2005.

[37] J. Sherman, "The drone wars," *Bull. Atomic Scientists*, pp. 28–37, 2005.

[39] R. Sparrow, "Building a better WarBot: Ethical issues in the design of unmanned systems for military applications," *Science and Engineering Ethics*, 2009, to be published.

[40] J. M. Sullivan, "Evolution or revolution? The rise of UAVs," *IEEE Technology & Society Mag.*, vol. 25, no. 3, pp. 43–49, Fall 2006. [41] D.L. Ulin, "When robots do the killing," *Los Angeles Times*, Jan. 30, 2005.

Robert Sparrow evidently joined the academic conversation about robotic technology shortly after newspaper and magazine journalism began to report on the expansion of its use during the American army's counterinsurgency in Iraq. As the first three sources cited in "Predators or Plowshares?" indicate, the *Boston Globe, Time,* and *Atlantic Monthly* all published articles on this topic in 2005–06. Appearing in 2009, "Predators or Plowshares?" draws upon subsequent publications that examine the political and strategic use of this technology, as well as upon publications that question the technology's ethical implications and moral consequences. Sparrow rejects the enthusiasm with which many greet its advances, and he asks where the advances might lead. The answer points to a future in which wars will be easier to conduct and hence more likely to occur, and in which the remoteness of combatants from their victims can weaken cognitive and emotional restraints against lethal outcomes. Sparrow then argues that we should design an arms control program that will limit the expansion and use of robotic weaponry.

Before Sparrow makes his argument, he informs his readers about the ongoing conversation. His opening paragraphs (1) familiarize readers with the issue by recounting the dynamics propelling the use of robotic weaponry in Iraq, Afghanistan, Pakistan, and elsewhere; (2) explain that he is responding to the vision of a dark future that will result from this turn of events; and (3) state his claim that "it is time to begin thinking about whether—and how—we might avoid [this future] by adopting an arms control regime designed to limit the development and deployment of robotic weapons" (paragraph 2). Sparrow is telling his readers, "This is what people are talking about. This is what they are saying. Here is why they are wrong. And here is why my proposal makes better sense." His reason for entering this conversation is to set readers straight. He wants them to see the situation as he sees it. Similarly, your goal as the writer of an argument-synthesis essay is to give your readers a better understanding of an issue that should interest them as much as you.

Sparrow's first move is to clarify the facts. Pointing out that popular newspapers and magazines have portrayed military uses of robotic weaponry in uplifting and future-oriented terms, Sparrow speculates that the distance between trigger and target will dissolve "psychological barriers to killing." He offers three general reasons to support his claim:

- Decisions about deployment will increasingly be left to robotic machines.
- Civilians will have little knowledge about what is happening.
- Dynamics motivating the scientific advancement of these machines imply that they will figure more and more prominently in military combat.

The remainder of the article develops and substantiates several particular, carefully researched reasons with evidence obtained from a wide range of sources recorded in the list of References. They include sources that report upon technological advances from a scientific and military point of view:

- *Parameters: U.S. Army War College Quarterly*
- *Aerospace Power Journal*
- *The Navy Unmanned Undersea Vehicle (UUV) Master Plan*
- *Air and Space Power Journal*
- *New Scientist*
- *Joint Robotics Program Master Plan*
- *Bulletin of Atomic Scientists*

And they include sources that report on ethical considerations from a political, philosophical, and moral point of view:

- *Governing Lethal Behavior*
- *Harper's*
- *New Statesman*
- *Science and Engineering Ethics*

All told, "Predators or Plowshares?" lists thirty-four sources. It is worth pointing out that Sparrow's format of documentation differs from ones that your professors will most likely expect you to use. We discuss the formats most commonly assigned in college courses, the MLA (humanities) and APA (sciences and social sciences) documentation styles, in Chapter 8 and in the Appendix. Here it is sufficient to note that in his section titled "References," Sparrow assigns a number to each of his sources, which he lists alphabetically according to the author's last name. In the body of his text, Sparrow

Overview of Robert Sparrow's "Predators or Plowshares?"

CENTRAL CLAIM

The widely reported development of robotic weaponry has greatly aided military combatants in pursuit of war. But it also carries risks relating to computer error, reduced levels of psychological resistance to killing, and heightened incentives to engage in warfare. It is time to begin thinking about whether—and how—we might avoid such risks by adopting an arms control regime designed to limit the development and deployment of robotic weapons.

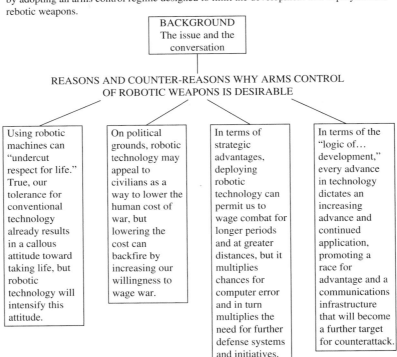

Figure 7–1

uses these numbers to direct the reader to specific titles in place of conventional foot-notes. Many journals and publication houses have developed their own "house styles" to record an author's sources, and this article from the *IEEE Technology and Society Magazine* offers a case in point.

Sparrow's references to sources perform a double function. The hallmark of a strong argument is the writer's acknowledgment of alternative views. In this article, the author's sources serve to document military applications of robotic technology in recent warfare and to raise moral and political questions about its ethical use. These sources consequently register competing claims about the desirability and undesirability of assigning lethal tasks to computerized machines. On the one hand, robotic machines help to protect our armed forces and alleviate the stress of their operations. On the other,

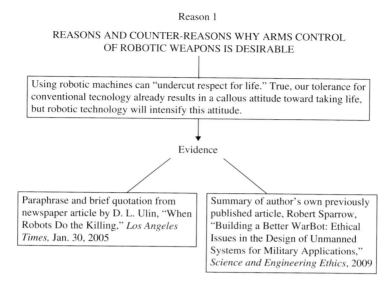

Figure 7–2

the possibilities of computer error increase chances of unintended devastation, the loss of human life, and an escalation of military conflict.

For example, in paragraph 3, Sparrow acknowledges the advantages of robotic technology in reducing the "'fog of war.'" In paragraph 4, he goes on to counter this view by arguing that "each nation's unrestrained pursuit of these advantages may result in a situation in which every nation is worse off than they would have been if none had set off on this path." In paragraph 5 he begins to enumerate specific reasons why this is so, in some cases qualifying his reasons with alternative arguments and competing claims. Here he argues that using robotic machines can "undercut warfighters' respect for human life," but he also points out that our tolerance for conventional technology already fosters a callous attitude toward life. In paragraph 6 he argues that on political grounds, robotic technology may appeal to civilians as a way to lower the human cost of war, but he also points out that lowering this cost can backfire by increasing our willingness to wage war. Similarly in paragraphs 8 through 11, Sparrow examines the strategic advantages and moral disadvantages of deploying robotic technology. Finally, in paragraphs 12 through 14, he examines the "logic of the development" whereby every advance in technology dictates an increasing use of that technology despite diminishing returns. Once technology advances, history shows that people use it willy-nilly for better or for worse. Consequently, Sparrow argues, we must institute responsible controls when using the new robotic technology.

In Figures 7–1, 7–2, and 7–3, we provide graphic overviews of Sparrow's argument. Study these maps. They are good templates for an argument-synthesis essay. Figure 7–1 depicts Sparrow's claim, his presentation of background information, and the four chief reasons he uses to support the claim. In Figures 7–2 and 7–3, we flesh out two of these reasons by displaying the evidence he incorporates from the source texts.

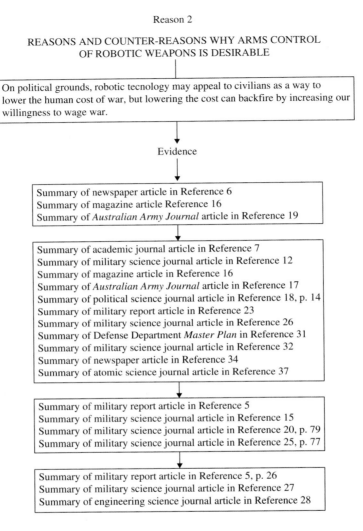

Figure 7–3

EXERCISE 7.1

- Review paragraphs 8–14 of Robert Sparrow's argument in "Predators or Plowshares?" Then break into small groups. Assign one of the following subsets of reasons to each group:

  - Robotic technology will make it possible to deploy unmanned weapons for longer periods and at a greater tempo of operations so as to conduct more dangerous missions than manned systems (paragraph 9)

  - Robotic systems multiply the need for further defense systems that aim to destroy or protect them, escalating the logic that demands further development (paragraphs 11–12).

  - The logic of development increasingly places decision-making in the control of robotic machines, promoting chances for computer error and for a competitive race in advancement among military nations (paragraph 13).

- Review Robert Sparrow's claim and then reread the paragraphs devoted to the reason you have been assigned.

- Sketch out a map or graphic overview comparable to the ones we present in Figure 7–2 and Figure 7–3. A member from each group will display the graphic overview and explain to the class the various ways Sparrow uses the sources to support his argument.

■ PROCESS OF WRITING AN ARGUMENT-SYNTHESIS ESSAY

■ Differentiate Between Issues and Topics

Think of a debatable issue on which you have a strong opinion. Note that we use the word *issue* here rather than *subject* or *topic*. A *topic* maps out a general area for discussion or inquiry. In and of itself, a topic is not contestable. An *issue* involves a specific point or matter for contention and debate. Abortion is a topic. Whether or not women should have free choice in the matter of abortion is an issue. Some people will say "Yes;" others will say "No." On every issue, there are alternative views.

EXERCISE 7.2

- Study the following list to be sure you understand the difference between a topic and an issue:

Topic	Issue
1. Imports	Whether we should buy American-made goods rather than imports
2. Rap or heavy metal music	Whether rap or heavy metal music promotes violence
3. Television	Whether excessive television viewing damages family life
4. Extension of the school year	Whether the United States should extend the school year
5. Experiments on animals	Whether cosmetics firms should experiment on animals

- In your writer's notebook, jot down your views on one of the issues or on an issue of your choice.

- Next, state the primary reason you hold your position. Ask yourself two questions:
  - What is the basis or main reason for my view?
  - Based on this reason, would anyone disagree with my reasoning?

  For example, you might claim that excessive television watching does not damage family life because when you were growing up, the TV was always on in your house and this didn't interfere with your family life. Your classmate sees things differently, claiming that excessive television watching was a distraction that prevented him from having serious discussions with his family.

- Think about how your readers or a larger audience might react to your position, and you will see how difficult it can be to construct a persuasive argument defending your views.

  We will return to this activity in a collaborative exercise after we have considered some strategies and techniques for fashioning strong arguments.

◼ Differentiate Between Claims and Evidence

The difference between the claim that you might make—what you propose to be true about your topic—and the evidence that you produce to support it might seem easy enough to understand. In practice, however, it proves to be enormously difficult to coordinate claims and their evidence. Trial judges and attorneys routinely dismiss many sorts of evidence as faulty, irrelevant, and inadmissible. Sometimes when the evidence itself is assumed without proof, it appears to be as presumptive as the claim that needs to be proved. Logicians call this situation "begging the question."

Rhetoricians who have dealt seriously with this problem usually make fine distinctions between factual evidence and reliable testimony and they question whether or not facts and testimony can furnish proof of an argument. Here we are concerned not so much with evidence or testimony as with how people use them. We need to examine every piece of evidence or testimony and ask whether it may supply possible, probable, reasonably certain, or largely uncertain proof for an argument.

The relationships among evidence, testimony, and proof depend upon generally accepted rules, laws, or scientific principles that validate the evidence or testimony as proof. Fingerprints on a weapon might constitute evidence about who used the weapon, but the proof that a particular culprit committed a crime would be complicated if the fingerprints belonged to more than one suspect. Links between evidence and proof demand a process of inquiry and reasoning to form what rhetoricians call a "warrant." An effective warrant summons belief because it persuasively connects evidence to a claim. Such a connection results in proof. An important writer who has designed tests for successful warrants is Stephen E. Toulmin, in his widely quoted book *The Uses of Argument*.

In "Predators or Plowshares?" Sparrow's evidence consists of psychological effects associated with "'killing at a distance'" (paragraph 5), strategic results of using robotic weapons (paragraphs 6–7), consequences of relying upon machines to make decisions (paragraph 8–11), and the logic of scientific development as it reaches into the future (paragraphs 12–14). He bases his evidence upon testimony from thirty-four published sources. The way he relates this testimony from his sources to his discussion of the evidence constitutes his warrant for the claim that we should design an arms control program to limit the use of robotic weapons.

Sparrow handles evidence and testimony so seamlessly in defense of his claim that it would be difficult to say whether he began with the evidence and arrived at his claim or whether he started with his claim and then looked for evidence. It's worth pointing out the soundness of a plan that starts with data or evidence before making a claim. Many inexperienced writers begin with a claim and then search for evidence to support it. Instead, the evidence-to-claim procedure almost always results in a stronger argument. Instead of reaching for a claim at the outset, design a reasonable hypothesis that may or may not turn out to be entirely true. As you assemble data and then analyze, interpret, and evaluate the evidence, you will arrive at a sharper, more precise view of your claim. As you work through your argument, you should periodically revise your claim so as to uncover a more convincing truth at the core of your presentation.

◼ Differentiate Between Opinions and Reasons

When you develop support for an argument, be sure to differentiate between opinions and reasons. An *opinion* is a belief that you cannot substantiate with direct proof, whereas a *reason* carries with it the weight of logic and reliable evidence. In the example in Exercise 7.2, one student's opinion about television watching is as good as another's. But neither will win an argument. Here are two additional examples of opinions:

> The school year should be lengthened because young kids usually waste away their summers anyway.
>
> From the time I was thirteen, I worked hard at a job all summer long. Kids should work during the summer and not go to school.

In both examples, the writers are expressing opinions about the productivity of kids on vacation. Both individuals define their points of view, but neither gives firm grounds of support. On the other hand, the student who writes

> Because our school year is 180 days and Japan's and West Germany's school years extend from 226 to 243 school days, Japanese and German children have more time to learn science and math. A lengthened school year will allow our students to spend as much classroom time on science and math as students in other industrialized countries and perhaps "catch up" with the competition.

has provided a rational ground of support for his or her view. This is called a *reason.* To make a strong argument, you have to support your position with substantial reasons. This will be easy if you have ample background knowledge of the issue. But if you know little about the issue, even if you have very strong opinions about it you must crack open reading sources that offer background information and present other people's arguments and views.

In some courses, professors will stipulate issues for you to discuss. At other times, you will be permitted to select your own issue. When this is the case, start with a topic and then convert your topic into an arguable issue by asking, "What is controversial about _____? What do people argue about?" Take "robotic weaponry," the topic we introduced earlier (see p. 193). If you have read about the dangers as well as the advantages of using this technology, you will know that this topic generates competing claims between the benefits of further technological development and the advisability of designing some controls over its application. Once you've acquired some background knowledge about the topic and have isolated some of its competing claims, you will have no trouble delving beneath the surface and discovering a number of specific issues. Your background knowledge of these issues will enable you to refine the topic and come up with an innovative slant on it. If you know very little about robotic weaponry, however, you will have to learn more about it by carefully reading the texts your professor recommends or by conducting library research. (Chapter 8 will assist you with library work.)

When you have determined what it is that people argue about, convert that information into an issue: Whether the advantages of using robotic weaponry are more important than the dangers of doing so. If you prefer, state your issue as a question: Which is better, the benefits that flow from this technology or the risks that it will escalate warfare of all against all?

Subject or Topic → What Do People Argue About? → Issue

You may have strong opinions on the issue from the outset ("No, the benefits of robotic technology are far more important than the problems that might arise from using it"; "Yes, we should design some controls upon the application of this technology before it exposes us to greater hazard"), but remember that opinions are not enough. To persuade someone else, you need convincing proof. Unless you are well-read and fully informed about the issue, you will need to consult published sources.

■ Probe Both Sides of the Issue

As you read the sources, you may uncover so much information that you decide to redefine and narrow your issue. Remember to probe both sides and read with an open mind, even if you have already taken a stand. A useful activity is what writing professor Peter Elbow calls the "believing game." As you encounter views that conflict with your own, try to see them through the holder's eyes. Even if the views are absurd or directly opposite to yours, put yourself in the other person's place. As Elbow points out, "To do this requires great energy, attention, and even a kind of inner commitment. It helps to think of it as trying to get inside the head of someone who saw things this way. Perhaps even constructing such a person for yourself. Try to have the experience of someone who made the assertion" (149). The following exercise will give you practice.

EXERCISE 7.3

To develop full, rich, rounded arguments requires some practice. You can get this practice by playing with controversial ideas in a creative and free-spirited way.

- Take a debatable issue, any issue, no matter how preposterous or absurd: For example, "Homelessness is a desirable way of life," "The U.S. government should allow no more immigrants to enter this country," "Recreational drugs should be freely available to anyone who wants them," "Communities should have the right to prohibit stores from selling questionable types of rock music," "Colleges and universities should enforce strict dress codes." Write down the issue in your own words.

- Write a statement expressing the opposite point of view.

- Brainstorm a list of possible reasons to explain the first statement. After that, brainstorm a list of possible reasons to explain the opposite point of view.

- Decide which reasons are most convincing for each position. Rank them in order of strength of importance.

- Decide which position is most convincing. State that position as the main clause of an independent sentence. Recast the other position as a subordinate clause linked to the main clause by "because," "although," "despite," or the like. Finally, try to express the relationship between both clauses: What is the connecting link that brings them together?

EXERCISE 7.4

Here we return to the activity that we initiated earlier in the chapter.

- In your writer's notebook, jot down your views on one of the following issues or on an issue of your choice:
    - Whether we should buy American-made goods rather than imports.
    - Whether rap or heavy metal music promotes violence.
    - Whether excessive television watching damages family life.
    - Whether the United States should extend the school year.
    - Whether cosmetics firms should experiment on animals.

- Next, state the primary reason you hold your position. Ask yourself two questions:
  - What is the basis for my view?
  - Would someone agree or disagree with my reasoning?
- Form collaborative learning groups and share your positions and reasons with your classmates.
- As each student explains the issue and gives his or her position and reason for holding it, the other group members should remain noncommittal. For example, if a student in your group explains why she is in favor of lengthening the school year, pretend that you have no opinion on the issue. From your neutral stance, evaluate your classmate's argument. Have you been persuaded to accept her view?
- When each student's argument has been examined, come to a consensus on what characteristics made arguments either strong or weak. Have the group recorder note your group's conclusions.
- Reconvene the entire class. Each group recorder should explain the characteristics of strong and weak arguments that the group identified.

After you have read through the sources, write a clear-cut statement of your position. Returning to Kenneth Burke's metaphor of the parlor conversation (p. 194), you are like the person who has just entered a roomful of people who are engaged in a lively conversation. You may feel like an outsider as you read the first few texts. Remember that the conversation started long before you arrived at the party, so you will have to hang in there until, as Burke says, you catch "the tenor of the argument." If your professor has supplied a set of readings as we have done in the anthology section of this book, you will have a much easier job conceptualizing the argument and analyzing its complexities than if you have to obtain your own sources through library research.

■ Question the Reading Sources

Earlier in this chapter, we explained that arguing is a habit of mind. We said the best way to devel op the disposition to argue is to ask questions. Essentially, argument-synthesis relies on the same questions for identifying relationships among texts as do other types of syntheses (see the questions on pp. 169–70), but argument-synthesis also calls for more pointed questions, such as the ones we present in the box below.

QUESTIONS FOR ARGUMENT-SYNTHESIS

- How does each text position itself with regard to the issue? List each author's thesis or claim.
- Do one or more texts serve as catalysts for the other texts in the sense that they spark debate?
- How do the texts talk to each other about the controversy?
  Does one author critique other authors' arguments?
  Does one author frame the issue in an entirely different way than the others?

(continued)

Do some of the authors offer the same evidence?

Do some authors support their claims with weak or questionable evidence?

Which authors agree with each other and which differ?

Do some authors come to the same conclusions?

- Which authors present single-minded arguments and which acknowledge and respond to alternative views?
- Which claims are the most convincing? Which are reasonable? Which are flawed?
- Which kinds of evidence are most persuasive? Which kinds of testimony are most persuasive?
- How do the evidence and the testimony warrant convincing proof of the author's claims? How does the author relate both evidence and testimony to the truth of what he or she wants to establish?
- Does the author need to back up what he or she warrants as proof of the claims? Is further support necessary to establish the relationship between evidence or testimony and the claims at stake?
- Does the author take account of possible rebuttals to his or her claims? Does the author carefully qualify these claims in light of the continuing controversy?
- Which published sources do the best job of contextualizing the current controversy? Which ones are up-to-date? Which ones are outdated?
- After synthesizing this background information, what aspects of the controversy still require further research?

■ State Your Claim

In the process of answering these questions, you will examine the complexities of the issue at hand, discover issues within the issue, and come to a deeper understanding. Your new understanding of the issue may lead you to formulate a position very different from the one you initially held. Or you may still hold the same position you expressed at the beginning of the process; however, you will have refined and solidified it. Either way, you are ready to point your oar toward the water, dip it in, and make a claim. To recap your progress, you have moved from a topic to an issue to a contestable claim.

Claim is another word for *thesis*; however, the claim of an argument-synthesis is more inclusive than the types of theses we have discussed previously in this book. The bottom line is that your thesis should include your position on the issue, your central reason for holding that position, and your acknowledgment of alternative views. If you tried to stuff all three of these elements into a single statement, you would end up with an awkward, unwieldy thesis.

EXAMPLE

CLAIM: In "Predators or Plowshares?" Robert Sparrow argues powerfully that robotic weaponry presents a great risk to human life and should be subject to careful controls. In my view, such controls alone are not enough. There needs to be better education for the entire military about how to use such weapons.

MAJOR REASON: Sparrow presents evidence from scientific bulletins, military journals, and operational studies that show that the deployment of these weapons creates a psychological distance from their effects and that their increased use heightens the chances of computer error and lethal malfunction. It stands to reason that a better-educated military would be better prepared to cope with the specialized problems that robotic technology presents.

ALTERNATIVE VIEW: Some observers respond by pointing out that the strategic advantages of using this technology are worth the current disadvantages.

An overstuffed thesis would dilute the clarity and force of this contrast by jamming further elements for discussion into the introductory paragraph:

DISTRACTING ELEMENTS IN AN OVERSTUFFED THESIS: Even if these advantages outweigh the disadvantages, we can still design a better educational program for the military to improve upon the military's weaknesses. Most of our current recruits have little more than high-school diplomas. The United States currently ranks twenty-fourth and seventeenth in math and science skills among high-school students in thirty countries. If our high schools did a better job of preparing students for a technological future that depends upon these skills, our servicemen and servicewomen would be better prepared to enter combat with math and science aptitude to operate robotic weaponry. I argue that the military ought to educate combat troops in advanced topics that a high-school education fails to cover.

Here is a more manageable presentation of the claim, major reason, and acknowledgment of an alternative view:

In "Predators or Plowshares?" Robert Sparrow argues powerfully that robotic weaponry presents great risk to human life and should be subject to careful controls. In my view, such controls alone are not enough. There needs to be better education for the entire military about how to use such weapons. Sparrow derives his evidence from scientific bulletins, military journals, and operational studies. All these studies show that the deployment of these weapons psychologically distances the user from their effects and that their increased use heightens the chances of computer error and lethal malfunction. Some observers point out that the strategic advantages of using this technology are worth the current disadvantages. It seems to me, however, that a better-educated military would be better prepared to respond to these disadvantages. I argue that a stronger program of education within the military can help combat troops to adjust to the demands of using the new technology.

As you read the anthology selections in Part II of this book, you will notice that authors' theses are not necessarily succinct and explicit, and sometimes authors make a series of claims that lead up to a major thesis. Despite our caveats about overstuffed thesis statements, we think it is good practice to use the graphic overview in Figure 7–4 to outline the major elements in your argument essay.

Your thesis—claim, main reason, and acknowledgement of alternative views— becomes an argument when you crack it open by adding two additional elements: *reasons* and *evidence*. Accordingly, your outline expands, as we illustrate in Figure 7–5.

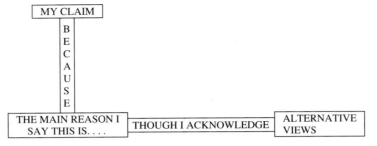

Figure 7–4 Sample Outline of Major Elements of Thesis

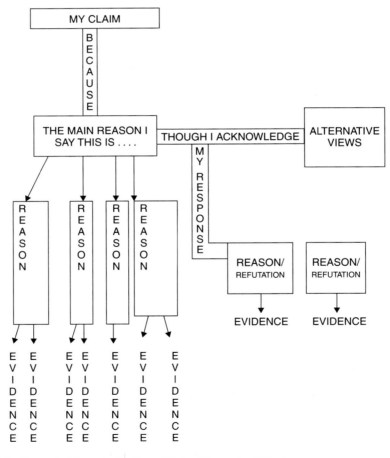

Figure 7–5 Expanded Sample Outline of Major Elements of Thesis

■ Support Reasons with Evidence from Reading Sources

As we noted earlier, a *reason* carries the weight of reliable evidence. We gave you a list of various types of supporting evidence on page 183. Additional techniques for supporting reasons are presented in the following box:

WAYS TO SUPPORT YOUR REASONS

- Examples:
  Based on a similarity to something that happened in the past.
  Based on a similar case.
  Based on a hypothetical situation.
- Relevant information:
  Facts
  Statistics
  Points of interest
- Statements, testimony, or other relevant information from acknowledged authorities.
- Personal experience (be sure the experience relates directly to the reason you are developing).

■ Acknowledge and Respond to Competing Claims

As Sparrow's synthesis illustrates, the supporting evidence comes from the reading sources. The challenge is to weave the evidence into your essay as gracefully and competently as you can. You can do this by using the vocabulary for attribution that we recommend on pages 64–65. When you are acknowledging and responding to competing claims, employ expressions comparable to the ones used by the authors in this book. In Figure 7–6, we list expressions that Robert Sparrow uses in "Predators or Plowshares?"

In addition to expressions gleaned from Sparrow's article, there are other stock expressions of concession to alternative points of view, such as:

Granted that _____, we still _____.

Even though _____, we nonetheless find that _____.

True, _____. Yet, _____.

On the one hand, _____. On the other hand, _____.

It is true that _____. Nonetheless, _____.

It is possible that _____, but it is also possible that _____.

These arguments are serious about _____. Yet, in my view they do not justify _____.

This may seem a good solution for _____, but it has several of its own problems: _____.

Some critics warn that _____. Others reply that _____.

• Now that we have had a glimpse of _____, it is time to begin thinking about whether—and how—we might avoid it by _____. (paragraph 2)

• I am in no way denying _____. However, the danger I wish to highlight here is ___. (paragraph 4)

• It is now possible for _____. However, the force of this objection… is greatly mitigated when we consider _____. (paragraph 5)

• A more powerful reason for considering arms control is _____. (paragraph 6)

• In part, this goal reflects the morally admirable desire to _____. However, it is difficult to avoid the suspicion that _____. (paragraph 7)

• The widespread use of UMS may also increase _____. … But these systems may, in turn, be shadowed by _____. (paragraph 11)

• Despite the insistence of military spokespeople that _____, there are significant reasons to doubt that _____. (paragraph 12)

• In one important regard, _____. … However, this superiority may well be challenged _____. (paragraph 15)

• However, most of these discussions settle for _____. I hope that…I can encourage other participants… to _____. (paragraph 16)

Figure 7–6   Sparrow's Expressions for Acknowledging and Responding to Competing Claims

Some experts explain that _____. However, they nowhere account for _____.

These observers are right about one thing: _____. They nonetheless go astray on other points: _____.

Contrary to the claims of _____, there is no _____.

Some advocate _____. There is some evidence for this view that _____. Other research, however, has found that _____.

If you have a vocabulary for acknowledging and responding to incompatible views, it will be easier to participate in a polite exchange of ideas in a gracious and intelligent way.

Point-by-Point Arrangement of Alternative Views

One important feature of argumentation to consider before we move on to examine an argument-synthesis paper written by a student concerns the point-by-point arrangement of alternative views. This point-by-point arrangement is usually the clearest way to present alternative views because it lists them in a summary format connected by transitional words or phrases, such as "some claim _____, yet evidence shows _____"; some propose _____, but we maintain _____"; "some have suggested _____, but critics object _____."

▓ Examination of Michael Crichton's "Patenting Life"

For an illustration of this point-by-point arrangement, we include Michael Crichton's "Patenting Life," an argument against the issuing of patents on human genes to scientists who are doing research on deadly diseases associated with these genes. The author, trained in medical research at Harvard Medical School, has written a series of highly successful novels that combine medical, scientific, and technological understanding with high action and thriller plots. His novels—many of them turned into block-buster movies—include *The Andromeda Strain* (1971), *Jurassic Park* (1993), and *Timeline* (2003), and he co-produced the long-running television series *ER* (1994–2009). In 2006 he published *Next*, a novel that deals with genetic research and legal complications.

As you read Crichton's "Patenting Life," examine its language, form, and logic. Pay special attention to the words and expressions that the author uses to introduce alternative views and respond to them. Beginning with the patent holders' claim in paragraph 3 that patents encourage further invention and discovery ("Couldn't somebody make a cheaper test?"), Crichton counters with his own argument, "Sure, but the patent holder blocks any competitor's test."

The article, originally published as an op-ed column in the *New York Times* (February 13, 2007), does not use specific sources to reinforce particular claims but instead relies upon the author's extensive knowledge of patent law and practices in medical research. After reading and commenting upon the general argument of "Patenting Life," we will move on to a student-written argument synthesis essay inspired by the essay.

▪ ▪ ▪ ▪ ▪ ▪ ▪ ▪ ▪ ▪ ▪ ▪

Patenting Life

Michael Crichton

You, or someone you love, may die because of a gene patent that should never have been granted in the first place. Sound far-fetched? Unfortunately, it's only too real. 1

Gene patents are now used to halt research, prevent medical testing and keep vital information from you and your doctor. Gene patents slow the pace of medical advance on deadly diseases. And they raise costs exorbitantly: a test for breast cancer that could be done for $1,000 now costs $3,000. 2

Why? Because the holder of the gene patent can charge whatever he wants, and does. Couldn't somebody make a cheaper test? Sure, but the patent holder blocks any competitor's test. He owns the gene. Nobody else can test for it. In fact, you can't even donate your own breast cancer gene to another scientist without permission. The gene may exist in your body, but it's now private property. 3

This bizarre situation has come to pass because of a mistake by an underfinanced and understaffed government agency. The United States Patent Office misinterpreted 4

previous Supreme Court rulings and some years ago began—to the surprise of everyone, including scientists decoding the genome—to issue patents on genes.

Humans share mostly the same genes. The same genes are found in other ani-   5
mals as well. Our genetic makeup represents the common heritage of all life on earth.
You can't patent snow, eagles or gravity, and you shouldn't be able to patent genes,
either. Yet by now one-fifth of the genes in your body are privately owned.

The results have been disastrous. Ordinarily, we imagine patents promote inno-   6
vation, but that's because most patents are granted for human inventions. Genes aren't
human inventions, they are features of the natural world. As a result these patents can
be used to block innovation, and hurt patient care.

For example, Canavan disease is an inherited disorder that affects children start-   7
ing at 3 months; they cannot crawl or walk, they suffer seizures and eventually become
paralyzed and die by adolescence. Formerly there was no test to tell parents if they
were at risk. Families enduring the heartbreak of caring for these children engaged a
researcher to identify the gene and produce a test. Canavan families around the world
donated tissue and money to help this cause.

When the gene was identified in 1993, the families got the commitment of a New   8
York hospital to offer a free test to anyone who wanted it. But the researcher's employer,
Miami Children's Hospital Research Institute, patented the gene and refused to allow any
health care provider to offer the test without paying a royalty. The parents did not believe
genes should be patented and so did not put their names on the patent. Consequently,
they had no control over the outcome.

In addition, a gene's owner can in some instances also own the mutations   9
of that gene, and these mutations can be markers for disease. Countries that don't
have gene patents actually offer better gene testing than we do, because when
multiple labs are allowed to do testing, more mutations are discovered, leading to
higher-quality tests.

Apologists for gene patents argue that the issue is a tempest in a teapot, that pat-   10
ent licenses are readily available at minimal cost. That's simply untrue. The owner of
the genome for Hepatitis C is paid millions by researchers to study this disease. Not
surprisingly, many other researchers choose to study something less expensive.

But forget the costs: why should people or companies own a disease in the first   11
place? They didn't invent it. Yet today, more than 20 human pathogens are privately
owned, including haemophilus influenza and Hepatitis C. And we've already mentioned that tests for the BRCA genes for breast cancer cost $3,000. Oh, one more thing:
if you undergo the test, the company that owns the patent on the gene can keep your
tissue and do research on it without asking your permission. Don't like it? Too bad.

The plain truth is that gene patents aren't benign and never will be. When SARS   12
was spreading across the globe, medical researchers hesitated to study it—because of
patent concerns. There is no clearer indication that gene patents block innovation,
inhibit research and put us all at risk.

Even your doctor can't get relevant information. An asthma medication only   13
works in certain patients. Yet its manufacturer has squelched efforts by others to develop
genetic tests that would determine on whom it will and will not work. Such commercial
considerations interfere with a great dream. For years we've been promised the coming
era of personalized medicine—medicine suited to our particular body makeup. Gene
patents destroy that dream.

Fortunately, two congressmen want to make the full benefit of the decoded ge- 14
nome available to us all. Last Friday, Xavier Becerra, a Democrat of California, and Dave
Weldon, a Republican of Florida, sponsored the Genomic Research and Accessibility
Act, to ban the practice of patenting genes found in nature. Mr. Becerra has been careful
to say the bill does not hamper invention, but rather promotes it. He's right. This bill will
fuel innovation, and return our common genetic heritage to us. It deserves our support.

We can readily see that in this essay, Crichton raises five premises upon which proponents of gene patenting base their claims, and point by point he counters each with an
argument that opposes the patenting of genes. In paragraph 3, he imagines a proponent
of patents asserting that competitors could still develop cheaper tests ("Couldn't somebody…"), but then he counters that the patent holder can still prevent these tests ("Sure,
but…"). In paragraph 6, he allows a proponent of patents to assert that we grant patents
for human inventions, including scientific discoveries ("Ordinarily, we imagine…"), and
then he counters this assertion with the statement that genes are not inventions or discoveries but rather "features of the natural world." In paragraph 9, he has a proponent of
patents offer the qualifying claim that patents concern not the invention of genes but the
discovery of gene mutations as "markers for disease." Here he remarks that in countries
without gene patents, multiple labs have a better record of discovering mutations and
designing higher-quality testing. In paragraph 10 he recounts the proponents' belief that
licenses to use patented genes are inexpensive and easy to obtain, and he counters bluntly
that "That's simply untrue." Finally, from paragraphs 11 to 13 he returns to the argument
about invention and discovery, and he shows with a series of examples that "patents block
innovation, inhibit research, and put us all at risk" (paragraph 12).

EXERCISE 7.5

- In addition to developing his argument in a point-by-point arrangement of alternative views,
  Crichton also supplements the arrangement with many examples of consequences or results that
  follow from the practice of gene patenting. Reread the article and underline these examples.

- Examine the language, form, and logic that Crichton uses in reporting these examples, and respond
  to them. Are they reasonable, well expressed, and convincing?

■■ ILLUSTRATION OF STUDENT'S PROCESS IN WRITING AN ARGUMENT-SYNTHESIS ESSAY

In the remainder of this chapter, we will illustrate the process of composing an argument-
synthesis essay by following a student, Sarah Allyn, as she works on an essay called "Patent
Protection: The Best Genes Money Can Buy." In a course on "Modern Social Issues,"
Sarah read Michael Crichton's "Patenting Life" as part of an assigned unit on "Issues in
Medical Care." For a final argument-synthesis research paper, Sarah decided to pursue
the topic on patented genes in medical testing.

Sarah began her research by consulting class notes for the assigned unit. From them,
she recalled that issues on patented genes had come to a head early in 2010. On March 29
of that year, a U.S. District Court judge invalidated patents on human genes when he ruled
that they involve a "law of nature" rather than laws of intellectual property. With the help of
her college librarians, Sarah located online newspaper accounts of this controversial ruling
and the appeal to it filed by a private biotechnological research foundation.

From these sources, Sarah learned that in 2009, the American Civil Liberties Union had supported many individuals and organizations in challenging such gene patents. She also learned that the defendant of these patents was a biotech firm named Myriad Genetics, represented by attorney Kenneth Chahine. With the help of her college librarians, she was able to find further accounts of the case on the Web sites of the American Civil Liberties Union <http://www.aclu.org/brca> and attorney Kenneth Chahine <http://bio.law.utah.edu/people/ken-chahine>, with their competing claims about the judge's decision and their respective bibliographies pro and con.

For her paper, Sarah supplemented Michael Crichton's "Patenting Life" with five other sources that she gleaned from these bibliographies:

Cook-Deegan, Robert. "Gene Patents." *From Birth to Death and Bench to Clinic: The Hastings Center Bioethics Briefing Book for Journalists, Policymakers, and Campaigns.* Ed. Mary Crowley. Harrison: The Hastings Center, 2008. 69–72. Web. 10 Oct. 2010.

Kesselheim, Aaron S., and Michelle M. Mello. "Gene Patenting: Is the Pendulum Swinging Back?" *New England Journal of Medicine* 362.20 (2010): 1855. Web. 10 Oct. 2010.

Koepsell, David. "The Ethics of Genetic Engineering." *Center for Inquiry,* Aug. 2007. Web. 14 Oct. 2010. <http://www.centerforinquiry.net/uploads/attachments/genetic-engineering-ethics_2.pdf>.

Schwartz, John, and Andrew Pollack. "Judge Invalidates Human Gene Patent." *New York Times.* New York Times, 29 Mar. 2010: B.1. Web. 14 Oct. 2010.

Venter, J. Craig. A *Life Decoded: My Genome, My Life.* New York: Penguin Books, 2007. Print.

Here are some drastically abridged portions of these sources. We include them here so that you can follow Sarah's progress as she read and responded to them; summarized, paraphrased, and quoted from them; and incorporated these materials into drafts of her argument-synthesis research paper. At the end of this chapter, we present the final draft of Sarah's paper as a student-written essay that exemplifies the genre of argument-synthesis.

From: Schwartz, John, and Andrew Pollack. "Judge Invalidates Human Gene Patent." *New York Times.* New York Times, 29 Mar. 2010: B.1. Web. 14 Oct. 2010. © 2010 The New York Times. All rights reserved. Used by permission and protected by the Copyright Laws of the United States. The printing, copying, redistribution, or retransmission of this Content without express written permission is prohibited.

A federal judge on Monday struck down patents on two genes linked to breast and ovarian cancer. The decision, if upheld, could throw into doubt the patents covering thousands of human genes and reshape the law of intellectual property. United States District Court Judge Robert W. Sweet issued the 152-page decision....

The American Civil Liberties Union and the Public Patent Foundation at the Benjamin N. Cardozo School of Law in New York joined with individual patients and medical organizations to challenge the patents last May: They argued that genes, products of nature, fall outside of the realm of things that can be patented. The patents, they argued, stifle research and innovation and limit testing options.

Myriad Genetics, the company that holds the patents with the University of Utah Research Foundation, asked the court to dismiss the case, claiming that the work of isolating the DNA from the body transforms it and makes it patentable. Such patents, it said, have been granted for decades; the Supreme Court upheld patents on living organisms in 1980. In fact, many in the patent field had predicted the courts would throw out the suit.

Judge Sweet, however, ruled that the patents were "improperly granted" because they involved a "law of nature."

From: Kesselheim, Aaron S., and Michelle M. Mello. "Gene Patenting: Is the Pendulum Swinging Back?" *New England Journal of Medicine* 362.20 (2010): 1855. Web. 10 Oct. 2010.

Are human genes and the process of comparing DNA sequences patentable?…As recently as the 1970s, the view among many medical researchers and legal scholars, as well as members of the USPTO, was that DNA sequences were not patentable, primarily because DNA is a naturally occurring substance rather than a human invention. This perception changed in 1980 with the Supreme Court's landmark ruling in Diamond v. Chakrabarty, which involved a dispute over the patentability of a microbe that dissolves oil and that had been specially constructed to include a DNA plasmid. The Court held that although the Patent Act did not authorize ownership of laws of nature, "products of nature," or physical phenomena, "anything under the sun made by man" was patentable, including the human-made bacterium at issue in the case.…

In invalidating Myriad's patents on the DNA sequences, U.S. District Court Judge Robert Sweet cited the Supreme Court's prior rulings that patentable products must have "markedly different characteristics" from what is found in nature. Purification alone, he held, does not change the essential characteristic of DNA—its nucleotide sequence. (p. 1855)

From: Cook-Deegan, Robert. "Gene Patents." *From Birth to Death and Bench to Clinic: The Hastings Center Bioethics Briefing Book for Journalists, Policymakers, and Campaigns.* Ed. Mary Crowley. Harrison: The Hastings Center, 2008. 69–72. Web. 10 Oct. 2010.

Areas of Controversy:

Most of the ethical as well as legal disputes over gene patenting have to do with patents for therapeutic proteins, genetic tests, and research. Each of these areas has its own set of concerns.

Therapeutic proteins:

Patents on inventions that enable production of a protein to treat a disease are among the most valuable because of their potential to lead to blockbuster drugs. They are also the targets of most of the litigation concerning gene patents.…

Diagnostics:

Genetic mutations can confer an inherited increased risk of cancer and other diseases. Patents are held on individual genes, their mutations, and on the tests developed to screen for the mutations. These patents have incited among the loudest and most widespread outcries against gene patenting. The controversy includes concern that monopolies on genetic tests make their prices unacceptably high and that these monopolies may reduce incentives to correct flaws in the tests or to adopt new technologies.…

Research:

One of the greatest fears about gene patents is that they could inhibit scientific progress. Making genes in the laboratory is essential for many kinds of research, and restrictions on the use of patented genes would be difficult to work around. In a 2002 case, *Madey v. Duke*, the Court of Appeals for the Federal Circuit made clear that academic institutions could be held liable for patent infringement even in nonprofit research.

In practice, however, no research institution has been sued for studying a gene or using it in academic research. This is partly because the patent holders stand to benefit from research that reveals how their patented genes work, and partly because of the difficulty in proving damages from mere use in research. But there has been litigation involving companies that supply transgenic animals, which incorporate patented genes and are themselves subject to patents, and companies using research tools aimed at creating commercial products and services. One gray zone is the use of materials or processes with gene patents in clinical research, such as genetic testing in the context of a clinical trial. Laboratories offering patented genetic tests for research studies have been asked to "cease and desist" unless they refer materials to or get a license from the patent holder. (pp. 69–71)

From: Koepsell, David. "The Ethics of Genetic Engineering." *Center for Inquiry*, Aug. 2007. Web. 14 Oct. 2010. <http://www.centerforinquiry.net/uploads/attachments/genetic-engineering-ethics_2.pdf>.

Beyond science-fiction examples, immediate issues involving access and social stratification impact on current notions of justice and should be worked out in public debate, perhaps legislation. As with any new and expensive medical technology, nonsocialized medical regimes in which genetic interventions become available will likely result in stratification of services and beneficiaries. There will be the class of those who can afford access to new technologies, and those who cannot. This will not be a unique situation, for already a number of elective and even necessary medical procedures are unavailable to the segment of the population that cannot afford them, or has inadequate or no health insurance. Inequality of access raises obvious social justice concerns where treatments or services are medically necessary which might not be available to everyone because of cost.

As with cosmetic enhancements presently available, genetic enhancements threaten to create a class division between the "haves" and "have-nots." Even now, cosmetic surgery confers some tangible economic and social benefits on those who can afford it. While a genetic underclass of slaves seems far-fetched, consider, for instance, parents who decide they want their child to be a NBA (National Basketball Association) player, so they select for traits conferring height, stamina and intense athleticism. Such a genetically enhanced individual will enjoy benefits that no amount of training could provide for the most motivated, unenhanced person. In such a possible future, one of the means by which poor yet motivated people now move from an underclass position to one of economic security may well disappear, given unfair competition from players whose parents could afford genetic enhancement. Similar scenarios can be envisioned for a range of abilities, including intelligence, musical ability, physical attractiveness, etc.

Although possession of these traits now confers some social and economic advantage, it is now the result of chance and evolution (which is largely unpredictable). In a world where genetic enhancement is available but not readily affordable, only the rich will be able to stack the deck in favor of their children. (p. 17)

From: Venter, J. Craig. *A Life Decoded: My Genome, My Life.* New York: Penguin Books, 2007. Print.

What was of real value was the complex analysis of the genetic code and to discuss what it means.... We wanted to sell access to the information that was gathered, packaged, organized in a comprehensive, user-friendly database. (p. 259)

■ Consider Audience

An important consideration for Sarah is the likely audience for her essay. If the issue is highly controversial, readers will have opinions of their own. A writer who addresses a single reader—say, a college professor or a public official whose confidence one seeks to engage—should estimate what the reader already knows and thinks about the issue. Members of a larger audience may hold conflicting points of view. Writers who address such an audience need especially to rely on the power and conviction of their argued proofs.

QUESTIONS ABOUT AUDIENCE FOR AN ARGUMENTATIVE ESSAY

- Am I writing for my professor, my classmates, a broader audience, or a special group of readers?
- What do my readers already know about the issue? Will I have to explain basic concepts and provide background information for my point of view to make sense?
- How do I want to come across to my audience—as an objective, scholarly authority, or as someone who identifies with my readers and shares their concerns?
- Is my audience noncommittal, or have my readers already taken a stand on the issue I am discussing?

Answers to the questions in the box above tell writers a number of things: (1) how much effort they should expend to attract their audience's attention with the lead sentence and introduction; (2) how much background information they should provide so that their readers will thoroughly understand the issue; (3) how they will address their readers (whether they will be totally objective or use pronouns such as "I," "you," or "we"); and (4) how they will order their presentation and how much space they will devote to opposing views.

■ Determine Issue, Thesis, and Competing Positions

After Sarah contemplates the audience for her essay, she reads the six assigned texts, looking first to identify the issue being discussed and second to determine how the texts are talking to each other.

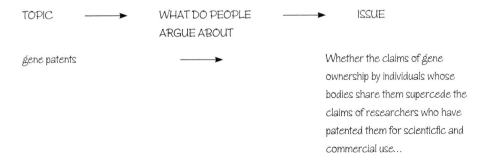

TOPIC ⟶ WHAT DO PEOPLE ARGUE ABOUT ⟶ ISSUE

gene patents ⟶ Whether the claims of gene ownership by individuals whose bodies share them supercede the claims of researchers who have patented them for scienticfic and commercial use…

Sarah then rereads the texts, interrogating them with In-Depth Questions for Identifying Relationships among Texts that appear on page 170 and the questions earlier in this chapter on pages 211–12. In the process of answering these questions, she refines the issue, stakes out her position, and acknowledges the major alternative positions. Here is Sarah's schematic outline of the issue.

Issue: Whether the claims of gene ownership by individuals whose bodies share them supercede the claims of researchers who have patented them for scientific and commercial use.

| My position: Since genes are products of nature and not the inventions of science, they should belong to the individuals who share them. | Alternative view: Since scientists have discovered useful properties of some genes, they should be able to patent those genes for therapeutic, diagnostic, and experimental purposes. |

Taking the two positions, Sarah composes a thesis statement that includes the main points of both sides:

Even though scientists have discovered useful properties of some genes, these genes are products of nature and should belong to the individuals who share them rather than to researchers who would patent them for private and commercial use.

Then Sarah returns to the reading sources to locate reasons she can use to substantiate her own position as well as the alternative position. She asks herself, "Which facts, examples, pieces of evidence, and citations by reliable authorities support my views and alternative views?" Sarah discovers reasons and jots them down in her writer's notebook.

SUPPORT FOR MY POSITIONS

- Crichton writes,"When multiple labs are allowed to do testing, more mutations are discovered, leading to higher-quality tests." (Paragraph 9)
- Crichton writes, "When SARS was spreading around the globe, medical researchers hesitated to study it—because of patent concerns." (paragraph 12)
- Cook-Deegan classifies the "areas of controversy" into three categories: "Most of the ethical as well as legal disputes over gene patenting have to do with patents for therapeutic proteins, genetic tests, and research. Each of these areas has its own set of concerns."
- Cook-Deegan considers "patents on inventions that enable production of a protein to treat a disease" as "among the most valuable."
- Cook-Deegan attributes the "loudest and most widespread outcries" to concerns "that monopolies on genetic tests make their prices unacceptably high and that these monopolies may reduce incentives to correct flaws in the tests or to adopt new technologies."
- Kesselheim and Mello summarize the view among many researchers that "DNA sequences were not patentable, primarily because DNA is a naturally occurring substance rather than a human invention.... From this perspective, DNA sequences are discovered, not invented, and are therefore quite different from genetically engineered products."
- Although he is an enthusiastic supporter of scientific progress and biotechnical advancement, David Koepsell urges us to take careful stock of "both short and long-term consequences" of genetic technology.

In particular, "long-term threats, known and unknown, must be considered as we move forward with research and genetic technologies" (p. 13). For example, "because of the complexity of most genomes, all the consequences of a particular gene's alteration often cannot be predicted" (p. 14).

- Koepsell warns that after "alteration is introduced into a species, evolution takes over for successive generations" and "evolution, as we know, is unpredictable" (p. 14). This argument provides all the more reason for scientific research to be open and collaborative rather than closed and privatized.

- Koepsell also emphasizes issues of justice and equity, providing examples that concern access and social availability: "There will be the class of those who can afford access to new technologies, and those who cannot....already a number of elective and even necessary medical procedures are unavailable to the segment of the population that cannot afford them, or has inadequate or no health insurance" (p. 17).

SUPPORT FOR THE OTHER SIDE (WITH MY REBUTTALS)

- Crichton writes,"Apologists for gene patents argue...that patent licenses are readily available at minimal cost" (paragraph 10). (But that is false. Crichton also writes that "a test for breast cancer that could be done for $1,000 now costs $3,000" (paragraph 2).)

- Kesselheim and Mello attribute the Supreme Court's upholding of gene patenting to its reasoning that "although the Patent Act did not authorize ownership of laws of nature, 'products of nature,' or physical phenomena, 'anything under the sun made by man' was patentable, including the human-made bacterium at issue in the case."

- Kesselheim and Mello report that according to Myriad, "insurance covers more than 90% of the cost of 90% of the tests it performs." (But insurance costs are already out of control, and this is certainly one area where they could be brought down if patents did not drive up prices for testing.)

- Kesselheim and Mello report that according to Myriad and its supporters, "gene patents are crucial to attracting private capital investment and stimulating research and development in fields such as personalized medicine."

- Venter unabashedly upholds the free-market position with respect to the commercial patenting and ownership of human genes.

- A counterargument to Koepsell's concern that high cost and the concentration of wealth give rise to "the possibility of a new genetic aristocracy" is that our society already has a sense of aristocracy about the availability of other expensive resources. "If use of one's money for a superior education is permissible, can we confidently say that the use of one's money to alter one's genes to obtain a higher IQ for oneself and one's offspring is impermissible?" (p. 18).

■ Organize Argument-Synthesis Essays

Some of the principles of argument that were taught in ancient Greece and Rome have been adapted for writers today. If you were a student in ancient times, you would have been taught to set up your argument in six parts:

1. Introduction (exordium)
2. Statement or exposition of the case under discussion (narratio)
3. Outline of the points or steps in the argument (divisio)

4. Proof of the case (confirmatio)

5. Refutation of the opposing arguments (confutatio)

6. Conclusion (peroratio) (Corbett 25)

Today's principles of organization are not quite so rigid or formulaic. Nevertheless, most modern writers of arguments use some variation of the following divisions: introduction, explanation of the issue and background information, writer's thesis, presentation of and response to alternative views, reasons and evidence for writer's thesis, conclusion. Two standard organizational formats are (1) acknowledge and respond to alternative views in separate, self-contained sections of the essay and (2) acknowledge and respond to objections in a point-by-point fashion.

Acknowledge and Respond to Alternative Views in Separate, Self-Contained Sections

The following template shows you how to construct an outline for sections of an essay in which you acknowledge and respond to alternative views.

ARRANGEMENT: ACKNOWLEDGE AND RESPOND TO ALTERNATIVE VIEWS IN SEPARATE, SELF-CONTAINED SECTIONS OF THE ESSAY

Introductory Section

- Opener: Introduce the issue and invite your readers into the conversation.
- Explanation and background: Familiarize your readers with the controversy. Give them the information they need to understand the issue at hand and make sense of the conversation.
- Thesis: Give your stand on the issue—your main claim.

Body of the Essay

- Acknowledge and respond to alternative views and offer reasons, substantiated by evidence, for your main claim.

Individual sections of essay (as many as needed throughout the essay: Repeat template for each section):

Variation A

1. Alternative view

2. Your response
Reasons (#1, #2, #3, etc.) and evidence to support your claim

Variation B

1. Reasons (#1, #2, #3, etc.) and evidence to support your claim

2. Alternative view

3. Your response

Conclusion

- Recap of argument
- Concluding technique

You can arrange your reasons in several different ways. Many writers prefer to present weaker reasons first and work to a climax by saving their strongest argument until the end of the composition. This movement from weak to strong provides a dramatic effect.

> Weakest reason + evidence
>
> Weaker reason + evidence
>
> Fairly strong reason + evidence
>
> Strongest reason + evidence
>
> Alternative views and objections
>
> Response to alternative views

Other writers start the body of the essay with the alternative views (Variation A in the preceding example); then, in sharp contrast, they present their strongest reasons; finally, they close with their weakest points. This movement begins the essay with an energetic claim that seizes the reader's attention.

> Alternative views and objections
>
> Response to alternative views
>
> Strongest reason + evidence
>
> Fairly strong reason + evidence
>
> Weaker reason + evidence
>
> Weakest reason + evidence

Still other writers think it best to present a relatively strong argument first, saving the strongest until last; in between, they arrange the weaker ones. This movement combines the dramatic effect of the first pattern with the attention-seizing aspect of the second.

Whether you choose to acknowledge and respond to alternative views before you give reasons for your own position or after you present your case depends on the situation and the nature of your audience. There is no rule that says you must arrange your essay one way or the other.

Acknowledge and Respond to Objections in a Point-by-Point Fashion

But what if you expect your readers to question or suggest alternative interpretations of multiple aspects of your argument? In that case, you may want to arrange the body of your essay in a different way. Instead of acknowledging and responding to alternative views in separate, self-contained sections of your essay, you can respond to the objections in a point-by-point fashion. The following box shows an outline of this alternating arrangement.

ARRANGEMENT: ACKNOWLEDGE AND RESPOND TO OBJECTIONS IN A POINT-BY-POINT FASHION

Introductory Section

- Opener: Introduce the issue and invite your readers into the conversation.
- Explanation and background: Familiarize your readers with the controversy. Give them the information they need to understand the issue at hand and make sense of the conversation.
- Thesis: Give your stand on the issue—your main claim.

Body of the Essay

- Alternative view on one aspect of the controversy
- Your refutation of this view
- Reason + evidence for your thesis
- Alternative view on another aspect of the controversy
- Your refutation of this view
- Reason + evidence for your thesis

(This pattern continues until you have covered all the aspects of the issue that you've chosen to focus on.)

Conclusion

- Recap of the argument
- Concluding technique

As you read Sarah Allyn's essay, note the paragraphs in which Sarah acknowledges and refutes opposing arguments and the paragraphs in which she provides further support for her own position. Here is Sarah's essay.

STUDENT'S ARGUMENT SYNTHESIS ESSAY

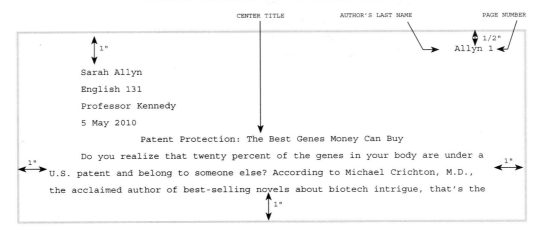

CENTER TITLE   AUTHOR'S LAST NAME   PAGE NUMBER

1/2"
Allyn 1

1"

Sarah Allyn

English 131

Professor Kennedy

5 May 2010

Patent Protection: The Best Genes Money Can Buy

Do you realize that twenty percent of the genes in your body are under a

1"   U.S. patent and belong to someone else? According to Michael Crichton, M.D.,   1"

the acclaimed author of best-selling novels about biotech intrigue, that's the

1"

INDENT FIVE SPACES   AUTHOR'S LAST NAME   PAGE NUMBER

1/2"
Allyn 2

percentage of everyone's genes currently patented by the United States Patent
and Trademark Office. These patents, however, are held not by those born with
the genes in question, but by private, commercial, and university researchers
who are experimenting with hereditary tissue for their own profit. It might seem
intuitive to argue that genes belong to those who share the gene pool encoded
in their particular DNA. The Unites States legal system apparently thinks otherwise. Since 1980 it has consistently protected individuals and corporations
who have patented some genes for therapeutic, diagnostic, and experimental purposes (Schwartz and Pollack). Those protected argue that because they have discovered useful properties in these genes, they ought to be able to profit from
their discoveries. In this paper I aim to counter their argument and some of the
abuses that result from it. In my view, even though scientists have discovered
useful properties in gene molecules, the genes in question are products of nature and should belong to those in the gene pool who share them rather than to
researchers who would patent them for profit in private or commercial use.

Over the past decade, this issue has attracted much attention. Its notori-
ety follows the many scientific advances that have resulted from the discovery
of DNA and from its medical applications. According to Robert Cook-Deegan in his
article "Gene Patents," there are three "areas of controversy" in public discussion about these patents: "Most of the ethical as well as legal disputes over
gene patenting have to do with patents for therapeutic proteins, genetic tests,
and research." Each area has its own concerns. Scientists discovered early on
that many of the proteins found in a DNA sequence could be useful to treat certain diseases. Cook-Deegan considers patents upon these therapeutic proteins to
be "among the most valuable." Medical technicians have meanwhile used these discoveries to design programs for genetic testing, and they've likewise obtained
patents for this testing. Cook-Deegan finds great public outcry in this area because "monopolies on genetic tests make their prices unacceptably high." Finally,
researchers have obtained further patents to prevent other researchers from beating them to the finish line. Many observers feel that this kind of patent-holding
will delay the advance of science rather than promote it. I will divide my discussion into three parts based upon these three major areas of controversy.

The therapeutic use of patented genes to treat certain diseases is an
area of controversy because patenting creates a monopoly for the patent holder
and consequently drives up the price of treatment. Defenders of this practice
such as J. Craig Venter argue that all drug therapies are protected by patents that create monopolies, so why shouldn't gene therapies be protected as
well? As Venter says in his own defense of patenting his scientific work on

Allyn 3

the human genome: "What was of real value was the complex analysis of the genetic code and to discuss what it means.... We wanted to sell access to the information that was gathered, packaged, organized in a comprehensive, user-friendly database" (259). I am in no way denying that inventors of gene therapy ought to be rewarded for their efforts. However, the materials that they use for this therapy—proteins derived from genetic sequences—are natural substances and not human inventions. Although procedures for applying them to therapy may be patentable, there are significant reasons to regard the proteins themselves as common property. For example, if one group of scientists owns a patent on certain genetic materials, the patent will prevent other scientists from discovering still further uses for those materials. All medical applications will be restricted to those designed by the patent-owning group, whether or not those are the best therapies or the ones that cover the broadest range of use.

Another source of controversy is the practice of genetic testing. Once again, the ownership of gene patents creates monopolies and drives up the price of testing. Michael Crichton reports the claim by supporters of gene patenting that test labs can always obtain special licenses from patent holders and that these licenses are "readily available at minimal cost." Crichton criticizes this claim as grossly misleading: "A test for breast cancer that could be done for $1,000 now costs $3,000." It would certainly be difficult to argue that such a rise in cost is "minimal." As David Koepsell at the Center for Inquiry points out, "There will be the class of those who can afford access to new technologies, and those who cannot." I am again not denying that designers of genetic testing should be rewarded. The problem is not with patenting their designs, but with patenting genes that they test. Testing designs are up for grabs and should therefore be patentable, but what's tested are genes, which are common property of all who share them.

There's another concern about testing that proponents of patenting likewise minimize. By creating monopolies and driving up prices for these tests, testing companies are contributing to the drain on our economy that worsens the recession affecting everyone. One testing company that has an exclusive monopoly over tests for a major type of breast cancer is Myriad Genetics. In the *New England Journal of Medicine*, Aaron Kesselheim and Michelle Mello report that this company justifies its policy by arguing that "insurance covers more than 90% of the cost of 90% of the tests it performs." That may be true, but insurance expenses have already spiraled out of control, and insurance providers more and more limit payments and decline claims. It is deceitful for testing companies to encourage customers by suggesting that someone else will pay the costs. Certainly genetic testing is one area where prices for medical treatment would be brought down if gene patents did not exist.

Allyn 4

The third area of controversy concerns research and experiment. Here it is not the general public but scientists who find themselves handicapped by patent law on human genes. In a sense, scientists have only themselves to blame for this, because they advocated for gene patenting in the early days of recombinant DNA experimentation. Kesselheim and Mello attribute the Supreme Court's upholding of gene patenting in December 1980 to its reasoning that "although the Patent Act did not authorize ownership of laws of nature, 'products of nature,' or physical phenomena, 'anything under the sun made by man' was patentable, including the human-made bacterium at issue in the case" (1855). What these scientists did not foresee was the extremes to which this reasoning would go in blocking experiment with so many genes from so many other scientists. Kesselheim and Mello summarize the current view among many researchers that "DNA sequences were not patentable, primarily because DNA is a naturally occurring substance rather than a human invention.... From this perspective, DNA sequences are discovered, not invented, and are therefore quite different from genetically engineered products" (1855). This argument by most of today's scientists clearly corrects their own earlier views supporting gene patents.

Unfortunately, commercial interests have meanwhile stepped in and have made gene therapy, genetic testing, and further experimentation a focus of profit-making big business. With respect to commercial patenting and the ownership of human genes, the scientist and human genome pioneer Venter unabashedly upholds a free-market position. On the other side of the ledger, however, a majority of scientists agree that out-of-control patents hold back their work. Michael Crichton alleges that during the SARS epidemic in 2002–03, "medical researchers hesitated to study it—because of patent concerns." Granted that scientists at that point were not lobbying for further patents. Still, big business had taken over and was looking to protect its market share on therapy, testing, and medication that could reduce the risk of a serious disease.

Among scientists and researchers, a concern about chain reactions following from new experimentation has aroused great anxiety. Although he is an enthusiastic supporter of scientific progress and biotechnical advancement, David Koepsell urges us to take careful stock of "both short and long-term consequences" of genetic technology. In particular, "long-term threats, known and unknown, must be considered as we move forward with research and genetic technologies" (13). For example, most genomes are highly complex, and it is extremely hard to foretell "all the consequences of a particular gene's alteration" (14). Koepsell further warns that after "alteration is introduced into a species, evolution takes over for successive generations" and "evolution, as we know, is unpredictable" (14). This argument provides all the more reason for scientific research to be open and collaborative rather than closed and privatized. When a great number of scientists

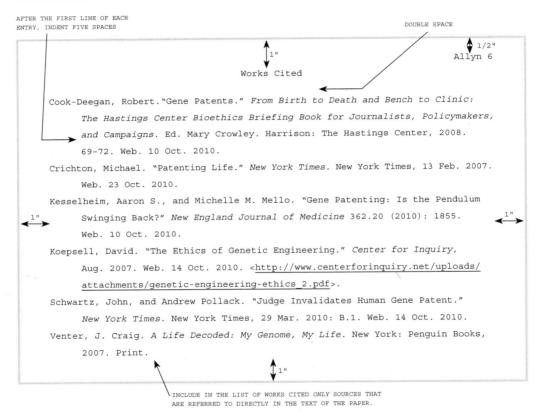

Allyn 5

with a variety of backgrounds and specializations are conducting research in a multiplicity of labs, they will discover more options and avert more problems.

For all these reasons, then, human genes should not be patented. Not only does gene patenting lead to monopolies in therapy and testing, with the result of high prices and restricted availability, but it also hampers the work of scientists and researchers who are willing to combine their forces in the name of progress. Scientists themselves have come around from filing for patents to urging their abolition. It is now time for U.S. lawmakers to reach the same conclusion.

AFTER THE FIRST LINE OF EACH ENTRY, INDENT FIVE SPACES

DOUBLE SPACE

1"

↕ 1/2"
Allyn 6

Works Cited

Cook-Deegan, Robert. "Gene Patents." *From Birth to Death and Bench to Clinic: The Hastings Center Bioethics Briefing Book for Journalists, Policymakers, and Campaigns.* Ed. Mary Crowley. Harrison: The Hastings Center, 2008. 69–72. Web. 10 Oct. 2010.

Crichton, Michael. "Patenting Life." *New York Times.* New York Times, 13 Feb. 2007. Web. 23 Oct. 2010.

Kesselheim, Aaron S., and Michelle M. Mello. "Gene Patenting: Is the Pendulum Swinging Back?" *New England Journal of Medicine* 362.20 (2010): 1855. Web. 10 Oct. 2010.

Koepsell, David. "The Ethics of Genetic Engineering." *Center for Inquiry,* Aug. 2007. Web. 14 Oct. 2010. <http://www.centerforinquiry.net/uploads/attachments/genetic-engineering-ethics_2.pdf>.

Schwartz, John, and Andrew Pollack. "Judge Invalidates Human Gene Patent." *New York Times.* New York Times, 29 Mar. 2010: B.1. Web. 14 Oct. 2010.

Venter, J. Craig. *A Life Decoded: My Genome, My Life.* New York: Penguin Books, 2007. Print.

1"   1"

1"

INCLUDE IN THE LIST OF WORKS CITED *ONLY* SOURCES THAT ARE REFERRED TO DIRECTLY IN THE TEXT OF THE PAPER.

Sarah Allyn's essay has followed many of the guidelines we've suggested for argumentative essays. It displays a broad knowledge of ideas; it outlines major areas of controversy on the topic, such as the status of gene therapy, genetic testing, and scientific research and experiment; and it articulates a strong thesis that expresses a particular point of view about the issues in question. Sarah's thesis argues in a positive vein that the genes in question are products of nature and should belong to those who share them rather than to researchers who wish to patent them for profit. In her conclusion, Sarah Allyn leaves no doubt that she has examined the issues and has considered how she wants her audience to respond.

■ Revising and Editing

Though we have presented Sarah's final draft, we want you to bear in mind that she produced this version of the paper after several preliminary drafts of its parts and their whole, and after a peer review session with a classmate. We present the peer review questions in the box on the following page.

Editing the Preliminary Draft

When you are satisfied with your revision, read your paper aloud. Then reread it line by line and sentence by sentence. Check for correct usage, punctuation, spelling, mechanics, manuscript form, and typos. If you are especially weak in editing skills, try getting a friend to read over your work.

QUESTIONS FOR HELPING WRITERS REVISE ARGUMENT ESSAYS

- Does the writer move beyond the purpose of simply synthesizing or comparing or contrasting opposing views? In other words, does the discussion have the discernible purpose of persuading or convincing an audience? If not, how might the writer sharpen the purpose?
- Is the argument two-dimensional, taking into account both sides of the issue, or is it one-sided?
- Does the writer use the conventions (not necessarily in this order) that the reader expects to find in an argument essay?

  Explanation of the issue?

  Arguable thesis?

  Background information?

  Support for the position being argued?

  Acknowledgment and response to alternative views?

  Conclusion?

- Does the writer present a sufficient number of solid reasons to back up his or her main claim? If not, what should be added?
- Are the reasons substantiated with reliable evidence? If not, what should be added?
- Does the writer draw on reliable sources? If not, which sources are questionable?
- Does the writer create a favorable, creditable impression of himself or herself? If not, how might the writer do this?
- Does the writer display an awareness of the audience's needs and set a context for the reader by:

  Giving appropriate background information?

  Mentioning authors and titles of sources when necessary?

  Supplying necessary documentation for sources?

  Providing clear connectives that differentiate his or her ideas from those of the writers of the sources?

EXERCISE 7.6

- Reread Sarah Allyn's paper.

- Note the structure of its presentation. After an introduction, Sarah questions current practices in gene therapy, genetic testing, and scientific research and experiment, which depend upon patenting people's genes for making commercial profit in these areas. She presents reasons why such patenting for profit violates the rights of those who share these genes and why, as products of nature, genes should not be patented.

- Write a brief critical analysis in which you evaluate the strength of her argument. Guidelines for writing critical analysis essays are presented in Chapter 3.

- Reconvene the entire class. Each group recorder should read the members' evaluations and respond to inquiries from the rest of the class about the effectiveness of Sarah's argument.

EXERCISE 7.7

- Form collaborative learning groups.

- Assign each member a paragraph from the body of Sarah Allyn's paper. Ask each to comment on Sarah's use of her sources.

- Reconvene the entire class. Each group recorder should read the members' evaluations and respond to inquiries from the rest of the class about the effectiveness of Sarah's use of sources.

WORKS CITED

Burke, Kenneth. *The Philosophy of Literary Form.* 3rd ed. Berkeley: U of California P, 1941. Print.

Cook-Deegan, Robert. "Gene Patents." *From Birth to Death and Bench to Clinic: The Hastings Center Bioethics Briefing Book for Journalists, Policymakers, and Campaigns.* Ed. Mary Crowley. Harrison: The Hastings Center, 2008. 69–72. Web. 10 Oct. 2010.

Corbett, Edward. *Classical Rhetoric for the Modern Student.* 3rd ed. New York: Oxford UP, 1990. Print.

Crichton, Michael. "Patenting Life." *New York Times.* New York Times, 13 Feb. 2007. Web. 23 Oct. 2010.

Eisenschitz, Aram. "Innocent Concepts? A Paradigmatic Approach to Argument." *Learning to Argue in Higher Education.* Ed. Sally Mitchell and Richard Andrews. Portsmouth: Boynton/Cook Heinemann, 2000. 12–25. Print.

Elbow, Peter. *Writing without Teachers.* New York: Oxford Up, 1973.

Kesselheim, Aaron S., and Michelle M. Mello. "Gene Patenting: Is the Pendulum Swinging Back?" *New England Journal of Medicine* 362.20 (2010): 1855. Web. 10 Oct. 2010.

Koepsell, David. "The Ethics of Genetic Engineering." *Center for Inquiry*, Aug. 2007. Web. 14 Oct. 2010. <http://www.centerforinquiry.net/uploads/attachments/genetic-engineering-ethics_2.pdf>.

Schwartz, John, and Andrew Pollack. "Judge Invalidates Human Gene Patent." *New York Times.* New York Times, 29 Mar. 2010: B.1. Web. 14 Oct. 2010.

Sparrow, Robert. "Predators or Plowshares? Arms Control of Robotic Weapons." *IEEE Technology and Society Magazine.* Fordham University, Spring 2009. Web. 10 Oct. 2010.

Toulmin, Stephen E. *The Uses of Argument.* Cambridge: Cambridge UP, 1958. Print.

Venter, J. Craig. *A Life Decoded: My Genome, My Life.* New York: Penguin Books, 2008. Print.

Eight

Writing Research Papers

■ THE RESEARCH PAPER: AN INTRODUCTION

Research involves collecting information from multiple sources and then acting on that information by analyzing, organizing, synthesizing, generalizing, and applying what you have learned. Often, we connect the term *research* with scientific and medical discoveries, but it applies to systematic investigation in any discipline, including the humanities and the social sciences. Professors typically assign research papers to make you an active, independent scholar who is able to locate other people's ideas, analyze and synthesize those ideas, and come to an independent conclusion. Studying research methods is learning how to learn.

In Chapters 1 through 7, we have stressed that the writing process requires active engagement, careful thought, and hard work. The same is true of research. Research involves more than just finding and recording information. A collection of facts will mean little to your readers without explanation, organization, and commentary. To locate appropriate sources in the library, you must plan ahead and think carefully about what you want to find.

Writing a research paper involves many of the writing processes and strategies you have learned in this book. The clerical work of compiling a list of sources is only a small part of the overall process. At the same time, the research paper differs from the other essays you have been practicing in this book because it is lengthier, more complex, and more scholarly. Although research begins with examining other people's ideas, it can develop into an extremely creative activity. When you synthesize information from various texts, you come to new conclusions that are entirely your own.

The process we describe in this chapter loosely follows the Cornell University Library guide for course-related research. When we speak of library-based research, we are referring to research conducted online in virtual libraries as well as in brick-and-mortar buildings. The overall process is outlined in the following box.

PROCESS OF WRITING A RESEARCH PAPER

- Identify a research topic.
- Find background information that will help you understand the broader context.
- Develop a research strategy.
- Determine your rhetorical purpose.
- Set a schedule.
- Decide on the specific questions your research paper will answer.
- Brainstorm a preliminary search vocabulary.
- Use catalogs to find books and media.
- Use indexes to find periodical articles.
- Find Internet resources.
- Evaluate what you find.
- Cite what you find using a standard format.

Cornell Steps for Conducting Course-Related Research

Steps	Resources
1. Identify a topic, phrase it as a question, and identify the main concepts and key words in your question.	Class instructor/assignment, reference librarian, library catalog
2. Find background information that will help you understand the broader context of your research and tell you in general terms what is known about your topic.	Subject encyclopedias and dictionaries, class textbooks, bibliographies
3. Use catalogs to find books and media.	Library catalog, Library of Congress, and OCLC WorldCat
4. Use indexes to find periodical articles.	Scholarly research databases
5. Find Internet resources.	Search engines (e.g., Google, Yahoo!Search, Ask.com
6. Evaluate what you find.	Guides for evaluating material found on the Web and distinguishing scholarly from nonscholarly sources
7. Cite what you find using a standard format.	Style guides such as those of the Modern Language Association (MLA) and the American Psychological Association (APA) and your college's code of academic integrity

Derived from "The Seven Steps of the Research Process." Olin Library Reference, Research & Learning Services, Cornell University Library, Ithaca, NY, USA. <http://olinuris.library.cornell.edu/ref/research/skill1.htm> Courtesy Cornell University Library.

■■ IDENTIFY A RESEARCH TOPIC: THE ROLE OF THE ASSIGNMENT

The process you go through to identify a research topic depends upon the specificity of your assignment. If your assignment defines the topic in pointed detail, you may be able to search for materials right away. If the assignment allows you to select your own topic, either from your personal storehouse of knowledge or from the professor's list, you'll have to choose a topic and narrow it before you begin your library search. Here are research assignments of varying degrees of specificity:

> *Specific assignment (from a psychology course):* Write a six-page research paper in which you draw upon the psychological literature on dance therapy published during the past decade.

> *Focused assignment (from a psychology course):* Write an eight- to ten-page research paper that expands upon one of the topics covered in our textbook or class lectures. Use at least ten sources of information, not including the textbook.

> *Open-ended assignment (from a first-year writing course):* Select a topic that truly interests you. Narrow the topic, convert it into a research question, and write a ten-page research paper.

The first assignment asks you to consult psychological journals published in the last ten years for articles on dance therapy. The second assignment allows you to select a topic from among the topics covered in the course textbook or class lectures. The third assignment leaves the choice of topic entirely up to you.

To illustrate, let's say you receive Assignment 3 in your first-year writing class. A subject that has been in the news lately is steroid use among athletes. You're interested in learning more about this issue, so you select steroids as your topic. Begin by stating your topic as a question: "What effect does the use of steroids have on the health of athletes?" Then identify the main concepts and keywords in the question: "steroids," "health," and "athletes."

Find Background Information That Will Help You Understand the Broader Context of Your Research and Tell You in General Terms What Is Known About Your Topic

The next thing you have to do is learn about your topic. Picture yourself standing on the threshold of a roomful of informed people who are discussing steroid use and the health of athletes. As we explained in Chapter 7, you have to thoroughly familiarize yourself with the topic and issues before you can join the conversation.

For basic background information, you consult an online encyclopedia such as *Funk & Wagnalls New World Encyclopedia* or another type of reference work. You look up *steroids*, read the entry, and narrow your topic to *anabolic steroids*, male hormones used to increase muscle mass. Next, you look up anabolic steroids in a specialized encyclopedia that will give you more in-depth, detailed information. Your library probably offers a number of special encyclopedias in print. You can also find specialized reference works online. For example, a search for *anabolic steroids* on *MedlinePlus*

<http://www.nlm.nih.gov/medlineplus/index.html> produces 187 entries. If you have difficulty locating a specialized reference, consult a reference librarian.

When looking for online reference sources, students are quick to use *Wikipedia* <http://en.wikipedia.org>. *Wikipedia* is worth consulting for general background information, but it is not a source you should include in your research paper. Anyone can contribute entries to *Wikipedia*; there is no academic oversight or review of entries' quality and accuracy. As a result, the usefulness of some of its articles is questionable and their validity is disputed.

ILLUSTRATION OF A STUDENT'S PROCESS OF WRITING A RESEARCH PAPER

Throughout the rest of this chapter, we will trace the process of our student Jennifer Piazza. In an upper-level psychology course entitled "Counseling: Theory and Dynamics," Jennifer received the assignment we mentioned previously:

> Write an eight- to ten-page research paper that expands upon one of the topics covered in our textbook or class lectures. Use at least ten sources of information, not including the textbook.

Select a Research Topic

Jennifer narrows the focus of her assignment by reviewing the subject areas covered in her psychology class and isolating a topic or, better yet, several potential topics, for her paper. She already knows a certain amount about psychological topics, so she bypasses the initial reference searches. If that were not the case, however, her first move would be to consult a few general reference works, such as specialized encyclopedias (e.g., *Encyclopedia of Psychology*).

Two prewriting strategies that we described in Chapter 1, freewriting and brainstorming, will help Jennifer to identify possible research topics. She could brainstorm a list of words and phrases in response to the assignment and then read over the list for similarities, patterns, and connections. Alternatively, she could freewrite nonstop for ten minutes, using cues in the assignment to generate ideas. Then she would search her freewriting for useful topics. The following is an excerpt from Jennifer's freewriting.

> The chapter on counseling trauma victims was especially interesting to me. I'm currently working as a volunteer with Suicide Prevention and Crisis Services, and many of the hotline calls I answer are from people who are coping with the result of a traumatic experience. Perhaps if I did my research paper on trauma, I would learn something that would be of direct benefit to my hotline clients. But I'm not sure how I could add anything to what the textbook presented except maybe to add more details about the theory. Perhaps I could write about how current ideas about dealing with trauma are different from what was previously believed. Our textbook chapter started with Freud, so I could research what was believed about trauma before Freud and try to show how the theory developed over time. One topic that I wish

the textbook had said more about was how talking through a traumatic experience is helpful in dealing with it. I know that my hotline clients feel better after they are able to get the experience off their chest by describing it. In my Personal Essay class, I wrote about a particularly traumatic event in my own life: When I was four, a close relative was diagnosed with cancer and in response to the news, my family really freaked out. I was terrified to see adults in this condition, and no one fully explained to me what was going on, so I couldn't make sense of it at all. I felt a strong sense of relief when, fifteen years later, I was able to relive the experience on paper and explain my emotions. Perhaps I could do research on the therapeutic effects of "reliving" traumatic experiences in conversation or on paper.

In the process of rereading her freewriting, Jennifer decides she would like to learn more about the history of psychic trauma theory and current therapies for trauma, particularly the use of verbal expression as a therapeutic response. She decides to focus her initial research on these two areas.

Another way to zero in on a research topic is to consult general subject headings in periodical indexes related to your broad subject area (biology, music, psychology, and so forth). You could also ask your professor to suggest topics. Whichever strategy you use, follow your own interests. The research and writing processes will be more successful and rewarding if you identify a topic that appeals to you.

It's a good idea to come up with several alternative subtopics because the one you initially select may not be practical for research. You might inadvertently select a topic that is treated only in scholarly texts that you would have difficulty understanding because of your unfamiliarity with their methodology, analytical techniques, and specialized vocabulary. You might choose a topic that requires a number of resources that are difficult to obtain from your college library. You might even identify a topic that cannot be researched because very few texts address it. If your preliminary research reveals that your initial research topic is naive and must be modified or abandoned, quickly turn to your alternative topics. We recap the procedure for selecting a topic in the box below.

SELECTING A RESEARCH TOPIC

- Identify a topic that interests you by:
  - Reviewing topics covered in the course textbook, assigned readings, and class lectures
  - Consulting general and specialized encyclopedias and other reference works related to your broad subject area
  - Asking you professor to suggest a topic
- Read up on your topic, narrow your focus, and come up with a list of alternative subtopics.
- Brainstorm a list of words or phrases associated with your topic. Then reread the list, looking for similarities, patterns, and connections.
  Or:
- Freewrite for ten minutes and then review your writing for useful ideas.

EXERCISE 8.1

Part A

Select a course you are taking this semester, excluding your writing course.

- Review the topics covered in the course textbook, readings, and lectures.
- Select a topic for a potential research paper.
- Brainstorm a list of words or phrases associated with your topic. Then reread the list, looking for similarities, patterns, and connections.
- Write one or two pages explaining how you selected and narrowed your research topic.

Part B

Select a topic you are interested in researching.

- First look up the topic in a general encyclopedia.
- Then look up the topic in a specialized encyclopedia or other reference work related to your subject.
- Brainstorm a list of words or phrases associated with your topic. Then reread the list, looking for similarities, patterns, and connections.

Or:

- Freewrite nonstop for ten minutes and then review your writing for useful ideas.
- Write one or two pages explaining how you selected and narrowed your research topic.

■ Develop a Research Strategy

You have a topic. Now you need a research strategy. Your most important consideration is your overall goal. Ask yourself the following questions:

- What am I trying to accomplish? What is my rhetorical purpose?
- What about a schedule? How long will the research and writing take me?
- What questions am I trying to answer?
- What are the most important words or phrases associated with my topic? How will this vocabulary help me to categorize my topic and find sources for my paper?
- Where will I find sources for my paper?

Determine Your Rhetorical Purpose

Research papers are synthesis essays such as the ones we discussed in Chapters 6 and 7. They incorporate more research than those, but they require the same operations. Library research will locate texts related to your topic. As with any synthesis, you must analyze these texts to determine what each contributes to the ongoing academic conversation. You read to learn what various authors have to say about the topic, how they bounce ideas off one another, and how they zero in on subtopics that run across the texts.

When you are well informed, you stake out your own position. Then you revisit the sources to extract relevant bits of information that will support your thesis. In the process of writing the paper, you weave together your own ideas with those you've gleaned from the sources. Depending on the research paper assignment, you have three options: (1) to write an exploratory synthesis, (2) to write a thesis-driven synthesis, or (3) to write an argument-synthesis. In the following box, we review each form of synthesis and its rhetorical purpose.

SYNTHESIS: FORMS AND RHETORICAL PURPOSE

Exploratory	The writer's goal is to unfold or unravel a topic or question to make it clearer to the readers. The synthesis might crack open a concept, place an issue in historical context, or clarify sides in a controversy. The synthesis is broad and nonjudgmental. The writer presents informative results in a straightforward manner. Such a synthesis often tries to define a topic or issue in an expository style that emphasizes the coverage of data rather than any further questioning or interpretation of the data.
Thesis-Driven	The writer's goal is to get the readers to understand his or her thesis and point of view. The writer takes a position on the topic or issue. The writer's position is explicit in a direct statement of judgment or opinion on the matter at hand. The thesis is supported by reasons that are based on evidence.
Argument	The writer's goal is to persuade readers that his or her position is reasonable and worthy of support. The synthesis focuses on a debatable issue or arguable question. The writer anticipates, acknowledges, and addresses alternative views.

In college courses, students are seldom called upon to write research papers in the form of exploratory syntheses. The sample assignment we provided earlier, "Write a six-page research paper in which you draw upon the psychological literature on dance therapy published during the past decade," implies a goal of presenting the psychological literature in a straightforward manner. But even though the professor phrased the assignment in this way, he or she probably expects students to articulate and support a position. Before you write an exploratory synthesis, we strongly suggest that you consult with your professor. Most professors expect students to fashion research papers that are thesis-driven and/or argumentative.

Despite our caveats about exploratory syntheses, this form of writing serves as an excellent precursor to a thesis-driven synthesis or an argument-synthesis. The student who presents straightforward coverage of ten years of research on dance therapy has already immersed herself in the academic conversation. She knows what the experts have said about dance therapy and she is aware of the issues they have yet to address and the questions they have yet to answer. She could easily propose an intelligent question or zero in on a pressing issue that would become the focal point of a research paper.

The preferred goal for research papers is either to get readers to understand your thesis or to persuade them of your argument. The goal you select depends on the assignment. If the assignment asks you to research a debatable issue—for example, whether the United States condones torture—then your paper will have an argumentative edge. If the assignment offers a topic rather than an issue, or if it leaves the choice of topic or issue up to you, you are free to determine your own purpose. Consider the progression we present below:

> **Thesis:** Psychologists experiment with different forms of trauma therapy.
>
> **Goal:** to inform readers about various forms of therapy.
>
> **Thesis:** Oral and written communication therapies are effective for victims of trauma.
>
> **Goal:** to get your readers to understand the effectiveness of oral and written therapies.
>
> **Thesis:** Therapeutic writing has a more beneficial effect for victims of trauma than other forms of verbal communication.
>
> **Goal:** to convince your readers that therapeutic writing has a more beneficial effect for victims of trauma than other forms of verbal communication.

The first statement lends itself to exploratory synthesis, the second to thesis-driven synthesis, and the third to argument-synthesis.

Keep in mind that you may not be able to make a firm decision about your purpose until you complete your library research. The more you read, the more your purpose will evolve. Midway through the process, you might express the purpose of reviewing and evaluating the various therapies for victims of trauma. Later, after you have amassed and read more sources, you might decide that your purpose is to argue that writing combined with oral communication is a more effective therapy than oral communication alone. Make sure that your research strategy is flexible enough to accommodate the unexpected. In practice, research often does not proceed as planned. You may need to change your goals during the research process.

Set a Schedule

A research paper is a major undertaking. Make sure you set aside enough time for it. The amount of time you need depends on the scope of your assignment. If your instructor provides a narrowed topic and requires only four or five sources, you may get by with a few visits to the library two or three weeks before the paper is due. If your instructor asks you to select your own topic and draw on ten or more sources, you need to begin six to eight weeks before the due date. Always allow for the unexpected in research assignments. Even knowledgeable researchers encounter difficulties that require more time than they had anticipated. You may discover your college library does not have important texts that you need. You will be able to obtain these sources through interlibrary loan, but you have to allow ample time for the transaction.

In our example, Jennifer has to select her own topic and locate at least ten sources, so she begins six weeks before the due date. She assumes that she will make at least five visits to the library. She establishes the following schedule:

RESEARCH PAPER DEADLINES

March 27	Select topic.
March 29	Read entries from general and specialized encyclopedias and narrow topic.
March 30	Write a list of questions I want my research to answer and brainstorm a list of key terms.
April 3–19	Conduct online searches; visit library; locate sources. (Leave time for interlibrary loan.)
April 21	Outline paper.
April 22–28	Write draft of paper; revisit library for needed sources.
April 30	Revise and edit draft.
May 1	Turn in final draft.

Decide on the Questions Your Research Will Answer

Throughout this book, we have emphasized the importance of developing a "questioning" frame of mind. Competent researchers do not merely look up information; they use research to answer questions about their topics. Before you begin the research process, at the point when you are reading entries in encyclopedias and reference sources or reviewing your course materials, list the questions that you hope your research will answer. Here are some of Jennifer's questions concerning trauma therapy:

1. To what extent do psychologists still accept Freud's theory concerning trauma?
2. How does current psychological theory explain the impact of traumatic experiences?
3. What therapies are available for victims of psychological trauma? Which are most effective?
4. According to psychologists and communication experts (writing and speech), what role does the verbal expression of traumatic experiences play in the recovery process?
5. Do victims of psychological trauma receive adequate attention in the mental health system?

In the process of conducting research, you will ask additional questions, refine the ones you started with, and drop questions that lead to dead ends. Questions will lead to questions and eventually you will have amassed enough information to write a draft of your paper.

Brainstorm a Preliminary Search Vocabulary

Before you search for books and articles, you need to come up with a preliminary list of words or phrases associated with your topic. Brainstorm words or phrases that might be used to describe or categorize the subject. These are the terms you will look up when you search catalogs and databases. Jennifer brainstorms the following list of search terms related to trauma therapy:

- Trauma or shock
- Traumatic experiences
- Freud and trauma
- Psychology and trauma
- Writing and trauma
- Verbal expression (communication) and trauma
- Trauma therapy
- Trauma counseling
- Post-traumatic stress disorder (or syndrome)
- Traumatic neuroses
- Trauma and the mental health system

When you brainstorm for such a list, be expansive and jot down as many terms as you can. As you locate sources, you will refine this preliminary list and add new terms. You need a rich list of search terms because it is often hard to guess which ones will give you access to the information you want.

EXERCISE 8.2

- Think of research papers you have written in the past. How did you select a topic? What planning did you do before attempting to locate sources? Were your activities during the early stages of the research process different from or similar to the ones we've described?
- Freewrite for ten minutes in response to these questions.
- Reread the paragraph you wrote for Exercise 8.1.
- Take the topic you already narrowed, and speculate about the questions your research will answer.
- Write a list of at least five questions.
- Brainstorm a list of words and phrases you might use as search terms for your topic.

EXERCISE 8.3

- Form small collaborative learning groups.
- Decide on a topic of mutual interest that your group might want to research. Do not take more than two or three minutes to come to a consensus. (The instructor may choose to assign research topics.)
- Working together, generate a list of research questions that pertain to your topic. Then brainstorm a list of search terms that will help you locate information on this topic.
- Reconvene the class. Each group recorder identifies the group's topic, reads the lists of research questions and search terms, and describes any problems that the group encountered.

Determine How You Will Find the Sources

Your college library will enable you to connect to online catalogs, periodical indexes, and databases to which the library subscribes. Sitting at your computer, you can compile lists of books, articles, and other sources relevant to almost any topic. If your library's online system provides the complete texts of sources, you can complete all the research for relatively short projects without leaving your room. As the access to full-text periodicals grows and more book-length works become available online, it will become possible to conduct more extensive research from homes and offices.

The search engine, Google, is already scanning the contents of five major research libraries. The ultimate goal is to assemble a digital library of everything that has ever been published. Writing about this new phenomenon in the *New York Times Magazine*, technology expert Kevin Kelly explains how books will eventually be linked to each other electronically:

> Once a book has been integrated into the new expanded library by means of this linking, its text will no longer be separate from the text in other books. For instance, today a serious nonfiction book will usually have a bibliography and some kind of footnotes. When books are deeply linked, you'll be able to click on the title in any bibliography or any footnote and find the actual book referred to in the footnote. The books referenced in that book's bibliography will themselves be available, and so you can hop through the library in the same way we hop through Web links, traveling from footnote to footnote to footnote until you reach the bottom of things. (45)

Although it will be a long time before the universal library moves from the realm of dream to the realm of reality, the explosive growth of technology has already affected how students conduct research. A vast collection of electronic texts, graphics, and sounds covers every imaginable topic, and sources that are appropriate for academic research are becoming available in full-text versions on the Web. A crucial word in the preceding sentence is "becoming." It will be a long time before we are able to access electronic versions of all the library sources we need. And some technology experts think this will never happen. So prepare yourself to visit the library and spend some time learning its ins and outs.

▨ Locate Sources in an Academic Library

Before you launch your search, familiarize yourself with your college library. Libraries vary dramatically in how they organize their collections and how they provide access to materials. Before you attempt to do any research, get a guide or a map that shows how your campus library is organized. Make sure you know where the reference desk is located. Do not confuse it with the circulation desk, the place where items are checked out. The librarians at the reference desk can provide one-on-one research assistance.

Your library reference department may also offer library-orientation sessions, reference-skills workshops, and credit-bearing courses on information resources. Take advantage of opportunities to learn about the library early in your academic career.

EXERCISE 8.4

Take a self-guided tour of your college library.

- Start by locating the reference desk. Find out what days and hours reference librarians are available and what services they provide.
- Find out how the collection is organized. Are periodicals shelved with books or separately? Are other formats (recordings, microfilms, and so on) shelved separately?
- Are there any subject-specific (music, science, and so forth) libraries on your campus?

You should be able to answer these questions based on materials that you can obtain at the reference desk. Now tour the library and make sure you can find the principal units in the collection.

EXERCISE 8.5

- Form collaborative learning groups.
- From the following list, pick an area of the library that your group will investigate. Groups should not duplicate one another's choices, so that as many areas as possible will be covered.

Reference collection

Book collection (main stacks)

Magazine and journal collection

Sound recordings collection

Video collection

Newspaper collection

Any discipline-specific collection

- Proceed to the library from class or arrange a time that your group can meet in the library for about an hour.
- When you arrive at the library, work together to answer the following questions concerning your area: What resources are available? What services are available?
- Reconvene the entire class. Each group recorder should read the group's answers to the two questions and respond to any inquiries from the class about the part of the library collection that the group investigated.

Your library houses computer workstations linked to the online catalog and databases. While you are at the library, sit down at a computer and click on the library's home page. We have reproduced the home page of the Cornell University Library below. (See Figure 8–1.)

Your library's home page is accessible from other computer workrooms across campus and from personal computers that can log into it with a network ID number. You will sign on using your ID number and a password. If you have questions about accessing the library site from off-campus locations, ask a reference librarian to help you.

As we mentioned earlier, you might begin the research for your topic by finding background information in encyclopedias and other reference books. Next, you should move on to books. Then, you can search for more timely information in the form of articles. Finally, if you need still more information, use the Web to find Internet resources.

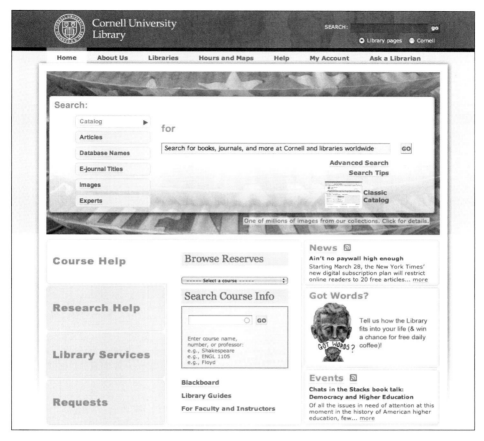

Figure 8–1   Cornell University Library Home Page. Courtesy Cornell University Library, Ithaca, NY, USA.

▇ Use Catalogs to Find Books

Online Public Access Catalog (OPAC)

Your college's online library catalog, also referred to as the Online Public Access Catalog (OPAC), contains a description of each item in the library's collection and indexes the items by subject, title, and author. Catalogs typically list books, periodicals (magazines, journals, and newspapers), pamphlets, sound recordings (reel-to-reel and cassette tapes, LPs, and compact discs), sheet music, microforms (microfilm, microfiche, and microcards), motion pictures, video recordings, computer data files, images (graphics and photos), three-dimensional artifacts, and maps.

The catalog provides titles of the journals and magazines the library subscribes to and the date range of holdings for periodicals, but it does not provide information about individual articles. In other words, if you look up *Newsweek* magazine, you may learn that the library includes the magazine in its collection. But in order to locate a particular article in *Newsweek*, you have to search a relevant index or database. We explain how to use these tools on page 249.

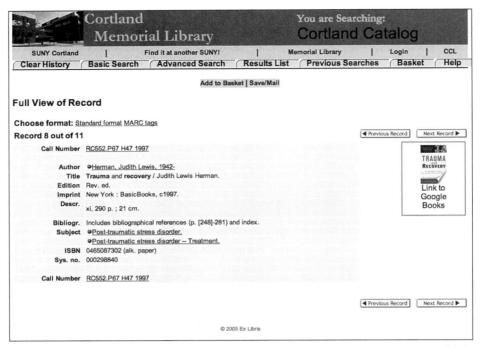

Figure 8–2   Sample Computer Catalog Entry. © 2005 Ex Libris. By permission of Ex Libris and Cortland Memorial Library, State University of New York at Cortland.

Online catalogs can be searched by subject, title, or author according to the principles described below. Figure 8–2 shows a sample computer catalog entry that Jennifer located in her research on trauma therapy. The entry describes a book by Judith Lewis Herman titled *Trauma and Recovery*.

The entry includes a *call number* for the book: RC552.P67 H47 1997. This number indicates the item's subject area and its shelving location. You are probably familiar with the Dewey decimal call numbers used in most primary and secondary schools. College libraries typically use the Library of Congress system, which is more comprehensive than the Dewey decimal system. The call number in Figure 8–2 is based on the Library of Congress system. Print versions of the Library of Congress subject headings are located in the reference section of the library. They are also published in the "Library of Congress Classification Outline," available online at <http://www.loc.gov/catdir/cpso/lcco/>. These subject headings provide a useful list of broad terms and narrow terms to use when searching for a topic. For example, "education" is divided into eleven categories, each of which is broken down into subtopics.

Books and other materials are shelved systematically by call numbers. As an example, let's consider the parts of the call number for Herman's *Trauma and Recovery*: RC552.P67 H47 1997. On the library shelves, books are alphabetized according to the letters indicating the general topic area—RC in the example above. Within each general topic area, items are arranged in ascending numerical order according to the topic subdivision, in this case 552.P67. For books, items within the subdivision are arranged alphabetically by the first letter of the author's last name and then numerically by an additional filing number. In our example, H is the first letter of Herman's name and 47 is the additional filing number. Finally, 1997 is the book's date of publication. Call numbers can get more complex than our example indicates, but the filing and shelving principles that we just described always apply. Call numbers provide a shelving address for an information source, and they also ensure that items on the same topic will be stored together. Thus, if you locate one item on your subject, you may find others shelved nearby.

College libraries differ in size. One of us teaches at SUNY Cortland, which has a single library collection of 412,000 volumes, and the other teaches at Cornell, where there are twenty different libraries containing more than seven million books. If your library does not own a source that you need, you will be able to acquire it through interlibrary loan. Your library probably has a link to Interlibrary Loan on its home page. Items may take anywhere from a day to a week or more to be delivered. That is why you must leave ample time when creating your research paper schedule.

Library of Congress and OCLC WorldCat
In addition to searching your college's online catalog, you can search the Library of Congress Online Catalog, a database of millions of records, at <http://catalog.loc.gov/>. A search for *trauma therapy* yields the titles of over 500 books. You can also search the Online Computer Library Center (OCLC) WorldCat, a catalog that includes the holdings of thousands of libraries worldwide, at <http://www.worldcat.org/>. A search for *trauma therapy* yields the titles of over 3,500 books. Your college won't have all these books, but you will be able to obtain the ones it lacks through interlibrary loan.

Bibliographic Details for Electronic Sources
As you locate sources that are potentially useful, be sure to keep a working bibliography that includes the elements we list in the Appendix on pages 591–608. Online sources require special attention because you must provide the date you access the electronic source. In some cases, you will provide the URL (Web address). See pages 592–604 in the Appendix. Find out if your campus library has a site license for citation management software such as *Refworks* or *Endnote*. If not, check out free citation programs such as *Zotero*, at <http://www.zotero.org>, and *Mendeley*, at <http://www.mendeley.com>.

EXERCISE 8.6

- Revisit the topic you narrowed in Exercise 8.1.
- Access the online catalog of your college library and locate at least five books related to your topic.
- Determine which books are available in your library and which you would have to request via interlibrary loan.
- Make a list of the books and include necessary bibliographic information.

Use Indexes to Find Periodical Articles
In academic libraries, you will find that magazines, journals, and newspapers are called *periodicals*. This term is used because they are published periodically—that is, at regular intervals (weekly, monthly, quarterly, annually) throughout the year. To locate articles, you will access a periodical

index, which is a searchable database containing thousands of articles. Periodical indexes provide bibliographic citations, abstracts, and, occasionally, the full text of the articles.

One such index is *Academic Search Premier.* It is a good place to begin your search because it is a general, multidisciplinary database that provides information on articles from hundreds of academic and popular journals, magazines, and newspapers. Another good starting point is *ProQuest Research Library.* To access these databases, look on your library's Web page for the link "Databases," "Articles," "Reference Tools," or "Subject Guides." Individual libraries may designate these listings by different names. If you have trouble locating a general interdisciplinary database, consult a reference librarian.

After you have searched the general database, look for a specialized disciplinary database, such as *ERIC (Educational Resource Information Center)* for education, *PsycFirst* for psychology, and the *MLA International Bibliography* for language courses and English, and search for your topic. Again, if you have difficulty locating a specialized database, ask a reference librarian for assistance.

When Jennifer accesses her college library's home page, she clicks on the link "Databases" and then on *Academic Search Premier.* One of the citations she locates is:

Disclosing Trauma Through Writing: Testing the Meaning-Making Hypothesis
   By: Park, Crystal L.; Blumberg, Carol Joyce. *Cognitive Therapy and Research* Oct 2002, Vol. 26 Issue, p597, 20p

When Jennifer clicks on the title of the article, she obtains the detailed display shown in Figure 8–3.

This detailed record provides a wealth of information. A click on the authors' names links to other relevant articles published by the authors. Jennifer finds forty-four articles by Crystal L. Park and three by Carol Blumberg. A click on the journal title links Jennifer to a page that allows her to search within all of the issues of *Cognitive Therapy and Research* published between 1993 and the present. Using the keywords "JN 'Cognitive Therapy & Research'" and "trauma," she locates an additional sixteen articles in this journal. Searches using the three "Subject Terms" provided by the database or the four terms provided by the authors and "trauma" will provide Jennifer with even more sources.

The detailed record in Figure 8–3 also includes an abstract of the article, information about copyright, and the academic affiliation of the authors. The column to the left of the display indicates that the article is available as full text ("PDF Full Text"). A click on "Check 360 Link for Full Text" takes Jennifer to a page that indicates other places the full text of the article is available, either in other databases or shelved by call number in her library's print periodical holdings. Sometimes back issues of periodicals are stored on microfiche. Check with your reference librarian. The left column also tells Jennifer the number of times "Disclosing Trauma Through Writing: Testing the Meaning-Making Hypothesis" has been cited in other articles in the database. The link takes her to the records of the ten articles.

The column to the right of the display provides tools for storing the article. Jennifer can temporarily keep it in a folder, print it, email it to herself, or save it to her computer. "Cite" is a feature that displays the article in popular citation formats. However, when you use the citation feature in library databases, always double-check that the bibliographic entries are correct. Consult a professional style guide or the Appendix of this book for exact punctuation and formatting guidelines.

If your library database does not provide the full text of an article, read the abstract and then decide if you will obtain the source through interlibrary loan. Abstracts are

Figure 8–3   *Academic Search Complete* Entry. © 2011 EBSCO Publishing, Inc. Reprinted with permission. Abstract reprinted with kind permission from Springer Science+Business Media: Park, Crystal L.; Blumberg, Carol Joyce. "Disclosing Trauma Through Writing: Testing the Meaning-Making Hypothesis." *Cognitive Therapy Research* 26.5 (2002): 597. Copyright © 2002 Springer Netherlands.

short summaries of articles' contents. Keep in mind that abstracts are intended to help researchers decide which articles are most relevant to their interests; they are not meant to circumvent careful reading of the complete text. Do not rely on abstracts as information sources; they are only access tools. Further, you should not cite an article in a research paper if you have read only the abstract and did not obtain the article's full text. For a detailed discussion of abstracts, see pages 55–57.

EXERCISE 8.7

- Select the topic you've been working on for Exercises 8.1, 8.2, and 8.6 or use a topic assigned by your professor.
- Go to the library and locate two books and two periodical articles on your topic.
- Use an online database to find two of these sources and print out the records.
- For the print sources, photocopy the table of contents of the book or periodical, and on the photocopy, circle the chapter or article that is relevant to your topic.
- Submit the computer printout and the photocopies to your instructor.

EXERCISE 8.8

- Form small groups.

- Come to a consensus on a topic you would like to research, or use one assigned by your instructor.

- Assign each group member one type of information resource: general reference, discipline-specific book, magazine, newspaper, or professional journal.

- Proceed to the library from class or go individually outside of class time. Find a source on your topic that represents the particular type of information resource that you were assigned. Photocopy or print out the table of contents of the book or periodical, and on the photocopy or printout, circle the chapter or article that is relevant to your topic.

- Reconvene your group at the next class meeting. Have each group member report on the source he or she found. Then discuss which types of resources seemed most useful for your topic and what further research would be necessary to actually write on your topic.

- Reconvene the entire class. Each group recorder should explain the group's topic and summarize the group's discussion of sources on this topic.

 A Word About Electronic Retrieval Systems

Electronic retrieval systems do not possess artificial intelligence. They are merely word-matching tools; they cannot make even the simplest inferences about your intentions. Don't expect the system to do any of your thinking for you. In addition, most retrieval systems cannot correct for misspelling or adjust for variations in spelling. Distinctions that may seem insignificant to you, such as the difference between "first" and "1st," may be crucial when using a computerized system.

To put retrieval systems to best use, whether you are searching your library's online catalog, an electronic database, or the World Wide Web, you need to understand basic principles of online searching. Students are sometimes under the impression that electronic searching is simple, that all they have to do is type in words or phrases that describe their topic and, voilà, they will receive a wealth of valuable information sources. However, to take maximum advantage of online searching, you need to know how search software operates.

You search a database by typing in a *query*, which is typically several words related to your topic. In response, the retrieval system matches the query with relevant information sources in the system's database. While systems vary in their precise search strategies, most compare the specific words in queries to indexes or word lists compiled from all the information sources.

Types of Searches

You can conduct either a **basic search** or an **advanced search**. Basic searches allow you to search by keyword, author, title, source, and year. Advanced searches permit you to search for other items, such as publication date, language, personal name, geographic name, and source type (book, video, sound recording, and so forth). Usually, you can examine several indexes with a single query; for example, you could search for sources on therapeutic writing that were published since the year 2000. In databases that provide the full texts of articles, the words used within each article are indexed so that you can search the articles' contents.

Let us return to our previous example of the database *Academic Search Premier.* When Jennifer begins her advanced search on this database, she sees a template comparable to the one in Figure 8–4.

She enters the words *trauma therapy* in the "Keyword" box and receives a list of 315 sources. She decides to narrow her search to sources published from January 2005 to December 2010, so she repeats the search entering these dates in the "Published Date from" boxes. This search produces 189 sources. Jennifer repeats the search again, narrowing it even further by limiting the results as follows: Full Text, Scholarly (Peer Reviewed) Journals, Publication Type—Periodical, Document Type—Article, and PDF Full Text. This search yields 45 results.

Whenever you use a scholarly database for the first time, take a few minutes to familiarize yourself with it. In Figure 8–4, you see that the banner at the top of the template has a button labeled "Help." This tab opens a comprehensive, searchable "how-to" manual.

Keyword Searching Unless you know the author or title of the source you are looking for, you will search by keyword. Keyword searches have advantages and disadvantages. A keyword search will locate one or more words in any position within the title or

Figure 8–4 Template for *Academic Search Premier* Advanced Search. © 2011 EBSCO Publishing, Inc. Reprinted with permission.

subject heading. When Jennifer types *trauma* in the title box of an electronic database, she will locate all titles that include the word *trauma*. It is often advantageous to use keywords or phrases to search for titles with those words in them since titles usually indicate the source's content. Keyword searching is likewise advantageous for subject indexes because it allows you to retrieve multiple references without knowing the exact wording of the subject heading. For instance, a keyword search for *welfare reform* would retrieve the subject headings *public welfare reform*; *reform, welfare*; and *reform, public welfare*, as well as *welfare reform* and *Welfare Reform Reconciliation Act of 1996*.

A disadvantage of keyword searching is that it has the potential to draw in a great many irrelevant sources because the words in the query are always matched to the index without regard to specific context. For instance, a keyword title search for *Grateful Dead* would retrieve the article entitled "Anti-Union Bill Dead in Committee: Autoworkers Grateful for Senator's Pivotal Vote." Some retrieval systems allow you to search for exact phrases—that is, for strings of words that appear in a particular order. For example, an exact phrase search for *Grateful Dead* would retrieve only the index items in which the word "Dead" immediately follows the word "Grateful." Exact phrase searches are usually specified by placing the target words in the query within quotation marks.

Truncation   Computerized retrieval systems often allow you to truncate or shorten search terms. Instead of typing in the search statement *politically correct movement*, you might enter *political* and *correct*. This query would retrieve *politically correct movement, political correctness*, and other variations on this terminology. It is often wise to truncate words in search statements, particularly when you are unsure of the precise indexing terms used in the database.

Refine Your Search by Using Boolean Logic   Sometimes searches retrieve far more sources than you need, as well as many sources that are unrelated to your topic. At other times a search will yield only a handful of sources. Boolean logic will enable you to link words and phrases to create a very specific request that takes full advantage of electronic searching. Boolean logic is named after the nineteeth-century British mathematician George Boole. The logic has many applications, one of which is computer searching. All you need to know is a very simplified version of the logic: how to connect your search terms by using the three Boolean operators AND, OR, and NOT.

If your search produces too many results, you can limit it by inserting the word AND (some systems require the + sign instead of AND) between your search terms. Suppose you want information on the national debate over welfare reform that occurred in 1996. You search with the term *welfare reform* and get hundreds of articles. If you enter *welfare reform AND 1996*, you will receive a list of all sources that have a subject heading "welfare reform" as well as a publication year of 1996. Don't let the Boolean AND confuse you. We usually associate AND with addition, so you would think that adding the word AND would increase the number of sources retrieved. The AND actually places more restrictions on searches and usually cuts down on the number of hits.

If your search produces a number of sources unrelated to the area you wish to study, insert the word NOT (some systems require the − sign instead of NOT) before words you would like to delete. Suppose your search for *welfare reform* results in a sizable number of articles dealing with occupational training, a topic you are not planning to investigate. If you enter *welfare reform NOT occupational training*, the computer will identify articles on welfare reform and exclude articles that concern job training.

If your search produces too few sources, insert the word OR between your search terms. Suppose you're interested in the topic of occupational training. The expression *welfare reform* OR *occupational training* will locate articles that focus just on welfare reform and articles that focus just on job training, along with articles that cover both topics.

You can also use Boolean operators in combination to piece together complex search statements such as the following: *welfare reform* OR *occupational training* AND *1996*. Most of the templates you will be offered for advanced searches already include Boolean operations (see Figure 8–4). Experiment with your search terms, but remember AND = narrow, NOT = limit, and OR = expand.

EXERCISE 8.9

Return to the topic you have been working with in the previous exercises in this chapter.

- Go to your library's home page and access an article database.
- Look for a general interdisciplinary database such as **Academic Search Premier** or a database recommended by your professor or reference librarian.
- Perform the following operations:

    Conduct a basic search and record the number of articles the search retrieves.

    Conduct an advanced search and record the number of articles the search retrieves.

    If the database allows, experiment with the Boolean AND, NOT, and OR.

■ Conduct Research on the World Wide Web

Advantages and Disadvantages of the Web

The explosion of the World Wide Web has made it easy to locate information on every imaginable topic. If you play the guitar, within seconds you can find Web sites that provide product information on new and used guitars, chords for the latest songs, and a discography for your favorite guitarist. This information would take hours to collect without the help of the Web. The Web works well in this case for several reasons. Since thousands of amateur musicians and music fans use the Web to share information, its popular music resources are vast and will probably cover any guitar, song, or guitarist that interests you. Search queries about guitars, guitar music, and guitarists are relatively easy to formulate, since they are based on straightforward names (Fender, "Voodoo Child," Jimi Hendrix) rather than descriptions of content. As an amateur guitarist, you are looking for information that is interesting or useful, and you may not be concerned with precise accuracy. In other words, you'd be satisfied with playable chord progressions that sound acceptably close to the original songs rather than completely authentic musical transcriptions.

The Web does not work as well for scholarly research as it does for topics of general interest. Books and scholarly journals remain the standard vehicles for academic communication, and many of these publications are not available on the Web. Another problem is that academic research usually involves searching by subject matter rather than by proper name, and the Web is not arranged for efficient subject searching. Given the Web's huge size, haphazard organization, and poor indexing, it may be difficult to locate material on your research topic.

Another drawback of the Web is that relevant information may be buried in long lists of information sources that contain the vocabulary in your search statement but are not actually useful to you. For example, if Jennifer, in her research on trauma therapy, used the search term *trauma* on the Web, it might steer her to the Web page of the Discoteca Trauma, a nightclub in Barcelona, Spain.

A final difficulty is that academic researchers care very much about reliability and accuracy, but the Web has no effective quality control. Any individual or group can establish a Web page and disseminate any information that he, she, or they choose, except for content that is in clear violation of the law. Some Web pages use very professional graphics but include content that is merely uninformed opinion. Of course, print sources can also contain unreliable content, but the Web has expanded tremendously the opportunity for "publishing" material that has no basis in fact. Consequently, subject searches conducted on the Web often direct the researcher to Web sites that do not provide reliable information.

The issues of reliability and objectivity are further complicated by the commercial nature of many Web sites. For instance, the search term "trauma" will likely provide a great many links to the dot-com (.com) business Web pages of psychologists, psychiatrists, and social workers who specialize in trauma therapy and use the Web to advertise their services. While some of these commercial sites may provide information that is useful to a researcher, others will be biased and manipulative. Keep in mind that standard Web search engines, the electronic retrieval systems that you use to search the Web, are commercial ventures. They may intentionally steer you to information providers who have paid the search engine companies to highlight their Web sites.

Advantages of College Libraries

In contrast to the World Wide Web, a college library collection is developed specifically to serve the needs of academic researchers. Books, periodicals, and other materials are chosen either by librarians who specialize in collection development or by faculty members who are experts in their fields of study. Because an academic library collection is built systematically, it is much more likely to include the seminal works in a particular discipline, whereas the Web does not discriminate between expert and uninformed opinion. Your library may also include special collections for certain programs of study that are highlighted at your college. Currently, relatively few books are available in full-text online versions; thus, with the exception of periodicals, most of the scholarly sources in your college library's collection are probably not available online.

Another advantage of conducting research in your college library is that you can get help from the reference librarians. The major responsibility of these information professionals is to help students and faculty members with their research questions. Reference librarians can show you how to access sources that are available online from remote sites, including material on the Web. In most cases, a few minutes spent discussing your research needs with a reference librarian will be more productive than hours of surfing the Web.

A final advantage of academic libraries is that they provide the sophisticated tools you need to conduct scholarly research. In your college library, you will find an online catalog and electronic links to other libraries from which you can obtain material via interlibrary loan. Your library provides specialized electronic databases and academic indexes that will help you locate information in journals, magazines, and newspapers and, consequently, conduct far more precise searches than is possible with the general access tools available on the World Wide Web.

ADVANTAGES OF THE WORLD WIDE WEB AND ACADEMIC LIBRARIES

Advantages of the Web for Researchers

- Uninterrupted availability
- Continuous updating
- Vast resources
- Coverage of virtually all topics (but without quality control)
- Convenience of one-stop shopping (but at risk of chaotic subject searching)

Advantages of Academic Libraries for Researchers

- Expert collection development and quality control
- Systematic organization and careful indexing of subject headings
- Increasingly available online resources for personal computer use at home
- Expert staff of reference librarians
- Extensive collections of book-length sources
- Commitment to scholarly inquiry and objectivity

Find Digital Resources on the Web

After you have conducted research in the library, you will be able to use the Web to good advantage. The primary research tools on the Web are subject directories and search engines.

Subject Directories

Subject directories are lists of Internet resources arranged by subject in a hierarchical order. The two most popular directories are *ipl2*, <http://www.ipl.org/>, and *WWW Virtual Library*, <http://vlib.org/>. In the acronym "ipl2," "ipl" stands for "Internet Public Library" and "2" represents the Librarians' Internet Index (LII). To search for *trauma therapy* on *ipl2*, Jennifer first clicks on "Resources by Subject," and then on the broad subject *Health and Medical Sciences*. When she enters "trauma therapy" in the search box, she receives over 150 sources. In other words, a search of subject directories uncovers layer after layer of material.

Subject directories are compiled by humans, whereas search engine data are collected by computers and robots. Some subject directories are components of search engines; examples include the Google Directory, <http://www.google.com/dirhp>, and the Yahoo Search Directory, <http://dir.yahoo.com/>. Others, like the five we list in the box below, are compiled by librarians and subject specialists. Future generations of the Web, sometimes called the Semantic Web, will replace searches conducted by humans with searches conducted by computer software. The Semantic Web will enable intelligent computers to create hierarchical subject directories comparable to the ones listed in the box below. Until that time, however, we have to rely on human judgment.

SUBJECT DIRECTORIES

Academic Info

<http://www.academicinfo.net/>

Infomine

<http://infomine.ucr.edu/>

Librarians' Internet Index

<http://www.ipl.org>

The WWW Virtual Library

<http://vlib.org/>

Intute

<http://www.intute.ac.uk/>

EXERCISE 8.10

- Form groups of five students. Select a topic from among the topics the group members have been working on in the previous exercises.
- Each student in the group will search for the topic in a different subject directory.
- As you search, keep a record of the various links you click as you uncover the layers of material.
- When the group reconvenes, the members should review one another's work and decide which subject directory produced the best results.

Search Engines

A Web search engine is a tool that combs the Internet looking for Web sites related to your search term. When you type your topic into a search engine, it responds with a list of Web sites that correspond as closely as possible to the words or phrases in your query. Search engines use a variety of methods for locating information. Entering the same words or phrases in two search engines can generate strikingly different search results. We suggest you begin with Google because it has the largest database. However, it does not search the entire Web. It is thus wise to search for your topic in two or three engines.

In the following box, we list four search engines and a multi-search engine. Multi-search engines search the databases of a number of search engines simultaneously.

The power of search engines is that they inspect billions of Web pages. The weakness is that they retrieve much more material than you need, and much of that material

---

SEARCH ENGINES

Alta Vista

<http://www.altavista.com/>

Ask.com

<http://www.ask.com>

Google

<http://www.google.com>

Yahoo! Search

<http://search.yahoo.com>

MULTI-SEARCH ENGINE

Metacrawler

<http://www.metacrawler.com/>

---

is inappropriate for college research papers. In the next section, we will explain how to increase the precision of your Web search.

How to Increase the Precision of Your Web Search

Our student Jennifer accesses Google, types the words *trauma therapy* into the search box, and in 0.20 second receives an overwhelming 6,860,000 results. Her first strategy for making the search more manageable is to move from a basic search to an advanced search. Jennifer clicks on the "Advanced Search" link. Before she enters her search terms, she clicks on "Advanced Search Tips" in order to learn about advanced search operations. After reading the tips, she returns to the advanced search template and fills it in, as we illustrate in Figure 8–5.

Since Jennifer has already conducted library-based research, she has acquired a respectable search vocabulary. In the "all these words" box, she types *trauma therapy*. Google does not require her to type in the Boolean operator AND. The search will narrowed because Google will locate documents that contain both the words *trauma* and *therapy*. In the "this exact wording or phrase" box, she types *therapeutic writing*, which will ensure that the results contain this exact phrase. She narrows the search further, asking for documents written in English. Lastly, in the "domain" box, she types ".edu" and consequently excludes Web sites with addresses ending in *.org* and *.com*. The narrowed search produces 120 results.

Web Addresses   Before we continue our discussion of search engines, we would like to say a few words about Web addresses. A Web address, also called a URL (uniform resource locator), reveals valuable information about the nature and purpose of the Web site. Let us look first at the composition of a URL, as detailed in Figure 8–6.

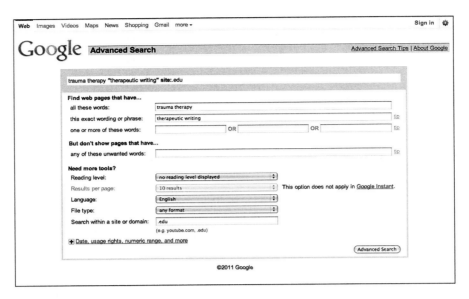

Figure 8–5   Template for Google Advanced Search. © 2011 Google. GOOGLE is a trademark of Google Inc.

Sometimes you don't have to type in the abbreviations *http://* and *www* even though they are still part of the official Web address. An important component of the Web address is the three-letter suffix following the domain name. This suffix, called the "domain type," indicates the nature and purpose of the Web site, for example, whether it is a commercial site (*com*), an educational site (*edu*), or a government site (*gov*). We list some common domains in the box below.

Let's return to our student: Jennifer conducts an additional search on Google Scholar, <http://scholar.google.com/>. The Google Scholar search retrieves ten sources

COMMON DOMAIN TYPES	
Domain Suffix	**Nature**
.com	Commercial and business entities
.net	Network organization or network administration
.org	Public and nonprofit organizations, businesses, and groups
.info	Nonprofit; intended for informative sites
.edu	Education: reserved for educational institutions (most are postsecondary)
.gov	Federal and local U.S. government sites
.mil	Department of Defense and military sites

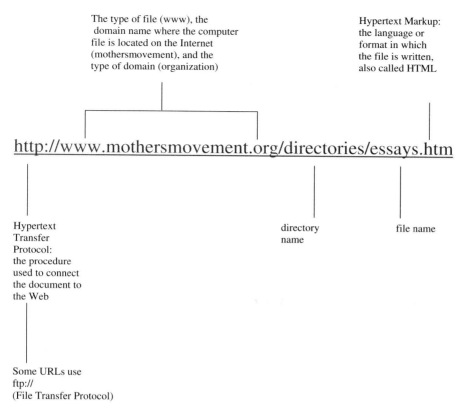

The type of file (www), the domain name where the computer file is located on the Internet (mothersmovement), and the type of domain (organization)

Hypertext Markup: the language or format in which the file is written, also called HTML

http://www.mothersmovement.org/directories/essays.htm

Hypertext Transfer Protocol: the procedure used to connect the document to the Web

directory name

file name

Some URLs use ftp:// (File Transfer Protocol)

Figure 8–6   Composition of a URL.

EXERCISE 8.11

Access each of the sites in the following list. In each case, predict what the domain type reveals about the nature of the site and its rhetorical purpose.

<http://www.archiva.net/footnote/index.htm>

<http://catalog.loc.gov/>

<http://wildlifecontrol.info/Pages/default1.aspx>

<http://www.womensenews.org/>

<http://www.carlisle.army.mil/ahec/>

<http://www.eightimprov.biz/Improv-Off-Broadway.html>

<http://www.library.cornell.edu/library/libweb.html>

published between 1990 and 2010. Figure 8–7 shows a copy of her Google Scholar Advanced Search page.

Google Scholar may link you to sites that require you to pay a fee for articles that you can otherwise obtain for free from your college library. After you search Google Scholar, return to

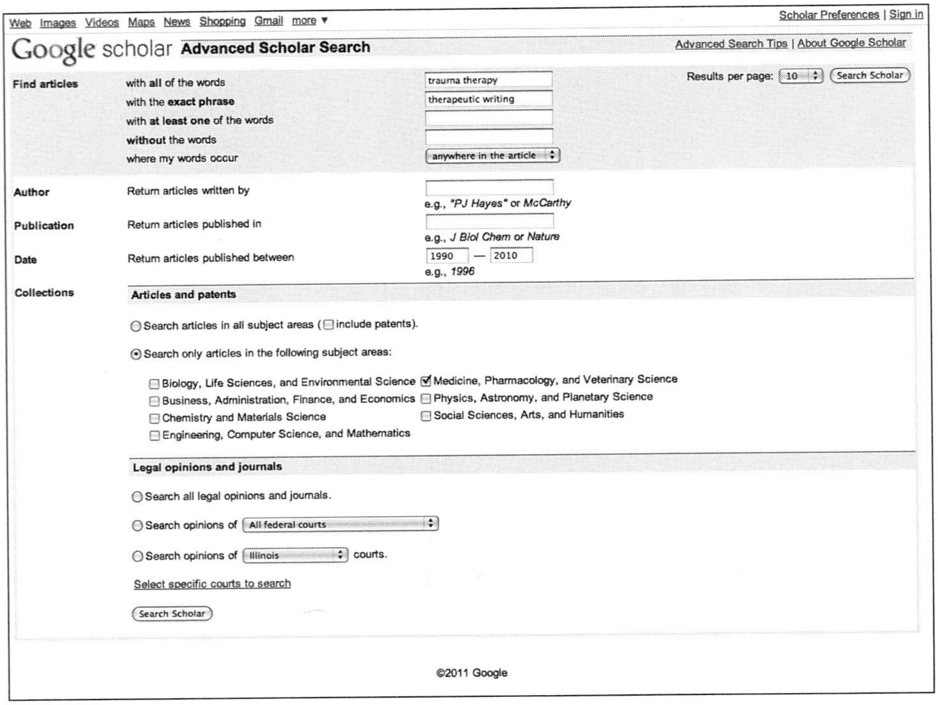

Figure 8–7 Template for Google Scholar Advanced Scholar Search. © 2011 Google. GOOGLE is a trademark of Google Inc.

your college library catalog to determine whether the articles that you've found on your Google search are also located there.

Another useful tool is the Google Book Search, <http://books/google.com>. As we mentioned earlier, Google has undertaken a library project that aims to digitalize the world's books. When Jennifer conducts an advanced book search, Google finds 105 books whose contents match her search terms, "trauma therapy" and "therapeutic writing." Google Book Search offers some books in their entirety and others with "previews" or "snippets."

EXERCISE 8.12

Reconvene the groups formed in Exercise 8.10 on page 258 and work with the same topic.

- As a group, decide which search terms and Boolean operations you will use to narrow or limit the topic.

- Each student will use these terms and operations to conduct an advanced search in one of the search engines we have listed on page 259. Assign a different search engine to each member of the group.

- When the group reconvenes, the members will review each other's work and decide which search engine produced the best results.

◼ EVALUATE WHAT YOU FIND

◼ Which Articles Are Most Appropriate?

In your database searching, you will find articles from popular magazines as well as from scholarly journals. Early in the research process, ask your professor if you may use articles from the popular press in your paper. Sometimes it is difficult to distinguish between popular and scholarly sources. The Cornell University Library Web site offers a useful research guide to four categories of periodicals: scholarly, substantive news or general interest, popular, and sensational. The box below provides an overview of these categories.

DISTINGUISHING SCHOLARLY FROM NONSCHOLARLY PERIODICALS

Scholarly

- Scholarly journals generally have a sober, serious look. They often contain many graphs and charts but few glossy pages or exciting pictures.
- Scholarly journals always cite their sources in the form of footnotes or bibliographies.
- Articles are written by a scholar in the field or by someone who has done research in the field.
- The language of scholarly journals is that of the discipline covered. It assumes some scholarly background on the part of the reader.
- The main purpose of a scholarly journal is to report on original research or experimentation in order to make such information available to the rest of the scholarly world.
- Many scholarly journals, though by no means all, are published by a specific professional organization.
- Examples of scholarly journals:

  American Economic Review

  Archives of Sexual Behavior

  JAMA: The Journal of the American Medical Association

  Journal of Marriage and the Family

  Modern Fiction Studies

  Sex Roles: A Journal of Research

Substantive News or General Interest

- These periodicals may be quite attractive in appearance, although some are in newspaper format. Articles are often heavily illustrated, generally with photographs.
- News and general interest periodicals sometimes cite sources, a scholar, or a freelance writer.
- The language of these publications is geared to any educated audience. There is no special training assumed, only interest and a certain level of intelligence.
- They are generally published by commerical enterprises or individuals, although some emanate from specific professional organizations.
- The main purpose of periodicals in this category is to provide information, in a general manner, to a broad audience of concerned citizens.

(continued)

- Examples of substantive news or general interest periodicals:

  Christian Science Monitor

  Economist

  National Geographic

  New York Times

  Scientific American

  Vital Speeches of the Day

Popular

- Popular periodicals come in many formats, although they are often somewhat slick and attractive in appearance. There are usually lots of graphics (photographs, drawings, etc.).
- These publications rarely, if ever, cite sources. Information published in such journals is often second- or thirdhand, and the original source is sometimes obscure.
- Articles are usually very short, written in simple language, and designed to meet a minimal education level. There is generally little depth to the content of these articles.
- Articles are written by staff members or freelance writers.
- The main purpose of popular periodicals is to entertain the reader, to sell products (their own or their advertisers'), and/or to promote a viewpoint.
- Examples of popular periodicals:

  Ebony

  Parents

  People Weekly

  Reader's Digest

  Sports Illustrated

  Time

  Vogue

Sensational

- Sensational periodicals come in a variety of styles, but often use a newspaper format.
- The language is elementary and occasionally inflammatory or sensational. They assume a certain gullibility in their audience.
- The main purpose of sensational magazines seems to be to arouse curiosity and to cater to popular superstitions. They often do so with flashy headlines designed to astonish (e.g., "Half-man Half-woman Makes Self Pregnant").
- Examples of sensational periodicals:

  Globe

  National Examiner

  Star

  Weekly World News

Research guide from: <<u>http://olinuris.library.cornell.edu/ref/research/skill20.html</u>> Courtesy of Olin Library Reference, Research & Learning Services, Cornell University Library, Ithaca, NY, USA.

Whenever you are in doubt about the appropriateness of a particular newspaper or magazine, consult your professor or a reference librarian.

EXERCISE 8.13

- Break into small groups.

- Review the records for the articles you selected for the individual and collaborative exercises on locating sources on page 262.

- As a group, speculate about the appropriateness of the articles. Use the Cornell guide "Distinguishing Scholarly from Nonscholarly Periodicals" to decide whether the articles are scholarly, substantive news or general interest, popular, or sensational.

- A reporter from each group will report the findings to the class.

How to Evaluate Web Sources

Question the reliability of all sources, even those that come from an academic library. It is particularly important to evaluate sources you obtain from the Web. Ask yourself the questions in the following box.

QUESTIONS FOR EVALUATING WEB SITES

- What is the overall goal of the Web site? Do the authors of the Web site have motives other than presenting scholarly truth? For instance, does the site attempt to advocate for a particular political agenda or to sell a product?

- Is the site produced by a reputable organization? Does it provide a mailing address and phone number? Does it invite inquiries?

- Do the authors of the Web site identify themselves? Do they provide any evidence of their expertise or credibility? For example, do they possess training or experience in the topic area covered by their site? Do they demonstrate that they are aware of the standard scholarly or professional literature in the topic area?

- Do the authors distinguish between opinion and fact? Do they provide nonanecdotal evidence to substantiate their conclusions? Do they cite published sources?

- When was the site created? How often is it updated? When was it last updated?

■ Evaluate Information Sources

As you locate source material, judge whether it has direct relevance to your topic. Don't excerpt information that is only remotely related. Ask yourself how the source fits in with your overall goals for the research paper. To what facet of the topic does the source pertain? What perspective on the topic does it represent? Make sense of each source as you examine it. Don't wait until you have completed your library research.

In addition to evaluating the source's relevance to your topic, you should judge its comparative quality. As we mentioned on page 265, you need to examine the reliability of everything you find on the Web. You also need to evaluate library materials. Too many students have complete confidence in sources they find in the library. Library sources come with no absolute guarantees.

As you analyze your sources, examine the author's rhetorical purpose. As we suggested in Chapter 1, ask yourself the Questions for Analyzing the Rhetorical Context of Texts on pages 28–31. The answers to these questions will help you to understand the source better and figure out whether it is appropriate for your paper. For instance, if you are writing for a science course on the future of nuclear power, you may be skeptical of information from lobby groups for the nuclear industry. If you think about writers' motives, you will be able to put their ideas in the proper perspective.

■ Collect Information on Your Own: Surveys and Interviews

The bulk of the material you use in research papers will come from published sources; however, depending on your assignment, it may be appropriate to use information that you collect personally through informal interviews and surveys. For example, suppose you are writing a research paper for a psychology class on how birth order (only child, firstborn, lastborn, and so on) affects personality. The psychological literature contains numerous studies on this topic, but you decide to supplement these publications by interviewing selected students in your class who represent each of the birth-order positions. You will use these cases as concrete illustrations of the conclusions reached in the psychological studies. You might also administer a survey to twenty-five students representing a range of birth orders to see if their perceptions of the relationship between birth order and personality match the research findings.

Informal surveys and interviews provide anecdotal information that is not a reliable basis for firm conclusions. Still, anecdotes are useful for explaining a concept to your readers or for framing an interesting introduction or closing for your research paper. Informal surveys may help you to sharpen your research question or identify trends that warrant more careful investigation. While an informal survey is not sufficient to challenge the conclusions of published studies, it can be useful to note a significant difference between informal and published research results. If the results of the informal classmate survey on the interaction between birth order and personality differ from published conclusions, then you might suggest in your paper that additional formal research should be conducted to see whether the published conclusions still hold for the current college-age population.

A final advantage of conducting informal surveys and interviews is that they get you directly involved with the topic you are researching. This hands-on approach increases interest, particularly for topics that seem rather dry based on the published sources alone. Even if you do not end up using any of the anecdotal information, the experience of getting actively involved with the topic will lead to a better final product.

Whenever you conduct informal interviews or surveys, adhere to the guidelines in the following box.

GUIDELINES FOR CONDUCTING INFORMAL INTERVIEWS AND SURVEYS

- Make sure you comply with college regulations concerning the use of human subjects. While these regulations typically apply to formal research studies, it is possible that your college has guidelines even for informal interviews and surveys. Check with your instructor if you are unsure of your college's human subject policies.

- Whatever your college's policies are, make sure you respect the privacy of your subjects. Do not repeat their responses in casual conversation, and do not use subjects' actual names in your research paper unless there is a clear reason to do so and you have their permission.

- Establish clear goals for your questions. Interview or survey questions should have one of the following goals:

  To establish facts

  To record beliefs about what is fact

  To record personal feelings or values

- Ask the same question worded in several different ways. Sometimes, a slight change in wording will prompt a different response from a subject. It is often difficult to predict wording that will convey the question most effectively.

- Don't ask questions that betray a bias. For example, suppose you are interviewing lastborn children to determine if there is a possible link between birth order and personality. You would indicate a bias if you asked, "In what ways did your parents and older siblings spoil you?" A more neutral question would be "What personality characteristics distinguish you from your older siblings?"

- Do not press anyone who is reluctant to undergo an interview or complete a survey. Many people do not want to discuss their personal lives, particularly when someone is taking notes on what they say.

▣ Modify Your Research Strategy

Research, by its very nature, is a creative process that exposes new approaches and gives rise to new ideas. As your research proceeds, you may modify your topic (if the assignment allows you to define your own topic), your research schedule (you may require more trips to the library than you had initially anticipated), your research questions, and your search vocabulary.

Consider how Jennifer modifies her search strategy. Recall her initial research questions:

1. To what extent do psychologists still accept Freud's theory concerning trauma?
2. How does current psychological theory explain the impact of traumatic experiences?
3. What therapies are available for victims of psychological trauma? Which are most effective?

4. According to psychologists and communication experts (writing and speech), what role does the verbal expression of traumatic experiences play in the recovery process?
5. Do victims of psychological trauma receive adequate attention in the mental health system?

Jennifer decides to drop Questions 3 and 5. She realizes that Question 3 is too broad for an eight- to ten-page paper, since it involves surveying and evaluating all the therapeutic techniques used in working with trauma victims, and she has found from her research that a wide range of treatments is available. She eliminates Question 5 because it is not addressed directly in any of the sources she has located so far. In addition, Jennifer has discovered that Questions 2 and 4 fit together because recent psychological theory, particularly theory grounded in research on brain physiology, highlights the therapeutic value of communication. And, as a result of the reading she has done so far, she has become particularly interested in these questions. She believes her research on Question 1 will fit into the introductory section of the paper, where she will provide historical context.

■ Excerpt Information from Sources and Cite What You Find Using a Standard Format

The basic tools for excerpting information from sources—paraphrasing, summarizing, and quoting—are covered in Chapter 2. Here we will discuss the special problems associated with the sheer number of sources required for a research paper.

One common problem is losing track of the exact source for an important piece of information. Each time you excerpt a passage from a source, whether you hand copy, reword, or photocopy, make sure that you carefully record a complete citation to the source. Be sure that you distinguish in your notes between passages that you have copied and passages that you have summarized or paraphrased in your own words (hint: always put direct quotations within quotation marks). Record the exact page numbers where specific pieces of text are located. Be especially careful about recording bibliographic information for electronic sources. (See our sample URL on p. 261.) When you draft your paper, you will cite the source as well as the page for each paraphrase, summary, and quotation. See the box below for information to record. (In the Appendix, we give more detailed information about citing and documenting sources, including essential citation formats.)

NECESSARY BIBLIOGRAPHIC INFORMATION

- For books, record author(s), title, publisher, city of publication, date of publication, and pages where the information you excerpted is located.
- For magazines and newspapers, record author(s), title of article, name of magazine or newspaper, date (day, month, year), inclusive pages for entire article, and pages where the information you excerpted is located (the section number or letter is needed for multisectioned newspapers).

- For scholarly journals, record the same information as for magazines and newspapers, as well as the volume number.
- For online sources, in addition to recording the items listed above, copy down the title and date of the Web site, the Web address (URL), the date you accessed the material online, and, when applicable, the name of the database or online subscription service and the library where you accessed the database.

Another problem is failing to distinguish adequately between paraphrases and quotations in research notes and thus including an author's exact words in your research paper without quotation marks. This is an unintentional yet serious form of plagiarism. Be very meticulous about your use of quotation marks as you take notes. Reread our comments on plagiarism on pages 47 and 53.

Warning: There is a danger of excerpting too much information. Some students compulsively collect every scrap of information that is remotely related to their topic, thinking they will make sense of it all at a later date. Don't bury yourself in paper, whether it consists of index cards, pages of notes, computer text files, or photocopies of sources. Excerpt only what you will use. Research is a sense-making process. It is hard to make sense of your research when you are overwhelmed with information.

Much has been written on how students should record the information they excerpt from sources. Some textbooks strongly recommend handwritten index cards for research notes because cards can be grouped and regrouped easily. Of course, you may prefer to record your research notes on your computer and use word-processing or outlining programs to organize the information. Try various methods of recording excerpts and find what works best for you. In addition to research notes, keep a separate set of notes for preliminary thesis statements, organizational plans, or other important ideas that occur to you during the writing process.

▇ Formulate a Working Thesis

After you have collected enough sources, formulate a working thesis. The purpose of the preliminary thesis or argument is to focus and direct your research. You may have a working thesis or argument in mind when you begin your research, or it may emerge as you collect information. The educational value of writing a research paper may in fact be that it enables you to derive an important thesis or argument from what you have learned through research. You are no longer blowing hot air on an opinion you've conceived, but instead elaborating a thesis or argument based on careful research.

To generate a thesis from your research notes: (1) scan the notes for general trends, main concepts, or overall patterns; (2) freewrite for ten minutes on what you think your research will tell your readers; and (3) reduce your freewriting to several sentences that explain what you want to say to your readers.

After scanning her research notes, Jennifer writes the following paragraph:

Freud's initial work on trauma led to the Seduction Hypothesis, the suggestion that hysteria resulted from the traumatic memories of sexual abuse. However, Freud abandoned this notion, and I don't want Freud to be the focus of my paper. Instead, I want to draw attention to the more current work by brain scientists that explains how trauma is etched into the human brain as an unprocessed memory. The research by van der Kolk best demonstrates this concept. Then I can go on to examine the evidence that shows that allowing these traumatic memories to be fully processed, through either speaking or writing, can provide relief from the trauma. The research done by Pennebaker will be helpful here. I still need more evidence on this point, but I think I will be able to back it up.

Jennifer rereads her freewriting and condenses it into a working thesis:

In our society, people are discouraged from expressing their feelings about traumatic events that happen to them and instead are encouraged to "keep your chin up." Despite this, there is increasing evidence that it is psychologically helpful to express feelings about trauma. Based on studies of the human brain, it has been established that allowing verbal analysis of traumatic experiences may allow processing of the experiences to take place and may aid in recovering from the impact of trauma.

The thesis is still preliminary. Compare it with Jennifer's final thesis, excerpted from the final version of her research paper:

Though we live in a culture where personal trauma and the lasting psychological effects of traumatic events are silenced, current research suggests that it should be otherwise. Verbal expression of pain, grief, and other responses to trauma speeds recovery. Psychologists and physiologists who study the brain have established that traumatic experiences are encoded in memory as images that are not fully processed by the conscious mind. Verbal analysis of the traumatic event, either through speech or writing, allows processing to take place and aids the person in recovering from the impact of trauma.

Jennifer's final thesis is refined, more fully developed, and more coherent than the earlier version. The main purpose of a working thesis is to focus your research activities, but you may find yourself departing from the initial thesis as you learn more about the topic.

◾ Planning the Research Paper

Select an Organizational Plan

A research paper can follow one organizational plan or a combination of the plans we have discussed in this book. Review the major organizational plans that we presented on pages 28–30 and 49–51. In many cases, a plan will occur to you as you conduct research. For instance, Jennifer has decided to write on how communicating about a traumatic event can help repair the psychological damage caused by the event. Thus, it occurs to her that a statement and response plan with a focus on problem and solution could work for her essay.

Outline

Because research writers must juggle multiple sources and deal with issues in depth, they need an outline that will keep them on task and provide a framework that unifies information from various sources. Review our explanation of free-form and formal outlining on pages 92–93. A pitfall of writing research papers is that you may become so bogged down in the details from the reading sources that you fail to clarify the relationships among major ideas. Your research paper will be easier to write if you draft it working from a detailed outline. In the end, your train of thought will be more evident to your readers.

As an example of a free-form outline, consider the one Jennifer develops for her research paper on trauma:

THESIS

— Psychologists and physiologists who study the brain have established that traumatic experiences are encoded in memory as images that are not fully processed by the conscious mind. Verbal analysis of the traumatic event, either through speech or writing, allows processing to take place and aids the person in recovering from the impact of trauma.

BACKGROUND

— After World War I, trauma came to the attention of researchers in studies of shell shock victims. Rivers encouraged those victims to talk and write about wartime experiences (Herman).

— Later, a link was made between war-induced trauma and trauma that resulted from domestic violence and sexual abuse (Herman).

CURRENT PHYSIOLOGICAL RESEARCH ON TRAUMA

— The brain responds to trauma through several distinct structures. The amygdala attaches emotional meaning to the experience, the hippocampus records the spatial dimensions of the experience and controls short-term memory of the experience, and the prefrontal cortex analyzes and categorizes the experience (van der Kolk, 1996).

— The information from a traumatic event goes first to the amygdala. If the emotional impact is too severe, the message cannot proceed to the hippocampus and prefrontal cortex for complete processing. Thus, the experience cannot be fully contextualized and understood (van der Kolk, 1996; LeDoux, Romanski, & Xagoraris). As a result, the traumatic experience is stored as images, not as a coherent narrative. The painful emotional feelings may remain over time, but the individual does not have a clear explanation for them and thus cannot cope with them.

RECOVERING FROM TRAUMA

— Victims must first understand what makes the memories resurface (Rauch). Then, they must find a way to describe the memories verbally and give them meaning.

WRITING AS THERAPY FOR TRAUMA

— Writing helps to integrate thoughts and feelings (Pennebaker).

— Writing can describe and give context to moments and images and help individuals make sense of incidents that initially were verbally indescribable.

— Writing has healing power and aids the immune system (Pennebaker).

— Writing provides an outlet to express the pain that our society masks in everyday life.

— Journaling is the most common form of writing. Focused Free Writing is another genre (Smyth & Helm).

OPPOSITION AND RESPONSE

— Some contemporary psychologists favor using beta-blockers to erase the memory of traumatic experience (Davis; Cahill). If this is done, the victims will never have a chance to fully process the experience, a necessary step on the road to recovery.

Write from Your Outline

Use your outline as a guide for drafting. Group your notes according to the points in your outline and draft the essay paragraph by paragraph. Be sure to record full bibliographic information in the first draft. It's easy to lose track of where the source information came from if you don't record it initially.

As you draft your essay, you may need to depart from your outline. An outline is supposed to guide your writing, not be a straitjacket. If you discover new patterns or ideas in the process of writing, don't hesitate to include them in your essay.

■ Revising

If your teacher agrees, make arrangements to have a classmate review your paper. If that is not possible, set the paper aside for a few days and then review it yourself. Respond to the questions in the following box.

PEER REVIEW QUESTIONS FOR REVISING A RESEARCH PAPER

- Is the paper written on a sufficiently narrow topic? If not, how might the topic be narrowed?
- Can you understand the writer's research goals? If not, how might the writer make the rhetorical purpose clearer to the reader?
- Does the writer present a clear thesis? If not, how might the writer sharpen the thesis?
- Is the research paper a thesis-driven synthesis or an argument-synthesis? If you are not sure, explain why.
- Are the writer's assertions substantiated with quotations, paraphrases, and summaries from sources? Which assertions need additional substantiation?
- Is the information from sources organized according to a clear plan? If not, what advice can you give the writer?
- Does the writer use information from sources convincingly? If not, what advice can you give the writer?

- Does the writer provide enough transitions and clearly differentiate between information from the sources and his or her own ideas? If not, what advice can you give the writer?
- Is the writer's voice appropriate for this type of essay? Why or why not?
- Is the paper opener satisfactory? Why or why not?
- Does the essay have an appropriate conclusion? Why or why not?
- Is the title suitable for the piece? Why or why not?
- Can you identify the source for each piece of information?
- Does the paper end with a list of works cited that includes all sources referred to in the text of the paper?

▣ Editing

When you are satisfied with your revision, read your paper aloud. Then reread it line by line and sentence by sentence. Check for correct usage, punctuation, spelling, mechanics, manuscript form, and typos. If you are especially weak in editing skills, get a friend to read over your work. Ask yourself the Questions for Editing on pages 113–14.

SAMPLE RESEARCH PAPER

The final draft of Jennifer Piazza's research paper appears on the following pages. Since Jennifer is writing her paper for a psychology class, she uses the American Psychological Association (APA) manuscript and documentation style rather than the MLA style given in our previous examples of student essays. APA style is used in many disciplines besides psychology.

Guidelines for the APA style are found in the *Publication Manual of the American Psychological Association*, 6th edition. We list the major guidelines for APA style in the box below.

GUIDELINES FOR FORMATTING RESEARCH PAPERS IN THE APA STYLE

1. Use a separate title page on which you center and double-space the title, your name, the course, the professor's name, and the date.

2. For each page, including the title page, use a shortened title and the page number as the header.

3. Use a separate page for a concise (no more than 120 words) summary of the research paper. Title the summary "Abstract." See pages 55–57 on guidelines for writing abstracts.

4. Repeat the title before the introductory paragraph.

5. Introduce source material by citing the author's name followed by the publication date in parentheses. Or provide the same material followed by a parenthetical citation of the author, publication date, and page number.

6. Begin the list of References on a new page.

We provide information for documenting sources according to the APA style in the Appendix.

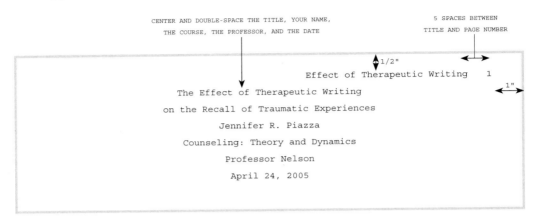

CENTER AND DOUBLE-SPACE THE TITLE, YOUR NAME, THE COURSE, THE PROFESSOR, AND THE DATE

5 SPACES BETWEEN TITLE AND PAGE NUMBER

1/2"

Effect of Therapeutic Writing   1

1"

The Effect of Therapeutic Writing
on the Recall of Traumatic Experiences
Jennifer R. Piazza
Counseling: Theory and Dynamics
Professor Nelson
April 24, 2005

1"   1/2"
Effect of Therapeutic Writing   2

Abstract

Though we live in a culture that does not encourage trauma victims to verbalize their suffering, research shows that verbal responses to trauma speed recovery. Trauma victims dissociate from or fail to recall the traumatic experience because they are unable to utilize explicit memory to tie past events to their present emotional states. Research has shown that writing serves to translate experiences individuals cannot express orally. Nonetheless, some psychologists question the value of verbal disclosure and advocate administering drugs that will erase memories of traumatic events.

1"   1"

The Effect of Therapeutic Writing on the
Recall of Traumatic Experiences

Trauma engulfs people suffering from abuse, grief, and loss of self. From war to domestic violence, from the death of a loved one to involvement in a tragic accident, from mental illness to physical disabilities, from a host of factors, trauma infiltrates lives. Yet, when trauma touches us on a personal level, we are sometimes taught that disclosing personal feelings is undesirable and unacceptable. The teachings come in the form of hushed words when a victim of trauma enters the room; they are evident when people look the other way as the widow of a spouse who committed suicide walks down the street; and the teachings are strengthened when the media focus on how a victim of a

1"

USE 8½" BY 11" PAPER FOR EACH PAGE. USE DOUBLE SPACES BETWEEN ALL LINES. LEFT-JUSTIFY ALL LINES IN THE TEXT OF THE PAPER. DO NOT RIGHT-JUSTIFY EVEN IF YOUR WORD PROCESSOR PROVIDES THIS FEATURE.

traumatic event could have prevented it. Those who contain their sorrow are viewed as the strong and resilient, while those who display reactions to trauma become the weak and insecure.

Though we live in a culture where personal trauma and the lasting psychological effects of traumatic events are silenced, current research suggests that it should be otherwise. Verbal expression of pain, grief, and other responses to trauma speeds recovery. Psychologists and physiologists who study the brain have established that traumatic experiences are encoded in memory as images that are not fully processed by the conscious mind. Verbal analysis of the traumatic event, either through speech or writing, allows processing to take place and aids the person in recovering from the impact of trauma.

During the late nineteenth century, Jean-Martin Charcot studied hysteria in an attempt to bring voices to those who have been silenced. Two of his students, Pierre Janet and Sigmund Freud, sought to surpass Charcot's work by finding the cause of hysteria (Herman, 1992). Both determined that trauma precipitated neuroses and that putting the traumatic experience into words was essential to moving past the trauma and dispelling neurotic symptoms. Freud discovered that everyday, trivial experiences seemed to trigger memories of childhood trauma in his patients. Freud stated that hysteria was the result of premature sexual experiences. This became known as the Seduction Hypothesis.

At the same time Freud was exploring the Seduction Hypothesis in Vienna, Janet was studying traumatic memory in France. Like Freud, he came to the conclusion that hysteria was the result of early childhood trauma. However, unlike Freud, Janet never abandoned his theory of hysteria and remained faithful to his patients. Soon after, the medical and psychological establishments accepted Freud, while Janet and his ideas of hysteria were forgotten. As a result, trauma research was halted for decades (Herman, 1992).

It was not until after World War I that trauma was once again in the forefront of research. Veterans who had undergone traumatic experiences returned from the war displaying symptoms of hysteria, or what was then called shell shock. A disease that was thought only to afflict women began to victimize large numbers of men who were once considered glorious and brave.

War-related trauma was publicized as a result of war, but the traumas of domestic violence, abuse, and rape were hidden. However, because both men and women displayed similar behaviors after their own personal traumas, the distinction between the trauma of war and the trauma of sexual assault and abuse began to blur. As a result of the recognition of psychological effects that occur both during and after traumatic events, the diagnosis of post-traumatic stress disorder (PTSD) was included in the *Diagnostic and Statistical Manual* in 1980 (Herman, 1992). Unfortunately, the battle fought by trauma survivors did not end when psychologists considered post-traumatic stress disorder legitimate. On the contrary, victims of trauma are still being silenced, and to this day the rift still exists between trauma survivors and those who do not understand the psychological and biological effects of trauma.

Dennis Charney, head of the clinical neuroscience division of the National Center for PTSD states:

> Victims of devastating trauma may never be the same, biologically. It does not matter if it was the incessant terror of combat, torture of repeated abuse in childhood, or a one-time experience, like being trapped in a hurricane or almost dying in an auto accident. All uncontrollable stress can have the same biological impact. (as cited in Butler, 1996, p. 41)

Individuals who have not experienced a major traumatic event or chronic trauma have the natural ability to prepare their bodies for danger. In a threatening situation, normal individuals' stress hormones increase, and the fight or flight response prepares them to escape the danger, either by resisting or by running. When the danger subsides, they return to a normal state because hormones have leveled off, and the nervous system is no longer in a state of arousal. It can be concluded, therefore, that normal, everyday stress does not permanently alter an individual's neurobiology (van der Kolk, McFarlene, & Weisaeth, 1996).

Unfortunately, this is not the case with trauma, especially trauma that occurs on a chronic basis. According to Bessel van der Kolk et al. (1996), "Chronic and persistent stress inhibits the effectiveness of the stress response and induces desensitization" (p. 222). Stress hormones in traumatized individuals are elevated because victims of trauma are in a state of constant hyperarousal and cannot modulate their bodies efficiently. Small stressors have the ability to trigger the release of a flood of hormones, which results in overreacting to everyday events. As a result, even in normal environments, the nervous system is always on alert.

It is evident that the neurochemistry of traumatized individuals is abnormal, and it is important to understand that traumatic experiences are also stored and processed differently from normal experiences. Bessel van der Kolk et al. (1996) state, "In the course of evolution, the human brain has developed three interdependent subanalyzers; the brainstem/hypothalamus, the limbic system and the prefrontal cortex" (p. 214). The authors go on to explain that the brainstem and hypothalamus are responsible for regulating internal homeostasis, and are partially dependent on the limbic system and prefrontal cortex to function properly. The limbic system, which maintains balance between the internal and external world, contains the hippocampus and the amygdala, two structures that are involved with processing traumatic events. The hippocampus records spatial dimensions of an experience and plays an important role in short-term memory; the amygdala is responsible for attaching emotional meaning to the sensory input of an experience. In other words, the hippocampus is responsible for the context of an experience, and the amygdala is responsible for the emotional weight of an experience. Finally, the prefrontal cortex analyzes the experience and categorizes it with past experiences (van der Kolk et al., 1996).

    According to van der Kolk et al. (1996), all information that we receive through our five senses reaches the amygdala before it travels to the hippocampus and the prefrontal cortex. Therefore, emotional responses occur before an actual experience can be interpreted and evaluated. When we experience a normal event, this is not a problem because the emotional weight is too weak to outweigh the actual experience. However, when we experience a traumatic event, the emotional impact is too extreme for further processing to occur. As demonstrated in animal studies (LeDoux, Romanski, & Xagoraris, 1989), if the amygdala is excessively stimulated, it interferes with the functioning of the hippocampus. If there is interference of the hippocampus, as in the case of trauma, it is impossible for a person to form a context for his or her experience. Thus, integration of the traumatic memory with a wide store of other memories never occurs (van der Kolk et al., 1996).

    Because integration does not occur, it is nearly impossible for people suffering from trauma to create a narrative that describes their traumatic memory. Instead, their experience exists in the form of images. Although the traumatic experience in its entirety may be hazy and difficult to retrieve, the images of certain moments remain frozen, untarnished. The pictures of the traumatic event are not organized. Traumatized victims cannot pick their mental photo albums off a shelf and note the manner in which the events occurred. Their pictures are scattered, bent, torn. There are no dates written on the back and no explanations as to why the event took place. Thus, trauma victims may dissociate from the experience. They are consciously unable to tie past events to their present emotional states.

    This inability to be consciously aware of the connection between events and emotions can be explained by the theory of implicit and explicit memory. According to van der Kolk et al. (1996), explicit or declarative memory is utilized to remember a particular moment and enables people to consciously tie their present behavior to an incident that occurred in their past. It is the memory of context, and it is tied closely to the hippocampus. Implicit memory, unlike explicit memory, does not rely on the hippocampus. It is utilized when perceptions, thoughts, and actions are unconsciously influenced by past experiences.

Traumatic experience interferes with explicit memory but does not interfere with implicit memory. Interference with explicit memory can be attributed to the fact that the hippocampus does not function properly during traumatic experience, due to excessive amygdala stimulation and elevated levels of neurohormones, such as corticosteroids. Since the hippocampus is essential for short-term memory, any damage to the hippocampus results in a person's inability to establish context for his or her experiences. Due to damage to the hippocampus, explicit memory cannot function properly. However, implicit memory is intact (van der Kolk et al., 1996).

For trauma victims to navigate through the aftermath of a traumatic event, they must acquire an understanding of how memories resurface; the purpose of this is so they understand why only feelings and fragments can be recalled rather than the entire incident. An inability to narrate a traumatic experience was examined by Rauch et al. in 1996. By playing to combat veterans and sexual abuse survivors with PTSD a tape of their most horrific memory, the three researchers were able to stimulate flashbacks. During recollection, positron emission tomography (PET) scans were used to record brain activity in these individuals. Results showed that areas of the brain's cortex involved in sensory memory were active, while Broca's area, which plays a large part in verbal articulation of experience, was inactive. When asked to recall a mundane experience, the opposite trend emerged: The sensory areas were inactive, while Broca's area was active (Rauch et al., 1996).

For some trauma victims, writing is an effective vehicle for communication (MacCurdy, 1999). For this reason, therapeutic writing has become an essential form of therapy in the mental health field. As Pennebaker (2000) puts it, "The act of converting emotions and images into words changes the way the person organizes and thinks about the trauma" (p. 8).

Writing is largely based on moments and images. Writers can make lists of things such as colors, feelings, and sounds. A piece of paper and a pen allow them to collect their thoughts; these inanimate objects, unlike people, are not impatient, nor do they become annoyed at images that do not form a story that makes sense. Writers have the power to write as quickly or as slowly as needed. Writers can arrange their pictures and take power over their prose until a story eventually emerges. The images are no longer uncontrollable; they are within the traumatized individual's control. The act of writing can be empowering to individuals as they try to make sense of incidents that initially seem indescribable.

Smyth and Helm (2003) point out that therapists have been using writing, especially journal writing, as a means of disclosure during the therapeutic process for decades. In addition to journaling, other types of writing may be valuable. Smyth and Helm are interested in a relatively recent type of therapeutic writing called Focused Free Writing (FEW):

> FEW involves asking participants to write about their deepest thoughts and feelings regarding the most stressful or traumatic event of their entire life. Typically, participants are brought into a research setting for several (typically three to five) sessions, usually on consecutive days. In these sessions, participants are asked to write about their assigned topic continuously for 20 to 30 min without regard for spelling or grammar. (p. 228)

Smyth and Helm believe FEW has great potential for trauma therapy.

In addition to the mental healing that writing provides, physical healing may also occur. Writing has been shown to enhance immune system functioning and reduce the number of physician visits (Pennebaker, Kiecolt-Glaser, & Glaser, 1988). Studies have shown that writing "increases antibody responses to the Epstein-Barr virus, and antibody response to hepatitis B vaccinations" (Pennebaker, 1997, p. 162). It also helps to increase t-helper cell growth (1997). Short-term changes in autonomic activity, such as lowered heart rate and electrodermal activity, are also produced by disclosure. Pennebaker (1997) has concluded that "the mere expression of trauma is not sufficient. Health gains appear to require translating experiences into language" (p. 164). Writing serves to translate experiences that an individual cannot express verbally. Writing also provides an outlet when no other outlet exists.

Without a supportive community, trauma victims bury their experiences beneath layers and layers of self-blame, guilt, and denial. The process of writing serves to integrate experience and document personal history. Memories, no matter how painful, make us who we are. By telling the story of our lives, we realize why we react the way we do in certain situations and why each of us is unique.

Unfortunately, some psychologists do not see the importance of community and disclosure. Instead, they would rather take the actual traumatic memory away by using drugs such as propranolol. According to Davis (1998), propranolol essentially blocks the ability to connect aversive emotions to traumatic

memories by acting as an antagonist on the B-adrenergic receptor. During
and after emotional experience, the B-adrenergic stress hormone systems are
activated, resulting in enhanced memory for the emotional event. In a study
conducted in 1994 (see Cahill, Prins, Weber, & McGaugh), participants were
given either propranolol or a placebo an hour before being shown a series of
slides accompanied by narratives. The emotionally neutral narrative described
a mother taking her son to visit his father, who worked as a laboratory tech-
nician in a hospital. The emotionally charged narrative started with the boy
and mother going to visit the boy's father at work, but in this version, the
two never made it to the lab because the boy was struck by a car and suffered
severe brain trauma. In addition, the boy's feet were severed, but a surgical team was able to reattach them. Participants were then given memory tests;
results showed that participants in the emotionally neutral scenario, regardless of whether they had received the propranolol, had similar recall. In the
emotionally charged condition, however, participants who were given propranolol scored significantly lower than participants who were given a placebo. The
results of this study show the profound impact beta-blockers can have in the
face of a traumatic event.

   According to Davis, the next step is to use propranolol to conduct a
controlled study with trauma victims. I think the thought of erasing a memory
from another human being is terrifying. The neurobiology of trauma victims may
leave them speechless, but with a supportive community and therapeutic writing,
their voices can return. Unfortunately, our society does not recognize this. It
was bad enough that we isolated victims from society; now we isolate them from
themselves.

References

Butler, K. (1996, March/April). The biology of fear. *Networker*, 39–45.

Cahill, L., Prins, B., Weber, M., & McGaugh, J. L. (1994). Beta-adrenergic
     activation and memory for emotional events. *Nature, 371*(6499), 702–704.

Davis, M. (1998). Neural systems involved in fear and anxiety. Symposium conducted
     at the University of Scranton, Scranton, PA.

Herman, J. L. (1992). *Trauma and recovery*. New York, NY: HarperCollins.

BEGIN YOUR ALPHABETICAL LIST OF REFERENCES ON A NEW PAGE. DOUBLE-SPACE THROUGHOUT. INCLUDE IN THE
LIST OF REFERENCES ONLY SOURCES THAT ARE REFERRED TO IN THE TEXT OF THE PAPER.

LeDoux, J. E., Romanski, L., & Xagoraris, A. (1989). Indelibility of subcorti-
    cal emotional memories. *Journal of Cognitive Neuroscience, 1*(3), 238–243.
    doi:10.1162/jocn.1989.1.3.238

MacCurdy, M. (1999). From trauma to writing: A theoretical model for practical
    use. In C. Anderson & M. MacCurdy (Eds.), *Writing and healing: Toward an
    informed practice.* Urbana, IL: National Council of Teachers of English.

Pennebaker, J. W. (1997). Writing about emotional experiences as a therapeutic
    process. *Psychological Science, 8*(3), 162–166. doi:970603308

Pennebaker, J. W. (2000). Telling stories: The health benefits of narrative.
    Literature and Medicine, 19(1), 3–18.

Pennebaker, J., Kiecolt-Glaser, J., & Glaser, R. (1988). Disclosure of trau-
    mas and immune function: Health implications for psychotherapy. *Journal
    of Consulting and Clinical Psychology, 56*(2), 239–245. doi:10.1037/
    0022-006X.56.2.239

Rauch, S. L., van der Kolk, B. A., Fisler, R. E., Alpert, N. M., Orr, S. P.,
    Savage, C. R.,...Pittman, R. K. (1996). A symptom provocation study of
    posttraumatic stress disorder using positron emission tomography and
    script-driven imagery. *Archives of General Psychiatry, 53*(5), 380–387.

Smyth, J., & Helm, R. (2003). Focused expressive writing as self-help for
    stress and trauma. *Journal of Clinical Psychology, 59*(2), 227–235.

van der Kolk, B. A., McFarlane, A. C., & Weisaeth, L. (1996). *Traumatic stress.*
    New York, NY: Guilford Press.

EXERCISE 8.14

Reread Jennifer Piazza's research paper and ask the following questions:

- What is her goal for writing?
- What is she trying to accomplish?
- What is the relationship between the sources of information she draws on and her own views?
Freewrite for ten minutes in response to these questions.

EXERCISE 8.15

- Form collaborative learning groups.
- Within your group, discuss the following questions: To what extent is Jennifer Piazza's paper an explanation of her own conclusions about the topic? To what extent is it an argument? Have the recorder note the high points of your deliberations.
- Reconvene the entire class. Each group recorder should explain the group's answers to the two questions. Then, discuss any disagreements among groups.

WORK CITED

Kelly, Kevin. "Scan This Book!" *New York Times Magazine* 14 May 2006: 43–49, 64, 71. Print.

An Anthology
of Readings

Natural Sciences and Technology

■ **The Scientific Method**

Science and technology are based on a **common methodology**, and thus scientific and technical researchers the world over share an approach to their work. Even though they may give conflicting answers to important questions in their disciplines, they rarely argue about the basic process of conducting scientific investigation. The specific means by which researchers discover, collect, and organize information is called **the scientific method**. This approach involves questioning, observing, experimenting, and theorizing. Drawing on previous knowledge and prior investigations, scientists ask questions not only about the unknown but also about phenomena that are supposedly understood. Often, they challenge commonly accepted beliefs as well as the conclusions of other scientists. Indeed, no fact or theory is exempt from legitimate inquiry. Even the most widely accepted ideas are continually reexamined. This questioning process helps make science self-correcting, since errors made by scientists can be detected and amended by subsequent investigation. The process is part of what we might call the "conversation" in scientific writing.

Scientific ideas must be confirmed through **verifiable observation** before they are considered fact. Assertions that cannot be supported by observation are generally greeted with skepticism by the scientific community. For phenomena that cannot be observed readily in nature, scientists design experiments that make events stand out more clearly. As with other information derived from observations, experimental findings are continually reexamined, and experiments are considered valid only if they can be repeated with identical results by different investigators. The "conversation" in scientific writing focuses upon this validation.

Scientists build **theories** to account for direct observations and experimental results. Theories are rules or models that explain a large body of separate facts. An example is the Bohr model of the atom, in which electrons orbit around the nucleus like moons around a planet. The Bohr model explains many basic observations made by physicists and chemists, but it is by no means the only theoretical description of the atom; quantum theory suggests an atomic model that does not include electrons in discrete orbits. Scientists often weigh competing theories that purport to explain the same facts. The other parts of the scientific method—questioning, observing, and experimenting—contribute to constructing and testing theories.

■ WRITING ABOUT SCIENCE AND TECHNOLOGY

Texts concerning science and technology can be separated into two groups: (1) **reports of original research**, which focus on a narrow topic, and (2) **summary or speculative articles**, which generalize about a body of specific information. Research reports are typically written for experts in scientific or technical disciplines. Footnotes in research reports generally focus on earlier studies directly related to the experiment in question. Summary and speculative articles are often directed to less specialized audiences. The footnotes in such academic articles may range far and wide as they address social, cultural, political, moral, or historical issues related to the topic. Consider, for example, the different sorts of documentation in Noel Sharkey's speculative article (Chapter 10), which considers the ethical consequences of using robots to care for children and the elderly, and in Thomas Colbridge's summary article (Chapter 11), which reviews the constitutional issues that arise from police use of thermal-imaging technology. Most of the articles in Chapters 9, 10, and 11 are summary and speculative articles written for a general audience rather than for an audience of professional scientists. These articles engage in conversation with one another and also with various forms of writing in other branches of science and technology, the social sciences, philosophy, law, religion, public policy, and so forth.

■ Organization

Research reports share **a common rhetorical pattern**. Scientists within specific disciplines have established standard methods for organizing research reports, and most journals that publish research results accept only articles written according to these formats. Summary and speculative articles, however, vary widely in rhetorical structure. Nonscientists who think the only aim of science writing is to relate established facts fail to recognize that much science writing argues a point. As you read through the next three chapters, notice that the majority of the articles are organized as arguments in conversation with the arguments of other writers. For example, the title of Kerry K. Howley's article "Who Owns Your Body Parts" (Chapter 9) indicates that the essay will touch upon concerns about bio-ethics and morality, and that it will do so from a legal point of view focused upon organ donation. The pursuit of science often gives rise to intense debate over what questions should be investigated, what observations are accurate, and what theories best explain particular observations. As a result, argumentative writing is common in science. In addition to argumentation, the full range of rhetorical patterns can be found in popular science writing.

Writing research reports according to a set organizational formula does have its drawbacks. In some cases, scientists may become so obsessed with fitting their work into a research report formula that they lose sight of the central goal of scientific research: an active pursuit of the truth. A similar problem sometimes surfaces in popular science writing in which the rhetorical pattern becomes more important than scientific accuracy. For example, Joseph Weizenbaum, an internationally known computer scientist, has noted that most essays about the societal impact of computer technology follow a set pattern. First, they survey the benefits to society of computers; then they consider some of the potential dangers of widespread computer use; finally, they claim that those dangers can be overcome with new technology and argue for a vigorous program to expand computer development and use. Weizenbaum implies that this simplistic, problem-solution approach to writing about computers may obscure the truth. Much popular writing about controversial science and technology follows a similar **problem-solution pattern**. To fit a set format, the science writer may ignore important facts or pass over alternative interpretations of certain facts. Consequently, analyzing rhetorical structure is an important element in comprehending science writing.

◼ Style

Although the tone of research report writing is almost always unemotional and authoritative, the tone as well as the style of summary and speculative science writing vary considerably. Once free from the constraints of the professional research report, scientists express emotions and personal attitudes, as do writers in other fields. As you read the article by Catherine Price in Chapter 11, notice that the writer uses a personal tone to discuss a technical issue: maintaining personal identity and privacy in an age of electronic surveillance.

No matter what the tone, a science writer establishes authority by providing **concrete evidence**. Even the most eminent scientists must support their theories with **verifiable observations**. In Chapters 9, 10, and 11, you will find that most of the authors include objective evidence to support major assertions. That evidence often comes from scientific investigation, but it also comes from **informal observations, anecdotes,** and **hypothetical cases**. For example, in Chapter 10, Sherry Turkle's "Alone Together: The Robotic Moment" offers personal observations about children's interaction with robotic pets and companions and then uses these observations as a basis for predicting how interactions between intelligent machines and humans will develop in the future. Most science writers are careful to build on evidence, even when they are writing for a general audience. Consequently, it is important for readers of science writing to identify and evaluate the evidence that authors provide in support of their claims.

Nonscientists are often amazed to find that different sources may present **conflicting versions of scientific "fact."** The same body of experimental evidence can lead to several different notions of what the truth is. When the experts disagree, science writers enter the conversation by describing precisely the various versions of the facts and, if possible, by trying to explain reasons for the differences of opinion. Sometimes, however, differences of opinion on scientific issues have nothing to do with scientific fact but, rather, reflect **conflicting personal or social values**. Science is not immune to the political and moral controversy that is part of other human activities. As you read the articles in Chapter 9 on human organ and tissue donation, you will see that the writers address social and moral issues. When writers do not support scientific claims with objective evidence, you should consider the moral, ideological, or emotional motivations behind their assertions.

Regardless of the specialized genre, writers in science and technology are expected to engage with one another in a sustained conversation on the topics they address. Most of the articles in the following chapters offer footnotes and bibliographies that report on the extent of the writers' conversation with others. Student papers in science and technology are likewise expected to join this kind of conversation. Here are some typical writing assignments in the sciences, as taken from exercises in the following chapters:

> In response to Kerry Howley's "Who Owns Your Body Parts?", draft an analysis essay in which you answer one or more of the following questions:
>
> - How might hospitals, insurance agencies, or the government set a price on human remains for "re-purposing"?
> - How might they guarantee the medical quality of human tissue for "re-purposing"?
> - How might they secure the legal acquisition and fair distribution of human tissue for "re-purposing"?

> It seems one thing to accept that an artificial-looking robot is not an authentic human being, despite its capabilities in executing humanoid tasks. But what happens when designers of robots can simulate fully convincing human appearances in a robotic android? Write a 500-word essay on how you might react to such human-looking androids when you suspend your disbelief and allow the robot to perform humanoid tasks.

> Do the events of September 11, 2001, justify employing technology that may violate individual privacy? Answer this question in a 1,250-word essay that draws on at least three of the articles in the chapter on "Privacy and Technology: Balancing Public Safety and Privacy."

Note that these assignments do not ask you to conduct original scientific research or even to draw inferences from scientific research or reports based on laboratory experiments. They do, however, require you to join the conversation about science and technology recorded in academic publications, summary and speculative studies, extended professional narratives, and journalistic reports.

Even nonscientists can evaluate intelligently many articles about science and technology addressed to a broad readership. As you read and think about the material in the next three chapters, keep in mind that many of the articles are organized as arguments and can be analyzed like other forms of argumentative writing. Ask yourself whether the article involves questioning, observing, experimenting, or theorizing—the basic components of the scientific method. Be sensitive to the author's tone. Look for evidence that supports the author's claims. Note the specific points on which the experts disagree, and try to account for those differences of opinion. Finally, consider the social or ethical questions that scientific advances raise. These procedures will help you read and write about science and technology with more understanding and better critical judgment.

WORK CITED

Weizenbaum, Joseph. "The Impact of the Computer on Society." *Science* 176 (1972): 609–14. Print.

Who Owns Your Body?

Ownership of one's body might seem the most natural and self-evident assumption that a person could make about his or her bodily tissue and organs. Modern science and technology have nonetheless complicated this assumption. With the development of life-enhancing procedures for tissue and organ transplants, the need for donor supply rises steadily, and with it a booming industry in the procurement, maintenance, and sale of appropriate body parts. From this industry, a host of social, moral, and legal consequences follows.

Because the supply and quality of available tissue and organ materials are always random and precarious, society has been reluctant to impose constraints that might limit tissue and organ availability. For vital organs such as kidneys, hearts, and livers, most world governments have designed strict procedures for their donation and procurement, and most governments have banned their sale for profit. The case is different with tissue donation because tissue is easier to come by and less difficult to transplant effectively. However, it is also more difficult to regulate and monitor. Consequently, donor agencies and tissue banks pursue aggressive recruitment policies unhampered by laws that prevent organ and tissue sale for profit.

Law and society both exercise less control over those who are willing to donate their tissue for research and medical recycling as well as over those who are willing to pay for tissue. A moral upshot is that compensation to donors and their families remains highly arbitrary and largely unregulated, while the task of obtaining donor tissue tends to favor those who are wealthy enough to pay any price to obtain what they want. As Kerry K. Howley writes in her article "Who Owns Your Body Parts?", we risk creating a system "in which the bodies of the poor are repurposed to serve the rich" (p. 300). At its worst extreme, such a system encourages desperately impoverished people to consider selling their own tissue and body parts as a last-resort means of survival. The traffic in such black-market matter exported from underdeveloped parts of the world to wealthy individuals in industrialized nations is already an ethical and moral problem of sizable proportions.

In addition to Kerry K. Howley's article, others in this chapter also focus upon controversies over the donation and sale of human substance across local, state, national, and international boundaries. In "Donors Have No Rights to Donated Tissue," Kristen E. Schleiter explores the consensus among legal experts that bodily donations no longer belong to the donors. Arthur Caplan argues in "The Trouble with Organ Trafficking" that financial incentives for such donations are unethical and will only compete with illegal black markets. "Why We Need a Market for Human Organs" by Sally Satel presents the case for establishing a public marketplace for donation as a legal counter to black-market practices. Student writer Caroline Rubin points out in her essay "The Gendered Language of Gamete 'Donation'" the surprising implications of sexist rhetoric in attracting donors. Such rhetoric may prove to be an illuminating point of entry when we examine the social, moral, and legal consequences of the new technologies that enhance as well as diminish our contemporary lives.

■ ■ ■ ■ ■ ■ ■ ■ ■ ■ ■

Who Owns Your Body Parts?
Everyone's Making Money in the Market for Body Tissue — Except the Donors

Kerry Howley

Kerry Howley is a senior editor at Defunct *magazine. She worked at* Reason Magazine *from 2005 to 2008 and was a senior editor at the magazine from 2007 to 2008. "Who Owns Your Body Parts?" received the 2008 Los Angeles Press Club Award for "Best Magazine News/Investigative Article."*

PREREADING

With advances in biomedical technology, the demand for human donor tissue has set a high price on the use of post-mortem human remains. What might be some of the moral, medical, and social consequences of this situation? How might hospitals, insurance agencies, or the government set a price on human remains, guarantee their medical quality, and secure their legal acquisition and fair distribution? Jot down some of your responses to these questions.

Alistair Cooke's body lay cold in the embalming room of an East Harlem funeral   1
home, suspended in the brief limbo between death and cremation. A "cutter" soon arrived to make a collection. He sliced open Cooke's legs, sawed the bones from the hip, and took them away. The quintessentially British presenter of *Masterpiece Theatre* and *Alistair Cooke's America*—the face of genteel, urbane Albion to millions of Americans—was being carved up for parts.

Howley, Kerry. "Who Owns Your Body Parts?" *Reason* 30.10 (Mar. 2007): 20–31. Print. *Reason* magazine and Reason.com. Reprinted with permission.

Cooke had died on March 30, 2004, the victim of a cancer that spread from   2
lung to bone. He left behind a 95-year-old disease-ridden corpse. Susan Kittredge,
Cooke's daughter, was mindful only of the potentially exorbitant funerary expenses
and flipped through the yellow pages in search of a good price. She eventually settled
on a funeral home with a $595 cremation fee.

The home, East Harlem's New York Mortuary Service, promised Kittredge a   3
box of ashes but said nothing of its bigger plans for her father, who would not make it
to the cremator whole. For a fee, the funeral director gave a New Jersey tissue procurement agency access to Cooke's remains. His bones, worth some $7,000, were prepped
for resale, and his records were falsified to alter his age and cause of death. Three days
later, as promised, Susan received a cardboard box of ashes by mail.

Alistair Cooke's remains were only the most famous of more than a thousand bod-   4
ies plundered by Michael Mastromarino, owner of Biomedical Tissue Services (BTS).
He had a simple business model: Pay funeral directors for access to bodies and resell
bones, heart valves, spines, and other tissues to biotech firms in need of spare parts.

A former dental surgeon, Mastromarino was familiar with the biotech industry   5
and its rising demand for transplantable tissue. While he was a legitimate practitioner,
he had co-authored a book about the benefits of replacing old with new, buoyantly titled
Smile: How Dental Implants Can Transform Your Life. He stopped transforming lives
through maxillofacial surgery six years ago, when his predilection for self-medication
led to trouble. He botched a surgery, and the patient charged that he was stoned on
Demerol as he did so. He lost the trust of his patients, and then he lost his license. BTS
was an attempt at fiscal redemption, and it proved very lucrative.

As the scandal unraveled in 2005, prosecutors revealed that Mastromarino had   6
netted $4.6 million in three years of back-room dissections. He paid undertakers
$1,000 a pop for providing access to the dead, paid cutters $300 to $500 for extract-
ing the most marketable parts, and, according to his lawyer, managed to take home
up to $7,000 per body. (One of Mastromarino's former employees contends the boss
was pulling in double that.) The New York Police Department later interviewed the
families of 1,077 people whose bodies were raided for spines, bones, tendons, and
other tissues. BTS had cut deals with funeral homes in New York City, Rochester,
Philadelphia, and New Jersey.

The company's work was amateurish at best, dangerous at worst. For families   7
who planned an open-casket funeral, BTS cutters would patch up gutted corpses as
best they could. Investigators later found legs stuffed with plastic piping of the kind
found at hardware stores. An employee said that he had used rolls of socks to the same
purpose, and police found surgical gloves sewn up inside hastily repaired remains.

Cooke's bones were sold to Regeneration Technologies, one of the country's   8
largest tissue banks. The company says Cooke's bones were deemed unsuitable
for implantation, but it can't say the same for other pieces of tissue it bought from
Mastromarino. The tissues BTS distributed ended up everywhere from a woman's
neck in Kentucky to a man's jaw in Tampa Bay. Hundreds of people wake up every
morning knowing that they are partly composed of stolen body parts.

In February 2005, Mastromarino and three others were indicted on 122   9
charges, including body stealing and opening graves. The grisly story received perhaps more media attention than any such scandal since a wave of body snatching in

the 18th century. A February 2006 *Paula Zahn Now* segment spun the story into the perfect media narrative, complete with a villain, a celebrity, and a whistleblower. But that telling, and many others, failed to point out that much of Mastromarino's basic business model was perfectly legal, common, and necessary to the biotech industry. If Mastromarino had been smarter, he could have made a fortune off body parts while staying well within the limits of the law.

Consider the massive market in which Mastromarino played but a tiny role. 10 Demand for human tissue has never been higher, and human remains have never been more valuable. According to the American Association of Tissue Banks, doctors perform more than 1 million tissue transplants each year, using everything from secondhand ligaments to hand-me-down heart valves. That fuels a thriving industry composed of tissue banks, biotech firms, and middlemen. Each year the industry takes in an estimated $1 billion in revenue, not a cent of which will go to the families or heirs of the donors who provide the raw material.

As the Cooke scandal deepened in early 2006, the Association of American 11 Tissue Banks sent its members a set of talking points, almost all of which emphasized the outlier status of Mastromarino's operation. There are important differences between BTS and legal banks, the association emphasized. Most crucially, Mastromarino never sought the consent of donor families before harvesting the tissue of their relatives. He conspired with funeral directors, lied about the quality of the tissue, and put transplant recipients in danger. "What these folks are alleged to have done violates everything we stand for and everything we are trying to do," says Robert Rigney, CEO of the association.

Yet a small but growing number of academics, doctors, and legislators believe 12 the Cooke scandal wasn't an aberration but an inevitability. They believe the tissue industry as a whole, even as it strives to distance itself from Mastromarino, is abusing families on a scale well beyond the reach of any one body broker. "The industry will argue that these are aberrant, isolated events that are irrelevant," says Todd Olson, a professor of anatomy and structural biology at the Albert Einstein School of Medicine. "My view is it's exactly the opposite. What we're really dealing with here is the tip of the iceberg."

Olson believes that the generosity of donors is being abused on an "epic scale" 13 by tissue procurement organizations, middlemen, and biotech companies that depend on tissue for their survival. With scientific advances there has emerged an enormously beneficial market in remains. But the players most fundamental to that market, donors, are locked out, prohibited by law from sharing in the benefits that others derive from their bodies. At the heart of this inequity is a confusion over to what extent we control our own persons—over whether we own our increasingly valuable component parts.

Resting in Pieces

Mastromarino found several buyers for his cadaveric contraband, among them a 14 highly profitable biotech firm known as LifeCell. The New Jersey-based corporation ranked 16 on *Fortune*'s list of fastest growing businesses in 2006, and with good reason: Its stock shot up 28 percent that year. The company owes much of the success to its flagship skin graft, AlloDerm.

"AlloDerm is a miraculous substance," says Maryland plastic surgeon Mark 15 Richards, "given its universal acceptance into the human body." Doctors have found that human bodies are far less likely to reject AlloDerm than previous skin substitutes. The graft melts into human flesh because it is *derived* from human flesh, the stripped-down product of bodies pulled apart after death.

Surgeons use AlloDerm for all manner of life-enhancing procedures, from re- 16 constructive breast surgery to hernia repair, as well as some perhaps less urgent operations. AlloDerm injections are a leading method of lip enhancement, an increasingly popular procedure among women. And the miracle substance is not without cosmetic benefit for men. "Some surgeons promote its use and employ it regularly for penis enlargement," says Stephen Giunta, a Virginia surgeon specializing in phalloplasty, "even though the manufacturer advises them not to do so."

AlloDerm is but one of many products that rely on donated bodies for their 17 manufacture. Another New Jersey company, Osteotech, processes donated bone into a putty surgeons use to patch small breaks. The publicly traded firm also sells demineralized bone as "dental dust," a product that accelerates healing after tooth extractions. DePuy Spine, a subsidiary of Johnson & Johnson, crafts raw tissue into specialized bio-implants for spinal surgery. The list of life-giving new technologies is long and growing.

Where bodies aren't mined for raw material, they're treasured for research. The 18 military buys cadavers to test explosive devices. Medical device companies buy them to test surgical equipment. Surgeons buy them to learn to use the same.

Tissue transplants range from the critical to the seemingly frivolous, but the in- 19 dustry's impact is clearly positive. The thriving market in tissue has enhanced the lives of millions of recipients, and it is a font of new products that will improve the lives of millions more. Tissue transplants can give sight to the blind and mobility to the bed-ridden. Before such operations were routine, limbs with cancerous bones would have to be amputated; now they can be replaced.

Law and custom both prohibit the sale of cadaveric tissue, a ban heartily sup- 20 ported by bioethicists like Arthur Caplan, the influential director of the University of Pennsylvania's Center for Bioethics. The prohibitionists warn of the degradation and commodification of human beings, but scientific progress has blurred the line between tissue and commodity. Doctors need a constant stream of remains to perform—and profit from—their work. The current compromise treats the body as property once it's in the hands of a corporation but as a "priceless" gift as it passes from a donor's family into the marketplace.

"We have a schizophrenic system," explains Lori Andrews, a professor of law at 21 Chicago-Kent College of Law who specializes in the legal implications of biotechnologies. Tissues, she says, "are being treated as property by the researchers and doctors secretly, and patients don't even realize that they have monetary value."

Current law proscribes the compensation of donors, ostensibly for their protec- 22 tion. But it also allows virtually anyone else to buy and sell tissue. Publicly traded companies are pumping out treatments that use the remnants of the dead to cure the bodies of the living; the preservation of life requires the commodification of death. "Bodies are in this stream of commerce, and that's not ultimately a bad thing," says Michele Goodwin, director of the Health Law Institute at DePaul University and author of the 2006 book *Black Markets: The Supply and Demand of Body Parts.* "But it's set up in such a way where only companies, brokers, and middlepersons receive compensation, and family members don't. It's an underhanded way of dealing with the public."

The Invisible Hand

The legal value of a human body, dead or alive, is zero dollars. "Under old English com- 23 mon law the body had no value at all," explains Ronn Wade, head anatomist for the state of Maryland. "Today if you look at not just transplantable tissue but the demand for body parts for medical research and training, and what the market will pay, the body certainly is valuable." The actual value of the body varies widely. A Brooklyn district attorney prosecuting the Mastromarino case says a single corpse can fetch $250,000, though most estimates are closer to a mere $100,000. One corpse can help heal 50 different people in the same number of countries; a tendon might be sent to Australia, a heart valve to India. Bones, skin, spines—all of it is worth something to someone. ↑ very quickly

The market is thriving and global demand has soared, but almost no one will cop 24 to buying and selling body parts. The 1984 National Organ Transplantation Act outlaws the transfer of "any human organ for valuable consideration" for use in transplantation, a proscription generally taken to include tissues as well as organs. But the law does al- low for "reasonable payments associated with the removal, transportation, implantation, processing, preservation, quality control, and storage of a human organ." Thus the tissue industry runs on what it deems to be "reasonable" terms. Those who strip skin for sales are "procurers," not vendors; their customers are "processors," not buyers. Tissues are not sold for prices based on demand but processed for a "reasonable price."

The first rule of the tissue market, in other words, is don't talk about the tissue 25 market. Patients would be far worse off if the trade in tissue were stanched, goes this line of thinking. The supply of life-enhancing materials would become as scarce as organs are now, creating shortages and jacking up prices. But to admit that the market exists, that profits are being made, is to risk violating the law and the social norms from which it springs.

Some donors have found ways to play along and make a buck, engaging the 26 language of donation even as they exact payment. Ova donors, for instance, can be "compensated" for their time at virtually any price the market will bear. Blood banks pay for plasma, sperm banks for semen. By contrast, the kin of deceased donors are never compensated, and they probably don't even know that their relatives' tissue will be sold.

Organs, unlike tissues, are not generally sold for profit, and the current donation 27 regime suffers from severe and deadly shortages. In 1986 the Uniform Anatomical Gift Act imposed a highly regulated system for managing organ donation. Kidneys, hearts, and lungs are tracked, waiting lists maintained. But supply is scarce, largely because the circumstances in which organ donation occurs are so limited. Organ donors must be young and healthy; typically they die of a catastrophic event such as a motorcycle crash. The government has also designated a single designated procurement organiza- tion for every locality. If you die at home and donate, the government knows exactly what organization gets to take your organs.

Tissue donation, by contrast, is lightly regulated and totally unmapped. The gov- 28 ernment never designated organizations for each area, and a variety of organizations compete for available bodies. Almost anyone of any age can be a tissue donor, and tissue never enters the tightly controlled, heavily regulated system of organ distribution. This relative freedom has huge advantages for burn victims and other patients who benefit from donor tissue, but it has upset established procurement organizations that, for the first time, have to compete for parts.

In the Washington, D.C., area, the local organ procurement organization— 29 the nonprofit with a monopoly on organs—also procures tissue. Hospitals notify the Washington Regional Transplant Consortium (WRTC) when someone is nearing death, and the nonprofit sends out family counselors to discuss donation with the next of kin. If consent is granted, WRTC sends a tissue recovery team to the hospital.

Where does the recovered tissue end up? According to Cindy Speas, WRTC's 30 director of community affairs, the organization is "not involved in any way with anything that is not a not-for-profit." And it's true that the consortium doesn't send tissue directly to corporations. Instead, WRTC provides tissue to LifeNet, another nonprofit, whose mission is to "improve the quality of human life" and "serve the community." LifeNet posted $107 million in revenues in 2004 for "tissue/organ procurement, processing fees, and reimbursements."

From LifeNet, the tissue enters the for-profit system. LifeNet has contracted with 31 LifeCell, the company that makes AlloDerm, along with other "alliance partners" such as Osteotech, the firm that makes bone putty. Standard and Poor's lists LifeCell's value at $888 million. From there, tissue can end up as replacement skin for a young burn victim or cosmetic filler for a thin-lipped socialite.

LifeNet is not alone in serving as the nonprofit face of a massive for-profit 32 industry. The Musculoskeletal Transplant Foundation is the world's largest tissue bank. Osteotech founded the bank to supply it with tissue in 1987. Osteotech and the bank are now separate entities, both pulling in a lot of cash. The Musculoskeletal Transplant Foundation reported more than $242 million in revenue in 2004.

Six years ago, two journalists at *The Orange County Register* undertook the 33 most extensive investigation to date of the legal tissue trade. They linked 59 non-profit tissue procurement agencies with publicly traded, for-profit firms. They also called each agency for comment, and the recorded answers are a jaw-dropping chronicle of deception and arrogance. The director of the nonprofit California Transplant Donor Network, which at the time was selling bone to Osteotech, ad-monished the *Register*, "It is not legal to sell organs and tissue." Others explained that families could not comprehend the distinction between nonprofit and for-profit. A spokesperson for the University of Miami Organ Procurement Agency, which sells skin and bone to the biotech company CryoLife, explained, "We can't be educating donors at the bedside."

Organizations like WRTC are among the most virulent critics of shady operators 34 like Mastromarino. They want higher barriers to entry for brokers: a stronger Uniform Anatomical Gift Act, a more heavily funded Food and Drug Administration with more stringent requirements. Ideally for them, the government would designate one tissue procurement agency per area, as it has done with organs, and leave the big play-ers with monopolies. "The FDA has very stringent requirements for tissue banking,"

Person who refuse customs & rule of a group.

says WRTC's Speas, "but they have not yet gotten the strictest requirements for tissue recovery agencies. Which is why we're seeing these mavericks out there."

Above all, such organizations emphasize the fact that they are nonprofit, blazon- 35 ing their tax status as incontrovertible evidence of ethical purity. Within the tissue business, these distinctions seem to hold little import. One industry expert, who wishes to remain anonymous because he is still heavily involved in tissue procurement, points out that employees of the nonprofit tissue banks generally make more money than those working at for-profit banks. Nonprofits simply turn earnings into salaries. "The companies are all run very similarly," Raj Denhoy, a medical device analyst with Piper Jaffray & Co., told the Associated Press in November. "It isn't as if the people in these companies aren't making a good living."

Selling the Gift of Life

Alistair Cooke never agreed to donate his body, but most tissues in the system come 36 from people who wanted their remains to be reused. Hospitals, hospices, and nursing homes have agreements with tissue procurement organizations, inviting them to contact the next of kin as a potential donor nears death.

About 30,000 Americans donated tissue in 2005, and the number rises every 37 year. Anecdotal evidence suggests that most of their families have no idea their tissue will be bought and sold. "There is a disincentive in alerting the families as to what might happen," says Goodwin, the DePaul University law professor, "because the families might—I think would—oppose their family members' ending up in the stream of commerce."

A 2001 report from the Department of Health and Human Services found that 38 tissue banking and processing practices have gradually diverged from donor families' expectations." Tissue banks have argued that grieving families are too fragile for hard-nosed talk about the marketplace, and no federal law requires tissue procurement organizations to tell donors that their loved ones may end up in a phalloplasty. The United Anatomical Gift Act includes stringent informed consent standards for organs [but] is silent on the matter of tissue.

Andrews, the biotech expert at Chicago-Kent College of Law, says a nonprofit 39 has asked her for legal advice on the extent to which it must inform donor families that tissue will be sold for profit. "The nonprofit tissue bank said, 'We don't want to mention [profits] because we're afraid people won't donate,'" she recalls. "But a key provision of informed consent is that you've got to tell people what's material to them. And if the tissue retrieval services think this is material, that people would do something different if they knew, then *of course* they have to tell them. But oftentimes they don't."

Donor recruitment agencies are famously aggressive, a phenomenon long 40 observed in organ procurement. As with organ donation, organizations can spend days coaxing a family into consenting. This process is probably best described by the University of Arizona sociologist Kieran Healy, who writes that we can think of procurement professionals as having industrialized altruism by turning it into a "resource-extraction problem." The marketing tactics are as rich as anything Jessica Mitford cataloged in her biting exposé of the funeral industry, *The American Way of Death*, four decades ago.

Tissue banks must recruit donors and avoid scaring away valuable, life-enhanc- 41
ing future parts; they need to give donors an account of what it means to donate.
Widely reported stories like the Alistair Cooke debacle threaten to lower the pool of
donors, so agencies have responded with media outreach. Like never before, organizations need to reassert control over the cultural narrative of donation. In large part,
that has meant taking control of the language, turning the lexicon of scandal into the
preferred patois of altruism. "I'd adore it if you'd look at the language we like to use,"
pleads Speas of the WRTC. "We don't like to use the word *harvest*."

The language WRTC *would* like journalists to use is compiled in a "reporter's 42
guide" available on the organization's website, a compact manual of right and wrong
words for journalists. The offending *harvest* has a line through it; the consortium suggests *recovery*. *Retrieval* is similarly verboten, as are *cadaveric* and *brain death*. The
preferred terms are described as "the correct media terminology," as if they've been
deemed acceptable by some centralized bureau of semantic and reportorial accuracy.

This is framing, and donor procurement agencies are well-versed in the art. 43
"How much will it cost my family to donate my tissue and organs?" reads a question
from a FAQ on the website of Community Tissue Services, an Ohio-based nonprofit.
"There is no cost," reads the reply, as if the organization were offering a valuable service at bargain rates.

At times, the language of donation and the language of medicine are just a 44
mouse click away. Take LifeNet, the Virginia nonprofit—not to be confused with
LifeBanc of Ohio, LifeGift of Texas, LifeSource of Minnesota, or LifeLink of Florida.
LifeNet runs two sites in two disparate languages, one donor-friendly and one doctor-
friendly. Accesslifenet.org is for customers looking to buy, not families looking to give.
The site stresses quality control, the engineering process, and service. "LifeNet's processing facilities," it explains, "are state of the art and have been designed to minimize
the risk of cross-contamination. They meet stringent regulatory, industry, and ISO
standards. LifeNet's allograft tissues undergo extensive development to ensure that the
products meet the surgeon's needs and preferences." Images of white-coated doctors
confer an air of clinical legitimacy, just above a note that customer service representatives are available "24 hours a day, 365 days a year."

LifeNet's "Donor Family Services Department" runs a very different site, hea- 45
lingthespirit.org, with a stated mission to "promote healing and peace for organ and
tissue donor families." The site's main image shows dappled light pouring through a
canopy of trees, the font of choice is a feminized cursive, and the sound of running
water loops endlessly in the background.

The Barnard anthropologist Lesley Sharp has called such framing "the greening 46
of the body." "Throughout the 1990s," she writes in the March 2001 issue of *American
Anthropologist*, "organ transfer has experienced an astounding proliferation of metaphorical language and ecological imagery." The imagery advances the idea that loved ones
are being recycled, reborn through the gift of tissue. Donor agencies spurn thoughts of
decay, death, and the loss of a specific person, steering patients toward highly generalized ideals of life and regeneration. The industry's websites and literature include far
more portraits of beaming toddlers than of the elderly who provide most of the tissue.

Where donor agencies do address loss, the language is elusive, metaphorical, 47
and almost comically devoid of content. A FAQ explains that "all grief is unique,"

and family members can send any questions about their own grief to a "bereavement specialist" by email. Customer service reps may be available 24/7, but the bereavement specialist requires at least one week to think up an answer. "You are brave to weather the pain of grief," reads one such long-awaited response. "It is a long road and a demanding journey, and not one that others can navigate for us." *mention*

48   Donor families are invited to add to an "online memory quilt," an oddly digital expression of grief suspended in cyberspace. Grieving family members are asked to choose from a list of greeting card-like messages, such as "Love so simple, so pure, so true...all in one precious bundle.../perfect beyond belief." They then choose from a set of brightly colored pictures—balloons, teddy bears, hearts—and add the square to the pixelated quilt.

The Disassembly Line *(a group of slaughtering dead body)* *computer network*

49   Predictably, the industry claims all of this is for the benefit of the donor family. Donor interests and those of the procurement organization are assumed to be identical. Speas says careful word use is necessary to protect grieving donor families from even more sorrow as they send a relative's body into the donation process. "With the BTS scandal, all the old words were used," she complains, "which makes the donor families who have given the gift just cringe. You know, it's really all about them."

50   P.R. machines like LifeNet and WRTC have well-established systems for recruiting and processing donors. WRTC has been around for 20 years, and for most of that period its monopoly on local organ donation prevented it from having to compete for the dead. But since no such monopolies are mandated for tissue donation, entrepreneurs have appeared, encouraged by insatiable demand.

51   One of those businessmen is Brent Bardsley, co-owner of the Anatomy Gifts Registry (AGR) in Hanover, Maryland. Brent and his brother Jim started out as tissue recovery coordinators at the Institute for the Advancement of Medicine, a nonprofit that recovers fetal tissue from terminated pregnancies for research purposes. In 1995 they decided to strike out on their own, founding AGR and eventually focusing on the recovery of adult cadaveric tissue, all of it gifted by altruistic donors.

52   AGR is officially a nonprofit, but it is also very much a start-up venture, and its operations reveal a lot about the tension between the rhetoric of altruism and the reality of the marketplace. Its headquarters sits in the last of a long row of single-story brick buildings near the Baltimore airport. Little distinguishes the outfit from its neighbors, most of which have chosen this location for the same reason: proximity to delivery planes. Some of the neighboring businesses are sending electronics all over the country and the world. Bardsley is doing the same with body parts.

53   Jim and Brent Bardsley process 40 to 50 donated bodies a month, extracting pieces and sending them off to medical device companies. Procuring tissue for research is less lucrative than selling parts for transplantation, but it is also subject to fewer regulations. When regulators complain that "you can start a tissue bank in a garage," they're talking about places like AGR. *producing money*

54   Indeed, AGR is part garage, part laboratory. As Jim and Brent show me the cavernous main storage site, a white van backs right into the facility. A woman jumps out, opens the back of the van, pulls out a covered body, and feeds it into a body cooler. One side

of the cooler opens at the drop-off point, and the other end opens into a dissection room. "We invented that system," says Brent, hands on his hips, ever the can-do business owner. Cracking open the body cooler to offer me a peek, Jim warns, "It's pungent in here."

The dissection room is small, cold, and filled with steel. A couple of sinks line one wall; dissection tables line the other. At harvest time, two of the Bardsleys' six technicians will dissect a body at once. The two will look to fill specific orders: limbs, internal organs, brain tissue, joints, and whatever else researchers have requested. "We try to customize the recovery to maximize the donation," Brent explains, "to use as many tissues as possible."

A steel specimen refrigerator holds extracted parts until the serological results come back, when they will be released for sale. Until then, the parts are wrapped in blue plastic and stored in freezers. The plastic package I'm staring at, Jim informs me, contains a pelvic girdle.

The Bardsleys are clearly more excited about an adjacent lab they're still preparing for use. As their business expands, they want a room to rent out so clinicians can train there in the facility, and they're building a sterile white space to meet the latest biosafety standards. At the same time, much in the facility is secondhand equipment cast off by medical schools. "That's a vintage autopsy sink," Jim says, pointing.

Back in the cavernous main facility, 20-odd freezers contain parts waiting to be shipped to medical device companies: spines, joints, whole torsos. On a raft above us are a set of Styrofoam containers for packing. The room is dominated by a tall, jet-black machine in its center. Brent flips it open to reveal a tiny pile of ashes and bone fragments. All the parts that don't make it to the airport come here, to the cremator. When the ashes are ready, they're scooped into a plastic black box for mailing, labeled with the tracking number.

AGR does not price parts based on demand. After all, on paper the Bardsleys aren't selling parts at all. They're selling recovery services at a "reasonable price." Because the same amount of effort goes into recovering a cadaver heart as a cadaver lung, internal organs cost one flat fee: The cost of a heart is the cost of a lung.

Brent says he hasn't made up his mind about whether donors should be paid for parts, but he understands the contention that donors deserve a piece of the pie. "Organizations are standing to make money, and why shouldn't the public be able to participate?" he reasons. But when money is involved, he adds, "the federal government views this as coercing people to donate. We can't be perceived as coercing people."

The Bardsleys have been criticized as unscrupulous simply for covering cremation costs for donors; they are assumed to "coerce" poor families into donating by absorbing the cost of disposal. The resistance to allowing cash for payment, says Brent Bardsley, would be far stronger.

But the Bardsleys do more than most to accommodate families; they're new and agile, making up the rules as they go along. Donor families worry about whether the ashes they get belong to their loved ones, so the Bardsleys have installed security cameras to record the drop-off-to-cremation cycle. Families sometimes want remains directed to certain research areas; when this is possible, AGR tries to comply. What families don't want, in many cases, is to know exactly what's going on—though the Bardsleys will show the facility upon request. "Most people," Brent comments, "don't ask for the grand tour."

an action or event regarded as morally or legally wrong & causing general public outrage.

Scandal and Reform   *make a change in order to improve it.*

During the last five years, scandals involving tissue procured and resold illegally   63
have chipped away at the neat separation between altruistic donation and big business. UCLA, Tulane, the University of Texas Medical Branch, and the University of
California at Irvine have all been accused of reselling bodies donated for research. To
get a sense of how many lawsuits are currently pending, consider the way corporations
have come to calibrate their legal troubles. "Of all the cases filed in state and federal
court," LifeCell attorney David Field recently boasted to the Associated Press, "it
appears less than five possibly involve LifeCell."

Doctors, journalists, and legislators are apt to blame the profusion of scandal on   64
the pursuit of profit. Calls for reform rarely suggest that donors should be compensated;
profit is perceived as the problem, not the solution. In April Sens. Charles Schumer
(D-N.Y.) and Patrick Leahy (D-Vt.) introduced the Safe Tissue Act, a bill that would,
among more defensible measures, require the secretary of health and human services to
"promulgate regulations defining 'reasonable payments'" for procuring and processing
tissue. Instead of letting middlemen set their own prices, the government would set the
cost of recovering tissue and thus the price of parts.

The bill never made it out of committee, though it is indicative of the quality   65
of solutions currently on the table. Price controls would do nothing to remove profit
from the system of exchange; biotech firms would still buy, manipulate, and resell
the tissue. While firms may find themselves paying less for donor tissue under such a
regime, families would remain uncompensated and uninformed. The market would
remain intact and unacknowledged, exploiting donors and their families.

The alternative reform—compensating donors, the crucial source of material   66
upon which life-giving treatments depend—has hardly been discussed. Tissue markets
are a well-kept secret, and when scholars talk about creating markets for body parts,
they're usually talking about kidneys, not skin and bone. The key difference between
tissue markets and organ markets is that the former don't have to be created; they are
already the primary means by which tissue finds its way from donor to recipient.

Compensation to donors might take a variety of forms, from reimbursement of   67
funeral expenses to charitable donation to direct payment. Tissue is already treated as
property once it is processed; if it were legal property before it left the donor's body,
sales would go to donors' estates along with other assets. Profits from their sale would
be willed along with the house and the car, left to favored grandchildren and pet
causes.

Many bioethicists worry that payment will create a two-tiered system, in which   68
the bodies of the poor are repurposed to serve the rich. This argument assumes that
those looking to sell tissue would be done material harm by actually selling it—that
the mere choice to sell is a form of coercion. Goodwin, the DePaul professor and
Black Markets author, argues that the poor have the most to gain. "I don't see any logic
in allowing companies to harvest individuals' body parts purely for financial gain,"
she says, "and meanwhile denying individuals the opportunity to pay off the costs of
funeral homes and medical expenses when their relatives die. Think about the cost
that poor families experience currently when they have to bury relatives. Their options
are, well, do we sell some furniture to pay for this funeral? Do we sell the car?"

The potential for wealth transfer is significant and, given the pace of biomedical 69 advance, sure to increase. And a formal market has another benefit, one whose necessity becomes more evident with each successive scandal: transparency. The same lack of transparency that discourages nonprofits from talk of moneymaking allowed Michael Mastromarino to strip-mine thousands of bodies, confident that potential donors wouldn't ask questions and biotech firms wouldn't look beyond the falsified records.

Exploitation and Repugnance

The history of transplantation has been one of overcoming visceral opposition — of 70 rejecting what the prominent bioethicist Leon Kass calls "the wisdom of repugnance." Kass, the former head of the President's Council on Bioethics, believes disgust to be "the emotional expression of deep wisdom." Wise or otherwise, repugnance has always fueled opposition to transplantation. When doctors performed the first successful kidney transplant in 1954, they were accused of playing God and cannibalizing the dead. When a South African doctor performed the first heart transplant 13 years later, he was met with the same refrain. Critics feared this new conceptual distance from the body; they warned of a future in which men and women treat the human machine like a run-down car, trading in old parts for new.

Half a century later, such predictions look less hysterical than prescient, less 71 nightmarish than benign. Other medical advances have accelerated the process by contributing to general longevity, increasing the likelihood that an individual will wear out old parts — shot knees, worn joints — and find himself needing a replacement. It wouldn't have comforted the critics to know it, but the ability to exchange human parts has become routine, its absence unthinkable. The slope has indeed been slippery, and the benefits have been incalculable.

What remains of that initial repugnance is arbitrary and inconsistent. Patients 72 have no problem paying for replacement parts, paying the surgeons who will implant them, paying the vast array of medical professionals who will nurse them back to health. For all the crowing over the benefits of altruism, no one has suggested that surgeons are tainted by the market that pays them so well; no one seems upset that biotech companies sell rather than donate their treatments. Patients and doctors cheer as new technologies find their way into the stream of commerce but recoil in revulsion at the thought of paying the donors at the source.

Beyond the visceral revulsion at Michael Mastromarino's ghoulish raids lies a 73 bigger and more important story, one that offends on another level. The tissue trade in its current form violates basic ideas of fair play, free exchange, equity, and honesty. These are wrongs at which our sense of repugnance has not diminished.

The Mastromarino scandal continues to unfold. In October 2006, Brooklyn 74 prosecutors issued yet another indictment, accusing Mastromarino of enterprise corruption. Two Philadelphia funeral homes were forced to close, and seven New York funeral directors pled guilty to related charges. A raft of post-transplant patients filed lawsuits, with others as far as Britain threatening to pile on.

Mastromarino, out on $1.5 million in bail, is looking at a possible 25 years in 75 prison. Meanwhile, LifeCell is set to report its most profitable year ever.

READING FOR CONTENT

1. List the types of scandal in paragraphs 1–18 that prompted the author to write this article.
2. Summarize Howley's explanation of the chief differences between human tissue donation and organ donation in paragraphs 24–35.
3. List the major issues raised by the testimony of scientists, social scientists, and lawmakers in paragraphs 20, 22, 38, 46, and 64.

READING FOR GENRE, ORGANIZATION, AND STYLISTIC FEATURES

1. How do paragraphs 36 and 41 mark a turning point in the author's development of her argument?
2. How do paragraphs 63–69 contribute to the author's argument?
3. Reread paragraphs 70–75. Do they offer a satisfying conclusion?

READING FOR RHETORICAL CONTEXT

1. Paragraphs 37–40 refer to academic opinions by professors of law, anthropology, and sociology about the marketing of tissue. How would these professors likely respond to the account of the Bardsley brothers' tissue-distribution business in paragraphs 51–62?
2. In paragraphs 70–75, what moral, social, and scientific contradictions remain unresolved?

WRITING ASSIGNMENTS

1. Use the "Prompts for Personal Response to the Text" on page 36 to write an informal response to Kerry Howley's "Who Owns Your Body Parts?" Then convert your informal response to a formal response essay. Use the tips we provide on page 39.
2. Draft an analysis essay in which you answer one or more of the following questions:

   - How might hospitals, insurance agencies, or the government set a price on human remains for "re-purposing"?
   - How might they guarantee the medical quality of human tissue for "re-purposing"?
   - How might they secure the legal acquisition and fair distribution of human tissue for "re-purposing"?

Donors Have No Rights to Donated Tissue

Kristen E. Schleiter, JD, LLM

Kristen E. Shleiter, JD, LLM, is a senior research associate for the Council on Ethical and Judicial Affairs for the American Medical Association in Chicago. She analyzes ethics policy and law and assists in developing and disseminating ethics policy and related materials.

Schleiter, Kristen E. "Donors Have No Rights to Donated Tissue." *American Medical Association Journal of Ethics* 11.8 (Aug. 2009): 621–25. Web. 28 Sept. 2010. <http://www.virtualmentor.org>

PREREADING

After reading the preceding article on differences between human organ donations and human tissue donations, jot down a few concerns that you might have about surrendering ownership of donated tissues of yourself or of persons close to you. What ownership rights seem most important to you as you reflect upon them?

Autonomy has been defined as "the quality or state of self-governing" [1]. In a health care context, respecting autonomy means allowing patients to make their own medical decisions. It also means allowing individuals to consent to participate in clinical research and to donate bodily tissues for research purposes. The boundaries of autonomy blur, however, once donated tissues leave the body, and the recipient researcher or university accepts the tissues.

The law has never established clear ownership rights in donated human tissues [2]. Historically, researchers and institutions have assumed that they retain the right to "collect, study, store, transfer, or dispose of tissue specimens and the associated patient data," such as patented gene lines or means of genetic testing [2]. Though the *Code of Medical Ethics* of the American Medical Association prohibits the use of human tissue and its products for commercial purposes without the informed consent of the donor, physicians and researchers have assumed that they can use patient tissues and other bodily substances to develop cell lines, genetic sequences, and other biologic products that may be financially rewarding [3]. Patents have been granted or patent applications filed for an estimated 20 percent of human genes [4]. Several court cases have challenged researchers' assumptions.

Moore v. Regents of the University of California

In the first case of its kind, the California Supreme Court held in *Moore v. Regents of the University of California* that individuals do not have an ownership interest in their cells after the cells are removed from their bodies. John Moore sought treatment from UCLA Medical Center (defendant) for hairy-cell leukemia. His attending physician, Dr. David Golde, recommended removal of Moore's spleen for therapeutic purposes. Golde and UCLA researcher Shirley Quan planned to use Moore's spleen tissue—which was "of great value in a number of commercial and scientific efforts"—for scientific study, a fact they never disclosed to Moore [5, 6].

Golde and Quan continued research on Moore for several years, causing him to incur inconvenience and expense associated with travel from Seattle to UCLA for visits that Golde misrepresented as medical appointments in the interest of Moore's health, when, in fact, the purpose of the visit was to draw samples for more research [2, 5-7]. Golde ultimately succeeded in developing a cell line from Moore's t-lymphocytes, and Golde, Quan, and the Regents of the University of California obtained a patent for the cell line then worth an estimated $3 billion [5, 6]. Golde also negotiated agreements for commercial development of the cell line and products to be derived from it.

Moore initiated a lawsuit against Golde, Quan, and the Regents, seeking to recover a share of the proceeds from the patented cell line. While the court recognized a physician's duty to disclose personal interests—research or economic—when seeking informed consent for a medical procedure, it ultimately found that the resulting patented cell line was the product of *invention*, not of the *donor* [5-7]. Even if the excised cells initially belonged to an individual, those cells were legally and factually distinct from the resulting research product [2, 5, 6]. Thus, the court held that individuals *do not* have an ownership interest in their cells after the cells are removed from their bodies [2, 5, 6].

The *Moore* decision remained the authority on a researcher's right to donated   6 human tissue until 2003, when the issue arose once again.

Greenberg v. Miami Children's Hospital Research Institute, Inc.

In *Greenberg v. Miami Children's Hospital Research Institute, Inc.*, the U.S. District   7 Court for the Southern District of Florida held that individuals have no property rights in body tissue and genetic material donated for research. The Greenberg family sued a physician-researcher and hospital after the researcher developed and patented a prenatal genetic test using blood and tissue samples donated by their family and others. The donated genetic material was used in the study of Canavan disease, a rare and fatal genetic disease that occurs most frequently in Ashkenazi Jewish families [8].

Daniel Greenberg had approached Dr. Rueben Matalon, a research physician,   8 to request his assistance in discovering the genes associated with Canavan so that tests could be administered to determine carrier status and allow for prenatal testing [6, 8]. Greenberg and other individual plaintiffs began supplying Matalon with genetic material including blood, urine, and tissue samples [6, 8]. Matalon soon identified an enzyme deficiency that was the cause of Canavan and developed a prenatal test to screen for the deficiency. After this discovery, several nonprofit groups began to promote Canavan disease testing.

In a second stage of research supported by Miami's Children's Hospital Research   9 Institute at Miami Children's Hospital (MCH), and using specimens donated by thousands of research participants, Matalon isolated and cloned the gene associated with Canavan. MCH Research Institute subsequently obtained a patent on the gene and related applications, including carrier and prenatal testing [6, 8]. In addition, MCH Research Institute enacted a marketing plan to enforce its intellectual property rights relating the tests. Annual royalties from the patent reached an estimated $375,000. To enforce its intellectual property rights, MCH Research Institute sent letters to clinical laboratories engaged in testing for Canavan and to the plaintiffs, informing them of the patent and MCH's intent to enforce the patent by charging a royalty fee of $12.50 per test [6, 8]. These letters informed Greenberg and others for the first time of MCH's intent to earn royalties from screening for Canavan [6, 8].

Greenberg and others filed a lawsuit in 2002 against Matalon, MCH, and MCH   10 Research Institute, claiming that the defendants had a continuing duty of informed consent to disclose any information that might influence the prospective subjects' decision to participate in the research [8]. Defendants breached this duty, Greenberg argued, when they failed to disclose the intent to patent the Canavan gene for their own economic benefit and by misrepresenting the research purpose on the written consent forms [8]. Plaintiffs alleged that they would have refused to participate in the research had they known of MCH's true intention to commercialize the genetic material and related testing [8].

While the court recognized that a medical researcher owes research participants   11 a duty of informed consent, it declined to extend this duty to cover disclosure of a researcher's economic interests [7]. The court noted in a footnote that the AMA *Code of Medical Ethics* required disclosure of a commercial interest, yet disregarded this opinion because it was enacted after the defendants' research had begun [3, 8]. The court reasoned that such a duty of informed consent would have a pernicious effect on medical research, in that "it would give each donor complete control over how medical research is used and who benefits from that research" [8]. Further, as a practical matter, retroactively imposing such a duty would "chill medical research," as it would force researchers to constantly evaluate whether a "discloseable event" had occurred [8].

Moreover, the court found as it had in *Moore* that a research product developed from human tissue is factually and legally distinct from the original excised tissue, such that a tissue specimen becomes the property of the researcher and thus prevents the donor from asserting rights in the resulting patent or commercial product [2]. Because the materials were voluntarily donated without a contemporaneous expectation of return, Greenberg and others had no acknowledged property interest in body tissue and genetic matter they had donated, even though commercial benefit accrued as a result [2, 6-8]. This holding was reaffirmed several years later in *Washington University v. Catalona*.

Washington University v. Catalona

In *Washington University v. Catalona*, an internationally known prostate cancer surgeon and researcher, William Catalona, at Washington University (WU) began asking patients to let him use for research the tissue removed during prostate surgery and other biologic samples [9]. Research participants were asked to sign one of various consent forms which included language: (1) acknowledging that the donor was making a "free and generous gift" of tissue to research that may benefit society, and (2) waiving ownership rights in the donated tissue or any medical or scientific product that resulted from research with the donated tissue [10]. All forms provided for patients' withdrawal from the research at will, a right also supported by the Uniform Anatomical Gift Act [9].

WU's biorepository amassed more than 30,000 tissue samples, 3,500 of which came from Catalona's patients [9]. WU considered the tissue samples not only a resource for prostate cancer advances, but also a source of capital for the university [9]. When Catalona wished to transfer 2,000 of the samples to a private laboratory for research, WU objected, noting that Catalona would essentially be appropriating materials "worth nearly $100,000 to the University" [9].

As the conflict escalated, Catalona left WU for a position at Northwestern University School of Medicine [9]. He informed his patients of his transfer and asked for permission to transfer their samples to Northwestern [9]. Six thousand patients consented to the transfer [9]. In response, WU both refused to authorize the transfer of samples and sued Catalona to enforce its refusal, claiming it owned the samples [9].

A group of patients added as necessary parties to the lawsuit claimed that they owned their tissue samples and advocated for their transfer to Northwestern to effectuate their original intent of having Catalona perform prostate cancer research [9]. The patients argued that Catalona's actions in transferring universities should not affect their ownership rights [9]. They argued that they donated to Catalona's prostate cancer reseach, not for the university to sell the samples to the highest bidder [9]. WU responded that the patients lacked ownership rights to the tissue, since the tissue was a gift to the university [9, 10]. Though the participants retained the right under federal law to withdraw from research and have their samples destroyed, the university argued, they did not have the right to direct and control use of the samples [9].

The Eighth Circuit Court of Appeals held that individuals who donate biospeci- 17 mens for research purposes *do not* retain ownership interest that would allow them to direct or authorize the transfer of those materials to a third party.

In this case, the research subjects had made informed and voluntary decisions 18 to participate in cancer research, and had donated their biological materials to WU as valid gifts [10]. This voluntary transfer of tissue and blood samples to WU demonstrated that the university owned the biological samples [10]. Whatever rights or interests the research subjects retained following their donation of biological materials, the right to direct or authorize the transfer of their biological materials from WU to another entity was not one of them [10].

The foregoing cases demonstrate that, while individuals have the right to donate 19 bodily tissues for research purposes, the right to own and control use of donated tissues vanishes once those tissues leave the body. The loss of ownership rights means loss of any claim to commercial benefit gained from cell lines or other commercial products derived from research on the donor's tissues. According to the AMA *Code of Medical Ethics*, however, potential commercial applications must be disclosed to a donor before a profit is realized on products developed from commercial materials [3]. Only with this knowledge can a donor truly make an autonomous decision to donate or not to donate his tissues.

References

[1] Merriam-Webster Online. Autonomy. <http://www.merriam-webster.com/dictionary/autonomy>. Accessed June 2, 2009.

[2] Hakimian R, Korn D. Ownership and use of tissue specimens for research. JAMA. 2004;292(20):2500–2505.

[3] American Medical Association. Opinion 2.08. Commercial use of human tissue. Code of Medical Ethics. Chicago, IL: American Medical Association. 2007. <http://www.ama-assn.org/ama/pub/physician-resources/medical-ethics/code-medical-ethics/opinion208.shtml>. Accessed July 2, 2009.

[4] Soini S, Ayme S, Matthijs G; Public and Professional Policy Committee and Patenting and Licensing Committee. Patenting and licensing in genetic testing: ethical, legal, and social issues. Eur J Hum Genet. 2008;16:S10–S50.

[5] Moore v Regents of the University of California, 793 P2d 479 (Cal 1990).

[6] Gitter DM. Ownership of human tissue: a proposal for federal recognition of human research participants' property rights in their biological material. Wash Lee Law Rev. 2004; 61(1):257–345.

[7] Piccolo KM. In the wake of Catalona: an alternative model to safeguard research participants' interests in their biological materials. Univ Pitts Law Rev. 2008;69:769–788.

[8] Greenberg v Miami Children's Hosp. Research Institute, Inc., 264 F Supp 2d 1064 (SD Fla 2003).

[9] Andrews L. Who owns your body? A patient's perspective on *Washington University v. Catalona. J Law Med Ethics.* 2006;34(2):398–407.

[10] *Washington University v Catalona*, 490 F3d 667 (8th Cir 2007).

READING FOR CONTENT

1. In paragraph 12, what clues does the author provide to be more precise about the time-line of legal decisions concerning donated tissue in three court cases, each separated from one another by "several years."

2. How does the case of *Washington University v. Catalona* differ from the two preceding cases about rights over donated tissue?

READING FOR GENRE, ORGANIZATION, AND STYLISTIC FEATURES

1. The author does not begin the article with any precise statement of thesis or argument. Why? Does she express any position or attitude about the issue she examines?

2. How would a preview of the article before reading it reveal its organizational pattern?

3. Summarize in your own words the legal reasoning implied in paragraphs 3 and 4, 11 and 12, and 16 and 17.

READING FOR RHETORICAL CONTEXT

1. Reread paragraphs 5, 12, and 18, which summarize the court's verdict for each case. Does the author express any position or attitude about these verdicts?

2. What might the author's brief professional biography prefacing the article imply from the outset about her position or attitude?

WRITING ASSIGNMENTS

1. Use the "Prompts for Personal Response to the Text" on page 36 to write an informal response to Kristen Schleiter's "Donors Have No Rights to Donated Tissue." Then convert your informal response to a formal response essay. Use the tips we provide on page 39.

2. Write a comparative analysis of Schleiter's essay and Kerry Howley's "Who Owns Your Body Parts?" How do the views in these two essays relate to one another as though they were part of a conversation or a give-and-take of interdependent ideas?

The Trouble with Organ Trafficking

Arthur Caplan

Rhetorical analysis p. 28

Abortion, women's rights

Why experience in high school about economics isn't sufficient. Needed to grow up to understand value of money more.

Arthur Caplan is the Emanuel and Robert Hart Professor of Bioethics and the director of the Center for Bioethics at the University of Pennsylvania. He is the author or editor of twenty-nine books and over 500 journal articles. He is currently the co-director of the Joint Council of Europe/United Nations Study on Trafficking in Organs and Body Parts.

Caplan, Arthur. "The Trouble with Organ Trafficking." *Free Inquiry* 29.6 (October/November 2009). Web. 15 Aug. 2010. <http://www.secularhumanism.org/index.php?section=library&page=caplan_29_6> Reprinted by permission of the author.

PREREADING

What might the title, the author's position as a professor of bioethics, and the name of the journal in which this article appears, *Free Inquiry*, suggest about its argument?

Levy Izhak Rosenbaum, an Orthodox Jewish rabbi in Brooklyn, New York, called   1
himself a "matchmaker." However, he was not arranging dates for his congregants.
Rosenbaum is one of five rabbis indicted for brokering the sale of black-market kidneys and livers. He found poor, vulnerable people in Israel and allegedly paid them
$10,000 to travel to the United States to sell their kidneys or a piece of their liver to
patients awaiting transplants in various U.S. medical centers. For a religious leader,
Rosenbaum was quite a businessman. He pocketed as much as $160,000 for serving as
a middleman in this organ-marketing scheme.

This is the first known instance of trafficked human organs reaching patients in the   2
United States, but many other cases of organ trafficking occur around the globe. In the
past few years, wealthy persons needing transplants have traveled from the United Arab
Emirates to Sri Lanka, from the United States to Azerbaijan, and from many nations
around the world to Pakistan, Egypt, China, and Iraq in pursuit of kidneys and livers.

In addition to moving sellers of organs to hospitals where their parts can be sold   3
to wealthy recipients, there is also a market in human tissues obtained from cadavers.
Corneas have been trafficked in Bulgaria. Skin obtained in the Netherlands has been
sold in the Czech Republic. Tissues from Pakistan have been sold for profit in the
Netherlands. Bone and fat from the United States has wound up in many nations and is
also sent across state borders in pay-for-parts schemes. Brains, bone, and other body parts
have been removed without adequate permission at funeral homes and morgues for transplant use, teaching, and research purposes in a number of locations in the United States.

One might think the reaction to this heinous trade in human beings and flesh   4
might elicit strong moral condemnation from all quarters. And, in one sense, these
practices do. It is clearly unethical to exploit the living by treating them as nothing
more than mobile parts farms—or the dead as a free-fire zone from which those who
deal with the bodies of the deceased can make money by pirating pieces and selling
them. It is very hard to find anyone willing to defend these black-market schemes,
especially when the outcomes for both those who sell and those who buy are much
worse than would be expected with legitimately obtained organs and tissue.

But some observers of the extensive illicit trade in persons to obtain organs, body   5
parts, and tissues argue that the problem is not harvesting the living or the dead for
money but rather that such activities are illegal. To them, the problem is not paying
people for their parts but the fact that the practice is outlawed and thus occurs underground where abuses can and do take place.

Proponents of markets in body parts argue that the only way to counter the   6
shortage of organs and tissues available for transplant is to legitimize the international
trade that is already occurring sub rosa in people, organs, and tissues. Given the gap
between supply and demand, those in need will do whatever they can to obtain organs
and tissues for themselves. Rather than try to battle an underground market, we should
simply legalize it and regulate it as necessary.

There are four major problems with the conclusion that the way to combat   7
organ trafficking is to make it legal. First, there is no reason to think that most nations

have the resources to regulate a market in organs effectively. After all, even the United States, Britain, and Germany proved unable to regulate their banking, housing, and securities sectors.

Second, there are other ways to expand the availability of organs and tissue that do not involve treating human beings as commercial body-parts factories. Nations could institute presumed-consent policies, asking those who do not want to be donors to carry cards or register their objection in computer registries. When supplemented with appropriate training and resources, these systems have proven very effective in Spain, Belgium, Austria, and other nations.

Third—and perhaps the greatest problem with legalizing organ and body-part markets—is that such markets prey on the grim circumstances of the poor. Fourth, they clearly violate the medical ethics of physicians and health-care workers.

Only the poor and desperate will want to sell their body parts. Faced with fiscal ruin or grinding poverty, it may be a "rational" decision to sell your body parts (or for that matter your baby or your body into prostitution or slavery), but that does not make it a matter of free, voluntary choice.

Having a wealthy person wave a wad of bills in your face while you watch your child go hungry because you have no job is not exactly a scenario that inspires confidence in the "choice" made by those with no options other than to sell vital body parts. Talk of individual rights and autonomy is hollow if those with no options must "choose" to sell their organs to purchase life's basic necessities. Choice requires information, options, and some degree of freedom, as well as the ability to reason about risks without being blinded by the prospect of short-term gain. If you have no real options, you have no real choice. All markets do is put a polite façade on exploitation.

Selling organs, even in a tightly regulated market, violates the existing bioethical framework of respect for persons since the sale is clearly being driven by profit. In the case of living persons it also violates the ethics of the health-care professions.

The core ethical norm of the medical profession is the principle "Do no harm." The only way removing an organ from someone seems even remotely morally defensible is if the donor has *chosen* to undergo the harm of surgery solely to make money. The creation of commerce in body parts puts medicine in the position of removing body parts from people exclusively to abet those people's interest in securing compensation as well as to let middlemen profit. Is this a role that the health professions can ethically countenance? In a market—even a regulated one—doctors and nurses still would be using their skills to help living people harm themselves solely for money. In a cadaver market, they would risk making families and patients uncertain about the degree to which appropriate care was being offered and continued if a person might be "worth more dead than alive." The resulting distrust and loss of professional standards is a high price to pay to gamble on the hope that a market may secure more organs and tissues for those in need.

Keeping trafficking in organs and tissues illegal is the only policy option that makes ethical sense. If transplant centers and surgeons are held accountable for knowing all they can about where their donors and organs come from, that will go a long way in making it possible to keep trafficking in check.

READING FOR CONTENT

1. Summarize the four major reasons why the author, in paragraphs 7–10, opposes the legalization of selling donor organs and tissues.

2. Construct a "graphic overview" of Caplan's arguments against the legalization of selling donor organs and tissues. (See Chapter 2 for suggestions about how to construct a graphic overview.)

READING FOR GENRE, ORGANIZATION, AND STYLISTIC FEATURES

1. Why does the author admit in paragraph 4 that it is hard to find people who defend black-market schemes that profit from donor harvesting?

2. Summarize the four arguments in paragraphs 7–9 against those who would legalize for-profit donation.

3. Why does the author focus in paragraph 13 upon the core norm of medical ethics, "Do no harm"?

READING FOR RHETORICAL CONTEXT

1. What rhetorical techniques does the author use to dramatize the problem of trafficking in body parts and for-profit donation?

2. Why does the author argue in paragraph 11, "If you have no real options, you have no real choice"?

WRITING ASSIGNMENTS

1. Take the graphic overview that you constructed in response to Question 2 in "Reading For Content" above and convert it into a 200- to 250-word summary of Caplan's essay.

2. Using your summary of Caplan's essay, write a comparative analysis of that essay and Kerry Howley's "Who Owns Your Body Parts?" What points of view emerge with regard to the topic?

Why We Need a Market for Human Organs

Sally Satel

Sally Satel, M.D., is a practicing psychiatrist. She is also a resident scholar at the American Enterprise Institute and editor of When Altruism Isn't Enough: The Case for Compensating Kidney Donors *(2009).*

PREREADING

After having read Caplan's objections to for-profit donations of human body organs, can you think of some morally cogent and socially just reasons to endorse the public sale of body parts by willing donors? Jot down your responses.

Gavin Carney, an Australian nephrologist, held a press conference in Canberra recently to urge that people be allowed to sell their kidneys. "The current system isn't working," he was quoted in the Sydney Morning Herald. "We've tried everything to drum up support" for organ donation, but "people just don't seem willing to give their organs away for free."   1

For $50,000, however, some Australians probably would donate organs. This is the amount that Dr. Carney, a professor at the Australian National University, suggests the federal government, "with proper ethical controls," should offer willing donors. He would have the government repeal the ban on kidney sales so it can purchase and distribute organs to patients languishing on dialysis.   2

Dr. Carney wants to keep desperate patients away from black markets. But until the kidney shortage is resolved, patients in Australia—along with those in countries all over the developed world—will continue to resort to them. The World Health Organization estimates that 5% to 10% of all transplants performed annually take place in the clinical netherworlds of China, Pakistan, Egypt, Colombia and the Philippines.   3

Because of the global organ shortage, thousands of patients die unnecessarily each year for want of a kidney. (In my case, I was lucky to have received a kidney from a friend.) And because organ sales are illicit, corrupt brokers may deceive indigent donors about the nature of transplant surgery, cheat them of payment, and ignore their postsurgical needs and long-term complications. The only way out is to increase the supply of available kidneys—whether by a cash payment to potential donors or through some other form of compensation.   4

Unfortunately, most of the world transplant establishment does not share this view. Instead, organizations such as the WHO and the international Transplantation Society focus on the obliteration of illicit markets.   5

The latest country to "get tough" is the Philippines. A few weeks ago, the government banned the sale of kidneys to foreigners. The reverberations are already being felt; a recent headline in the Jerusalem Post read, "Kidney Transplant Candidates in Limbo after Philippines Closes Gates." (Israel has one of the lowest rates of donation in the world, so the government pays for transplant surgery performed outside the country.)   6

Similarly, patients from Qatar who traveled to Manila are "looking for alternative solutions," according to The Peninsula. Many had turned to the Philippines because countries such as China, India and Pakistan have begun cracking down on illicit organ sales.   7

But the prohibition policy urged on these countries will only end up pushing organ markets further underground, or cause them to blossom elsewhere. World health authorities should direct their passion toward promoting a legal apparatus for exchange.   8

To do so, they'll have to relinquish some gross misconceptions.   9

One is that a legal system of exchange will inevitably replicate the sins of unau- 10 thorized markets. "We don't want to open up that type of exploitation," warned Nicola Roxon, Australia's federal minister for health, when she heard Dr. Carney's proposal. But he is not promoting a free-for-all. His goal is a regulated, transparent regime backed by the rule of law and devoted to donor protection.

Another misconception is that a compensation system inevitably preys on des- 11 perate people. "They will be the only ones who would put up their hands," said Dr. Tim Matthews, the head of the advocacy group Kidney Health Australia.

One way to circumvent this risk is by not catering to desperate people. A model 12 system could establish a months-long period of medical screening and education. By providing in-kind rewards financed by the government—such as a down payment on a house (one of Dr. Carney's suggestions), a contribution to a retirement fund, or lifetime health insurance—the program would not be attractive to people who might otherwise rush to flawed judgment (and surgery) on the promise of a large sum of instant cash.

Would prospective donors lie about their health to be eligible for compensation? 13 An irrelevant worry in the context of regulated exchanges, since they would have to undergo rigorous medical testing over several months, which is the standard of care for altruistic donors. And donors or health-care professionals would be legally liable for any harm suffered by a patient as the result of receiving a diseased or substandard organ.

The way to stop illicit transactions—and the depredations of underground 14 markets—is to sanction legal exchanges.

READING FOR CONTENT

1. Summarize the information that Satel provides in paragraphs 1–7 about the social problems of black-market practices.
2. Paraphrase from paragraphs 10–12 the misconceptions about legal compensation for body parts that Satel urges us to address.

READING FOR GENRE, ORGANIZATION, AND STYLISTIC FEATURES

1. Do the figures and statistics that Satel presents in paragraphs 2–3 seem reasonable and reliable?
2. What argument does Satel formulate in paragraphs 5–8 to refute the view that financial incentives for voluntary donation are unethical?
3. How do the misconceptions that Satel puts forth in paragraphs 10–12 argument for establishing a public marketplace for organ donation?

READING FOR RHETORICAL CONTEXT

1. What is the effect of the author's personal remark in paragraph 4, "In my case, I was lucky to have received a kidney from a friend"?
2. In paragraphs 10–12, how does the author develop a positive argument about the value of legalizing for-profit organ donations?

WRITING ASSIGNMENTS

1. Write a 150-word précis of Sally Satel's "Why We Need a Market for Human Organs." Use the "Procedure for Writing a Précis" in Chapter 2.

2. Using your précis, write a 500-word formal response to Satel's article, either endorsing her proposals or rejecting them on critical grounds of your own.

one of the cells that join together to begin making a person

The Gendered Language of Gamete "Donation"

Caroline Rubin

Caroline Rubin is a graduate of MIT. She received the Kampf Prize from the university's Program in Women's and Gender Studies for this essay submitted in 2008 when she was a senior majoring in brain and cognitive science and anthropology.

PREREADING

Reproductive science has advanced to levels of sophistication that invite commercial applications of its discoveries. College students seem particularly vulnerable to requests for donating their reproductive services for commercial uses. Jot down some of your observations about differences between appeals to male students and appeals to female students in this regard.

Advertisements soliciting gamete donors have become such a ubiquitous fact of   1 university life that for most college students, the brightly colored flyers proclaiming "Egg Donors Wanted!" and "Donate Your Sperm!" are hardly worth a second look. But we should stop to examine these seemingly innocuous pieces of bulletin board clutter, because beneath their glossy surface lie subtle messages about gender roles, sexuality, and morality. Here I wish to examine the public discourse surrounding gamete donation in accordance with the Foucauldian tradition of analyzing discourse as it relates to knowledge/power, a relation that is especially interesting as gamete donation discourse subtly reflects and reinforces the ideologies of wage labor and gender under capitalism, and a sexist sociobiology. I do not wish to make any implications about the motivations and experiences of actual gamete donors (for an ethnography of donor motivations and experiences, see Ragone 1999).

Gamete donation refers to the process by which men or women provide gametes   2 (sperm or eggs, respectively) for the express purpose of creating a baby, often for an infertile couple. The use of the term "donation" to describe what is ostensibly a commercial transaction—the "donor" provides a product, the recipient pays for it, and the transaction is complete—attempts to mask the commodification of human tissue implied by these transactions, in much the same way blood and organ donation are described in terms of giving the "gift of life" to ameliorate societal discomfort with the "commodification of life" (Layne 1999:3). But unlike blood and organ donation, the tissue changing hands in gamete donation is gendered—androgynous donors do not provide generic gametes; men provide sperm to replace the sperm of other men, and women provide eggs to replace the eggs of other women. Emily Martin has shown that the language used to describe sperm and eggs in bioscientific discourse (e.g., in scientific textbooks and papers) is highly gendered (1991), and so it is not surprising to find that the everyday language surrounding sperm and egg donation is highly gendered as well. The types of ads used to recruit gamete donors, the criteria they must meet to donate, and the language surrounding gamete donation are all different for male versus female donors. These differences reflect pervasive societal views about sexuality, morality, and gender roles.

both male female CXS

advertisment

Gendered Advertisements: "Supplementing Your Income" Versus "Donating Your Heart"

Sperm and egg donors are targeted through different types of advertisements, and careful examination of these differences reveals their basis in both reflecting and reinforcing differential attitudes towards men and women as sexual beings and as potential parents.   3

Typically, ads soliciting sperm donors prominently feature the amount of   4
money being offered per "donation," as well as a list of additional donor benefits offered by the particular agency, such as "minimal time commitment," "receive free health and genetic screening," "supplement your income," or "many extras, including movie tickets and gift certificates." These financial benefits are spoken about in terms of "earning" or "making," and correspondingly, a quick internet search of "sperm donation" produces links not just to sperm banks, but to job listings. Sperm donation ads are also typically very illustrative, and often feature decorative cartoon images of sperm intended to be amusing or otherwise attention-grabbing. For example, a recurring MIT campus newspaper advertisement reads "got sperm?" in a large font, but the question mark has been replaced with the image of a sperm with a tail curved into the shape of a question mark. A poster on the T features a large dollar sign being swarmed with sperm on all sides, similar to the way sperm are typically portrayed as swarming an egg.

In contrast, ads soliciting egg donors typically emphasize the philanthropic   5
aspects of egg donation, with phrases such as "Help loving couples who want to have a baby!" or "You're not just donating your eggs, you're donating your heart." Instead of offering commercial incentives such as free medical exams and movie tickets, egg donation agencies offer emotional incentives such as being able to choose the couple receiving the eggs and whether to be a known or anonymous donor. The monetary offer in egg donation ads is not an "earnings," it is a "compensation," and internet queries for "egg donation" produce many egg donation agencies, but no job listings. Egg donation ads do not feature pithy catchphrases, and they certainly do not feature cartoon eggs in the shape of a dollar sign. If they feature any non-verbal component at all it is a picture of a cooing baby, often accompanied by a portion of

a smiling adult female face, a type of familial portrait that is altogether lacking from sperm donation ads.

Why is it that sperm donation ads use amusing cartoons to target men looking   6
to "earn" a little extra spending money, but egg donation ads use photos of babies to target women looking to help infertile couples "realize their dreams," and only incidentally receive monetary "compensation"?

A simplistic explanation is that different procedures are required to donate   7
sperm versus eggs; it is difficult to imagine the necessity of "compensating" a man for the inconvenience of masturbating to produce donor sperm, but easy to imagine why women, who must undergo invasive and unpleasant medical and surgical interventions to produce donor eggs, deserve to be compensated for their efforts. But this difference cannot explain the reverse asymmetry in remuneration language — if men earn money for the sperm they produce, why cannot women earn money for their eggs?

A deeper factor contributing to this difference is rooted in the historical Euro-   8
American ideal of "separate spheres" for men and women, which suggests that commodity exchange and wage labor should occur exclusively in the public sphere of men, while reproduction and family should be located securely in the private sphere of women. While women are no longer confined to the private sphere and men are no longer exempt from it, ideology does not always evolve at the same rate as the behavior it purports to explain. Accordingly, male gamete donors are targeted with advertising techniques similar to those used to market any public sphere commodity, and are told they will earn money based on how much product they produce. Women are targeted with private sphere images of babies and families, and told they will be compensated for their inconvenience, not paid for their product (Ragone 1999). This rhetoric of "compensation," however, is clearly only a superficial attempt to obscure that donated eggs, like donated sperm, are bought and sold on the market like any other commodity. If the remuneration offered to egg donors was only compensation for their inconvenience, we would not see ranges in remuneration offers from $5,000 for "average" eggs to $100,000 for the eggs of a woman who is "5'9 or taller, Caucasian, very attractive (modeling experience is a plus)...college educated, [and with] a history of participating in athletics or dance" (http://www.elitedonors.com/index3.html), since surely the latter woman is not inconvenienced twenty times more by egg donation than the former. It is also telling that the payment scheme at the first egg donation facilities in the early 1980s was not a flat compensation, but a base fee plus a bonus for every egg that was successfully recovered (Corea 1985). Again, it is difficult to imagine that a woman is proportionately inconvenienced based on how many eggs she produces, given that the procedure she must undergo to produce them is the same if she ends up with zero eggs or with twenty.

The separate spheres argument alone cannot explain the difference in donation   9
language, however, since even if men as workers belong in the public sphere of work, their sperm belongs in the private sphere of reproduction. Yet as we have seen, male gametes can more easily make the transition from private to public sphere than female gametes can. To understand the origin of this difference, it is necessary to examine the screening process male and female gamete donors must go through, and the qualities of what makes a "proper" sperm or egg donor these processes reveal.

Limited by gender

Gendered Donation Criteria: Seeking Income Versus Accepting Compensation

As we have seen, ads soliciting gamete donors target the financial interests of men 10 and the humanitarian interests of women. However, this distinction does not stop at recruiting donors; it is also used as a selection criteria for weeding out "appropriate" donors from the sea of "inappropriate" ones. While both egg and sperm donation applications include questions about physical features, college attendance, occupation, and medical history, only egg donor applications include questions such as "Why would you like to become a donor?" (conceptualoptions.com), or "Please describe how religion affects your egg donation" (aplusegg.com). Women's answers to these questions are instrumental to whether or not they will pass the screening (Ragone 1999); women who express any motive besides helping infertile families are routinely not selected as donors, despite the fact that after being accepted as donors, 76% of women admit that their decision to donate was at least in part financially motivated (ibid.).

Donation agencies are not unique in questioning the motives of egg, but not 11 sperm, donors. The rising "compensation" rates paid to egg donors have led to public concerns about the ethics of paying money for gametes (e.g., Kolata 1998, Irvine 2007), but largely, if not entirely, absent from these discussions is the fact that sperm donors also receive money in exchange for gametes, a practice which both predates and outnumbers egg donation for money. Tellingly, the Wikipedia entry on egg donation includes a subheading on "Donor Motivation" (with "altruism" listed first), while the entry on sperm donation does not.

feelong interest

Why this insistence that egg donation be motivated by altruistic instead of 12 financial interests? A partial explanation can be found in the separate spheres ideology previously discussed, and the resulting "moral threat" of allowing the "invasion of the human and sacralized world of kinship by economistic principles deemed appropriate only to the world of things" (Kopytoff 2004: 272). But why then is only selling eggs a moral threat, and not selling sperm? The answer lies in the gendered division of reproductive roles. Motherhood is seen as central to womanhood to a much larger extent than fatherhood is to manhood, and female sexuality is seen as much more directly linked to female reproduction than male sexuality is to male reproduction—hence the difficulty of members of the "voluntary motherhood" movement of the early twentieth century in promoting a female-controlled method of birth control, despite the availability and moral acceptance of male-controlled methods (Gordon 1974). Popular scientific discourse is full of evolutionary accounts that attempt to naturalize this socially created distinction. Many people are by now familiar with the sociobiological narrative of the prolific caveman looking to spread his seed as far and wide as possible evolving into the modern sexually voracious and paternally challenged man, while the cavewoman attempts to save her limited reproductive resources for a powerful mate and evolves into the contemporary sexually choosey and inherently maternal woman (e.g., Rhoads 2004). This narrative, combined with the fact that sperm donations are produced through masturbation and egg donations are not, explains the ease with which sperm can easily leave the private sphere while eggs cannot—men's sperm were already in the public sphere to some extent, or at least their sexuality was, because it is assumed to be too voracious to be satisfied by just one woman, neatly confined within the private sphere. Women's sexuality, on the other hand, is confined within the private sphere (or must be made to appear that way), thereby making the free market availability of their fertility (and the sexuality it is frequently conflated with) morally unacceptable. To further illustrate this point, let us turn to the popular discourse surrounding gamete donation.

Gendered Discourse: "Manly Urges" Versus "Prostituted Maternity"

The conflation of fertility with sexuality pervades the popular discourse of gamete donation, often in quite overt ways. Cartoons depicting the sexual voraciousness of sperm donors and the sexual satisfaction they derive from donation are omnipresent, as is sperm donation-themed pornography. An article on the shortage of sperm donors in the UK is topped with a photograph of an attractive woman wearing a tight-fitting shirt that says "we want your sperm," and a fake advertisement to recruit sperm donors in the UK features pictures of four women and is titled "These women want to have your babies." These cartoons and ads "make sense" because they appeal to the notion that sperm donors, as men, are motivated by a primitive urge to impregnate as many (hopefully attractive) women as possible, without having to commit to fatherhood. The caption of the fake advertisement directly appeals to this logic by listing potential reasons for donating sperm: "Maybe you want to become a father with none of the moral or financial responsibilities. It could be because you're a man. And a man's biological imperative is to carry on his legacy." In contrast, cartoons about egg donors, in addition to being less prevalent than cartoons about sperm donors, do not make light of the donors' overactive sexuality and reproductive urges. Instead they ridicule the improper maternity of women who donate eggs, such as one cartoon showing a woman in a hospital bed being presented with a slip of paper by a doctor exclaiming, "Congratulations! It's a cheque." The clear message here is that women who donate their eggs are prostituting their maternity, which is in line with Helena Ragone's observation that egg donors do occasionally feel "trashy" and "like a prostitute" after completing the donation cycle, often because of the reaction of their friends and family (1999). So far as I have been able to ascertain, there is no niche market of egg donation pornography, nor any fake egg donor advertisements with pictures of handsome men labeled "These men want to impregnate you." This is not surprising, as such jokes would not make sense within the narrative of women as strict gatekeepers of their reproductivity and men as the invaders trying to break down those gates with a battering ram. Within this cultural logic, women who not only voluntarily provide their reproductive capabilities to strangers, but do so for money, can readily be interpreted as prostitutes (it is surely not accidental that the first woman to serve as a contracted surrogate mother in the UK was indeed an actual prostitute [Corea 1985]). Therefore, egg donors must be "compensated" instead of "paid" not only to avoid allowing the sacred private sphere to leak into the unholy public sphere, but to attempt to minimize the implication that by selling their reproductive ability, egg donors are prostituting themselves.

Conclusion: Towards a New Direction in Gamete Donation Discourse *final discussion*

Gamete donation is like other types of bodily tissue donation in that it relies heavily 14 on narratives of gift-giving to avoid being associated with the morally distressing idea of commodification of the human body. But unlike organ or blood donation, the tissue exchanged in gamete donation is given in exchange for money, and furthermore, it is sex-specific tissue. Accordingly, the gifting rhetoric used to make gamete donation morally acceptable differs for egg donors versus sperm donors, from the advertisements used to recruit them, to the application process they must go through to be deemed acceptable donors, to the public discourse surrounding their donations. Egg donors are recruited with images of babies and families and appeals to altruism, while sperm donors are recruited with cartoon sperm and promises of high earnings potential and other personal benefits. Egg donors must profess a desire to help infertile couples start a family (even if in reality they are financially motivated) if they are to be accepted into a donation program, whereas sperm donors must simply have their medical history check out. Egg donors receive "compensation" for their inconvenience, despite the logical inconsistency of greater compensations for more desirable egg donors, although they are not actually more inconvenienced by the procedure than less desirable donors. In contrast, sperm donors receive a straightforward payment for a product. These gender differences reflect underlying differences in gender roles and expectations for men and women. Historically men have been the sole members of the public sphere, where business exchanges take place, while women have been confined to the private sphere of reproduction and family—hence the need to prevent the entrance of women's reproductive abilities into the public sphere by narrating egg donors as philanthropists who happen to be compensated for their trouble. But the separate spheres ideology alone cannot account for why men's reproductive abilities can so easily transition to the public sphere. To understand this phenomenon it is necessary to understand the cultural logic which holds that men are driven by primitive urges to spread their seed as far as possible (possibly through sperm donation), while women with similar urges are sexually deviant, and women who do so for money are prostitutes. This cultural logic is pervasive to the point of hegemony, but perhaps one way to start undermining this double standard for men and women is to start questioning the gendered discourse of gamete donation, so that one day women can unabashedly "earn" money for providing their eggs to others just as easily as men currently earn it for providing their sperm.

Works Cited

Corea, Gina. *The Mother Machine*. New York: Harper, 1985. Print.

Gordon, Linda. *Woman's Body, Woman's Right: Birth Control in America*. Penguin, 1974. Print.

Irvine, Martha. "Increase in Egg Donors Raises Concerns." *New York Times*, 18 Feb. 2007. Print.

Kolata, Gina. "Price of Donor Eggs Soars; Setting Off a Debate on Ethics." *New York Times*, 25 Feb. 1998. Print.

Kopytoff, Igor. "Commoditizing Kinship in America." *Consuming Motherhood*. Eds. Janelle Taylor, Linda Layne, and Danielle Wozniak. New Brunswick: Rutgers UP, 2004. 271–78. Print.

Layne, Linda. "The Child as Gift: New Directions in the Study of Euro-American Gift Exchange." *Transformative Motherhood: On Giving and Getting in a Consumer Culture.* Ed. Linda L. Layne. New York: New York University P, 1999. 1–28. Print.

Martin, Emily. "The Egg and the Sperm: How Science Has Constructed a Romance Based on Stereotypical Male-Female Roles." *Signs: Journal of Women in Culture and Society* 16.3 (1991): 485–501. Web. 1 Dec. 2007.

Ragone, Helena. "The Gift of Life: Surrogate Motherhood, Gamete Donation, and Constructions of Altruism." *Transformative Motherhood: On Giving and Getting in a Consumer Culture.* Ed. Linda L. Layne. New York: New York University P, 1999. 65–88. Print.

Rhoads, Steven. *Taking Sex Differences Seriously.* San Francisco: Encounter, 2004. Print.

READING FOR CONTENT

1. Paraphrase the transitional remarks in paragraph 10 leading from the discussion of advertisements for donors in the preceding section to a discussion of differences between compensating men and women as donors in this new section.

2. Summarize the conclusion in paragraph 14.

READING FOR GENRE, ORGANIZATION, AND STYLISTIC FEATURES

1. What kinds of evidence does the author rely upon to highlight differences between the ways in which men and women are treated as gamete donors?

2. How do the headings preceding paragraphs 3, 10, and 13 help to organize the essay?

3. What kinds of stylistic revision might you offer to the writer for improving her essay?

READING FOR RHETORICAL CONTEXT

1. Does the author's analysis of local advertisements found on campus strengthen or narrowly limit the evidence that she brings to bear upon her argument?

2. How does the semantic difference between the words "compensated" and "paid" at the end of paragraph 13 epitomize the argument?

WRITING ASSIGNMENTS

1. Visit the Google home page, <http://www.google.com>, and click on "images" in the menu at the top of the page. Search Google Images with the terms "sperm donor" and "egg donor." Select an image from each category and, using Caroline Rubin's analysis of her images as a guide, write your own 500-word analysis of the images you have selected.

2. Using the images you have selected from the Google Images site, write a 500-word critique of Rubin's essay in which you express your agreement or your disagreement with her analysis.

3. Explore bulletin boards on your own campus to look for ads for other services (such as tutoring, help for local projects, recruitment for public service, job prospects) and examine them for evidence of appeals to different gender interest. Use your evidence to write a short essay in the manner of Rubin's analysis with respect to gendered language.

SYNTHESIS WRITING ASSIGNMENTS

1. Write a 1,000-word essay that comments on the desirability or undesirability of gene patenting with respect to genetic testing. Draw on at least two articles from this chapter to support your commentary.

2. Write a 1,000-word essay that comments on the desirability or undesirability of gene patenting with respect to gene therapy. Draw on at least two articles from this chapter to support your commentary.

3. Write a 1,000-word essay that comments on the desirability or undesirability of gene patenting with respect to further research in genetic science. Draw on at least two articles from this chapter to support your commentary.

4. Synthesize material from the readings in this chapter to describe, in a 1,000-word essay, how the legalization of gene patenting can either help or hinder genetic testing, gene therapy, and research in genetic science. Evaluate the potential advantages or disadvantages of changing the current policy.

5. Drawing on the selections in this chapter and resources you locate on your own, write a 1,250-word argumentative research paper in response to the question "Who owns and controls genetic information?" Begin by visiting the government Web site of the Human Genome Project, <http://www.ornl.gov/sci/techresources/Human_Genome/project/about.shtml>.

6. Drawing on the selections in this chapter and resources you locate on your own, write a 1,250-word argumentative research paper in response to the question "Who owns your genes?" Give some consideration to the issues associated with genetic testing, gene therapy, and research in genetic science, or else concentrate on a set of issues associated with only one of those topics.

Ten

Human/Robot Interaction

system or group of electric circuits

unfriendly.

Most Americans are accustomed to relationships with machines. For example, we talk to our cars, feel betrayed when they break down, and sometimes grieve when they are hauled to the junkyard. As a nation, we spend more time in front of the television than we do with family and friends. Video games have captivated a generation of adolescents, and many of their parents spend workdays in front of computer screens. The development of virtual-reality systems that emulate the real world may signal a new era in our relationship with machines, wherein circuitry may be an important source of "life" experiences.

Technology is often described as a double-edged sword that can work to our benefit or detriment, depending upon how it is applied. Some commentators argue that our relationships to machinery and electronics will provide us with greater control over our lives; others claim such relationships will alienate us from human experience. These viewpoints and others are presented in the conversation about human/machine interaction in this chapter.

The first selection, Sherry Turkle's "Alone Together: The Robotic Moment," explores the topic with detached observation, personal experience, and wry humor. Turkel considers the possibilities of regarding robots as human or animal substitutes by contrasting their artificial intelligence with authentic thinking and feeling in the human and animal worlds. The next selection is written by Hiroshi Ishiguro and Minoru Asada, pioneers in simulating human appearances among robots. Titled "Humanoid and Android Science," it outlines differences between humanoid robots and android robots. The form and shape of humanoid robots, based abstractly upon human anatomy, allow for goal-directed interaction with living persons, while those of android robots, based concretely upon human features, project life-like human appearances.

Social, cultural, and moral concerns about using robots as substitutes for human functions dominate the remaining three selections. Glenda Shaw-Garlock's "Looking Forward to Sociable Robots" asks why Western societies usually deny robots companionate equivalence with human beings while conversely, Asian societies often prize robots for their companionable qualities. Noel Sharkey calls these robotic qualities into question in "The Ethical

Frontiers of Robotics." There he explicitly warns about entrusting humanoid machines with caregiving functions for the young and the elderly and with military combat responsibilities in times of war. Finally, Kenneth W. Goodman and Norman G. Einspruch devote their essay "The Way Forward in the World of Robotics" to criticizing Sharkey for highlighting worst-case scenarios in his warning about using robotic technology. In these essays, the conversation among those concerned with ethical implications of developing robotic science proves vibrant and robust.

■ ■ ■ ■ ■ ■ ■ ■ ■ ▨ ▨

Alone Together: The Robotic Moment

Sherry Turkle

Sherry Turkle is Abby Rockefeller Mauzé Professor in the Program in Science, Technology, and Society at MIT and the founder and current director of the MIT Initiative on Technology and Self. She is the author of Psychoanalytic Politics: Jacques Lacan and Freud's French Revolution, The Second Self: Computers and the Human Spirit, *and* Life on the Screen: Identity in the Age of the Internet.

PREREADING

Until recently, a major distinction between human beings and robots that are capable of performing certain human actions turned on the idea that, unlike humans, robots have no states of mind or emotions that confer upon them a human psychology. But what if designers of robots manage to expand robots' domains of sociability and companionate interaction? Freewrite for ten minutes on how you might react to a robot that offers to be your friend.

In late November 2005, I took my daughter Rebecca, then fourteen, to the Darwin   1
exhibition at the American Museum of Natural History in New York. From the moment you step into the museum and come face-to-face with a full-size dinosaur, you become part of a celebration of life on Earth, what Darwin called "endless forms most beautiful." Millions upon millions of now lifeless specimens represent nature's invention in every corner of the globe. There could be no better venue for documenting Darwin's life and thought and his theory of evolution by natural selection, the central truth that underpins contemporary biology. The exhibition aimed to please and, a bit defensively in these days of attacks on the theory of evolution, wanted to convince.

At the exhibit's entrance were two giant tortoises from the Galápagos Islands,   2
the best-known inhabitants of the archipelago where Darwin did his most famous

eager to know

investigations. The museum had been advertising these tortoises as wonders, curiosities, and marvels. Here, among the plastic models at the museum, was the life that Darwin saw more than a century and a half ago. One tortoise was hidden from view; the other rested in its cage, utterly still. Rebecca inspected the visible tortoise thoughtfully for a while and then said matter-of-factly, "They could have used a robot." I was taken aback and asked what she meant. She said she thought it was a shame to bring the turtle all this way from its island home in the Pacific, when it was just going to sit there in the museum, motionless, doing nothing. Rebecca was both concerned for the imprisoned turtle and unmoved by its authenticity.

It was Thanksgiving weekend. The line was long, the crowd frozen in place. I began to talk with some of the other parents and children. My question—"Do you care that the turtle is alive?"—was a welcome diversion from the boredom of the wait. A ten-year-old girl told me that she would prefer a robot turtle because aliveness comes with aesthetic inconvenience: "Its water looks dirty. Gross." More usually, votes for the robots echoed my daughter's sentiment that in this setting, aliveness didn't seem worth the trouble. A twelve-year-old girl was adamant: "For what the turtles do, you didn't have to have the live ones." Her father looked at her, mystified: "But the point is that they are real. That's the whole point." 3

Refuse to change one's mind

The Darwin exhibition put authenticity front and center: on display were the actual magnifying glass that Darwin used in his travels, the very notebook in which he wrote the famous sentences that first described his theory of evolution. Yet, in the children's reactions to the inert but alive Galápagos tortoise, the idea of the original had no place. What I heard in the museum reminded me of Rebecca's reaction as a seven-year-old during a boat ride in the postcard-blue Mediterranean. Already an expert in the world of simulated fish tanks, she saw something in the water, pointed to it excitedly, and said, "Look, Mommy, a jellyfish! It looks so realistic!" When I told this story to a vice president at the Disney Corporation, he said he was not surprised. When Animal Kingdom opened in Orlando, populated by "real"—that is, biological— animals, its first visitors complained that they were not as "realistic" as the animatronic creatures in other parts of Disneyworld. The robotic crocodiles slapped their tails and rolled their eyes—in sum, they displayed archetypal "crocodile" behavior. The biological crocodiles, like the Galápagos tortoises, pretty much kept to themselves. 4

I believe that in our culture of simulation, the notion of authenticity is for us what sex was for the Victorians—threat and obsession, taboo and fascination. I have lived with this idea for many years; yet, at the museum, I found the children's position strangely unsettling. For them, in this context, aliveness seemed to have no intrinsic value. Rather, it is useful only if needed for a specific purpose. Darwin's endless forms so beautiful were no longer sufficient unto themselves. I asked the children a further question: "If you put a robot instead of a living turtle in the exhibit, do you think people should be told that the turtle is not alive?" Not really, said many children. Data on aliveness can be shared on a "need-to-know basis"—for a purpose. But what are the purposes of living things? 5

Only a year later, I was shocked to be confronted with the idea that these purposes were more up for grabs than I had ever dreamed. I received a call from a *Scientific American* reporter to talk about robots and our future. During that conversation, he accused me of harboring sentiments that would put me squarely in the camp 6 of those who have for so long stood in the way of marriage for homosexual couples. I was stunned, first because I harbor no such sentiments, but also because his accusation was prompted not by any objection I had made to the mating or marriage of people. The reporter was bothered because I had objected to the mating and marriage of people to robots.

The call had been prompted by a new book about robots by David Levy, a [7] British-born entrepreneur and computer scientist. In 1968 Levy, an international chess master, famously wagered four artificial intelligence (AI) experts that no computer program would defeat him at the game in the subsequent decade. Levy won his bet. The sum was modest, 1,250 British pounds, but the AI community was chastened. They had overreached in their predictions for their young science. It would be another decade before Levy was bested in chess by a computer program, Deep Thought, an early version of the program that beat Gary Kasparov, the reigning chess champion in the 1990s.[1] These days, Levy is the chief executive officer at a company that develops "smart" toys for children. In 2009, Levy and his team won—and this for the second time—the prestigious Loebner Prize, widely regarded as the world championship for conversational software. In this contest, Levy's "chat bot" program was best at convincing people that they were talking to another person and not to a machine.

Always impressed with Levy's inventiveness, I found myself underwhelmed by [8] the message of this latest book, *Love and Sex with Robots*.[2] No tongue-in-cheek science fiction fantasy, it was reviewed without irony in the *New York Times* by a reporter who had just spent two weeks at the Massachusetts Institute of Technology (MIT) and wrote glowingly about its robotics culture as creating "new forms of life."[3] *Love and Sex* is earnest in its predictions about where people and robots will find themselves by mid-century: "Love with robots will be as normal as love with other humans, while the number of sexual acts and lovemaking positions commonly practiced between humans will be extended, as robots will teach more than is in all of the world's published sex manuals combined."[4] Levy argues that robots will teach us to be better friends and lovers because we will be able to practice on them. Beyond this, they will substitute where people fail. Levy proposes, among other things, the virtues of marriage to robots. He argues that robots are, of course, "other" but, in many ways, better. No cheating. No heartbreak. In Levy's argument, there is one simple criterion for judging the worth of robots in even the most intimate domains: Does being with a robot make you feel better? The master of today's computerspeak judges future robots by the impact of their behavior. And his next bet is that in a very few years, this is all we will care about as well.

I am a psychoanalytically trained psychologist. Both by temperament and profession, I place high value on relationships of intimacy and authenticity. Granting that [9] an AI might develop its own origami of lovemaking positions, I am troubled by the idea of seeking intimacy with a machine that has no feelings, can have no feelings, and is really just a clever collection of "as if" performances, behaving as if it cared, as if it understood us. Authenticity, for me, follows from the ability to put oneself in the place of another, to relate to the other because of a shared store of human experiences: we are born, have families, and know loss and the reality of death.[5] A robot, however sophisticated, is patently out of this loop.

So, I turned the pages of Levy's book with a cool eye. What if a robot is not a [10] "form of life" but a kind of performance art? What if "relating" to robots makes us feel "good" or "better" simply because we feel more in control? Feeling good is no golden rule. One can feel good for bad reasons. What if a robot companion makes us feel good but leaves us somehow diminished? The virtue of Levy's bold position is that it forces reflection: What kinds of relationships with machines are possible, desirable, or ethical? What does it mean to love a robot? As I read *Love and Sex*, my feelings on these matters were clear. A love relationship involves coming to savor the surprises and the rough patches of looking at the world from another's point of view, shaped by history, biology, trauma, and joy. Computers and robots do not have these experiences to share. We look at mass media and worry about our culture being intellectually "dumbed down." *Love and Sex* seems to celebrate an emotional dumbing down, a willful turning away from the complexities of human partnerships—the inauthentic as a new aesthetic.

I was further discomforted as I read *Love and Sex* because Levy had interpreted 11 my findings about the "holding power" of computers to argue his case. Indeed, Levy dedicated his book to Anthony,* an MIT computer hacker I interviewed in the early 1980s. Anthony was nineteen when I met him, a shy young man who found computers reassuring. He felt insecure in the world of people with its emotional risks and shades of gray. The activity and interactivity of computer programming gave Anthony—lonely, yet afraid of intimacy—the feeling that he was not alone.[6] In *Love and Sex*, Levy idealizes Anthony's accommodation and suggests that loving a robot would be a reasonable next step for people like him. I was sent an advance copy of the book, and Levy asked if I could get a copy to Anthony, thinking he would be flattered. I was less sure. I didn't remember Anthony as being at peace with his retreat to what he called "the machine world." I remembered him as wistful, feeling himself a spectator of the human world, like a kid with his nose to the window of a candy store. When we imagine robots as our future companions, we all put our noses to that same window.

I was deep in the irony of my unhappy Anthony as a role model for intimacy 12 with robots when the *Scientific American* reporter called. I was not shy about my lack of enthusiasm for Levy's ideas and suggested that the very fact we were discussing marriage to robots at all was a comment on human disappointments—that in matters of love and sex, we must be failing each other. I did not see marriage to a machine as a welcome evolution in human relationships. And so I was taken aback when the reporter suggested that I was no better than bigots who deny gays and lesbians the right to marry. I tried to explain that just because I didn't think people should marry machines didn't mean that any mix of adult people wasn't fair territory. He accused me of species chauvinism: Wasn't I withholding from robots their right to "realness"? Why was I presuming that a relationship with a robot lacked authenticity? For me, the story of computers and the evocation of life had come to a new place.

At that point, I told the reporter that I, too, was taking notes on our conversa- 13 tion. The reporter's point of view was now data for my own work on our shifting cultural expectations of technology—data, that is, for the book you are reading. His analogizing of robots to gay men and women demonstrated that, for him, future

---

*This name and the names of others I observed and interviewed for this book are pseudonyms. To protect the anonymity of my subjects, I also change identifying details such as location and profession. When I cite the opinions of scientists or public figures, I use their words with permission. And, of course, I cite material on the public record.

intimacy with machines would not be a second-best substitute for finding a person to love. More than this, the reporter was insisting that machines would bring their own special qualities to an intimate partnership that needed to be honored in its own right. In his eyes, the love, sex, and marriage robot was not merely "better than nothing," a substitute. Rather, a robot had become "better than something." The machine could be preferable—for any number of reasons—to what we currently experience in the sometimes messy, often frustrating, and always complex world of people.

This episode with the *Scientific American* reporter shook me—perhaps in part 14 because the magazine had been for me, since childhood, a gold standard in scientific publication. But the extravagance of the reporter's hopes for robots fell into a pattern I had been observing for nearly a decade. The encounter over *Love and Sex* most reminded me of another time, two years before, when I met a female graduate student at a large psychology conference in New Orleans; she had taken me aside to ask about the current state of research on robots designed to serve as human companions. At the conference, I had given a presentation on *anthropomorphism*—on how we see robots as close to human if they do such things as make eye contact, track our motion, and gesture in a show of friendship. These appear to be "Darwinian buttons" that cause people to imagine that the robot is an "other," that there is, colloquially speaking, "somebody home."

During a session break, the graduate student, Anne, a lovely, raven-haired woman 15 in her mid-twenties, wanted specifics. She confided that she would trade in her boyfriend "for a sophisticated Japanese robot" if the robot would produce what she called "caring behavior." She told me that she relied on a "feeling of civility in the house." She did not want to be alone. She said, "If the robot could provide the environment, I would be happy to help produce the illusion that there is somebody really with me." She was looking for a "no-risk relationship" that would stave off loneliness. A responsive robot, even one just exhibiting scripted behavior, seemed better to her than a demanding boyfriend. I asked her, gently, if she was joking. She told me she was not. An even more poignant encounter was with Miriam, a seventy-two-year-old woman living in a suburban Boston nursing home, a participant in one of my studies of robots and the elderly.

I meet Miriam in an office that has been set aside for my interviews. She is a 16 slight figure in a teal blue silk blouse and slim black pants, her long gray hair parted down the middle and tied behind her head in a low bun. Although elegant and composed, she is sad. In part, this is because of her circumstances. For someone who was once among Boston's best-known interior designers, the nursing home is a stark and lonely place. But there is also something immediate: Miriam's son has recently broken off his relationship with her. He has a job and family on the West Coast, and when he visits, he and his mother quarrel—he feels she wants more from him than he can give. Now Miriam sits quietly, stroking Paro, a sociable robot in the shape of a baby harp seal. Paro, developed in japan, has been advertised as the first "therapeutic robot" for its ostensibly positive effects on the ill, elderly, and emotionally troubled. Paro can make eye contact by sensing the direction of a human voice, is sensitive to touch, and has a small working English vocabulary for "understanding" its users (the robot's Japanese vocabulary is larger); most importantly, it has "states of mind" affected by how it is treated. For example, it can sense whether it is being stroked gently or with aggression. Now, with Paro, Miriam is lost in her reverie, patting down the robot's soft fur with care. On this day, she is particularly depressed and believes that the robot is depressed as well. She turns to Paro, strokes him again, and says, "Yes, you're sad, aren't you? It's tough out there. Yes, it's hard." Miriam's tender touch triggers a warm response in Paro: it turns its head toward her and purrs approvingly. Encouraged, Miriam shows yet more affection for the little robot. In attempting to provide the comfort she believes it needs, she comforts herself.

Because of my training as a clinician, I believe that this kind of moment, if it 17 happens between people, has profound therapeutic potential. We can heal ourselves by giving others what we most need. But what are we to make of this transaction between a depressed woman and a robot? When I talk to colleagues and friends about such encounters—for Miriam's story is not unusual—their first associations are usually to their pets and the solace they provide. I hear stories of how pets "know" when their owners are unhappy and need comfort. The comparison with pets sharpens the question of what it means to have a relationship with a robot. I do not know whether a pet could sense Miriam's unhappiness, her feelings of loss. I do know that in the moment of apparent connection between Miriam and her Paro, a moment that comforted her, the robot understood nothing. Miriam experienced an intimacy with another, but she was in fact alone. Her son had left her, and as she looked to the robot, I felt that we had abandoned her as well.

Experiences such as these—with the idea of aliveness on a "need-to-know" basis, 18 with the proposal and defense of marriage to robots, with a young woman dreaming of a robot lover, and with Miriam and her Paro—have caused me to think of our time as the "robotic moment." This does not mean that companionate robots are common among us; it refers to our state of emotional—and I would say philosophical—readiness. I find people willing to seriously consider robots not only as pets but as potential friends, confidants, and even romantic partners. We don't seem to care what these artificial intelligences "know" or "understand" of the human moments we might "share" with them. At the robotic moment, the performance of connection seems connection enough. We are poised to attach to the inanimate without prejudice. The phrase "technological promiscuity" comes to mind.

As I listen for what stands behind this moment, I hear a certain fatigue with the 19 difficulties of life with people. We insert robots into every narrative of human frailty. People make too many demands; robot demands would be of a more manageable sort. People disappoint; robots will not. When people talk about relationships with robots, they talk about cheating husbands, wives who fake orgasms, and children who take drugs. They talk about how hard it is to understand family and friends. I am at first surprised by these comments. Their clear intent is to bring people down a notch. A forty-four-year-old woman says, "After all, we never know how another person really feels. People put on a good face. Robots would be safer." A thirty-year-old man remarks, "I'd rather talk to a robot. Friends can be exhausting. The robot will always be there for me. And whenever I'm done, I can walk away."

The idea of sociable robots suggests that we might navigate intimacy by skirting 20 it. People seem comforted by the belief that if we alienate or fail each other, robots will be there, programmed to provide simulations of love.[7] Our population is aging; there will be robots to take care of us. Our children are neglected; robots will tend to them. We are too exhausted to deal with each other in adversity; robots will have the energy.

Robots won't be judgmental. We will be accommodated. An older woman says of her robot dog, "It is better than a real dog. . . . It won't do dangerous things, and it won't betray you. . . . Also, it won't die suddenly and abandon you and make you very sad."[8]

The elderly are the first to have companionate robots aggressively marketed to 21 them, but young people also see the merits of robotic companionship. These days, teenagers have sexual adulthood thrust upon them before they are ready to deal with the complexities of relationships. They are drawn to the comfort of connection without the demands of intimacy. This may lead them to a hookup—sex without commitment or even caring. Or it may lead to an online romance—companionship that can always be interrupted. Not surprisingly, teenagers are drawn to love stories in which full intimacy cannot occur—here I think of current passions for films and novels about high school vampires who cannot sexually consummate relationships for fear of hurting those they love. And teenagers are drawn to the idea of technological communion. They talk easily of robots that would be safe and predictable companions.[9]

These young people have grown up with sociable robot pets, the companions 22 of their playrooms, which portrayed emotion, said they cared, and asked to be cared for.[10] We are psychologically programmed not only to nurture what we love but to love what we nurture. So even simple artificial creatures can provoke heartfelt attachment. Many teenagers anticipate that the robot toys of their childhood will give way to full-fledged machine companions. In the psychoanalytic tradition, a symptom addresses a conflict but distracts us from understanding or resolving it; a dream expresses a wish.[11] Sociable robots serve as both symptom and dream: as a symptom, they promise a way to sidestep conflicts about intimacy; as a dream, they express a wish for relationships with limits, a way to be both together and alone.[12]

Some people even talk about robots as providing respite from feeling over- 23 whelmed by technology. In Japan, companionate robots are specifically marketed as a way to seduce people out of cyberspace; robots plant a new flag in the physical real. If the problem is that too much technology has made us busy and anxious, the solution will be another technology that will organize, amuse, and relax us. So, although historically robots provoked anxieties about technology out of control, these days they are more likely to represent the reassuring idea that in a world of problems, science will offer solutions.[13] Robots have become a twenty-first-century deus ex machina. Putting hope in robots expresses an enduring technological optimism, a belief that as other things go wrong, science will go right. In a complicated world, robots seem a simple salvation. It is like calling in the cavalry. — *horse man*

But my argument is not about robots. Rather, it is about how we are changed 24 as technology offers us substitutes for connecting with each other face-to-face. We are offered robots and a whole world of machine-mediated relationships on networked devices. As we instant-message, e-mail, text, and Twitter, technology redraws the boundaries between intimacy and solitude. We talk of getting "rid" of our e-mails, as though these notes are so much excess baggage. Teenagers avoid making telephone calls, fearful that they "reveal too much." They would rather text than talk. Adults, too, choose keyboards over the human voice. It is more efficient, they say. Things that happen in "real time" take too much time. Tethered to technology, we are shaken when that world "unplugged" does not signify, does not satisfy. After an evening of avatar-to-avatar talk in a networked game, we feel, at one moment, in possession of a full social life and, in the next, curiously isolated, in tenuous complicity with strangers. We build a following on Facebook or MySpace and wonder to what degree our followers are friends. We recreate ourselves as online personae and give ourselves new bodies, homes, jobs, and romances. Yet, suddenly, in the half-light of virtual community, we may feel utterly alone. As we distribute ourselves, we may abandon ourselves. Sometimes people experience no sense of having communicated after hours of connection. And they report feelings of closeness when they are paying little attention. In all of this, there is a nagging question: Does virtual intimacy degrade our experience of the other kind and, indeed, of all encounters, of any kind?

The blurring of intimacy and solitude may reach its starkest expression when a robot is proposed as a romantic partner. But for most people it begins when one creates a profile on a social-networking site or builds a persona or avatar for a game or virtual world.[14] Over time, such performances of identity may feel like identity itself. And this is where robotics and the networked life first intersect. For the performance of caring is all that robots, no matter how sociable, know how to do.

I was enthusiastic about online worlds as "identity workshops" when they first appeared, and all of their possibilities remain.[15] Creating an avatar—perhaps of a different age, a different gender, a different temperament—is a way to explore the self. But if you're spending three, four, or five hours a day in an online game or virtual world (a time commitment that is not unusual), there's got to be someplace you're not. And that someplace you're not is often with your family and friends—sitting around, playing Scrabble face-to-face, taking a walk, watching a movie together in the old-fashioned way. And with performance can come disorientation. You might have begun your online life in a spirit of compensation. If you were lonely and isolated, it seemed better than nothing. But online, you're slim, rich, and buffed up, and you feel you have more opportunities than in the real world. So, here, too, better than nothing can become better than something—or better than anything. Not surprisingly, people report feeling let down when they move from the virtual to the real world. It is not uncommon to see people fidget with their smartphones, looking for virtual places where they might once again be more.

Sociable robots and online life both suggest the possibility of relationships the way we want them. Just as we can program a made-to-measure robot, we can reinvent ourselves as comely avatars. We can write the Facebook profile that pleases us. We can edit our messages until they project the self we want to be. And we can keep things short and sweet. Our new media are well suited for accomplishing the rudimentary. And because this is what technology serves up, we reduce our expectations of each other. An impatient high school senior says, "If you really need to reach me, just shoot me a text." He sounds just like my colleagues on a consulting job, who tell me they would prefer to communicate with "real-time texts."

Our first embrace of sociable robotics (both the idea of it and its first exemplars) is a window onto what we want from technology and what we are willing to do to accommodate it. From the perspective of our robotic dreams, networked life takes on a new cast. We imagine it as expansive. But we are just as fond of its constraints. We celebrate its "weak ties," the bonds of acquaintance with people we may never meet. But that does not mean we prosper in them.[16] We often find ourselves standing depleted in the hype. When people talk about the pleasures of these weak-tie relationships as "friction free," they are usually referring to the kind of relationships you can have without leaving your desk. Technology ties us up as it promises to free us up. Connectivity technologies once promised to give us more time. But as the cell phone and smartphone eroded the boundaries between work and leisure, all the time in the world was not enough. Even when we are not "at work," we experience ourselves as "on call"; pressed, we want to edit out complexity and "cut to the chase."

Notes

1. On this, see "The Making of Deep Blue," IBM Research, www.research.ibm.com/deepblue/ meet/html/d,3.1.html (accessed June 10, 2010).
2. David L. Levy, *Love and Sex with Robots: The Evolution of Human-Robot Relationships* (New York: Harper Collins, 2007).
3. The book review is Robin Marantz Henig, "Robo Love," *New York Times*, December 2, 2007, www.nytimes.com/2007/12/02/books/review/Henig-t.html (accessed July 21, 2009). The original article about the MIT robot scene is Robin Marantz Henig, "The Real Transformers," *New York Times*, July 29, 2007, www.nytimes.com/2007/07/29/magazine/29robots-t.html (accessed July 21, 2009).
4. Levy, *Love and Sex*, 22.
5. On "alterity," the ability to put oneself in the place of another, see Emmanuel Lévinas, *Alterity and Transcendence*, trans. Michael B. Smith (London: Athlone Press, 1999).
6. Sherry Turkle, *The Second Self: Computers and the Human Spirit* (1984; Cambridge, MA: MIT Press, 2005), 183–218.
7. The way here is paved by erotic images of female robots used to sell refrigerators, washing machines, shaving cream, and vodka. See, for example, the campaign for Svedka Vodka (Steve Hall, "Svedka Launches Futuristic, Un-PC Campaign," Andrants.com, September 20, 2005, www.adrants.com/2005/09/svedka-launches-futuristic-unpc.php [accessed September 1, 2009]) and Phillip's shaving system ("Feel the Erotic Union of Man and Shavebot," AdFreak.com, August 21, 2007, http://adweek.blogs.com/adfreak/2007/08/feel-the-erotic. html [accessed September 1, 2009]).
8. Sharon Moshavi, "Putting on the Dog in Japan," *Boston Globe*, June 17, 1999, A1.
9. As preteens, the young women of the first Google generation (born roughly from 1987 to 1993) wore clothing widely referred to as "baby harlot"; they listened to songs about explicit sex well before puberty. Their boomer parents had few ideas about where to draw lines, having spent their own adolescences declaring the lines irrelevant. Boomer parents grew up rejecting parental rules, but knowing that there were rules. One might say it is the job of teenagers to complain about constraints and the job of parents to insist on them, even if the rules are not obeyed. Rules, even unheeded, suggest that twelve to fifteen are not good ages to be emotionally and sexually enmeshed.

    Today's teenagers cannot easily articulate any rules about sexual conduct except for those that will keep them "safe." Safety refers to not getting venereal diseases or AIDS. Safety refers to not getting pregnant. And on these matters teenagers are eloquent, unembarrassed, and startlingly well informed. But teenagers are overwhelmed with how unsafe they feel in relationships. A robot to talk to is appealing—even if currently unavailable—as are situations that provide feelings of closeness without emotional demands. I have said that rampant fantasies of vampire lovers (closeness with constraints on sexuality) bear a family resemblance to ideas about robot lovers (sex without intimacy, perfect). And closeness without the possibility of physical intimacy and eroticized encounters that can be switched off in an instant—these are the affordances of online encounters. Online romance expresses the aesthetic of the robotic moment. From a certain perspective, they are a way of preparing for it. On the psychology of adolescents' desire for relationships with constraint, I am indebted to conversations with child and adolescent psychoanalyst Monica Horovitz in August 2009.
10. Commenting on the insatiable desire for robot pets during the 2009 holiday season, a researcher on social trends comments, "A toy trend would be something that reflects the

broader society, that tells you where society is going, something society needs." Gerald Celente, founder of the Trends Research Institute, cited in Brad Tuttle, "Toy Craze Explained: A Zhu Zhu Pet Hamster Is Like a 'Viral Infection,'" *Time*, December 9, 2009, http://money.blogs.time.com/2009/12/07/toy-craze-explained-a-zhu-zhu-pet-hamster-is-like-a- viral-infection (accessed December 9, 2009).

11. For classic psychodynamic formulations of the meaning of symptoms, see Sigmund Freud, "The Unconscious," in *The Standard Edition of Sigmund Freud*, ed. and trans. James Strachey et al. (London: Hogarth Press, 1953–1974), 14:159–204; "Introductory Lectures on Psychoanalysis," in *The Standard Edition*, vols. 15 and 16; "From the History of an Infantile Neurosis," in *The Standard Edition*, 17:1–122; "Inhibitions, Symptoms, and Anxiety," in *The Standard Edition*, 20:75–172; and Sigmund Freud and Joseph Breuer, "Studies on Hysteria," in *The Standard Edition*, 2:48–106. For Freud on dreams as wishes, see "The Interpretation of Dreams," in *The Standard Edition*, vol. IV.

12. For an argument about the pleasures of limited worlds in another technological realm, see Natasha Schüll's work on gambling, *Addiction by Design: Machine Gambling in Las Vegas* (Princeton, NJ: Princeton University Press, forthcoming).

13. See, for example, Bill Gates, "A Robot in Every Home," *Scientific American*, January 2007, www.scientificamerican.com/article.cfm?id=a-robot-in-every-home (accessed September 2, 2009).

14. See Sherry Turkle, *Life on the Screen: Identity in the Age of the Internet* (New York: Simon and Schuster, 1995). On life as performance, the classic work is Erving Goffman, *The Presentation of Self in Everyday Life* (Garden City, NY: Doubleday Anchor, 1959).

15. The apt phrase "identity workshop" was coined by my then student Amy Bruckman. See "Identity Workshop: Emergent Social and Psychological Phenomena in Text Based Virtual Reality" (unpublished essay, Media Lab, Massachusetts Institute of Technology, 1992), www.cc.gatech.edu/~asb/papers (accessed September 2, 2009).

16. Sociologists distinguish between strong ties, those of family and close friendship, and weak ties, the bonds of acquaintanceship that make us comfortable at work and in our communities. Facebook and Twitter, friending rather than friendship—these are worlds of weak ties. Today's technology encourages a celebration of these weak ties as the kind we need in the networked life. The classic work on weak ties is Mark S. Granovetter, "The Strength of Weak Ties," *American Journal of Sociology* 78, no. 6 (May 1973): 1360–1380.

READING FOR CONTENT

1. In paragraphs 2–5, how do the children at the Darwin exhibit explain their preference for robotic animals rather than real ones?

2. In your own words, explain what Turkle means by "authenticity" (paragraph 9), "anthropomorphism" (paragraph 14), and the "robotic moment" (paragraph 18).

3. Why does Turkle state in paragraph 24 that "the problem is not about robots"?

READING FOR GENRE, ORGANIZATION, AND STYLISTIC FEATURES

1. What purposes do the narrative anecdotes about Anne and Miriam serve in paragraphs 14–18?

2. Point to some ways in which Turkle organizes her essay by comparing past responses to robotic life with present responses to it.

3. Why does Turkle end her essay with the abrupt conclusion, "Pressed, we want to edit out complexity and 'cut to the chase'" (paragraph 28)?

READING FOR RHETORICAL CONTEXT

1. Why does Turkle characterize the incident at the Darwin exhibit (paragraphs 1–5) as one that seems "strangely unsettling" to her (paragraph 5)?

2. How does Turkle's response to David Levy's book on *Love and Sex with Robots* in paragraph 10 help to contextualize her strong feelings about having affective relationships with robots?

3. Turkle refers to a generation of young people who have grown up with robotic toys and in paragraph 22 she epitomizes their defense of sociable robots as "both symptom and dream." What leads her to this conclusion?

WRITING ASSIGNMENTS

1. Write a 500-word response to Turkle's surprise in finding that today's young people accept robots as a substitute for living things more than people did a generation ago. Do young people really accept robotic substitutes as Turkle thinks they do, or do they have a strong understanding of robotic difference that diverges from Turkle's understanding? Frame your argument in relation to this question.

2. Visit the Google home page <http://www.google.com/>, and click on "images" in the menu at the top of the page. Search Google Images with the term "human robot interaction" or "assistive robot" or "robot nanny." Based upon your analysis of the images you find, write a 1,000-word essay in response to Turkle's criticism that robotic facsimiles of living creatures are predictable and conform to expectations, offering none of the challenges that authentic creatures incur. Do you think that robotic facsimiles are devoid of "authenticity"? Frame your argument in relation to this question.

3. Write a 1,000-word essay that draws on Turkle's article and attempts to define criteria for "authenticity" in comparing human and robotic characteristics.

■ ■ ■ ■ ■ ■ ■ ■ ■ ■

Humanoid and Android Science

Hiroshi Ishiguro and Minoru Asada

Hiroshi Ishiguro and Minoru Asada are research scientists at Osaka University in Japan. They specialize in the design of interactive humanoids and the development of synergistic intelligence in robots.

PREREADING

Visit the *Google* home page, <http://www.google.com/>, and click on "images" in the menu at the top of the page. Search Google Images with the term "human robot interaction" or "assistive robot" or "robot nanny." Based upon your analysis of the images you find, freewrite about

Ishiguro, Hiroshi, and Minoru Asada. "Humanoid and Android Science." *IEEE Intelligent Systems*, July/Aug. 2006: 74–76. Web. 15 Aug. 2010. <http://www.computer.org/intelligent> © 2006 IEEE. Reprinted with permission.

whether you think that you or people you know might ever express a preference for android companionship over human relationships in certain situations, such as for company on long automobile trips or for assistance in performing monotonous household tasks.

W hy are we attracted to humanoids and androids? The answer is simple: we tend to anthropomorphize nonhuman things. Humans always anthropomorphize targets of communication and interaction, so we expect much from humanoids. In other words, we find a human in the humanoid. Recently, robotics researchers have begun shifting from traditional studies on navigation and manipulation to studying interaction with robots.

The study of human-robot interaction has been neglecting an issue — appearance and behavior. The interactive robots that have been developed thus far are nonandroid types, so the researchers who developed them didn't focus on the robots' appearances. Evidently, a robot's appearance influences subjects' impressions, and it's an important factor in evaluating the interaction. Although many technical reports compare robots with different behaviors, they haven't focused on the robots' appearances. There are many empirical discussions on simplified robots, such as dolls. However, designing a robot's appearance, particularly to make it appear humanoid, has always been the industrial designers' role rather than that of researchers and engineers. This is a serious problem for developing and evaluating interactive robots. Appearance and behavior are tightly coupled.

Bridging Science and Engineering

One way to tackle the issue is to use a humanlike robot—an android—to study human-robot interaction Figure 1a is a humanoid developed by Mitsubishi Heavy Industry, and figure 1b shows an android that Hiroshi Ishiguro and his colleagues developed in cooperation with Kokoro. The android has 42 air actuators for the upper torso, excluding fingers. During development, we determined the actuators's positions by analyzing a human's movements using a precise 3D motion-capture system. The actuators can represent unconscious movements such as chest movements due to breathing, in addition t large, conscious movements of the head and arms. Furthermore, the android can generate facial expressions that are important for interaction with humans. When we publicized the android through the media, we were anxious about ordinary Japanese people' reactions. However, it wasn't uncanny for them; they just praised the quality and technology.

Developing androids requires contributions from both robotics and cognitive science To realize a more human like android, knowledge from human science (that is, from studying humans) is necessary. This new interdisciplinary frame work between engineering and cognitive science is called *android science.*[1]

In the past, robotics research used knowledge from cognitive science, and cognitive science research utilized robots to verify hypotheses for understanding humans. However, robotics' contribution to cognitive science has been inadequate. Appearance and behavior couldn't be handled separately, and nonandroid type robots weren't sufficient as cognitive science tools. We expect that using androids with a humanlike appearance can solve this problem. Robotics research based on cues from cognitive science faces a similar problem, because it's difficult to recognize whether

(a)

(b)

Figure I   Humanoid and android robots. (a) Humanoid Eveliee P1 is based on WAKAMURU, developed by Mitsubishi Heavy Industry. (b) Android Repliee Q2 was developed in cooperation with KOKORO (www.kokoro-dreams.co.jp). Courtesy of Hirosi-i Ishiguro.

the cues pertain solely to a robot's behavior, isolated from its appearance, or to the combination of its appearance and behavior. In the framework of android science, androids enable us to directly share knowledge between the development of androids in engineering and the understanding of humans in cognitive science.

So, android science has several major research issues. The issues in robotics are   6 to develop a humanlike appearance using silicon, humanlike movement and human-like perception by integrating ubiquitous sensor systems. In cognitive science, the issue is conscious and subconscious recognition. When we observe objects, various modules are activated in our brain. Each of these matches the input sensory data with our brains' models of human faces, voices, and so on, which affect our reactions. So, even if we recognize that a robot is an android, we react to it as if it were human. Android sience's goal is to find the essential factors of humanlikeness and realize a humanlike robot.

How can we define humanlikeness? Furthermore, how do we perceive it? That   7 humans have both conscious and unconscious recognition is fundamental for both the engineering and scientific approaches. It will be an evaluation criterion in androids' development, and it provides us cues for understanding the human brain mecharism of recognition.

From Android Science to Humanoid Science

The history of intelligent robotics started with Shakey, a robot developed at SRI in   8 1965. Shakey provided robotics researchers with several important research questios. We focused on the fundamental issues for making Shakey more intelligent, suchas AI, computer vision, and language recognition. Since Shakey's development, wve been using these technologies to create new humanoids and androids, which prove us with important new research questions as Shakey did. These questions are in inter-disciplinary areas among robotics, cognitive science, neuroscience, and social science.

Android science is also an interdisciplinary framework, but it's rather limited. 9 In addition to humanlike appearance and movement, we must consider the internal mechanisms, such as humanlike dynamic and adaptive mechanisms and complicated sensorimotor mechanisms, for more tightly coupling engineering and science. As we mentioned earlier, what we wish to know is what a human is. We can understand this by developing humanoids comprising humanlike hardware and software. We call this extended framework *humanoid science.*

Our project, JST ERATO (Japan Science and Technology Agency, Exploratory 10 Research for Advanced Technology) Asada Synergistic Intelligence (www.jeap.org), is based on the humanoid-science framework. *Synergistic intelligence* means intelligent behaviors that emerge through interaction with the environment, including humans. Synergistic effects are expected in brain science, neuroscience, cognitive science, and developmental psychology. Synergistic intelligence provides a new way of under-standing ourselves and a new design theory of humanoids through mutual feedback between the design of humanlike robots and human-related science.

Synergistic intelligence adopts *cognitive developmental robotics,*[2] a methodology 11 that comprises the design of self-developing structures inside the robot's brain and environmental design (how to set up the environment so that the robots embedded therein can gradually adapt to more complex tasks in more dynamic situations). Here, one of the most formidable issues is nature versus nurture. To what extent should we embed the self-developing structure, and to what extent should we expect the environ-ment to trigger development? We're approaching this issue using the kinds of topics in Figure 2 (on the next page).

References

H. Ishiguro, "Interactive Humanoids and Androids as Ideal Interfaces for Humans," *Proc. 11th Int'l Conf. Intelligent User Interfaces*, ACM Press, 2006, pp. 2–9; www.ed.ams.eng.osaka-u.ac.jp/research/Android/android_eng.htm.

M. Asada et al., "Cognitive Developmental Robotics as a New Paradigm for the Design of Humanoid Robots," *Robotics and Autonomous Systems*, vol. 37, 2001, pp. 185–193.

READING FOR CONTENT

1. Paraphrase what the authors define in paragraph 6 as the goal of android science. How does it abet what the authors in paragraph 9 call the "extended framework *humanoid science*"?

2. What do the authors mean by "synergistic intelligence" in paragraph 10? How does it relate to what they call "cognitive developmental robotics" in paragraph 11?

READING FOR GENRE, ORGANIZATION, AND STYLISTIC FEATURES

1. How does the authors' use of illustrations clarify their discussion?

2. How do the authors signal that their project is an interdisciplinary one?

3. Which specific disciplines constitute its base?

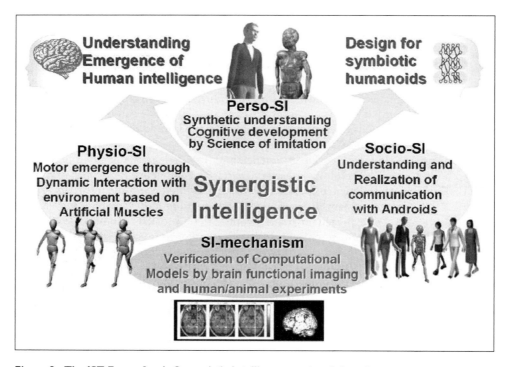

Figure 2   The JST ERATO Asada Synergistic Intelligence project is based on a humanoid-science framework. Courtesy of Hiroshi Ishiguro.

READING FOR RHETORICAL CONTEXT

1. Why do the authors approach the end of their essay with a question in paragraph 11?
2. Do the authors express optimism about the outcome of their experiment?

WRITING ASSIGNMENTS

1. It seems one thing to accept that an artificial-looking robot is not an authentic human being, despite its capabilities in executing humanoid tasks. But what happens when designers of robots can simulate fully convincing human appearances in a robotic android? Write a 500-word essay on how you might react to such human-looking androids when you suspend your disbelief and allow the robot to perform humanoid tasks.

2. Visit the Google home page, <http://www.google.com/>, and click on "images" in the menu at the top of the page. Search Google Images with the term "human robot interaction" or "assistive robot" or "robot nanny." After analyzing these images, write a 500-word essay on whether or not designers of robots can simulate fully convincing human appearances and movements in a robotic android. What good might such simulation eventually succeed in bringing about?

Looking Forward to Sociable Robots

Glenda Shaw-Garlock

Glenda Shaw-Garlock is completing her doctoral dissertation at Simon Fraser University on the topic of human and robotic communication.

PREREADING

We are all familiar with utilitarian robots that perform useful but tedious or risky jobs. The preceding essays have familiarized us with affective robots that interact with human beings in performing other useful tasks. Might there be a hybrid category that performs yet different tasks? Freewrite for ten minutes on the possiblities. In "Looking Forward to Sociable Robots," Shaw-Garlock describes two robots named Kismet and Repliée-Q2. Before you read the article, take a look at photos of Kismet and Repliée-Q2. Kismet has its own Web site at <http://www.ai.mit.edu/projects/humanoid-robotics-group/kismet/kismet.html>. For a view of Repliée-Q2, visit Professor Hiroshi Ishiguro's laboratory at Osaka Univeristy: <http://www.is.sys.es.osaka-u.ac.jp/development/0006/index.en.html>.

Abstract

This work examines humanoid social robots in Japan and the North America with a view to comparing and contrasting the projects cross culturally. In North America, I look at the work of Cynthia Breazeal at the Massachusetts Institute of Technology and her sociable robot project: Kismet. In Japan, at the Osaka University, I consider the project of Hiroshi Ishiguro: Repliée-Q2. I first distinguish between utilitarian and affective social robots. Then, drawing on published works of Breazeal and Ishiguro I examine the proposed vision of each project. Next, I examine specific characteristics (embodied and social intelligence, morphology and aesthetics, and moral equivalence) of Kismet and Repliée with a view to comparing the underlying concepts associated with each. These features are in turn connected to the societal preconditions of robots generally. Specifically, the role that history of robots, theology/spirituality, and popular culture plays in the reception and attitude toward robots is considered.

I. Introduction

This work examines the emergence of the humanoid social robot in Japan and the United States with a view to comparing and contrasting two prominent social robot   1

Shaw-Garlock, Glenda. "Looking Forward to Sociable Robots." *International Journal of Social Robotics* 1.3 (2009): 249–60. *SpringerLink*. Web. 29 Aug. 2010. <http://www.springerlink.com/content/1875-4791> © Springer Science & Business Media BV 2009. With kind permission from Springer Science+Business Media.

projects (MIT's *Kismet* and Osaka University's *Repliée*). Western rationalist philosophers of science once imposed an unassailable boundary between nature and culture, wherein the natural world was regarded as separate from society. An alternative perspective to this bounded view of the world involves (re)conceptualizing objects, such as humans and machines, as existing un-antagonistically along a continuum. Different views about machines exist in other regions of the world, Japan for example, wherein robots have historically occupied a legitimate, indeed sometimes sacred, space within society alongside human beings.

Two humanoid social robot projects are considered in this paper. In the American case, I look at the work of Cynthia Breazeal at the Massachusetts Institute of Technology (MIT) and her social robot, Kismet. In the Japanese case, at the Osaka University, I consider the work of Hiroshi Ishiguro and the humanoid social robot Repliée-Q2. I first distinguish between the utilitarian and the affective social robot and situate Kismet and Repliée within the latter category. Then, drawing on video interviews, text interviews, and the published works of Breazeal and Ishiguro I examine the proposed vision of each researcher. Next, I examine specific characteristics (embodied and social intelligence, morphology and aesthetics, and moral equivalence) of Kismet and Repliée with a view to comparing the underlying concepts associated with each. These features are in turn connected to the societal preconditions of each robot's emergence. Specifically, the role that the history of robots, theology/spirituality, and popular culture plays in the reception and attitude toward social robots is considered. Finally, in light of the profound reconfigurations of the boundaries between human beings and their machines, I propose a revised set of conceptual strategies from which we may critique and respond to our emerging social robots.

2. Utilitarian Versus Affective Robots

Generally speaking, there are two classes of social robots: the *utilitarian* humanoid social robot and the *affective* humanoid social robot [11, 77]. Utilitarian social robots are sometimes referred to as domestic robots or service robots and are designed to interact with humans mainly for instrumental or functional purposes. Examples familiar to North Americans include: ATMs, vending machines, and automated telephone and answering systems. Less familiar examples include: help desk receptionists, salespersons, private tutors, travel agents, hospital food servers, and museum tour guides. This category of social robot typically involves regarding robots as "very sophisticated appliances that people use to perform tasks" [11].

Affective humanoid social robots on the other hand, are robots that are designed to interact with humans on an emotional level through play, sometimes therapeutic play, and perhaps even companionship. Contemporary examples include, Tiger Electronic's hamsters-like *Furby* and Sony's puppy-like robot *AIBO*. Japan's National Institute of Advanced Industrial Science and Technology created Paro, a harp seal robot, to serve as companions for Japan's expanding number of senior citizens [40] and therapeutic playmates for children with Autism [19]. Turkle refers to this class of robot as *relational artifacts*, defining them as "artifacts that present themselves as having 'states of mind' for which an understanding of those states enriches human encounters with them" [67]. Unlike the utilitarian robot, this category of robot demands a more social form of human-robot interaction, meaning this class of robot requires a level of functionality and usability that will allow it to interact with human agents within the context of natural social exchange.

Kismet and Repliée, the robots under consideration in this paper, fall into the category of affective social robot in that they are capable of interacting with humans using facial expression, gaze direction, and vocalization and thereby engage in the affective dynamics of human relationships. Upon reviewing the literature it seems clear that in the future social robots will increasingly fall into the hybrid category (yet unnamed) between strictly utilitarian and affective. For example, Heerink et al. [35] consider therapeutic social robots, such as Paro, as a hybrid category that is utilitarian because it functions as an assistive technology and affective or "hedonic" in that it serves an affective or emotional function. As such, the tasks that social robots will be expected to perform will become more complex and in turn so shall the robots themselves.

3. Project Visions

Cynthia Breazeal's Kismet is an expressive infant-like anthropomorphic robot designed specifically to engage "physically, affectively, and socially with humans in order to ultimately learn from them" [8, 12]. Anthropomorphism refers to the ascription of human forms, characteristics or behaviors to a non-human entity such as robots, computers and animals. Kismet is capable of displaying[1] and perceiving[2] a broad range of social cues. Its design is inspired by infant development with computational models drawn from psychology, ethology, and cognitive development. Kismet is a socially situated robot designed to engage in emotional and inter-personal dimensions of human-robot social interaction [13]. Kismet utilizes facial expressions, eye to eye contact, and close intimate interaction to convey emotion, communicate, and learn [9]. For example, Kismet can differentiate between skin tones and bright colors and therefore distinguish between people and toys [60]. Breazeal articulates her vision of social robots,

> For me, a sociable robot is able to communicate and interact with us, understand and even relate to us, in a personal way. It should be able to understand us and itself in social terms. We, in turn, should be able to understand it in the same social terms—to be able to relate to it and to empathize with it. Such a robot must be able to adapt and learn throughout its lifetime, incorporating shared experiences with other individuals into its understanding of self, of others, and of the relationships they share. In short, a sociable robot is socially intelligent in a human-like way, and interacting with it is like interacting with another person. At the pinnacle of achievement, they could befriend us, as we could them. [8]

Less formally, Breazeal asks, "How do you make something that's not alive appear lifelike?" [63]. To convey human-like perceptual ability, Kismet's visual, auditory, and proprioceptive input sensors are *concentrated* upon the robot's body which allows it to perceive and reciprocate social signals through gaze direction, facial expression, body posture, and vocal babbles [1]. Kismet perceives and maintains eye contact with the aid of nine computers that govern its vision process, representing the most computationally extensive processing that must be undertaken. This is because gaze is given a central role in Breazeal's project. "Gaze is probably one of the most critical powerful social cues we have" [60]. Further, in teaching scenarios, the caregiver is interested in focusing Kismet's attention on something the teacher-caregiver wants it to learn.

Hiroshi Ishiguro is a pioneer in researching the significance of the aesthetic appearance of social robots upon human-robot interactions. Ishiguro takes intelligence to be a "subjective phenomena among humans or between humans and robots" [38]. Further, Ishiguro is interested in the conveyance of *sonzai-kan,* or human presence, and the best way to evoke the sensation of "presence" within the social robot's human social partner. He questions if it will be found that highly anthropomorphic social robot are always regarded as uncanny and strange, as roboticist Masahiro Mori predicted [48]? "Simply put, what gives something a social presence? Is it mainly behavior, or is there instead some complex interplay between appearance and behavior?" [46]. For Ishiguro appearance *and* behavior are the critical factors in creating sufficiently believable humanoid robots.

Repliée differs from Kismet in terms of the way it achieves and conveys human-like perceptual abilities. Repliée utilizes a system of ubiquitous and *distributed* sensors to address this issue [37]. This strategy allows the social robot to become aware of its environment and the human activities within it through the use [of] multiple, coordinated, and distributed cameras, microphones, infrared motion sensors, floor sensors, and ID tag readers within the interactive human-robot setting. Repliée Q2 uses environmental and omni-directional vision sensors to recognize where people are (in the environment) in order to make eye contact while addressing them during conversation.

Kismet and Repliée represent the view that learning and intelligence is first and foremost an embodied experience which is expanded further in the next section. It should be noted however, that Kismet is a unique project within the field of North American robotics that has historically invested negligible attention to the physical features of humanoid robots. The field tends to favor instead sophisticated AI programming and computational speed over non-computational engineering facets (aesthetics) of humanoid body construction. The western privileging of the mind (programming and computation) over the body (engineering) is subtly expressed through Kismet's mechanistic head (the site of the mind) upon a platform, lacking any compelling connection to organicism at all.

Conversely, Repliée's synthetic body seems to convey a dual attendance to engineering and artificial intelligence features, suggestive of a scientific perspective that "acknowledges no necessary contradiction between animism and modern scientism" [26]. The following section examines other aspects of these social robots, considering in turn: embodied and social intelligence, morphology and aesthetics, and moral equivalence.

4. Underlying Assumptions: Embodied and Social Intelligence, Morphology and Aesthetics, Moral Equivalence

to represent clear & obvious way

relating to art & beauty.

4.1. Embodied and Social Intelligence

From the early stage of Kismet's development, there was the explicit assumption that embodiment is connected to intelligence and learning. "The point was, if you really wanted to understand human intelligence, it was important to have a human-like body, to have human-like interactions with the world. . . [and] that in order to learn from experience, you have to have something to get experience through, and that of course is this body situated in this environment" [8, 60]. Similarly, a distinguishing feature within Japanese robotics is the idea of embodied intelligence, consistent with the behavior-based approach which guides the research project Kismet. The central idea here is a shift from AI projects that 'think' intelligently to projects that 'act' intelligently. Under this view, intelligence may not be abstracted to some algorithmic equation but requires physical grounding or a material foundation (body). In this way, "embodied intelligence blurs the conceptual distinction between life and cognition, and between living and intelligent behavior" [57]. Ishiguro's project takes the principles underlying Kismet's project a step beyond being embodied (a material basis in the world) and being situated (sensory input effecting behavior) and to it adds an extremely sophisticated level of human like verisimilitude [36]. [11]

We can also distinguish between Kismet and Repliée in terms of *social intelligence* or the degree to which each may be considered "a full-fledged social participant" [10]. [12]

> If the robot's observable behaviour adheres to a person's social model for it during unconstrained interactions in the full complexity of the human environment, then we argue that the robot is socially intelligent in a genuine sense. Basically, the person can engage the robot as one would another socially responsive creature, and the robot does the same. At the pinnacle of performance, this would rival human–human interaction. [10]

Comparing the social intelligence realized by the two robots under consideration, it may be concluded that Kismet is a highly convincing socially intelligent creature but less compelling aesthetically as a humanoid agent. Breazeal describes the rich interaction between test subjects and Kismet as taking "place on a physical, social, and affective level. In so many ways, they treat Kismet as if it were a socially aware, living creature" [8].

Repliée on the other hand, is highly believable in terms of her aesthetic appearance, indeed she passes as a human 70% of time in short interval (2 second) recognition tests [37, 38, 45]. However, in terms of her ability to engage with humans as a genuine social agent Repliée is quite limited relative to Kismet. Utilizing Breazeal's [10] matrix of humanoid social robots, Repliée falls into the 'social interface' category, [13]

> This subclass of robots uses human-like social cues and communication modalities in order to facilitate interactions with people (i.e., to make the interactions more natural and familiar). . . commonly, an interface model is used, such as robot museum tour

guides, where information is communicated to people using speech and sometimes with reflexive facial expressions. Because this class of robot tends to value social behaviour only at the interface, the social model that the robot has for the person tends to be shallow (if any) and the social behavior is often pre-canned or reflexive. [10]

Conversely, Kismet is a fully "sociable creature" in that it possesses its "own internal goals and motivations . . . proactively engage[s] people in a social manner not only to benefit the person (e.g., to help perform a task, to facilitate interaction with the robot, etc.), but also to benefit itself" [10]. In conclusion, we can say that the degree of social intelligence achieved in each project highlights the artificial intelligence bias (associated with the view that behavior is of primary importance in human-robot interaction) in Kismet and the aesthetic bias (associated with the view that appearance is at least as important as behavior in human-robot interaction) in Repliée.

4.2. Morphology and Aesthetics

An immediately identifiable difference between the projects of Breazeal and Ishiguro 14 is their robots' morphology. Kismet is creature-like, but clearly a nonhuman social robot; whereas Repliée is a human-like social robot, modeled after a Japanese media figure (Anyako Fujii) of a very sophisticated kind. Kismet is consciously designed to *not* look like a human [8] yet successfully evokes an infant-caregiver response from those interacting with it. Breazeal notes that she engages in close face-to-face interaction that emulates what happens "between a mother and her infant" [60]. Kismet is designed to "tug on your emotional heartstrings" and induce nurturing and care giving responses [60]. "[Kismet] has a highly expressive face with an infant-like appearance. This encourages people to naturally interact with Kismet as if it were a baby (approx. 6 months) and to teach it social skills commensurate with that age" [13]. In selecting specific design features of Kismet, Breazeal decided to create a youthful and appealing, believable infant-like "fanciful robotic creature" [8].

Sophisticated humanoid robots such as Repliée Q2 [22, 39] are very humanlike 15 in appearance and behavior and in MacDorman and Ishiguro's [45] view, "[only] humanlike appearance and behavior can elicit fully humanlike communication, which is why androids will be one of the most useful platforms for investigating human behavior." Woods and Dautenhahn's [75] study of children's perception of robots may partly support this view in that they found "children were extremely clear in their distinction between a machine looking robot not having any feelings and human looking robots as possessing feelings." It is widely held that Repliée Q1 (Repliée Q2's earlier version) is "the closest thing yet to a machine copy of a human being" [2]. Repliée Q1 made her first appearance at the 2005 *World Expo* in Japan and is described as follows,

> She gestured, blinked, spoke, and even appeared to breathe . . . the android is partially covered in skin like silicone. Q1 is powered by a nearby air compressor, and has 31 points of articulation in its upper body. Internal sensors allow the android to react "naturally." It can block an attempted slap, for example. But it's the little, "unconscious" movements that give the robot its eerie verisimilitude: the slight flutter of the eyelids, the subtle rising and falling of the chest, the constant, nearly imperceptible shifting so familiar to humans.[3]

Breazeal notes, "[h]ow the human perceives the robot establishes a set of expectation that fundamentally shape how the human interacts with it" [8]. The fact that Kismet resembles an immature dependent creature situates it within a specific set of culturally shaped expectations and responses.[4] Similarly, MacDorman and Ishiguro [45] point out that, "The fact that Uando [Repliée 2] looks and is beginning to act like a Japanese woman sets off a slew of culturally-dependent expectations and responses."

Within the nascent field of social robotics, issues of appropriate human-robot   16
expectation, behavior, and response are growing increasing[ly] complicated, raising questions of ethics and morality in relation to ever more complex human-robot relationships. Our evolving human-robot relationships inevitably open up to larger debates relating to the obligations and responsibilities we ought to have toward our machines and our machines toward us. Such a dialogue has already begun, evidenced in the emergence of such initiatives as the *Euron Roboethic Roadmap* [69], developed by scientists from the European robotics community who are responding to the perceived need for discussion and development of an ethical framework that may eventually serve as a useful guideline for the design, manufacturing, and use of robots. Similarly, the *South Korean Robot Ethics Charter* is a highly anticipated document set to be released sometime in 2009. The South Korean Charter is a first attempt by a panel of futurists, science fiction authors, government officials, robotics professors, psychology experts, and medical doctors to develop a preliminary "set of ethical guidelines concerning the roles and functions of robots, as robots are expected to develop strong intelligence in the near future" [15, 76].

4.3. Moral Equivalence

The emergence of ubiquitous robot companions begins to raise complex ethical ques-   17
tions connected to notions of humanity and humanness. The Christian world enforces a strict division between creatures that have a soul and objects that do not. From this view, without an ensoulment event, social robots remain non-human and incapable of ever assuming a position of moral equivalence with humans [14]. Some researchers have begun to question the moral veracity of human-robot relationships, suggesting that such relations risk being psychologically impoverished from a moral perspective [41], or are disconcertingly inauthentic and therefore morally problematic [67]. Kahn et al. [41] question a robot's ontological status as 'social' or its ability to engage in *truly* social behavior, doubting that they can really interpret the world around them in terms of their own experience. Their study of owners of AIBO (a dog-like robot) found that while AIBO successfully evoked a sense of presence or lifelike essence, it evoked conceptions of moral standing only 12% of the time [41]. Turkle's study examined the interaction between seniors and Paro (a robotic baby harp seal) and found that Paro elicited feelings of admiration, loving behaviour, and curiosity but felt that the robot seal raised difficult "questions about what kind of authenticity we require of our technology. Do we want robots saying things that they could not possibly 'mean'? What kinds of relationships do we think are most appropriate for our children and our elders to have with relational artifacts?" [67]

From a cultural perspective, Harvey [33] argues that ". . . the historical record   18
indicates that the whole notion of 'humanity' is an intensely constructed cultural

product. There is no such thing as 'naturally' human; there is only what a given culture defines as 'human' at a given historical moment." Indeed, there seems to be strong evidence that scientists and engineers are in the midst of a social, cultural, and perceptual shift that may well redefine our present understanding [of] humanity, evident within conflicting views about the future moral status of robots. Each outlook on the moral standing of social robots suggests a unique ethical frame. For example, if robots are regarded as nothing more than *smart machines* or *clever tools* (utilitarian social robots), questions of consciousness, free will, and agency simply do not emerge and neither do questions of obligation and responsibility. Under such a view, Asimov's three laws of robotics would suffice as a guiding ethical outline. On the other hand, some roboethicists insist that these tenets are not appropriate "for our magnificent robots. These laws are for slaves" [18, 27].

Robots imagined as a magnificent new social species (affective social robots) presumes that machines may ultimately *"exceed in the moral as well as the intellectual dimension"* [69]. Therefore, we require ethical approaches and frames that move beyond classical moral theory and are better able to deal with unexpected, yet to be resolved, ethical/moral problems related to the emergence of new technological subjects that can no longer be easily classified as mere tools but perhaps as new species of agents, companions, and avatars [23].

It is difficult for some to imagine that robots could genuinely be regarded as serious companion surrogates. However, research has clearly shown that humans "will generally apply a social model when observing and interacting with autonomous robots" [8]. Ishiguro notes, "In our experience, the participants react to the android as if it were human even if they consciously recognize it as an android. The reaction is very different from reactions to robot-like robots" [37]. Says Robert J. Sawyer, Canadian science fiction writer, "What's weird is how biological entities change their behaviour when in the company of robots. When robots start interacting with us, we'll probably show as much resistance to their influence as we have to iPods, cell phones, and TV" [51]. In other words, provide appropriate cues (i.e. make the robot socially intelligent) and humans will instinctively engage in social behaviour with social robots. Alun Anderson provides a vivid description of his first encounter with Ishiguro's female android Repliée Q2 that is worth quoting in full,

> If my experience is anything to go by, when you meet an android you should prepare for reactions outside of your control. Walking across Ishiguro's lab, I can see android Repliée Q2 in the distance. Originally created from a body cast of a TV announcer, she seems nothing more than a shop-window mannequin. Close up, I can see that her skin is silicone and I imagine the steel skeleton and networks of pneumatic actuators that lie beneath it. But as Ishiguro switches on the control computers, I am in for a surprise. Repliée Q2 comes to life: she breathes, fidgets, gestures, blinks and looks around her—movements copied from video analysis of the real person's behavior. Then she makes eye contact with me and I unconsciously drop my eyes, move to a more correct social distance, and blurt out an instinctive "excuse me" for staring at her. And while the incongruity of apologizing to a brainless android is flashing through my mind, I also notice that I've begun mirroring her body posture. [3]

Cynthia Breazeal also confides that she feels a strong emotional connection to Kismet. She claims to be quite attached and never tires of her interaction with this engaging social robot. "To me Kismet is very special because when you interact with Kismet, you feel like you're interacting with Kismet. You know, there's someone home so to speak [laughs]. There's someone behind those eyes that you're interacting with. That's very different from most other robots which you observe as being this cool mechanical thing." [60]. This surprising instance of anthropomorphization by Dr. Breazeal is consistent with Nass et al.'s [49] findings that "individuals engage in social behavior towards technologies even when such behavior is entirely inconsistent with their beliefs about the machines." These authors suggest that when confronted with an entity that behaves in human-like ways, such as using language and responding based on prior inputs our brain's default response is to unconsciously treat the encountered object as human. Further, it is suggested that the more we "like" the encountered object, the more this encounter is likely to "lead to secondary consequences in interpersonal relationships (e.g. trust, sustained friendship, etc.). . . " [66].

Compounding the social robot's capacity to elicit unconscious, natural, and 21 intuitive responses within human-robot interaction, is its ability to generate an effect Breazeal refers to as *social amplification* [8]. For example, if an object is too close for Kismet's cameras to distinguish clearly, the robot will physically pull back and away. In this context, Kismet's behavior is really an aid for the internal system emulating human visual behavior to adjust to its social situation. However, this compensatory behavior also has a secondary, often magnifying effect. Kismet's backing up also provides the human partner with a strong social cue to back away "since it is analogous to the human response to invasions of 'personal space'" [8]. Breazeal's tests with social amplification found that when Kismet engaged in compensatory behaviours many social partners responded with reciprocating compensatory behaviour. For example, one robot partner queried "Am I too close to you? I can back up," while another backed up immediately and apologized. This preliminary finding adds to the evidence that people "readily and willingly read these cues to adapt their behavior" to accommodate the perceived need of the robot.

Cultures vary with regard to their attitudes toward robot companionship based 22 on a range of factors including religion, history, exposure to robots through media, and personal experience [4]. In the preceding section it was perhaps noted that western responses to highly anthropomorphic social robots is sometimes experienced as unsettling, surprising and even incongruous. The following section considers cultural and spiritual factors that contribute the reception and impact of ubiquitous social robots.

5. Social Preconditions: The East

One of the best well-known episodes among Shinto myths is the tale of the vanishing of 23 Amaterasu O-mi Kami, the sun goddess. The goddess, offended by her brother's provocations, decided to withdraw to a cave. As a result, the world was turned into darkness. To convince her to come back, the other deities decided to set up a spectacle with music, theatre and dance. The party was not a real one, but all the guests pretended to have fun, laughed and made a great amount of noise. Driven by curiosity, Amaterasu O-mi Kami decided to take a look at what was going on and came out of her cave. As soon as she was out, the other Gods blocked the entrance: the sun was back for good. The world was saved by a simple masquerade, a fake party and forced laughter, set up to fool a goddess. In the Shinto tradition, artificiality is licit: it saved the world. [42]

In Japan, erotic love dolls or 'Dutch Wives,' as they are still sometimes called, hold a unique and legitimate cultural space. Love dolls utilized for sexual pleasure among men were first written about in Japanese literature in the late seventeenth century. The mechanism described was an artificial vulva, called *azumagata*, Japanese for woman substitute. Formed out of tortoiseshell or leather with an entrance lined with velvet or silk, this mechanism replicated a woman's labia major. Some versions of the azumagata were of entire female bodies. These versions were sometimes called *doningyo*, meaning doll body [44]. Paul Tabori describes the *doningyo*: "A man who is forced to sleep alone can obtain pleasure with a doningyo. This is the body of a female doll, the image of a girl of thirteen or fourteen with a velvet vulva. But these dolls are only for people of high rank. Another name of the doll body is even more outspoken: *tahi-joro*—'traveling whore'" [61].

These dolls (Dutch Wives) are believed to have originated with the leather dolls 24 brought aboard Dutch merchant ships starting at around the seventeenth century. The Japanese interacted with Dutch merchants on the trade island of Deshima, established by the Dutch East India Company in 1641. Through the relationship between traders, the Japanese became familiar with this sexual practice [44, 52]. Today, discarded dolls are even afforded respectful funeral rites at a special bodhisattva for dolls at the Shimizu Kannondo (Goddess of Mercy) in Ueno Park. This park was founded in the seventeenth century as a place where the souls of dolls are consecrated. Hideo Tsuchiya, president of Orient Industries the leading manufacturer of love dolls in Japan, says the following about love dolls, "A Dutch wife is not merely a doll, or an object. She can be an irreplaceable lover, who provides a sense of emotional healing" [44].

Ishiguro observes that the receptiveness of robot integration into human society 25 is culturally determined and that Japanese people generally embrace "the idea of a human-like android as a companion and we are quite serious about developing helper robots for old people" [3]. The history of the humanoid robot in Japan can be traced back to the Edo Period (1600–1867) and the masterful craft of constructing *karakuri* (meaning 'trick,' 'mechanism' or 'gadget') that were widely known and adored by the Japanese public [36]. The most famous karakuri depicts a delightful child engaged in a traditional Japanese act of hospitality: green tea service. Thus, the character of the relationship between human and robot from this very early period was interactive and social. "This unique interactivity makes the windup tea-serving doll a social-machine, in which the main purpose, like the Japanese humanoid robots that are its natural descendents, is communication with human beings" [36]. Yoshikazu Suematsu, Dean of Tokyo National College of Technology, makes clear the way in which early social robots informed the way Japanese culture subsequently came to regard robots.

To put it simply, the difference between *Might Atom* [Japan's equivalent of the North American Mickey Mouse] and the *Terminator* show the differences between how Japanese and Westerners view robots. Japanese are unique in the world for their strong love and affinity for robots. [36]

The Euro-American automata emerging at around the same time as the Japanese ka[r]akuri were lucrative and wildly popular entertainment for the masses, but they were also engaged with the central debates of their time. The mechanisms of master automaton builder Jacques de Vaucanson and other mechanicians represented "philosophical experiments" that explored the outer boundaries of mechanical simulation and sought to learn what these mechanical contrivances "might reveal about their natural subjects" [55]. The entertainment value of automata lay principally in their dramatic representation of a philosophical preoccupation engaging laymen, philosophers and royalty throughout this period: the problem of whether or not human processes and functions were essentially mechanical. The goal of Japanese karakuri on the other hand, according to Suematsu, "was not realism but charm—art for its own sake rather than the advancement of scientific knowledge" [36].

The view of robots as extension of family is also evident in very early robot 26 history as well as the view held by Makoto Nishimura, creator of Japan's first modern robot (1928), "[if] one considers humans as the children of nature, artificial humans created by the hand of man are thus nature's grandchildren" [36]. In Japan, humanoid robots are regarded as and referred to 'as' persons, not 'as if' they were persons. This sensibility is evident in the lexicon of the Japanese language and the use of certain suffixes, such as *kun* (for boys) and *chan* (for girls and boys). These suffixes express a sense of endearment, intimateness, sweetness, and child-like or diminutive status and are often reflected in the names of Japanese social robots. In short, humanoid social robots are conceived and marketed "as adopted members of a household" [36].

In addition [to] the early history of the robot, Japanese spiritual teachings may 27 have also had a shaping influence on the positive development of robot culture in Japan. Geraci [26] notes, "Shinto and Buddhism have played easily recognized roles in the development of the Japanese robotics industry. For example, engineer Masahiro Mori believes that a robot could someday become a Buddha." According to Shinto Buddhism, God is in everything, including humans, animals, plants, rocks, and machines.

> . . . tools and machines, while appearing to be separate from us, are in truth only functions that have been cut away from us, but are essentially part of us. . . In my opinion, the Buddha's most basic teaching i[s] that we must not consider as separate that which is one. To commit this fallacy is what is called in Buddhism sinful or unclean. [47]

According to Shinto, robots are not that different from humans and share the same vital energies or forces called *kami* that are present in all aspects of the world and universe [57]. This perspective is particularly evident in such popular culture forms as Japanese Manga and the beloved "poster child for benevolent technology"—Atom (Astro) Boy.

> The effect of this small, pointy-headed superhero on Japanese attitudes toward humanoid robots is incaculable. . . Atom embodies a deeply ingrained postwar vision of pacifism and technology, representing the well spring of an almost universal agreement among theorists, researchers and engineers that robots can not only be friends with human beings but even be, perhaps, the country's salvation. [36]

In short, within Japanese popular culture good and the evil are not simplistically mapped such that robots (and technology generally) are positioned as mankind's enemy and humans positioned as some superior and benevolent race. Rather, technology and humans are taken to be equally capable of good and bad and therefore distributed equally between imperfect humans and machines [4, 36]. This technological perspective, as we will see, is *not* shared in western culture.

6. Social Preconditions: The West

> I was now about to form another being of whose dispositions I was alike ignorant; she   28
> might become ten thousand times more malignant than her mate and delight, for its
> own sake, in murder and wretchedness . . . and she . . . might refuse to comply with
> a compact made before her creation. . . She might also turn with disgust from him
> to the superior beauty of man. . . Even if they were to leave . . . one of the first results
> of these sympathies for which the demon thirsted would be children, and a race of
> devils would be propagated upon the earth. . . I left the room, and locking the door,
> made a solemn vow in my own heart to never resume my labours. [59]

The western dream of creating life through moving statues, golem, homunculi, automata, androids, cyborgs, and humanoid social robots is evident within myths and superstitions from antiquity, through the Middle Ages, and up to our contemporary moment [16, 17]. That humans desire to create simulacra of the human body is indisputable; however, the motivation, purpose, and significance propelling scientists and roboticists forward are not well understood.

In 1832, David Brewster, noted scholar and inventor, asserted that life like   29 automata were produced merely as *entertainment for the masses.* "Ingenious and beautiful as all these pieces of mechanisms are, and surprising as their effect appear even to scientific spectators, the principal object of their inventions was to astonish and amuse the public" [25]. Derek de Solla Price and Silvio Bedini [5], historians of science, posit an *innate and deeply rooted desire* within "man to simulate the world about him through the graphic and plastic arts," [20] as motivation for the building of automata and that such creations reflect the creator's desire to better understand his external world [5]. Norbert Wiener, father of North American cybernetics, writes similarly (in terms of desire) about the historic quest to create life, "At every stage of technique . . . the ability of the artificer to produce a working simulacrum of a living organism has always intrigued people" [71]. Robert Plank's scholarship on the literary treatment of the robot theme from medieval legend to our contemporary moment, suggests that the motivation to create artificial life represents a *symbolic desire* of the male artificer to reproduce without female participation in the process [54]. In this way, argues Ksenija Bilbija, the artificer may "prove that men have the sole power in creation" [7]. JP Telotte, film studies scholar, asserts that the "human penchant for artifice," that is to say that the desire to study, comprehend, and recreate the world about him (including himself) reflects *a quest to reduce human life itself to artifice* [62]. For Michel Foucault, Enlightenment automata represented *"small-scale models of power"* [24] in an age where the body became increasingly docile as it was subjected to intensifying practices of power and control. Gaby Wood [74], historian of eighteenth century mechanical life, regards the quest to imitate life as instances of rational science pushing beyond the "bounds of reason" [74], at times bordering upon *madness*. In contrast, Jessica Riskin [55, 56], historian of Enlightenment science, regards the drive to recreate life as an undertaking continually shaped and *reshaped by the evolving relationship between humans and the nonhumans*. Jennifer Gonzalez [28], historian of art and visual culture, argues that shifting representations of *artificial life reflect abrupt changes* in the social and cultural attitudes related to our understanding of what it means to be human.

But even as the quest to simulate life proceeds unencumbered, the project 30 remains deeply rooted and inflected with the cultural anxiety that these masterful mechanical contrivances initially evoked [58]. This apprehension is related to the fact that mechanized models of life, automata for example, seem to animate of their own accord and therefore appear to be endowed with a spirit of their own and this elicited fear and anxiety. "The horror and fear provoked by appearances in nature of monstrous births moved over to the horror and fear provoked by our own artificial creations, where these affects have remained lodged to this day" [31]. The echoes of this anxiety are also bound up in the West's enduring "Frankenstein Mythology." Mary Shelley's [59] narrative gave early voice to fears and desires about modernity, especially in relation to violations of the body wherein it was exposed as "both a stable ground for experience in a time of unprecedentedly rapid change and a fragile, limited vessel, which we yearn to remake" [68]. Shelley's narrative also stands as a cautionary cultural myth that explored tensions and concerns related to the (re)production of new life forms that we may or may not be able to control and raises important questions of agency and whether our creations will be (or should be) endowed with the desire for (and right to) independence and agency.

I suggest that the dual aspects of this contradictory disposition toward creating 31 artificial-life outlined above (e.g. desire on one hand and anxiety on the other) are evident in the design choices of Kismet. Recall Breazeal's statement, "There's someone behind those eyes that you're interacting with." On one hand, Breazeal is highly engaged and attached to her creation to the degree that she imbues it with a generous measure of animism. On the other, her aesthetic design choices are informed by research that suggests humans are sensitive "in a negative way" to robots that seek to imitate humans to high degree but fail [8]. This perspective (referred to as *the uncanny valley* effect) was forwarded by Masahiro Mori [48], an influential roboticist, who cautioned against building robots that appear too humanlike because they would be perceived as too eerie or unsettling.

I propose that the deeply embedded cultural fear of machines resembling 32 humans lay at the heart of Breazeal's design choices; choices which ensure that her creation will not evoke *Frankenstein* fears about monsters out of control. As the quest to create life artificially pushes forward we are in need of critical concepts and strategies and language that move us beyond Frankenstein mythology and take into account the shifting ontological ground between humans and machines. The closing section of this work offers a set of concepts that may prove instructive in this regard.

7. Conclusion: New Conceptual Tools—Ontology, Stories and Language

Speaking about the potential benefits of social robots, roboethicists predict that 33 intelligent machines will behave like realistic and reliable companions and that they will be highly adaptable and therefore fit easily into a variety of human situations and circumstances [69]. Further, as humanoid creatures are introduced into a wide range of human environments, workplaces, homes, schools, hospitals, public places, offices (and more) their presence promises to "dramatically change our society" [69]. In short, social robots of the twenty-first century are creatures which merge disparate elements of the biological and technological into an image that is situated at the outer boundary of human and nonhuman interface. They are at once provocative expressions of the height of human, scientific, and technological prowess as well as complex sites that demand reconceptualised ontological categories, stories, and language.

Donna Haraway has argued that in an increasingly cyborg society the ontological 34 separation of the human from the nonhuman entrenched during the Modern period is no longer tenable.

> The cyborg age is here and now, everywhere there's a car or a phone or a VCR. Being a cyborg isn't about how many bits of silicon you have under your skin or how many prosthetics your body contains. It's about. . . going to the gym, looking at a shelf of carbloaded bodybuilding foods, checking out the Nautilus machines, and realizing that [we're] in a place that wouldn't exist without the idea of the body as a high-performance machine. [43]

Jennifer Gonzalez [28] has noted that when the existing ontological model of human *being* does not fit an emerging paradigm, a hybrid model of existence is needed and emerges to take in a new, complex and contradictory lived experience. Similarly, Elaine Graham [29], cultural critic of post humanism, argues that each era has its own unique creatures that negotiate the margins and boundaries separating the human from the non-human. According to Graham, Western imagination has fashioned an assortment of "fantastical, monstrous and alien beings," who simultaneously demonstrate and destabilize "ontological hygiene by which cultures have distinguished nature from artifice, human from non-human, normal from pathological" [29]. Social robots exhibit the power to demonstrate and destabilize, evidenced by the ambivalent feelings of wonder and admiration these objects seem to evoke through their ability to simulate the complexity of life but also disturb and threaten because of their disinclination to fit easily into either/or (alive or dead; human or nonhuman) ontological categories.

Katherine Hayles [34] suggests that one of the ways in which scientific enter- 35 prises gain credence for their visions is to tell stories about the world; yet, as Donna Haraway [32] has remarked, not all stories are equal. In researching the Japanese perspective on social robots, I was particularly struck by the impact that Atom/Astro Boy has had on Japanese society through his ability to act as a mediator between humans and machines, while at the same time interfacing between culture and science.

Science fiction writer Hideaki Sena believes Atom's role as intermediary goes even farther, spanning the gap between fantasy and reality. "We may be able to gain a realistic view of the environment for robots in Japan by thinking of robot stories as interfaces between culture and science," he writes. "Images are being passed back and forth between fiction and real life science, and these two realms are closely interconnected. [36]

Thus, in a Western context if we take seriously the idea that movies, magazines, newspapers, and television represent critical locations in society wherein myth making and meaning making are exchanged, then we may also realize that these same cultural spaces permit us to construct new stories to tell ourselves about the shifting and changing relationships humans have with technology. Contemporary anxieties associated with social robots are bound up with historical "themes, scripts, and metaphors" such as the *Frankenstein myth*. These themes, scripts, and metaphors in turn contribute to contemporary attitudes toward scientific advancements [50]. This would seem a vital moment in which to revise aspects of the Frankenstein mythology that has haunted the social robot for the past three centuries. Thus, we might ask what stories we would tell ourselves if we (re)imagine Victor Frankenstein *not* abandoning his prodigal son. What lessons would he have taught his unnamed creation about being a human, about being a machine, and perhaps more importantly about being not quite either?

Ishiguro refers to Repliée as an *android* to foreground her aesthetic kinship with human beings. Breazeal refers to Kismet as a *social robot* to highlight its capacity to engage with humans in complex social contexts. Turkle uses the term *relational artefact* to draw attention to the psychological dimensions of human-robot interactions. Kuhn et al. [41], favour the term *robotic others* because this term "makes less of a commitment to the ontological social status of a robot (whether it is actually social or not) and less of a commitment to the ways in which people interpret the social standing of a robot." Indeed, Kuhn and collaborators stress the importance of new language to suitably capture the shifting ontological status of machines and the new social relationships arising from our increasing interaction with robotic others.

> As an analogy, we do not normally present people with an orange object and ask, "Is this object red or yellow?" It is something of both, and we call it orange. Similarly, it may not be the best approach to keep asking if these emerging technological agents are, for example, "alive" or "not alive" if from the person's experience of the subject object interaction, the object is alive in some respects and not alive in other respects, and is experienced not simply as a combination of such qualities. . . . [41]

Numerous people who have had an opportunity to interact with Kismet have admitted to Breazeal that this social robot has *real* presence, variously referred to in the social robot literature as essence, presence, or animism. Breazeal notes, "It seems to really impact them on an emotional level, to the point where they tell me that when I turn Kismet off, it's really jarring. That's powerful. It means that I've really captured something in this robot that's special" [63]. Indeed, Breazeal confesses to sensing 'something' behind Kismet's eyes herself. And even if she is reluctant to bequest a gendered pronoun upon her creation, she does submit that being in its presence gives her a feeling that she [is] interacting with a 'someone.' I found this admission an interesting counter point to the fact that Breazeal consistently refers to Kismet as 'it' in papers and interviews. In studies involving interaction between children and Kismet a similar space betwixt human and nonhuman emerges in the children's language [67], coming through in statements like Kismet seems "sort of alive." These ideas taken together suggest that we are in critical need of revitalized language to capture the complexities and contradictions of emerging social agents and our relationship to them.

The quest to create ever more sophisticated social robots will inevitably inten- 37 sify. The UK's National Health Service has already used robots called *Da Vinci* and *Zeus* to perform surgeries at Guy's and St. Thomas Foundation Trust in London [30, 72]. Advanced versions of humanoid robots are expected to assume domestic responsibilities and assist in the care of the elderly and children in as few as 20 years. At Tokyo's University of Science, visitors are greeted by a *robo-receptionist* dressed in a university uniform who is capable of answering questions and appears to grow bored in the absence of something to occupy herself [21]. So-called *nursebots* are expected to be functioning in Japanese hospital wards and will be capable of ensuring patients have taken their medication and alert other medical staff if a patient's vital signs appear to deteriorate [21]. It seems clear that as social robots become ubiquitous and enter into therapeutic, emotional, social, companion, and surrogate relationships with humans, the Western tendency to see the world in terms of strictly bounded categories ordered by hierarchical and divisive binary relations will become increasingly untenable.

To date, there has been a lack of sociological interest in human–humanoid 38 relationships and very few have examined the social impact of human–humanoid interaction [64, 65, 70, 73, 77]. In my view what is required is a set of conceptual tools that are capable of engaging with the boundary contradictions that robot-human relations evoke. That is to say, tools that take into consideration the ontological blurring between social actors (i.e. between humans and nonhumans); creates a conceptual space for new kinds of stories about human-machine interaction to be told; and facilitates the emergence of a new language to speak about new social actors and our relationships with them. This requires that we begin by using a mode of thought that situates us at the confluence of conceptual categories that see contradictory. We might call this mode of thinking dialectical. To think dialectically is to interrogate ideas which coexist in the tension between things, "a location where our knowledge can be both stable and on the move" [6]. Donna Haraway also argues for a middle position which she refers to as "within the belly of the monster" [53]. From this dialectic location, a shifting space betwixt and between, concepts that question rather than presuppose dichotomous categories can be employed so as to create knowledge that is "situated" [32], meaning knowledge that is produced by positioned actors who work in/between all kinds of locations and work up/on/through all kinds of research relationships [6]. As the future increasingly looks like a scene out of Asimov's *I-Robot*, it is my fervent hope that we take seriously Donna Haraway's plea that we take pleasure as well as responsibility in our coupling with new technology. As our evolving social robots increasingly pass as living creatures, it demands that we answer the question: "what is it to be alive?" And as our humanoid machines eventually transcend the final boundary separating humans from machines it becomes ever more problematic to regard such objects as mere machines.

Notes

1. Kismet can express through tone of voice such emotional states as anger, fear, disgust, happiness, sadness, and surprise.
2. Kismet can perceive through tone of voice such emotional cues as praising, scolding, and soothing. It should be noted however, that Breazeal's project "totally side steps the issue of conscious experience and awareness of the emotional state which we consider to be feelings" [10].
3. http://news.nationalgeographic.com/news/2005/06/0610_050610_robot.html.
4. Kismet's design was guided by the findings of Eibli-Eibesfeldt, who identified a set of cross culturally consistent facial characteristics thought to evoke nurturing responses from adults. These features include an enlarged head (relative to body size), enlarged eyes (relative to face size), a large or high forehead, and lips which suggest suckling [8].

References

[1] Kismet. Available at: http://www.ai.mit.edu/projects/humanoid-robotics-group/kismet/kismet.html. Accessed March 2008
[2] Alford P (2007) In search of the perfect tin. In: The Australian, July 4:23
[3] Anderson A (2007) Interview: The shape of android robots to come. N Sci 195(2614): 46–47
[4] Bartneck C et al (2005) Cultural differences in attitudes toward robots. In: Proceedings of the symposium on robot companions: Hard problems and open challenges in HRI, 2005. AISB'05 Convention, Hatfield, UK, April 12–15, 2005. The Society for the Study of Artificial Intelligence and the Simulation of Behaviour, The University of Hertfordshire, Hatfield, pp 1–4
[5] Bedini S (1964) The role of automata in the history of technology. Technol Cult 5(1):24–42
[6] Berg A-J, Lie M (1995) Feminism and constructivism: Do artifacts have gender? Sci, Technol Hum Values 20(3):332–351
[7] Bilbija K (1994) Rosario Ferre's "The youngest doll": On women, dolls, golems and cyborgs. Callaloo 17(3):878–888
[8] Breazeal C (2002) Designing sociable robots. Intelligent robots and autonomous agents. MIT Press, Cambridge
[9] Breazeal C (2003) Emotion and sociable humanoid robots. Int J Hum-Comput Stud 29:119–155
[10] Breazeal C (2003) Toward sociable robots. Robot Auton Syst 42:167–175
[11] Breazeal C, Scassellati B (1999) How to build robots that make friends and influence people. In: Proceedings of the international conference on intelligent robots and systems, IROS'99. Kyongju, South Korea, October 17–21, 1999. IEEE Press, Piscataway, pp 858–863
[12] Breazeal C, Scassellati B (2000) Infant-like social interactions between a robot and a human caregiver. Adapt Behav 8(1):49–74
[13] Breazeal C, Velasquez J (1999) Robot in society: Friend or appiiance? In: Proceedings of agents '99 workshop on emotion based architectures, Seattle, Washington, 1999, pp 18–26
[14] Calverley D (2006) Android science and animal rights, does an analogy exist? Connect Sci 18(4):403–417
[15] Chang-Won L (2007) South Korea draws up code of ethics for robots. Available at: http://www.forbes.com/markets/feeds/afx/2007/08/06/afx3992827.html. Accessed August 2008

[16] Chapuis A, Droz E (1958) Automata: A historical and technological study. Neuchatel, Switzerland

[17] Cohen J (1967) Human robots in myth and science. AS Barnes, South Brunswick

[18] Coleman KG (2001) Android arete: Toward a virtue ethic for computational agents. Eth Inf Technol 3:247–265

[19] Dautenhahn K, Billard A (2002) Proceedings of the 1st Cambridge workshop on universal access and assistive technology. In: 1st Cambridge workshop on universal access and assistive technology, London, March 2002

[20] de Solla Price D (1964) Automata and the origins of mechanism and mechanistic philosophy. Technol Cult 5(1):9–23

[21] Doherty G (2007) Rise of the machines [Newspaper Database]. May 16, 2007. Available at: http://www.independent.ie/unsorted/features/rise-of-the-machines-677434.html. Accessed December 2008

[22] Dwyer M (2006) Monster mash is out of this world. In: The Age:4

[23] Floridi L, Sanders JW (2001) Artificial evil and the foundation of computer ethics. Ethics Info Technol 3:55–66

[24] Foucault M (1995) Discipline and punish: Birth of the prison. Random House, New York

[25] Fryer D, Marshall J (1979) The motives of Jacques de Vaucanson. Technol Cult 20(2):257–269

[26] Geraci R (2006) Spiritual robots: Religion and our scientific view of the natural world. Theol Sci 4(3):229–246

[27] Gips J (1995) Towards the ethical robot. In: Ford K et al (eds) Android epistemology. AAAI Press/MIT Press, Menlo Park, pp 243–252

[28] Gonzalez J (2000) Envisioning cyborg bodies: Notes from current research. In: Kirkup G et al (eds) The gendered cyborg: A reader. Routledge in association with the Open University. London, pp 58–73

[29] Graham E (1999) Cyborgs or goddesses? Becoming divine in a cyberfeminist age. Inf Commun Soc 2(4):419–438

[30] Habershon E. Woods R (2006) No sex please, robot, just clean the floor. In: Sunday Times, June 18, 2006:11

[31] Hanafi Z (2000) The monster in the machine: Magic, medicine, and the marvelous in the time of the scientific revolution. Duke University Press, Durham

[32] Haraway D (1991) Simians, cyborgs, and women: The reinvention of nature. Free Association Books, London

[33] Harvey LSC (1994) Mr. Jefferson's wolf: Slavery and the suburban robot. J Am Cult 17(4):79–89

[34] Hayles NK (1999) How we became posthuman: Virtual bodies in cybernetics, literature, and informatics. University of Chicago Press, Chicago

[35] Heerink M et al (2008) Enjoyment intention to use and actual use of a conversational robot by elderly people. In: Proceedings of the 3rd ACM/IEEE international conference on human robot interaction, 2008, Amsterdam, The Netherlands, pp 113–120

[36] Hornyak T (2006) Loving the machine: The art and science of Japanese robots. Kodansha International, New York

[37] Ishiguro H (2006) Android science: Conscious and subconscious recognition. Connect Sci 18(4):319–332

[38] Ishiguro H (2007) Android science: Toward a new cross-interdisciplinary framework. Robot Res 28:118–127

[39] Ishiguro H (2009) Androids. Available at: http://www.ed.ams.eng.osaka-u.ac.jp/research/0007/. Accessed November 1, 2007

[40] Johnstone B (1999) Japan's friendly robots. Tech Rev 102(3):64–69

[41] Kahn P et al (2004) Social and moral relationships with robotic others? In: Proceedings of the 13th international workshop on robot and human interactive communication, RO-MAN '04. Kurashiki, Okayama, Japan. September 20–22, 2004. IEEE Press, Piscataway, pp 545–550

[42] Kaplan F (2004) Who is afraid of the humanoid? Investigating cultural differences in the acceptance of robots. Int J Hum Robot 1(3):1–16

[43] Kunzri H (1997) You are cyborg: Interview with Donna Haraway [Online Magazine]. Available at: www.wired.com/wired/archive//5.02/ffharaway.html?person=donna_haraway&topic_set=wiredpeople. Accessed December 20, 2004

[44] Levy D (2007) Love + sex with robots: The evolution of human-robot relationships. Harper Collins, New York

[45] MacDorman K, Ishiguro H (2006) The uncanny advantage of using androids in cognitive and social science research. Interact Stud 7(3):297–337

[46] MacDorman K et al (2005) Assessing human likeness by eye contact in an android testbed. In: Proceedings of the 27th annual meeting of the cognitive science society, Stresa, Italy, September 21–23, 2005

[47] Mori M (1999) The Buddha in the robot: A robot engineer's thoughts on science and religion. Kosei Publishing Co, Tokyo

[48] Mori M (1970) The uncanny valley. Energy 7(4):33–35

[49] Nass C et al (1997) Computers are social actors: A review of current research. In: Friedman B (ed) Human values and the design of computer technology. CSLI Press, Stanford, pp 137–162

[50] Nerlich B et al (2001) Fictions, fantasies, and fears: The literary foundations of the cloning debate. J Lit Semant 30:37–52

[51] Nickerson C (2007) With robotic bugs, larger ethical questions: Advances affect ties of human, machine. In: The Boston Globe, November 16:A1

[52] Pate AS, Gardiner L (2005) Ningyo: The art of the Japanese doll. Tuttle Publishing, Boston

[53] Penley C, Ross A (1990) Cyborgs at large: Interview with Donna Haraway. Soc Text 25(26):8–23

[54] Plank R (1965) The golem and the robot. Lit Psychol 15(1):12–28

[55] Riskin J (2003) The defecating duck, or, the ambiguous origins of artificial life. Crit Inq 29:599–633

[56] Riskin J (2003) Eighteenth-century wetware. Represent 83:97–125

[57] Robertson J (2007) Robo sapiens japanicus: Humanoid robots and the posthuman family. Crit Asian Stud 39(3):369–398

[58] Shaw-Garlock GR (2006) Descartes' daughters: Monstrous machine-women through time. Simon Fraser University, Burnaby

[59] Shelley M (1983) Frankenstein: Or, the modern Prometheus. Penguin, New York. First published 1818

[60] Stork D, O'Connell M (2001) Emotional intelligence: Cynthia Breazeal interview. Available at: http://www.2001halslegacy.com/interviews/breazeal.html. Accessed March 3, 2008

[61] Tabori P (1969) The humor and technology of sex. Julian Press, New York

[62] Telotte JP (2004) Human artifice and the science fiction film. In: Redmond S (ed) Liquid metal. Wallflower Press, London, pp 57–63. First published 1983

[63] Thomson E (2001) MIT team building social robot. Available at: http://web.mit.edu/newsoffice/2001/kismet.html. Accessed March 20

[64] Turkle S (1984) The second self: Computers and the human spirit. Simon & Schuster, New York

[65] Turkle S (1995) Life on the screen: Identity in the age of the internet. Simon & Schuster, New York

[66] Turkle S et al (2006) Encounters with kismet and cog: Children respond to relational artifacts. In: Messaris P, Humphreys L (eds) Digital media: Transformations in human communication. Peter Lang, New York, pp 313–330

[67] Turkle S et al (2006) Relational artifacts with children and elders: The complexities of cybercompanionship. Connect Sci 18(4):347–361

[68] Turney J (1998) Frankenstein's footsteps: Science, genetics and popular culture. Yale University Press, New Haven

[69] Veruggio G (2006) Euron roboethics roadmap. In: Proceedings of the 6th IEEE-RAS international conference on humanoid robots, Genoa, Italy, December 4–6, 2006, pp 612–617

[70] Wessels MG (1990) The human use of human beings. Prentice-Hall, Englewood Cliffs

[71] Wiener N (1948) Cybernetics or control and communication in the animal and the machine, 2nd edn. MIT Press, Cambridge

[72] Wilson D (2006) Rise of the robot. In: The Age, November 9:4

[73] Wolfe A (1991) Mind, self, society and computer: Artificial intelligence and the sociology of mind. Am J Sociol 96(5):1073–1096

[74] Wood G (2002) Living dolls: A magical history of the quest for mechanical life. Faber and Faber, London

[75] Woods S et al (2004) The design space of robots: Investigating children's views. In: Proceedings of the 13th IEEE international workshop on robot and human interactive communication, RO-MAN, Okayama, Japan, September 20–22, 2004, pp 47–52

[76] Yoon-Mi K (2007) Korea drafts robot ethics charter. [Online Newspaper] April 28, 2007. Available at: www.koreaherald.co.kr. Accessed March, 2008

[77] Zhao S (2006) Humanoid social robots as a medium of communication. New Media Soc 8(3):401–419

READING FOR CONTENT

1. Summarize the chief differences that Shaw-Garlock draws between Breazeal's Kismet robot and Ishiguro's Repliée robot in paragraphs 11–16.

2. Summarize the chief moral and cultural differences between Kismet and Repliée as suggested in paragraphs 17–27.

READING FOR GENRE, ORGANIZATION, AND STYLISTIC FEATURES

1. The genre of critique relies upon comparison and contrast to clarify differences between competing systems. List the comparisons and contrasts that seem most important to you in this essay.

2. List the chief conceptual categories within which the author compares and contrasts Kismet and Repliée.

3. Describe the framework of cultural reference in the author's style.

READING FOR RHETORICAL CONTEXT

1. How does the author's broad cultural reference enable her to respond to the different robotic systems of Breazeal and Ishiguro?

2. What attitudes does the author project toward these different robotic systems?

WRITING ASSIGNMENTS

Shaw-Garlock draws distinctions between Breazeal's Kismet robot and Hiroshi Ishiguro's Repliée robot.

1. In a 500-word essay, write a critical response to Shaw-Garlock's description of Breazeal's Kismet robot. How accurately does Shaw-Garlock describe it? How sympathetic is she to Breazeal's aims? How might Breazeal criticize Shaw-Garlock's aims?

2. In a 500-word essay, write a critical response to Shaw-Garlock's description of Hiroshi Ishguro's Repliée robot. How accurately does Shaw-Garlock describe it? How sympathetic is she to Hiroshi Ishiguro's aims? How might Hiroshi Ishiguro criticize Shaw-Garlock's aims?

3. In a 1,000-word essay that draws upon Shaw-Garlock's discussion of Eastern and Western cultural differences (paragraphs 23–31), write an argument-synthesis that attempts to define criteria for acceptable tasks that affective robots might perform in our society while interacting with human beings. For example, might the work of robots be limited to routine, mechanized tasks, or might it cross the line into sharing companionable feelings and emotions with human beings?

The Ethical Frontiers of Robotics

Noel Sharkey

Noel Sharkey is a professor of computer science at the University of Sheffield in England. He appears frequently on British television and radio as an expert on robot science and techno games.

PREREADING

Would you entrust the care of aging relatives to industrial robots? If you were a parent, would you entrust the care of young children to robots? Do you think the military should deploy autonomous robot weaponry? Freewrite for ten minutes on reasons why you would or would not approve of using robots for these purposes.

Robots have been used in laboratories and factories for many years, but their uses are changing fast. Since the turn of the century, sales of professional and personal service robots have risen sharply and are estimated to total ~5.5 million in 2008. This number, which far outstrips the 1 million operational industrial robots on the planet, is estimated to reach 11.5 million by 2011 (*1*). Service robots are good at dull, dangerous, and dirty work, such as cleaning sewers or windows and performing domestic duties in the home. They harvest fruit, pump gasoline, assist doctors and surgeons, dispose of bombs, and even entertain us. Yet the use of service robots poses unanticipated risks and ethical problems.

1

Sharkey, Noel. "The Ethical Frontiers of Robotics." *Science* 322.5909 (19 Dec. 2008): 1800–01. Web. 3 Sept. 2010. <http://www.sciencemag.org> Reprinted with permission from AAAS.

Two main areas of potential ethical risk are considered here: the care of children and the elderly, and the development of autonomous robot weapons by the military.

The widespread availability of service robots has resulted from several developments that allowed robots to become mobile, interactive machines. Artificial intelligence has not met its early promise of truly intelligent machines, but researchers in the emerging field of human-robot interaction have implemented artificial intelligence techniques for the expression of emotion, language interaction, speech perception, and face recognition (2,3).

Sophisticated control algorithms have been developed (4) and have been combined with advances in sensor technology, nanotechnology, materials science, mechanical engineering, and high-speed miniaturized computing. With the prices of robot manufacture falling—robots were 80% cheaper in 2006 than they were in 1990—service robots are set to enter our lives in unprecedented numbers.

In the area of personal-care robots, Japanese and South Korean companies have developed child-minding robots that have facilities for video-game playing, conducting verbal quiz games, speech recognition, face recognition, and conversation. Mobility and semiautonomous function are ideal for visual and auditory monitoring; radio-frequency identification tags provide alerts when children move out of range. The robots can be controlled by mobile phone or from a window on a PC that allows input from camera "eyes" and remote talking from caregivers.

Research on child-minding robots in the United States (5) using the Sony Qurio and large-scale testing by NEC in Japan with their PaPeRo have demonstrated close bonding and attachment by children, who, in most cases, prefer a robot to a teddy bear. Short-term exposure can provide an enjoyable and entertaining experience that creates interest and curiosity. In the same way, television and computer games may be used by parents as an entertainment or distraction for short periods. They do not provide care and the children still need human attention. However, because of the physical safety that robot minders provide, children could be left without human contact for many hours a day or perhaps for several days, and the possible psychological impact of the varying degrees of social isolation on development is unknown.

What would happen if a parent were to leave a child in the safe hands of a future robot caregiver almost exclusively? The truth is that we do not know what the effects of the long-term exposure of infants would be. We cannot conduct controlled experiments on children to find out the consequences of long-term bonding with a robot, but we can get some indication from early psychological work on maternal deprivation and attachment. Studies of early development in monkeys have shown that severe social dysfunction occurs in infant animals allowed to develop attachments only to inanimate surrogates (6).

Despite these potential problems, no international or national legislation or policy guidelines exist except in terms of negligence, which has not yet been tested in court for robot surrogates and may be difficult to prove in the home (relative to cases of physical abuse). There is no guidance from any international Nanny code of ethics, nor even from the U.N. Convention on the Rights of Children (7) except by inference. There is a vital need for public discussion to decide the limits of robot use before the industry and busy parents make the decision themselves.

At the other end of the age spectrum, the relative increase in many countries in the population of the elderly relative to available younger caregivers has spurred the development of sophisticated elder-care robots. Examples include the Secom "My Spoon" automatic feeding robot, the Sanyo electric bathtub robot that automatically washes and rinses, and the Mitsubishi Wakamura robot for monitoring, delivering messages, and reminding about medicine. These robots can help the elderly to maintain independence in their own homes (8), but their presence could lead to the risk of leaving the elderly in the exclusive care of machines. The elderly need the human contact that is often only provided by caregivers and people performing day-to-day tasks for them (9).

Robot companions such as Paro the seal are marketed as pets because they are soft and cuddly and are designed to imitate some of the features of pets, such as purring when touched—they are exploiting human zoomorphism. They are being touted as a solution to the contact problem, but these are still toys that do not alleviate elder isolation, even if they may relieve some of the guilt felt by relatives or society in general about this problem. The success of these robots may stem from people being systematically deluded about the real nature of their relation to the devices (10, 11).

A different set of ethical issues is raised by the use of robots in military applications. Coalition military forces in Iraq and Afghanistan have deployed more than 5000 mobile robots. Most are used for surveillance or bomb disposal, but some, like the Talon SWORD and MAARS, are heavily armed for use in combat, although there have been no reports of lethality yet. The semiautonomous unmanned combat air vehicles, such as the MQ1 Predator and MQ9 Reapers, carry Hellfire missiles and bombs that have been involved in many strikes against insurgent targets that have resulted in the deaths of many innocents, including children.

Currently, all these weapons have a human in the loop to decide when to apply lethal force. However, there are plans to create robots that can autonomously locate targets and destroy them without human intervention (12)—a high-priority agenda item for all the U.S. armed services (13,14). Ground-based unmanned autonomous vehicles (UAVs) such as DARPA's Unmanned Ground Combat Vehicle (the PerceptOR Integration System) are already being created (15). The military contractor, BAE Systems, has "completed a flying trial which, for the first time, demonstrated the coordinated control of multiple UAVs autonomously completing a series of tasks" (16). These developments fit with a major goal of the Future Combat Systems project, with estimated costs to exceed $230 billion, to use robots as force multipliers; one soldier can be a nexus for initiating large-scale ground (17) and aerial robot attacks (13). Robot autonomy is required because one soldier cannot control several robots.

The ethical problems arise because no computational system can discriminate between combatants and innocents in a close-contact encounter. Computer programs require a clear definition of a noncombatant, but none is available. The 1944 Geneva Convention suggests common sense, while the 1977 Protocol 1 update defines a civilian as someone who is not a combatant (18). Even with a definition, sensing systems are inadequate for the discrimination challenge, particularly in urban insurgency warfare. These complexities are difficult to resolve even for experienced troops in the field. No computational inference systems yet exist that could deal with the huge number of circumstances where lethal force is inappropriate. These systems should not be confused with smart bombs or submunitions that require accurate human targeting.

Robots for care and for war represent just two of many ethically problematic areas that will soon arise from the rapid increase and spreading diversity of robotics applications.

Scientists and engineers working in robotics must be mindful of the potential dangers of their work, and public and international discussion is vital in order to set policy guidelines for ethical and safe application before the guidelines set themselves.

References and Notes

1. IFR Statistical Department, *World Robotics Report 2008* (www.worldrobotics.org).
2. C. Breazeal, *Robot. Auton. Sys.*, **42**, 167 (2003).
3. T. Fong, I. Nourbakhsh, K. Dautenhahn, *Robot. Auton. Sys.* **42**, 143 (2003).
4. R. A. Brooks, *IEEE. Robot. Automat.* **2**, 14 (1986).
5. F. Tanaka, A. Cicourel, J. R. Movellan, *Proc. Natl. Acad. Sci. U.S.A.* **194**, 46 (2007).
6. D. Blum, *Love at Goon Park: Harry Harlow and the Science of Affection* (Wiley, Chichester, UK, 2003).
7. Convention on the Rights of the Child, adopted and opened for signature, ratification, and accession by U.N. General Assembly Resolution 44/25, 20 November 1989.
8. J. Forlizzi, C. DiSalvo, F. Gemperte, *Hum. Comput. Interact.* **19**, 25 (2004).
9. R. Sparrow, L. Sparrow, *Minds Machines* **16**, 141 (2004).
10. R. Sparrow, *Ethics Inform. Technol.* **4**, 305 (2002).
11. N. E. Sharkey, A. J. C. Sharkey, *Artif. Intell. Rev.* **25**, 9 (2007).
12. N. E. Sharkey, *IEEE Intell. Sys.* **23**, 14 (July–August 2008).
13. U.S. Department of Defense, *Unmanned Systems Roadmap 2007–2032* (10 December 2007).
14. National Research Council, Committee on Autonomous Vehicles in Support of Naval Operations, *Autonomous Vehicles in Support of Naval Operation* (National Academies Press, Washington, DC, 2005).
15. Fox News, "Pentagon's 'Crusher' Robot Vehicle Nearly Ready to Go," 27 February 2008 (www.foxnews.com/story/0,2933,332755,00.html).
16. United Press International, "BAE Systems Tech Boosts Robot UAV's IQ," Industry Briefing, 26 February 2008 (http://bae-systems-news.newslib.com/story/3951-3226462).
17. U.S. Department of Defense, LSD (AT&L) *Defense Systems/Land Warfare and Munitions 3090, Joint Robotics Program Master Plan FY2005* (2005).
18. Protocol 1 Additional to the Geneva Conventions, 1977 (Article 50).
19. Supported by a fellowship from the Engineering and Physical Sciences Research Council, UK.

READING FOR CONTENT

1. How does paragraph 6 define the ethical problem of using robots for caregiving?
2. How does paragraph 12 define the ethical problem of using autonomous robots for warfare?

READING FOR GENRE, ORGANIZATION, AND STYLISTIC FEATURES

1. Does the evidence in paragraph 1 encourage you to think that using robots for caregiving is practical and useful?
2. Does the admission in paragraph 10 that the use of robots for military purposes differs from the use of robots for caregiving alert you to adjust your thinking to a wider set of problems?

READING FOR RHETORICAL CONTEXT

1. Evaluate the footnote documentation in this article.
2. What characterizes the author's style in this article?

WRITING ASSIGNMENTS

1. Use the "Prompts for Personal Response to the Text" on page 36 to write an informal response to Sharkey's essay. Then convert your informal response to a formal response essay. Use the tips we provide on page 36.
2. Draft a critical analysis of Sharkey's essay. Use the Questions for Helping a Writer Revise a Critical Analysis Essay in Chapter 3 to revise your essay.
3. Write a 1,000-word argument that draws support from other articles in this chapter to either defend or attack Sharkey's criticism of using affective robots for caregiving and military combat in ways that interact with human beings in potentially dangerous situations.

■ ■ ▦ ▦ ▨ ■ ■ ▨ ▨ ▦ ▨

The Way Forward in the World of Robotics

Kenneth W. Goodman and Norman G. Einspruch

Kenneth W. Goodman is a professor of ethics at the University of Miami, Miami. Norman G. Einspruch is a professor of electrical and computer engineering at the University of Miami, Coral Gables.

PREREADING

What objections might you make to Noel Sharkey's argument in the preceding article about the danger of using robots? List as many objections as you can.

N. Sharkey exaggerated the dangers of robotics use in his Perspective on "The   1
ethical frontiers of robotics" (19 December 2008, p. 1800). Although the number of
child-minding robots has increased in some countries, such technology should perhaps be regarded as a special case of ubiquitous medical computing, smart homes,
and telemedicine; these are sources of ethical challenges, to be sure, but they do not
warrant preying on emotions by invoking threats of child neglect and abuse (*1, 2*).

Goodman, Kenneth W., and Norman G. Einspruch. "The Way Forward in the World of Robotics."
Science 324.5926 (24 Apr. 2009): 463–64. Web. 3 Sept. 2010. <http:www.sciencemag.org> ©
2009 Kenneth W. Goodman and Norman G. Einspruch. Reprinted by permission of Kenneth W.
Goodman.

Intuitively, we also suspect that nannybots are not good for the psychological development of children left in their care, but until empirical research demonstrates this, we must suspend judgment; such research might, in fact, find no harm at all. Similarly, we are as horrified and angry as Sharkey is when noncombatants are harmed by military robots, but whether such devices generally increase or reduce the number of civilian casualties is also an empirical question.

The job of applied ethics is not limited to warning about worst-case scenarios.   2 Rather, it must include the identification and analysis of challenges raised by new technologies and the identification of suitable precautions, constraints, and trade-offs required to protect safety, privacy, and liberty.

Sharkey has made a start as regards robotics, but much more needs to be done.   3 The agencies that fund these technologies should ensure that adequate resources are devoted to the analysis of concomitant ethical, legal, and social issues.

Kenneth W. Goodman and Norman G. Einspruch

References

K. W. Goodman, in *Ethics, Computing, and Medicine: Informatics and the Transformation of Health Care*, K. W. Goodman, Ed. (Cambridge Univ. Press, Cambridge, 1998), pp. 1–31.

K. W. Goodman, in *The Handbook of Information and Computer Ethics*, K. E. Himma, H. T. Tavani, Eds. (Wiley, Hoboken, NJ, 2008), pp. 293–309.

RESPONSE

I thank Goodman and Einspruch for their thoughtful comments on my paper. I agree   4 that the job of applied ethics should not be limited to worst-case scenarios, but I feel that the issues I raised about robotics in care and in the military need to be dealt with urgently before we sleepwalk into a world of neglect and indiscriminate killing.

I disagree with Goodman and Einspruch's suggestion that we should wait for the   5 empirical evidence before placing ethical constraints on the use of autonomous weapons. There is an ongoing and accelerating proliferation of military robots in research, development, and application. What evidence there is about the development of smart bombs and weapons technology since World War II indicates an increase rather than a decrease in the numbers of civilian casualties (*I*). I value empirical methods, but not when it comes to betting on the lives of innocent civilians. Moreover, I am doubtful as to the impact of empirical findings about noncombatant deaths. Until these weapons can be shown to discriminate between civilians and combatants, I believe that they belong in the same class as mines and sensor-fuzed weapons that have been banned by many countries.

In addition, I do not regard child-minding robots "as a special case of ubiquitous   6 medical computing, smart homes, and telemedicine." It is the mobility and exploitation of the children's anthropomorphic projection to create bonding, trust, and attachment that makes robots different from other smart sensing systems. Again, I think that waiting for empirical research to demonstrate psychological harm to children is dangerous. Suspending judgment about possible harm when many empirical studies show the lasting effects of neglect is not a good option.

Goodman and Einspruch and I agree that considerably more ethical appraisal is 7 required before and at the time of developing new technologies rather than waiting to see the outcomes. History has taught us that once a technological genie is out of the bottle, we can't get it back in again.

Noel Sharkey

Reference

S. Peterson, "Smarter bombs still hit civilians," *The Christian Science Monitor*, 22 October 2002 <www.csmonitor.com/2002/1022/p01s01-wosc.html>.

READING FOR CONTENT

1. Summarize the authors' negative criticism of Sharkey's argument.
2. Summarize the positive suggestion that they offer about Sharkey's argument.

READING FOR RHETORICAL CONTEXT

1. Describe the organization and style of Sharkey's response.

WRITING ASSIGNMENTS

1. Write a 750-word critical response to Goodman and Einspruch's essay in which you develop your own commentary in support of Sharkey's argument against using affective robots for caregiving and military combat in ways that interact with human beings in potentially dangerous situations.
2. Write a 750-word critical response to Goodman and Einspruch's essay in which you develop your own commentary attacking Sharkey's argument against using affective robots for caregiving and military combat in ways that interact with human beings in potentially dangerous situations.

SYNTHESIS WRITING ASSIGNMENTS

1. Draw on at least four of the articles in this chapter to develop a 1,250-word essay that projects the future of human/robotic interactions.
2. Draw on at least four of the articles in this chapter to develop a 1,250-word argument on what limits of decision-making should be assigned to robots that display humanlike reason and emotions.

3. Commentators in this chapter such as Turkle and Sharkey imply skeptical attitudes toward assigning affective robots decision-making powers in many tasks that involve interacting with humans. Others such as Hiroshi Ishiguro and Minoru Asada, Shaw-Garlock, and Goodman and Einspruch display more permissive attitudes. Use the articles in this chapter to write a 1,250-word synthesis argument defending one or the other of these points of view.

4. Draw on the readings in this chapter to write a 1,000-word critical analysis of relationships between humans and machines in a work of fiction that you have read or seen (such as *The Matrix*, *The Hurt Locker*, *Avatar*). What issues does the fiction address? Are they the same as those raised in the articles of this chapter?

5. Try to imagine a future in which humans and robotic machines interact in ways the articles in this chapter suggest. How would this future differ from the present? What would life be like for human beings? What moral or ethical issues might arise with respect to risk-taking, responsibility, and concern for consequences? Write a 1,000-word thesis-driven synthesis in response to these questions. You might organize your essay as a comparative analysis of human and robotic decision-making in relation to affective response.

6. Visit the Web sites of Kismet and Repliée. Kismet's site at MIT is <http://www.ai.mit .edu/projects/humanoid-robotics-group/kismet/kismet.html>. You will find Repliée at the site of Professor Hiroshi Ishiguro's laboratory at Osaka University: <http://www.is.sys .es.osaka-u.ac.jp/development/0006/index.en.html>. Draw on the guidelines in Chapter 4 to write a comparative analysis essay of the two Web sites.

7. Return to Chapter 3, pages 81–85, and reread "Dry Your Eyes: Examining the Role of Robots for Childcare Applications." In this article, David Feil-Seifer and Maja J. Matarić's critique Noel Sharkey and Amanda Sharkey's "The Crying Shame of Robot Nannies: An Ethical Appraisal." Write an essay in which you compare Feil-Seifer and Matarić's views with those of one of the authors presented in Chapter 10.

8. Return to Chapter 7, pages 197–202, and reread Robert Sparrow's "Predators or Plowshares? Arms Control of Robotic Weapons." Write an essay in which you compare Sparrow's views with those of another author presented in Chapter 10.

Privacy and Technology

Balancing Public Safety and Privacy

Modern technology has created challenges to civil liberties that the framers of the Constitution did not envision. Audio and visual surveillance, monitoring of electronic communications, duplication of private or copyrighted computer files, DNA finger-printing, and a host of other innovations make it much easier for government agencies, employers, and anyone else who takes an interest in our activities to find out what we are doing and thinking. When these technologies are employed to reduce crime, they usu-ally receive support from the public. Since the attacks on the World Trade Center and the Pentagon on September 11, 2001, many Americans want the police and military to use any means available to reduce the risk of terrorism. On the other hand, Americans are quick to assert their personal rights, particularly their right to privacy. Although inva-sive technologies do assist police investigations, some commentators wonder if, by opting for technological quick fixes, we enter into a Faustian bargain that will eventually result in the loss of important constitutional rights.

The readings in this chapter focus on how our constitutional rights to privacy and to protection from illegal searches might be affected by technological innovations. The conversation recruits writers from the fields of best-selling fiction, legal history, FBI forensic science, civil rights advocacy, investigative journalism, and economics. The award-winning novelist Jonathan Franzen reflects upon invasions of his privacy in a de-nunciation of public cell-phone usage in "'I Just Called to Say I Love You.'" Humorous but also poignant in its recall of the private personal lives of the author's parents, Franzen's essay provides a contrast to the sober examinations of legal concerns and per-sonal liberties that follow. In his essay "*Kyllo v. United States*: Technology v. Individual Privacy," FBI agent and instructor Thomas D. Colbridge analyzes the implications of a modern Supreme Court decision about barring the use of thermal-imaging technology to detect illegal indoor marijuana-growing operations. Colbridge's detailed footnotes evoke a host of legal precedents that furnish a context for his argument about the limits of forensic science.

From experimental, activist, and economic perspectives, the next three articles challenge common assumptions about civil liberties in early twenty-first-century America. "The Anonymity Experience" by Catherine Price narrates the lengths to which its author went—usually in vain—to remain anonymous for just a single week. Wendy Kaminer, the author of "Trading Liberty for Illusions," focuses upon the response to September 11, 2001, and posits that Americans should not surrender civil liberties in exchange for a false sense of security. Kaminer develops her legal argument in a nontechnical style that complements her broad references to scientific development in defense of her position. Finally, in "If Looks Could Kill," the anonymous author of this article from *The Economist* foregrounds perils that a reliance upon image-detecting technology can induce. Currently unreliable in its application, this technology can lead to false arrests, unwarranted convictions, and even wrongful capital punishment. The sobering conclusion puts life and death in the unfathomable balance.

■ ■ ■ ■ ■ ■ ■ ■ ■ ■

"I Just Called to Say I Love You"

Jonathan Franzen

Jonathan Franzen is a celebrated author of fiction and nonfiction whose prize-winning novels include The Twenty-Seventh City, Strong Motion, The Corrections, *and* Freedom.

PREREADING

Visit Google, <http://www.google.com/>, and click on "images" in the menu at the top of the page. Search Google Images with the terms "privacy," "cell phone usage," and "surveillance technology." You will note that images associated with "privacy" and "cell phone usage" are often humorous as they depict individuals in awkward or embarrassing situations. Images associated with "surveillance technology" are largely serious, often terrifying as they depict individuals in dangerous or menacing situations. Think for a few minutes about why this should be so and freewrite on the implications of this difference.

Cell Phones, Sentimentality, and the Decline of Public Space

One of the great irritations of modern technology is that when some new development   1 has made my life palpably worse and is continuing to find new and different ways to bedevil it, I'm still allowed to complain for only a year or two before the peddlers of coolness start telling me to get over it already, Grampaw—this is just the way life is now.

I'm not opposed to technological developments. Digital voice mail and caller ID, which together destroyed the tyranny of the ringing telephone, seem to me two of the truly great inventions of the late 20th century. And how I love my BlackBerry, which lets me deal with lengthy, unwelcome e-mails in a few breathless telegraphic lines for which the recipient is nevertheless obliged to feel grateful, because I did it with my thumbs. And my noise-canceling headphones, on which I can blast frequency-shifted white noise ("pink noise") that drowns out even the most determined woofing of a neighbor's television set: I love them. And the whole wonderful world of DVD technology and high-definition screens, which have already spared me from so many sticky theater floors, so many rudely whispering cinema-goers, so many open-mouthed crunchers of popcorn: yes.

Privacy, to me, is not about keeping my personal life hidden from other people. It's about sparing me from the intrusion of other people's personal lives. And so, although my very favorite gadgets are actively privacy enhancing, I look kindly on pretty much any development that doesn't force me to interact with it. If you choose to spend an hour every day tinkering with your Facebook profile, or if you don't see any difference between reading Jane Austen on a Kindle and reading her on a printed page, or if you think Grand Theft Auto IV is the greatest Gesamtkunstwerk since Wagner, I'm very happy for you, as long as you keep it to yourself.

The developments I have a problem with are the insults that keep on insulting, the injuries of yesteryear that keep on giving pain. Airport TV, for example: it seems to be actively watched by about one traveler in ten (unless there's football on) while creating an active nuisance for the other nine. Year after year; in airport after airport; a small but apparently permanent diminution in the quality of the average traveler's life. Or, another example, the planned obsolescence of great software and its replacement by bad software. I'm still unable to accept that the best word-processing program ever written, WordPerfect 5.0 for DOS, won't even run on any computer I can buy now. Oh, sure, in theory you can still run it in Windows' little DOS-emulating window, but the tininess and graphical crudeness of that emulator are like a deliberate insult on Microsoft's part to those of us who would prefer not to use a feature-heavy behemoth. WordPerfect 5.0 was hopelessly primitive for desktop publishing but unsurpassable for writers who wanted only to write. Elegant, bug-free, negligible in size, it was bludgeoned out of existence by the obese, intrusive, monopolistic, crash-prone Word. If I hadn't been collecting old 386s and 486s in my office closet, I wouldn't be able to use WordPerfect at all by now. And already I'm down to my last old 486. And yet people have the nerve to be annoyed with me if I won't send them texts in a format intelligible to all-powerful Word. We live in a Word world now, Grampaw. Time to take your GOI pill.

But these are mere annoyances. The technological development that has done lasting harm of real social significance—the development that, despite the continuing harm it does, you risk ridicule if you publicly complain about today—is the cell phone.

Just 10 years ago, New York City (where I live) still abounded with collectively maintained public spaces in which citizens demonstrated respect for their community by not inflicting their banal bedroom lives on it. The world 10 years ago was not yet fully conquered by yak. It was still possible to see the use of Nokias as an ostentation or affectation of the affluent. Or, more generously, as an affliction or a disability or a crutch. There was unfolding, after all, in New York in the late 1990s, a seamless city-wide transition from nicotine culture to cellular culture. One day the lump in the shirt pocket was Marlboros, the next day it was Motorola. One day the vulnerably unaccompanied pretty girl was occupying her hands and mouth and attention with a cigarette, the next day she was occupying them with a very important conversation with a person who wasn't you. One day a crowd gathered around the first kid on the playground with a pack of Kools, the next day around the first kid with a color screen. One day travelers were clicking lighters the second they were off an airplane, the next day they were speed-dialing. Pack-a-day habits became hundred-dollar monthly Verizon bills. Smoke pollution became sonic pollution. Although the irritant changed overnight, the suffering of a self-restrained majority at the hands of a compulsive minority, in restaurants and airports and other public spaces, remained eerily constant. Back in 1998, not long after I'd quit cigarettes, I would sit on the subway and watch other riders nervously folding and unfolding phones, or nibbling on the teatlike antennae that all the phones then had, or just quietly clutching their devices like a mother's hand, and I would feel something close to sorry for them. It still seemed to me an open question how far the trend would go: whether New York truly wanted to become a city of phone addicts sleepwalking down the sidewalks in icky little clouds of private life, or whether the notion of a more restrained public self might somehow prevail.

Needless to say, there wasn't any contest. The cell phone wasn't one of those 7 modern developments, like Ritalin or oversized umbrellas, for which significant pockets of civilian resistance hearteningly persist. Its triumph was swift and total. Its abuses were lamented and bitched about in essays and columns and letters to various editors, and then lamented and bitched about more trenchantly when the abuses seemed only to be getting worse, but that was the end of it. The complaints had been registered, some small token adjustments had been made (the "quiet car" on Amtrak trains; discreet little signs poignantly pleading for restraint in restaurants and gyms), and cellular technology was then free to continue doing its damage without fear of further criticism, because further criticism would be unfresh and uncool. Grampaw.

But just because the problem is familiar to us now doesn't mean steam stops 8 issuing from the ears of drivers trapped behind a guy chatting on his phone in a passing lane and staying perfectly abreast of a vehicle in the slow lane. And yet: everything in our commercial culture tells the chatty driver that he is in the right and tells everybody else that we are in the wrong—that we are failing to get with the attractively priced program of freedom and mobility and unlimited minutes. Commercial culture tells us that if we're sore with the chatty driver it must be because we're not having as good a time as he is. What is wrong with us, anyway? Why can't we lighten up a little and take out our own phones, with our own Friends and Family plans, and start having a better time ourselves, right there in the passing lane?

Socially retarded people don't suddenly start acting more adult when social critics 9 are peer-pressured into silence. They only get ruder. One currently worsening national plague is the shopper who remains engrossed in a call throughout a transaction with a checkout clerk. The typical combination in my own neighborhood, in Manhattan, involves a young white woman, recently graduated from someplace expensive, and a local black or Hispanic woman of roughly the same age but fewer advantages. It is, of course, a liberal vanity to expect your checkout clerk to interact with you or to appreciate the scrupulousness of your determination to interact with her. Given the repetitive and low-paying nature of her job, she's allowed to treat you with boredom or indifference; at worst, it's unprofessional of her. But this does not relieve you of your own moral obligation to acknowledge her existence as a person. And while it's true that some clerks don't seem to mind being ignored, a notably large percentage do become visibly irritated or angered or saddened when a customer is unable to tear herself off her phone for even two seconds of direct interaction. Needless to say, the offender herself, like the chatty freeway driver, is blissfully unaware of pissing anybody off. In my experience, the longer the line behind her, the more likely it is she'll pay for her $1.98 purchase with a credit card. And not the tap-and-go microchip kind of credit card, either, but the wait-for-the-printed-receipt-and-then-(only then)-with-zombiesh-clumsiness-begin-shifting-the-cell-phone-from-one-ear-to-the-other-and-awkwardly-pin-the-phone-with-ear-to-shoulder-while-signing-the-receipt-and-continuing-to-express-doubt-about-whether-she-really-feels-like-meeting-up-with-that-Morgan-Stanley-guy-Zachary-at-the-Etats-Unis-wine-bar-again-tonight kind of credit card.

There is, to be sure, one positive social consequence of these worsening misbehav- 10 iors. The abstract notion of civilized public spaces, as rare resources worth defending, may be all but dead, but there's still consolation to be found in the momentary ad hoc micro-communities of fellow sufferers that bad behaviors create. To look out your car window and see the steam coming out of another driver's ears, or to meet the eyes of a pissed-off checkout clerk and to shake your head along with her: it makes you feel a little less alone.

Which is why, of all the worsening varieties of bad cell-phone behavior, the one 11 that most deeply irritates me is the one that seems, because it is ostensibly victimless, to irritate nobody else. I'm talking about the habit, uncommon 10 years ago, now ubiquitous, of ending cell-phone conversations by braying the words "LOVE YOU! Or, even more oppressive and grating: "I LOVE YOU!" It makes me want to go and live in China, where I don't understand the language. It makes me full of hate.

The cellular component of my irritation is straightforward. I simply do not, while 12 buying socks at the Gap, or standing in a ticket line and pursuing my private thoughts, or trying to read a novel on a plane that's being boarded, want to be imaginatively drawn into the sticky world of some nearby human being's home life. The very essence of the cell phone's hideousness, as a social phenomenon—the bad news that stays bad news—is that it enables and encourages the inflicting of the personal and individual on the public and communal. And there is no higher-caliber utterance than "I love you"—nothing worse that an individual can inflict on a communal public space. Even "Fuck you, dickhead" is less invasive, since it's the kind of thing that angry people do sometimes shout in public, and it can just as easily be directed at a stranger.

My friend Elisabeth assures me that the new national plague of love yous is a 13 good thing: a healthy reaction against the repressed family dynamics of our Protestant childhoods some decades ago. What could be wrong, Elisabeth asks, with telling your mother that you love her, or with hearing from her that she loves you? What if one of you dies before you can speak again? Isn't it nice that we can say these things to each other so freely now?

I do here admit the possibility that compared with everyone else on the air- 14 port concourse, I am an extraordinarily cold and unloving person; that the sudden overwhelming sensation of loving somebody (a friend, a spouse, a parent, a sibling), which to me is such an important and signal sensation that I'm at pains not to wear out the phrase that best expresses it, is for other people so common and routine and easily achieved that it can be re-experienced and re-expressed many times in a single day without significant loss of power.

It's also possible, however, that too-frequent habitual repetition empties phrases 15 of their meaning. Joni Mitchell, in the last verse of "Both Sides Now," referenced the solemn amazement of saying I love you "right out loud": of giving vocal birth to such intensity of feeling. Stevie Wonder, in lyrics written 17 years later, sings of calling somebody up on an ordinary afternoon simply to say "I love you," and, being Stevie Wonder (who probably really is a more loving person than I am), he half succeeds in making me believe in his sincerity—at least until the last line of the chorus, where he finds it necessary to add: "And I mean it from the bottom of my heart." No such avowal is thinkable for the person who really does mean something from the bottom of his heart.

And, just so, when I'm buying those socks at the Gap and the mom in line 16 behind me shouts "I love you!" into her little phone, I am powerless not to feel that something is being performed; overperformed; publicly performed; defiantly inflicted. Yes, a lot of domestic things get shouted in public which really aren't intended for public consumption; yes, people get carried away. But the phrase "I love you" is too important and loaded, and its use as a sign-off too self-conscious, for me to believe I'm being made to hear it accidentally. If the mother's declaration of love had genuine, private emotional weight, wouldn't she take at least a little care to guard it from public hearing? If she truly meant what she was saying, from the bottom of her heart, wouldn't she have to say it quietly? Overhearing her, as a stranger, I have the feeling of being made party to an aggressive assertion of entitlement. At a minimum, the person is saying to me and to everyone else present: "My emotions and my family are more important to me than your social comfort." And also, often enough, I suspect: "I want you all to know that unlike many people, including my cold bastard of a father, I am the kind of person who always tells my loved ones that I love them."

Or am I, in my admittedly now rather lunatic-sounding irritation, simply pro- 17 jecting all this?

The cell phone came of age on September 11, 2001. Imprinted that day on our 18 collective consciousness was the image of cell phones as conduits of intimacy for the desperate. In every too-loud I love you that I hear nowadays, as in the more general national orgy of connectedness—the imperative for parents and children to connect by phone once or twice or five or ten times daily—it's difficult not to hear an echo of those terrible, entirely appropriate, heartbreaking I love yous uttered on the four doomed planes and in the two doomed towers. And it's precisely this echo, the fact that it's an echo, the sentimentality of it, that so irritates me.

My own experience of 9/11 was anomalous for the lack of television in it. At 19 nine in the morning, I got a phone call from my book editor, who, from his office window, had just seen the second plane hit the towers. I did immediately go to the nearest TV, in the conference room of the real-estate office downstairs from my apartment, and watch with a group of agents as first one tower and then the other went down. But then my girlfriend came home and we spent the rest of the day listening to the radio, checking the Internet, reassuring our families, and watching from our roof and from the middle of Lexington Avenue (which was filled with pedestrians streaming uptown) as the dust and smoke at the bottom of Manhattan diffused into a sickening pall. In the evening, we walked down to 42nd Street and met up with an out-of-town friend and found an unremarkable Italian restaurant in the West 40s which happened to be serving dinner. Every table was packed with people drinking heavily; the mood was wartime. I got another brief glimpse of a TV screen, this one showing the face of George W. Bush, as we were departing through the restaurant's bar. "He looks like a scared mouse," somebody said. Sitting on a 6 train at Grand Central, waiting for it to move, we watched a New York commuter angrily complain to a conductor about the lack of express service to the Bronx.

Three nights later, from 11:00 p.m. to nearly 3:00 a.m., I sat in a frigid room 20 at ABC News from which I could see my fellow New Yorker David Halberstam and speak by video link to Maya Angelou and a couple of other out-of-town writers while we waited to offer Ted Koppel a literary perspective on Tuesday morning's attacks. The wait was not short. Footage of the attacks and the ensuing collapses and fires was shown again and again, interspersed with long segments on the emotional toll on ordinary citizens and their impressionable children. Every once in a while, one or two of us writers would have 60 seconds to say something writerly before the coverage reverted to more carnage and wrenching interviews with friends and family of the dead and the missing. I spoke four times in three and a half hours. The second time, I was asked to confirm widespread reports that Tuesday's attacks had profoundly changed the personality of New Yorkers. I could not confirm these reports. I said that the faces I had seen were somber, not angry, and I described seeing people shopping in the stores in my neighborhood on Wednesday afternoon, buying fall clothes. Ted Koppel, in his response, made clear that I'd failed at the task I'd been waiting half the night to perform. With a frown, he said that his own impression was very different: that the attacks had indeed profoundly changed the personality of New York City.

Naturally, I assumed that I was speaking truth and Koppel merely retransmitting 21 received opinion. But Koppel had been watching TV and I had not. I didn't understand that the worst damage to the country was being done not by the pathogen but by the immune system's massive overresponse to it, because I didn't have a TV. I was mentally comparing Tuesday's death toll with other tallies of violent death—3,000 Americans killed in traffic accidents in the 30 days preceding September 11—because, not seeing the images, I thought the numbers mattered. I was devoting energy to imagining, or resisting imagining, the horror of sitting in a window seat while your plane came in low along the West Side Highway, or of being trapped on the 95th floor and hearing the steel structure below you begin to groan and rumble, while the rest of the country was experiencing actual real-time trauma by watching the same footage over and over. And so I was not in need of—was, for a while, not even aware of—the national televised group therapy session, the vast techno-hugathon, that unfolded in the following days and weeks and months in response to the trauma of exposure to televised images.

What I could see was the sudden, mysterious, disastrous sentimentalization of 22 American public discourse. And just as I can't help blaming cellular technology when people pour parental or filial affection into their phones and rudeness onto every stranger within earshot, I can't help blaming media technology for the national foregrounding of the personal. Unlike in, say, 1941, when the United States responded to a terrible attack with collective resolve and discipline and sacrifice, in 2001 we had terrific visuals. We had amateur footage and could break it down frame by frame. We had screens to bring the violence raw into every bedroom in the country, and voice mail to record the desperate final calls of the doomed, and late-model psychology to explicate and heal our trauma. But as for what the attacks actually signified, and what a sensible response to them might look like, attitudes varied. This was the wonderful thing about digital technology: No more hurtful censoring of anybody's feelings! Everybody entitled to express his or her own opinion! Whether or not Saddam Hussein had personally bought plane tickets for the hijackers therefore remained open to lively debate. What everybody agreed to agree on, instead, was that the families of 9/11's victims had a right to approve or veto plans for the memorial at Ground Zero. And everybody could share in the pain experienced by the families of the fallen cops and firefighters. And everybody agreed that irony was dead. The bad, empty irony of the '90s was simply "no longer possible" post-9/11; we'd stepped forward into a new age of sincerity.

On the plus side, Americans in 2001 were a lot better at saying "I love you" to 23
their children than their fathers or grandfathers had been. But competing economically? Pulling together as a nation? Defeating our enemies? Forming strong international alliances? Perhaps a bit of a minus side there.

My parents met two years after Pearl Harbor, in the fall of 1943, and within a few 24
months they were exchanging cards and letters. My father worked for the Great Northern Railway and was often on the road, in small towns, inspecting or repairing bridges, while my mother stayed in Minneapolis and worked as a receptionist. Of the letters from him to her in my possession, the oldest is from Valentine's Day 1944. He was in Fairview, Montana, and my mother had sent him a Valentine's card in the style of all her cards in the year leading up to their marriage: sweetly drawn babies or toddlers or baby animals voicing sweet sentiments. The front of her valentine (which my father likewise saved) shows a pigtailed little girl and a blushing little boy standing beside each other with their eyes bashfully averted and their hands tucked bashfully behind their backs.

> I wish I were a little rock,
> 'Cause then when I grew older,
> Maybe I would find some day
> I was a little "boulder."

Inside the card is a drawing of the same two kids, but holding hands now, with my mother's cursive signature ("Irene") at the feet of the little girl. A second verse reads:

> And that would really help a lot
> It sure would suit me fine,
> For I'd be "bould" enough to say,
> "Please be my Valentine."

My father's letter in response was postmarked Fairview, Montana, February 14. 25

Tuesday Evening

Dear Irene,

I'm sorry to have disappointed you on Valentine's Day; I did remember but after not being able to get one at the drugstore, I felt a little foolish about asking at the grocery or hardware store. I'm sure they have heard about Valentine's Day out here. Your card fit the situation out here perfectly and I'm not sure if it were intentional or accidental, but I guess I did tell about our rock troubles. Today we ran out of rock so I'm wishing for little rocks, big rocks or any kind of rocks as there is nothing we can do until we get some. There is little enough for me to do when the contractor is working and now there is nothing at all. Today I hiked out to the bridge where we are working just to kill time and get a little exercise; it's about four miles which is far enough with a sharp wind blowing. Unless we get rock on the freight in the morning, I'm going to sit right here and read philosophy; it hardly seems right that I should get paid for putting in that kind of day. About the only other pastime around here is to sit in the hotel lobby and take in the town gossip, and the old timers who haunt the place can sure put it out. You would get a kick out of it because there is sure a broad cross section of life represented here—from the local doctor down to the town drunk. And the last is probably the most interesting; I heard that he taught at the University of N.D. at one time, and he seems really to be quite an intelligent person, even when drunk. Normally the talk is pretty rough, about like Steinbeck must have used for a pattern, but this evening there came in a great big woman who made herself right at home. It all sort of makes me realize how sheltered a life we city people live. I grew up in a small town and feel quite at home here but I somehow now seem to view things differently. You will hear more of this.

I hope to get back to St. Paul on Saturday night but cannot tell for certain now. I'll call you when I get in.

With all my love,
Earl

My father had recently turned 29. It's impossible to know how my mother, in 26 her innocence and optimism, received his letter at the time, but in general, considering the woman I grew up knowing, I can say that it was absolutely not the sort of letter she would have wanted from her romantic interest. Her valentine's cutely punning conceit taken literally as a reference to *track ballast*? And she, who spent her whole life shuddering free of the hotel bar where her father had worked as a bartender, *getting a kick out of* hearing "rough talk" from the *town drunk*?! Where were the endearments? Where were the dreamy discussions of love? It was obvious that my father still had a lot to learn about her.

To me, though, his letter seems full of love. Love for my mother, certainly: he's 27 tried to get her a valentine, he's read her card carefully, he wishes she were with him, he has ideas he wants to share with her, he's sending all his love, he'll call her as soon as he's back. But love, too, for the larger world: for the varieties of people in it, for small towns and big cities, for philosophy and literature, for hard work and fair pay, for conversation, for thinking, for long walks in a sharp wind, for carefully chosen words and perfect spelling. The letter reminds me of the many things I loved in my father, his decency, his intelligence, his unexpected humor, his curiosity, his conscientiousness, his reserve and dignity. Only when I place it alongside the valentine from my mother, with its big-eyed babies and preoccupation with pure sentiment, does my focus shift to the decades of mutual disappointment that followed my parents' first few years of half-seeing bliss.

Late in life, my mother complained to me that my father had never told her that 28 he loved her. And it may literally be true that he never spoke the big three words to her—I certainly never heard him do it. But it's definitely not true that he never wrote

the words. One reason it took me years to summon the courage to read their old correspondence is that the first letter of my father's that I glanced at, after my mother died,
began with an endearment ("Irenie") that I had never heard him utter in the 35 years
I knew him, and it ended with a declaration ("I love you, Irene") that was more than
I could stand to see. It sounded nothing like him, and so I buried all the letters in a
trunk in my brother's attic. More recently, when I retrieved the letters and managed to
read through them all, I discovered that my father had in fact declared his love dozens
of times, using the big three words, both before and after he married my mother. But
maybe, even then, he'd been incapable of saying the words out loud, and maybe this
was why, in my mother's memory, he'd never "said" them at all. It's also possible that
his written declarations had sounded as strange and untrue to his character in the
1940s as they now sound to me, and that my mother, in her complaints, was remembering a deeper truth now concealed by his seemingly affectionate words. It's possible
that, in guilty response to the onslaught of sentiment he was getting from her notes to
him ("I love you with all my heart," "With oh so much love," etc.), he'd felt obliged
to perform romantic love in return, or to try to perform it, the way he'd tried (sort of) to
buy a valentine in Fairview, Montana.

"Both Sides Now," in the Judy Collins version, was the first pop song that ever 29
stuck in my head. It was getting heavy radio play when I was eight or nine, and its
reference to declaring love "right out loud," combined with the crush I had on Judy
Collins's voice, helped to ensure that for me the primary import of "I love you" was
sexual. I did eventually live through the '70s and become capable, in rare accesses of
emotion, of telling my brothers and many of my best male friends that I loved them.
But throughout grade school and junior high, the words had only one meaning for
me. "I love you" was the phrase I wanted to see scrawled on a note from the cutest girl
in the class or to hear whispered in the woods on a school picnic. It happened only a
couple of times, in those years, that a girl I liked actually said or wrote this to me. But
when it did happen, it came as a shot of pure adrenaline. Even after I got to college
and started reading Wallace Stevens and found him making fun, in "Le Monocle de
Mon Oncle," of indiscriminately love-seeking people like me—

> If sex were all, then every trembling hand
> Could make us squeak, like dolls, the wished-for words

—those wished-for words continued to signify the opening of a mouth, the offering of a
body, the promise of intoxicating intimacy.

And so it was highly awkward that the person I constantly heard these words 30
from was my mother. She was the only woman in a house of males, and she lived with
such an excess of unrequitable feeling that she couldn't help reaching for romantic
expressions of it. The cards and endearments that she bestowed on me were identical
in spirit to the ones she'd once bestowed on my father. Long before I was born, her
effusions had come to seem intolerably babyish to my father. To me, though, they
weren't nearly babyish enough. I went to elaborate lengths to avoid reciprocating
them. I survived many stretches of my childhood, the long weeks in which the two
of us were alone in the house together, by clinging to crucial distinctions in intensity
between the phrases "I love you"; "I love you, too"; and "Love you." The one thing
that was vital was never, ever to say "I love you" or "I love you, Mom." The least
painful alternative was a muttered, essentially inaudible "Love you." But "I love you,

too," if pronounced rapidly enough and with enough emphasis on the "too," which implied rote responsiveness, could carry me through many an awkward moment. I don't remember that she ever specifically called me out on my mumbling or gave me a hard time if (as sometimes happened) I was incapable of responding with anything more than an evasive grunt. But she also never told me that saying "I love you" was simply something she enjoyed doing because her heart was full of feeling, and that I shouldn't feel I had to say "I love you" in return every time. And so, to this day, when I'm assaulted by the shouting of "I love you" into a cell phone, I hear coercion.

My father, despite writing letters filled with life and curiosity, saw nothing wrong 31
with consigning my mother to four decades of cooking and cleaning at home while he was enjoying his agency out in the world of men. It seems to be the rule, in both the small world of marriage and the big world of American life, that those without agency have sentimentality and vice versa. The various post-9/11 hysterias, both the plague of I love yous and the widespread fear and hatred of the ragheads, were hysterias of the powerless and overwhelmed. If my mother had had greater scope for accomplishment, she might have tailored her sentiments more realistically to their objects.

Cold or repressed or sexist though my father may appear by contemporary 32
standards, I'm grateful that he never told me, in so many words, that he loved me. My father loved privacy, which is to say: he respected the public sphere. He believed in restraint and protocol and reason, because without them, he believed, it was impossible for a society to debate and make decisions in its best interest. It might have been nice, especially for me, if he'd learned how to be more demonstrative with my mother. But every time I hear one of those brayed parental cellular I love yous nowadays, I feel lucky to have had the dad I did. He loved his kids more than anything. And to know that he felt it and couldn't say it; to know that he could trust me to know he felt it and never expect him to say it: this was the very core and substance of the love I felt for him. A love that I in turn was careful never to declare out loud to him.

And yet: this was the easy part. Between me and the place where my dad is 33
now—i.e., dead—nothing but silence can be transmitted. Nobody has more privacy than the dead. My dad and I aren't saying a whole lot less to each other now than we did in many a year when he was alive. The person I find myself actively missing— mentally arguing with, wanting to show stuff to, wishing to see in my apartment, making fun of, feeling remorse about—is my mother. The part of me that's angered by cellular intrusions comes from my father. The part of me that loves my BlackBerry and wants to lighten up and join the world comes from my mother. She was the more modern of the two of them, and although he, not she, was the one with agency, she ended up on the winning side. If she were still alive and still living in St. Louis, and if you happened to be sitting next to me in Lambert Airport, waiting for a New York-bound flight, you might have to suffer through hearing me tell her that I love her. I would keep my voice down, though.

READING FOR CONTENT

1. Why does the author compare cell-phone culture with "nicotine culture" in paragraph 6?
2. Why does the author in paragraphs 22–32 compare the public and private expressions of love in his parents' generation with those of the present?

READING FOR GENRE, ORGANIZATION, AND STYLISTIC FEATURES

1. Why does the author introduce the subjective views of his parents and friends into his own personal essay on privacy?
2. Why does the author in paragraph 24 shift dramatically from September 11, 2001, to Valentine's Day, 1944?
3. In paragraphs 24–32, what different stylistic features of his own writing and behavior does the author associate with those of his father and those of his mother? How does he situate his own writing and behavior between them?

READING FOR RHETORICAL CONTEXT

1. Does the author express hope that cell-phone culture might correct itself toward a greater exercise of civility once cell-phoning becomes a universal practice?
2. Why does the author claim in paragraphs 18–23 that our shared experience of September 11, 2001, marked the "coming of age" of the cell phone and the invasion of privacy?

WRITING ASSIGNMENTS

1. Write a 500-word essay on the following topic: Privacy includes the right not only to keep one's personal affairs hidden from others but also the duty to spare everyone from witnessing in public the personal affairs of others. You may take either a serious or a humorous approach.
2. Use the "Prompts for Personal Response to the Text" on page 36 to write an informal response to Franzen's personal essay. Then convert your informal response to a 700-word formal response essay that delineates serious issues underlying Franzen's concern with public rudeness, venting personal affairs in common view, and the right to privacy in an age of increasing surveillance.

■ ■ ■ ■ ■ ■ ■ ■ ■ ■ ■

Kyllo v. United States: Technology v. Individual Privacy

Thomas D. Colbridge

Thomas Colbridge is an FBI agent and a legal instructor at the FBI Academy.

PREREADING

Do police officials need expanded powers to help them combat drug dealers? Freewrite for ten minutes in response to this question.

Colbridge, Thomas D. "*Kyllo v. United States*: Technology v. Individual Privacy." *FBI Law Enforcement Bulletin* (October 2001): 25–32. Print.

Few issues evoke as much passionate debate as police use of new technologies to combat crime. As noted in a previous article regarding thermal imaging,[1] the introduction of any advanced crime-fighting device into law enforcement's arsenal of weapons raises public concern about the erosion of constitutional rights. The specter of "Big Brother" looms large in the public mind. The debate is an honest one, raising basic issues regarding the proper balance between the personal privacy of individuals and the government's obligation to enforce the law and ensure public safety. Recently, the U.S. Supreme Court decided another skirmish in this ongoing philosophical battle in the case of *Kyllo v. United States*,[2] involving police use of thermal imaging.

This article discusses the Court's holding in the Kyllo case and its restrictions on police use of thermal-imaging devices.[3] The article also explores major themes developed by federal courts when assessing the impact of new police technologies on traditional Fourth Amendment search law.

Fourth Amendment Search

The Fourth Amendment to the Constitution of the United States prohibits unreasonable searches.[4] The drafters of the Constitution never defined the concepts of "unreasonable" and "search" as used in the Fourth Amendment. The Supreme Court struggled with these constitutional definitions for many years. Finally, in 1967 in the famous case of *Katz v. United States*,[5] the Supreme Court formulated the modern definition of a search for purposes of the Constitution. The Court said that a Fourth Amendment search occurs whenever the government intrudes into an individual's reasonable expectation of privacy.[6] Supreme Court Justice Harlan, in a concurring opinion, established a useful two-prong test to determine if a reasonable expectation of privacy exists: (1) Do individuals have an actual (subjective) expectation that their activities will remain private? and (2) Is their subjective expectation of privacy one that society is willing to accept as reasonable (objectively reasonable)?[7] If the answer to both questions is yes, then a reasonable expectation of privacy exists, and any governmental invasion of that expectation is a search for Fourth Amendment purposes.

However, the Fourth Amendment does not prohibit all government searches, only unreasonable ones. Assuming the government does conduct a search as defined in *Katz*, is it reasonable or unreasonable? Unlike the question of whether a search has occurred, which can be difficult, the question of the reasonableness of the search is straightforward. If the search is conducted under the authority of a search warrant, or one of the recognized exceptions to the warrant requirement, the search is reasonable for Fourth Amendment purposes.[8]

Thermal-Imaging Technology

Thermal imaging is not a new technology. It has been used by both the military and law enforcement for years. The public is accustomed to seeing thermal images of battlefields on the nightly news and thermal images of the streets on popular police reality television programs.

All objects with a temperature above absolute zero emit infrared radiation, which is invisible to the naked eye. The warmer an object is, the more infrared radiation it emits. The thermal imager detects this infrared radiation and converts it into a black-and-white picture. The hotter areas (i.e., those areas emitting more infrared radiation) appear lighter in the picture; the cooler areas appear darker. The device does not measure the actual temperature of objects, only the relative temperatures of the surfaces of objects scanned. It emits no rays or beams that penetrate the object viewed. Law enforcement has found several uses for the device, including locating bodies, tracking fleeing persons, and detecting possible indoor marijuana-growing operations. Using the thermal imager in the battle against indoor marijuana-growing operations brought Danny Kyllo and the thermal imager to the attention of the U.S. Supreme Court.

The Kyllo Case

The facts of the Kyllo case are typical of these types of investigations. An agent of the U.S. Bureau of Land Management developed information that Kyllo might be growing marijuana inside his home. Among the information he gathered were the facts that Kyllo's ex-wife, with whom he still was apparently living, was arrested the previous month for delivery and possession of a controlled substance; that Kyllo told a police informant that he could supply marijuana; and that other individuals suspected of drug trafficking lived in the same triplex occupied by Kyllo and his ex-wife. The agent subpoenaed Kyllo's utility records and concluded that his utility use was abnormally high. Finally, at the request of the investigator, a member of the Oregon National Guard scanned Kyllo's home using a thermal imager. The scan was made at approximately three o'clock in the morning from the streets in front of and behind the Kyllo residence. No search warrant authorizing the scan was sought. The scan revealed what investigators believed to be abnormally high amounts of heat coming from Kyllo's home. Investigators concluded that the facts of the case gave them probable cause to believe Kyllo was growing marijuana in his house. Investigators applied for and obtained a warrant to search Kyllo's home, using the results of the thermal scan as part of their probable cause. The search revealed marijuana plants, weapons, and drug paraphernalia.

After his indictment for manufacturing marijuana,[9] Kyllo moved to suppress the evidence gathered in his home on several grounds, including the use of the thermal imager without a search warrant. Kyllo argued that targeting his home with a thermal imager was an unreasonable Fourth Amendment search because there was no warrant authorizing it, and the government could not justify the lack of a search warrant under one of the warrant exceptions. The trial court denied his motion and Kyllo was convicted. The case was appealed to the U.S. Court of Appeals for the Ninth Circuit.

The Circuit Court's View

The U.S. Court of Appeals for the Ninth Circuit heard the Kyllo case three times before it reached a final conclusion. The Ninth Circuit's struggle to decide this case is a reflection of the divergence of opinion that had developed in the courts regarding the warrantless thermal scanning of a home. It also is an interesting study of the difficulty that courts have in dealing with the impact of advancing technology on Fourth Amendment privacy issues.

The first time the Ninth Circuit considered Kyllo's appeal, it made no decision 10 regarding the constitutionality of a warrantless scan of a home with a thermal imager. Instead, it sent the case back to the trial court for additional hearings on the capabilities of the thermal imager.[10] The trial court found that the imager used by police in this case recorded no intimate details of life inside Kyllo's home; did not invade any personal privacy inside the home; could not penetrate walls or windows to reveal human activities or conversations; and recorded only heat escaping from the house.[11] On that basis, the trial court decided that the thermal scan did not invade a reasonable expectation of privacy and therefore was not a search within the meaning of the Fourth Amendment. It again refused to suppress the evidence. The case went back to the Ninth Circuit for a second time.

This time, a three-judge panel of the Ninth Circuit decided that the warrantless 11 thermal scan of Kyllo's home was an unconstitutional search.[12] The court adopted the view that using a thermal imager to target a private home is a Fourth Amendment search, requiring probable cause and authorization of a search warrant or one of the exceptions to the warrant requirement.[13] Its decision was clearly a minority view among federal circuit courts at the time.[14] However, the Ninth Circuit's debate over the issue was not finished. In July 1999, the court withdrew this opinion[15] and decided to reconsider the issue.

On its third and final consideration of this case, the Ninth Circuit reversed 12 itself and held that a thermal scan of a residence is not a search under the Fourth Amendment.[16] It joined the majority of other federal circuit courts[17] in deciding that Kyllo had no actual (subjective) expectation of privacy in the "waste heat"[18] radiating from the surface of his home because he made no effort to conceal the emissions. Even if he could demonstrate an actual expectation of privacy in the escaping heat, the court reasoned that privacy expectation was not objectively reasonable. The court said that the crucial question to be answered in judging the impact of new technologies on privacy issues is whether the technology used to enhance the senses of the police officer is "so revealing of intimate details as to raise constitutional concerns."[19] This court decided thermal imaging was not so revealing. To resolve the conflicting views among federal circuit courts regarding the constitutionality of residential thermal scans, the U.S. Supreme Court agreed to hear the case.[20]

The Supreme Court's View

The Supreme Court disagreed with the majority of the federal circuit courts. In a 5 to 13 4 decision, it ruled that targeting a home with a thermal imager by police officers is a search under the Fourth Amendment[21] and therefore requires probable cause and a search warrant unless the government can forego the warrant under one of the Court's recognized exceptions to the warrant requirement.[22]

The majority and dissenting opinions in this case reflect the difficulty courts in 14 general have resolving the tension between individual privacy and governmental use of technology to combat crime. Several themes emerged in the opinion that echoed arguments made in previous rulings involving police use of emerging technologies.

The first theme involves the area that actually was searched. The majority opin- 15 ion argued that the surveillance in this case was of the interior of a private home. The

Court made it clear that the interior of a home indeed is still a castle. It said, "'[A]t the very core' of the Fourth Amendment 'stands the right of a man to retreat into his own home and there be free from unreasonable governmental intrusion.'"[23] While the Court often has held that naked-eye surveillance of the exterior of a home and its curtilage by the police is not objectionable as long as police have a lawful vantage point from which to see the home,[24] this case involved more. Using the thermal imager, the majority felt, police were able to explore details of the interior of Kyllo's house that they could not have gotten otherwise without going inside.[25]

The dissent disagreed. It distinguished between technology permitting "through-the-wall surveillance," a search it admitted is presumptively unconstitutional,[26] and "off-the-wall surveillance," a search it assumed to be constitutional.[27] The thermal imager in this case, according to the dissent, passively measured heat emissions from the exterior surfaces of Kyllo's home. There was no penetration into the interior of the residence by the police or by rays or beams emitted by the imager. The dissent argued that police simply gathered information exposed to the public from the outside of Kyllo's home. [16]

A second theme discussed by the Court is the public availability of the technology used. This issue was raised in 1986 in the Dow Chemical Company[28] case. In that case, the Supreme Court noted in passing that "It may well be,...that surveillance of private property by using highly sophisticated surveillance equipment not generally available to the public...might be constitutionally proscribed absent a warrant."[29] It was significant to the majority in the Kyllo case that thermal-imaging technology is not widely available to the general public.[30] [17]

While the dissent did not specifically disagree,[31] it criticized the majority for not providing guidance regarding how much use constitutes general public use. It is difficult to discern from the opinion why public availability is important or how important it actually is. It may be a recognition on the part of the Court that as technology makes its way into everyday life, it becomes more difficult for individuals to claim a reasonable expectation to be shielded from its impact. [18]

A third theme that emerges in this case is the debate over the nature and quality of the information supplied to the police by the thermal imager. The Court framed its discussion of this issue in terms of whether or not the technology enabled police to gather information regarding "intimate details"[32] of human activities in the home. This debate also arose in the Dow Chemical Company case. The issue there was the government's use of an aerial mapping camera to photograph a Dow Chemical plant to look for environmental violations. In its opinion, the Court said, "...but the photographs here are not so revealing of intimate details as to raise constitutional concerns."[33] The obvious corollary of that statement is that technology in the hands of the government that reveals intimate details of in-home activities does raise constitutional concerns. [19]

The Kyllo majority rejected the government's contention that because the imager used in this case did not provide exacting detail regarding activities inside Kyllo's home, it should not be of constitutional concern. As the majority opinion put it, "In the home, our cases show all details are intimate details because the entire area is held safe from prying government eyes."[34] The majority reasoned, for example, that the imager used in this case might reveal when a person inside the home regularly [20] took a bath each night. Several previous Supreme Court cases were cited to support this view. In *United States v. Karo*,[35] where government agents simply detected the presence of a can of ether in a private residence by monitoring a beeper placed in the can, the Court found that the agents had conducted an unconstitutional search. In *Arizona v. Hicks*,[36] an officer lawfully inside a home moved a record player to see its serial number. The Court said that was an unlawful search because it went beyond what the officer could see in plain view. In both cases, the information gathered by the police was relatively insignificant, but because it was information about the inside of a home, the majority felt it was intimate enough to warrant protection from the government.

The dissent argued that the thermal scan here provided scant detail regarding 21 the exterior of Kyllo's home and certainly no information concerning its interior. In the dissent's view, the only information gathered by police was an indication that some areas of Kyllo's roof and outside walls were hotter than others. That kind of information, the dissent argued, is unworthy of Fourth Amendment protection because anyone can tell the warmth of a home's walls and roof by looking at evaporation or snowmelt patterns on the roof, and because most people do not care if the amount of heat escaping from their homes is made public.[37]

These major themes are important for law enforcement for two reasons. The 22 first reason is practical—the Kyllo case will have an immediate impact on the use of thermal imaging in criminal investigations. The second reason is less immediate but more far-reaching. The Supreme Court has given law enforcement important clues regarding the government's future use of technology to gather criminal evidence.[38]

Limitations on the Use of the Thermal Imager

The most immediate impact of the Kyllo case is the elimination of the thermal 23 imager as an investigative tool in residential indoor marijuana-growing cases. The majority opinion makes it clear that using a thermal imager to surveil a home is a search under the Fourth Amendment, requiring a search warrant supported by probable cause or justified by one of the search warrant exceptions. If officers have probable cause to believe marijuana is being grown inside a house (or any premises where there is a reasonable expectation of privacy), they will get the warrant and search, not get a warrant and conduct a thermal scan. Consequently, thermal imagers have been rendered superfluous in indoor residential marijuana-growing investigations.

However, the thermal imager still is a valuable tool for use where there is no 24 expectation of privacy or when police are excused from the warrant requirement. For example, using the device to search for fleeing fugitives in an open field, where there is no expectation of privacy, is permissible. In addition, using the thermal imager to target even a private residence still is arguably permissible in emergency situations where the search warrant requirement is excused.[39] For example, if faced with a dangerous barricaded subject or a hostage situation and officers decide an entry is necessary, no warrant would be necessary to thermally scan a premises as long as officers have reasonable suspicion to believe a threat to life exists.[40] Of course, if time permits, officers always should seek a warrant before entering a private area.

Larger Implications of *Kyllo*

Law enforcement officers have sworn to uphold the Constitution of the United States   25
and of their respective states. The oath includes the obligation to assess their actions in
light of ever-changing interpretations of the law by the courts. That assessment must
include the increasing use of sophisticated technology to ferret out crime.

In *Kyllo*, the Supreme Court provided some guidance to law enforcement re-   26
garding when its use of technology unreasonably infringes personal privacy. In light of
Kyllo, law-enforcement officers should ask themselves certain questions before using
sophisticated devices in their investigations.

What Is Being Targeted?

Kyllo confirms the familiar proposition that anytime police invade a reasonable expec-   27
tation of privacy, it is a Fourth Amendment search requiring a warrant or an exception
to the warrant requirement. That is true whether the invasion is physical or technological as in the Kyllo case. If the target of the technological surveillance is the interior of a
home, the Supreme Court has made it clear that there is an expectation of privacy, and
it is reasonable.[41] The same conclusion must be reached where the target of the surveillance is the interior of a commercial building inaccessible to the public. Where the target is the exterior of a premises, there likely is no expectation of privacy as long as police
have a lawful vantage point from which to conduct their technological surveillance,
and the results of the surveillance reveal nothing regarding the interior of the premises.

Similarly, if the thermal imager is used to search a person (as opposed to search   28
for a person in an area where there is no expectation of privacy), a reasonable expectation of privacy must be assumed. For example, using a thermal imager, it is theoreti-
cally possible to detect the presence of objects concealed under a person's clothing.
Such a use of the thermal imager is a Fourth Amendment search and must comply
with the constitutional requirements.

What Information Is Gathered?

It is clear from the *Kyllo* decision that the Supreme Court is concerned about the col-   29
lection by the police of what it calls "intimate details" or "private activities occurring
in private areas."[42] The Court did not define what details are intimate and private
and what details are not, and wants to avoid deciding the issue on a case-by-case basis.
Instead, the Court opted for a rule that within the confines of a home, "all details are
intimate details"[43] and protected by the Fourth Amendment. Consequently, if officers
are considering using a device that will enable them to gather any information regarding the interior of a home (or any area in which there is a reasonable expectation of
privacy) from outside, they must comply with the provisions of the Fourth Amendment.

Is the Device Generally Available to the Public?

As noted above, the Supreme Court often limits its reservations regarding police use   30
of technological devices to those devices not generally available to the public. It did

so in its opinion in the Dow Chemical Company[44] case and in *Kyllo*.[45] It is unclear how important this consideration is to the Court. The implication seems to be that individuals cannot claim a reasonable expectation of privacy against technological intrusions that are widely known to occur and happen on a regular basis. The Court in *Kyllo* acknowledged that. It said, "It would be foolish to contend that the degree of privacy secured to citizens by the Fourth Amendment has been entirely unaffected by the advance of technology. For example … the technology enabling human flight has exposed to public view (and, hence, we have said, to official observation) uncovered portions of the house and its curtilage that once were private."[46]

Does that mean if thermal imagers become commonplace the Court will permit 31 police to routinely scan the interior of homes without warrants? Probably not, for two reasons. The Court has long distinguished between police surveillance of the exterior of homes and the interior of homes: "We have said that the Fourth Amendment draws a firm line at the entrance to the house, [citation omitted]. That line, we think, must be not only firm but also bright. …"[47] Given the strong language in the *Kyllo* opinion, it is unreasonable for police to assume that governmental intrusions into private areas are permissible simply because everyone is doing it. In addition, private (nongovernmental) and commercial use of new technologies does not raise constitutional concerns. The Constitution was written to limit the authority of the government, not private citizens.[48] Consequently, the Supreme Court will not question the use of a thermal imager by an insulation company to demonstrate homeowners' need to insulate their homes, but put the same thermal imager into the hands of the police investigating a crime, and a multitude of weighty legal issues will arise. When assessing the Fourth Amendment implications of using technological devices to gather information about the interior of premises, officers should not rely on the fact that the device is widely available.

Why Is the Device Being Used?

Using technology to gather evidence of criminal activity obviously raises Fourth 32 Amendment concerns. However, criminal investigation is not always the goal. Often, technology is employed by the government for the broader purpose of public safety. The most obvious example is the use of X-ray and magnetic screening devices at airports and government office buildings. Courts have long recognized that such warrantless searches are permissible because they are administrative in nature, not criminal, and are not very intrusive. They serve the valid governmental purpose of securing public safety rather than gathering evidence of criminal activity.[49] So long as the technological search is narrowly limited to serve only that public safety purpose, it will pass constitutional muster.

Where and When Is the Device Being Used?

Another factor courts consider when assessing police use of technology is where and 33 when the device is used. If the device is used in public areas, such as airports and public buildings, where people are aware of its presence, courts generally have fewer constitutional reservations regarding its use. Under those conditions, people can make a choice to enter the screening area or not. If they choose to enter, some courts have reasoned that they have consented to be searched by the device in use.[50] If the device is used in the dead of night, as happened in the Kyllo case, consent obviously is impossible.

Conclusion

Historically, modern technology in the hands of the police has raised well-founded 34 fears in the public mind concerning the erosion of privacy rights. The police, how-ever, have an obligation to protect the public safety through whatever constitutional means are available to them. Criminal elements are quick to adopt the latest tech-nological gadgets in order to stay one step ahead of the police. Police quickly must respond in kind. The tension between these two legitimate interests has created some of the most difficult issues faced by U.S. courts.

In *Kyllo v. United States*, the U.S. Supreme Court drew a bright line around the 35 home and announced a rule that warrantless police use of technology stops at the front door. Simply put, the Court stated that if police use technology from outside the home to gather information they could not otherwise obtain without going inside, they have conducted a search within the meaning of the Constitution, which must be supported by a warrant or a recognized exception to the warrant requirement.

While the Kyllo case dealt specifically with thermal-imaging technology, it has 36 much larger implications. Law-enforcement officers have an obligation to assess all technological devices in their arsenal in light of the lessons delivered in this case.

Notes

1. Thomas D. Colbridge, "Thermal Imaging: Much Heat but Little Light." *The FBI Law Enforcement Bulletin*, December 1997, 18–24.
2. 121 S. Ct. 2038 (2001).
3. While the Kyllo case dealt with a thermal imaging device, the legal principles discussed in this article apply equally to the Forward Looking Infrared Radar (FLIR) device, an adapta-tion of the thermal imager for use on aircraft.
4. U.S. Const. Amend IV: "The right of the people to be secure in their persons, houses, papers, and effects against unreasonable searches and seizures shall not be violated...."
5. 389 U.S. 347 (1967).
6. Id.
7. Supra note 5 at 361 (J. Harlan, concurring).
8. Supra note 5 at 357. The exceptions to the search warrant requirement recognized by the Supreme Court are the consent search (*Schneckloth v. Bustamonte*, 412 U.S. 218 [1973]); the search incident to arrest (*U.S. v. Robinson*, 414 U.S. 218 [1973]); the emergency search or exigent circumstances search (*Warden v. Hayden*, 387 U.S. 394 [1967]); the motor ve-hicle search (*Carroll v. U.S.*, 267 U.S. 132 [1925]); the inventory search (*South Dakota v. Opperman*, 428 U.S. 364 [1976]); certain administrative searches of regulated businesses (*New York v. Berger*, 482 U.S. 691 [1987]); and "special needs" searches (*Veronia School District 47 J v. Acton*, 515 U.S. 646 [1995]).
9. 21 U.S.C. 841(a)(1).
10. *United States v. Kyllo*, 37 F.3d 526 (9th Cir. 1994).
11. *United States v. Kyllo*, No. CR 92-051-FR (D.Or. March 15, 1996).
12. *United States v. Kyllo*, 140 F.3d 1249 (9th Cir. 1998).
13. Id. at 1255.
14. The U.S. Court of Appeals for the Tenth Circuit held in 1995 that a thermal scan of a home was a search: *United States v. Cusumano*, 67 F.3d 1497 (10th Cir. 1995), vacated

on other grounds, 83 F.3d 1247 (10th Cir. 1996). Two states also had adopted this minority view: *State v. Young*, 867 P.2d 593 (Wash. 1994) and *State v. Siegel*, 934 P.2d 176 (Mont. 1997).

15. *United States v. Kyllo*, 184 F.3d 1059 (9th Cir. July 29, 1999).
16. *United States v. Kyllo*, 190 F.3d 1041 (9th Cir. 1999).
17. See *United States v. Ishmael*, 48 F.3d 850 (5th Cir. 1995); *United States v. Myers*, 46 F.3d 668 (7th Cir. 1995); *United States v. Pinson*, 24 F.3d 1056 (8th Cir. 1994); *United States v. Robinson*, 62 F.3d 1325 (11th Cir. 1995).
18. Supra note 16 at 1046.
19. Supra note 16 at 1047 (quoting *Dow Chemical Co. v. United States*, 476 US 227 (1986) at 238).
20. *Kyllo v. United States*, 530 U.S. 1305 (2000).
21. *Kyllo v. United States*, 121 S. Ct. 2038 at 2043.
22. Supra note 8 lists the exceptions to the search warrant requirement.
23. Kyllo, 121 S. Ct. at 2043 quoting *Silverman v. United States*, 365 U.S. 505 (1961) at 511.
24. *California v. Ciraolo*, 476 U.S. 207 (1986); *Florida v. Riley*, 488 U.S. 445 (1989).
25. Kyllo, 121 S. Ct. at 2043.
26. Kyllo, 121 S. Ct. at 2048 (J. Stevens, dissenting), citing *Payton v. New York*, 445 U.S. 573 (1980).
27. Kyllo, 121 S. Ct. at 2048 (J. Stevens, dissenting), citing *California v. Ciraolo*, supra note 24; *Florida v. Riley*, supra note 24; *California v. Greenwood*, 486 U.S. 35 (1988); *Dow Chemical Co. v. United States*, supra note 19; and *Air Pollution Variance Board of Colorado v. Western Alfalfa Corporation*, 416 U.S. 861 (1974).
28. Supra note 19.
29. *Dow Chemical Company*, 476 U.S. at 238 (1986).
30. Kyllo, 121 S. Ct. at 2043.
31. The dissent did point out in a footnote that thousands of thermal imagers had been manufactured and are available for rental by anyone. See Kyllo, 121 S. Ct. at 2050, note 5. (J. Stevens, dissenting).
32. Kyllo, 121 S. Ct. at 2045.
33. *Dow Chemical Company*, 476 U.S. at 238 (1986).
34. Kyllo, 121 S. Ct. at 2045 (emphasis in original).
35. 468 U.S. 705 (1984).
36. 480 U.S. 321 (1987).
37. Kyllo, 121 S. Ct. at 2048 (J. Stevens, dissenting).
38. Regarding certain technology in development, the Court offered more than clues. In a footnote, the majority specifically named surveillance devices under development and implied they would raise Fourth Amendment concerns. Those technologies are the Radar-Based Through-the-Wall Surveillance System, Handheld Through-the-Wall Surveillance, and a Radar Flashlight enabling officers to detect people through interior building walls. See Kyllo, 121 S.Ct. at 2044, footnote 3.
39. See *United States v. Johnson*, 9 F.3d 506 (6th Cir. 1993).
40. See *Terry v. Ohio*, 392 U.S. 1 (1968); *United States v. Menard*, 95 F.3d 9 (8th Cir. 1996).
41. Kyllo, 121 S. Ct. at 2043. Of course, even inside the home, there is no expectation of privacy regarding matters that individuals choose to expose to the public: *Katz v. United States*, 389 U.S. 347 at 351 (1967), and cases cited at supra note 27.
42. Kyllo, 121 S. Ct. at 2045.
43. Kyllo, 121 S. Ct. at 2045.
44. Supra note 29.
45. Supra note 30.
46. Kyllo, 121 S. Ct. at 2043.
47. Kyllo, 121 S. Ct. at 2046, citing *Payton v. New York*, 445 U.S. 573 (1980).
48. *United States v. Jacobson*, 466 U.S. 109 (1984); *United States v. Knoll*, 16 F. 3rd 1313 (2nd Cir.), cert. denied 115 S. Ct. 574 (1994).

49. *United States v. Bulalan*, 156 F. 3rd 963 (9th Cir. 1998); *United States v. John Doe, aka Geronimo Pizzaro-Calderon*, 61 F.3d 107 (1st Cir. 1995); *United States v. $124,570 U.S. Currency*, 873 U.S. 1240 (9th Cir. 1989).
50. *United States v. DeAngelo*, 584 F.2d 46 (4th Cir. 1978), cert. denied 440 U.S. 935 (1979); *United States v. Miner*, 484 F.2d 1075 (9th Cir. 1973).

READING FOR CONTENT

1. Summarize the definition of privacy that emerged from *Katz v. United States*.
2. Summarize how thermal imagers function.
3. Summarize briefly the events that led up to Kyllo's arrest.
4. Explain briefly the basis for each of the three separate opinions on the Kyllo case that were issued by the U.S. Court of Appeals for the Ninth Circuit.
5. Summarize the basis for the majority opinion of the Supreme Court on the Kyllo case.
6. Summarize the basis for the dissenting opinions of the Supreme Court on the Kyllo case.
7. In the wake of the Kyllo decision, what options remain for police use of thermal imagers?
8. Summarize briefly what Colbridge believes are the implications of *Kyllo* for police searches that do not involve thermal imaging.

READING FOR GENRE, ORGANIZATION, AND STYLISTIC FEATURES

1. Characterize Colbridge's use of language.
2. Comment on Colbridge's use of section headings to divide his article.
3. Explain Colbridge's extensive use of endnotes.
4. Does Colbridge's conclusion capture the essence of the Supreme Court's ruling in the Kyllo case? Explain your answer.

READING FOR RHETORICAL CONTEXT

1. Who do you imagine is the target audience for the *FBI Law Enforcement Bulletin*, the publication in which Colbridge's article appears?
2. How does Colbridge establish his authority?
3. What is Colbridge's goal in writing?
4. How does Colbridge's job as an FBI agent complicate his role as author of an article on the Kyllo case?

WRITING ASSIGNMENTS

1. Write a 500-word summary of the most important elements in the case against Kyllo and in the Supreme Court's ruling in *Kyllo v. United States*.
2. Write a 1,000-word essay that defends or attacks the Supreme Court's ruling in *Kyllo v. United States*.
3. In the movie *E.T.*, government agents use high-power listening devices to monitor conversations taking place within private homes in a neighborhood where they suspect children might be hiding an alien creature. Do you think the audio monitoring in *E.T.* would pass the standards for police searches set forth in *Kyllo*? Defend your answer in a 750-word essay.

unknown to most people.

The Anonymity Experiment

Catherine Price

Catherine Price lives in an undisclosed location in Oakland, California.

PREREADING

Visit the Google home page, <http://www.google.com/>, and click on "images" in the menu at the top of the page. Search Google Images with the term "anonymity." As with the images of "privacy," "cell phone usage," and "surveillance technology" that you explored earlier, you will note a discrepancy between humorous depictions of "anonymity" and terrifying ones. Freewrite for ten minutes on the differences between them and on the implications of these differences.

> Too often, privacy has been equated with anonymity. . . . But in our interconnected and wireless world, anonymity—or the appearance of anonymity—is quickly becoming a thing of the past.
>
> —DONALD M. KERR, PRINCIPAL DEPUTY DIRECTOR OF NATIONAL INTELLIGENCE, OCTOBER 2007

In 2006, David Holtzman decided to do an experiment. Holtzman, a security consultant and former intelligence analyst, was working on a book, about privacy, and he wanted to see how much he could find out about himself from sources available to any tenacious stalker. So he did background checks. He pulled his credit file. He looked at Amazon.com transactions and his credit-card and telephone bills. He got his DNA analyzed and kept a log of all the people he called and e-mailed, along with the Web sites he visited. When he put the information together, he was able to discover so much about himself—from detailed financial information to the fact that he was circumcised—that his publisher, concerned about his privacy, didn't let him include it all in the book.

I'm no intelligence analyst, but stories like Holtzman's freak me out. So do statistics like this one: Last year, 127 million sensitive electronic and paper records (those containing Social Security numbers and the like) were hacked or lost—a nearly 650 percent increase in data breaches from the previous year. Also last year, news broke that hackers had stolen somewhere between 45 million and 94 million credit- and debit-card numbers from the databases of the retail company TJX, in one of the biggest data breaches in history. Last November, the British government admitted losing computer discs containing personal data for 25 million people, which is almost half the country's population. Meanwhile, some privacy advocates worry that the looming merger between Google and the Internet ad company DoubleClick presages an era in which corporations regularly eavesdrop on our e-mail and phone calls so they can personalize ads with creepy precision. Facebook's ill-fated Beacon feature, which notifies users when their friends buy things from Facebook affiliates, shows that in the information age, even our shopping habits are fit for public broadcast. Facebook made Beacon an opt-in service after outraged users demanded it do so, but the company didn't drop it completely.

Then we have Donald Kerr, the principal deputy director of National Intelligence, who proclaimed in a speech last October that "protecting anonymity isn't a fight that can be won." Privacy-minded people have long warned of a world in which an individual's every action leaves a trace, in which corporations and governments can peer at will into your life with a few keystrokes on a computer. Now one of the people in charge of information-gathering for the U.S. government says, essentially, that such a world has arrived. 3

So when this magazine suggested I try my own privacy experiment, I eagerly agreed. We decided that I would spend a week trying to be as anonymous as possible while still living a normal life. I would attempt what many believe is now impossible: to hide in plain sight. 4

A Gallup poll of approximately 1,000 Americans taken in February 1999 found that 70 percent of them believed that the Constitution "guarantees citizens the right to privacy." Wrong. The Constitution doesn't even contain the word. And in a fully wired world, that's an unnerving fact. 5

A number of amendments protect privacy implicitly, as do certain state and federal laws, the most significant of which is the Privacy Act of 1974, which prohibits disclosure of some federal records that contain information about individuals.(1) Unfortunately, the law is full of exceptions. As Beth Givens, founder and director of the nonprofit Privacy Rights Clearinghouse, put it, the Privacy Act has "so many limitations that it can barely be called a privacy act with a straight face." 6

In the U.S., privacy law is sectoral, which means that we don't have broad, generally applicable laws to protect our personal information. We've got federal laws that safeguard very specific types of data, like student records, credit reports and DVD rentals. But those have loopholes too.(2) 7

In addition, technological advances are quickly rendering many of these laws useless. What good is strong protection for cable records when a technology like TiVo comes along that is not, technically, a "cable service provider"?(3) Or a statute about postal mail in a world where most communication now takes place online? "We're way behind the curve," says Richard Purcell, CEO of the Corporate Privacy Group and former chief privacy officer for Microsoft. "Technology is way ahead of our ability as a society to think about the consequences." 8

Navigating this technological and legal maze wouldn't be easy; I needed professional help, a privacy guru who could guide me through my week. That man was Chris Jay Hoofnagle, a privacy expert and lawyer who used to run the West Coast office of the Electronic Privacy Information Center (EPIC), a public-interest research center in Washington, D.C., that focuses on privacy and civil-liberties issues. 9

Hoofnagle had tried his own version of the same thing, partly for fun and partly because of fears of retribution from private investigators he had irritated in his previous job at EPIC. "When moving to San Francisco two years ago, I deliberately gave my 10 new address to no business or government entity," he told me. "As a result, no one really knows where I live." His bills are in aliases, and despite set-backs—like having his power turned off because the company didn't know where to send the statement—he's been successful at concealing his home address.

Now that he's a senior fellow at the University of California at Berkeley's Boalt Hall School of Law, Hoofnagle doesn't keep his office location a secret, so on a sunny afternoon, I set off to meet him there.

Tall and friendly, Hoofnagle has an enthusiastic way of talking about privacy violations that could best be described as "cheerful outrage." He laid out my basic tasks: Pay for everything in cash. Don't use my regular cellphone, landline or e-mail account. Use an anonymizing service to mask my Web surfing. Stay away from government buildings and airports (too many surveillance cameras), and wear a hat and sunglasses to foil cameras I can't avoid. Don't use automatic toll lanes. Get a confetti-cut paper shredder for sensitive documents and junk mail. Sign up for the national do-not-call registry (ignoring, if you can, the irony of revealing your phone number and e-mail address to prevent people from contacting you), and opt out of prescreened credit offers. Don't buy a plane ticket, rent a car, get married, have a baby, purchase land, start a business, go to a casino, use a supermarket loyalty card, or buy nasal decongestant.(4) By the time I left Hoofnagle's office, a week was beginning to sound like a very long time.

After withdrawing seven days' worth of cash, I officially began my experiment by attempting to buy an anonymous cellphone. This was a crucial step. My cellphone company keeps records of every call I make and receive. What's more, my phone itself can give away my location. Since 1999, the Federal Communications Commission has required that all new cellphones in the U.S. use some form of locating technology that makes it possible to find them within 1,000 feet 95 percent of the time; the technology works as long as your phone is on, even if it isn't being used. This is to help 911 responders locate you, but the applications are expanding. Advertisers hope to use cellphone GPS to send text-message coupons to lure you into stores as you pass by, and services such as Loopt and Buddy Beacon allow you to see a map of where your friends are, in real time, using either their cellphone signals or GPS.(5) I left an outgoing message explaining that I wasn't going to be using my normal cellphone for a week and then turned it off.

Wearing a baseball cap and sunglasses, I walked into an AT&T store and immediately noticed several black half-globes suspended from the ceiling: surveillance cameras. I needed to keep my head down. When I tried to pay for my new phone, the cashier swiped its bar code, looked up at me with her fingers poised above her keyboard, and asked me for identification. "I don't have any on me," I lied.

She seemed mildly annoyed and asked for my name and address.

"I'm sorry," I said, "but I don't really want my information in the system."

"We need your information."

"Why?"

"For billing purposes."

"But it's a prepaid card. You don't need to bill me."

This, apparently, was irrelevant. "We need to put your information into the system," she said again. "Otherwise you can't buy the phone."

I didn't buy the phone. Instead I walked across the street to a generic cellphone 17 store where a young clerk with pink hair and black-framed glasses was sitting behind the cash register, text messaging. "So do you want me to, like, just put in some random name?" she asked. Before I knew it, she'd christened me Mike Smith, born October 18, 2007.(6) As she charged minutes to my phone, I overheard a young man next to me tell a different clerk that he wanted to activate a cellphone that was registered under his mother's name. "That's no problem at all," said the clerk. "We just need her Social Security number." Unfazed, the man called his mom. He was dictating the number to the clerk as Mike Smith walked out the door.

My new phone was anonymous, but I still needed to be careful. If I didn't want it to 18 be traceable back to me, I had to disguise my outgoing calls and minimize the number of calls that I received; records of both could be used to identify me. I changed the phone's settings so that its number wouldn't show up when I placed calls(7) and bought a prepaid calling card to use on top of my cellphone. That way, if anyone were to pull a record of my outgoing calls, they would just see the calling-card number.

If masking your cellphone number is difficult, hiding your online activity is 19 nearly impossible. Anytime you access the Internet, your Internet service provider (ISP) knows you're online, and it might soon keep track of more. In 2005, the European Parliament passed legislation requiring phone and Internet providers to retain records of calls and online activity for between six months and two years. In 2006, then–U.S. attorney general Alberto Gonzales and FBI director Robert Mueller met privately with America's major ISPs to request that they, too, hold on to these records for two years. Search engines already keep records of queries, a practice that's become enough of a concern among users that in December, Ask.com launched AskEraser, a service that deletes your searches within hours. When you send an unencrypted e-mail, it can be intercepted and read and may be stored indefinitely on a server, even if you've deleted it. And Web sites routinely retain such information as how you got there, how long you lingered on each page, and your scrolling, clicks and mouse-overs.

But I'm getting ahead of myself. My first challenge was to figure out how to con- 20 nect to the Internet. I subscribed to Anonymizer, a service that uses a technique called secure-shell tunneling to create a virtual link between your computer and Anonymizer's proxy servers (that is, the servers that act as middlemen between your computer and the sites you're visiting). That meant my ISP wouldn't know what Web sites I was visiting, and the sites I visited wouldn't know it was me.

Anonymizer has two potential weaknesses, though. First, Anonymizer itself knows 21 what sites you're visiting, although the company claims not to retain this information. And then there's the conspiracy theory. "There are reports that the government has sneakily had people volunteer to run Anonymizer server nodes who are actually 'quislings'—traitors—Holtzman told me. "I don't know if it's true," he said. "But if it were my job to spy on people, I'd be doing it."

There are Anonymizer alternatives (the freeware Tor is probably the best-known), 22 but according to Holtzman, if you want to be sure of anonymity, "you just cannot use your own computer. The only way to do so is if it's brand-new and you never put it online." Unfortunately, I didn't have a brand-new computer, and I needed to use the Internet. I decided to avoid using my own ISP whenever possible. Instead I needed to either piggyback on neighbors' open connections or use public Wi-Fi hotspots.(8)

Once I got online, I had other challenges, such as the notorious "cookie," a small 23
text file that Web sites leave on your computer so that you can be identified when you return. Cookies often make the Internet easier to use; they remember your login name, for
example, and some sites now deny access to visitors who refuse cookies. But if you want
to remain anonymous online, you've got to toss your cookies. When I looked through
my cookie cache, I found them from all sorts of places, including one from a site called
Vegan Porn (it's not as naughty as it sounds) and another, from Budget Rent A Car, that
wasn't set to expire until 2075.

Lastly, there was the question of e-mail. I set my usual address to forward to a 24
Hotmail account I'd created with fake user information and signed up for a free account
through Hushmail, a service that allows you to send encrypted, anonymous e-mail.
I figured that if I monitored my messages through Hotmail but responded using only
Hushmail, no one would be able to connect the two accounts—or know definitively that
the person checking the Hotmail was me. Only later did I discover that even Hushmail
has occasionally spilled information to the feds.

I started marking items off Hoofnagle's to-do list. I signed up for the do-not-call 25
registry to avoid telemarketers and sent a letter opting out of all prescreened offers of
credit. I called my bank and opted out of its information sharing.(9) Then I called
my phone company and told them I didn't want them to share my CPNI—customer
proprietary network information.

Your CPNI includes records of what services you use, what types of calls you 26
make, when you place them, and a log of the numbers you've called. Before 1996,
phone companies were allowed to freely sell this information to third parties for marketing purposes. Today, thanks to legislation limiting what they can do without your
permission, CPNI is mainly used to sell you other services offered by your phone company, such as a new long-distance plan.

When my phone company's automated system picked up, a voice announced that 27
my call might be monitored or recorded but that I could ask to be on an unrecorded line.
So I did. "Uh, OK," the representative said. "But all the lines are recorded automatically.
If you don't want to be recorded, I'm going to have to call you back."

"How long will that take?" I asked, having already spent 10 minutes on hold. 28

"We'll call you as soon as we have a chance," he said. "Probably within an hour." 29
In other words, the cost of privacy would be an hour of my time.

I told him that a recorded line was fine and then asked him to stop using my 30
CPNI to market things to me. He agreed. Then he asked if I had a few minutes to
talk about my phone service and proceeded to use my CPNI to try to sell me a unified
messaging system.

This was getting exhausting. I'd thought a yoga class would be a nice break, but 31
I'd forgotten one thing: The yoga studio I go to has a computer system that keeps track
of all its students' names. I scrawled "CPrice" illegibly on the sign-in sheet and paid
in cash. I thought I'd gotten away with my ploy until the end of class when, just after
our final "om," the teacher picked up a piece of paper that the front desk had slipped
under the door. "Would whomever signed in as number 19 please stop by the front on
the way out?" he asked. "They couldn't read your signature."

I doubt the young Buddhists behind the yoga-studio desk are profit-minded 32
enough to sell my personal information, but many other businesses are. Data-broker

Web sites sell lists of information you never thought would be for sale—records of 750,000 people who signed up for medical alert services, for example, or a list of 11,418 people, mostly men over the age of 55, who bought a particular herbal sexual-potency product in September or October. Private investigators buy phone records from pizza-delivery places, and a few years ago, data aggregator LexisNexis advertised that it, too, used pizza-delivery records to get hard-to-find phone numbers. If you want to invalidate some of the information on the lists, you could move, but you'd have to carry your own boxes—moving companies sell lists of new addresses to marketers.

More disturbing is the fact that this relatively disparate information is frequently 33 rounded up by other data-aggregator companies such as ChoicePoint and Acxiom. Acxiom's databases contain records on 96 percent of American households. Its newest customer intelligence database, InfoBase-X, includes 199 million names and can draw on 1,500 "data elements" to help companies market to potential customers, including "Life Event, Buying Activity, Travel, Behavior, Ethnicity, Lifestyle/Interests, Real Property, Automotive and more."

These companies are only minimally regulated, in part because the government 34 itself is one of their largest clients. Contracting data-collection projects to outside companies allows the government to purchase data that would be illegal for it to collect itself. Take, for example, what happened in 2002 when a now-defunct information-mining company and Department of Defense contractor called Torch Concepts got five million itinerary records for JetBlue passengers—records that included names, addresses and phone numbers—for a project whose goal was ostensibly to identify high-risk airline passengers. Torch Concepts then bought demographic data from Acxiom on about 40 percent of the passengers whose records JetBlue had released.

This demographic data included passengers' genders, home-ownership status, 35 occupations, length of time spent at their residence, income level, vehicle information, Social Security numbers and how many kids they had. The company used the information to create detailed profiles of the passengers, including one (with the name stripped off but all other information still intact) that it used as part of a presentation to pitch potential clients.

Transportation was tricky. I'd been wearing my hat and sunglasses so I couldn't be 36 recognized on cameras, but to take buses or the train would be to willingly subject myself to heavy surveillance, and that was against my rules. I couldn't drive my car through toll plazas—they're covered in cameras, and if you have an automatic toll-payment system that uses a pre-paid account, like E-ZPass or, in the Bay Area, FasTrak, you leave behind a record.(10)

I'd also learned about EDRs, or event data recorders, small devices installed 37 in most new passenger vehicles that monitor things like speed, steering-wheel angle, acceleration, braking and seatbelt use. EDRs were first developed in the 1970s and began to be installed as part of airbag systems in the 1990s.(11) If safety sensors in your car detect a sudden deceleration, they trigger the airbag, and the EDR retains a record of what happened in the seconds preceding and following the collision.

But today, EDRs are part of sophisticated systems that do much more. If you 38 subscribe to GM's OnStar service, for example, and get in a wreck, your car will notify OnStar so a representative can contact you through the speaker system in your car and medics can respond to the scene more quickly.

It's hard to complain about a voluntary service that could save your life, but other features are more intrusive. Starting in 2009, OnStar will be able to remotely deactivate a car's accelerator, forcing it to drive at a top speed of five miles an hour—which is great if your car is stolen but not so good if someone were to hack into OnStar's computers. Plus, systems like these include a two-way microphone and speakers that the company can activate remotely, which means they can be used for eavesdropping. 39

The FBI took advantage of this capability a few years ago, when it got court authority to compel a company (which was unnamed in court documents) to turn on the microphone in a suspect's car to monitor conversations. The FBI eventually lost the case on appeal, but only when a court decided that the agency had forced the company to breach its contract with the suspect, because using the car's microphone for surveillance rendered it useless in case of emergency. 40

Fortunately, my car is old enough that it doesn't have an EDR. If I were to just drive around my neighborhood, I'd only have to worry about traffic and red-light cameras, whose images generally aren't archived unless something noteworthy happens. But I needed to go to San Francisco—the International Association of Privacy Professionals was having a conference. The problem was that attending it would require getting across the Bay Bridge. 41

At first I thought this might be impossible. Then I remembered Casual Carpool, an informal system in which drivers can use toll-free lanes by picking up passengers throughout the East Bay and dropping them off in San Francisco. 42

Up to that point, I'd been wearing a cap and sunglasses every time I went outside.(12) I liked my camouflage. It made me feel like I could be mistaken for J. Lo. But I thought that for my grand trip into surveillance-camera-dense San Francisco, I should try something different. I decided to wear my visor. 43

Let me be clear: This was no ordinary face visor. Designed to provide complete sun protection, it was more of a mask, with a wraparound piece of dark plastic that extended from my forehead all the way down to my chin. It made me look like a welder. It also made it difficult to see. But I still managed to find a car, and surprisingly, no one commented on the visor. In fact, they didn't talk to me at all. 44

At the conference, I switched from visor to hat, which made it easier to blend into the crowd of more than 900 "privacy professionals" (whose existence is a sign that more companies are taking privacy seriously). Here I listened to lectures on two technologies—IPv6 and RFID—that have significant privacy implications. IPv6, which stands for Internet Protocol Version 6 and is an eventual replacement for our current Internet protocol, IPv4, would allow mobile devices to connect to one other directly without any need for a server; it also means that your camera, PDA or just about any other gadget could have a unique identifier that would make it possible to track you in real time. 45

And then there are RFID (radio-frequency identification) chips, small devices that consist of a microchip and an antenna that use radio waves to identify objects and people.(13) About five years ago, these chips (often called tags) were the obsession of conspiracy theorists everywhere. But the time to really worry about RFID may be near. Experts like Holtzman predict that soon the price of the tags will drop enough that they will be attached to almost everything we buy and will become so small as to basically be invisible. "You couldn't get away with this experiment in a couple years because of the RFID chips," Holtzman told me later. "You'd literally have to get rid of everything you 46 own and start over, since every artifact you'd bought from a major manufacturer would probably have a chip embedded in it that could identify you as the buyer."

Just before the conference ended, I tracked down Richard Purcell, the former CPO   47
of Microsoft. After dodging security cameras in the hallway, we ducked into an empty ballroom to talk. He was not encouraging. "The thing is, surveillance is a fact of our electronic society," he said. "You are going to be tracked. One has to be thoughtful about that." He's right. No one knows exactly how many surveillance cameras are being used in the U.S. right now, but consider that the much-smaller U.K. has three to four million.

And more cameras arrive all the time. The New York City Police Department,   48
for instance, aims to install an additional 3,000 public and private security cameras below Canal Street, with video feeds that could broadcast directly to the Department of Homeland Security and the FBI. That's understandable—once the Freedom Tower goes up at the World Trade Center site, lower Manhattan will once again be home to one of the most conspicuous terrorist targets in the world. But the surveillance-camera craze has begun to veer into absurdity: The British government recently approved funding to pay for cameras in the hats of more than 2,000 police officers.

The problem with Casual Carpool is that it primarily runs into the city, which   49
left me without a way to get home. I decided to take a cab but then noticed a plastic decal that read "Smile, you're on camera!" Whatever. By that point, one more camera was the least of my worries. Instead, I spent the cab ride mulling the most common counterargument to concerns over lost privacy: So what? If giving up personal information makes it easier for me to shop online, so be it. If total surveillance can prevent terrorist attacks, bring on Big Brother.

Here's the thing, though—We don't know what information is being collected   50
about us, whom it's being shared with, what it's being used for, or where it's being held. As companies and the government collect more and more data on us, some of it will inevitably be incorrect, and the effect of those errors could range from trivial to severe. It's not a big deal to get coupons for products you don't want, but if a mistake in your file or an identity theft caused by a data breach drives down your credit score, you could find yourself knocked into the subprime-mortgage market. And privacy-invading safeguards don't just catch bad guys. Anyone could end up like Senator Ted Kennedy, who was erroneously placed on a do-not-fly list because a terrorist had once used the alias "T. Kennedy."

For now, few systems are in place to help us understand what data is being gath-   51
ered or correct the inevitable mistakes, and in the absence of laws that define punishments for data breaches—and judges who enforce them—companies can walk away from serious privacy violations with nothing more than a slap on the wrist.

Case in point: When EPIC filed a complaint with the FTC against JetBlue   52
for disclosing passenger information to Torch Concepts, the agency never publicly opened an investigation; in response to a separate suit filed by JetBlue passengers, a federal judge agreed that the company had violated its privacy policies but dismissed the lawsuit because passengers weren't able to prove that anything had happened to them as a result of the profiling, and that JetBlue hadn't "unjustly enriched" itself by sharing the information. And because this kind of news is so often met with no more than a collective shrug, such privacy violations are likely to keep happening.

At the end of my week of paranoia, I met Hoofnagle at the Yerba Buena Center   53
of the Arts in San Francisco so he could grade me on my performance.

His verdict: I did a pretty good job. But his approval seemed less satisfying when 54
I considered all the aspects of my life that made it easier to minimize my digital trail.
I don't use pay-per-view or FasTrak. I don't work in an office, which would require an
ID card and logging on to and e-mailing from company computers. I don't use Instant
Messenger, play online games, visit chatrooms, or sell things on eBay. I've never been
married or arrested, or owned property or a business, so few public records are associated
with my name.

Also, spending one week undercover doesn't do anything about information that's 55
already out there—information that, for the most part, I volunteered. Countless Web
sites have records on me. UPS, FedEx and the Department of Motor Vehicles know
where I live. My bank, credit-card company, gym and phone company all have me in
their records, and my information is in alumni databases. Both my college and graduate
school have lost laptops containing my Social Security number.

I was reminded of something Holtzman had told me earlier that week. "No mat- 56
ter what you do, you'll never really know if you're successful at keeping private," he
said. "There are all sorts of trails you leave that you'll never even know about."

Once Hoofnagle had left, I walked through an exhibit, "Dark Matters," that 57
happened to feature—no kidding—pieces about surveillance. One installation in particular captivated me. Called Listening Post, it was a darkened room with gray walls,
empty except for a large lattice hanging from the ceiling made from 231 small screens,
each the shape and size of a dollar bill. The screens displayed scrolling blue-green
sentence fragments that were being culled, in real time, from Internet chatrooms.
Occasionally the program would search for sentences that began with key words—
"I am," "I like," "I love"—and the results would roll across the screens. "I love my new
cellphone." "I love you and your sexy hair." "I love Quark."

It was strangely calming, standing in this dim room, watching the words and 58
thoughts of strangers reveal themselves to me. I still had my hat on, but for once there
were no surveillance cameras, so I sat down on a bench in the room and pulled out my
notebook, grateful to finally be the observer rather than the observed. And then, out
of the corner of my eye, I saw her: a security guard standing in the room's darkened
corner—silent, motionless, watching.

Notes

1. California, where I live, leads the nation in privacy protection. If I'd conducted my experiment elsewhere in the U.S., it would have been even more difficult.
2. One oft-cited loophole is in the Driver's Privacy Protection Act of 1994. It was created after a
series of crimes linked to Department of Motor Vehicles records, the most notorious of which
occurred in 1989: An obsessed fan hired a private investigator to get actress Rebecca Schaeffer's
home address from her DMV record and then tracked her down and killed her. Now DMV
employees aren't allowed to release personal information. The only problem is that the law has
14 exemptions, including one that allows the release of information to licensed private investigators if they say they're using it for purposes listed in the other 13 exemptions.
3. TiVo actually has a strict privacy policy—but it's the company's own doing. Legally, it's
allowed to sell a minute-by-minute record of users' viewing habits.
4. Pseudoephedrine can be used to make methamphetamine, and thanks to a federal law
passed in 2006, your name goes into a log when you buy products that contain it.
5. These services are voluntary, but they vividly illustrate the privacy-killing potential of cellphone GPS.

6. She'd asked for my birth date to use as an activation code, but it turned out she really just needed any eight-digit series of numbers.

7. Because of something called "automatic number identification," there's no way to stop your information from showing up when you call toll-free or 900 numbers.

8. Even then, I still wouldn't be entirely anonymous. Every networking device in every computer is assigned a media access control (MAC) address, a unique identifying number picked up by your router when you go online. To learn how to find your MAC address, go to www-dcn.fnal.gov/DCG-Docs/mac/index.html.

9. Banks sell lists of information that you'd think would be kept private—transaction histories, bank balances, where you've sent payments—and can continue to do so even if your account is closed. But banks are better than they used to be: Until the Gramm-Leach-Bliley Act in 1999, banks could even sell account and credit-card numbers to unaffiliated third parties.

10. Some states have sensors along the road that use toll passes to identify cars as they pass through two points. This information is used to make calculations about traffic speed and feed electronic billboards that provide up-to-the-minute estimated driving times to various locations. This information could also be used, hypothetically, to automatically issue speeding tickets.

11. If you want to see whether your car has an EDR, check your owner's manual—it's usually disclosed in the section about airbags. But EDRs aren't the only thing to be aware of. Car-rental companies have used GPS to tell when customers violated the terms of their contracts by speeding or crossing state lines.

12. The quality of the images taken by most surveillance cameras—at least the surveillance cameras of today—is unrefined enough that you don't need too much of a disguise.

13. Starting last year, all new U.S. passports are embedded with RFID chips that contain the person's identifying information and a photo, and research is under way on how to embed the chips in paper currency. RFID tags are already used to "microchip" pets. One company, VeriChip, has implanted 500 people in the U.S. with RFID chips and it has proposed replacing military dog tags by implanting the chips into American soldiers. It sounds far-fetched, but this is a real enough possibility that last October, California governor Arnold Schwarzenegger signed a bill forbidding employers to force employees to have RFID chips implanted under their skin.

READING FOR CONTENT

1. Underline the basic precautions listed in paragraph 12 to ensure privacy.

READING FOR GENRE, ORGANIZATION, AND STYLISTIC FEATURES

1. Does the author cover all the bases in trying to establish her anonymity?

2. Reread the exchange of dialogue in paragraph 15. What does the author's use of dialogue contribute to her argument?

3. What is the effect of the author's casual style and use of popular common expressions such as "Whatever" and "Here's the thing, though" (paragraphs 49–50)?

READING FOR RHETORICAL CONTEXT

1. What is the effect of the author's use of examples such as purchasing cell phones and arranging transportation through the busy San Francisco Bay Area?

2. Does the author feel proud about her accomplishment in remaining anonymous for an entire week?

WRITING ASSIGNMENTS

1. Reread paragraphs 5–8 in Price's essay and reflect upon their implications for legal action to ensure personal privacy in everyday dealings with others. Based upon your reflections, write a 500-word essay on the following topic: The Constitution does not guarantee any right to privacy; some amendments (such as the Privacy Act of 1974) protect privacy implicitly, but most privacy laws are not federal, and the few that exist protect only very specific types of data.

2. Use the "Prompts for Personal Response to the Text" on page 36 to write an informal response to Price's personal essay. Then convert your informal response to a 700-word formal response essay that delineates serious issues underlying Price's attempt to maintain her anonymity for a single week. Following Price's approach, you may take either a serious or a humorous approach.

■ ■ ■ ■ ■ ■ ■ ■ ■ ■ ■

Trading Liberty for Illusions

Wendy Kaminer

Wendy Kaminer is a lawyer and has written several books, including Sleeping with Extra-Terrestrials: The Rise of Irrationalism and the Perils of Piety.

PREREADING

How have the events of September 11, 2001, affected your own views about crime detection efforts? Freewrite for ten minutes in response to that question.

Only a fool with no sense of history would have been sanguine about the prospects for civil liberties after the September 11 attack. Whenever Americans have felt frightened or under siege, they have responded by persecuting immigrants, members of suspect ethnic groups, or others guilty only of real or apparent sympathy for unpopular ideologies. Our most revered, or at least respected, presidents have been among the worst offenders: John Adams supported the Alien and Sedition Acts, which criminalized opposition to the government (and was used to imprison his political foes); Abraham Lincoln suspended habeas corpus and presided over the arrests of thousands of people for crimes like "disloyalty" (which sometimes consisted of criticizing the president); Woodrow Wilson imprisoned Eugene Debs for speaking out against America's entry into the First World War; Franklin Roosevelt famously and shamefully interned Japanese-Americans during

1

World War II. Liberty was trampled by all of these measures, while security was enhanced by none of them.

But the cruelty and folly of imprisoning people for their political views or their ethnicity is usually acknowledged only in hindsight. During World War II some people no doubt felt safer knowing that their Japanese-American neighbors were interned. The Supreme Court ruled at the time that the internment was justified on national security grounds. People felt safer last fall when the Bush administration swept up and detained over one thousand immigrants in the wake of the September 11 attack, even though the vast majority of them had no apparent connection to terrorism. History shows that frightened people tend to assume that restrictions on liberty make them safe. They support repressive measures instinctively in the expectation that other people will be targeted by them, and ask questions only decades later.

Consider the false promise of many electronic surveillance measures, like facial-recognition systems. A recent report by the American Civil Liberties Union reveals that the widely publicized facial-recognition system used on the streets by police in Tampa, Florida, "never identified even a single individual contained in the department's database of photographs." Instead, "the system made many false positives, including such errors as confusing what were to a human easily identifiable male and female images." The ACLU report was based on a review of police logs obtained through Florida's open-records law.

Technological inaccuracies like these were coupled with human errors and abuses of discretion. A facial-recognition system can only be as good as its database in identifying terrorists or other violent criminals, and in Tampa the photographic database was not limited to known criminals: It included people the police were interested in questioning in the belief that they might have "valuable intelligence." Under guidelines like this, ordinary law-abiding citizens who venture out in public might find themselves setting off alarms in facial-recognition systems (should they ever work properly).

Whether or not your photograph is in the database, your privacy is likely to be invaded by a facial-recognition system. Cameras scan crowds and, as the ACLU observes, in Britain, where electronic surveillance is becoming routine, camera operators are apt to focus disproportionately on racial minorities or while away the hours peering up women's skirts. In Michigan, according to a report by the *Detroit Free Press*, police used a database to stalk women and intimidate other citizens.

Considering the ways facial-recognition systems have been used and abused so far, it's fair to say that they constitute a threat—to privacy, liberty and even physical safety—not a promise of security. But we are beginning to use them more, not less. Several cities have decided to deploy the kind of system that failed so miserably in Tampa, and of course, facial recognition is being touted as an important airport security tool. Airports in cities including Boston, Providence, and Palm Beach are installing facial-recognition systems. Meanwhile, precautions that might actually enhance security, like screening all checked bags and carry-ons, are as far from implementation as ever.

Why do a majority of Americans tolerate and support invasive or repressive faux   7
security measures? I suspect we're simply too frightened and uninformed to challenge
them. People who want or need to continue flying, for example, can't bear to devote
much thought to the continuing inadequacies of airport security; instead they take
comfort in whatever false promise of security they're offered. So, the problem for civil
libertarians isn't the tendency of people to trade liberty for security. It's their tendency
to trade liberty for mere illusions of security. Liberty would benefit greatly from a logical, pragmatic approach to safety. In our frightened, irrational world, freedom may be
threatened most by wishful thinking.

What is it?

READING FOR CONTENT

1. Paraphrase the first sentence of Kaminer's article.
2. According to Kaminer, how, in the past, have Americans responded when they felt threatened?
3. How does facial-recognition technology function?
4. According to Kaminer, how successful has facial recognition been in reducing crime?
5. What specific dangers of facial-recognition technology does Kaminer identify?
6. Why, according to Kaminer, do Americans accept "invasive or repressive faux security measures"?

READING FOR GENRE, ORGANIZATION, AND STYLISTIC FEATURES

1. Describe Kaminer's opening strategy.
2. Describe Kaminer's organizational plan.
3. Comment on the length of Kaminer's piece.

READING FOR RHETORICAL CONTEXT

1. Characterize Kaminer's attitude toward the government.
2. Who is Kaminer's intended audience? What assumptions does she make about her audience?
3. How do you think police officers would respond to Kaminer's article?

WRITING ASSIGNMENTS

1. Write a 1,000-word essay that weighs the pros and cons of using facial-recognition tech-nology to monitor the general public.
2. Write a 1,000-word essay of response to Kaminer's assertion that "freedom may be threat-ened most by wishful thinking."
3. Write a 1,000-word essay that compares and contrasts facial-recognition technology with one or more of the other infringements on personal freedom that are mentioned in Kaminer's first and second paragraphs.

If Looks Could Kill

The Economist

The Economist is a weekly magazine published in England by The Economist Group. Begun in 1843 and employing many famous editors throughout the years, the magazine is known for its international perspective on links between economic issues, current affairs, business, finance, science, technology, and the arts. Most articles are published with no authorial byline.

PREREADING

This article's first sentence states that "monitoring surveillance cameras is tedious work." Technology might be able to develop computerized systems that relieve humans of monotonous observation tasks. But less-than-perfect systems can result in a great deal of confusion and harm. Try to imagine a few instances in which you might be apprehended on false charges even though you are entirely innocent of them. Jot them down with personal comments.

Monitoring surveillance cameras is tedious work. Even if you are concentrating, 1 identifying suspicious behaviour is hard. Suppose a nondescript man descends to a subway platform several times over the course of a few days without getting on a train. Is that suspicious? Possibly. Is the average security guard going to notice? Probably not. A good example, then—if a fictional one—of why many people would like to develop intelligent computerised surveillance systems.

The perceived need for such systems is stimulating the development of devices 2 that can both recognise people and objects and also detect suspicious behaviour. Much of this technology remains, for the moment, in laboratories. But Charles Cohen, the boss of Cybernet Systems, a firm based in Ann Arbor, Michigan, which is working for America's Army Research Laboratory, says behaviour-recognition systems are getting good, and are already deployed at some security checkpoints.

Human gaits, for example, can provide a lot of information about people's 3 intentions. At the American Army's Aberdeen Proving Ground in Maryland, a team of gait analysts and psychologists led by Frank Morelli study video, much of it conveniently posted on the internet by insurgents in Afghanistan and Iraq. They use special object-recognition software to lock onto particular features of a video recording (a person's knees or elbow joints, for example) and follow them around. Correlating those movements with consequences, such as the throwing of a bomb, allows them to develop computer models that link posture and consequence reasonably reliably. The system can, for example, pick out a person in a crowd who is carrying a concealed package with the weight of a large explosives belt. According to Mr Morelli, the army plans to deploy the system at military checkpoints, on vehicles and at embassy perimeters.

Guilty

Some intelligent surveillance systems are able to go beyond even this. Instead of merely learning what a threat looks like, they can learn the context in which behaviour is probably threatening. That people linger in places such as bus stops, for example, is normal. Loitering in a stairwell, however, is a rarer occurrence that may warrant examination by human security staff (so impatient lovers beware). James Davis, a video-security expert at Ohio State University in Columbus, says such systems are already in use. Dr Davis is developing one for America's Air Force Research Laboratory. It uses a network of cameras to track people identified as suspicious—for example, pedestrians who have left a package on the ground—as they walk through town. 4

As object- and motion-recognition technology improves, researchers are starting to focus on facial expressions and what they can reveal. The Human Factors Division of America's Department of Homeland Security (DHS), for example, is running what it calls Project Hostile Intent. This boasts a system that scrutinises fleeting "micro-expressions", easily missed by human eyes. Many flash for less than a tenth of a second and involve just a small portion of the face. 5

Terrorists are often trained to conceal emotions; micro-expressions, however, are largely involuntary. Even better, from the researchers' point of view, conscious attempts to suppress facial expressions actually accentuate micro-expressions. Sharla Rausch, the director of the Human Factors Division, refers to this somewhat disturbingly as "micro-facial leakage." 6

There are about 40 micro-expressions. The DHS's officials refuse to describe them in detail, which is a bit daft, as they have been studied for years by civilian researchers. But Paul Ekman, who was one of those researchers (he retired from the University of California, San Francisco, in 2004) and who now advises the DHS and other intelligence and law-enforcement agencies in the United States and elsewhere, points out that signals which seem to reveal hostile intent change with context. If many travellers in an airport-screening line are running late, telltales of anguish—raised cheeks and eyebrows, lowered lips and gaze—cause less concern. 7

Supporters of this sort of technology argue that it avoids controversial racial profiling: only behaviour is studied. This is a sticky issue, however, because cultures—and races—express themselves differently. Judee Burgoon, an expert on automated behaviour-recognition at the University of Arizona, Tucson, who conducts research for America's Department of Defence, says systems should be improved with cultural input. For example, passengers from repressive countries, who may already be under suspicion because of their origins, typically display extra anxiety (often revealed by rigid body movements) when near security officials. That could result in a lot of false positives and consequent ill-will. Dr Burgoon is upgrading her software, called Agent 99, by fine-tuning the interpretations of body movements of people from about 15 cultures. 8

Another programme run by the Human Factors Division, Future Attributable Screening Technology, or FAST, is being developed as a complement to Project Hostile Intent. An array of sensors, at a distance of a couple of metres, measures skin temperature, 9 blood-flow patterns, perspiration, and heart and breathing rates. In a series of tests, including a demonstration last month with 140 role-playing volunteers, the system detected about 80% of those who had been asked to try to deceive it by being hostile or trying to smuggle a weapon through it.

A number of "innocents," though, were snagged too. The trial's organisers are 10 unwilling to go into detail, and are now playing down the significance of the testing statistics. But FAST began just 16 months ago. Bob Burns, the project's leader, says its accuracy will improve next year thanks to extra sensors that can detect eye movements and body odours, both of which can provide further clues to emotional states.

Until Proved Innocent

That alarms some civil-libertarians. FAST, they say, amounts to a forced medical ex- 11 amination, and hostile-intent systems in general smack of the "pre-crime" technology featured in Philip K. Dick's short story "The Minority Report" and the film based on it. An exaggeration, perhaps. But the result of using these devices, according to Barry Steinhardt, the head of technology and liberty at the American Civil Liberties Union in Washington, DC, will inevitably be that too many innocents are entangled in intrusive questioning or worse with "voodoo science" security measures.

To the historically minded it smacks of polygraphs, the so-called lie-detectors 12 that rely on measuring physiological correlates of stress. Those have had a patchy and controversial history, fingering nervous innocents while acquitting practised liars. Supporters of hostile-intent systems argue that the computers will not be taking over completely, and human security agents will always remain the final arbiters. Try telling that, though, to an innocent traveller who was in too much of a hurry—or even a couple smooching in a stairwell.

READING FOR CONTENT

1. List some of the reasons that behavior-recognition systems are getting good at classifying types of behavior.
2. List some of the circumstances in which behavior-recognition systems might fail to analyze behavior properly.

READING FOR GENRE, ORGANIZATION, AND STYLISTIC FEATURES

1. This article was published in a relatively mainstream magazine. Does its argument suffer from a lack of documentation and extensive footnoting?
2. Describe the effect of beginning the article with a survey of new technological devices (paragraph 3) and concluding it with an analogy to how old techniques (such as polygraphs) misidentified suspects of crime.

READING FOR RHETORICAL CONTEXT

1. What persuasive effects does the final paragraph aim for?
2. What audience does the article hope to attract?

WRITING ASSIGNMENTS

1. Draw upon this article to write a 1,000-word essay that compares and contrasts the level of privacy you think people should have in their homes to the level of privacy you think they should have while driving cars and riding on the street.

2. In paragraphs 3, 5, and 9, the article refers to technology that analyzes human behavior with respect to determining people's motivations. In a 900-word essay, explain the assertions implied in these analyses and respond to them based upon your own views.

3. Do you think that the views in this essay are consistent with constitutional guarantees of civil liberties? Defend your views in a 1,000-word essay.

SYNTHESIS WRITING ASSIGNMENTS

1. Write a comparative analysis of Colbridge's and Kaminer's attitudes toward the development of advanced technology and its effects on individual rights.

2. Many private citizens and law-enforcement officers maintain that if you've done nothing wrong, then you have nothing to fear from surveillance of your activities or searches of your home or car. Respond to this belief in an argument-synthesis essay that draws from at least three readings in this chapter.

3. Are amendments to the Constitution sufficient to protect our individual rights, given recent advances in surveillance technology? Respond to this question in a 1,000-word synthesis essay that draws on at least three articles in this chapter.

4. Under what circumstances, if any, should we give up our right to privacy? Answer this question in a 1,000-word argument essay that draws on at least three articles in this chapter.

5. Do the events of September 11, 2001, justify employing technology that may violate individual privacy? Answer this question in a 1,000-word essay that draws on at least three articles in this chapter.

6. Drawing upon the articles in this chapter, write an exploratory synthesis essay that distinguishes between types of high-tech evidence that should be admitted in court and types that should be excluded. Refer to the various sorts of crime-fighting technology described in this chapter.

7. In the first paragraph of his article, Colbridge points out that it is difficult to maintain "the proper balance between the personal privacy of individuals and the government's obligation to enforce the law and ensure public safety." Draw on at least two other articles in this chapter to write a 1,250-word response to Colbridge's statement.

Social Sciences

▪️ SUBJECTS AND METHODS OF STUDY IN THE SOCIAL SCIENCES

Anthropology, economics, education, political science, psychology, sociology, and geography are called social sciences because they use the process of scientific inquiry to study various aspects of society, such as human behavior (psychology), human relationships (family studies), social conditions (sociology), political conduct (government), and cultural practices (anthropology). Social scientists begin their inquiry by **asking questions or identifying problems** related to particular phenomena. In Chapter 12, Pauline Irit Erera asks, "What Is a Family?" and Rebecca M. Blank asks, "Absent Fathers: Why Don't We Ever Talk about the Unmarried Men?"

Such questions reveal the sorts of conversation conducted by social scientists. The writers posing those questions identify possible causes of the phenomena they are studying and then form a **hypothesis** based on certain assumptions they have made. They next try to verify the hypothesis by making a series of **careful observations**, assembling and analyzing **data**, and determining a clear **pattern of response**. If the data verify their hypothesis, they will declare it confirmed. Many social scientists conduct investigations "**in the field**," testing their hypotheses in actual problem situations by making on-site observations, interviewing, conducting case studies and cross-sectional and longitudinal studies, collecting surveys and questionnaires, examining artifacts and material remains, and studying landscapes and ecology. Barbara Ehrenreich derives "Serving in Florida" (Chapter 13) from field work that she conducted by living as a low-wage worker in Florida. Other social scientists, such as experimental psychologists, work under carefully controlled conditions in laboratory settings.

SPECIAL TYPES OF SOCIAL SCIENCE WRITING

When researchers complete their studies, they present their findings in official reports, organized in accordance with the scientific method (see the introductory section on the natural sciences). A format commonly found in research articles is introduction with background and problem statement; method; results; discussion; summary. An **abstract** (a brief summary of the article) may precede the study. Usually, the study begins with a **literature review** in which the writer recapitulates previous research. Social scientists regard this acknowledgment of their predecessors' work and of divided opinion about it to be crucial to the development of any new thesis or interpretation. Often, when they publish their work, they designate it as a "**proposal**" or a "**work in progress**" because they have not yet arrived at conclusions that they are willing to consider final. They view this kind of publication as a means of receiving feedback or peer review that will enable them to continue with new insights and perspectives. They believe that a community of scholars cooperating within a complex system of checks and balances will ultimately arrive at some statement of truth.

Advanced social science courses teach students how to evaluate these formal reports of research findings. Meanwhile, all students should be familiar with less specialized forms of writing in the social sciences, such as summaries of research; reviews of the literature; case studies; proposals; position papers; presentations of new theories and methods of analysis; commentaries, reviews, analyses, critiques, and interpretations of research.

For examples of various genres of social science writing, consult the following sources:

Review of the literature: Robert L. Barret and Bryan E. Robinson's "Children of Gay Fathers," Chapter 12; Pauline Irit Erera's "What Is a Family?" Chapter 12.

Case study: Barret and Robinson's "Children of Gay Fathers," Chapter 12; Barbara Ehrenreich, "Serving in Florida," Chapter 13.

Theory: James Q. Wilson's "Cohabitation Instead of Marriage," Chapter 12.

Position paper: Herbert Gans's "The War Against the Poor Instead of Programs to End Poverty," Chapter 13.

Interpretation of research: The Economist, "Middle of the Class," Chapter 13.

Historical analysis: Andrew J. Cherlin, "The Origins of the Ambivalent Acceptance of Divorce," Chapter 12.

Proposal: Rebecca M. Blank, "Absent Fathers: Why Don't We Ever Talk about the Unmarried Men?" Chapter 12.

Regardless of the specialized genre, writers in the social sciences are expected to engage in a spirited conversation with other writers on the topic they address. Most of the articles mentioned offer footnotes and bibliographies that report on the parameters of their conversation with others.

Student papers in the social sciences are likewise expected to engage in this kind of conversation. Here are some typical writing assignments in the social sciences, drawn from exercises in the following chapters:

Use Pauline Irit Erera's arguments in "What Is a Family?" to write a defense of the family arrangements described in Barret and Robinson's "Children of Gay Fathers." (p. 448)

How widespread are the class discrimination and prejudice that Gans discusses in "The War Against the Poor Instead of Programs to End Poverty"? Use the selections by Angela Locke and Charmion Browne to write an essay in response. (p. 489)

Write an essay in which you agree or disagree with *The Economist's* assessment in "Middle of the Class" that equality of opportunity is under threat in the United States. (p. 486)

Note that these assignments do not ask you to do original data research or draw statistical inferences from data already collected. They do, however, require you to join the conversation recorded in academic publications, field studies, personal narratives, and journalistic reports.

■ PERSPECTIVES ON SOCIAL SCIENCE WRITING

In this anthology, we present reading selections on social science topics by journalists and other popular writers as well as by social scientists. As with scientific writers of research reports and summary or speculative articles, these social science writers treat a common subject matter, but their approaches differ. Take, for example, Angela Locke, whose article in the feminist news-journal *off our backs*, "Born Poor and Smart," appears on pages 450–52, and Charmion Browne, whose *New York Times* article "When Shelter Feels Like a Prison" appears on pages 486–88. These writers do not use special modes of social science writing, nor do they rely heavily on other sources or write for specialized readers. Still, their writing is very important for social scientists because it reflects the very stuff of everyday life that social scientists study. Likewise, consider Barbara Ehrenreich's "Serving in Florida" from her popular book *Nickel and Dimed: On (Not) Getting By in America*. Ehrenreich treats an issue that social scientists find extremely important as a barometer of public feeling, and not surprisingly, her book has generated extensive conversation among journalists and popular writers as well as among academic scholars in the social sciences.

■ SOCIAL SCIENCE WRITERS' ORGANIZATIONAL PLANS

Social science writers rely on a variety of organizational plans: time order, narration, process; antecedent-consequent, cause-effect; description; statement-response; comparison and contrast; analysis, classification; definition; problem-solution; question-answer. You will find that some plans appear more frequently than others. Given the nature of the inquiry process, social scientists use the **statement-response, problem-solution, question-answer** plans with some regularity. Notice that in Rebecca M. Blank's "Absent Fathers: Why Don't We Ever Talk About the Unmarried Men?" (Chapter 12), the title indicates a question that will be answered. Also popular is the **antecedent-consequent** plan, because it enables writers to analyze and explain the causes of behaviors and events. Notice how Matt Yglesias structures "A Great Time to Be Alive" (Chapter 13) according to this plan. When you are reading social science writing, look for overlapping organizational plans. Very few social science writers rely on only one; more often they use networks of different plans, often intermeshing them in a single piece.

■ AUTHORS' LITERARY TECHNIQUES

Did you ever wonder why some writers are clear and easy to understand and others are pedantic and inaccessible? Clear writers process their information and ideas in an organized and modulated sequence, and they articulate their thinking in crisp, uncluttered prose. Pedantic and inaccessible writers often presume that their readers know a great deal of specialized terminology and thus don't need explanations, examples, and illuminating details. Writers make themselves understood by defining new terms, concepts, and specialized vocabulary; providing examples, scenarios, and illustrations; and using figurative language.

You will find that many of the selections in this unit display a specialized vocabulary. In some cases, familiar terms are often given new, specialized meanings. Take, for example, the various definitions of "family" in Chapter 12. As you read, pay close attention to the different ways writers handle vocabulary. Some use specialized words with impunity, assuming that their readers have sufficient background knowledge for comprehension. Other writers provide helpful contexts that give clues to verbal meaning. Still others supply definitions of specialized vocabulary. Definitions may take the form of explanations of causes, effects, or functions; synonyms; negations; analogies; descriptions; or classifications. Some definitions are brief, like the following from Pauline Irit Erera's "What Is a Family?"

> Only half of American children live in families that the Census Bureau defines as the traditional nuclear family: a married couple living with their biological children and no one else (Vobejda, 1994). (p. 417)

Other definitions are long, extended ones, such as Herbert Gans's definition of "undeserving poor" in "The War Against the Poor Instead of Programs to End Poverty" (Chapter 13).

Another technique social science writers use to make specialized subjects more accessible to nonspecialized readers is to provide concrete examples and illustrations. Notice the effective examples found in the writing of Robert L. Barret and Bryan E. Robinson and Barbara Ehrenreich.

Writing in the social sciences, then, invites a wide variety of approaches, organizational plans, styles, authorial presences, and literary techniques. Although the selections in this unit do not always exemplify wholly academic social science writing, they do suggest the range of types, modes, and styles in that discourse. Writers in the social sciences often vary their own range from the extreme impersonality of technical reports to the impassioned concern of urgent social issues. The social sciences, after all, study people and their interactions in society. The diversity of the social sciences, therefore, is as broad as the diversity of the people and institutions examined and as broad as the conversations that are swirling around in the public forum and in the academic ivory tower.

Twelve

The Changing American Family

Drawing on research in sociology, psychology, and social psychology, the six readings in this chapter focus on the dramatic challenges confronting American families. Our traditional views of families come into question as families are being transformed and re-defined by forces such as single parenting, divorce, maternal employment, delayed child-bearing, adult independent living, and homosexual parenting couples. As the authors in this chapter point out, the American family is both vulnerable and resilient in the face of these forces.

In the opening selection, "Children of Gay Fathers," Robert L. Barret and Bryan E. Robinson discuss the ramifications of homosexual parents for children's development. Their essay is the product of studies of attitudes toward homosexuality and children raised by gay fathers, which the authors analyze and interpret in light of a specialized bibliog-raphy of twenty-six academic books and articles. Next, Pauline Irit Erera traces the rise and fall of the traditional family in "What Is a Family?" Central to Erera's discussion is a defense of diverse, nontraditional families. Her study presents data about such families gleaned from a specialized bibliography of thirty-seven academic books and articles.

Alarmed by the dissolution of the nuclear family, James Q. Wilson writes the third essay, on the pros and cons of "Cohabitation Instead of Marriage." A distinguished profes-sor of government and of management and public policy, Wilson weighs the costs and benefits of cohabitation as an alternative to marriage and concludes that living together is less socially advantageous than being married. His essay, an analysis of concepts and ideas rather than of data or statistics, provides an example of theoretical writing in the social sciences. In the next selection, "The Origins of the Ambivalent Acceptance of Divorce," sociologist Andrew J. Cherlin turns his attention to the long history in American culture of divided opinions about tolerance of divorce and divorced parenthood. According to Cherlin in his carefully documented article, Americans came slowly to recognize divorce and remarriage as an individual right in cases where the original marriage had become unsatisfactory. The increasing attention of family law to individual rights has likewise afforded protections for childbearing outside marriage. From this evidence, Cherlin concludes that, like divorce, nonmarital childbearing will also gain broader acceptance in coming years.

In "Absent Fathers: Why Don't We Ever Talk about the Unmarried Men?", Rebecca M. Blank deploys the conventional methodology of the social sciences, but she directs it toward a wholly unexpected question. While most academic studies of single parenting focus on unmarried mothers, Blank's study focuses on unmarried fathers and produces the surprising conclusion that many of them have contact with their children but provide meager child support because employment opportunities have passed them by. Evolving methodologies and approaches in the social sciences have enriched academic conversations about the changing American family, and these conversations have in turn contributed to a renewed discussion of the topic in the public arena. The concluding essay in this chapter provides documentation for a sociological argument about problems and historical advances in the plight of working mothers. In "The Ballad of a Single Mother," Lynn Olcott depicts challenges in her life as a wage-earning mother—and eventually as a divorced mother—over a period of thirty years. She acknowledges many difficulties throughout, but also the gradual progress in the availability of support services and the communal acceptance of mothers in the workforce, and she concludes on the hopeful note that coming generations will experience even greater progress.

■ ■ ■ ■ ■ ■ ■ ■ ■ ■ ■

Children of Gay Fathers

Robert L. Barret and Bryan E. Robinson

Robert L. Barret is a professor of counseling at the University of North Carolina at Charlotte, a psychologist, a gay father, and a grandfather of five. His current writings include Gay Fathers: Encouraging the Hearts of Gay Dads and Their Families, *co-authored with Bryan E. Robinson;* Counseling, Gay Men and Lesbians, *co-authored with Colleen Logan; and* Ethical Issues in HIV-Related Psychotherapy *co-authored with Jon Anderson.*

Bryan E. Robinson, a professor of counseling, special education, and child development at the University of South Carolina, has authored over 25 books and more than 100 articles. His most recent books include Gay Fathers: Encouraging the Hearts of Gay Dads and Their Families, *co-authored with Robert L. Barret;* Don't Let Your Mind Stunt Your Growth; *and* A Guidebook for Workaholics, Their Partners and Children and the Clinicians Who Treat Them.

PREREADING

Comment on your familiarity with the issue of homosexual parenting. Has the idea of a gay man choosing to be an active parent and visible father ever occurred to you? Why or why not? Freewrite your response.

Barret, Robert L., and Bryan E. Robinson. "Children of Gay Fathers." In *Redefining Families: Implications for Children's Development*, ed. Adele Eskeles Gottfried and Allen W. Gottfried, pp. 162–70. © 1994 Plenum Press, New York. With kind permission from Springer Science+Business Media B.V.

The children of gay fathers are like children from all families. Some are academically talented, some struggle to get through school, some are model students, and some are constantly in trouble. In thinking about the children of gay fathers, it is essential to recognize that many of them have experienced the divorce of their parents, others have grown up in single-parent homes, and still others have been caught in major crossfire between their parents, grandparents, and perhaps their community over the appropriateness of gay men serving in the father role. Much of any distress that one sees in a child living with a gay father may in fact be the result of the divorce or other family tensions. Legitimate concerns about the impact of living with a gay father include the developmental impact of the knowledge that one's father is gay, reasonable worries about the timing of coming out to children, and creating sensitivity to how the children will experience society's generally negative attitudes towards homosexuality.

Coming out to children is usually an emotion-laden event for gay fathers. The disclosure of one's homosexuality creates anxiety about rejection, fear of hurting or damaging the child's self-esteem, and grieving over the loss of innocence. Some gay fathers never accomplish this task and remain deeply closeted, citing legal and emotional reasons (Bozett, 1980, 1981; Humphreys, 1979; Spada, 1979). Recent publications report the intricacies of this question (Corley, 1990). Those who never disclose their homosexuality often lead deeply conflicted lives and present parenting styles that are characterized by psychological distance (Miller, 1979). Those who do come out to their children do so in the desire to be more of a whole person as a father. As they try to merge their gayness with the father role, they encounter a different kind of conflict: deciding how open to be about their sexual relationships and how much exposure to the gay community to offer their children (Robinson & Barret, 1986).

Fathers report that the first concern they have about coming out is the well-being and healthy adjustment of their children. Many gay fathers seek the help of counselors or specialists in child development as they decide when and how to tell their children about their homosexuality. Research studies indicate that fathers and children report that they are closer after self-disclosure about the father's sexual orientation (Bozett, 1980; Miller, 1979). Bigner and Bozett (1989) studied the reasons that gay fathers give for coming out to their children. Among the most cited were wanting their children to know them as they are, being aware that children will usually discover for themselves if there is frequent contact, and the presence of a male lover in the home.

Gay fathers may come out indirectly by showing affection to men in front of their children or by taking them to gay community events. Others choose to come out verbally or by correspondence (Maddox, 1982). Factors in disclosure are the degree of intimacy between the father and his children and the obtrusiveness of his gayness (Bozett, 1988). By and large, the research suggests that children who are told at an earlier age have fewer difficulties with the day-to-day issues that accompany their father's homosexuality (Bozett, 1989).

The parenting styles of gay fathers are not markedly different from those of other single fathers, but gay fathers try to create a more stable home environment and more positive relationships with their children than traditional heterosexual parents (Bigner & Jacobsen, 1989a; Bozett, 1989). One study found that homosexual fathers differed from their heterosexual counterparts in providing more nurturing and in having less traditional parenting attitudes (Scallen, 1981). Another study of gay fathers found no differences in paternal involvement and amount of intimacy (Bigner & Jacobsen, 1989b). In general, investigators have found that gay fathers feel an additional responsibility to provide effective fathering because they know their homosexuality causes others to examine their parenting styles more closely (Barret & Robinson, 1990). This is not to say that no risk is involved in gay fathering. Miller (1979) found that six daughters of the gay fathers in his study had significant life problems. Others have reported that the children of gay fathers must be prepared to face ridicule and harassment (Bozett, 1980; Epstein, 1979) or may be alienated from their agemates, may become confused about their sexual identity, and may express discomfort with their father's sexual orientation (Lewis, 1980). Most researchers have concluded that being homosexual is compatible with effective parenting and is not usually a major issue in parental relationships with children (Harris & Turner, 1986).

As Chip reveals (Figure 12–1), dealing with the outside world is a task that gay 6
fathers and their children must master. Gay families live in a social system that is generally uncomfortable with homosexuality and that certainly does not overtly support gay parenting. One reality for gay fathers is figuring out how to interact successfully with the world of schools, after-school activities, PTAs, churches, and their children's social networks. Many gay fathers see no choice other than to continue living relatively closeted lives (Bozett, 1988; Miller, 1979). Others, fearing the damage that exposure may bring to their children and/or possible custody battles involving their homosexuality, live rigidly controlled lives and may never develop a gay identity. Those who are more

---

CASE STUDY—CHIP SPEAKS

My name is Chip and I'm seventeen and in twelfth grade. When we first moved to Indianapolis, I learned my dad was gay. I was twelve. I didn't really think much about it. There was a birthday coming up and Dad said we were going to go out and buy a birthday card. He went out, drove around the block and then parked in front of our house. Then he took me to the park and told me the facts of life. He asked me if I knew what it meant to be gay. I told him, "Yeah, it means to be happy and enjoy yourself." Then he started to explain to me about being homosexual. I really didn't know what it was at that point, until he explained it to me.

It's an accepted part of my life now. I've been growing up with it almost five years. When he invites another guy into the house it's OK. I don't bring other kids home then. One of my friends is extremely homophobic and he lets that fact be known. I wouldn't dare risk anything or it would be like "goodbye" to my friend. My other two friends, I don't know how they would react. So I have to be careful about having certain friends over. To me it's blatantly obvious. Having been exposed to so many gay people, I know what to look for and what I'm seeing. Sometimes it's kind of hard because people make fun of gay people. And, if I stick up for their rights, then I get ridiculed. So I just don't say anything at school. It's kind of hard sometimes.

The good thing is that you get a more objective view of people in general, being raised by someone who's so persecuted by society. You begin to sympathize with anyone who is persecuted by society. You tend not to be as prejudiced. You need to appreciate people for what they are personally, not just in terms of color, religion, or sexual preference. That's the

---

Figure 12–1

best thing. The hardest thing is hearing all those people making cracks or jokes on TV or at school and not being really able to do anything about it. Because he's my dad after all, it makes me kind of sad. I never feel ashamed or embarrassed, but I do feel a little pressured because of this. One time a friend of mine made a joke about gay people. I just played it off like I thought it was funny, but I didn't. You have to pretend you think the same thing they do when you don't. That makes me feel like a fraud.

When my dad puts his arm around another man, the first thing I think is, "I could never do that." It makes me a little bit uncomfortable, but I'm not repulsed by it. There are times I wish he wouldn't do it, but other times I'm glad he can have the freedom to do it. When he first came out to me, the only question I asked him was, "What are the chances of me being gay?" He couldn't answer it. But today, to the best of my knowledge, I'm not gay. I like chasing after girls.

Sometimes I feel like I'm keeping a big secret. My dad had a holy union with a man once. My friends had big plans and we were all going out on the day of the big event. And I couldn't go and couldn't explain why. Things like that have happened a number of times. I can't go and I can't tell why. They start yelling at me and get mad. They'll get over it; it's none of their business.

As fathers go, mine tends to be a little nicer—almost a mother's temperament. A friend of mine's father doesn't spend much time with him. They just seem to have stricter parents than mine. I don't know if that's just because of his personality in general or if it's because he's gay. He's a very emotional person; he cries easily. I love him. He's a good dad. He's more open than other dads. He doesn't let me get away with a lot. He tends to be more worried about me and a girl together than some other fathers are about their sons—more worried about my having sex. Whenever I go out on a date, he always says something like, "Don't do anything I wouldn't do," only he doesn't say it jokingly. Sometimes he's just overly cautious.

If I could change my dad and make him straight, I wouldn't do it. It might make things easier for me in some ways, but I wouldn't have grown up the way I have. Being exposed to the straight world and gay world equally has balanced me out more than some of the other people I know. The only things I'd want to change is society's treatment of him. (Barret & Robinson, 1990, pp. 14–15)

Figure 12–1   (continued)

(*Note:* Chip's dad died of AIDS two years after this interview took place.)

open about their gayness struggle to help their children develop a positive attitude toward homosexuality while simultaneously cautioning them about the dangers of disclosure to teachers and friends. Teaching their children to manage these two tasks is a major challenge for gay fathers (Morin & Schultz, 1978; Riddle, 1978). Accomplishing this task when there are virtually no visible role models frequently leaves these fathers and their children feeling extremely isolated.

Bozett (1988) identified several strategies that these children use as they experience both their own and the public's discomfort with their gay fathers. The children of gay fathers in his study used boundary control, nondisclosure, and disclosure as they interacted with their fathers and the outside world. For example, some children limited or attempted to control the content of their interactions with their father. One father we talked with (Barret & Robinson, 1990) reported that he had offered to introduce his teenaged daughter to some of his gay friends in the hope that she would see how normal they were. Her reply was a curt "Dad, that will never happen!" Another father told of trying to reconcile with his son but being rebuffed by the comment, "I don't want to hear anything about your personal life. I can't handle it." Such boundary control limits the ability of the relationship to grow. Other ways that children control boundaries are by not introducing their friends to their fathers or by carefully managing the amount of time they spend together, as Chip reveals in his interview.

Some children do learn to let their friends know carefully about their father's homosexuality. These disclosures have a potential for both increased intimacy and rejection. Helping children discriminate when and how to inform their friends is a critical challenge of gay parenting. As children grow up, these issues may become more complex, as families struggle to involve gay fathers in events such as weddings, graduations, and birth celebrations, where the presence of the gay father and his partner may raise questions. 8

Children of gay fathers do sometimes worry that their sexual orientation may become contaminated by their father's homosexuality. Either they or their friends may begin to question whether they are gay as well. Those children who do disclose their father's homosexuality report being harassed by the use of such terms as *queer* and *fag*. Naturally, this concern is greatest during their teenage years (Riddle & Arguelles, 1981). Obviously, the children of gay fathers need to consider carefully the consequences of disclosure. Keeping this aspect of their lives secret may have the same negative impact on their development as isolation, alienation, and compartmentalization does on gay men. 9

This is not to say that the responses of social support networks are universally negative. Many children with gay fathers report that their friends are both curious and supportive. It is important to recognize that coming out is a process rather than a discrete event. Fathers, children, and their friends need time to move into the process and to examine their own feelings and attitudes so that acceptance and understanding replace confusion and fear. One child of a gay father said: 10

> At first, I was really angry at my dad. I couldn't figure out how to tell my friends what was going on, so I said nothing. My dad and I had terrible fights as he put pressure on me to say it was OK. I thought what he was doing was sinful and embarrassing. But over time, I began to realize that he is the same dad he has always been, and now we are closer than ever. My friends have also got used to the idea and like to spend time with him, too.

State of Research on Children of Gay Fathers

In reviewing the impact of gay fathering on children, it is important to acknowledge that most children who live with gay fathers are also the products of divorce and may show the psychological distress that typically accompanies the experience of marital dissolution. All too often, the emotional distress of children with gay parents is solely attributed to the parents' sexual orientation and is not seen as a complex mixture of family dynamics, divorce adjustment, and the incorporation of the parents' sexual coming out. 11

Only two studies have directly addressed the children of gay fathers (Green, 1978; Weeks, Derdeyn, & Langman, 1975). In both studies, the researchers gave psychological tests to the children. The findings from this testing have been used to support the notion that a parent's homosexuality has little bearing on the child's sexual orientation. Children showed clear heterosexual preferences or were developing them. Green concluded that "The children I interviewed were able to comprehend 12 and verbalize the atypical nature of their parents' lifestyles and to view their atypicality in the broader perspective of the cultural norm" (p. 696). Our interviews with children have also supported this finding (Barret & Robinson, 1990). Still, the problem is that the observations of Weeks and his colleagues (1975) are based on the clinical assessment of only two children, and the Green study (1978) observed only the children of lesbian mothers and the children of parents who had experienced sex-change surgery. None of the parents in that sample were classified as gay fathers. The findings of these two studies and others of lesbian mothers (e.g., Goodman, 1973; Hoeffer, 1981; Kirkpatrick, Smith, & Roy, 1981) are frequently generalized to include the gay father's children, even though important differences exist between transsexuals and gay men as well as between gay men and lesbians.

Conclusions

The profile we use to understand and describe gay fathers and their children is far from conclusive. Clearly, the literature has improved, after 1982, in its use of comparison groups and a more diverse, nationwide sampling. Still, until researchers can obtain larger, more representative samples and use more sophisticated research designs, caution must be exercised in making sweeping generalizations about gay fathers and their families. Meanwhile, it is possible to speculate from some limited data that, although not fully developed, provides an emerging picture of the children of gay fathers:

1. They are like all kids. Some do well in just about all activities; some have problems; and some are well adjusted.
2. They live in family situations that are unique and must develop strategies to cope with these situations.
3. They need help sorting out their feelings about homosexuality and their anxieties about their own sexual orientation.
4. They may be isolated and angry and may have poor relationships with their fathers.
5. They are in little danger of sexual abuse and unlikely to "catch" homosexuality.
6. Many of them adjust quite well to their family situation and use the family as a means to develop greater tolerance of diversity.
7. Some of them become involved in the human rights movement as they promote gay rights.
8. Their relationships with their fathers have a potential for greater honesty and openness.

References

Barret, R., & Robinson, B. (1990). *Gay fathers*. New York: Free Press.

Bigner, J., & Bozett, F. (1989). Parenting by gay fathers. *Marriage and Family Review, 14*, 155–175.

Bigner, J., & Jacobson, R. (1989a). Parenting behaviors of homosexual and heterosexual fathers. *Journal of Homosexuality, 18*, 173–186.

Bigner, J., & Jacobsen, R. (1989b). The value of children to gay and heterosexual fathers. *Journal of Homosexuality, 18*, 163–172.

Bozett, F. (1980). Gay fathers: How and why they disclose their homosexuality to their children. *Family Relations: Journal of Applied Family and Child Studies, 29*, 173–179.

Bozett, F. (1981). Gay fathers: Evolution of the gay father identity. *American Journal of Orthopsychiatry, 51*, 552–559.

Bozett, F. (1988). Social control of identity of gay fathers. *Western Journal of Nursing Research, 10,* 550–565.

Bozett, F. (1989). Gay fathers: A review of the literature. *Journal of Homosexuality, 18,* 137–162.

Corley, R. (1990). *The final closet: The gay parent's guide to coming out to their children.* Miami: Editech Press.

Epstein, R. (1979, June). Children of gays. *Christopher Street,* 43–50.

Goodman, B. (1973). The lesbian mother. *American Journal of Orthopsychiatry, 43,* 283–284.

Green, R. (1978). Sexual identity of 37 children raised by homosexual or transsexual parents. *American Journal of Psychiatry, 135,* 692–697.

Harris, M., & Turner, P. (1986). Gay and lesbian parents. *Journal of Homosexuality, 18,* 101–113.

Hoeffer, B. (1981). Children's acquisition of sex-role behavior in lesbian-mother families. *American Journal of Orthopsychiatry, 51,* 536–544.

Humphreys, L. (1979). *Tearoom trade.* Chicago: Aldine.

Kirkpatrick, M., Smith, C., & Roy, R. (1981). Lesbian mothers and their children. *American Journal of Orthopsychiatry, 51,* 545–551.

Lewis, K. (1980). Children of lesbians: Their point of view. *Social Work, 25,* 200.

Maddox, B. (1982, February). Homosexual parents. *Psychology Today,* 62–69.

Miller, B. (1979, October). Gay fathers and their children. *The Family Coordinator, 28,* 544–551.

Morin, S., & Schultz, S. (1978). The gay movement and the rights of children. *Journal of Social Issues, 34,* 137–148.

Riddle, D. (1978). Relating to children: Gays as role models. *Journal of Social Issues, 34,* 38–58.

Riddle, D., & Arguelles, M. (1981). Children of gay parents: Homophobia's victims. In I. Stuart & L. Abt (Eds.), *Children of separation and divorce.* New York: Van Nostrand Reinhold.

Robinson, B., & Barret, R. (1986). *The developing father.* New York: Guilford Press.

Scallen, R. (1981). *An investigation of paternal attitudes and behaviors in homosexual and heterosexual fathers.* Doctoral dissertation, California School of Professional Psychology, San Francisco, CA. (*Dissertation Abstracts International, 42,* 3809B).

Spada, J. (1979). *The Spada report.* New York: Signet Books.

Weeks, R. B., Derdeyn, A. P., & Langman, M. (1975). Two cases of children of homosexuals. *Child Psychiatry and Human Development, 6,* 26–32.

READING FOR CONTENT

1. Why do Barret and Robinson mention repeatedly that most children of gay fathers have experienced their parents' divorce? Why is that an important consideration?
2. Why is it that some gay fathers never disclose their homosexuality to their children?
3. List the three strategies that children of gay fathers use when they have to interact with the outside world.
4. Summarize what the research reveals about the effect of parents' homosexuality on their children.
5. According to Barret and Robinson, why must we exercise caution in making generalizations about gay fathers and their children?

READING FOR GENRE, ORGANIZATION, AND STYLISTIC FEATURES

1. Underline and identify the various types of data, research findings, and authorities Barret and Robinson cite to support their view.

2. Which features of Barret and Robinson's writing are particularly scholarly or "academic"?

3. Compare Barret and Robinson's writing style with that of Chip in the case study. How are the two styles similar or different?

4. Notice how Barret and Robinson conclude the selection. Explain whether or not you think the ending is effective.

READING FOR RHETORICAL CONTEXT

1. What is Barret and Robinson's rhetorical purpose? What is the central point they want to communicate to their readers?

2. Why do you think the authors include the case study of Chip? What is the effect on the reader? What would be gained or lost if the case study were left out?

3. Why do you think Barret and Robinson refer to Chip only twice? Why don't they analyze or respond to Chip's story?

WRITING ASSIGNMENTS

1. Write a brief summary of the barriers that gay parents and their children must overcome.

2. For an audience who has not read "Children of Gay Fathers," write an essay in which you discuss the problems that children of gay fathers face and explain how these children turn out.

3. Go to the library and research the topic of homosexual parenting. Write a three- to four-page paper answering questions like the following: How do gay men and lesbians become parents? Are the numbers of homosexual families increasing? What is the reaction of conservative groups to gay parenting? What are the views of the gay community concerning gay parenting?

■ ■ ■ ■ ■ ■ ■ ■ ■ ■ ■ ■

What Is a Family?

Pauline Irit Erera

Pauline Irit Erera, associate professor at the University of Washington School of Social Work, has written extensively about family diversity, focusing on step-, foster, and lesbian families, and on noncustodial fathers. This selection is from her most recent book, Family Diversity: Continuity and Change in the Contemporary Family.

PREREADING

Respond to the title "What Is a Family?" by writing out your definition of a family. Share your definition with the other students in your class.

Families have always come in various forms, reflecting social and economic con- 1
ditions and the cultural norms of the times. However, since the 1960s, the increasing
diversity among families in the United States and most other Western nations has
been especially striking. At a dizzying pace, the traditional, two-parent, heterosexual
family has given way to a variety of family arrangements. Today, most adults no longer
live in a coresident nuclear family (Hill, 1995). The first-married, heterosexual family
we have cherished since at least Victorian times is but one of numerous alternative
family structures (Csikszentmihalyi, 1997).

In 1998, just 26 percent of American households were composed of married 2
couples with children. This was down from 45 percent in the early 1970s (University
of Chicago National Opinion Research Center, 1999). Only half of American children
live in families that the Census Bureau defines as the traditional nuclear family: a
married couple living with their biological children and no one else (Vobejda, 1994).
Furthermore, family arrangements differ considerably according to race and ethnicity.
Although about 56 percent of white American children live in a traditional nuclear
family, only about 26 percent of African American children and 38 percent of Hispanic
children do (Vobejda, 1994).

In this [reading] I examine alternative constructions of what a family is. I trace 3
the rise and decline of the traditional family, outline the subsequent increase in
family diversity, and examine reactions to family diversity as expressed in the debate
about "family values." I also discuss the continuing influence of the traditional family
model. Finally, I consider the strengths and promise of family diversity, and set forth
the perspectives that inform the analysis of the families in this book.

Defining Families

The family is not simply a social institution. It is an ideological construct laden with 4
symbolism and with a history and politics of its own. As Jagger and Wright (1999)
put it, "The groupings that are called families are socially constructed rather than
naturally or biologically given" (p. 3). In studying families, we need to keep clear
the distinctions between the institutionalized family, the ideology of the family, and
the lives of actual families. Although social and economic forces shape family life,
our understanding of family is shaped by the evolving patterns of the actual families
around us. Furthermore, conceptions of what constitutes a family are necessarily
rooted in time and place. White, Western, two-parent families have generally been
regarded, explicitly or implicitly, as the model or template against which we compare
all families, regardless of culture, ethnicity, race, or class. This parochial view distorts
our understanding of diverse families by considering them deviations from the norm
(Smith, 1995; Thorne, 1982).

One early definition of the family was that offered by the anthropologist George 5
Peter Murdock (1949), based on his survey of 250 ethnographic reports:

> The family is a social group characterized by common residence, economic coopera-
> tion, and reproduction. It includes adults of both sexes, at least two of whom maintain
> a socially approved sexual relationship, and one or more children, own or adopted, of
> the sexually cohabiting adults. (p. 1)

Murdock identified the basic family unit found in about one quarter of the societies he surveyed as "a married man and woman with their offspring" (p. 1), which he termed a nuclear family. Another quarter of the societies were predominantly polygamous, with families based on plural marriages of a spouse, hence, in his view, constituting two or more nuclear families. In the remaining half surveyed, the families were extended in that the nuclear family resided with the bride's or the groom's parents and/or other relatives. Murdock, reflecting the prevailing orthodoxy of the times, concluded that the nuclear family was universal and inevitable, the basis for more complex family forms.

Given the diversity of families and the political debates about them, a single, all- 6 encompassing definition of "family" is impossible to achieve. Families are defined in a variety of ways depending on the purposes and circumstances (Smith, 1995; Sprey, 1988). Although traditionalists have held blood ties or consanguinity to be a defining characteristic of the family, others argue that we should define families according to the attachments and intimacy that individuals have toward significant people in their lives. This latter definition shifts the focus from the family's structure or legal status to the nature and meaning of relationships (Dowd, 1997).

Diverse families challenge our definition and perceptions of what a family is. 7 These families also "challenge gender roles and influence gender typing by what they say and what they do" (Dowd, 1997, p. 110). They force us to reconsider our conceptions of what a mother, father, parent, and sibling are. Is a family defined by genes and blood relationships? Shared residence? Is it a group of people who provide one another social, emotional, and physical support, caring, and love? Does a family necessarily involve two adults? Are these adults necessarily of the opposite sex? Must families be based on marriage? Can a child have two or more mothers or fathers? Is a parent more "real" by virtue of biological or legal status? Does a family have to share a common residence, economic cooperation, and reproduction to be a family? Such questions are the subject of heated debates about the family and "family values."

The Rise and Decline of the Traditional Family: The Heyday of the Traditional Family

The 1950s saw a surge in family formation associated with the end of the depression 8 and World War II. Although few Americans ever enjoyed family lives as harmonious, wholesome, or predictable as the ones portrayed in those beloved fifties television sitcoms, such programs symbolized a definition of ideal family life that was widely shared in that decade. Three fifths of U.S. households in that period fit the model of the nuclear family structure, with its breadwinner-husband and homemaker-wife, of their pop culture icons. The economy was booming and even many working-class men earned enough to support such families. Yet this upsurge in marriage and childbearing proved to be a short-lived experiment. Starting in the 1960s, fertility rates began to decline, and the trend to early marriage was reversed (Silverstein & Auerbach, 1999).

Family life in the 1950s was hardly ideal. Families were not as well off economi- 9 cally as they would become by the end of the 1960s; African Americans in particular had higher rates of poverty than they do now. Women, minorities, lesbians, gays, and nonconforming groups were subject to discrimination, and family problems got little attention or social assistance (Coontz, 1997).

In some ways, the decline of the 1950s family grew out of the trends and contradic- 10 tions of the fifties themselves. The main reason for family change was the breakdown of the postwar social compact between government, corporations, and workers. The 1950s were years of active government assistance to families. Government-backed home mortgages financed many of the new family homes, and the minimum wage was set high enough to support a family of three above the poverty level. Large numbers of workers joined unions, received pensions and health benefits, and worked a relatively short workweek. Corporations and the wealthy were taxed at high rates to support high levels of spending on veterans benefits and public works (Coontz, 1997).

Family Diversity in the 1960s and 1970s

The affluence and optimism that explains the family behavior of the postwar generation were challenged by America's new economic problems, whose impact was felt at the family level in the form of inflation and lower real earnings. Public policies aggravated these problems by cutting taxes for corporations and the wealthy while cutting spending for services, public works, and investments in human capital (Coontz, 1997). This meant that families had to modify the socially valued form of the family to try to protect their socially valued lifestyle: the standard of living to which they had become accustomed. Economic pressures made women's employment more a matter of necessity than of choice (Coontz, 1997). Today's politicians are being disingenuous when they advocate a return to the 1950s family while opposing the kinds of social and political supports that helped make it possible (Coontz, 1997). 11

Along with the economic shifts in the late 1950s and early 1960s came technological developments and social movements that also contributed to the stunning increase in family diversity. The example of African Americans' struggle to secure civil rights inspired other minorities and marginalized groups—women, gay men and lesbians, the disabled—to fight for their rights. The 1960s and 1970s became an era of diversity and identity politics as a host of "others" sought recognition and liberation from the constraints of discriminatory laws, social policies, and negative stereotypes. Foremost among those claiming their rights were women. 12

The struggle for women's liberation was advanced by the availability of the birth control pill and other methods that gave women control over reproduction. These changes generated an increased acceptance of sexual behavior not necessarily linked with marriage, for women as well as for men (Riley, 1997). While white feminists began to claim the right to control and limit their fertility through the use of contraception and abortion, women of color started claiming the right to have their fertility not be controlled by forced contraception and sterilization (Hargaden & Llewellin, 1996). By 1973, many women in the United States and other industrialized countries were able to prevent pregnancies, had access to legal abortion, and could end unwanted pregnancies before birth (Riley, 1997). 13

The movement for gender equality led to increased employment opportunities for women, while at the same time declining wage rates for unskilled male workers made them less desirable marriage partners. Although paid far less than their male counterparts, an increasing number of women were now employed and financially independent. Consequently, more women who were unhappy in their marriages were able to divorce (Coontz, 1997; Riley, 1997). The changing roles of women, their increasing participation in the labor force, and their economic independence had undercut the economic basis of marriage (Lichter & McLaughlin, 1997). With divorce 14 becoming more available, community norms regarding divorce, single parenthood, and nonmarital childbearing began to change. More people were themselves the product of diverse families, and were more accepting of divorce, single parenthood, and women's right to live independently.

Single-parent families were in many respects the pioneers of family diversity, pav-   15 ing the way for the recognition of other families. The growing acceptance of divorced, single-parent families facilitated the emergence of yet another form of single parenthood: that resulting not from divorce but from women electing to give birth while remaining single. Women increasingly saw motherhood without marriage as offering greater satisfaction and security than a marriage of questionable stability (Mann & Roseneil, 1999). Increasingly, women chose to cohabit rather than formally marry, to postpone marriage and childbearing, and to live alone. Still others chose to give birth, adopt, or foster children as single parents. Many women, defying the stigma attached to childless women, elected not to have children at all, thus creating a new family configuration: childless families by choice.

With fewer unwanted pregnancies and fewer unwanted births, and with more   16 white, single mothers keeping their babies as had African American mothers in the past, fewer white babies were available for adoption (Riley, 1997). The decline in the number of babies placed for adoption precipitated an increased interest in international adoptions as an alternative. Because these adoptions often involved children who were racially and/or ethnically different from their adoptive parents, the adoption could not be kept secret as had been the practice in the past. The growing acceptance of adoptive families, in turn, facilitated a greater acceptance of stepfamilies and other families not related by blood.

With the increasing numbers and visibility of single-parent, step-, and adoptive   17 families, the gay liberation movement opened the way for the emergence of gay and lesbian families. Some gay men and lesbians were divorced and had custody of the children, becoming in the process single-parent families. Others chose to give birth to a child within the lesbian/gay relationship.

Another factor contributing to family diversity since the 1970s, and especially to   18 foster families and grandmother-headed families, has been a dramatic increase in the imprisonment of women and mothers, a legacy of the war on drugs with its harsh sentencing policies. Most of the women in prison are there for drug-related offenses, often because of the activities of a male partner. This, together with the growing number of women, especially women of color, infected by HIV (the human immunodeficiency virus) has contributed to an increasing number of children whose mothers are not able to parent them. In addition, many children, and especially African American children, are removed from homes considered unfit and placed in foster care, sometimes with relatives. Increasingly, grandmothers are assuming responsibility for raising their grandchildren.

Finally, innovations in reproductive technology have vastly opened up the pos-   19 sibilities for people to create new kinds of families, further challenging conventional definitions of family. New reproductive technologies (NRTs) include donor insemination, embryo freezing and transfer, ovum extraction, and *in vitro* fertilization (IVF). The first test-tube baby, conceived through *in vitro* fertilization, was born in England in 1978, and the first surrogate birth, in which an embryo was transferred to a woman with no genetic connection to it, took place in 1986. In 1992, a postmenopausal grandmother gave birth to her own granddaughter in South Africa, having served as a surrogate for her daughter's embryo.

To protect marriages, the law in most jurisdictions recognizes husbands of inseminated women as the "real" fathers (Benkov, 1997) while denying parental rights to donors (Bartholet, 1993). Although NRTs reflect a preference for biological reproduction over social parenting through adoption, fostering, or informal care of relatives (McDaniel, 1988), social parenting has become a powerful force in family diversity. NRTs were originally administered to support traditional nuclear families, and were denied to unmarried women. However, as they became increasingly available through for-profit laboratories seeking to expand their markets, they were offered to single women, including lesbians. To date, about one million children have been conceived in laboratories in the United States (Benkov, 1997). The NRTs have undermined the cultural norm that blood relations are the *sine qua non* of families, and that nonbiological members are not "real" family members. Families created through reproductive technologies, similar to adoptive-foster families, and to some extent like stepfamilies, defy the notion that biological conception has to be the basis for family formation. This disjunction between reproduction and parenting, between the biological and social aspects of parenting, alters the meaning of parenthood, kinship, and family (Benkov, 1997; Gross, 1997; Stacey, 1996).

Families in the 1980s and 1990s: The Backlash Against Family Diversity

The 1980s and 1990s were, in many respects, a period of regression in the United States with respect to civil rights and policies supporting diversity. The family became, and continues to be, a battleground over contending visions of what a family ought to be. Voices on the right blame changes in the family for a wide range of social problems, while voices on the left look to the family to provide the basis for a more communitarian society. At one extreme, we hear claims that the family is obsolete, a reactionary institution destined to disappear. At the other, conservatives strive to uphold "family values," advocating a return to the conventional family arrangements enshrined in midcentury television sitcoms (Csikszentmihalyi, 1997). Across the political spectrum, invoking "family values" is a way of idealizing the traditional nuclear family to the exclusion of other family forms (Jagger & Wright, 1999).

Family values proponents offer a simple and dangerous misdiagnosis of what they consider wrong in America—the "family breakdown" thesis (Stacey, 1998). Family breakdown—namely the high divorce rates, the decline of the two-parent married family, and the increase in family diversity—has been blamed for everything from child poverty, declining educational standards, substance abuse, high homicide rates, AIDS (acquired immune deficiency syndrome), infertility, and teen pregnancy to narcissism and the Los Angeles riots (Coontz, 1997; Jagger & Wright, 1999; Wright & Jagger, 1999). Family breakdown is in turn attributed to a generalized decline in family values, which is often blamed on a lack of commitment to marriage, an acceptance of female-headed families as a way of life, feminism, the sexual revolution, and gay liberation (Beca Zinn, 1997; Coontz, 1997). Hence women's desire for personal fulfillment is described by conservatives as an egotistic abandonment of parental obligations that sacrifices the well-being of children (Council on Families in America, 1996). Ironically, the current emphasis on family self-sufficiency and the pressure on single mothers to be self-supporting are in direct conflict with conservatives' traditional preference for full-time mothers (Wright & Jagger, 1999).

In keeping with the family breakdown thesis, political discourse in the 1990s   23 blamed single motherhood for the perpetuation of an "underclass" in British and American society. Although there is little consensus among scholars about the under-class, or whether it exists at all, under the label of the underclass debate, researchers returned to old questions about the relationship between family structure, race, and poverty. In the 1960s and early 1970s, the discussion focused on how poor families adapted to poverty; current discussions, in contrast, are primarily concerned with the failure of women-headed families to lift themselves and their children out of poverty (Jarrett, 1994). For example, American conservative Charles Murray, who played a prominent role in blaming single motherhood for poverty and violence, argued (in Wright & Jagger, 1999) that more young women were choosing unwed motherhood because the sexual revolution had destigmatized it and the welfare system was reward-ing it. Though welfare costs have always been a very small portion of the federal bud-get, single-parent families were also held responsible for a "crisis" of the welfare state (Beca Zinn, 1997; Mann & Roseneil, 1999; Wright & Jagger, 1999).

Although single mothers were being attacked, they suffered high rates of poverty,   24 a legacy of social policies that especially disadvantages women and children. Welfare benefits to impoverished single mothers and their children in the United States de-clined markedly from the 1970s to the 1990s, and in 1996, the federal welfare entitle-ment was abolished in favor of a drastically limited employment-based program. The attacks on welfare were, in effect, attacks against struggling and vulnerable families (Stacey, 1996).

The attack on single mothers is partly a backlash against feminism, an attempt   25 to restore fathers to their "rightful role." It is also motivated by concerns over how women are exercising their agency and their freedom of choice to become mothers or not. Instead of viewing disadvantaged women as committed, responsible mothers who assume custody and care of their children, the rhetoric portrays them as oppressors of the fathers. The fathers, on the other hand, who are at least as responsible for the cre-ation of poor single-parent families, are often viewed as the victims. If they pay child support, they are heralded as responsible fathers, even though the child support is usually insufficient to meet the expense of raising the children, and even though they generally forgo the daily responsibilities of caring for the children. This rhetoric justi-fies reductions in government assistance to single mothers and their children, making their situations even worse (Mann & Roseneil, 1999).

The Family Values Agenda

Family values proponents define the family as an institution comprising people re-   26 lated by blood and marriage that performs specific social functions. The majority of family values advocates use "the family" to mean a heterosexual, conjugal, nuclear, domestic unit, ideally one with a male breadwinner, female homemaker, and their dependent offspring—a version of the 1950s television Ozzie-and-Harriet family, sometimes updated to include employed wives and mothers (Stacey, 1998). This prescriptive definition of what constitutes a proper family obscures racial, class, and sexual diversity in domestic arrangements, as well as masking the inequities within the traditional family (Stacey, 1998). Pluralism, so commonly recognized in other aspects of American society, has yet to be fully accepted when it comes to the family (Klee, Schmidt, & Johnson, 1989).

A striking feature of our contemporary family politics is the chasm between 27 behavior and ideology. Most family values enthusiasts still judge our "brave new families" by a fifties standard to which only a minority of citizens would wish to return (Stacey, 1998). In a 1999 national survey, for example, only a third of the respondents thought that parents should stay together just because they have children (University of Chicago National Opinion Research Center, 1999).

Support for "traditional family values" serves political purposes. It provides a ra- 28 tionale for family surveillance and intervention, focuses attention on individual moral solutions to social problems rather than costly public solutions, and offers a simple alternative to dealing with the real complexities of social change. The new call for family values represents an effort to reduce collective responsibility and increase the dependency of family members on one another (Wright & Jagger, 1999).

Pro-family values stories are appearing in the press, in popular magazines, on 29 radio and television talk shows, and in scholarly journals. During the late 1980s, a network of research and policy institutes, think tanks and commissions, began mobilizing to forge a national consensus on family values and to shape the family politics of the "new" Democratic Party. Central players were the Institute for American Values and the Council on Families in America, whose goal is to restore the privileged status of lifelong, heterosexual marriage.

The Council on Families in America (1996) urges marriage counselors, family 30 therapists, and family life educators to approach their work "with a bias in favor of marriage" and to "link advocacy for children to advocacy for marriage" (p. 311). It advocates a revision of the federal tax code "to provide more favorable treatment for married couples with children" (p. 313), and advocates a "bias in favor of marriage-with-children in the allocation of subsidized housing loans and public housing" (p. 314).

Marriage has become increasingly fragile with the increase in women's em- 31 ployment and their reduced economic dependency on men. It has also become less obligatory, particularly for women. In all cultures and eras, stable marriage systems have rested upon coercion—overt or veiled—and on inequality. Proposals to restrict access to divorce and parenting implicitly recognize this. Without coercion, divorce and single motherhood will remain commonplace. It seems a poignant commentary on the benefits to women of modern marriage that even when women retain chief responsibility for supporting children, raising them and caring for them, when they earn much less than men with similar "cultural capital," and when they and their children suffer major economic loss after divorce, so many regard divorce as the lesser evil.

Rather than examining and solving the problems of traditional marriages that 32 so often end up in divorce, advocates of family values aim to coerce women to stay in marriages by erecting barriers to divorce. They wish to restore fault criteria to divorce proceedings and impose new restrictions, like mandatory waiting periods and compulsory counseling. Claiming that divorce and unwed motherhood inflict devastating harm on children, they seek to revive the social stigma that once marked these "selfish" practices. They advocate restricting adoption to married couples, and they oppose welfare payments to unmarried mothers. However, in their staunch advocacy of marriage, they avoid examining what might be lacking in a traditional marriage, especially for women, or questioning why so many women choose to divorce or not to marry.

What is primarily at stake in the debate over the family is the relationship between the sexes. Advocates of family values assign responsibilities to families without explicitly acknowledging the burdens that family life places on women or the gender conflicts resulting from unequal roles. At the same time, they place most of the blame for family problems on "deviant" women, especially those who raise children alone.   33

The Significance of Family Structure

Contrary to the claims of family values advocates, there is no empirical basis for granting privileged status to the heterosexual, nuclear, two-parent family (Acock & Demo, 1994; Dowd, 1997; Silverstein & Auerbach, 1999). Few social scientists would agree that a family's structure is more important than the quality of the relationships between parents and children. Revisionists employ academic sleights of hand to evade this consensus. For example, they rest claims on misleading comparison groups and on studies that do not use any comparison groups at all. In fact, most children from both divorced or nondivorced families turn out reasonably well; and when other parental resources—like income, education, self-esteem, and a supportive social environment—are roughly similar, signs of two-parent privilege largely disappear. Most research indicates that a stable, intimate relationship with one responsible, nurturing adult is a child's surest path to becoming a nurturing adult as well (Furstenberg & Cher lin, 1991). As Dowd (1997) points out, "Dysfunctional families come in all shapes and sizes; so do healthy families" (p. xv). There is no question that two responsible, loving parents generally can offer children more than one parent can. However, three or four might prove even better. Putting the case against the essential significance of structure, Dowd (1997) concludes,   34

> Children need love, care, and parenting. Structure neither produces nor insures that those things will be present. We need to put children first, structure second. It makes no sense to punish children or separate them from their families as the consequence of structure that they had no hand in creating and that are unconnected to their well-being. (p. xix)

The "Essential Father"

With many mothers no longer at home full time, and in the absence of universal child care and policies to help families integrate work and caregiving, the conservative stance taps into widespread anxiety about "who will raise the children" (Silverstein & Auerbach, 1999). Attacks on single-parent families are also based on claims that families without fathers cannot socialize sons into civilized manhood (Charles Murray, in Wright & Jagger, 1999). These concerns about the well-being of children, and especially boys, represent a reaction against the women's movement, the perceived loss of male privilege, and the gay liberation movement (Silverstein & Auerbach, 1999). As expressed by the Council on Families in America (1996), "The explosion of never-married motherhood in our society means that fathers are increasingly viewed as superfluous, unnecessary, and irrelevant" (pp. 302–303). Men have lost their position at   35 the center of family life. With marriage losing its normative force and with increasing numbers of women working, men have seen their economic ascendancy over the family being eroded, and most are expected to share at least some of the domestic tasks. The conservative concern about the necessity of the "essential father" can be seen as an effort to reestablish male dominance by rescuing the traditional family based on traditional gender roles (Silverstein & Auerbach, 1999).

Conservatives have it backward when they argue that the collapse of traditional 36 family values is at the heart of our social decay. The losses in real earnings and in breadwinner jobs, the persistence of low-wage work for women, global economic restructuring, and corporate greed have wreaked far more havoc on Ozzie-and-Harriet land than have the combined effects of feminism, the sexual revolution, gay liberation, the counterculture, narcissism, and every other value flip of the past half-century. There is no going back to the "good old 1950s," when breadwinner-husbands had unpaid homemaker wives who tended dependent children and the household full time. The modern family has been decisively replaced by the post-modern family of working mothers, high divorce rates, and diverse family arrangements (Coontz, 1997; Stacey, 1998). Nevertheless, the traditional family continues to cast its shadow over other family forms.

The Hegemony of the Traditional Family

The overpowering strength of the paradigm of the first-married, heterosexual family 37 lingers even though this family style has long since lost its place as the most prevalent (Glick, 1989). Despite the diversity, society's institutions continue to support a single family structure that is no longer applicable to the majority of families. As Dowd (1997) states,

> We as a society, through law, support nuclear marital families in significant material and ideological ways. We provide resources including financial support, fringe benefits, tax breaks, and housing. We facilitate the use of reproductive technology or adoption for favored families. We define our vision of family, ideologically and practically ... by limiting recognition of non-marital families. (p. 4)

The supremacy and the idealization of the traditional family model are expressed in 38 laws, policies, and institutional practices, attitudes, and behaviors. Nuclear families have historically provided a model of normalcy for which family specialists, such as psychologists, social workers, family researchers and theorists, have based their ideals (Adams & Steinmetz, 1993). Increased social tolerance for diversity has, to some extent, modified the notion that nuclear families offer an exemplary family structure. Nevertheless, social policies and attitudes still favor the traditional family. This puts enormous pressures on diverse families to play down their uniqueness and to act like the traditional family, as if this is the only "right" kind of family, irrespective of the differences in structure and style. Despite its demographic decline, "The image of this idealized form [of the traditional nuclear family] persists in the social consciousness and remains the standard against which all other configurations are compared" (Allen & Baber, 1992, p. 379).

Viewed against a template of the first-married, heterosexual family, other fam- 39 ily structures tend to fall into two broad stereotypical categories: the deviant and the variant. A deviant stereotype is assigned to families that seem much too different to be regarded as a variation of the first-married, heterosexual family. In the past, this included the single-parent family, and now includes lesbian and gay families, teenage single-parent families, and childless families, among others. Deviant implies not only that these families are different, but that they are bad or wrong in some way. Therefore, "deviant" families need somehow to prove their legitimacy.

The variant family stereotype views diverse families more positively, consider- 40
ing them more or less like first-married, heterosexual families, but with a difference. Families considered variant usually have two parents of the opposite sex who reside with children in the same household; notable examples are adoptive and stepfamilies. Although lacking the negative connotation of deviance, this positive stereotype is also problematic. It establishes unrealistic expectations based on the model of the traditional nuclear family. Because such families are not quite the same when measured against the template, they may be left feeling that they are falling short in some respects. The stereotypes exert pressures on families to try to function in the same mold as the traditional family, or to "pass" in order to gain the legitimacy and resources reserved for traditional families. The appeal of assimilation is especially attractive for those families that most resemble a traditional family. "Passing," however, creates tensions between the actual and idealized lifestyles of family members. As Eheart and Power (1995) found in their study of adoptive families, "failure occurs when families live stories that differ in acceptable ways from their expectations of what their family life should be like" (p. 211). It engenders a falsehood that may lead family members to experience a sense of failure, shame, and identity confusion. At the same time, it restricts their creativity, flexibility, and uniqueness (Biddle, Kaplan, & Silverstein, 1998). In contrast, when families manage to let go of myths of the ideal family life, their lives are experienced as appropriate and fitting.

It is therefore not surprising that with the exception of stepfamilies and single- 41
parent families, families…have rarely been examined as family structures in their own right. To the extent that they have been considered at all, it has been from a particular academic or practice perspective. Foster families, viewed as nuclear families temporarily hosting an additional child, are examined from the standpoint of child welfare; gay and lesbian families, under gender or women's studies; and grandmother-headed families, within gerontology or race and gender studies. Furthermore, these families are often characterized as lacking something. Single-parent families are deemed deficient for lack of a father. Grandparents raising grandchildren are discounted because they are old, are not the parents, and are frequently people of color and poor. Gay and lesbian families are not considered as families at all because the partners are of the same sex and because they are not married. The refusal to acknowledge them as families is a denial that their relationships count, regardless of their stability, duration, or quality.

Family theories do not sufficiently account for families in their diversity. New 42
perspectives are needed that value family plurality and resilience (Demo & Allen, 1996; McAdoo, 1998). As Weitzman (1975) noted a quarter of a century ago, in a diverse society, a single family form cannot fit the needs of all. Rather than shaping concepts of the family from a single mold, we must recognize the diversity and fluidity of family and household arrangements, and acknowledge change in families as a sign of strength.

References

Acock, A. C., & Demo, D. H. (1994). *Family diversity and well-being*. Thousand Oaks, CA; Sage.

Adams, B. N., & Steinmetz, S. K. (1993). Family theory and methods in the classics. In P. G. Boss & W. J. Doherty (Eds.), *Sourcebook of family theories and methods: A contextual approach* (pp. 71–94). New York: Plenum.

Allen, K. R., & Baber, K. M. (1992). Starting the revolution in family life education: A feminist vision. *Family Relations, 41*, 378–384.

Bartholet, E. (1993). *Family bonds: Adoption and the politics of parenting*. Boston: Houghton Mifflin.

Beca Zinn, M. B. (1997). Family, race, and poverty. In A. S. Skolnick & J. H. Skolnick (Eds.), *Family in transition* (9th ed., pp. 316–329). New York: HarperCollins.

Benkov, L. (1997). Reinventing the family. In A. S. Skolnick & J. H. Skolnick (Eds.), *Family in transition* (9th ed., pp. 354–379). New York: HarperCollins.

Biddle, C., Kaplan, S. R., & Silverstein, D. (1998). *Kinship: Ties that bind*. Available at: http://www.adopting.org/silveroze/html/kinship.html.

Coontz, S. (1997). *The way we really are: Coming to terms with America's changing families*. New York: Basic Books.

Council on Families in America. (1996). Marriage in America: A report to the nation. In D. Popenoe, J. Bethke-Elshtain, & D. Blankenhorn (Eds.), *Promises to keep: Decline and renewal of marriage in America* (pp. 293–317). Lanham, MD: Rowman & Littlefield.

Csikszentmihalyi, M. (1997). *Finding flow: The psychology of engagement with everyday life*. New York: Basic Books.

Demo, D. H., & Allen, K. R. (1996). Diversity within lesbian and gay families: Challenges and implications for family theory and research. *Journal of Social and Personal Relationships, 13*(3), 415–434.

Dowd, N. E. (1997). *In defense of single-parent families*. New York: New York University Press.

Eheart, B. K., & Power, M. B. (1995). Adoption: Understanding the past, present, and future through stories. *Sociological Quarterly, 36*(1), 197–216.

Furstenberg, F. F., Jr., & Cherlin, A. J. (1991). *Divided families: What happens to children when parents part*. Cambridge, MA: Harvard University Press.

Glick, P. C. (1989). Remarried families, stepfamilies, and stepchildren: A brief demographic analysis. *Family Relations, 38*, 24–27.

Gross, H. E. (1997). Variants of open adoptions: The early years. *Marriage and Family Review, 25*(1–2), 19–42.

Hargaden, H., & Llewellin, S. (1996). Lesbian and gay parenting issues. In D. Davies & C. Neal (Eds.), *Pink therapy: A guide for counselors and therapists working with lesbian, gay and bisexual clients* (pp. 116–130). Buckingham, England: Open University Press.

Hill, M. S. (1995). When is a family a family? Evidence from survey data and implications for family policy. *Journal of Family and Economic Issues, 16*(1), 35–64.

Jagger, G., & Wright, C. (1999). Introduction: Changing family values. In G. Jagger & C. Wright (Eds.), *Changing family values* (pp. 1–16). London: Routledge.

Jarrett, R. L. (1994). Living poor: Family life among single parent, African-American women. *Social Problems, 41*(1), 30–49.

Klee, L., Schmidt, C., & Johnson, C. (1989). Children's definitions of family following divorce of their parents. In C. A. Everett (Ed.), *Children of divorce: Developmental and clinical issues* (pp. 109–127). New York: Haworth.

Lichter, D. T., & McLaughlin, D. K. (1997). Poverty and marital behavior of young women. *Journal of Marriage and the Family, 59*(3), 582–595.

Mann, K., & Roseneil, S. (1999). Poor choices? Gender, agency and the underclass debate. In G. Jagger & C. Wright (Eds.), *Changing family values* (pp. 98–118). London: Routledge.

McAdoo, H. P. (1998). African-American families: Strengths and realities. In H. I. McCubbin, E. A. Thompson, A. I. Thompson, & J. A. Futrell (Eds.), *Resiliency in African-American families* (pp. 17–30). Thousand Oaks, CA: Sage.

McDaniel, S. A. (1988). Women's roles, reproduction, and the new reproductive technologies: A new stork rising. In N. Mandell & A. Duffy (Eds.), *Reconstructing the Canadian family: Feminist perspectives* (pp. 175–206). Toronto, Ontario: Butterworths.

Murdock, G. P. (1949). *Social structure*. New York: Free Press.

Riley, N. (1997). American adoptions of Chinese girls: The socio-political matrices of individual decisions. *Women's Studies International Forum, 20*(1), 87–102.

Silverstein, L. B., & Auerbach, C. F. (1999). Deconstructing the essential father. *American Psychologist, 54*(6), 397–407.

Smith, T. E. (1995). What a difference a measure makes: Parental-separation effect on school grades, not academic achievement. *Journal of Divorce and Remarriage, 23*(3–4), 151–164.

Sprey, J. (1988). Current theorizing on the family: An appraisal. *Journal of Marriage and the Family, 50*(4), 875–890.

Stacey, J. (1996). *In the name of the family: Rethinking family values in the postmodern age.* Boston: Beacon.

Stacey, J. (1998). *Brave new families: Stories of domestic upheaval in late twentieth century America* (Rev. ed.). New York: Basic Books.

Thorne, B. (1982). Feminist rethinking of the family: An overview. In B. Thorne & M. Yalom (Eds.), *Rethinking the family: Some feminist questions* (pp. 1–24). New York: Longman.

University of Chicago National Opinion Research Center. (1999, November 24). *The emerging 21st century American family.* Available at: http://www.norc.uchicago.edu/new/homepage.htm.

Vobejda, B. (1994). Study alters image of "typical" family. *Seattle Times.* Available at: http://seattletimes.nwsource.com.

Weitzman, L. J. (1975). To love, honor, and obey? Traditional legal marriage and alternative family forms. *Family Coordinator, 24*(4), 531–547.

Wright, C., & Jagger, G. (1999). End of century, end of family? Shifting discourses of family "crisis." In G. Jagger & C. Wright (Eds.), *Changing family values* (pp. 17–37). London: Routledge.

READING FOR CONTENT

1. Explain what Erera means when she says, "The main reason for family change was the breakdown of the postwar social compact between government, corporations, and workers" (paragraph 10).

2. Make a list of the various complaints about single mothers. Explain how Erera defends single moms against each attack.

3. Summarize Erera's argument against proponents of family values.

4. Does Erera view fathers as "essential" to the well-being of children? Why or why not?

5. Explain the distinction Erera makes between deviant and variant families.

READING FOR GENRE, ORGANIZATION, AND STYLISTIC FEATURES

1. Use Chapter 7 to explain how Erera has fashioned an argument in which she accounts for both sides of the problem.

2. What devices or aids help the reader follow Erera's argument?

3. What types of sources does Erera draw upon, and what functions do those sources serve?

READING FOR RHETORICAL CONTEXT

1. Toward the beginning of the selection, Erera provides a number of alarming statistics. What purpose do they serve?

2. What is the function of the questions in paragraph 7?

3. How do you think readers will be affected by Erera's argument? After reading the selection, would you support her position? Why or why not?

WRITING ASSIGNMENTS

1. After reading the selection, respond to the question "What is a family?" Compare your postreading response to the definition you wrote for your prereading. Write a brief essay comparing and/or contrasting the two definitions.

2. How do the statistics in paragraph 2 compare to your experience? Is your family included in the 26 percent of American households with married couples and children? Write an essay that describes your family.

3. Interview an individual or couple who are representative of one of the nontraditional structures or lifestyles—single-parent families, lesbian and gay families, teenage single-parent families, childless families, grandmother-headed families, foster families—that Erera discusses. Ask the interviewee(s) to explain what he or she sees as the advantages and disadvantages of the particular lifestyle. Then write an essay in which you compare your interviewee's explanations with those presented by Erera. Draw your own conclusions.

4. Using Erera's explanation of the family breakdown thesis and her description of the attack on single mothers as a base, conduct some research on separated, divorced, never-married, and widowed single-parent families. Drawing on the guidelines for synthesis essays in Chapter 6, write an essay addressed to your classmates explaining the rewards and difficulties of single parenting today.

Cohabitation Instead of Marriage

James Q. Wilson

James Q. Wilson served as the Shattuck Professor of Government at Harvard University and the James Collins Professor of Management and Public Policy at UCLA. He is the author or co-author of 14 books, including Moral Judgement, Moral Sense, American Government, Bureaucracy, Thinking About Crime, Varieties of Police Behavior, Political Organizations, *and* Crime and Human Nature *(co-authored with Richard J. Herrnstein). This selection is from his 2002 book,* The Marriage Problem: How Our Culture Has Weakened Families.

PREREADING

In your view, is marriage a prerequisite to living with a partner? Why do you think increasing numbers of people are deciding to live together rather than marry? Respond to these questions in your writer's notebook.

If marriage is designed to help solve a society's need to maintain family, and if   1
modern societies such as ours have created ways of raising children that are independent of family life, then family life ought not to be very important. If a child can be raised by a nanny or a day-care center, if its education can be left in the hands of public and private schools, if its physical well-being can be entrusted to police officers and social workers, then marriage does not offer much to the father and mother. And if the couple has no wish for children, then marriage offers nothing at all. Perhaps men and women can simply decide to live together—to cohabit—without any formalities that define a "legal" marriage.

But cohabitation creates a problem that most people will find hard to solve. If   2
people are free to leave cohabitation (and they must be, or it would be called a marriage instead), then in many cases, neither the man nor the woman has any strong incentive to invest heavily in the union. Marriage is a way of making such investments plausible by telling each party that they are united forever, and if they wish to dissolve this union that they will have to go through an elaborate and possibly costly legal ritual called divorce. Marriage is a way of restricting the freedom of people so that investing emotionally and financially in the union makes sense. I can join my money with yours because, should we ever wish to separate, we would have to go through a difficult process of settling our accounts. That process, divorce, makes merged accounts less risky. If a cohabiting couple has a child, its custody can be decided by one parent taking it. If we marry, however, the custody of the child will be determined by a judge, and so each of our interests in its custody will get official recognition. This fact makes it easier for us to have a child.

And love itself is helped by marriage. If we cohabit and I stop loving you, I walk   3
away. This means that you have less of an incentive to love me, since your affection may not be returned by me for as long as you would like and hence your love might be wasted. But if we promise to live together forevermore (even though we know that we can get a divorce if we are willing to put up with its costs), each of us is saying that since you have promised to love me, I can afford to love you.

Cohabiting couples in the United States tend to keep separate bank accounts   4
and divide up the expenses of their life together. And this financial practice signals a potential social burden. While married couples with unequal incomes are less likely to get a divorce than those with more equal ones, cohabiting ones with unequal incomes are likely to split apart. If our money is kept in separate accounts, then your having more (or less) money than I makes a difference. If it is kept in merged accounts, then nobody observes differences in income.

Cohabitation ordinarily does not last very long; most such unions in America   5
break up (sometimes with a split, sometimes with a marriage) within two years. Scholars increasingly regard cohabitation as a substitute to being single, not an alternative to marriage. And a good thing, since people seem to bring different

expectations to the former than to the latter. When high-school seniors were followed into their early thirties, women who highly valued having a career and men who greatly valued leisure were more likely to cohabit than were people with the opposite views. Women seemed to think that cohabitation helps their careers, men to think it helps them spend more time with "the boys." Neither view makes much sense, since cohabitation not only does not last very long, most people think cohabiting couples are doing something odd. Like it or not, the couple living together will discover in countless ways that society thinks they should either get married or split apart. And society's opinion makes sense. As Linda Waite and Maggie Gallagher put it,

> ...marriage makes you better off, because marriage makes you very important to someone. When you are married you know that someone else not only loves you, but needs you and depends on you. This makes marriage a contract like no other.

Until recently, cultures set rules for marriage that were not only designed to 6 protect the child but to achieve a variety of other goals as well. A family was a political, economic, and educational unit as well as a child-rearing one. It participated in deciding who would rule the community and (except in wandering hunter-gatherer groups) control or have privileged access to land that supplied food and cattle. Until the modern advent of schools, families educated their children, not with books, but by demonstrating how to care for other children, perform certain crafts, and mind cattle and agricultural fields. These demonstrations sometimes took the form of games and sometimes depended simply on show-and-tell, but a child's life in either event was governed by the need to demonstrate, year by year, that it had learned how to watch, carry, feed, hunt, fish, and build. These tutorial, educational, and economic families were linked together in kinship groupings that constituted the whole of the small society—often no more than two hundred people, and sometimes even fewer—that lived together in a settlement.

These social functions did not prevent married men and women from caring 7 for each other, even in arranged marriages. Affection existed, though of course it was sometimes interrupted by quarrels and beatings. This affection and the companionship it entailed were valuable supports to family life, but they were not until recently the chief, much less the sole, grounds for maintaining the union.

Today, the family has lost many of these functions. Politically, the family has 8 been replaced by the voting booth and the interest group, economically by the office and the factory, and educationally by the school and the Internet. Modernity did not simply produce these changes: Capitalism did not change the family (the family first changed in ways that made capitalism possible), and schools did not make families less relevant (families changed in ways that made schools more valuable).

It is important to observe that the family now rests almost entirely on affection 9 and child care. These are powerful forces, but the history of the family suggests that almost every culture has found them to be inadequate to producing child support. If we ask why the family is, for many people, a weaker institution today than it once was, it is pointless to look for the answer in recent events. Our desire for sexual unions and romantic attachments is as old as humankind, and they will continue forever.

But our ability to fashion a marriage that will make the union last even longer than the romance that inspired it depends on cultural, religious, and legal doctrines that have slowly changed. Today people may be facing a challenge for which they are utterly unprepared: a vast, urban world of personal freedom, bureaucratized services, cheap sex, and easy divorce.

Marriage is a socially arranged solution for the problem of getting people   10 to stay together and care for children that the mere desire for children, and the sex that makes children possible, does not solve. The problem of marriage today is that we imagine that its benefits have been offset by social arrangements, such as welfare payments, community tolerance, and professional help for children, that make marriage unnecessary. But as we have already seen, the advantages of marriage—personal health, longer lives, and better children—remain great. The advantages of cohabitation are mostly illusory, but it is an illusion that is growing in its appeal.

READING FOR CONTENT

1. What does Wilson say about the longevity of cohabitation?
2. Do women and men cohabit for the same reasons?
3. According to Wilson, the family has lost many of its traditional functions. What has been lost?
4. Summarize Wilson's explanation of the problem of marriage today.

READING FOR GENRE, ORGANIZATION, AND STYLISTIC FEATURES

1. What effect does Wilson achieve with the sequence of "If … then" constructions in the first paragraph?
2. How would you describe the overall organizational structure of the selection? What other organizational patterns do you notice in the various paragraphs?

READING FOR RHETORICAL CONTEXT

1. Explain Wilson's rhetorical purpose. What is the main point he is trying to get across?
2. Notice that Wilson draws heavily on one particular source. How strong would his argument be if he did not use that source to bolster his case?

WRITING ASSIGNMENTS

1. Write an essay in which you compare and contrast a marriage contract and a cohabitation arrangement.
2. Write an essay in response to Wilson's definition of marriage as "a socially arranged solution for the problem of getting people to stay together and care for children" (paragraph 10). If you wish, you may draw upon other sources in this chapter.

The Origins of the Ambivalent Acceptance of Divorce

Andrew J. Cherlin

Andrew J. Cherlin is professor of sociology at Johns Hopkins University and the author of several books on the changing profiles of American family life, including Public and Private Families: An Introduction *(2008) and* The Marriage-Go-Round: The State of Marriage and the Family in America Today *(2009).*

PREREADING

Cherlin's historical analysis begins as a response to a sociological study by Margaret Usdansky on depictions of single-parent families in popular magazines during the 1990s. Visit the Debatepedia Web site at <http://debatepedia.idebate.org/> and search with the term "single parents." Examine the various arguments pro and con about single parenthood and ask yourself how many of these arguments might have been standard in the early 1900s and how many are still standard in the early 2000s. Freewrite for ten minutes about whether an historical awareness of conditions a century ago can enlighten us about conditions that we accept or reject now.

In her informative analysis of the content of magazine and journal articles, Usdansky (2009) finds that depictions of single-parent families resulting from divorce became less critical during the 20th century, but depictions of single-parent families resulting from a nonmarital birth remained just as critical as in the early 1900s. By the end of the century, she writes, Americans showed an "ambivalent acceptance" of divorce-based single parents while still finding fault with nonmarital births. What explains the different responses to divorce and nonmarital childbearing? Usdansky suggests that the relatively greater acceptance of divorce-based single parenthood may have resulted from its higher prevalence compared to nonmarital-birth-based single parenthood. Because divorce was the more common route to single parenthood, she hypothesizes, writers and social scientists—an increasing share of whom were themselves divorced—may have been reluctant to criticize divorced single parents, whereas they may have been less reluctant to criticize mothers who had children outside of marriage.

Although the commonness-of-divorce explanation is plausible, it is at best incomplete. It is true that rates of divorce increased throughout most of the 20th century and that the rise occurred in all social classes (although divorce remained more common among the less educated; Cherlin, 1992). But the percentage of children born outside of marriage also increased greatly, rising from 4% in the 1950s to 33% in 2000 (U.S. National Center for Health Statistics, 2005). Both divorce and nonmarital childbearing

Cherlin, Andrew J. "The Origins of the Ambivalent Acceptance of Divorce." *Journal of Marriage and Family* 71.2 (2009): 226–229. *SocINDEX.* Web. 15 July 2010. © National Council on Family Relations, 2009. Reprinted by permission of John Wiley & Sons, Inc.

became much more common, in other words, yet the increases in divorce were accepted less critically by Americans. Why is that? I would argue that the less critical view of divorce was able to draw upon a long tradition in American culture of ambivalence toward divorce, whereas there is no such tradition concerning nonmarital childbearing. The differing depictions of divorce and nonmarital childbearing have roots in American values and law that extend back to the colonial era—back to a time when divorce rates, although worrisome to observers at the time, were tiny compared to today. From that era forward to the mid-20th century, Americans have shown a moral and legal ambivalence toward divorce. In contrast, Americans at all times prior to the mid-20th century showed a moral and legal rejection of nonmarital births. Examining the historical picture may help us place Usdansky's late-20th-century findings in context.

Divorce in the American Past

The New England colonists brought to the New World a Protestantism formed in dissension from both the Catholic Church and the Church of England. Part of that dissension concerned divorce. The Catholic Church did not allow divorce, although if a marriage had been formed in a way that violated church rules, it could be annulled, that is, treated as if it never happened. For instance, if either partner had been forced to consent to the marriage, it was invalid under Church rules and subject to annulment. There was, consequently, no tradition of divorce in Catholic Europe. Except for a brief period during the French revolution, for example, France did not legalize divorce until 1884 (Phillips, 1988). The Church of England also did not allow divorce. When Pope Clement denied Henry VIII the annulment he desired in order to marry Ann Boleyn, Henry withdrew his kingdom from the Catholic Church and established the Church of England, also known as the Anglican Church (and later, in the United States, as the Episcopalian Church). Yet Henry VIII never divorced anyone. He either annulled his marriages or simply beheaded his wives. Divorce remained illegal in England, except by Act of Parliament, until 1857 (Phillips). [3]

The New England colonists, however, followed the theology of John Calvin, who, in turn, based much of his thought on the writings of Martin Luther. As part of his break from Catholicism, Luther proposed that divorce, while always deplorable, ought to be allowed in two circumstances: adultery or desertion. In these cases, he argued, the innocent partner should be allowed to divorce and remarry. He wrote of divorce, "Frequently something must be tolerated even though it is not a good thing to do, to prevent something even worse from happening" (Witte, 1997, p. 67), a sentiment that sounds similar to the tone Usdansky (2009) finds in some contemporary American articles about divorce. Calvin derived his position on divorce largely from Luther. He, too, believed that divorce was justifiable in cases of adultery and desertion. In fact, Calvin served as the counsel to his brother Antoine, who requested a divorce from the Genevan authorities on grounds of adultery. Although Antoine's wife denied the charges—even after being imprisoned and tortured—the brothers persevered and the divorce was granted (Kingdon, 1995). [4]

The New England colonies allowed divorce along Calvinist lines, and a small but steady stream of divorces ensued. In Connecticut, prominent clergy and [5] academics expressed their dismay at levels of divorce that contemporary observers would regard as extremely modest. In the 1800s, some states liberalized their divorce laws, establishing Indiana and later the Dakotas and Arkansas as the first "divorce mills"—states to which Americans in search of divorces migrated. Some states expanded the grounds for divorce to include wife-beating and mental cruelty. A few even enacted so-called omnibus clauses that allowed divorce for any misconduct that permanently destroyed the happiness of the petitioner (Phillips, 1988). To be sure, divorce was still frowned upon. Public unease eventually led Connecticut and Indiana to withdraw their omnibus clauses. New York retained adultery and desertion as the only permissible grounds for divorce. Public concern grew as the divorce rate rose from about 1 in 20 marriages just after the Civil War to about 1 in 10 in the 1890s (Cherlin, 1992). President Theodore Roosevelt wrote to Congress in 1895, after commissioning a study of divorce, "There is widespread conviction that the divorce laws are dangerously lax and indifferently administered in some of the states, resulting in a diminished regard for the sanctity of the marriage relation" (O'Neill, 1967, pp. 245–246). Yet despite Roosevelt's call for tightening the divorce laws, few states took action.

Thus, the ambivalence that Usdansky (2009) found in 20th-century articles about divorced single parents was present all along in American history. Divorce was always seen as unfortunate but in some circumstances necessary and even, as time passed, acceptable. Although presidents and blue-ribbon panels complained about growing rates of divorce, little was done about it. This tolerance of divorce set the stage for its ambivalent embrace during the last half of the 20th century, as shown by Usdansky. What was new in the last half of the 20th century, I would suggest, was the spread of the idea that divorce is an individual right. Until the end of the 19th century, according to legal historian Hendrik Hartog (2000, p. 84), "Divorce was not a right, only a remedy for a wrong." That changed dramatically after California passed the first so-called no-fault divorce law in 1969 and nearly all the other states quickly followed with similar legislation. Since then, an individual may obtain a divorce for any reason merely by citing irreconcilable differences, whether or not a spouse agrees. The individual's wishes also became more important in other aspects of family law, such as the emerging right to marry, the right to be free from family violence, and the right to reject the unwanted sexual advances of a spouse, leading one observer to name the recognition and protection of individual rights as "the most important event that has occurred in family law that has affected family relationships in the last fifty years" (Katz, 2000, p. 621). 6

The movement toward unilateral divorce, then, reflected the spread of a more individualistic view of family life. I have argued elsewhere (Cherlin, 2004) that the companionate marriage of the mid-20th century morphed into the individualized marriage of the late 20th century, in which self-development and personal growth were paramount. A divorce might still be seen as unfortunate, but Americans were less likely to criticize someone for wanting one—not just because divorce was common but because wanting a divorce was consistent with the individualistic way that more and more Americans viewed family life. By the end of the 20th century, a person who was deeply unhappy in his or her marriage was almost expected to seek a divorce. 7

Nonmarital Childbearing in the American Past

No such ambivalence, however, characterized attitudes in the past toward childbear-   8
ing outside of marriage. The American colonies followed English common law,
which held that an "illegitimate" child had almost no legal rights. The underlying
principle was that childbearing should always occur within the framework of marriage. Children were a source of valuable labor for families—they could help tend
the farm or assist a craftsman from a young age. And that labor was under the control
of the husband, who had almost complete legal authority over his wife and offspring.
The norm that the husband controlled his children's labor was so strong that if a married woman gave birth to a child, her husband became the legal father even if it could
be shown that he was not the biological father—a rule that still applies in many states.
It may seem odd by contemporary standards to consider children mainly as sources of
labor, but that was the dominant legal interpretation until the 20th century. In 1896,
for instance, the parents of a 2-year-old child who was killed by a train sued for damages not because of the love they lost but because of the valuable services the child
supposedly performed in the household: "going upon errands to neighbors ... watching and amusing ... younger child" (Zelizer, 1985).

Case law concerning the position of children born outside of marriage was largely   9
unchanged through the mid-20th century (Hartog, 2000). An illegitimate child, for example, still could not recover damages in the case of the wrongful death of his or her
father. The father of an illegitimate child was still a legal stranger to the child and bore
no responsibility to provide support. In 1972, however, the U.S. Supreme Court considered the case of an Illinois man who had fathered children with a woman he had never
married. After the mother died, a state agency seized the children under its established
rule that children of deceased unwed mothers became wards of the state. The agency
denied the father's attempts to gain access to the children because he had not married
the mother, and state courts sided with the agency. The Supreme Court, however, over-
ruled the lower courts. Justice Byron R. White, writing for the majority, stated: "The
private interest here, that of a man in the children he has sired and raised, undeniably
warrants deference and, absent a powerful countervailing interest, protection" (Stanley
v. Illinois, 1972). Yet, until this point, courts had not considered the "private interest"
of the father to be stronger than the countervailing interest in protecting the position of
marriage as the sole legal basis for children's rights. A series of important decisions since
then has affirmed not only the rights of biological fathers but also their responsibility to
provide support to their children. By the end of the 20th century, the fact of fatherhood,
whether or not the father was married to the mother, mattered greatly in assigning legal
rights and responsibilities for parents and children (Douglas, 2000).

It is only in the last several decades, then, that the laws governing childbearing   10
outside of marriage have moved away from a firm rejection of legal rights and responsibilities. Moreover, only within the past half century has childbearing outside of
marriage become common, as I noted earlier. So-called shotgun marriages were still
a part of the culture at mid-century, and unmarried pregnant teenagers might be sent
to a home for unwed mothers to deliver their babies. Unlike divorce, then, there is no
long-term social and legal tradition of ambivalence toward, let alone acceptance of,
single parents who have borne children without marrying.

Contemporary Views

The different responses to divorce and nonmarital childbearing can be seen today 11
not just in magazine and journal articles but also in the moral language that has suddenly reappeared in political discussions of family life. The moralistic view of "the
marriage relation" expressed by Roosevelt was common among public officials in the
19th century. In 1888, for example, Supreme Court Justice Stephen Field wrote that
"marriage, as creating the most important relation in life, as having more to do with
the morals and civilization of a people than any other institution, has always been subject to the control of the legislature" (Hartog, 2000, p. 261). During most of the 20th
century, this moralistic language was replaced by the more value-neutral language of
social science (Cott, 2000). But at century's end, it was revived by social conservatives
and their adherents in the Congress and the presidency. For instance, the preamble
to the landmark welfare reform bill of 1996 (Personal Responsibility Act, 1996) said
that "[m]arriage is the foundation of a successful society" and that "[t]he increase in
the number of children receiving public assistance is closely related to the increase in
births to unmarried women." It went on to document that increase in detail and to articulate strategies to reduce it. The preamble had much less to say about divorce, even
though it acknowledged that many children were receiving public assistance because
they lived with single parents who had divorced.

Yet, if family researchers were to replicate Usdansky's study a generation from 12
now, I doubt that they would still find a lesser acceptance of nonmarital childbearing than of divorce. Criticism of divorced single parents will probably remain
low, although a steady counter-current of concern about the effects of divorce on
children may remain. But I think it unlikely that the historically strong criticism
of nonmarital childbearing will remain high. Family law has finally changed—a
development that both influences and reflects the family values of our time. The
principle of individual rights is ascendant. Moreover, there are signs that among
at least some segments of the population, the stigma of having a child outside
of marriage is fading. In low-income neighborhoods, most mothers express the
opinion that having a child without marrying, although not ideal, is quite acceptable (Cherlin, Cross-Barnet, Burton, & Garrett-Peters, 2008; Edin & Kefalas, 2005).
Among the middle class, some stigma seems to remain. In a decade or two, we may
see the ambivalent embrace of divorced single parents extend to those who have had
their children outside of marriage.

References

Cherlin, A. J. (1992). *Marriage, divorce, remarriage*. Cambridge, MA: Harvard University Press.

Cherlin, A. (2004). The deinstitutionalization of American marriage. *Journal of Marriage and Family*, 66, 848–861.

Cherlin, A., Cross-Barnet, C., Burton, L. M., & Garrett-Peters, R. (2008). Promises they can keep: Low-income women's attitudes toward motherhood, marriage, and divorce. *Journal of Marriage and Family*, 70, 919–933.

Cott, N. F. (2000). *Public vows: A history of marriage and the nation*. Cambridge, MA: Harvard University Press.

Douglas, G. (2000). Marriage, cohabitation, and parenthood—From contract to status? In S. N. Katz, J. Eekelaar, & M. Maclean (Eds.), *Cross currents: Family law and policy in the US and England* (pp. 211–233). Oxford, UK: Oxford University Press.

Edin, K., & Kefalas, M. J. (2005). *Promises I can keep: Why poor women put motherhood before marriage*. Berkeley: University of California Press.

Hartog, H. (2000). *Man and wife in America: A history*. Cambridge, MA: Harvard University Press.

Katz, S. N. (2000). Individual rights and family relationships. In S. N. Katz, J. Eekelaar, & M. Maclean (Eds.), *Cross currents: Family law and policy in the US and England* (pp. 621–635). Oxford, UK: Oxford University Press.

Kingdon, R. M. (1995). *Adultery and divorce in Calvin's Geneva*. Cambridge, MA: Harvard University Press.

O'Neill, W. L. (1967). *Divorce in the Progressive Era*. New York: New Viewpoints.

Personal Responsibility and Work Opportunity Reconciliation Act of 1996. Pub.L. 104–193, 110 Stat. 2105.

Phillips, R. (1988). *Putting asunder: A history of divorce in Western society*. Cambridge, UK: Cambridge University Press.

Stanley v. Illinois, 405 645 (U.S. 1972).

Usdansky, M. L. (2009). A weak embrace: Popular and scholarly depictions of single-parent families, 1900–1998. *Journal of Marriage and Family, 71*, 209–225.

U.S. National Center for Health Statistics. (2005). Vital statistics of the United States. Vol. 1, Natality. Number and percent of births to unmarried women, by race and Hispanic origin: United States, 1940–2000. Retrieved October 13, 2008, from www.cdc.gov/nchs/data/statab/t001x17.pdf

Witte, J. J. (1997). *From sacrament to contract: Marriage, religion, and law in the Western tradition*. Louisville, KY: Westminster John Knox Press.

Zelizer, V. (1985). *Pricing the priceless child: The changing social value of children*. New York: Basic Books.

READING FOR CONTENT

1. In surveying the history of American attitudes toward divorce, what attitude does the author find to be genuinely new at the end of the twentieth century, and what impact does it have on changing ideas about family life?

2. What legal attitude toward children, whether born in wedlock or not, does the author find to be prevalent before the late twentieth century? How has this attitude changed in recent decades?

READING FOR GENRE, ORGANIZATION, AND STYLISTIC FEATURES

1. What sorts of historical evidence does the author use to construct his history of attitudes toward marriage, children, and single parenting?

2. Which historical finding do you find to be the strongest in this essay? How does the author use this finding to reinforce his historical claim about changing attitudes toward marriage, children, and single parenting?

3. What conclusion does the author reach when he draws together all his historical information in the final paragraph?

READING FOR RHETORICAL CONTEXT

1. What persuasive effects does the author's analysis of the language of court decisions have in paragraph 9?

2. How does the final paragraph revise the apparent conclusion about the resurgence of moralistic attitudes in paragraph 11?

WRITING ASSIGNMENTS

1. Visit Google at <http://www.google.com> and click on "images" in the menu at the top of the page. Search with the terms "single parent," "single-parent families," "single parenthood," and the like. Select several images related to one another by a topic such as "single parents past and present," "single divorced parents," "single widowed parents," "single teenage parents," "single gay parents," or some other topic of your choice. Based upon these images and some further research, write a research paper on current varieties of single parenthood in the United States.

2. As outlined in the preceding assignment, visit Google Images and search for related images of single parenthood with your own or one of the suggested topics in mind. Based upon these images and some further research, write a research paper on the current state of single parenthood in the United States.

■ ■ ■ ■ ■ ■ ■ ■ ■ ■ ■

Absent Fathers: Why Don't We Ever Talk About the Unmarried Men?

Rebecca M. Blank

Rebecca M. Blank is professor of economics at Northwestern University, where she has directed the Joint Center for Poverty Research. During the Clinton administration, she served on the Council of Economic Advisors. Her publications include Why Were Poverty Rates So High in the 1980s? *(1991),* It Takes a Nation: A New Agenda for Fighting Poverty *(1997),* The Clinton Legacy for America's Poor *(2001), and* The New World of Welfare *(2001).*

PREREADING

Turn to the table on page 442. What might the statistics imply about Rebecca Blank's topic and argument? Her title focuses on "Absent Fathers" and "Unmarried Men," but the graph focuses on "Child Support Awards among Women with Children Whose Father Is Not Present in the Household." Despite its focus on mothers, what might the graph tell us about absent fathers and unmarried men? Freewrite your response.

Blank, Rebecca M. *It Takes a Nation: A New Agenda for Fighting Poverty*, pp. 42–47. © 1997 Russell Sage Foundation, published by Princeton University Press. Reprinted by permission of Princeton University Press.

Summary. *The lives of poor single men are much less well understood, since these men typically have less contact with the public and private organizations that serve the poor. By most accounts, poor unmarried men exhibit far more behavioral problems than single mothers, despite the fact that much of the policy discussion focuses on the mothers. A high share of younger men are under the supervision of the judicial system in this country. Child support payments from absent fathers to their children are extremely low, and this lack of parental support is a major factor contributing to the poverty of single mothers and their children. These problems are correlated with the larger economic trends that have affected these men's lives: Less-skilled men have faced declines in wages, the changing location of jobs in cities, and high and persistent unemployment rates.*

For every single mother, there is a father who is not living with his children. For every unwed mother, there is a father who did not marry her. The public discussion about growing numbers of divorced and never-married mothers too rarely mentions the missing men in these families. Here we will focus on the absent fathers and their behavior. 1

We know surprisingly little about the lives of the low-income single men who father the children in low-income single-mother families. This is true for at least two reasons. First, because these men are much less publicly visible than the mothers of their children, they are often ignored in the policy discussion. Because we provide little public assistance to single men, they have less contact with the public and private organizations that serve low-income families. Disproportionately, it is the mothers who show up at schools, who bring their children in for health care, or who apply for public assistance. Thus, these men appear to cost society nothing; it is mothers and children whom we support. Of course, as any economist will tell you, this is a false notion. To the extent that *both* the men and the women choose to divorce or not marry, the resulting social costs are due to the men's behavior as much as the women's. 2

Second, because none of the data the government collects links absent fathers with their children, they are often ignored in the research literature. The data collected on family and child poverty are based on information about all family members who *live together*, thus we know little about the absent fathers. As noted below, a substantial number of fathers in out-of-wedlock births are not identified on birth certificates. Some of these fathers may not even know they have children. Among those who are known, the fathers typically do not live in the household. It is not possible to study absent fathers without collecting new data that will help identify and contact men who are not living with their children. This is an expensive undertaking. 3

As a result, we know very little about how absent fathers behave, or even about who they are. At best, we can talk about less-skilled and low-income unmarried men, assuming that many of them are part of the absent-fathers population. In general, this group exhibits more behavioral problems than single mothers. 4

These men are at greater risk of homelessness, and they are more likely to be involved in crime or illegal drug-related activities. By the mid-1990s, the number of men under the supervision of the judicial system (either in jail or on probation or parole) relative to the male workforce was 7 percent, that is, there was one man under court 5 supervision for every twelve men working; this is higher than the unemployment rate for this group. Among young men between the ages of 18 and 34, 11 percent are under the supervision of the judicial system; among black men between these ages, the share under judicial supervision is an amazing 37 percent.[1] Why are these numbers so high? There is evidence of increasing criminal involvement among younger men, and this interacts with stronger sentencing laws and a growing willingness to incarcerate those involved with drug dealing.

6   All of this has led to soaring prison populations and large increases in the number of men on probation or parole. These numbers are disturbing not just because of what they signal about current behavioral problems, but also because of the long-term problems they create for these men in finding employment as ex-offenders.[2]

7   Without excusing these behavioral problems, it is important to recognize that the world has changed for the worse for many less-skilled, low-income men. Less-skilled men have faced major declines in their earning ability, and high rates of unemployment. These economic changes are strongly correlated with both declines in work effort in the mainstream labor market and increases in criminal activity.

8   Among African American and Latino men, these problems are greatest and overlap with ongoing problems of discrimination and job access. A number of authors have described the many ways in which young black men are treated hostilely by white society, learn distrust and anger, and develop a responding culture of hostility and violence.[3] The result is a downward cycle, in which problematic behavior and economic and social constraints interact with and reinforce each other.

9   It is also worth emphasizing that these problems are concentrated among a minority of the poor men. Most poor men are employed at least part-time or part-year or are actively searching for work. Most are not in jail or on probation. Many are married to the mothers of their children. We should not let the real problems of some low-income men shape our image of all low-income men.

Child Support and Absent Fathers

10   Many less-skilled single mothers find it difficult to escape poverty through their own earnings. One obvious way for these families to obtain more income is through support from absent fathers. Whether divorced or never married, fathers should bear their fair share of the financial responsibility for raising their children.

11   The growth in never-married mothers has exacerbated the problems of nonsupport from fathers, although many divorced women also receive little support. Of all children born to unmarried women, less than one-third have paternity established at time of birth.[4] That means that if support from the father is sought at a later stage, he first must be found and identified, not always an easy process.

12   The level of child support collected among single women in this country is extremely low. Table 12–1 presents the data, showing child support receipt among poor and nonpoor women in 1989.[5] Only 43 percent of poor mothers with children whose father lives outside the household have ever received a child support award by the courts, ordering the father to pay ongoing support. Among never-married women, less than one quarter have such an award. Among women who are divorced or married to a man who is not the father of their children, about 70 percent have an award. While

TABLE 12–1   Child Support Awards Among Women with Children Whose Father Is Not Present in the Household, 1989

	Current Marital Status			
	All	Divorced	Never Married	Married*
Poor Mothers				
Percent with child support award	43.3	70.4	24.5	72.2
Percent with child support award and receiving payments	25.4	42.4	14.4	40.4
Average payments among recipients	$1,889	$2,112	$1,553	$2,275
Nonpoor Mothers				
Percent with child support award	64.5	79.1	23.2	79.5
Percent with child support award and receiving payments	43.1	57.5	14.5	48.6
Average payments among recipients	$3,304	$3,649	$2,276	$2,972

*The "Married" column shows women who are currently married to a man who is not the father of their children.
Source: U.S. Bureau of the Census (1991).

nonpoor women do slightly better, Table 12–1 indicates that substantial numbers of nonpoor women are also without child support assistance.

Simply having an award does not guarantee that the father will make regular 13 payments, however. Only 25 percent of poor women actually receive child support payments, and only 14 percent of never-married poor women receive payments. Many women who receive payments do not receive the full amount of their support order, but get only partial amounts. This is reflected in the fact that the amounts of money received are quite low. Among those poor single parents who do receive child support payments, the average payment received for all children is under $2,000 per year.

Teenage men who father children are particularly unlikely to live with the 14 mother of their children, unlikely to pay child support, and have low earnings and employment levels. Thus, the problems of teen fatherhood are closely related to the problems of teen motherhood. Many teen fathers, however, receive higher earnings as they move into their twenties. While they may be able to pay little child support initially, if teen fathers are followed by the child support system, they may be able to contribute more as their children grow older.[6]

The rise in single parenting has not simply led to an increase in the number of 15 children who physically live with and are primarily raised by their mothers. It has also meant massive financial desertion of these children by their fathers. This is a major reason why the women who raise children on their own are so likely to be poor.

One caveat on this statement needs to be noted: at least some financial support 16 from absent fathers to their children goes unreported. For men whose children receive public assistance, the incentives to provide much in the way of financial support are minimal. The first fifty dollars that a man pays in child support each month increases the income of the mother and her children. After that, any additional money goes to offset the cost of public assistance. The result is that child support payments above fifty dollars per month result in absolutely no additional income to the mother and children. This provides a strong incentive for under-the-table payments by men to their girlfriends and children. In-depth interviews with women on welfare in a few selected cities indicate that about one-quarter of welfare recipients in poor urban neighborhoods receive unreported contributions from absent fathers. The average amount of unreported income from children's fathers was relatively small, however, averaging thirty dollars per month.[7]

Of course, many less-skilled women with limited earning ability have children 17 with men of similar economic backgrounds. Thus, the absent fathers of many poor children are themselves poor, suggesting that these men would not be able to pay substantial amounts of child support. Researchers have tried to simulate the effect on poverty among single-parent families of substantially increased enforcement of child support orders, assuming that the absent fathers have the same educational background as the mothers. The results indicate that this would help lessen the depth of poverty among single-mother families but, by itself, would move only some families out of poverty entirely. The amounts that the noncustodial fathers could afford to pay are limited, because many of these fathers are not employed or because they have very low earnings. But these studies also conclude that better child support enforcement would make many single-mother families less poor, raising their income closer to the poverty line. For mothers living on $6,000 per year with their children, an additional $1,000 per year in child support payments provides a substantial increase in income.[8]

Finally, it is worth underscoring the fact that nonpayment of child support 18 awards and nonidentification of fathers among unwed mothers are not problems solely among poor women. A substantial number of single mothers who are well above the poverty line receive little ongoing support from the fathers of their children. Most of the billions of dollars in unpaid child support is owed to nonpoor single women from men who have steady jobs with good incomes. Demanding that fathers accept financial responsibility for their children is not just an antipoverty agenda, but a move that will benefit working women and their children at all income levels.

Lack of financial involvement does not necessarily mean lack of parental involve- 19 ment. While few men provide much financial support, particularly to low-income mothers, many of them remain in contact with their children. Sociologists Sara McLanahan and Gary Sandefur indicate that two-thirds of all children who live apart from their fathers have contact with them.[9] Surprisingly, this number is only slightly lower among children of unmarried versus divorced women. About one-third of the children who do not live with their father report seeing him once per week.

This information suggests that a substantial number of "absent fathers" are not 20 entirely absent. They are present in their children's lives, even if they do little of the primary parenting and provide only minimal or irregular child support payments. Clearly, many fathers do feel ongoing responsibility and love for their children.

It is worth putting all of this into the context of larger economic changes. The 21 decline in marriage and the decreased support for children by their fathers are both intimately linked to the economic changes of the last two decades. Less-skilled men — exactly the group most likely to father the children in poor single-mother families — are the group most affected by the changing economy. They have experienced big declines in wages, high and persistent unemployment rates, and (particularly among

African American men) a loss of jobs from the changing location of employment in urban areas. Judging their changing parental behavior without these economic trends in mind is to miss an important component of the picture. Demanding that men be more responsible with regard to their children—particularly asking them to provide more financial support—is a harder demand to make when these men are more and more pressed by limited economic opportunities. Though their behavior may not be excusable, ordering them to get a job and/or pay more in child support may not be as easily accomplished as in years past.

Finally, it is important to keep in mind that there is a great deal of variability in the behavior of fathers of poor children. In almost 40 percent of all poor families with children *both* parents are present. Many fathers do *not* desert their children. And of those children whose parents are divorced or never married, there are a substantial minority of fathers who stay in their children's lives, spend time with them, and contribute regularly to their financial well-being. While worrying about the missing fathers, we should not forget to appreciate those who are present. 22

Notes

1. These numbers are from Freeman (1995). Similar data are in Mauer and Huling (1995).
2. For a review of the problem relating criminal involvement to labor market earnings and participation, see Freeman (1992, 1995). Wilson and Petersilia (1995) provide a range of evidence on recent changes in criminal behavior, its causes and implications.
3. For instance, see Mincy (1994).
4. U.S. House of Representatives (1994), page 470.
5. Data in Table 12–1 and the textual discussion from U.S. Bureau of the Census (1991).
6. See Pirog-Good and Good (1995).
7. Edin and Lein (forthcoming).
8. For a discussion of the estimated impact of child support enforcement on poverty status, see Robins (1986) or U.S. House of Representatives (1994), pp. 500–502. More extensive child support assurance systems would do more to reduce poverty, as Meyer et al. (1992) indicate.
9. McLanahan and Sandefur (1994), fig. 12.

Works Cited

Edin, Kathryn, and Laura Lein. 1997. *Making Ends Meet: How Single Mothers Survive Welfare and Low-Wage Work*. New York: Russell Sage Foundation.

Freeman, Richard B. 1992. "Crime and the Employment of Disadvantaged Youths." In *Urban Labor Markets and Job Opportunity*, George E. Peterson and Wayne Vroman, editors. Washington, D.C.: The Urban Institute Press.

Freeman, Richard B. 1995. "The Labor Market." In *Crime*, James Q. Wilson and Joan Petersilia, editors. San Francisco: ICS Press.

Mauer, Marc, and Tracy Huling. 1995. *Young Black Americans and the Criminal Justice System: Five Years Later*. Washington, D.C.: The Sentencing Project.

McLanahan, Sara, and Gary Sandeful. 1994. *Growing Up with a Single Parent: What Hurts, What Helps*. Cambridge, Mass.: Harvard University Press.

Meyer, Daniel R., et al. 1992. "Who Should Be Eligible for an Assured Child Support Benefit?" In *Child Support Assurance*, Irwin Garfinkel, et al., editors. Washington D.C.: The Urban Institute Press.

Mincy, Ronald B. 1994. *Nuturing Young Black Males*. Washington, D.C.: The Urban Institute Press.

Pirog-Good, Maureen A., and David H. Good. 1995. "Child Support Enforcement for Teenage Fathers: Problems and Prospects." *Journal of Policy Analysis and Management* 14 (1, Winter): 25–42.

Robins, Philip K. 1986. "Child Support, Welfare Dependency, and Poverty." *American Economic Review* 76 (4, September): 768–88.

U.S. Bureau of the Census. 1991. *Child Support and Alimony, 1989*. Current Population Reports, Series P60–173. Washington, D.C.: U.S. Government Printing Office.

U.S. House of Representatives. 1994. *1994 Green Book: Overview of Entitlement Programs*. Washington, D.C.: U.S. Government Printing Office.

Wilson, James Q., and Joan Petersilia, editors. 1995. *Crime*. San Francisco: ICS Press.

READING FOR CONTENT

1. In paragraph 7, how does the comment on declining economic opportunities among low-income men contribute to the author's argument?

2. In paragraphs 19–20, how do the comments that differentiate financial uninvolvement from parental uninvolvement contribute to the author's argument?

READING FOR GENRE, ORGANIZATION, AND STYLISTIC FEATURES

1. In paragraph 21, how does the focus on the context of larger economic changes reinforce the author's claim that she is writing an economic essay about absent fathers rather than a sociocultural or moral essay?

2. In paragraphs 5, 12, 13, 16, and 17, underline the statistics that Blank uses to organize her argument about economic motivations for absent fatherhood.

3. In paragraphs 7, 9, 16, 18, 21, and 22, how do such stylistic markers as "it is important to recognize" and "one caveat needs to be noted" accentuate Blank's argument?

READING FOR RHETORICAL CONTEXT

1. What social conditions do paragraphs 2 and 3 evoke as a rhetorical context for Blank's argument?

2. What cultural conditions does paragraph 22 evoke as a rhetorical context for Blank's argument?

WRITING ASSIGNMENTS

1. Use the "Prompts for Personal Response to the Text" on page 36 to write an informal response to Rebecca M. Blank's "Absent Fathers." Then convert your informal response to a formal response essay. Use the tips we provide on page 39.

2. Draft a critical analysis of Rebecca M. Blank's "Absent Fathers." Use the Questions for Helping a Writer Revise a Critical Analysis Essay in Chapter 3 to revise your essay.

The Ballad of a Single Mother

Lynn Olcott

Lynn Olcott is a teacher at the Auburn Correctional Facility in upstate New York, and an author who has written about her experiences as an educator conducting GED programs for jailed adolescent women. Her article "I Want to Go Back to Jail" appeared in Phi Delta Kappan, *December 2004.*

PREREADING

The following personal essay written by a single mother reflects upon her three decades of balancing the responsibilities of family and career. Do you think it is easier to balance these responsibilities nowadays than it was thirty years ago? Freewrite your responses for ten minutes.

This year my youngest child turns 18. I can almost see the finish line. I no longer rush anyone to the doctor with ear infections, or stay home with kids who are sick. Of course, there is still the need to support the family, to keep us insured, to keep up with the college bills. But compared with the old days, it's a piece of cake.

I am lucky. I love being a mother and I love the work I do. My oldest son was born in 1977. Every morning, returning to work after a short maternity leave, I would put my little baby, screaming, into the arms of my neighbor, Rosalyn. She would call me later and tell me he was fine. Then I could work.

When my youngest child was a baby, I took him to another neighbor, Janice, whose voice overflowed with softness. She knew I missed being home with my baby, and one day she called me at work to tell me he was standing up in his crib for the first time. I sat at my desk and wept. Over the years I used every child-care arrangement known to woman. I missed a lot of milestones. Day-care workers toilet-trained my babies and wrote me notes about their days. During some of those years I was married, but I always worked to pay the bills.

By 1989 1 had been a single parent for a few years, trying to go back to school, trying to support my family, feeling overwhelmed and exhausted. A minister helped me put things in perspective. She told me cheerfully, "Nowadays, bread winner, bread maker, it's all the same thing." I began to see myself as a mother who supported her family. I began to be proud of myself.

Money was always a problem. Like most working women, I was underpaid and so were the women who cared for my children. When I was finally able to put my youngest child in a preschool, it took a quarter of my monthly take-home salary. But the program was good, and the workers there had health insurance. Most of them were working moms like me, carrying the family benefits package.

Once, during a job interview, the men interviewing me asked if there was any- 6
thing I wanted to add. From somewhere came the courage to be blunt. "I have school-
age children," I said. "When they are sick, I stay home with them." Nonetheless, I was
offered the job.

For several years I worked in a county agency with about 30 other people, most 7
of us working mothers. Summers were the hardest. We were at work and the kids were
running loose doing God knows what. Several times a day, a child or teen would call
and say, "Can I talk to my mom?" We learned the voices of each other's kids. We
dropped what we were doing to find the right moms for them. They called about
broken eggs and broken legs and brushes with the police. We were all relieved when
school started again in the fall.

Fortunately, my salary usually covered the basics, but extra things were hard 8
sometimes. One year, I lost my job. I quickly took another, but at a much lower salary.
My son was a talented soccer player, and I could no longer afford the fee for him to
play. Some of the men who managed the league were noble enough to take care of the
fee for me. They hatched their plan to keep my son on the team in such a way that my
pride allowed me to accept their generosity. And they didn't do it for the kudos; to this
day, I don't know who actually paid.

For almost three decades I have been a working mother, managing to support 9
my family in a society that routinely underpays women, undervalues child care and
ties family health-care access to employment level. There are millions like me. Yet we
are practically invisible.

I have been blessed with a 1-year-old granddaughter. I don't doubt that she 10
too will one day be a working mom, like her mother and her grandmother before
her. I wish for her success, and a career that thrills her heart. I wish her wage equity.
I wish her adequate family health benefits. It's essential that working mothers have
better tools and more support for coping with the responsibilities of supporting
a family. But I have to be realistic. I do not see mothers being relieved of bread-
winning to concentrate on child-rearing any time soon. So what can we do? Plan as
if for a marathon. Pace ourselves. Drink plenty of fluids and try to get enough rest.
Notice the flowers. And hand off a water bottle to another working mother as she
runs by.

READING FOR CONTENT

1. In paragraph 4, how does the minister help the author to put her harried life into perspective by saying, "Nowadays, bread winner, bread maker, it's all the same thing"?
2. How does paragraph 9 summarize the author's reflections upon her decades as a working
   mother?

READING FOR GENRE, ORGANIZATION, AND STYLISTIC FEATURES

1. The genre of personal reflection relies upon vivid accounts of private frustration and individual success. Which incidents in this essay strike you as most interesting? Freewrite for
   a few minutes on why you think they are so interesting.

READING FOR RHETORICAL CONTEXT

1. Describe the author's tone in her concluding paragraph. Is it hopeful? resigned? ambivalent? some combination of each?

WRITING ASSIGNMENTS

1. Using Pauline Irit Erera's analysis of the many different types of family in modern American society, write an analytical essay on how Olcott's account of working-mother parenthood before and after her divorce relates to Erera's typology of family structures.

2. Using Olcott's narrative in this article, write a critical response essay to Andrew J. Cherlin's article on changing attitudes toward single parenthood in the United States. Does Olcott's experience suggest that single parenthood has become easier in her working lifetime and that there is now a greater support system for the conditions she has described?

SYNTHESIS WRITING ASSIGNMENTS

1. In "What Is a Family?" Erera explains how new reproductive technologies have enabled people to create various forms of alternative, nontraditional families. Write an argument-synthesis essay in which you examine how some of these technologies affect current structures of marriage and the family. Draw upon selections in Chapters 9, 10, 11, and 12 to support your argument.

2. Use Erera's arguments about alternative family structures in "What Is a Family?" to write a defense of the parenting arrangements described in Barret and Robinson's "Children of Gay Fathers."

3. In response to the question of whether cohabitation is a testing ground for marriage or simply "playing house" as explored in Wilson's "Cohabitation Instead of Marriage," write a synthesis argument based upon your views. Support your position by drawing on other selections in this chapter.

4. Write a comparative analysis in which you compare and contrast Wilson's sociological argument and Cherlin's historical argument about greater tolerance for alternative family and parental structures in the contemporary United States. How do the views in these two articles relate to one another as though they were part of a conversation or give-and-take of interdependent ideas?

5. Write a critical response to Lynn Olcott's narrative of her experience as a working mother. Draw upon selections in this chapter to situate your response in relation to current thinking on the state of parenthood, single parenthood, divorce, and the future of the American family.

Social Class and Inequality

The selections in Chapter 13 examine ideas about social class from different perspectives and offer explanatory principles for the unequal distribution of income, power, and prestige. The authors discuss class conflict, examine factors that profoundly affect the existence and continuance of poverty, and offer solutions for dealing with these persistent problems. The evidence these authors supply has political, psychological, cultural, and moral ramifications as well as social consequences.

In the first selection, "Born Poor and Smart," Angela Locke interprets the unexamined assumptions that poor people aren't smart and that smart people aren't poor from her own experience of being both smart and poor. Her account initiates our conversation on poverty by challenging stereotypes that limit our full understanding of its reality, its causes, and its consequences. Next, the conservative writer Brink Lindsey turns attention away from poverty and economic resources as he explores the topic of his article "Culture of Success." Lindsey argues that neither wealth nor a lack of money accounts for unequal outcomes in college acceptance and completion rates or in subsequent job success and wage earning. Instead he claims that cultural factors associated with hard work, disciplined training, and long-term persistence provide better indicators of social mobility. From exactly the opposite perspective, the distinguished sociologist Herbert J. Gans demonstrates the inequalities that result from impoverished resources in his essay "The War Against the Poor Instead of Programs to End Poverty," and he offers a cultural and intellectual defense of poor people. Drawing upon a spectrum of theoretical tenets that are themselves derived from various sorts of statistical studies, Gans formulates an argument on behalf of job-centered economic growth that creates better public and private employment. Matt Yglesias extends this argument in "A Great Time to Be Alive?" by asking how we can better support job-centered economic growth. He answers that higher taxes for the very wealthy would not only help to reduce the gap in social equality but would also help to finance public services that would benefit everyone. He sees a focus on family policy and early childhood education as the keys to remedy inequality. This focus cannot resolve every problem, but it at least gets disadvantaged people off to a good start.

The fifth selection is "Serving in Florida," Barbara Ehrenreich's riveting account of her experiences as a low-wage worker trying to survive on six to seven dollars an hour as a server in restaurants in Key West, Florida. Recording personal observations and linking them in a narrative of her day-to-day hardships and frustrations, Ehrenreich provides abundant evidence of worker exploitation in some of America's largest and most well-known service industries. A magazine article from *The Economist* entitled "Middle of the Class" frames Ehrenreich's experiences in a larger context as it argues that equality of opportunity is increasingly diminishing in the United States. Gathering and interpreting a vast amount of statistic evidence, this article exemplifies the technical precision of academic writing in the social sciences while nonetheless addressing a general readership of intelligent, concerned, and educated citizens.

Finally, Charmion Browne brings the conversation to a striking academic level in her personal account of living in homeless shelters, "When Shelter Feels Like a Prison." Browne, herself a young college student, draws upon her teenage experiences as the child of a homeless single parent, and she contrasts these experiences with her current campus activities in a large university. The approaches to poverty illustrated in this chapter by factual reports, narrative accounts, statistical gathering, statistical interpretations, and theoretical speculations represent different aspects of source study in the social sciences. Each of them contributes to the academic conversation about poverty in an important way.

Born Poor and Smart

Angela Locke

Angela Locke is a writer for the feminist news journal off our backs.

PREREADING

Preview the article by reading paragraph 2. What does the author mean when she writes, "Oppression can't perpetuate itself without the cooperation of the oppressed"? Explain the sentence in your own words and elaborate it with examples from your own experience.

My mother was smart, and she was poor. She did things that poor people aren't   1
supposed to do. Between working at the E-Z Bargain Center and cleaning up the messes that my father made around town and her four children made around the

house, she read. She read to me when I was young. Later, she always wanted to know what I was reading, and she taught me how to talk about what I was reading. She didn't read romances or crime novels from the Five and Dime. Just a glance at one of her bookshelves shows Martin Buber, Carl Jung, John Gardner, John Barth, Margaret Atwood, Germaine Greer. She bought most of her books at yard sales and library sales, and she actually read them. She didn't just put them on her shelf for show.

Oppression can't perpetuate itself without the cooperation of the oppressed. 2 One way that cooperation works with class is that intelligence is scorned within the ranks of the poor. I still hear the voices in my head—"Don't show off." "She thinks she's better than the rest of us." "Let me slap that superior look right off your face." "Don't get it into your head that you're going to college." "Learn something practical, so you can take care of yourself."

My mother would have been lucky to find a friend at her dead-end nonunion 3 job to talk to about books, but she didn't. She worked her ass off all her life, eventually leaving the E-Z Bargain Center for the halls of the Nestle factory. At least it had a union and some procedures for raises. She worked for years on the assembly line, finally landing a position in the lab, where she made coffee for her male coworkers just to get along with them well enough to work without conflict. Even if one of those guys had been interested in discussing what Carl Jung said about dream imagery, he wouldn't have been interested in discussing it with the woman who made his coffee.

But her intelligence paid off with her kids. Two out of four got college degrees, 4 and I was one of them. Class accompanied me all the way.

It took me years longer to finish college than it took others whose parents and 5 social class supported them. I paid my own way in between having children and working low-end jobs. I only finished when a wealthier partner of mine helped with the finances.

Attending college put me in the company of women with class advantages. But 6 rather than finding a home there, I felt like an outsider in two worlds. What I had heard and feared was true. The price I paid for trying to break the class pattern I was raised with was that I belonged nowhere.

Something I struggle with to this day is that I never developed the sense of 7 entitlement that distinguishes the rich from the poor. Success is a given in upper-class families, a habit as nonnegotiable as brushing one's teeth. I have never been able to convince myself that I am "worthy" of success, whereas my wealthier friends have never questioned that they are. And that feeling can make the difference between accomplishment and failure.

So my relationship to class isn't only about a relationship to money. It's about a 8 relationship to success. My definition of success has something to do with money, but everything to do with class.

Success is not only living by the values that you believe in, but being in some 9 way recognized in the world for those values. Success is not only discovering your talents and your interests, but being able to make a living using them.

In my extended working-class family, there are no models of success. My mother 10 fulfilled the first terms of my definition, but she couldn't fulfill the second. It remains to be seen if I can.

READING FOR CONTENT

1. Paraphrase in your own words and then elaborate upon what Locke means when she writes that "intelligence is scorned within the ranks of the poor" in paragraph 2.

2. Paraphrase in your own words and then elaborate upon Locke's definition of success in paragraph 9. How does her definition relate to her argument about social class?

READING FOR GENRE, ORGANIZATION, AND STYLISTIC FEATURES

1. How does Locke use her personal experience to strengthen her argument about entitlement in paragraph 7?

2. How does Locke organize her definition of success in paragraph 9 around her personal experience in the rest of the essay?

READING FOR RHETORICAL CONTEXT

1. In paragraph 2, Locke writes that oppressed people cooperate in their own oppression. To what audience does she direct this comment? How might a nonoppressed person understand this comment? How might an oppressed person understand it?

2. In paragraph 6, Locke writes that she felt like an outsider among both her college classmates and her family. To what audience does she direct this comment? How might a person who has experienced only one social class understand it? How might a person who has experienced class differences understand it?

WRITING ASSIGNMENTS

1. Write a 500-word personal essay recounting your experiences of class difference.

2. Write a 500-word commentary on Locke's essay arguing that, besides class, other factors such as gender or ethnic identity have some bearing upon attitudes toward intelligence and success.

Culture of Success

Brink Lindsey

Brink Lindsey is vice-president for research at the conservative Cato Institute. He is the author of Against the Dead Hand: The Uncertain Struggle for Global Capitalism *(2002) and* The Age of Abundance: How Prosperity Transformed America's Politics and Culture *(2007).*

Lindsey, Brink. "The Culture of Success." *The New Republic* 12 Mar. 2008: 30–31. Print.

PREREADING

The "college wage premium" measures the differences in wage earning between those who have college degrees and those who don't. Aside from specialized skills learned in particular career-oriented courses, what might account for these differences? Freewrite your response.

Inside an Inequality Riddle

Something is holding back lower-income Americans from going to college. It's not 1 that there aren't major incentives for them to go. In fact, the college wage premium — the difference between the average wages of college grads and those of high school grads — has climbed to around 85 percent, up from less than 50 percent in 1980. At the same time, according to Harvard economists Claudia Goldin and Lawrence Katz, the relative supply of college grads grew an average of only 2 percent per year between 1980 and 2005 — down sharply from an average growth rate of 3.8 percent per year between 1960 and 1980. As you would expect, slowing supply growth (in graduates) has led to higher prices (in wages). But the next step should be a supply boom in response to the higher wages — and it's not happening.

In particular, it's not happening for kids from lower-income families — kids who 2 are disproportionately black or Hispanic. As of 2003, 80 percent of high school seniors from families in the top 20 percent of income enrolled in college the fall after graduation, while only 49 percent from families in the lowest 40 percent did so. That class divide translates directly into big disparities along ethnic lines. In 2006, 34 percent of white Americans aged 25–29 held college degrees, compared to 19 percent of African Americans and only 10 percent of Hispanics.

The obvious reason for this education gap is that college is too expensive. After 3 all, tuition costs have galloped far ahead of inflation, while many in the working class have seen their incomes stagnate or slip. But, in truth, the source of the problem lies much deeper: in the way parents raise their children.

A lack of money is the most common explanation for why lower-income 4 children don't go to college, and it's the impetus for proposals, like those put forward by Hillary Clinton and Barack Obama, to increase tuition subsidies. But James Heckman, the Nobel Prize-winning economist from the University of Chicago, is convinced that additional subsidies would do little good. Heckman recognizes the strong correlation between family income and college matriculation, but he argues that income is just a proxy for more fundamental differences in family and environmental conditions — like parental education — that ultimately show up in test scores and scholastic achievement. In a 2001 study co-authored with Stephen Cameron from Columbia University, Heckman tested the attendance gap between blacks, whites, and Hispanics, controlling for academic ability using scores from the Armed Forces Qualification Test (AFQT), and found that family income did not really matter when it came to getting kids into college. In fact, "at the same AFQT level Blacks and Hispanics enter college at rates that are substantially higher than the White rate," regardless of how much money their families made. The problem was that relatively few blacks and Hispanics reached a sufficiently high AFQT level in the first place. In other words, the main reason fewer African Americans and Hispanics go to college isn't that they can't afford it. It's that they lack the skills to do the work.

Not all scholars share Heckman's skepticism about additional tuition assis-   5
tance. David Ellwood and Thomas Kane of Harvard are two prominent proponents of improving access to college financing. Yet even they concede that "the single most powerful determinant of college-going remains high school achievement."

Of course, even if lack of money isn't preventing many well-qualified students   6
from matriculating, it could still explain why less-advantaged kids aren't gaining the abilities that going to college requires. For one thing, lower-income kids tend to go to under-funded schools that offer a poorer quality education. However, going back to the Civil Rights Act-sponsored Coleman report of 1966 (named for its principal investigator, sociologist James S. Coleman), study after study has shown that most of the variation in scholastic achievement occurs within schools, not among them. The abilities students bring with them to class matter more than any differences in school programs.

On the other hand, those same studies show that students' abilities correlate strongly   7
with their families' socioeconomic status. So another possibility is that wealthier parents invest more financially in their children, spending money on tutors, extracurricular travel, and so forth, thus helping them get better grades. Alternatively, more money could mean less stressed-out parents—parents with more time and energy to help with homework, go to school events, and just generally be around.

But University of Chicago sociologist Susan E. Mayer has found otherwise. In   8
her book What Money Can't Buy, she examined the connection between parental income and child outcomes, including school performance. She concluded that, "once children's basic material needs are met, characteristics of their parents become more important to how they turn out than anything additional money can buy." The condition is emphasized for a reason. Mayer is not suggesting that existing government programs for the poor ought to be cut. Rather, she is saying that those programs have been relatively successful at meeting kids' basic needs. Consequently, having the government or parents spend more money on children is unlikely to have much impact on how they do in school and beyond.

If more money isn't the answer, what does have an impact? In a word: culture.   9
Everything we know about high performance in all fields of endeavor tells us that, while natural talent is a plus, there is no substitute for long hours of preparation and hard work. That commonsense notion has been confirmed by the findings of the so-called "Expert Performance Movement," led by Florida State University psychologist Anders Ericsson. Ericsson and fellow researchers have spent years studying top performers in a whole host of different domains, and they've found a common denominator: practice. Chess grandmasters, concert pianists, and other superstars are distinguished from less-accomplished performers by two main things: starting their chosen fields earlier in life, and logging more hours per day of training over the course of many years.

Apply these lessons to doing well in school, and it becomes clear that the class   10
divide in academic achievement is fundamentally a cultural divide. To put it in a nutshell, the upper-middle-class kid grows up in an environment that constantly pushes him to develop the cognitive and motivational skills needed to be a good

student; the low-income kid's environment, on the other hand, pushes in the opposite direction.

Child psychologists Betty Hart and Todd Risley have tested the effect of class 11 on the differences in how parents interact with their young children. After observing several dozen families with toddlers over the course of a couple of years, they were able to document dramatic differences in the intensity and nature of the verbal stimulation the kids were getting: Professional parents directed an average of 487 "utterances" per hour toward their children, as compared to 301 for working-class parents and only 176 for welfare parents. The quality of those utterances was also very different: Among professional parents, the ratio of encouraging to discouraging utterances was six to one; for working-class parents, the ratio slipped to two to one; and welfare parents made two discouraging utterances for every encouraging one. The consequences were predictable: By the time the children in the study were around three years old, the ones from professional families had average vocabularies of 1,116 words; the working-class ones averaged 749; the welfare kids, 525.

Money isn't the issue here, since talking to your kids is free. What does matter 12 is the parents' inclination to nurture their child's development and the resulting verbal practice that the child gets. Kids from well-off homes get more chances to interact verbally, and that practice is an essential ingredient of developing a large vocabulary.

Once kids reach school age, the growing influence of peer groups reinforces 13 the early patterns established at home. The relative clout of parents and peers in shaping personality and values is a subject of hot debate, but here they generally work in concert. College-educated professional parents make sure their kids are in college-bound peer groups, while working-class and underclass kids tend to gravitate toward others like them. Consequently, children on either side of the class divide grow up with very different attitudes about the importance of school achievement—which leads to different expectations about future life plans and different self-conceptions in relation to larger society.

The "acting white" stigma reported among groups of black students was recently 14 tested by Harvard economist Roland Fryer. Fryer used data on high school friendship groups to determine that, while white kids were more popular the higher their GPA, blacks and Hispanics whose average exceeded a certain level were increasingly unpopular.

These findings are controversial, to be sure. Other quantitative studies, using dif- 15 ferent methods, have reached different conclusions. But the phenomenon identified by Fryer has been corroborated by a large number of ethnographic studies—not only of blacks and Hispanics, but also of other less-advantaged groups, such as the Buraku outcastes in Japan, the Maori in New Zealand, the British working class, and Italian immigrants in 1950s Boston. It's a bedrock fact of social psychology: Humans have a powerful and universal tendency to form self-policing social groups. With groups that are marginal to begin with, the tendency to enforce group solidarity can express itself through stigmatizing anything that looks like mainstream success.

The idea that class-based cultural differences contribute to academic under- 16 achievement is cause for consternation across the ideological spectrum. Let's start with me and my fellow libertarians. We insist on the central importance of individual responsibility for the healthy functioning of a free society. Yet, by the time people become legally responsible adults, circumstances not of their own choosing—namely, how they were raised and whom they grew up with—may have prevented them from ever developing the capacities they need to thrive and flourish. Which raises the possibility that government intervention to improve those circumstances could actually expand the scope of individual autonomy.

For example, preschool enrichment programs—along the lines of Head Start,   17 but more intensive and beginning with even younger kids—offer some promise in counteracting the negative influences of a disadvantaged upbringing. So do housing programs that encourage relocation from areas of concentrated poverty. Meanwhile, additional wage subsidies for low-skilled workers might help to shrink the underclass and promote the gradual assimilation of middle-class norms. Progressives, for their part, should recognize that libertarians have their own good ideas for boosting human capital and fostering assimilation. Among them are: greater competition in the school system, cessation of the drug war that so needlessly fosters criminality, and elimination of occupational licensing restrictions that block opportunities for entrepreneurship among the less credentialed.

Furthermore, progressives need to understand that the rise in skill-based inequal-   18 ity is not some populist morality play of capitalism run amok. On the contrary, in many ways it can be seen as a capitalist success story. For a generation now, our economy has been creating more opportunities for the productive use of highly developed cognitive skills than there are people able to take advantage of them. That is what the run-up in the college wage premium is telling us. Economic development has raced ahead of cultural development; as a result, culture is now acting as a brake on upward mobility. So, instead of railing against the economic system, we need to do a better job of helping people to adapt to it and rise to its challenges. The rules of the game aren't the problem—we just need more skillful players.

READING FOR CONTENT

1. In paragraph 9, underline and explain what the author defines as the chief characteristics that distinguish high wage earners from lower wage earners.
2. In paragraph 15, underline and explain what the author defines as the "group solidarity" distinguishing high wage earners from low wage earners.

READING FOR GENRE, ORGANIZATION, AND STYLISTIC FEATURES

1. Why does the author in paragraphs 4, 6, and 15 cite conclusions from such government-sponsored sources as the Armed Forces Qualification Test, the Coleman report of 1966, and studies of the British working class and Italian immigrants in 1950s Boston?
2. Why does the author move from an argument based on sociology in paragraphs 4–8 to one based on child psychology and group psychology in paragraphs 11–15?
3. In paragraph 17, how does the author try to appeal to progressive readers about the value of his conservative agenda?

READING FOR RHETORICAL CONTEXT

1. In paragraph 4, the author reveals the conservative underpinnings of his argument when he claims that the answer to explaining why lower-income people don't go to college is not a lack of money. What does he propose as an alternative answer?
2. In paragraph 6, the author disparages the idea that higher-income families pay for supplementary college-prep programs to raise their children's scores. How might a college student who has not benefited from these programs respond?

WRITING ASSIGNMENTS

1. Use the "Prompts for a Personal Response to the Text" on page 36 to write an informal response to Brink Lindsey's "Culture of Success." Then convert your informal response to a formal response essay. Use the tips we provide on page 39.
2. Draft a critical analysis of "Culture of Success." Use the Questions to Help a Writer Revise a Critical Analysis Essay in Chapter 3 to revise your essay.

■ ■ ■ ■ ■ ■ ■ ■ ■ ■ ■

The War Against the Poor Instead of Programs to End Poverty

Herbert J. Gans

Herbert J. Gans is a professor of sociology at Columbia University. He has written numerous articles and books on the subject of poverty, including The Urban Villagers, The Levittowners, People and Plans, Popular Culture and High Culture, Deciding What's News, The War against the Poor, *and* Making Sense of America.

PREREADING

Before you read the article, take a few minutes to write a response to the title. Do you think we are making a serious effort to end poverty in the United States? Can you think of why we might be accused of engaging in a war against the poor instead of a battle to improve their condition?

While liberals have been talking about resuming the War on Poverty, elected 1 officials are doing something very different: waging a war on the poor. Even the riot that took place in Los Angeles in early May [1992] did not interrupt that war, perhaps because the riot was a mixture of protest, looting, and destruction.

Gans, Herbert J. "The War Against the Poor Instead of Programs to End Poverty," *Dissent*, Fall 1992, pp. 461–65. Reprinted with permission of the University of Pennsylvania Press.

The war on the poor was initiated by dramatic shifts in the domestic and world   2
economy, which have turned more and more unskilled and semiskilled workers into
surplus labor. Private enterprise participated actively by shipping jobs overseas and by
treating workers as expendable. Government has done its part as well, increasingly
restricting the welfare state safety net to the middle class. Effective job-creation schemes,
housing programs, educational and social services that serve the poor—and some of the
working classes—are vanishing. Once people become poor, it becomes ever harder for
them to escape poverty.

Despite the willingness to help the poor expressed in public opinion polls, other,   3
more covert, attitudes have created a political climate that makes the war on the poor
possible. Politicians compete with each other over who can capture the most headlines with new ways to punish the poor. However, too many of their constituents see
the poor not as people without jobs but as miscreants who behave badly because they
do not abide by middle-class or mainstream moral values. Those judged "guilty" are
dismissed as the "undeserving poor"—or the underclass in today's language—people
who do not deserve to escape poverty.

True, *some* people are indeed guilty of immoral behavior—that is, murderers, street   4
criminals, drug sellers, child abusers.

Then there are poor people whose anger at their condition expresses itself in   5
the kind of nihilism that cannot be defined as political protest. Even so, most of those
labeled "undeserving" are simply poor people who for a variety of reasons cannot live
up to mainstream behavioral standards, like remaining childless in adolescence, finding and holding a job, and staying off welfare. This does not make them immoral.
Because poor adolescents do not have jobs does not mean they are lazy. Because their
ghetto "cool" may deter employers does not mean they are unwilling to work. Still, the
concept of an underclass lumps them with those who are criminal or violent.

Why do Americans accept so many untruths about the poor and remain un-   6
willing to accept the truth when it is available? The obvious answer is that some of
the poor frighten or anger those who are better off. But they also serve as a lightning
rod—scapegoats—for some problems among the better off. Street criminals rightly
evoke fears about personal safety, but they and the decidedly innocent poor also
generate widespread anger about the failure of government to reduce "urban" and
other problems.

Among whites, the anger is intertwined with fears about blacks and "Hispanics,"   7
or the newest immigrants, reflecting the fear of the stranger and newcomer from
which their own ancestors suffered when they arrived here. (Few remember that at the
start of the twentieth century, the "Hebrews" then arriving were sometimes described
as a "criminal race"—as the Irish had been earlier in the nineteenth century.)

The hostility toward today's welfare recipients is a subtler but equally revealing   8
index to the fears of the more fortunate. This fear reflects a historic belief that people who
are not economically self-sufficient can hurt the economy, although actual expenditures
for welfare have always been small. Welfare recipients are also assumed to be getting
something for nothing, often by people who are not overly upset about corrupt governmental or corporate officials who get a great deal of money for nothing or very little.

Welfare recipients possibly provoke anger among those concerned about their   9
own economic security, especially in a declining economy. Welfare recipients are

seen as living the easy life while everyone else is working harder than ever—and thus become easy scapegoats, which does not happen to the successful, who often live easier lives.

The concern with poor unmarried mothers, especially adolescents, whose number and family size have in fact long been declining, epitomizes adult fears about the high levels of sexual activity and the constant possibility of pregnancy among *all* adolescent girls. In addition, the notion of the "undeserving poor" has become a symbol for the general decline of mainstream moral standards, especially those celebrated as "traditional" in American society.

Ironically, however, the "undeserving poor" can be forced to uphold some of these very standards in exchange for welfare, much as some Skid Row homeless still get a night's dinner and housing in exchange for sitting through a religious service. The missionaries in this case are secular: social workers and bureaucrats. But the basic moralistic expectations remain the same, including the demand that the poor live up to values that their socioeconomic superiors preach but do not always practice. Thus, social workers can have live-in lovers without being married, but their clients on welfare cannot. Members of the more fortunate classes are generally free from moral judgments altogether; no one talks about an undeserving middle class or the undeserving rich.

The war on the poor is probably best ended by job-centered economic growth that creates decent public and private jobs. Once poor people have such jobs, they are almost automatically considered deserving, eligible for a variety of other programs to help them or their children escape poverty.

The most constructive way to supply such jobs would be an updated New Deal that repairs failing infrastructures, creates new public facilities (including new databases), and allows the old ones to function better—for example, by drastically reducing class size in public schools. Equally important are ways of reviving private enterprise and finding new niches for it in the global economy. Without them, there will not be enough well-paying jobs in factories, laboratories, and offices—or taxes to pay for public programs. Such programs are already being proposed these days, by Bill Clinton and in the Congress, but mainly for working-class people who have been made jobless and are now joining the welfare rolls.

Last but not least is a new approach to income grants for those who cannot work or find work. The latest fashion is to put welfare recipients to work, which would be a good idea if even decent entry-level jobs for them could be found or created. (Alas, when taxpayers discover how much cheaper it is to pay welfare than to create jobs, that remedy may end as it has before.)

Also needed is a non-punitive, universal income grant program, which goes to all people who still end up as part of the labor surplus. If such a program copied the European principle of not letting the incomes of the poor fall below 60 to 70 percent of the median income—in the United States, welfare recipients get a fifth of the median on average—the recipients would remain integral members of society, who could be required to make sure their children would not become poor. (Such a solution would also cut down the crime rate.)

However, even minimal conventional antipoverty programs are politically unpopular at the moment. The 1992 Democratic presidential candidates paid little attention to the poor during the primaries, except, in passing, in New York City and, then again, after Los Angeles. The future of antipoverty programs looks no brighter than before.

The time may be ripe to look more closely at how nonpoor Americans feel about 17 poverty, and try to reduce their unwarranted fear and anger toward the poor—with the hope that they would then be more positive about reviving antipoverty efforts.

The first priority for reducing that anger is effective policies against drugs and 18 street crime, though they alone cannot stem all the negative feelings. Probably the only truly effective solution is a prosperous economy in which the anger between all groups is lessened; and a more egalitarian society in which the displacement of such anger on the poor is no longer necessary, and the remaining class conflicts can be fought fairly.

This ideal is today more utopian than ever, but it ought to be kept in mind. 19 Every step toward it will help a little. Meanwhile, in order to bring back antipoverty programs, liberals, along with the poor and others who speak for the poor, could also try something else: initiating an intellectual and cultural defense of the poor. In a "sound bite": to fight *class* bigotry along with the racial kind.

Anti-bigotry programs work slowly and not always effectively, but they are as 20 American as apple pie. Class bigotry is itself still a novel idea, but nothing would be lost by mounting a defense of the poor and putting it on the public agenda. Ten such defenses strike me as especially urgent:

1. *Poverty is not equivalent to moral failure.* That moral undesirables exist 21 among the poor cannot be denied, but there is no evidence that their proportion is greater than among the more fortunate. "Bums" can be found at all economic levels. However, more prosperous miscreants tend to be less visible; the alcoholic co-worker can doze off at his desk, but the poor drunk is apt to be found in the gutter. Abusive middle class parents may remain invisible for years, until their children are badly hurt, but violent poor parents soon draw the attention of child-welfare workers and may lose their children to foster care.

Troubled middle-class people have access to experts who can demonstrate that 22 moral diagnoses are not enough. The abusive mother was herself abused; the school dropout has a learning disability; the young person who will not work suffers from depression. Poor people, on the other hand, rarely have access to such experts or to clinical treatment. For the poor, the explanations are usually moral, and the treatment is punitive.

2. *"Undeservingness" is an effect of poverty.* Whatever else can be said about 23 unmarried mothers on welfare, school dropouts, and people unwilling to take minimum-wage dead-end jobs, their behavior is almost always *poverty-related.*

This is, of course, also true of many street criminals and drug sellers. Middle-class 24 people, after all, do not turn into muggers and street drug dealers any more than they become fifteen-year-old unmarried mothers.

People who have not been poor themselves do not understand how much of 25 what the poor do is poverty-related. Poor young women often do not want to marry the fathers of their children because such men cannot perform as breadwinners and might cope with their economic failures by battering their wives. Although a great deal of publicity is given to school dropouts, not enough has been said about the peer pressure in poor, and even working-class, neighborhoods that discourages doing well in school.

3. *The responsibilities of the poor.* Conservatives, often mute about the responsi- 26
bilities of the rich, stress the responsibilities of the poor. However, poor people sometimes feel no need to be responsible to society until society treats them responsibly.
Acting irresponsibly becomes an angry reaction to, even a form of power, over that
society. Those whose irresponsibility is criminal deserve punishment and the clearly
lazy deserve to lose their benefits. But who would punish an unmarried mother who
goes on welfare to obtain medical benefits that a job cannot supply? Is she not acting
responsibly toward her child? And how well can we judge anyone's responsibility
without first knowing that choices, responsible and irresponsible, were actually open?
Being poor often means having little choice to begin with.

4. *The drastic scarcity of work for the poor.* Many Americans, including too many 27
economists, have long assumed that there are always more jobs than workers, that the
properly eager can always find them, hence the jobless are at fault. This is, however, a
myth—one of many Ronald Reagan liked to promote when he was president. The facts
are just the opposite. Decent jobs that are open to the poor, especially to blacks, were
the first to disappear when our deindustrialization began. This helps to explain why so
many poor men have dropped out of the labor force, and are no longer even counted as
jobless.

Incidentally, the myth that the unemployed are unwilling to work is never attached 28
to the rising number of working- and middle-class jobless. But, then, they are not yet poor
enough to be considered undeserving.

5. *Black troubles and misbehavior are caused more by poverty than by race.* Because 29
the proportion of blacks who are criminals, school dropouts, heads of single-parent
families, or unmarried mothers is higher than among whites, blacks increasingly have to
face the outrageous indignity of being considered genetically or culturally undesirable.
The plain fact is that the higher rates of nearly all social problems among blacks are the
effects of being poor—including poverty brought about by discrimination. When poor
whites are compared with poor blacks, those with social problems are not so different,
although black proportions remain higher. Even this difference can be attributed to
income disparity. Black poverty has been worse in all respects and by all indicators ever
since blacks were brought here as slaves.

6. *Blacks should not be treated like recent immigrants.* Black job-seekers sometimes 30
face the additional burden of being expected, both by employers and the general public,
to compete for jobs with recently arrived immigrants. This expectation calls on people
who have been in America for generations to accept the subminimum wages, long hours,
poor working conditions, and employer intimidation that are the lot of many immigrants.
Actually, employers prefer immigrants because they are more easily exploited or more
deferential than native-born Americans. To make matters worse, blacks are then blamed
for lacking an "immigrant work ethic."

7. *Debunking the metaphors of undeservingness.* Society's word-smiths—academics, 31
journalists, and pundits—like to find, and their audiences like to hear, buzzwords that
caricature moral failings among the poor; but it should not be forgotten that these terms
were invented by the fortunate. *Not only is there no identifiable underclass, but a class
"under" society is a social impossibility.* Welfare "dependents" are in that condition mainly
because the economy has declared them surplus labor and because they must rely on
politicians and officials who determine their welfare eligibility.

Such metaphors are never applied to the more affluent. There are no hard-core 32 millionaires, and troubled middle-class people will never be labeled an under-middle class. Women who choose to be financially dependent on their husbands are not described as spouse-dependent, while professors who rely on university trustees for their income are not called tenure-dependent.

8. *The dangers of class stereotypes.* Underclass and other terms for the undeserving 33 poor are class stereotypes, which reinforce class discrimination much as racial stereotypes support racial discrimination. The many similarities between class and racial stereotypes still need to be identified.

Stereotypes sometimes turn into everyday labels that are so taken for granted 34 that they turn into self-fulfilling prophecies—and then cause particular havoc among the more vulnerable poor. For example, boys from poor single-parent families are apt to be punished harder for minor delinquencies simply because of the stereotype that they are growing up without paternal or other male supervision. Once they, and other poor people, are labeled as undeserving, public officials who are supposed to supply them with services feel justified in not being as helpful as before—though depriving poor people of an emergency rent payment or food grant may be enough to push them closer to homelessness or street crime.

The recent display of interest in and appeals for affirmative action along class 35 lines—even by conservatives like Dinesh D'Souza—suggests that the time may be ripe to recognize, and begin to fight, the widespread existence of class discrimination and prejudice. The confrontation has to take place not only in everyday life but also in the country's major institutions, politics, and courts. The Constitution that is now interpreted as barring racial discrimination can perhaps be interpreted to bar class discrimination as well.

9. *Blaming the poor reduces neither poverty nor poverty-related behavior.* Labeling 36 the poor as undeserving does not attack the causes of street crime, improve the schools of poor children, or reduce adult joblessness. Such labels are only a way of expressing anger toward the poor. Blaming the victim solves nothing except to make blamers feel better temporarily. Such labeling justifies political ideologies and interests that oppose solutions, and thus increases the likelihood that nothing will be done about poverty—or crime.

10. *Improving reporting and scholarship about the poor.* Most poverty news is 37 about crime, not poverty. How many reporters ever ask whether economic hardship is part of the crime story? The government's monthly jobless rate is reported, but not the shortage of jobs open to the poor. Likewise, the percentage of people below the poverty rate is an annual news story, but the actual income of the poor, often less than half the poverty line, or about $6,000 a year, is not mentioned.

The "spins," both in government statistics and in journalism, carry over into 38 scholarship. Millions were spent to find and measure an underclass, but there is little ethnographic research to discover why the poor must live as they do. Researchers on homelessness look at mental illness as a cause of homelessness; they do not study it as a possible *effect!*

There are also innumerable other studies of the homeless, but too few about the 39 labor markets and employers, housing industry and landlords, and other factors that create homelessness in the first place.

The Americans who feel most threatened by the poor are people from the working 40 class, whom journalists currently call the middle class. They are apt to live nearest the poor. They will suffer most, other than the poor themselves, from street crime, as well as from the fear that the poor could take over their neighborhoods and jobs. Indeed, as inexpensive housing and secure jobs requiring little education become more scarce, the people only slightly above the poor in income and economic security fear that their superior status will shrink drastically. Viewing the poor as undeserving helps to maintain and even widen that status gap.

No wonder, then, that in the current economic crisis, the journalists' middle 41 class and its job problems are the big story, and the poor appear mainly as the underclass, with candidates ignoring poverty. The political climate being what it is, this may even be unavoidable. Indeed, if the winner's margin in the coming elections comes from that middle class, the candidate must initiate enough economic programs to put *its* jobless back to work and to solve its health care, housing, and other problems.

That winner should be bold enough to make room in the program for the poor 42 as well. Poverty, racial polarization, crime, and related problems cannot be allowed to rise higher without further reducing morale, quality of life, and economic competitiveness. Otherwise, America will not be a decent, safe, or pleasant place to live, even for the affluent.

READING FOR CONTENT

1. Summarize how the economy, the government, and the political climate have participated in the war against the poor.
2. Paraphrase Gans's objections to the concept of the "underclass" (paragraphs 33 and 34).
3. Discuss why people who are better off are frightened and angered by the poor. Do you agree with Gans's explanation?
4. List Gans's solutions for ending the war on the poor. Do you think they are workable?
5. What is the ideal way of reducing the anger directed against the poor?
6. In your own words, explain which of Gans's ten defenses against class bigotry are the most workable.
7. React to Gans's forecast for the future.

READING FOR GENRE, ORGANIZATION, AND STYLISTIC FEATURES

1. Explain Gans's overall organizational plan. What other organizational patterns does he use?
2. What is the function of paragraphs 11, 21, 22, and 32?
3. Describe the features of the article that help the reader to follow Gans's train of thought.
4. Why do you think Gans concludes the article as he does? What effect did the conclusion have on you as a reader?

READING FOR RHETORICAL CONTEXT

1. What do you think prompted Gans to write this article?
2. Do you think Gans provides his readers with enough background to support his premise about the war against the poor? What additional information would be useful?
3. What impact does Gans want to have on his audience? Do you think he is successful?

WRITING ASSIGNMENTS

1. Write a two- to three-page essay explaining why you agree or disagree with Gans's observation, "The Americans who feel most threatened by the poor are people from the working class" (paragraph 40).

2. Write an essay in which you argue for or against Gans's claim that Americans need to fight against class bigotry as well as racial discrimination and prejudice.

3. For a two-week period, keep a written record of how poor people are treated in a daily newspaper or a daily news broadcast. Then, use your notes to write an essay explaining whether or not the media stereotype poor people as undeserving.

■ ■ ■ ■ ■ ■ ■ ■ ■ ■ ■

A Great Time to Be Alive?

Matt Yglesias

Matt Yglesias is a Fellow at the Center for American Progress, a staff writer at the American Prospect, *and a blogger on* thinkprogress.org.

PREREADING

If income taxes were redistributed so that the wealthiest Americans would pay more rather than less to the federal government and the proceeds were spent on public services for all, what services do you think should receive priority? List these services in order of usefulness and need.

For all the disastrousness of the current recession in the developed world, examined   1 more broadly the early twenty-first century has been one of the greatest times to be alive in the history of mankind. The cause is the enormous improvement in living standards of the people in China, India, Brazil and other large developing nations. On the moral balance sheet, this betterment of some of the globe's poorest people more than outweighs the continued stagnation of middle-class wages in the United States.

But the fact remains that here, in what's still the wealthiest large nation on earth,   2 things have not been improving in a nearly commensurate manner. And yet it's not as if global economic growth has passed the country by. Instead, a wildly dispropor- tionate share of the material gains of recent technological progress and economic globalization has been captured by a tiny, already rich slice of the population. The causes of this are complicated and controversial, and the solutions can be complicated if we want; but they can also be simple—the government can and should deploy its tax

Yglesias, Matt. "A Great Time to Be Alive?" *The Nation* 291.5 (July 19, 2010): 22–23. Print. Reprinted with permission from the July 19, 2010 issue of *The Nation*. For subscription informa- tion, call 1-800-333-8536. Portions of each week's Nation magazine can be accessed at <http:// www.thenation.com>.

authority to capture a larger share of this wealth and spend it on useful services for the broad public.

Higher taxes to finance more and better public services is not the only conceivable method of curbing inequality, but it is the best one because it directly tackles the most objectionable aspect of high inequality in the economy—its tendency to perpetuate itself in the form of unequal access to basic social goods and unequal access to opportunities in the next generation.

The goal should be a country where every neighborhood features safe, well-paved streets, excellent schools, functioning mass transit and a healthy environment. Families should have equal access to medical treatment if they fall ill, to preschool and to decent nutrition for their children, and to a secure retirement after a few decades in the workforce. Those with skills that are more highly valued in the marketplace would still have fancier cars, larger televisions, more upscale clothing. But the main conditions for human flourishing would be available across the board, and no family would need to worry that broadening America's circle of social and economic opportunity by allowing foreigners to move here or sell goods across national borders imperils their fundamental interests.

To get from here to there is going to be a difficult task in a country where the public is averse to any increase in taxation on the nonrich and where elites are equally hostile to the hiking of taxes on the wealthiest. Ultimately, doing some of both will be essential. That's because it's important to conceive of future expansion in public services in terms similar to those of our existing and highly successful insurance programs for retirees, Social Security and Medicare. These programs are redistributive in their impact, guaranteeing for all things that the rich could afford on their own, but they're not narrow antipoverty efforts, nor are they targeted giveaways. Instead, the idea is that everyone pays a share and everyone gets to participate in the benefits. This invests middle-class and even wealthy people in the notion of ensuring the quality of services and shifts the conversation away from the concept of "handouts."

Programs of this kind probably can't be funded exclusively through taxes on high earners. But the $250,000-and-over crowd would be a good place to start. Conventional wisdom sometimes holds that the public opposes even taxes on the richest, but the polling data don't support that conclusion. The problem is that politicians have shied away from raising taxes. There's also a strong case for increasing the number of tax brackets so the system can become more progressive at the higher end, and prosperous professionals earning "only" $500,000 a year would not be treated the same as multimillionaires. Another promising source of revenue is an excise tax on undesirable behavior. Greenhouse gas pollution should be taxed; the declining real value of federal alcohol taxes should be reversed; taxes on public health hazards like sugary drinks and junk food should be considered.

For the moment, however, fighting the recession must be the top priority, so tax increases should be deferred. The main thing now is to defend existing services against the apostles of austerity and, where possible, make the case that expansion of services can boost the economy and lay the groundwork for future prosperity.

One particularly promising set of opportunities lies in early childhood education and general well-being. Americans understand that a temporary economic downturn is not a good reason to permanently scar a generation of kids. As recession makes more children than ever dependent on food assistance, it's a good time to highlight the reality that subsidized school lunches suddenly become unavailable during summer vacation, although children need to eat whether or not school is open. More broadly, a family security agenda centered on assuring the availability of paid family leave and high-quality preschool has the potential to appeal to the streak of cultural conservatism that runs deep in working-class America. It would certainly connect the inequality agenda to the everyday concerns of American families.

What's more, a focus on family policy and early childhood has the virtue of work-   9 ing on two sides of the problem simultaneously. In other words, not only do expenditures in this realm directly mitigate the inequities of the market distribution of income; they serve to reduce inequality of opportunity and thus the tendency of unequal outcomes to reinscribe themselves on the next generation. On its own, that's inadequate to the full scope of the inequality challenge, but it's an excellent place to start.

READING FOR CONTENT

1. In paragraphs 3 and 4, what argument does the author present for raising taxes on the wealthy as a way to curb inequality?
2. In paragraphs 8 and 9, why does the author argue that a particularly promising area to spend tax monies on is early childhood education and family security? Paraphrase his reasoning.

READING FOR GENRE, ORGANIZATION, AND STYLISTIC FEATURES

1. Why does the author admit in paragraph 3 that higher taxes are not the only way to curb inequality, and how does he defend his claim that higher taxes may be the best way to do so?
2. In paragraph 4, underline the particular services that the author mentions as the best ones to target for funding from higher taxes on the wealthy. Why does he select these services?
3. How would the author further refine the current tax system for the very wealthy?

READING FOR RHETORICAL CONTEXT

1. In paragraph 5, how does the author try to enlist the sympathies of wealthy people, whom his plan targets for higher taxes?
2. In the concluding paragraphs, how does the author try to enlist the sympathies of social conservatives who usually resist imposing higher taxes?

WRITING ASSIGNMENTS

1. Use the "Prompts for a Personal Response to the Text" on page 36 to write an informal response to "The Inequality Challenge." Then convert your informal response to a formal response essay. Use the tips we provide on page 39.
2. Draft a critical analysis of "The Inequality Challenge." For support, refer to materials in the preceding articles by Locke, Lindsey, and Gans. Use the Questions for Helping a Writer Revise a Critical Analysis Essay in Chapter 3 to revise your essay.

Serving in Florida

Barbara Ehrenreich

Barbara Ehrenreich has contributed articles to many magazines and written twelve books, including The Worst Years of Our Lives, Blood Fires, Fear of Falling, *and* Nickel and Dimed: On (Not) Getting By in America, *from which this selection was taken.*

PREREADING

From 1998 to 2000, Ehrenreich went undercover and became a low-wage worker in order to experience firsthand what it is like to survive on six to seven dollars an hour. Before Ehrenreich embarked on the project, she set three rules for herself: that in her search for jobs, she would not rely on her education or her former occupation; that she would accept the highest-paying job she was given; and that she would lower her expenses by taking the cheapest housing she could find. Over the course of the project, Ehrenreich took jobs in Key West, Florida; Portland, Maine; and Minneapolis, Minnesota.

In this selection Ehrenreich relates her experiences as a server, first at the Hearthside Restaurant, where she worked from 2:00 p.m. to 10:00 p.m. for $2.43 per hour plus tips, and then at Johnny's Restaurant. She also worked briefly as a housekeeper in the hotel attached to Johnny's.

What is the lowest-paid job you have ever held? Take ten to fifteen minutes to write a journal entry explaining what it entailed. In small groups, share your experience with your classmates.

I still flinch to think that I spent all those weeks under the surveillance of men (and later women) whose job it was to monitor my behavior for signs of sloth, theft, drug abuse, or worse. Not that managers and especially "assistant managers" in low-wage settings like this are exactly the class enemy. Mostly, in the restaurant business, they are former cooks still capable of pinch-hitting in the kitchen, just as in hotels they are likely to be former clerks, and paid a salary of only about $400 a week. But everyone knows they have crossed over to the other side, which is, crudely put, corporate as opposed to human. Cooks want to prepare tasty meals, servers want to serve them graciously, but managers are there for only one reason—to make sure that money is made for some theoretical entity, the corporation, which exists far away in Chicago or New York, if a corporation can be said to have a physical existence at all. Reflecting on her career, Gail tells me ruefully that she swore, years ago, never to work for a corporation again. "They don't cut you no slack. You give and you give and they take." 1

Managers can sit—for hours at a time if they want—but it's their job to see that   2
no one else ever does, even when there's nothing to do, and this is why, for servers, slow
times can be as exhausting as rushes. You start dragging out each little chore because
if the manager on duty catches you in an idle moment he will give you something far
nastier to do. So I wipe, I clean, I consolidate catsup bottles and recheck the cheese-
cake supply, even tour the tables to make sure the customer evaluation forms are all
standing perkily in their places—wondering all the time how many calories I burn in
these strictly theatrical exercises. In desperation, I even take the desserts out of their
glass display case and freshen them up with whipped cream and bright new maraschino
cherries; anything to look busy. When, on a particularly dead afternoon, Stu finds me
glancing at a *USA Today* a customer has left behind, he assigns me to vacuum the
entire floor with the broken vacuum cleaner, which has a handle only two feet long,
and the only way to do that without incurring orthopedic damage is to proceed from
spot to spot on your knees.

On my first Friday at Hearthside there is a "mandatory meeting for all res-   3
taurant employees," which I attend, eager for insight into our overall marketing
strategy and the niche (your basic Ohio cuisine with a tropical twist?) we aim to
inhabit. But there is no "we" at this meeting. Phillip, our top manager except for
an occasional "consultant" sent out by corporate headquarters, opens it with a
sneer: "The break room—it's disgusting. Butts in the ashtrays, newspapers lying
around, crumbs." This windowless little room, which also houses the time clock
for the entire hotel, is where we stash our bags and civilian clothes and take our
half-hour meal breaks. But a break room is not a right, he tells us, it can be taken
away. We should also know that the lockers in the break room and whatever is in
them can be searched at any time. Then comes gossip; there has been gossip; gossip
(which seems to mean employees talking among themselves) must stop. Off-duty
employees are henceforth barred from eating at the restaurant, because "other
servers gather around them and gossip." When Phillip has exhausted his agenda
of rebukes, Joan complains about the condition of the ladies' room and I throw in
my two bits about the vacuum cleaner. But I don't see any backup coming from
my fellow servers, each of whom has slipped into her own personal funk; Gail, my
role model, stares sorrowfully at a point six inches from her nose. The meeting ends
when Andy, one of the cooks, gets up, muttering about breaking up his day off for
this almighty bullshit.

Just four days later we are suddenly summoned into the kitchen at 3:30 P.M.,   4
even though there are live tables on the floor. We all—about ten of us—stand around
Phillip, who announces grimly that there has been a report of some "drug activity" on
the night shift and that, as a result, we are now to be a "drug-free" workplace, meaning
that all new hires will be tested and possibly also current employees on a random basis.
I am glad that this part of the kitchen is so dark because I find myself blushing as hard
as if I had been caught toking up in the ladies' room myself: I haven't been treated this
way—lined up in the corridor, threatened with locker searches, peppered with care-
lessly aimed accusations—since at least junior high school. Back on the floor, Joan
cracks, "Next they'll be telling us we can't have *sex* on the job." When I ask Stu what
happened to inspire the crackdown, he just mutters about "management decisions"
and takes the opportunity to upbraid Gail and me for being too generous with the

rolls. From now on there's to be only one per customer and it goes out with the dinner, not with the salad. He's also been riding the cooks, prompting Andy to come out of the kitchen and observe—with the serenity of a man whose customary implement is a butcher knife—that "Stu has a death wish today."

Later in the evening, the gossip crystallizes around the theory that Stu is himself the drug culprit, that he uses the restaurant phone to order up marijuana and sends one of the late servers out to fetch it for him. The server was caught and she may have ratted out Stu, at least enough to cast some suspicion on him, thus accounting for his pissy behavior. Who knows? Personally, I'm ready to believe anything bad about Stu, who serves no evident function and presumes too much on our common ethnicity, sidling up to me one night to engage in a little nativism directed at the Haitian immigrants: "I feel like I'm the foreigner here. They're taking over the country." Still later that evening, the drug in question escalates to crack. Lionel, the busboy, entertains us for the rest of the shift by standing just behind Stu's back and sucking deliriously on an imaginary joint or maybe a pipe.

The other problem, in addition to the less-than-nurturing management style, is that this job shows no sign of being financially viable. You might imagine, from a comfortable distance, that people who live, year in and year out, on $6 to $10 an hour have discovered some survival stratagems unknown to the middle class. But no. It's not hard to get my coworkers talking about their living situations, because housing, in almost every case, is the principal source of disruption in their lives, the first thing they fill you in on when they arrive for their shifts. After a week, I have compiled the following survey:

> Gail is sharing a room in a well-known downtown flophouse for $250 a week. Her roommate, a male friend, has begun hitting on her, driving her nuts, but the rent would be impossible alone.
>
> Claude, the Haitian cook, is desperate to get out of the two-room apartment he shares with his girlfriend and two other, unrelated people. As far as I can determine, the other Haitian men live in similarly crowded situations.
>
> Annette, a twenty-year-old server who is six months pregnant and abandoned by her boyfriend, lives with her mother, a postal clerk.
>
> Marianne, who is a breakfast server, and her boyfriend are paying $170 a week for a one-person trailer.
>
> Billy, who at $10 an hour is the wealthiest of us, lives in the trailer he owns, paying only the $400-a-month lot fee.
>
> The other white cook, Andy, lives on his dry-docked boat, which, as far as I can tell from his loving descriptions, can't be more than twenty feet long. He offers to take me out on it once it's repaired, but the offer comes with inquiries as to my marital status, so I do not follow up on it.
>
> Tina, another server, and her husband are paying $60 a night for a room in the Days Inn. This is because they have no car and the Days Inn is in walking distance of the Hearthside. When Marianne is tossed out of her trailer for subletting (which is against trailer park rules), she leaves her boyfriend and moves in with Tina and her husband.

Joan, who had fooled me with her numerous and tasteful outfits (hostesses wear their own clothes), lives in a van parked behind a shopping center at night and showers in Tina's motel room. The clothes are from thrift shops.[1]

It strikes me, in my middle-class solipsism, that there is gross improvidence in   7
some of these arrangements. When Gail and I are wrapping silverware in napkins—the only task for which we are permitted to sit—she tells me she is thinking of escaping from her roommate by moving into the Days Inn herself. I am astounded: how she can even think of paying $40 to $60 a day? But if I was afraid of sounding like a social worker, I have come out just sounding like a fool. She squints at me in disbelief: "And where am I supposed to get a month's rent and a month's deposit for an apartment?" I'd been feeling pretty smug about my $500 efficiency, but of course it was made possible only by the $1,300 I had allotted myself for start-up costs when I began my low-wage life: $1,000 for the first month's rent and deposit, $100 for initial groceries and cash in my pocket, $200 stuffed away for emergencies. In poverty, as in certain propositions in physics, starting conditions are everything.

There are no secret economies that nourish the poor; on the contrary, there are   8
a host of special costs. If you can't put up the two months' rent you need to secure an apartment, you end up paying through the nose for a room by the week. If you have only a room, with a hot plate at best, you can't save by cooking up huge lentil stews that can be frozen for the week ahead. You eat fast food or the hot dogs and Styrofoam cups of soup that can be microwaved in a convenience store. If you have no money for health insurance—and the Hearthside's niggardly plan kicks in only after three months—you go without routine care or prescription drugs and end up paying the price. Gail, for example, was doing fine, healthwise anyway, until she ran out of money for estrogen pills. She is supposed to be on the company health plan by now, but they claim to have lost her application form and to be beginning the paperwork all over again. So she spends $9 a pop for pills to control the migraines she wouldn't have, she insists, if her estrogen supplements were covered. Similarly, Marianne's boyfriend lost his job as a roofer because he missed so much time after getting a cut on his foot for which he couldn't afford the prescribed antibiotic.

My own situation, when I sit down to assess it after two weeks of work, would not   9
be much better if this were my actual life. The seductive thing about waitressing is that you don't have to wait for payday to feel a few bills in your pocket, and my tips usually cover meals and gas, plus something left over to stuff into the kitchen drawer I use as a bank. But as the tourist business slows in the summer heat, I sometimes leave work with only $20 in tips (the gross is higher, but servers share about 15 percent of their tips with the busboys and bartenders). With wages included, this amounts to about the minimum wage of $5.15 an hour. The sum in the drawer is piling up but at the present rate of accumulation will be more than $100 short of my rent when the end of the month comes around. Nor can I see any expenses to cut. True, I haven't gone the lentil stew route yet, but that's because I don't have a large cooking pot, potholders, or a ladle to stir with (which would cost a total of about $30 at Kmart, somewhat less at a thrift store), not to mention onions, carrots, and the indispensable bay leaf. I do make my lunch almost every day—usually some slow-burning, high-protein combo like frozen chicken patties with melted cheese on top and canned pinto beans on the side.

Dinner is at the Hearthside, which offers its employees a choice of BLT, fish sand-wich, or hamburger for only $2. The burger lasts longest, especially if it's heaped with gut-puckering jalapeños, but by midnight my stomach is growling again.

So unless I want to start using my car as a residence, I have to find a second 10 or an alternative job. I call all the hotels I'd filled out housekeeping applications at weeks ago—the Hyatt, Holiday Inn, Econo Lodge, HoJo's, Best Western, plus a half dozen locally run guest houses. Nothing. Then I start making the rounds again, wasting whole mornings waiting for some assistant manager to show up, even dipping into places so creepy that the front-desk clerk greets you from behind bullet-proof glass and sells pints of liquor over the counter. But either someone has exposed my real-life housekeeping habits—which are, shall we say, mellow—or I am at the wrong end of some infallible ethnic equation: Most, but by no means all, of the working housekeepers I see on my job searches are African Americans, Spanish-speaking, or refugees from the Central European post-Communist world, while servers are almost invariably white and monolingually English-speaking. When I finally get a positive response, I have been identified once again as server material. Jerry's—again, not the real name—which is part of a well-known national chain and physically attached here to another budget hotel, is ready to use me at once. The prospect is both exciting and terrifying because, with about the same number of tables and counter seats, Jerry's attracts three or four times the volume of customers as the gloomy old Hearthside.

Picture a fat person's hell, and I don't mean a place with no food. Instead there is 11 everything you might eat if eating had no bodily consequences—the cheese fries, the chicken-fried steaks, the fudge-laden desserts—only here every bite must be paid for, one way or another, in human discomfort. The kitchen is a cavern, a stomach leading to the lower intestine that is the garbage and dishwashing area, from which issue bizarre smells combining the edible and the offal: creamy carrion, pizza barf, and that unique and enigmatic Jerry's scent, citrus fart. The floor is slick with spills, forcing us to walk through the kitchen with tiny steps, like Susan McDougal in leg irons. Sinks everywhere are clogged with scraps of lettuce, decomposing lemon wedges, water-logged toast crusts. Put your hand down on any counter and you risk being stuck to it by the film of ancient syrup spills, and this is unfortunate because hands are utensils here, used for scooping up lettuce onto the salad plates, lifting out pie slices, and even moving hash browns from one plate to another. The regulation poster in the single unisex rest room admonishes us to wash our hands thoroughly, and even offers instructions for doing so, but there is always some vital substance missing—soap, paper towels, toilet paper—and I never found all three at once. You learn to stuff your pockets with napkins before going in there, and too bad about the customers, who must eat, although they don't realize it, almost literally out of our hands.

The break room summarizes the whole situation: There is none, because 12 there are no breaks at Jerry's. For six to eight hours in a row, you never sit except to pee. Actually, there are three folding chairs at a table immediately adjacent to the bathroom, but hardly anyone ever sits in this, the very rectum of the gastroarchi-tectural system. Rather, the function of the peri-toilet area is to house the ashtrays in which servers and dishwashers leave their cigarettes burning at all times, like votive candles, so they don't have to waste time lighting up again when they dash back here for a puff. Almost everyone smokes as if their pulmonary well-being depended on it—the multinational mélange of cooks; the dishwashers, who are all Czechs here; the servers, who are American natives—creating an atmosphere in which oxygen is only an occasional pollutant. My first morning at Jerry's, when the hypoglycemic shakes set in, I complain to one of my fellow servers that I don't understand how she can go so long without food. "Well, I don't understand how *you* can go so long without a cigarette," she responds in a tone of reproach. Because work is what you do for others; smoking is what you do for yourself. I don't know why the antismoking crusaders have never grasped the element of defiant self-nurturance that makes the habit so endearing to its victims—as if, in the American workplace, the only thing people have to call their own is the tumors they are nourishing and the spare moments they devote to feeding them.

Now, the Industrial Revolution is not an easy transition, especially, in my 13 experience, when you have to zip through it in just a couple of days. I have gone from craft work straight into the factory, from the air-conditioned morgue of the Hearthside directly into the flames. Customers arrive in human waves, sometimes disgorged fifty at a time from their tour buses, peckish and whiny. Instead of two "girls" on the floor at once, there can be as many as six of us running around in our brilliant pink-and-orange Hawaiian shirts. Conversations, either with customers or with fellow employees, seldom last more than twenty seconds at a time. On my first day, in fact, I am hurt by my sister servers' coldness. My mentor for the day is a supremely competent, emotionally uninflected twenty-three-year-old, and the others, who gossip a little among themselves about the real reason someone is out sick today and the size of the bail bond someone else has had to pay, ignore me completely. On my second day, I find out why. "Well, it's good to see *you* again," one of them says in greeting. "Hardly anyone comes back after the first day." I feel powerfully vindicated—a survivor—but it would take a long time, probably months, before I could hope to be accepted into this sorority.

I start out with the beautiful, heroic idea of handling the two jobs at once, and for 14 two days I almost do it: working the breakfast/lunch shift at Jerry's from 8:00 till 2:00, arriving at the Hearthside a few minutes late, at 2:10, and attempting to hold out until 10:00. In the few minutes I have between jobs, I pick up a spicy chicken sandwich at the Wendy's drive-through window, gobble it down in the car, and change from khaki slacks to black, from Hawaiian to rust-colored polo. There is a problem, though. When, during the 3:00–4:00 o'clock dead time, I finally sit down to wrap silver, my flesh seems to bond to the seat. I try to refuel with a purloined cup of clam chowder, as I've seen Gail and Joan do dozens of time, but Stu catches me and hisses "No *eating!*" although there's not a customer around to be offended by the sight of food making contact with a server's lips. So I tell Gail I'm going to quit, and she hugs me and says she might just follow me to Jerry's herself.

But the chances of this are minuscule. She has left the flop-house and her 15 annoying roommate and is back to living in her truck. But, guess what, she reports to me excitedly later that evening, Phillip has given her permission to park overnight in the hotel parking lot, as long as she keeps out of sight, and the parking lot should be totally safe since it's patrolled by a hotel security guard! With the Hearthside offering benefits like that, how could anyone think of leaving? This must be Phillip's theory, anyway. He accepts my resignation with a shrug, his main concern being that I return my two polo shirts and aprons.

Gail would have triumphed at Jerry's, I'm sure, but for me it's a crash course in 16 exhaustion management. Years ago, the kindly fry cook who trained me to waitress at a Los Angeles truck stop used to say: Never make an unnecessary trip; if you don't have to walk fast, walk slow; if you don't have to walk, stand. But at Jerry's the effort of distinguishing necessary from unnecessary and urgent from whenever would itself be too much of an energy drain. The only thing to do is to treat each shift as a one-time-only emergency: You've got fifty starving people out there, lying scattered on the battlefield, so get out there and feed them! Forget that you will have to do this again tomorrow, forget that you will have to be alert enough to dodge the drunks on the drive home tonight—just burn, burn, burn! Ideally, at some point you enter what servers call a "rhythm" and psychologists term a "flow state," where signals pass from the sense organs directly to the muscles, bypassing the cerebral cortex, and a Zen-like emptiness sets in. I'm on a 2:00–10:00 P.M. shift now, and a male server from the morning shift tells me about the time he "pulled a triple"—three shifts in a row, all the way around the clock—and then got off and had a drink and met this girl, and maybe he shouldn't tell me this, but they had sex right then and there and it was like *beautiful*.

But there's another capacity of the neuromuscular system, which is pain. I start 17 tossing back drugstore-brand ibuprofens as if they were vitamin C, four before each shift, because an old mouse-related repetitive-stress injury in my upper back has come back to full-spasm strength, thanks to the tray carrying. In my ordinary life, this level of disability might justify a day of ice packs and stretching. Here I comfort myself with the Aleve commercial where the cute blue-collar guy asks: If you quit after working four hours, what would your boss say? And the not-so-cute blue-collar guy, who's lugging a metal beam on his back, answers: He'd fire me, that's what. But fortunately, the commercial tells us, we workers can exert the same kind of authority over our painkillers that our bosses exert over us. If Tylenol doesn't want to work for more than four hours, you just fire its ass and switch to Aleve.

True, I take occasional breaks from this life, going home now and then to catch 18 up on email and for conjugal visits (though I am careful to "pay" for everything I eat here, at $5 for a dinner, which I put in a jar), seeing *The Truman Show* with friends and letting them buy my ticket. And I still have those what-am-I-doing-here moments at work, when I get so homesick for the printed word that I obsessively reread the six-page menu. But as the days go by, my old life is beginning to look exceedingly strange. The emails and phone messages addressed to my former self come from a distant race of people with exotic concerns and far too much time on their hands. The neighborly market I used to cruise for produce now looks forbiddingly like a Manhattan yuppie emporium. And when I sit down one morning in my real home to pay bills from my past life, I am dazzled by the two- and three-figure sums owed to outfits like Club Body Tech and Amazon.com.

Management at Jerry's is generally calmer and more "professional" than at the 19 Hearthside, with two exceptions. One is Joy, a plump, blowsy woman in her early thirties who once kindly devoted several minutes of her time to instructing me in the correct one-handed method of tray carrying but whose moods change disconcertingly from shift to shift and even within one. The other is B.J., aka B.J. the Bitch, whose contribution is to stand by the kitchen counter and yell, "Nita, your order's up, move it!" or "Barbara, didn't you see you've got another table out there? Come *on*, girl!" Among other things, she is hated for having replaced the whipped cream squirt cans with big plastic whipped-cream-filled baggies that have to be squeezed with both hands—because, reportedly, she saw or thought she saw employees trying to inhale the propellant gas from the squirt cans, in the hope that it might be nitrous oxide. On my third night, she pulls me aside abruptly and brings her face so close that it looks like she's planning to butt me with her forehead. But instead of saying "You're fired," she says, "You're doing fine." The only trouble is I'm spending time chatting with customers: "That's how they're getting you." Furthermore I am letting them "run me," which means harassment by sequential demands: You bring the catsup and they decide they want extra Thousand Island; you bring that and they announce they now need a side of fries, and so on into distraction. Finally she tells me not to take her wrong. She tries to say things in a nice way, but "you get into a mode, you know, because everything has to move so fast."[2]

I mumble thanks for the advice, feeling like I've just been stripped naked by the   20
crazed enforcer of some ancient sumptuary law: No chatting for *you*, girl. No fancy service ethic allowed for the serfs. Chatting with customers is for the good-looking young college-educated servers in the downtown carpaccio and ceviche joints, the kids who can make $70–$100 a night. What had I been thinking? My job is to move orders from tables to kitchen and then trays from kitchen to tables. Customers are in fact the major obstacle to the smooth transformation of information into food and food into money—they are, in short, the enemy. And the painful thing is that I'm beginning to see it this way myself. There are the traditional asshole types—frat boys who down multiple Buds and then make a fuss because the steaks are so emaciated and the fries so sparse—as well as the variously impaired—due to age, diabetes, or literacy issues—who require patient nutritional counseling. The worst, for some reason, are the Visible Christians—like the ten-person table, all jolly and sanctified after Sunday night service, who run me mercilessly and then leave me $1 on a $92 bill. Or the guy with the crucifixion T-shirt (SOMEONE TO LOOK UP TO) who complains that his baked potato is too hard and his iced tea too icy (I cheerfully fix both) and leaves no tip at all. As a general rule, people wearing crosses or WWJD? ("What Would Jesus Do?") buttons look at us disapprovingly no matter what we do, as if they were confusing waitressing with Mary Magdalene's original profession.

I make friends, over time, with the other "girls" who work my shift: Nita, the   21
tattooed twenty-something who taunts us by going around saying brightly, "Have we started making money yet?" Ellen, whose teenage son cooks on the graveyard shift and who once managed a restaurant in Massachusetts but won't try out for management here because she prefers being a "common worker" and not "ordering people around." Easy-going fiftyish Lucy, with the raucous laugh, who limps toward the end of the shift because of something that has gone wrong with her leg, the exact nature of which cannot be determined without health insurance. We talk about the usual girl things—men, children, and the sinister allure of Jerry's chocolate peanut-butter cream pie—though no one, I notice, ever brings up anything potentially expensive, like shopping or movies. As at the Hearthside, the only recreation ever referred to is partying, which requires little more than some beer, a joint, and a few close friends. Still, no one is homeless, or cops to it anyway, thanks usually to a working husband or

boyfriend. All in all, we form a reliable mutual-support group: If one of us is feeling sick or overwhelmed, another one will "bev" a table or even carry trays for her. If one of us is off sneaking a cigarette or a pee, the others will do their best to conceal her absence from the enforcers of corporate rationality.[3]

But my saving human connection—my oxytocin receptor, as it were—is George, 22 the nineteen-year-old Czech dishwasher who has been in this country exactly one week. We get talking when he asks me, tortuously, how much cigarettes cost at Jerry's. I do my best to explain that they cost over a dollar more here than at a regular store and suggest that he just take one from the half-filled packs that are always lying around on the break table. But that would be unthinkable. Except for the one tiny earring signaling his allegiance to some vaguely alternative point of view, George is a perfect straight arrow—crew-cut, hardworking, and hungry for eye contact. "Czech Republic," I ask, "or Slovakia?" and he seems delighted that I know the difference. "Vaclav Havel," I try, "Velvet Revolution, Frank Zappa?" "Yes, yes, 1989," he says, and I realize that for him this is already history.

My project is to teach George English. "How are you today, George?" I say at the 23 start of each shift. "I am good, and how are you today, Barbara?" I learn that he is not paid by Jerry's but by the "agent" who shipped him over—$5 an hour, with the agent getting the dollar or so difference between that and what Jerry's pays dishwashers. I learn also that he shares an apartment with a crowd of other Czech "dishers," as he calls them, and that he cannot sleep until one of them goes off for his shift, leaving a vacant bed. We are having one of our ESL sessions late one afternoon when B.J. catches us at it and orders "Joseph" to take up the rubber mats on the floor near the dishwashing sinks and mop underneath. "I thought your name was George," I say loud enough for B.J. to hear as she strides off back to the counter. Is she embarrassed? Maybe a little, because she greets me back at the counter with "George, Joseph—there are so many of them!" I say nothing, neither nodding nor smiling, and for this I am punished later, when I think I am ready to go and she announces that I need to roll fifty more sets of silverware, and isn't it time I mixed up a fresh four-gallon batch of blue-cheese dressing? May you grow old in this place, B.J., is the curse I beam out at her when I am finally permitted to leave. May the syrup spills glue your feet to the floor.

I make the decision to move closer to Key West. First, because of the drive. 24 Second and third, also because of the drive: Gas is eating up $4–$5 a day, and although Jerry's is as high-volume as you can get, the tips average only 10 percent, and not just for a newbie like me. Between the base pay of $2.15 an hour and the obligation to share tips with the busboys and dishwashers, we're averaging only about $7.50 an hour. Then there is the $30 I had to spend on the regulation tan slacks worn by Jerry's servers—a setback it could take weeks to absorb. (I had combed the town's two downscale department stores hoping for something cheaper but decided in the end that these marked-down Dockers, originally $49, were more likely to survive a daily washing.) Of my fellow servers, everyone who lacks a working husband or boyfriend seems to have a second job: Nita does something at a computer eight hours a day; another welds. Without the forty-five-minute commute, I can picture myself working two jobs and still having the time to shower between them.

So I take the $500 deposit I have coming from my landlord, the $400 I have 25 earned toward the next month's rent, plus the $200 reserved for emergencies, and use the $1,100 to pay the rent and deposit on trailer number 46 in the Overseas Trailer Park, a mile from the cluster of budget hotels that constitute Key West's version of an industrial park. Number 46 is about eight feet in width and shaped like a barbell inside, with a narrow region—because of the sink and the stove—separating the bedroom from what might optimistically be called the "living" area, with its two-person table and half-sized couch. The bathroom is so small my knees rub against the shower stall when I sit on the toilet, and you can't just leap out of the bed, you have to climb down to the foot of it in order to find a patch of floor space to stand on. Outside, I am within a few yards of a liquor store, a bar that advertises "free beer tomorrow," a convenience store, and a Burger King—but no supermarket or, alas, Laundromat. By reputation, the Overseas park is a nest of crime and crack, and I am hoping at least for some vibrant multicultural street life. But desolation rules night and day, except for a thin stream of pedestrians heading for their jobs at the Sheraton or the 7-Eleven. There are not exactly people here but what amounts to canned labor, being preserved between shifts from the heat.

In line with my reduced living conditions, a new form of ugliness arises at Jerry's. 26 First we are confronted—via an announcement on the computers through which we input orders—with the new rule that the hotel bar, the Driftwood, is henceforth off-limits to restaurant employees. The culprit, I learn through the grapevine, is the ultraefficient twenty-three-year-old who trained me—another trailer home dweller and a mother of three. Something had set her off one morning, so she slipped out for a nip and returned to the floor impaired. The restriction mostly hurts Ellen, whose habit it is to free her hair from its rubber band and drop by the Driftwood for a couple of Zins before heading home at the end of her shift, but all of us feel the chill. Then the next day, when I go for straws, I find the dry-storage room locked. It's never been locked before; we go in and out of it all day—for napkins, jelly containers, Styrofoam cups for takeout. Vic, the portly assistant manager who opens it for me, explains that he caught one of the dishwashers attempting to steal something and, unfortunately, the miscreant will be with us until a replacement can be found—hence the locked door. I neglect to ask what he had been trying to steal but Vic tells me who he is—the kid with the buzz cut and the earring, you know, he's back there right now.

I wish I could say I rushed back and confronted George to get his side of the story. 27 I wish I could say I stood up to Vic and insisted that George be given a translator and allowed to defend himself or announced that I'd find a lawyer who'd handle the case pro bono. At the very least I should have testified as to the kid's honesty. The mystery to me is that there's not much worth stealing in the dry-storage room, at least not in any fenceable quantity: "Is Gyorgi here, and am having 200—maybe 250—catsup packets. What do you say?" My guess is that he had taken—if he had taken anything at all—some Saltines or a can of cherry pie mix and that the motive for taking it was hunger.

So why didn't I intervene? Certainly not because I was held back by the kind of 28 moral paralysis that can mask as journalistic objectivity. On the contrary, something new—something loathsome and servile—had infected me, along with the kitchen odors that I could still sniff on my bra when I finally undressed at night. In real life I am moderately brave, but plenty of brave people shed their courage in POW camps, and maybe something similar goes on in the infinitely more congenial milieu of the low-wage American workplace. Maybe, in a month or two more at Jerry's, I might have regained my crusading spirit. Then again, in a month or two I might have turned into a different person altogether—say, the kind of person who would have turned George in.

But this is not something I was slated to find out. When my monthlong plunge 29 into poverty was almost over, I finally landed my dream job—housekeeping. I did this by walking into the personnel office of the only place I figured I might have some credibility, the hotel attached to Jerry's, and confiding urgently that I had to have a second job if I was to pay my rent and, no, it couldn't be front-desk clerk. "All *right*," the personnel lady fairly spits, "so it's *housekeeping*," and marches me back to meet Millie, the housekeeping manager, a tiny, frenetic Hispanic woman who greets me as "babe" and hands me a pamphlet emphasizing the need for a positive attitude. The pay is $6.10 an hour, and the hours are nine in the morning till "whenever," which I am hoping can be defined as a little before two. I don't have to ask about health insurance once I meet Carlotta, the middle-aged African American woman who will be training me. Carlie, as she tells me to call her, is missing all of her top front teeth.

On that first day of housekeeping and last day—although I don't yet know it's 30 the last—of my life as a low-wage worker in Key West, Carlie is in a foul mood. We have been given nineteen rooms to clean, most of them "checkouts," as opposed to "stay-overs," and requiring the whole enchilada of bed stripping, vacuuming, and bathroom scrubbing. When one of the rooms that had been listed as a stay-over turns out to be a checkout, she calls Millie to complain, but of course to no avail. "So make up the motherfucker," she orders me, and I do the beds while she sloshes around the bathroom. For four hours without a break I strip and remake beds, taking about four and a half minutes per queen-sized bed, which I could get down to three if there were any reason to. We try to avoid vacuuming by picking up the larger specks by hand, but often there is nothing to do but drag the monstrous vacuum cleaner—it weighs about thirty pounds—off our cart and try to wrestle it around the floor. Sometimes Carlie hands me the squirt bottle of "Bam" (an acronym for something that begins, ominously, with "butyric"—the rest of it has been worn off the label) and lets me do the bathrooms. No service ethic challenges me here to new heights of performance. I just concentrate on removing the pubic hairs from the bathtubs, or at least the dark ones that I can see.

I had looked forward to the breaking-and-entering aspect of cleaning the 31 stay-overs, the chance to examine the secret physical existence of strangers. But the contents of the rooms are always banal and surprisingly neat—zipped-up shaving kits, shoes lined up against the wall (there are no closets), flyers for snorkeling trips, maybe an empty wine bottle or two. It is the TV that keeps us going, from Jerry to Sally to *Hawaii Five-0* and then on to the soaps. If there's something especially arresting, like "Won't Take No for an Answer" on Jerry, we sit down on the edge of a bed and giggle for a moment, as if this were a pajama party instead of a terminally dead-end job. The soaps are the best, and Carlie turns the volume up full blast so she won't miss anything from the bathroom or while the vacuum is on. In Room 503, Marcia confronts Jeff about Lauren. In 505, Lauren taunts poor cheated-on Marcia. In 511, Helen offers Amanda $10,000 to stop seeing Eric, prompting Carlie to emerge from the bathroom to study Amanda's troubled face. "You take it, girl," she advises. "I would for sure."

The tourists' rooms that we clean and, beyond them, the far more expensively 32 appointed interiors in the soaps begin after a while to merge. We have entered a better world—a world of comfort where every day is a day off, waiting to be filled with sexual intrigue. We are only gate-crashers in this fantasy, however, forced to pay for our presence with backaches and perpetual thirst. The mirrors, and there are far too many of them in hotel rooms, contain the kind of person you would normally find pushing a shopping cart down a city street—bedraggled, dressed in a damp hotel polo shirt two sizes too large, and with sweat dribbling down her chin like drool. I am enormously relieved when Carlie announces a half-hour meal break, but my appetite fades when I see that the bag of hot dog rolls she has been carrying around on our cart is not trash salvaged from a checkout but what she has brought for her lunch.

Between the TV and the fact that I'm in no position, as a first dayer, to launch 33 new topics of conversation, I don't learn much about Carlie except that she hurts, and in more than one way. She moves slowly about her work, muttering something about joint pain, and this is probably going to doom her, since the young immigrant housekeepers—Polish and Salvadoran—like to polish off their rooms by two in the afternoon, while she drags the work out till six. It doesn't make any sense to hurry, she observes, when you're being paid by the hour. Already, management has brought in a woman to do what sounds like time-motion studies, and there's talk about switching to paying by the room.[4] She broods, too, about all the little evidences of disrespect that come her way, and not only from management. "They don't care about us," she tells me of the hotel guests; in fact, they don't notice us at all unless something gets stolen from a room—"then they're all over you." We're eating our lunch side by side in the break room when a white guy in a maintenance uniform walks by and Carlie calls out, "Hey you," in a friendly way, "what's your name?"

"Peter Pan," he says, his back already to us.   34

"That wasn't funny," Carlie says, turning to me. "That was no kind of answer. 35 Why did he have to be funny like that?" I venture that he has an attitude, and she nods as if that were an acute diagnosis. "Yeah, he got a attitude all right."

"Maybe he's a having a bad day," I elaborate, not because I feel any obligation to 36 defend the white race but because her face is so twisted with hurt.

When I request permission to leave at about 3:30, another housekeeper warns 37 me that no one has so far succeeded in combining housekeeping with serving at Jerry's: "Some kid did it once for five days, and you're no kid." With that helpful information in mind, I rush back to number 46, down four Advils (the name brand this time), shower, stooping to fit into the stall, and attempt to compose myself for the oncoming shift. So much for what Marx termed the "reproduction of labor power," meaning the things a worker has to do just so she'll be ready to labor again. The only unforeseen obstacle to the smooth transition from job to job is that my tan Jerry's slacks, which had looked reasonably clean by 40-watt bulb last night when I hand washed my Hawaiian shirt, prove by daylight to be mottled with catsup and ranch-dressing stains. I spend most of my hour-long break between jobs attempting to remove the edible portions of the slacks with a sponge and then drying them over the hood of my car in the sun.

I can do this two-job thing, is my theory, if I can drink enough caffeine and 38 avoid getting distracted by George's ever more obvious suffering.[5] The first few days after the alleged theft, he seemed not to understand the trouble he was in, and our chirpy little conversations had continued. But the last couple of shifts he's been list-less and unshaven, and tonight he looks like the ghost we all know him to be, with dark halfmoons hanging from his eyes. At one point, when I am briefly immobilized by the task of filling little paper cups with sour cream for baked potatoes, he comes over and looks as if he'd like to explore the limits of our shared vocabulary, but I am called to the floor for a table. I resolve to give him all my tips that night, and to hell with the experiment in low-wage money management. At eight, Ellen and I grab a snack together standing at the mephitic end of the kitchen counter, but I can only manage two or three mozzarella sticks, and lunch had been a mere handful of McNuggets. I am not tired at all, I assure myself, though it may be that there is simply no more "I" left to do the tiredness monitoring. What I would see if I were more alert to the situation is that the forces of destruction are already massing against me. There is only one cook on duty, a young man named Jesus ("Hay-Sue," that is), and he is new to the job. And there is Joy, who shows up to take over in the middle of the shift dressed in high heels and a long, clingy white dress and fuming as if she'd just been stood up in some cocktail bar.

Then it comes, the perfect storm. Four of my tables fill up at once. Four tables 39 is nothing for me now, but only so long as they are obligingly staggered. As I bev table 27, tables 25, 28, and 24 are watching enviously. As I bev 25, 24 glowers because their bevs haven't even been ordered. Twenty-eight is four yuppyish types, meaning every-thing on the side and agonizing instructions as to the chicken Caesars. Twenty-five is a middle-aged black couple who complain, with some justice, that the iced tea isn't fresh and the tabletop is sticky. But table 24 is the meteorological event of the century: ten British tourists who seem to have made the decision to absorb the American experience entirely by mouth. Here everyone has at least two drinks—iced tea *and* milk shake, Michelob *and* water (with lemon slice in the water, please)—and a huge, promiscuous orgy of breakfast specials, mozz sticks, chicken strips, quesadillas, burgers with cheese and without, sides of hash browns with cheddar, with onions, with gravy, seasoned fries, plain fries, banana splits. Poor Jesus! Poor me! Because when I arrive with their first tray of food—after three prior trips just to refill bevs—Princess Di refuses to eat her chicken strips with her pancake and sausage special since, as she now reveals, the strips were meant to be an appetizer. Maybe the others would have accepted their meals, but Di, who is deep into her third Michelob, insists that everything else go back while they work on their starters. Meanwhile, the yuppies are waving me down for more decaf and the black couple looks ready to summon the NAACP.

Much of what happens next is lost in the fog of war. Jesus starts going under. 40 The little printer in front of him is spewing out orders faster than he can rip them off, much less produce the meals. A menacing restlessness rises from the tables, all of which are full. Even the invincible Ellen is ashen from stress. I take table 24 their reheated main courses, which they immediately reject as either too cold or fossilized by the microwave. When I return to the kitchen with their trays (three trays in three trips) Joy confronts me with arms akimbo: "What *is* this?" She means the food—the plates of rejected pancakes, hash browns in assorted flavors, toasts, burgers, sausages, eggs. "Uh, scrambled with cheddar," I try, "and that's—" "*No*," she screams in my face, "is it a traditional, a super-scramble, an eye-opener?" I pretend to study my check for a clue, but entropy has been up to its tricks, not only on the plates but in my head, and I have to admit that the original order is beyond reconstruction. "You don't know an eye-opener from a traditional?" she demands in outrage. All I know, in fact, is that my legs have lost interest in the current venture and have announced their intention to fold. I am saved by a yuppie (mercifully not one of mine) who chooses this moment to charge into the kitchen to bellow that his food is twenty-five minutes late. Joy screams at him to get the hell out of her kitchen, *please*, and then turns on Jesus in a fury, hurling an empty tray across the room for emphasis.

I leave. I don't walk out, I just leave. I don't finish my side work or pick up my   41
credit card tips, if any, at the cash register or, of course, ask Joy's permission to go. And the surprising thing is that you *can* walk out without permission, that the door opens, that the thick tropical night air parts to let me pass, that my car is still parked where I left it. There is no vindication in this exit, no fuck-you surge of relief, just an overwhelming dank sense of failure pressing down on me and the entire parking lot. I had gone into this venture in the spirit of science, to test a mathematical proposition, but somewhere along the line, in the tunnel vision imposed by long shifts and relentless concentration, it became a test of myself, and clearly I have failed. Not only had I flamed out as a housekeeper/server, I had forgotten to give George my tips, and, for reasons perhaps best known to hardworking, generous people like Gail and Ellen, this hurts. I don't cry, but I am in a position to realize, for the first time in many years, that the tear ducts are still there and still capable of doing their job.

When I moved out of the trailer park, I gave the key to number 46 to Gail and   42
arranged for my deposit to be transferred to her. She told me that Joan was still living in her van and that Stu had been fired from the Hearthside. According to the most up-to-date rumors, the drug he ordered from the restaurant was crack and he was caught dipping into the cash register to pay for it. I never found out what happened to George.

READING FOR CONTENT

1. Explain why affordable housing is the principal problem for low-wage workers.
2. Paraphrase the passage (paragraph 18) in which Ehrenreich contrasts her life as a low-wage worker with her middle-class life.
3. Did any of the working conditions Ehrenreich describes shock you? Give some examples.
4. In your own words, explain why Ehrenreich did not intervene on behalf of the dishwasher, George.
5. Ehrenreich describes a number of humiliations she was subjected to as a low-wage worker. Cite some examples.

READING FOR GENRE, ORGANIZATION, AND STYLISTIC FEATURES

1. Ehrenreich breathes life into her story by including rich, vivid detail. Divide the class into small groups, each of which is responsible for a certain number of pages of the text. Identify details and explain why they are effective.
2. Reread paragraph 11 and comment on the effectiveness of the imagery Ehrenreich uses to describe Jerry's Restaurant.

3. What function do Ehrenreich's footnotes serve?

4. Throughout the selection, Ehrenreich uses humor to convey some serious thoughts to the reader. Cite five to ten examples.

READING FOR RHETORICAL CONTEXT

1. Whom do you think Ehrenreich visualizes as her audience? What role does she assume in relation to these readers?

2. How would you describe Ehrenreich's tone: complacency? moral outrage? or something in between? Explain.

WRITING ASSIGNMENTS

1. Write an essay in which you compare and contrast your work experiences with those of Ehrenreich and her coworkers. Consider questions such as the following:
   What types of obstacles did you have to overcome?
   How were you treated by your boss?
   Did you get along with your coworkers?
   Was your workplace environment satisfactory and safe?
   Did you experience any type of class bigotry or discrimination?
   Were your working conditions reasonable?

2. Ehrenreich's experiences take place from 1998 to 2000, years of unprecedented prosperity in the United States. What does this say about the growing economic chasm between the rich and the poor that the following article from *The Economist* discusses? Respond in essay form.

3. In "The War Against the Poor Instead of Programs to End Poverty," Herbert Gans writes, "People who have not been poor themselves do not understand how much of what the poor do is poverty-related" (paragraph 25). What insights did you gain from Ehrenreich's experiences? Write an essay in response.

Notes

1. I could find no statistics on the number of employed people living in cars or vans, but according to a 1997 report of the National Coalition for the Homeless, "Myths and Facts about Homelessness," nearly one-fifth of all homeless people (in twenty-nine cities across the nation) are employed in full- or part-time jobs.

2. In *Workers in a Lean World: Unions in the International Economy* (Verso, 1997), Kim Moody cites studies finding an increase in stress-related workplace injuries and illness between the mid-1980s and the early 1990s. He argues that rising stress levels reflect a new system of "management by stress" in which workers in a variety of industries are being squeezed to extract maximum productivity, to the detriment of their health.

3. Until April 1998, there was no federally mandated right to bathroom breaks. According to Marc Linder and Ingrid Nygaard, authors of *Void Where Prohibited: Rest Breaks and the Right to Urinate on Company Time* (Cornell University Press, 1997), "The right to rest and void at work is not high on the list of social or political causes supported by professional or executive employees, who enjoy personal workplace liberties that millions of factory workers can only dream about.... While we were dismayed to discover that workers lacked an acknowledged right to void at work, [the workers] were amazed by outsiders' naïve belief that their employers would permit them to perform this basic bodily function when necessary.... A factory worker, not allowed a break for six-hour stretches, voided into pads worn inside her uniform; and a

kindergarten teacher in a school without aides had to take all twenty children with her to the bathroom and line them up outside the stall door while she voided."

4. A few weeks after I left, I heard ads on the radio for housekeeping jobs at this hotel at the amazing rate of "up to $9 an hour." When I inquired, I found out that the hotel had indeed started paying by the room, and I suspect that Carlie, if she lasted, was still making the equivalent of $6 an hour or quite a bit less.

5. In 1996 the number of persons holding two or more jobs averaged 7.8 million, or 6.2 percent of the workforce. It was about the same rate for men and for women (6.1 versus 6.2). About two-thirds of multiple jobholders work one job full-time and the other part-time. Only a heroic minority—4 percent of men and 2 percent of women—work two full-time jobs simultaneously (John F. Stinson Jr., "New Data on Multiple Jobholding Available from the CPS," *Monthly Labor Review*, March 1997).

Middle of the Class

The Economist

The Economist is a weekly magazine published in England by The Economist Group. Begun in 1843 and employing many famous editors throughout the years, the magazine is known for its international perspective on links between economic issues, current affairs, business, finance, science, technology and the arts. Most articles are published with no authorial byline.

PREREADING

Scan the article for its topical subdivisions. What do the headings "Equality of Opportunity is Under Threat," "A Harder Climb," and "The Trouble with Being Poor" lead you to expect about its argument? Because the magazine originates as a British publication, what might you expect about its attitude toward society in the United States—which professes to be class free? Freewrite your responses to these questions.

Equality of Opportunity Is Under Threat

For the past three years, the most successful shows on American television have been   1
American Idol and *The Apprentice*. This spring, millions tuned in to watch Carrie Underwood, a 21-year-old country-and-western singer from small-town Oklahoma, win the entertainment contest and to see Bill Rancic, who put himself through university by cleaning boats, land a six-figure salary as Donald Trump's chosen sidekick. The success of these shows in America testifies to the endurance and popularity of the American Dream—the idea that anything is possible if you work at it hard enough.

America's founding document declares all men to be created equal. From   2
Benjamin Franklin, the 15th child of a candlemaker, to Bill Clinton, whose mother

"Middle of the Class." *The Economist* 376.8435 (14 July 2005): 12. Print. © The Economist Newspaper Limited, London, July 14, 2005.

was widowed before he was born, the American creed proclaims that the ladder of success can be climbed by all. A decline in social mobility would run counter to Americans' deepest beliefs about their country. Unfortunately, that is what seems to be happening. Class is reappearing in a new form.

For the quarter-century after the second world war, income growth in America   3
was fairly evenly spread. According to a study by the Economic Policy Institute (EPI), the poorest fifth of the population saw its income increase by as much as the next-poorest fifth, and so on in equal steps to the top. But in the past quarter-century, the rich have been doing dramatically better than the less well off. Since 1979, median family incomes have risen by 18% but the incomes of the top 1% have gone up by 200%. In 1970, according to the Census Bureau, the bottom fifth received 5.4% of America's total national income and the richest fifth got 40.9%. Twenty-five years later, the share of the bottom fifth had fallen to 4.4% but that of the top fifth had risen to 46.5%.

A Harder Climb

This makes America unusual. Thomas Piketty and Emmanuel Saez examined the   4
incomes of the top 0.1% of people in America, France and Britain from 1913 to 1998. The fortunes of the three countries' super-rich kept fairly closely in step for most of the 20th century, until America began to diverge in the late 1970s. Now the top 0.1% of Americans earn two or three times as much as their peers in Britain and France. If America is a ladder, the rungs have been moved further apart.

Perhaps Americans think the rich deserve their success. They certainly work   5
more than they used to. In the 1970s, the top 10% worked fewer hours than the bottom 10%; now the reverse is true. Back in 1929, 70% of the income of the extremely rich (the top 0.01%) came from capital (dividends, rent and interest). Now, 80% comes from wages and stock options, which is earned income of a sort.

Or perhaps what really matters is how the poor are doing in absolute terms rather   6
than in relation to the wealthy. Americans' average salaries have risen over the past 30 years, though admittedly not by much. A far smaller share of the population lives in poverty now than in the supposedly golden age of equality in the 1950s (12% compared with 22%). Moreover, a surge of immigrants on minimum wages tends to bring down the average: home-grown Americans are probably better off than the figures suggest. The rich have not got richer at the expense of the poor. The rising tide has lifted dinghies as well as yachts.

Anyway, what Americans seem to mind about most is equality of opportunity—   7
and people do not feel there is any less of it now than there used to be. Some 80% (a higher proportion than in the 1980s) think it is possible to start out poor, work hard and become rich. A poll for the *New York Times* found that twice as many Americans reckon that their chances of moving up a notch have improved over the past 30 years than think their chances have gone down. Most Americans say their standard of living is higher than that of their parents, and that their children will do better than they are doing.

So, on the face of it, rising inequality is not affecting the optimism and ambition   8
of average Americans, and these are what matter to the country's entrepreneurial spirit and social cohesion. But there are three big problems with this rosy view. The first is that America has never been as socially mobile as Americans like to believe. According

to a long-term research project carried out at the University of Michigan, led by Gary Solon, America's score on social mobility is not particularly high or low, but middling.

That does not sound too bad. But it means that, if you are among the poorest 5% of the population, your chances of achieving an average income are only one in six. If you are among the poorest 1%, they become very dim indeed. Moreover—and this was the most surprising thing about the study—despite America's more flexible labour markets, social mobility there is no longer greater than in supposedly class-ridden Europe, and if anything it seems to be declining. 9

A study by Katharine Bradbury and Jane Katz for the Federal Reserve Bank of Boston found that in the 1970s, 65% of people changed their social position (that is, moved out of the income bracket in which they had started the decade). In the 1990s, only 60% did. Not a huge change, but consistent with Mr Solon's study showing that the correlation between parents' and children's income is even closer now than it was in the 1980s. The authors also found decreasing amounts of social mobility at the top and the bottom. This is squeezing the middle class. Americans may be sorting themselves into two more stable groups, haves and have-nots. This is the same trend that geographical mobility has been encouraging. Decreasing mobility may one day come to erode Americans' faith in the fairness of their economy. 10

The second reason for pessimism is that mobility may continue to decline because it is rooted in fundamental changes to the economy. These explain both the big rise in income inequality and the smaller shift in social mobility. Over the past 25 years, globalisation has increased rewards for intellectual skills, pushing up the value of a degree. The income gap between college graduates and those without university degrees doubled between 1979 and 1997. 11

This has gone hand in hand with changes in the nature of work. It used to be possible to start at the bottom of a big firm and work your way up. But America's corporate giants have got rid of their old hierarchies. Lifetime employment is at an end, and managers hop from job to job. That makes a degree essential. In the 1930s and 1940s, only half of all American chief executives had a college degree. Now almost all of them do, and 70% also have a higher degree, such as an MBA. People with a university degree are now more likely to move up an income bracket than those without. This is a big change since the 1970s, when income rises were distributed equally across all educational levels. America is becoming a stratified society based on education: a meritocracy. 12

But what if education itself becomes stratified? Historically, America's education system has been the main avenue for upward mobility. Mass secondary education supplied the workforce of the world's most successful industrial economy in the late 19th century; mass university education did the same for the period of American economic dominance after the second world war. But now, worries Lawrence Summers, the president of Harvard University, what had been engines of social mobility risk becoming brakes. 13

At secondary-school level, American education is financed largely by local property taxes. Naturally, places with big houses paying larger property taxes have schools with more resources. At university level, the rise in the cost of education has taken Ivy League universities out of the reach of most middle-class and poor families. The median income of families with children at Harvard is $150,000. The wealthy have always dominated elite schools, but their representation is rising. Between 1976 14 and 1995, according to one study, students from the richest quarter of the population increased their share of places at America's elite universities from 39% to 50%.

Even outside elite schools, students from poor backgrounds are becoming rarer. The budget squeeze on states in 2001–04 forced them to increase fees at state colleges, traditionally the places where the children of less wealthy parents went. Those children also face increasing competition from richer kids squeezed out of the Ivy League. As a result, a student from the top income quarter is six times more likely to get a BA than someone from the bottom quarter. American schools seem to be reinforcing educational differences rather than reducing them.

The third reason for gloom is perhaps the most worrying. It is the possibility that, as Isabel Sawhill of the Brookings Institution argues, your chances of a good education, good job and good prospects—in other words, of moving upwards—are partly determined by family behaviour. On this view, the rich really are different, and not just because they have more money; moreover, these differences are becoming embedded in the structure of the family itself. Class stratification, in other words, is more than a matter of income or inherited wealth.

College graduates tend to marry college graduates. Both go out to work, so in the households of the most educated the returns to a university education are doubled. College-educated women are also postponing children for the sake of their careers. On average, they have their first child at 30, five years later than in the 1970s and eight years later than their contemporaries who have not been to college.

The Trouble with Being Poor

At the bottom of the heap, you see the opposite: women have children younger, often out of wedlock and without a job. True, out-of-wedlock births are falling and welfare reform has increased the chances of mothers holding down jobs, but the gap is still vast. If, as Ms Sawhill argues, the key to upward mobility is finishing your education, having a job and getting and staying married, then the rich start with advantages beyond money.

This does not mean that America's meritocracy is a fake, or that nothing can be done. The country faced a similar rise in inequality in the early 20th century and rallied against it. President Roosevelt sought to save American capitalism from its own excesses so that "malefactors of great wealth" would not become a hereditary aristocracy.

Today, policy changes, such as reforming the way schools are financed, or giving federal help to poorer college students, would lessen social inequality. But for that to happen, American politicians and the public must first acknowledge that there is a problem. At the moment, they do not.

READING FOR CONTENT

1. The article points out that average Americans do not seem alarmed by rising levels of inequality in the United States. What three problems does the article expose about this attitude in paragraphs 8, 11, and 16? Summarize these problems in your own words.

2. Summarize the threat to social mobility presented by changes in university and secondary-school education discussed in paragraphs 11–15.

READING FOR GENRE, ORGANIZATION, AND STYLISTIC FEATURES

1. The genre of economic analysis relies upon statistics and their interpretation. How does the article interpret its statistics in paragraphs 3, 6, 9, 12, and 15?

2. How do the headings before paragraphs 1, 4, and 18 organize the argument?

3. How do the statistics in paragraphs 4, 5, 7, 10, 11, and 14 explain features of American society for an international audience? Do these statistics surprise you?

READING FOR RHETORICAL CONTEXT

1. *The Economist* is a British publication, but it addresses its articles to an international readership. How does paragraph 3 use an elementary lesson in American history to prepare readers for its argument that in the United States, class is reappearing in a new form?

2. How does paragraph 20 use an appeal to American politicians and the public to conclude the argument about the threat to equality of opportunity in recent U.S. history?

WRITING ASSIGNMENTS

1. Write a letter to the editor of *The Economist* explaining that, as a North American college student, you agree or disagree with the article's assessment of the role that class differences play in American education. Use statistics given in the article to defend your argument even if you arrive at conclusions that differ from the ones presented in the article.

2. Write a letter to the administration of your college about the problems raised by this article. Draw upon your own experience at the college to illustrate these problems and formulate some provisional advice about what the college can do to resolve some of them before they get out of hand.

■ ■ ■ ■ ■ ■ ■ ■ ■ ■ ■

When Shelter Feels Like a Prison

Charmion Browne

When Charmion Browne wrote this article, she was a senior at Cornell University.

PREREADING

In an article published in the *New York Times* on March 24, 2002, Jennifer Egan writes, "Today, families make up 75 percent of New York's homeless-shelter population, with more than 13,000 children having slept in city shelters and temporary apartments most nights this winter" (Egan, Jennifer. "Be Young and Homeless." *New York Times* 24 Mar. 2002, Sunday Magazine:

32–35, 58–59. Print). Egan goes on to say, "In an era regarded as generally prosperous, the numbers are staggering: Between 900,000 and 1.4 million children in America are homeless for a time in a given year" (34–35). Were you aware that children make up a large percentage (up to Forty percent) of the nation's homeless population? Respond in your writer's notebook.

During my early childhood I lived in four or five different homeless shelters in New York City. It's a good thing my mother found employment when she did; otherwise I, too, might have been like one of the homeless children in the city today, left without even a shelter to live in because of overcrowding. Last week some of these children were sent to an unused jail in the Bronx—and then removed when lead paint was found there—because the city could find nowhere else for them to live.

From a house to a shelter to a former jail—not the most desirable pathway to take in life. I only had to deal with having to write down an address in school that was never going to be my own, living in a "house" where I had an extended family of one-hundred strangers, being cramped in a room as small as a bathroom with three other families besides my own, with no sense of privacy—ever. Some homeless children in New York can now add to their childhood memories the time they had no place else to live but a former jail.

My mother had financial difficulties as a single mother taking care of my brother and me on her own. She worked very hard to move us from a small one-bedroom apartment to a two-bedroom apartment. We finally did move into that bigger apartment when I was around 8, but after living there a week we discovered that the place was infested with centipedes and we had to move out before my mother could find us another apartment. So we ended up in a shelter. I think my mother thought it was only going to be a temporary situation until she could find someplace else to go.

On that first night without a home, I fell asleep as we waited in line at the department of homeless services to find out which shelter would take us. There were no more seats available and we were there for over five hours before my mother even got to talk to someone. We then had to wait another two hours before a van came to pick us up and take us to the shelter in downtown Manhattan where we would be spending the next two months.

It still puzzles me how so many beds could fit in the room we stayed in. There were four bunk beds crammed into one tiny room. I shared a top bunk with my brother, with my mother sleeping below. Every time we wanted to get to our bed, we had to jump across someone else's bed. Since we had been the last to arrive at the shelter, we had no choice; we got the bed farthest back in the room.

My brother and I learned quickly that there were unspoken rules for living in these places. In a way, living there was like living in a kind of prison. You had to fit in fast or someone would take advantage of you. There weren't any curtains in the bathrooms and everyone on the floor—100 or more people—had to use the same facility. My mother quickly picked up the habit of waking us at 4 a.m. to make sure we took a shower before anyone else awakened. Later, we learned that if you didn't start lining up for meals at least two hours before the kitchen was open, you might as well forget about eating. We had to watch our things at all times, because if you weren't careful someone might take your things and you'd never see them again.

I was in high school when I finally accepted the fact that I was homeless. Until 7 that point I was in complete denial. During those miserable times, my brother and I learned how to become expert liars. We never let our friends in school know where we were living. In some cases we were lucky enough not to be going to the local school, so no one ever walked home with us. If the shelter was near our school or one of our friends caught us coming out of the "bums" building, as the kids in the neighborhood used to call it, then we would tell them our mother worked there and we had to meet her there after school. It is difficult enough to fit in when you are a kid, and worse yet when you can never invite anyone home to visit because you don't have a home.

Being in those shelters, though, helped me to see that the biggest cause of 8 homelessness is not lack of money to pay rent. There were a lot of broken families in these shelters: broken by drugs, alcohol abuse, divorce, AIDS, early pregnancy, lack of education and, most important, lack of information about how to get out of these troubles. Many of the kids I knew at the shelter really wanted to change their circumstances, but few of them did—few of them knew how. There weren't many social workers around, and even when they were around and noticed a problem, they rarely followed up. The children in these situations need a listening ear, someone to turn to consistently.

Sure, having a bed to sleep on is better than having no bed at all. But sleeping 9 on a bed in a shelter that was once a jail doesn't help ease the psychological burden of being homeless in the first place. I understand that Mayor Michael Bloomberg's administration is trying to make sure that the new shelter in the Bronx is safe, but is it working to make it seem less prison-like? A line for food, cramped space, no privacy— sounds a lot like a prison to me. The only difference now is that the city is calling a homeless shelter what it really is.

READING FOR CONTENT

1. What event prompted Browne to write this piece?
2. In your own words, explain why living in a homeless shelter is like living in a prison.

READING FOR GENRE, ORGANIZATION, AND STYLISTIC FEATURES

1. Explain how the opening paragraph informs the reader of the direction Browne will take in the remainder of the selection.
2. Describe the type of evidence Browne uses to support her position. Is the evidence effective?

READING FOR RHETORICAL CONTEXT

1. Describe Browne's purpose. What is she trying to get across to the readers of the *New York Times*?
2. How would you characterize Browne's tone of voice? Is it appropriate for her rhetorical purpose?

WRITING ASSIGNMENTS

1. In response to Charmion Browne's article, write a letter to the editor of the *New York Times.*

2. In "Serving in Florida," Barbara Ehrenreich provides insights into the problem of homelessness when she discusses the acute shortage of affordable housing for extremely low-income families. Write an essay in which you draw upon Barbara Ehrenreich as well as other authors in Chapter 13 to explain Charmion Browne's childhood of homelessness.

SYNTHESIS WRITING ASSIGNMENTS

1. Conduct research on the Personal Responsibility and Work Opportunity and Reconciliation Act (PRWORA) that Congress enacted as part of welfare reform in 1996. Your objective is to determine whether or not Herbert Gans's forecast, written in 1992, was accurate:

   The latest fashion is to put welfare recipients to work, which would be a good idea if even decent entry-level jobs for them could be found or created. (Alas, when taxpayers discover how much cheaper it is to pay welfare than to create jobs, that remedy may end as it has before.) (paragraph 14)

   Write an essay in which you assess the extent to which the reform has made a long-term difference in lifting poor people, especially women, out of poverty.

2. At the end of her book *Nickel and Dimed*, Barbara Ehrenreich writes:

   When someone works for less pay than she can live on—when, for example, she goes hungry so that you can eat more cheaply and conveniently—then she has made a great sacrifice for you, she has made you a gift of some part of her abilities, her health, and her life. The "working poor," as they are approvingly termed, are in fact the major philanthropists of our society. They neglect their own children so that the children of others will be cared for; they live in substandard housing so that other homes will be shiny and perfect; they endure privation so that inflation will be low and stock prices high. To be a member of the working poor is to be an anonymous donor, a nameless benefactor, to everyone else. (221)

   Drawing on *The Economist*'s "Middle of the Class" and other selections in this chapter, write an essay in response to Ehrenreich's statement.

3. Both Lindsey and Gans write about upper-class success and lower-class poverty and make an effort to explain reasons for the difference between the two, even though their reasoning differs dramatically. Write a comparative analysis essay in which you examine their differing views and, in the end, explain why one of them persuades you more than the other.

4. Matt Yglesias argues on behalf of redistributing wealth by increasing the taxes on the very wealthy, and he proposes using the revenue from such taxation to fund a number of educational programs that will help impoverished families to improve their economic standing. Drawing upon other articles in this chapter, write a critical analysis of Yglesias's proposals and explain why you evaluate them either positively or negatively.

5. How widespread are the class discrimination and prejudice that Gans discusses in "The War Against the Poor Instead of Programs to End Poverty"? Use the selections by Angela Locke and Charmion Browne to write an essay in response.

6. Show how Ehrenreich's "Serving in Florida" communicates the exploitation, prejudice, discrimination, and injustice that are discussed by the other writers in this chapter. Write an essay addressed to your classmates.

Humanities

The subjects that humanists study have cultural, historical, critical, and theoretical orientations. There is a great deal of overlap among these subjects because, for example, music or the visual arts can be studied from a performance or a creative practitioner's perspective, from a cultural perspective in terms of their impact upon social life, from an historical perspective in terms of their development over time, from a critical perspective in terms of their formal structures, or from a theoretical perspective in terms of their relationship to other discourse.

- The **historical** subjects are history; various area studies such as ancient classical civilization, Latin American studies, and Asian studies; and historical studies of particular disciplines, such as the history of science, the history of art, and historical linguistics. Humanists approach these subjects by studying the causes, effects, developments, and interactions of peoples, nations, institutions, ideas, fashions, styles, and the like.

- The **critical** subjects are literature, drama, music, the visual arts, and other expressive arts. Humanists approach them by analyzing, interpreting, and evaluating "texts," understood in the broadest sense of the term as novels, poems, plays, films, paintings, sculpture, dance, musical scores, musical performances, and so forth.

- The **theoretical** subjects are philosophy, linguistics, and semiotics. Humanists approach them from a broad perspective and at close range by examining thought, language, structures of meaning and expression, and other significant evidence of human rationality.

The conversation among students and scholars in these subjects can be intense. An array of approaches defines this conversation through cultural studies, gender studies, media studies, and critical theory in its various historical, philosophical, linguistic, social, and psychoanalytical forms.

■ METHODS OF STUDY IN THE HUMANITIES

The cultural, historical, critical, and theoretical orientations of the humanities also describe the methods that humanists use. The study of history, for example, requires a **critical reading** of documents from the past as well as a theoretical probing of their importance. The study of literature and the arts usually emphasizes **critical interpretation**, but it also calls for some cultural study of how styles, forms, and themes developed, and for a theoretical study of how we understand them. When you are reading in the humanities, therefore, you need to recognize how the various theoretical, historical, and critical approaches work in the various disciplines. The chapters on the humanities in this anthology provide examples from the cultural, historical, critical, and sociological study of music (Chapter 14); a literary study of some short stories about ethnic diversity in the United States (Chapter 15); and examples from the cultural, historical, critical, and analytic study of photographic images (Chapter 16).

■ WRITING IN THE HUMANITIES

Assignments for writing in the humanities require you to exercise your analytical judgment. In this anthology, for example, writing assignments in the humanities run the gamut from critical summary to theoretical speculation. Shorter assignments may call for various types of writing: a summary or **précis** of an article, chapter, or book; a critical report on an article, chapter, or book; or a review of research in several publications. Each of these assignments requires you to select important issues from the content of your source text, to focus upon the author's treatment of them, and to analyze the author's argument as it is shaped by stylistic and rhetorical turns of phrase and idea.

Here, for example, is a writing assignment in music criticism. It requires you to analyze and evaluate a professional critic's argument about current pop music. Note that it also requires you to develop your own argument about the value of such music.

> Write a 750-word critical response to Scruton's article in which you counter his attack on metal and DJ styles by elaborating upon their positive features. Extend the "conversation" that his article initiates by referring to other champions of these musical forms. (p. 516)

In selecting issues to write about, you would want them to amount to something more than random observations drawn from the text. You would aim to trace a **pattern of thought** that conveys the author's dominant argument. As you explore relationships among these ideas, you would be constructing your own argument about the author's contribution to the conversation that engages music critics. When you organize your treatment of these issues, you would decide whether to write about them in the order in which the source text presents them, in the order of importance that you attribute to them, or in a logical or sequential order that advances your own argument about them.

Longer assignments may require a close analysis of several texts. Here's an example from Chapter 15 of this anthology:

> Drawing on short stories by Mukherjee, Viramontes, and Saunders, write a five- to six-page essay in which you compare and contrast the experiences of different ethnic groups as they interact with one another in North America. What conditions drive members of these groups to different forms of economic survival? Address your essay to an audience of students who have not read these texts. (p. 575)

Note that, because this assignment asks you to "address your essay to an audience of students who have not read these texts," it implicitly requires you to summarize and paraphrase portions of the authors' stories, indicating their thematic concerns and stylistic features. It also implicitly requires you to speculate on the stories' common engagement with representations of economic survival. For this purpose, you will have to think about how Mukherjee, Viramontes, and Saunders might contribute to a conversation about such survival if they were brought together to discuss the topic.

◼️ PERSPECTIVES ON WRITING IN THE HUMANITIES

Most writing assignments in the humanities will call upon you to use critical skills in one way or another, but some higher-level writing assignments may also require you to use historical and theoretical skills as well. You may be asked to examine a certain problem in its historical context or to discuss the theoretical implications of another problem on a broad scale. Other writing assignments in the humanities will call upon you to analyze a creative text such as a work of music, visual art, or literature. In such assignments, you will focus your critical skills directly upon the musical or visual or literary text in order to analyze, interpret, and evaluate it as deeply as you can. In Chapters 3, 4, and 5, we presented models for approaching such texts and writing papers about them.

◼️ Organizational Patterns of Writing in the Humanities

Organizational patterns for writing in the humanities follow models similar to those in the natural and social sciences. In the most common pattern, the writer explains each proposition, event, or detail in its order of occurrence from his or her perspective. The good writer, however, will vary this basic pattern in many subtle ways. Sometimes he or she may take a number of points from the same source and classify them under general headings—for example, all the negative arguments against a certain moral or ethical position; or all the long-term and short-term implications of an argument based on analyzing current political conditions. Or the writer may endorse and appropriate some conclusions from a given source but contest and refute others from the same source. In "Toward an Aesthetic of Popular Music" (Chapter 14), Simon Frith organizes his argument by introducing a seemingly unlikely sociological approach that avoids aesthetic value judgment and then by aligning his aesthetic theory directly with this approach so that one illuminates the other:

> My particular concern is to suggest that the sociological approach to popular music does not rule out an aesthetic theory but, on the contrary, makes one possible. At first sight this proposition is unlikely. There is no doubt that sociologists have tended to

explain away pop music.... And yet for ten years or more I have also been a working rock critic, making such judgments as a matter of course, assuming, like all pop fans, that our musical choices matter. (p. 498)

Other organizational patterns may contrast statement with response or question with answer, each time penetrating deeper into the problem being investigated. The same writer, Simon Frith, examines popular music by posing questions that require sustained analysis:

> Are such judgments spurious—a way of concealing from myself and other consumers the ways in which our tastes are manipulated? Can it really be the case that my pleasure in a song by the group Abba carries the same aesthetic weight as someone else's pleasure in Mozart? ... The question facing sociologists and aestheticians in both cases is the same: how do we make musical value judgments? How do such value judgments articulate the listening experiences involved? (p. 498)

The rest of Frith's essay pursues answers to these questions.

Still other organizational patterns may establish cause-and-effect relationships in their critical assessment of diverse sources. In Chapter 15, Ronald Takaki reviews several sources and finds that "by 1900, 60 percent of Japan's industrial laborers were women" (p. 544). He therefore speculates, "While it is not known how many of the women who emigrated had been wage-earners, this proletarianization of women already well under way in Japan paved the way for such laborers to consider working in America" (p. 544). Takaki then considers the impact of such research upon his own argument.

◼ Styles of Writing in the Humanities

Some styles of writing in the humanities suggest—within limits—the tone of the author's personal and idiosyncratic voice. This quality distinguishes it radically from impersonal styles of writing in the natural and social sciences. The major evidence for critical assessments of texts in the humanities is direct observation of details in the texts themselves, close reference to them, and pointed quotation from them. How the author of an article projects an attitude toward these texts often counts as much as what he or she directly says about them.

In "Toward an Aesthetic of Popular Music," Simon Frith poses the difficult question of how we can analyze and evaluate some forms of music as being more worthwhile than others, and whether we can disparage certain forms as being detrimental to us:

> My starting question was how is it that people (myself included) can say, quite confidently, that some popular music is better than others? (p. 505)

Later Frith provides an answer by referring to the way in which valued music "seems to provide an experience that transcends the mundane, that 'takes us out of ourselves.'" He goes on to describe this quality by dissociating particular kinds of music from comparisons to either more or less critically praised forms, and by associating it instead with self-recognition and social expectations. His voice is analytical and respectful, even if he disagrees with one or another style of music:

> It is special, that is, not necessarily with reference to other music, but to the rest of life. This sense of specialness, the way in which music seems to make possible a new kind

of self-recognition, frees us from the everyday routines and expectations that encumber our social identities, is a key part of the way in which people experience and thus value music. (p. 506)

Music thus acquires value by performing functions that are both personal and social.

▨ Personal Voice

Writing in the humanities not only tolerates the development of a personal voice but also encourages it. Listen to Roger Scruton's voice as he tries to counter an enthusiasm for popular music such as Frith's by arguing in "Music and Morality" that some of its forms lack the complexities of melody and harmony that elevate other forms:

> The essence of pop is not form, structure, or abstract musical relationships. It is rhythm, and rhythm is something to which you move, not something to which you listen. (p. 513)

Scruton then goes on to disparage pop music in a tone that leaves no doubt about his attitude toward it:

> The complaints that might be made against the worst form of pop apply also to the lame attempts at dancing that generally are produced by it—attempts that involve no control of the body, no attempt to dance *with* another person, but at best only the attempt to dance *at* him or her, by making movements that are sliced up and atomized like the sounds that provoke them. (p. 513)

For Scruton, pop is not music, but only a "lame" attempt at issuing "sounds" to dance to. Agree or disagree with his reasoning—and many will cogently disagree—you have to admit that the author knows how to turn a phrase. Frith and Scruton stand on opposing sides of the question about the value of pop music, and their differing voices reinforce their differing perspectives.

Because the humanities propose to exercise and develop critical thinking, the issue of "what you think and why" becomes crucial. The "what" and "why" seldom generate straightforward, unequivocal answers. To the casual observer, some answers may seem curious, whimsical, arbitrary, entirely subjective. To others more deeply acquainted with the humanistic disciplines, open-endedness confers its own rewards. Among them is the light it casts upon our processes of thought, our understanding of complex issues, and the wide-ranging and often contradictory interpretations of them. In "A Different Mirror" (Chapter 15), Ronald Takaki begins his essay on American multiculturalism with a personal account of how his Asian facial features led a taxi driver in Virginia to mistake him for a foreign visitor:

> He glanced at me in the mirror. Somehow I did not look "American" to him; my eyes and complexion looked foreign. (p. 539)

Takaki's anecdote proves as germane to his historical argument as statistical data would to a scientific argument.

A writer in the humanities measures the success of an argument by how it accommodates divergent explanations and shows their relationships. Significantly, most writers in the humanities do not agree on the universal applicability of any single formula, method, or approach for solving problems. The best solutions usually entail a combination of formulas, methods, and approaches.

Reading and writing in the humanities, therefore, requires a tolerance for ambiguity and contradiction. Oddly enough, however, most writers in the humanities defend their assertions with a strong and aggressive rhetoric. At best, this rhetoric scrupulously avoids bloat, pomposity, and roundabout ways of saying things. Instead of "It was decided that they would utilize the sharp instrument for perforating and unsealing aluminum receptacles," it prefers "They decided to use the can opener." It uses technical vocabulary when necessary, but it usually prefers clear, precise, intelligible diction to stilted, awkward jargon. It uses figurative language and analogy, but not for their own sake; it uses them to express meanings and relationships that literal language sometimes obscures.

In Chapter 15, Ronald Takaki concludes his study of Japanese immigration with a poem that expresses the emotions of young women leaving their place of birth for the uncertainties of a marriage in America. As their ships sailed from the harbor, many women gazed at the diminishing shore:

> With tears in my eyes
> I turn back to my homeland
> Taking one last look. (p. 546)

Writing in the humanities strives for a richness of texture and implication but at the same time, it highlights important threads in that texture and designates them as central to the unraveling. Readers, however, should not allow assertiveness to fool them. Few examples of good writing in the humanities are completely intolerant of opposing views. There's always room for another perspective.

Fourteen

Rock Music and Cultural Values

In the mid-1950s, when rock and roll was born, much of it was considered countercultural, and most of it found a hostile reception. A half-century later, it is consumed by the masses and solidly established as a major component of popular culture. As the essays in this chapter suggest, however, even though rock has been integrated into the mainstream culture and become respectable, it is still a subject of controversy. These essays exemplify some of the arguments in the controversy. Though the conversation unfolds with civility and academic decorum, the old antagonisms still haunt the boundaries of the discourse. An academic footnote or two mutes but does not tame the combatants.

The selections in this chapter begin with a discussion of aesthetics. Simon Frith's "Toward an Aesthetic of Popular Music" asks, "How do we make value judgments about popular music?" Frith explains that we value music when it fulfills such social functions as giving us an identity, enabling us to manage our feelings, and offering us a sense of time and place. The next two articles present a modern version of the old debate for or against the respectability of rock music. In "Music and Morality," the conservative commentator Roger Scruton argues that music can encourage virtue but also vice, and he disparages forms of music such as Metal and DJ for their violence and lewdness. Countering Frith's aesthetic argument about an experience of music that takes us outside of ourselves, Scruton deploys a philosophical argument about moral character that positions us either with or against others. In his view, pop music shouts at us and moves us to shout at others rather than act in concert with them to advance social harmony. In "Redeeming the Rap Music Experience," Venise Berry examines the sex, violence, and racism of its lyrics in the context of urban Afro-American youth. She contends that the genre "serves as a bridge from favorite songs and artists to personal and social realities" and in so doing empowers low-income black youth.

The final two articles attempt to delineate not only changes in musical taste over time, but also changes in social personality among people who deploy new technologies to access their music. Lane Jennings, a writer who has devoted much attention to Futurist innovations, points out in "Digital Music: You Are What You Listen To" that the sharing of musical playlists among students and coworkers has the desirable effect of creating a community within public space. At the same time, it has the questionable effect of encouraging conformity and a loss of private individuality. Fox News correspondent James Rosen devotes "Of iPods and Dirty Underwear" to examining his own hidden motivations for downloading particular kinds of music to his iPod collection. Often these motivations do not concern his personal likes or dislikes of certain kinds, but rather his fears about judgment by others as to his tastes and whether they meet social approval or not. He humorously compares this apprehension to fears about being caught in public wearing dirty underwear. Even as the conversation about the cultural value of rock music continues outside the walls of academe, it develops with robust energy worthy of critical analysis.

Towards an Aesthetic of Popular Music

Simon Frith

Simon Frith holds the Tovey Chair of Music at Edinburgh University, Scotland. He has published numerous articles on the sociology of music and major studies of popular music institutions and aesthetics, including Sound Effects *and* Performing Rites.

PREREADING

What is your preferred style of music? Who are your favorite musicians, singers, or groups? Why does their sound appeal to you more than the sound of others? Do you think some types of music are better than others? Why or why not?

Introduction: The "Value" of Popular Music

Underlying all the other distinctions critics draw between "serious" and "popular" music   1 is an assumption about the source of musical value. Serious music matters because it transcends social forces; popular music is aesthetically worthless because it is determined by them (because it is "useful" or "utilitarian"). This argument, common enough among academic musicologists, puts sociologists in an odd position. If we venture to suggest that the value of, say, Beethoven's music can be explained by the social conditions determining its production and subsequent consumption we are dismissed as philistines—aesthetic theories of classical music remain determinedly non-sociological.

Popular music, by contrast, is taken to be good only for sociological theory. Our very success in explaining the rise of rock' n' roll or the appearance of disco proves their lack of aesthetic interest. To relate music and society becomes, then, a different task according to the music we are treating. In analyzing serious music, we have to uncover the social forces concealed in the talk of "transcendent" values; in analyzing pop, we have to take seriously the values scoffed at in the talk of social functions.

In this paper I will concentrate on the second issue; my particular concern is to suggest that the sociological approach to popular music does not rule out an aesthetic theory but, on the contrary, makes one possible. At first sight this proposition is unlikely. There is no doubt that sociologists have tended to explain away pop music. In my own academic work I have examined how rock is produced and consumed, and have tried to place it ideologically, but there is no way that a reading of my books (or those of other sociologists) could be used to explain why some pop songs are good and others bad, why Elvis Presley is a better singer than John Denver, or why disco is a much richer musical genre than progressive rock. And yet for ten years or more I have also been a working rock critic, making such judgments as a matter of course, assuming, like all pop fans, that our musical choices matter. 2

Are such judgments spurious—a way of concealing from myself and other consumers the ways in which our tastes are manipulated? Can it really be the case that my pleasure in a song by the group Abba carries the same aesthetic weight as someone else's pleasure in Mozart? Even to pose such a question is to invite ridicule—either I seek to reduce the "transcendent" Mozart to Abba's commercially determined level, or else I elevate Abba's music beyond any significance it can carry. But even if the pleasures of serious and popular musics are different, it is not immediately obvious that the difference is that between artistic autonomy and social utility. Abba's value is no more (and no less) bound up with an experience of transcendence than Mozart's; the meaning of Mozart is no less (and no more) explicable in terms of social forces. The question facing sociologists and aestheticians in both cases is the same: how do we make musical value judgments? How do such value judgments articulate the listening experiences involved? 3

The sociologist of contemporary popular music is faced with a body of songs, records, stars and styles which exists because of a series of decisions, made by both producers and consumers, about what is a successful sound. Musicians write tunes and play solos; producers choose from different sound mixes; record companies and radio programmers decide what should be released and played; consumers buy one record rather than another and concentrate their attention on particular genres. The result of all these apparently individual decisions is a pattern of success, taste and style which can be explained sociologically. 4

If the starting question is why does this hit sound this way, then sociological answers can be arranged under two headings. First, there are answers in terms of technique and technology: people produce and consume the music they are capable of producing and consuming (an obvious point, but one which opens up issues of skill, background and education which in pop music are applied not to individual composers but to social groups). Different groups possess different sorts of cultural capital, share different cultural expectations and so make music differently—pop tastes are shown to correlate with class cultures and subcultures; musical styles are linked to specific age 5 groups; we take for granted the connections of ethnicity and sound. This is the sociological common sense of rock criticism, which equally acknowledges the determining role of technology. The history of twentieth-century popular music is impossible to write without reference to the changing forces of production, electronics, the use of recording, amplification and synthesizers, just as consumer choices cannot be separated from the possession of transistor radios, stereo hi-fis, ghetto blasters and Walkmen.

While we can thus point to general patterns of pop use, the precise link (or 6 homology) between sounds and social groups remains unclear. Why is rock 'n' roll youth music, whereas Dire Straits is the sound of Yuppie USA? To answer these questions there is a second sociological approach to popular music, expressed in terms of its functions. This approach is obvious in ethnomusicology, that is in anthropological studies of traditional and folk musics which are explained by reference to their use in dance, in rituals, for political mobilization, to solemnize ceremonies or to excite desires. Similar points are made about contemporary pop, but its most important function is assumed to be commercial—the starting analytical assumption is that the music is made to sell; thus research has focused on who makes marketing decisions and why, and on the construction of "taste publics." The bulk of the academic sociology of popular music (including my own) implicitly equates aesthetic and commercial judgments. The phenomenal 1985 successes of Madonna and Bruce Springsteen are explained, for example, in terms of sales strategies, the use of video, and the development of particular new audiences. The appeal of the music itself, the reason Madonna's and Springsteen's fans like them, somehow remains unexamined.

From the fans' perspective it is obvious that people play the music they do 7 because it "sounds good," and the interesting question is why they have formed that opinion. Even if pop tastes are the effects of social conditioning and commercial manipulation, people still explain them to themselves in terms of value judgment. Where, in pop and rock, do these values come from? When people explain their tastes, what terms do they use? They certainly know what they like (and dislike), what pleases them and what does not. Read the music press, listen to band rehearsals and recording sessions, overhear the chatter in record shops and discos, note the ways in which disc jockeys play records, and you will hear value judgments being made. The discriminations that matter in these settings occur *within* the general sociological framework. While this allows us at a certain level to "explain" rock or disco, it is not adequate for an understanding of why one rock record or one disco track is better than another. Turn to the explanations of the fans or musicians (or even of the record companies) and a familiar argument appears. Everyone in the pop world is aware of the social forces that determine "normal" pop music—a good record, song, or sound is precisely one that transcends those forces!

The music press is the place where pop value judgments are most clearly ar- 8 ticulated. A reading of British music magazines reveals that "good" popular music has always been heard to go beyond or break through commercial routine. This was as true for critics struggling to distinguish jazz from Tin Pan Alley pop in the 1920s and black jazz from white jazz in the 1930s as for critics asserting rock's superiority to teen pop in the late 1960s. In *Sound Effects*[1] I argued that rock's claim to a form of aesthetic autonomy rests on a combination of folk and art arguments: as folk music rock is heard to represent the community of youth, as art music rock is heard as the sound of individual, creative sensibility. The rock aesthetic depends, crucially, on an argument about authenticity. Good music is the authentic expression of something—a person, an idea, a feeling, a shared experience, a *Zeitgeist*. Bad music is inauthentic—it expresses nothing. The most common term of abuse in rock criticism is "bland"—bland music has nothing in it and is made only to be commercially pleasing.

"Authenticity" is, then, what guarantees that rock performances resist or subvert 9 commercial logic, just as rock-star quality (whether we are discussing Elvis Presley or David Bowie, the Rolling Stones or the Sex Pistols), describes the power that enables certain musicians to drive something individually obdurate through the system. At this point, rock criticism meets up with "serious" musicology. Wilfrid Mellers' scholarly books on the Beatles and Bob Dylan,[2] for example, describe in technical terms their subjects' transcendent qualities; but they read like fan mail and, in their lack of self-conscious hipness, point to the contradiction at the heart of this aesthetic approach. The suggestion is that pop music becomes more valuable the more independent it is of the social forces that organize the pop process in the first place; pop value is dependent on something outside pop, is rooted in the person, the *auteur*, the community or the subculture that lies behind it. If good music is authentic music, then critical judgment means measuring the performers' "truth" to the experiences or feelings they are describing.

Rock criticism depends on myth—the myth of the youth community, the myth 10 of the creative artist. The reality is that rock, like all twentieth-century pop musics, is a commercial form, music produced as a commodity, for a profit, distributed through mass media as mass culture. It is in practice very difficult to say exactly who or what it is that rock expresses or who, from the listener's point of view, are the authentically creative performers. The myth of authenticity is, indeed, one of rock's own ideological effects, an aspect of its sales process: rock stars can be marketed as artists, and their particular sounds marketed as a means of identity. Rock criticism is a means of legitimating tastes, justifying value judgments, but it does not really explain how those judgments came to be made in the first place. If the music is not, in fact, made according to the "authentic" story, then the question becomes how we are able to judge some sounds as more authentic than others: what are we actually listening for in making our judgments? How do we know Bruce Springsteen is more authentic than Duran Duran, when both make records according to the rules of the same complex industry? And how do we recognize good sounds in non-rock genres, in pop forms like disco that are not described in authentic terms in the first place? The question of the value of pop music remains to be answered.

An Alternative Approach to Music and Society

In an attempt to answer these questions I want to suggest an alternative approach to 11 musical value, to suggest different ways of defining "popular music" and "popular culture." The question we should be asking is not what does popular music *reveal* about "the people" but how does it *construct* them. If we start with the assumption that pop is expressive, then we get bogged down in the search for the "real" artist or emotion or belief lying behind it. But popular music is popular not because it reflects something, or authentically articulates some sort of popular taste or experience, but because it creates our understanding of what popularity is. The most misleading term in cultural theory is, indeed, "authenticity." What we should be examining is not how true a piece of music is to something else, but how it sets up the idea of "truth" in the first place—successful pop music is music which defines its own aesthetic standard.

A simple way to illustrate the problems of defining musical popularity is to   12 look at its crudest measure, the weekly record sales charts in the British music press and the American *Billboard*. These are presented to us as market research: the charts measure something real—sales and radio plays—and represent them with all the trimmings of an objective, scientific apparatus. But, in fact, what the charts reveal is a specific definition of what can be counted as popular music in the first place—record sales (in the right shops), radio plays (on the right stations). The charts work not as the detached measure of some agreed notion of popularity, but as the most important determination of what the popularity of popular music means—that is, a particular pattern of market choice. The charts bring selected records together into the community of the market place; they define certain sorts of consumption as being collective in certain sorts of ways.

The sales charts are only one measure of popularity; and when we look at   13 others, it becomes clear that their use is always for the creation (rather than reflection) of taste communities. Readers' polls in the music press, for example, work to give communal shape to disparate readers; the Pazz 'n' Jop poll in *The Village Voice* creates a sense of collective commitment among the fragmented community of American rock critics. The Grammy awards in the United States and the BPI awards in Britain, present the industry's view of what pop music is about—nationalism and money. These annual awards, which for most pop fans seem to miss the point, reflect sales figures and "contributions to the recording industry" measures of popularity no less valid than readers' or critics' polls (which often deliberately honor "unpopular" acts). In comparing poll results, arguments are really not about who is more popular than whom empirically (see rock critics' outrage that Phil Collins rather than Bruce Springsteen dominated the 1986 Grammys) but about what popularity means. Each different measure measures something different or, to put it more accurately, each different measure constructs its own object of measurement. This is apparent in *Billboard*'s "specialist" charts, in the way in which "minority" musics are defined. "Women's music," for example, is interesting not as music which somehow expresses "women," but as music which seeks to define them, just as "black music" works to set up a very particular notion of what "blackness" is.

This approach to popular culture, as the creation rather than the expression of   14 the people, need not be particular to music. There are numerous ways in our everyday life in which accounts of "the people" are provided. Turn on the television news and notice the ways in which a particular mode of a ddress works, how the word "we" is used, how the word "you." Advertisers in all media are clearly in the business of explaining to us who we are, how we fit in with other people in society, why we necessarily consume the way we do. Each mass medium has its own techniques for addressing its audience, for creating moments of recognition and exclusion, for giving us our sense of ourselves. Pop music does, though, seem to play a particularly important role in the way in which popular culture works. On the one hand, it works with particularly intense emotional experiences—pop songs and pop stars mean more to us emotionally than other media events or performers, and this is not just because the pop business sells music to us through individual market choices. On the other hand, these musical experiences always contain social meaning, are placed within a social context—we are not free to read anything we want into a song.

The experience of pop music is an experience of placing: in responding to a song, 15 we are drawn, haphazardly, into affective and emotional alliances with the performers and with the performers' other fans. Again this also happens in other areas of popular culture. Sport, for example, is clearly a setting in which people directly experience community, feel an immediate bond with other people, articulate a particular kind of collective pride (for a non-American, the most extraordinary aspect of the 1984 Olympics was the display/construction of the Reagan ideology of both the United States and patriotism). And fashion and style—both social constructions—remain the keys to the ways in which we, as individuals, present ourselves to the world: we use the public meanings of clothes to say "this is how I want to be perceived."

But music is especially important to this process of placement because of some- 16 thing specific to musical experience, namely, its direct emotional intensity. Because of its qualities of abstractness (which "serious" aestheticians have always stressed) music is an individualizing form. We absorb songs into our own lives and rhythms into our own bodies; they have a looseness of reference that makes them immediately accessible. Pop songs are open to appropriation for personal use in a way that other popular cultural forms (television soap operas, for example) are not—the latter are tied into meanings we may reject. At the same time, and equally significant, music is obviously rule-bound. We hear things as music because their sounds obey a particular, familiar logic, and for most pop fans (who are, technically, non-musical) this logic is out of our control. There is a mystery to our musical tastes. Some records and performers work for us, others do not—we know this without being able to explain it. Somebody else has set up the conventions; they are clearly social and clearly apart from us.

This interplay between personal absorption into music and the sense that it 17 is, nevertheless, something out there, something public, is what makes music so important in the cultural placing of the individual in the social. To give a mundane example, it is obviously true that in the last thirty years the idea of being a "fan," with its oddly public account of private obsessions, has been much more significant to pop music than to other forms of popular culture. This role of music is usually related to youth and youth culture, but it seems equally important to the ways in which ethnic groups in both Britain and the United States have forged particular cultural identities and is also reflected in the ways in which "classical" music originally became significant for the nineteenth-century European bourgeoisie. In all these cases music can stand for, symbolize *and* offer the immediate experience of collective identity. Other cultural forms—painting, literature, design—can articulate and show off shared values and pride, but only music can make you *feel* them.

The Social Functions of Music

It is now possible to move back to the starting point of this essay—the social func- 18 tions of music and their implications for aesthetics. I will begin by outlining the four most significant ways in which pop is used and then suggest how these uses help us to understand how pop value judgments are made.

The first reason, then, we enjoy popular music is because of its use in answering questions of identity: we use pop songs to create for ourselves a particular sort of self-definition, a particular place in society. The pleasure that pop music produces is a pleasure of identification—with the music we like, with the performers of that music, with the other people who like it. And it is important to note that the production of identity is also a production of nonidentity—it is a process of inclusion and exclusion. This is one of the most striking aspects of musical taste. People not only know what they like, they also have very clear ideas about what they don't like and often have very aggressive ways of stating their dislikes. As all sociological studies of pop consumers have shown, pop fans define themselves quite precisely according to their musical preferences. Whether they identify with genres or stars, it seems of greater importance to people what they like musically than whether or not they enjoyed a film or a television program.

The pleasure of pop music unlike the pleasures to be had from other mass cultural forms, does not derive in any clear way from fantasy: it is not mediated through day-dreams or romancing, but is experienced directly. For example, at a heavy metal concert you can certainly see the audience absorbed in the music; yet for all the air-guitar playing they are not fantasizing being up on stage. To experience heavy metal is to experience the power of the concert as a whole—the musicians are one aspect of this, the amplification system another, the audience a third. The individual fans get their kicks from being a necessary part of the overall process—which is why heavy metal videos always have to contain moments of live performance (whatever the surrounding story line) in order to capture and acknowledge the kind of empowerment that is involved in the concert itself.

Once we start looking at different pop genres we can begin to document the different ways in which music works to give people an identity, to place them in different social groups. And this is not just a feature of commercial pop music. It is the way in which all popular music works. For example, in putting together an audience, contemporary black-influenced pop clearly (and often cynically) employs musical devices originally used in religious music to define men's and women's identity before God. Folk musics, similarly, continue to be used to mark the boundaries of ethnic identity, even amidst the complications of migration and cultural change. In London's Irish pubs, for example, "traditional" Irish folk songs are still the most powerful way to make people feel Irish and consider what their "Irishness" means. (This music, this identity, is now being further explored by post-punk London Irish bands, like the Pogues.) It is not surprising, then, that popular music has always had important nationalist functions. In Abel Gance's "silent" film, *Napoleon*, there is a scene in which we see the *Marseillaise* being composed, and then watch the song make its way through the Assembly and among the crowds until everyone is singing it. When the film was first shown in France, the cinema audience rose from their seats and joined in singing their national anthem. Only music seems capable of creating this sort of spontaneous collective identity, this kind of personally felt patriotism.

Music's second social function is to give us a way of managing the relationship between our public and private emotional lives. It is often noted but rarely discussed that the bulk of popular songs are love songs. This is certainly true of twentieth-century popular music in the West; but most non-Western popular musics also feature romantic, usually heterosexual, love lyrics. This is more than an interesting statistic; it is a centrally important aspect of how pop music is used. Why are love songs so important? Because people need them to give shape and voice to emotions that otherwise cannot be expressed without embarrassment or incoherence. Love songs are a way of giving emotional intensity to the sorts of intimate things we say to each other (and to ourselves) in words that are, in themselves, quite flat. It is a peculiarity of everyday language that our most fraught and revealing declarations of feeling have to use phrases—"I love/hate you," "Help me!," "I'm angry/scared"—which are boring and banal; and so our culture has a supply of a million pop songs, which say these things for us in numerous interesting and involving ways. These songs do not replace our conversations—pop singers do not do our courting for us—but they make our feelings seem richer and more convincing than we can make them appear in our own words, even to ourselves.

The only interesting sociological account of lyrics in the long tradition of American content analysis was Donald Horton's late 1950s study[3] of how teenagers used the words of popular songs in their dating rituals. His high school sample learned from pop songs (public forms of private expression) how to make sense of and shape their own inchoate feelings. This use of pop illuminates one quality of the star/fan relationship: people do not idolize singers because they wish to be them but because these singers seem able, somehow, to make available their own feelings—it is as if we get to know ourselves via the music. 23

The third function of popular music is to shape popular memory, to organize our sense of time. Clearly one of the effects of all music, not just pop, is to intensify our experience of the present. One measure of good music, to put it another way, is, precisely, its "presence," its ability to "stop" time, to make us feel we are living within a moment, with no memory or anxiety about what has come before, what will come after. This is where the physical impact of music comes in—the use of beat, pulse and rhythm to compel our immediate bodily involvement in an organization of time that the music itself controls. Hence the pleasures of dance and disco; clubs and parties provide a setting, a society, which seems to be defined only by the time-scale of the music (the beats per minute), which escapes the real timepassing outside. 24

One of the most obvious consequences of music's organization of our sense of time is that songs and tunes are often the key to our remembrance of things past. I do not mean simply that sounds—like sights and smells—trigger associated memories, but, rather, that music in itself provides our most vivid experience of time passing. Music focuses our attention on the feeling of time; songs are organized (it is part of their pleasure) around anticipation and echo, around endings to which we look forward, choruses that build regret into their fading. Twentieth-century popular music has, on the whole, been a nostalgic form. The Beatles, for example, made nostalgic music from the start, which is why they were so popular. Even on hearing a Beatles song for the first time there was a sense of the memories to come, a feeling that this could not last but that it was surely going to be pleasant to remember. 25

It is this use of time that makes popular music so important in the social organization of youth. It is a sociological truism that people's heaviest personal investment 26 in popular music is when they are teenagers and young adults—music then ties into a particular kind of emotional turbulence, when issues of individual identity and social place, the control of public and private feelings, are at a premium. People do use music less, and less intently, as they grow up; the most significant pop songs for all generations (not just for rock generations) are those they heard as adolescents. What this suggests, though, is not just that young people need music, but that "youth" itself is defined by music. Youth is experienced, that is, as an intense presence, through an impatience for time to pass and a regret that it is doing so, in a series of speeding, physically insistent moments that have nostalgia coded into them. This is to reiterate my general point about popular music: youth music is socially important not because it reflects youth experience (authentically or not), but because it defines for us what "youthfulness" is. I remember concluding, in my original sociological research in the early 1970s, that those young people who, for whatever reasons, took no interest in pop music were not really "young."

The final function of popular music I want to mention here is something more 27 abstract than the issues discussed so far, but a consequence of all of them: popular music is something possessed. One of the first things I learned as a rock critic—from abusive mail—was that rock fans "owned" their favorite music in ways that were intense and important to them. To be sure, the notion of musical ownership is not peculiar to rock—Hollywood cinema has long used the clichéd line, "they're playing our song"—and this reflects something that is recognizable to all music lovers and is an important aspect of the way in which everyone thinks and talks about "their" music. (British radio has programs of all sorts built around people's explanations of why certain records "belong" to them.) Obviously it is the commodity form of music which makes this sense of musical possession possible, but it is not just the record that people think they own: we feel that we also possess the song itself, the particular performance, and its performer.

In "possessing" music, we make it part of our own identity and build it into our 28 sense of ourselves. To write pop criticism is, as I have mentioned, to attract hate mail; mail not so much defending the performer or performance criticized as defending the letter writer: criticize a star and the fans respond as if you have criticized them. The biggest mail bag I ever received was after I had been critical of Phil Collins. Hundreds of letters arrived (not from teenyboppers or gauche adolescents, but from young professionals) typed neatly on headed notepaper, all based on the assumption that in describing Collins as ugly, Genesis as dull, I was deriding their way of life, undermining their identity. The intensity of this relationship between taste and self-definition seems peculiar to popular music—it is "possessable" in ways that other cultural forms (except, perhaps, sports teams) are not.

To summarize the argument so far: the social functions of popular music are in 29 the creation of identity, in the management of feelings, in the organization of time. Each of these functions depends, in turn, on our experience of music as something which can be possessed. From this sociological base it is now possible to get at aesthetic questions, to understand listeners' judgments, to say something about the value of pop music. My starting question was how is it that people (myself included) can say, quite confidently, that some popular music is better than others? The answer can now be related to how well (or badly), for specific listeners, songs and performances fulfill the suggested functions. But there is a final point to make about this. It should be apparent by now that people do hear the music they like as something special: not, as orthodox rock criticism would have it, because this music is more "authentic" (though that may be how it is described), but because, more directly, it seems to provide an experience that transcends the mundane, that takes us "out of ourselves." It is special, that is, not necessarily with reference to other music, but to the rest of life. This sense of specialness, the way in which music seems to make possible a new kind of self-recognition, frees us from the everyday routines and expectations that encumber our social identities, is a key part of the way in which people experience and thus value music: if we believe we possess our music, we also often feel that we are possessed by it. Transcendence is, then, as much a part of the popular music aesthetic as it is of the serious music aesthetic; but, as I hope I have indicated, in pop, transcendence marks not music's freedom from social forces but its patterning by them. (Of course, in the end the same is true of serious music, too.)

The Aesthetics of Popular Music

I want to conclude with another sort of question: what are the factors in popular music that enable it to fulfill these social functions, which determine whether it does so well or badly? Again, I will divide my answer into four points; my purpose is less to develop them in depth than to suggest important issues for future critical work. 30

My first point is brief, because it raises musicological issues which I am not competent to develop. The most important (and remarkable) feature of Western popular music in the twentieth century has been its absorption of and into Afro-American forms and conventions. In analytical terms, to follow the distinction developed by Andrew Chester at the end of the 1960s, this means that pop is complex "intentionally" rather than, like European art music, "extensionally." In the extensional form of musical construction, argues Chester, "theme and variations, counter-point, tonality (as used in classical composition) are all devices that build diachronically and synchronically outwards from basic musical atoms. The complex is created by combination of the simple, which remains discrete and unchanged in the complex unity." In the intentional mode, "the basic musical units (played/sung notes) are not combined through space and time as simple elements into complex structures. The simple entity is that constituted by the parameters of melody, harmony and beat, while the complex is built up by modulation of the basic notes, and by inflexion of the basic beat."[4] Whatever the problems of Chester's simple dichotomy between a tradition of linear musical development and a tradition of piled-up rhythmic interplay, he does pose the most important musicological question for popular music: how can we explain the *intensity* of musical experience that Afro-American forms have made possible? We still do not know nearly enough about the musical language of pop and rock: rock critics still avoid technical analysis, while sympathetic musicologists, like Wilfrid Mellers, use tools that can only cope with pop's non-intentional (and thus least significant) qualities. 31

My second point is that the development of popular music in this century has increasingly focused on the use of the voice. It is through the singing voice that people are most able to make a connection with their records, to feel that performances are theirs in certain ways. It is through the voice that star personalities are constructed 32 (and since World War II, at least, the biggest pop stars have been singers). The tone of voice is more important in this context than the actual articulation of particular lyrics—which means, for example, that groups, like the Beatles, can take on a group voice. We can thus identify with a song whether we understand the words or not, whether we already know the singer or not, because it is the voice—not the lyrics—to which we immediately respond. This raises questions about popular non-vocal music, which can be answered by defining a voice as a sign of individual personality rather than as something necessarily mouthing words. The voice, for example, was and is central to the appeal of jazz, not through vocalists as such but through the way jazz people played and heard musical instruments—Louis Armstrong's or Charlie Parker's instrumental voices were every bit as individual and personal as a pop star's singing voice.

Today's commercial pop musics are, though, song forms, constructing vocal 33 personalities, using voices to speak directly to us. From this perspective it becomes possible to look at pop songs as narratives, to use literary critical and film critical terms to analyze them. It would be fairly straightforward, for example, to make some immediate genre distinctions, to look at the different ways in which rock, country, reggae, etc. work as narratives, the different ways they set up star person- alities, situate the listener, and put in play patterns of identity and opposition. Of course, popular music is not simply analogous to film or literature. In discussing the narrative devices of contemporary pop in particular, we are not just talking about music but also about the whole process of packaging. The image of pop performers is constructed by press and television advertisements, by the routines of photo-calls and journalists' interviews, and through gesture and performance. These things all feed into the way we hear a voice; pop singers are rarely heard "plain" (without mediation). Their vocals already contain physical connotations, associated images, echoes of other sounds. All this needs to be analyzed if we are going to treat songs as narrative structures; the general point, to return to a traditional musicological concern, is that while music may not represent anything, it nevertheless clearly communicates.

The third point is an elaboration of the suggestion I have just made: popular 34 music is wide open for the development of a proper genre analysis, for the classifica- tion of how different popular musical forms use different narrative structures, set up different patterns of identity, and articulate different emotions. Take, for example, the much discussed issue of music and sexuality. In the original article on rock and sexuality I wrote with Angela McRobbie at the end of the 1970s,[5] we set up a distinc- tion between "cock" rock and teenybop narratives, each working to define masculin- ity and femininity but for different audiences and along different contours of feeling. Our distinctions are still valid but we were looking only at a subdivision of one pop genre. Other musical forms articulate sexuality in far more complicated ways; thus it would be impossible to analyze the sexuality of either Frank Sinatra or Billie Holiday, and their place in the history of crooning and torch singing, in the terms of the "cock" rock/teenybop contrast. Even Elvis Presley does not fit easily into these 1970s accounts of male and female sexuality.

The question these examples raise is how popular musical genres should be 35 defined. The obvious approach is to follow the distinctions made by the music industry which, in turn, reflect both musical history and marketing categories. We can thus divide pop into country music, soul music, rock 'n' roll, punk, MOR, show songs, etc. But an equally interesting way of approaching genres is to classify them according to their ideological effects, the way they sell themselves as art, community or emotion. There is at present, for example, clearly a form of rock we can call "authentic." It is represented by Bruce Springsteen and defines itself according to the rock aesthetic of authenticity which I have already discussed. The whole point of this genre is to develop musical conventions which are, in themselves, measures of "truth." As listeners we are drawn into a certain sort of reality: this is what it is like to live in America, this is what it is like to love or hurt. The resulting music is the pop equivalent of film theorists' "classic realist text." It has the same effect of persuading us that this is how things really are—realism inevitably means a non-romantic account of social life, and a highly romantic account of human nature.

What is interesting, though, is how this sort of truth is constructed, what it rests 36 on musically; and for an instant semiotic guide I recommend the video of *We Are the World*. Watch how the singers compete to register the most sincerity; watch Bruce Springsteen win as he gets his brief line, veins pop up on his head and the sweat flows down. Here authenticity is guaranteed by visible physical effort.

To approach pop genres this way is to look at the pop world in terms rather 37 different from those of the music industry. Against the authentic genre, for instance, we can pitch a tradition of artifice: some pop stars, following up on David Bowie's and Roxy Music's early 1970s work, have sought to create a sense of themselves (and their listeners) as artists in cool control. There is clearly also an avant-garde within popular music, offering musicians and listeners the pleasures of rule breaking, and a sentimental genre, celebrating codes of emotion which everyone knows are not real but carry nostalgic weight—if only they were! What I am arguing here is that it is possible to look at pop genres according to the effects they pursue. Clearly we can then judge performers within genres (is John Cougar Mellencamp's music as truthful as Springsteen's?), as well as use different genres for different purposes (the sentimental genre is a better source of adult love songs than the avant-garde or the artificers). To really make sense of pop genres, though, I think we need to place this grid of ideologies over the industry's grid of taste publics. To understand punk, for example, we need to trace within it the interplay of authenticity and artifice; to understand country we need to follow the interplay of authenticity and sentiment.

In everyday life we actually have a rather good knowledge of such conventional 38 confusions. To know how to listen to pop music is to know how to classify it. One thing all pop listeners do, whether as casual fans or professional critics, is to compare sounds—to say that A is like B. Indeed, most pop criticism works via the implicit recognition of genre rules, and this brings me to my final point. Our experience of music in everyday life is not just through the organized pop forms I have been discussing. We live in a much more noisy soundscape; music of all sorts is in a constant play of association with images, places, people, products, moods, and so on. These associations, in commercial and film soundtracks, for example, are so familiar that for much of the time we forget that they are "accidental." We unthinkingly associate particular sounds with particular feelings and landscapes and times. To give a crude example, in Britain it is impossible now for a ballet company to perform the *Nutcracker Suite* for an audience of children without them all, at the key moment, breaking into song: "Everyone's a fruit and nut case," has been instilled into them as a Cadbury's jingle long before the children hear of Tchaikovsky. Classical or "serious" music, in short, is not exempt from social use. It is impossible for me, brought up in post-war popular culture, to hear Chopin without immediately feeling a vaguely romantic yearning, the fruit of many years of Chopinesque film soundtracks.

There is no way to escape these associations. Accordions played a certain way 39 mean France, bamboo flutes China, just as steel guitars mean country, drum machines the urban dance. No sort of popular musician can make music from scratch—what we have these days instead are scratch mixers, fragmenting, unpicking, reassembling music from the signs that already exist, pilfering public forms for new sorts of private vision. We need to understand the lumber-room of musical references we carry about with us, if only to account for the moment that lies at the heart of the pop experience, when, from amidst all those sounds out there, resonating whether we like them or not, one particular combination suddenly, for no apparent reason, takes up residence in our own lives.

Conclusion

In this paper I have tried to suggest a way in which we can use a sociology of popular 40 music as the basis of an aesthetic theory, to move, that is, from a description of music's social functions to an understanding of how we can and do value it (and I should perhaps stress that my definition of popular music includes popular uses of "serious" music). One of my working assumptions has been that people's individual tastes—the ways they experience and describe music for themselves—are a necessary part of academic analysis. Does this mean that the value of popular music is simply a matter of personal preference?

The usual sociological answer to this question is that "personal" preferences are 41 themselves socially determined. Individual tastes are, in fact, examples of collective taste and reflect consumers' gender, class and ethnic backgrounds; the "popularity" of popular music can then be taken as one measure of a balance of social power. I do not want to argue against this approach. Our cultural needs and expectations are, indeed, materially based; all the terms I have been using (identity, emotion, memory) are socially formed, whether we are examining "private" or public lives. But I do believe that this derivation of pop meaning from collective experience is not sufficient. Even if we focus all our attention on the collective reception of pop, we still need to explain why some music is better able than others to have such collective effects, why these effects are different, anyway, for different genres, different audiences and different circumstances. Pop tastes do not just derive from our socially constructed identities; they also help to shape them.

For the last fifty years at least, pop music has been an important way in which 42 we have learned to understand ourselves as historical, ethnic, class-bound, gendered subjects. This has had conservative effects (primarily through pop nostalgia) and liberating ones. Rock criticism has usually taken the latter as a necessary mark of good music but this has meant, in practice, a specious notion of "liberation." We need to approach this political question differently, by taking seriously pop's individualizing effects. What pop can do is put into play a sense of identity that may or may not fit the way we are placed by other social forces. Music certainly puts us in our place, but it can also suggest that our social circumstances are not immutable (and that other people—performers, fans—share our dissatisfaction). Pop music is not in itself revolutionary or reactionary. It is a source of strong feelings that because they are also socially coded can come up against "common sense." For the last thirty years, for example, at least for young people, pop has been a form in which everyday accounts of race and sex have been both confirmed and confused. It may be that, in the end, we want to value most highly that music, popular and serious, which has some sort of collective, disruptive cultural effect. My point is that music only does so through its impact on individuals. That impact is what we first need to understand.

READING FOR CONTENT

1. What are Frith's views on the "authenticity" of rock music? What should we be examining instead of authenticity?
2. List the four social functions of popular music cited in the essay.
3. Frith says that four factors determine whether music will fulfill its social functions. What are these factors?
4. Summarize Frith's conclusion in paragraphs 40 to 42.

READING FOR GENRE, ORGANIZATION, AND STYLISTIC FEATURES

1. Describe the contrasts Frith sets up in the first paragraph.
2. Frith divides the article into five parts. How does each part contribute to his argument?
3. Do you think that Frith is addressing his article to a wide, general audience or to specialized, scholarly readers? How did you come to that conclusion?

READING FOR RHETORICAL CONTEXT

1. Explain Frith's purpose for writing the article. What does he want to achieve?
2. Find the places in the article where Frith refers to his previous work. What function do these references serve?
3. In a number of paragraphs (3, 6, 7, 10, 22, 29, 30, 31, 40), Frith poses questions. What function do the questions serve? How do they affect the reader?

WRITING ASSIGNMENTS

1. Frith says that for all people, the most significant pop songs "are those they heard as adolescents" (paragraph 26). Which songs are most memorable to you? What memories do these songs trigger? Write an essay in which you recall songs and experiences and reflect upon the meanings they hold for you.

2. As a prereading question, we asked you to explain whether you think some types of music are better than others. Reread your response. Rewrite your response in light of Frith's argument, explaining how well specific songs and performances fulfill various social functions for you.

3. Write an essay in which you agree or disagree with Frith's statement "Pop tastes do not just derive from our socially constructed identities; they also help shape them" (paragraph 41).

Notes

1. Simon Frith, *Sound Effects: Youth, Leisure and the Politics of Rock 'n' Roll* (New York, 1981).
2. Wilfrid Mellers, *Twilight of the Gods: The Beatles in Retrospect* (London, 1973), and *A Darker Shade of Pale: A Backdrop to Bob Dylan* (London, 1984).
3. Donald Horton, "The Dialogue of Courtship in Popular Songs," *American Journal of Sociology*, 62 (1957), pp. 569–78.
4. Andrew Chester, "Second Thoughts on a Rock Aesthetic: The Band," *New Left Review*, 62 (1970), pp. 78–9.
5. Simon Frith and Angela McRobbie, "Rock and Sexuality," *Screen Education* 29 (1978/9), pp. 3–19.

■ ■ ■ ■ ■ ■ ■ ■ ■ ■ ■

Music and Morality

Roger Scruton

Roger Scruton, professor of moral philosophy at St. Andrews University, Scotland, has taught at Cambridge and Oxford and is the author of books on such topics as animal rights, political thought, and the nation-state and the United Nations. His most recent books are Beauty *(2009) and* Understanding Music *(2009).*

PREREADING

Freewrite a response the question of whether Metal or DJ music plays only to oppressive rhythms without harmony or melody, and whether it alienates us, compels our submission, and limits our social horizons.

Plato Remains Our Finest Rock Critic

"The ways of poetry and music are not changed anywhere without change in the most   1
important laws of the city." So wrote Plato in the *Republic* (4.424c). Music, for Plato, was not a neutral amusement. It could express and encourage virtue—nobility, dignity,

Scruton, Roger. "Music and Morality." *The American Spectator* 43.1 (Feb. 2010): 42–45. Print. Reprinted by permission of The American Spectator, www.spectator.org.

temperance, chastity. But it could also express and encourage vice—sensuality, belligerence, indiscipline.

Plato's concern was not so very different from that of a modern person worrying 2 about the moral character, and moral effect, of Death Metal, say, or musical kitsch of the Andrew Lloyd Webber kind. "Should our children be listening to this stuff?" is the question in the mind of modern adults, just as "should the city permit this stuff?" was the question in the mind of Plato. Of course, we have long since given up on the idea that you can forbid certain kinds of music by law. Nevertheless, it is still common to believe that music has—or can have—a moral character, and that the character of a work or style of music can "rub off" in some way on its devotees.

We don't forbid musical idioms by law, but we should remember that our laws 3 are made by people who have musical tastes; Plato may be right, even in relation to a modern democracy, that changes in musical culture go hand in hand with changes in the laws, since changes in the laws so often reflect pressures from the culture. There is no doubt that popular music today enjoys a status higher than any other cultural product. Pop stars are first among celebrities, idolized by the young, taken as role models, courted by politicians, and in general endowed with a magic aura that gives them power over crowds. It is surely likely, therefore, that something of their message will rub off on the laws passed by the politicians who admire them. If the message is sensual, self-centered, and materialistic (which it generally is), then we should not expect to find that our laws address us from any higher realm than that implies.

However, ours is a "nonjudgmental" culture. To criticize another's taste, whether 4 in music, entertainment, or lifestyle, is to assume that some tastes are superior to others. And this, for many people, is offensive. Who are you, they respond, to judge another's taste? Young people in particular feel this, and since it is young people who are the principal devotees of pop music, this places a formidable obstacle in the path of anyone who undertakes to criticize pop in a university. This is especially so if the criticism is phrased in Plato's idiom, as an analysis and condemnation of the moral vices exemplified by a musical style. In the face of this a teacher might be tempted to give up on the question of judgment, and assume that anything goes, that all tastes are equally valid, and that, insofar as music is an object of academic study, it is not criticism, but technical analysis and know-how that should be imparted. Indeed this is the line that seems to be followed in academic departments of musicology, at least in the Anglophone world.

The question of the moral character of music is also complicated by the fact that 5 music is appreciated in many different ways: people dance to music, they work and converse over a background of music, they perform music, and they listen to music. People happily dance to music that they cannot bear to listen to—a fairly normal experience these days. You can talk over Mozart, but not over Schoenberg; you can work to Chopin, but not to Wagner. And it is sometimes argued that the melodic and rhythmic contour of pop music both fits it for being overheard, rather than listened to, and also encourages a *need* for it in the background. Some psychologists wonder whether this need follows the pattern of addictions; more philosophical critics like Theodor Adorno raise questions of a deep kind as to whether the human ear has not changed entirely under the impact of jazz and its musical successors, and whether music can ever be for us what it was for Bach or Mozart.

Adorno attacked something that he called the "regression of listening," which 6
he believed had infected the entire culture of modern America. He saw the culture of
listening as a deep spiritual resource of Western civilization. For Adorno the habit of
listening to long-range musical thought, in which themes are subjected to extended
melodic, harmonic, and rhythmic development, is connected to the ability to live
beyond the moment, to transcend the search for instant gratification, to set aside the
routines of the consumer society, with its constant pursuit of the "fetish," and to put
real values in the place of fleeting desires. And there is something persuasive here
that needs to be rescued from Adorno's intemperate and over-politicized critique of
just about everything he found in America. But Adorno reminds us that it is very hard
to criticize a musical idiom without standing in judgment on the culture to which it
belongs. Musical idioms don't come in sealed packets, with no relation to the rest of
human life. And when a particular kind of music surrounds us in public spaces, when
it invades every café, bar, and restaurant, when it blares at us from passing motor cars
and dribbles from the open taps of radios and iPods all over the planet, the critic may
seem to stand like the apocryphal King Canute before an irresistible tide, uttering useless cries of indignation.

Do we then give up on pop music, regard it as beyond criticism, and the culture 7
expressed in it as a fact of life? That seems to be the received view among musicologists.
Pop, they tell us, is music to be danced to, and those who judge it by the standards of
the concert hall, which is a place of silent listening, have simply lost the plot. The essence of pop is not form, structure, or abstract musical relationships. It is rhythm, and
rhythm is something to which you move, not something to which you listen.

That is certainly a fair response to the more curmudgeonly forms of criticism, 8
but it raises a question of profound importance in the study of music, which is that of
the nature of rhythm. Many of the most successful types of pop today (DJ music, for
example, or synthetic products like Crystal Castles' "Alice Practice") are computer
generated. In such pieces you do not hear rhythm, but rather a slicing of time by an
electric cheese-wire. Rhythm is not the same thing as measure. It is not simply a matter of dividing time into repeatable units. It is a matter of organizing sound into movement, so that one note invites the next into the space that it has vacated. This is exactly
what goes on in dancing—real dancing, I mean. And the complaints that might be
made against the worst form of pop apply also to the lame attempts at dancing that
generally are produced by it—attempts that involve no control of the body, no attempt
to dance *with* another person, but at best only the attempt to dance *at* him or her, by
making movements that are sliced up and atomized like the sounds that provoke them.

A simple contrast is provided by the eightsome reel. Nothing could be more 9
metrically regular than this, but there is an audible sense of transition between sections as the gestures change—sometimes the hands are in the air, sometimes around
the middle of the body; sometimes the legs are freely crossing, at other times more
inclined to stamp. The melody is slightly varied with each change of partner, and the
excitement builds with every closure of the melodic line.

The rhythm in Heavy Metal, or in the DJ music, is shot *at* you; the rhythm in 10
the reel invites you to move *with* it. The difference between "at" and "with" is one
of the deepest differences we know, and is exemplified in all our encounters with
other people—notably in conversation and in sexual gambits. And the "withness" of

the eightsome reel reflects the fact that this is a social dance, in which people move consciously with others. The human need for this kind of dancing is still with us, and explains the current craze for salsa as well as the periodic revivals of ballroom dancing.

Metal is shouted at its devotees, and the loss of melody from the vocal line 11 emphasizes this. Not that melody is entirely absent, of course; it is allowed in with the guitar solo, which is often a poignant reflection on its own loneliness—the ghost of the community that has vanished from this harshly enameled world. The world of this music is one in which people talk, shout, dance, and feel at each other, without ever doing those things *with* them. You dance to Heavy Metal by head-banging, slam-dancing, or "moshing" (pushing people around in the crowd). Such dancing is not really open to people of all ages, but confined to the young and the sexually available. Of course, there is nothing to forbid the old and the shriveled from joining in, but the sight of their doing so is an embarrassment, all the greater when they themselves seem unaware of this.

In other words, what seems like rhythm, and the foregrounding of rhythm, is 12 often in fact an absence of rhythm, a drowning out of rhythm by the beat. Rhythm divorced from melodic organization becomes inert; it loses its quality as gesture and hence loses the plasticity of gesture. Mechanical and computer-synthesized beats collapse into sound effects and cease to wear the human smile that can be heard in all true dance music, from the steel bands of the Caribbean to the waltzes of Johann Strauss.

Melody has been the fundamental principle of the traditional popular song; it 13 is what makes it possible to memorize the words and to join in the singing. All folk traditions contain a repertoire of song-melodies, built from repeatable elements. The American songbook is similar, though using the new melodic and harmonic language that arose out of jazz, and many of its tunes have endured to become known all over the world. By contrast, there is very little emerging from contemporary pop that shows either melodic invention or even an awareness of why melody matters—that is to say, an awareness of its social meaning and its ability to give musical substance to a strophic song. Countless pop songs give us permutations of the same stock phrases, diatonic or pentatonic, but kept together not by any intrinsic power of adhesion but only by a plodding measure in the background and a banal sequence of chords.

This returns me to Adorno's attack on the "regression of listening." This surely 14 accurately describes the way in which contemporary pop—from Crystal Castles to Lady Gaga—is received by its devotees. I am not talking of the words. I am talking about the musical experience. It is surely right to speak of a new kind of listening, maybe a kind of listening that is not listening at all, when there is no melody to speak of, when the rhythm is machine made, and when the only invitation to dance is an invitation to dance with oneself. And it is easier to imagine a kind of pop that is not like that: pop that is *with* the listener and not *at* him. There is no need to go back to Elvis or the Beatles to find examples.

Faced with youth culture we are encouraged to be nonjudgmental. But to be 15 nonjudgmental is already to make a kind of judgment: it is to suggest that it really doesn't matter what you listen to or dance to, and that there is no moral distinction between the various listening habits that have emerged in our time. That is a morally charged position, and one that flies in the face of common sense. To suggest that people who live with a metric pulse as a constant background to their thoughts and movements are living *in the same way*, with the same kind of attention and the same pattern of challenges and rewards, as others who know music only from sitting down to listen to it, clearing their minds, meanwhile, of all other thoughts—such a suggestion is surely implausible.

Likewise, to suggest that those who dance in the solipsistic way encouraged by   16
metal or indie music share a form of life with those who dance, when they dance, in disciplined formation, is to say something equally implausible. The difference is not merely in the kind of movements made; it is a difference in social valency, and in the relative value placed on being with your neighbor rather than over and against him. The externalized beat of pop is shoved at us. You cannot easily move *with* it, but you can submit to it. When music organized by this kind of external movement is played at a dance it automatically atomizes the people on the dance floor. They may dance at each other, but only painfully with each other. And the dance is not something that you do, but something that happens to you—a pulse on which you are suspended.

When you are in the grip of an external and mechanized rhythm your freedom   17
is overridden, and it is hard then to move in a way that suggests a personal relation to a partner. The I-Thou relation on which human society is built has no place on the disco dance floor. Plato was surely right, therefore, to think that when we move in time to music we are educating our characters. For we are learning an aspect of our embodiment as free beings.

And he was right to imply that embodiment can have virtuous and vicious forms.   18
To take just one example, there is a deep distinction, in the matter of sexual presentation, between modesty and lewdness. Modesty addresses the other as someone whom you are with. Lewdness is pointed at the other, but is certainly not with him or her, since it is an attempt to impede the other's freedom to withdraw. And it is very clear that these traits of character are displayed in music and dancing. Plato's thought was that if you display lewdness in the dances that you most enjoy, then you are that much nearer to acquiring the habit.

There is plenty of tuneful popular music, and plenty of popular music with   19
which one can sing along and to which one can dance in sociable ways. All this is obvious. Yet there is growing, within pop, another kind of practice altogether, one in which the movement is no longer contained in the musical line but exported to a place outside it, to a center of pulsation that demands not that you listen but that you submit. If you do submit, the moral qualities of the music vanish behind the excitement; if you listen, however, and listen critically as I have been suggesting, you will discern those moral qualities, which are as vivid as the nobility in Elgar's Second Symphony or the horror in Schoenberg's *Erwartung*. And then you might be tempted to agree with Plato that if this music is permitted, then the laws that govern us will change.

READING FOR CONTENT

1. Paraphrase what Scruton means by the "'regression of listening'" in paragraphs 6 and 14.
2. Paraphrase what Scruton means by the differences between "at" and "with" in paragraph 10, with reference also to the way he uses these words in paragaphs 8, 11, 15, and 16.

READING FOR GENRE, ORGANIZATION, AND STYLISTIC FEATURES

1. How would you classify the genre of Scruton's article?
2. What features characterize its organization?
3. How would you describe the style and the tone that it projects?

READING FOR RHETORICAL CONTEXT

1. In paragraphs 8 and 9, Scruton offers a response to what he calls "curmudgeonly forms of criticism," which condemn rock music for its emphasis on rhythm. Here he claims that pop music is, after all, mostly dance music that relies chiefly on rhythm to which you move. To which kinds of readers does he address his response: those who enjoy pop music or those who hate it? Why does he adopt this strategy as part of his argument?
2. To what specific kind of reader does Scruton address the major argument that he formulates about the moral qualities of music?

WRITING ASSIGNMENTS

1. Write a 750-word critical response to Scruton's article in which you counter his attack on Metal and DJ styles by elaborating upon their positive features. Extend the "conversation" that his article initiates by referring to other champions of these musical forms.
2. Write a critical response essay in which you agree or disagree with Scruton's argument. Analyze its strengths and weaknesses and explain how well Scruton supports his points even if you disagree with them.
3. Write a comparative analysis in which you compare Scruton's comments about the antisocial nature of current pop music with Frith's evaluation of it in "Toward an Aesthetic of Popular Music." How do the views of these two authors relate to each other as though they were part of a conversation or a give-and-take of independent ideas?

■ ■ ■ ■ ■ ■ ■ ■ ■ ■

Redeeming the Rap Music Experience

Venise Berry

Venise Berry is an assistant professor in the School of Journalism and Mass Communication at the University of Iowa. She is the co-editor of Mediated Messages and African-American Culture: Contemporary Issues. *She has published book chapters in* Adolescents and Their Music, Cecilia Reclaimed: Feminist Perspectives on Gender and Music, Viewing War: How the Media Handled the Persian Gulf, *and* Men, Masculinity, and the Media; *she is also the author of the novel* So Good (1996).

Berry, Venise. "Redeeming the Rap Music Experience." *Adolescents and Their Music: If It's Too Loud, You're Too Old.* Ed. Jonathon S. Epstein. New York: Garland, 1994. 165–87. Print. Copyright 1994 by Jonathon S. Epstein. Reproduced with permission of Taylor & Francis Group LLC – Books in the format Textbook via Copyright Clearance Center.

PREREADING

React to the title of the article. What is your opinion of rap music? Do you think it needs to be redeemed? Freewrite your reactions.

Introduction

When rap music first appeared on the scene, music critics said it wouldn't last, record 1
companies felt it was too harsh and black-oriented to cross over, and parents dismissed
it as the latest fad. Ten years later, rap has become a powerful and controversial force
in American popular culture. Rap music has grown significantly from its humble
street beginnings in Harlem and the South Bronx. It now encompasses a dominant
media paradigm through traditional music vehicles like cassettes and CDs, as well as
television coverage in videos and talk shows, rappers as actors, film themes, concerts,
advertising, and other promotional components.

On *Billboard*'s top 200 album list on January 18, 1992, rappers were found as 2
high as #3 and as low as #184. Despite, or maybe because of, the controversies, groups
such as Hammer, Public Enemy, Ice Cube, Ghetto Boyz, Salt N' Pepa, 2 Live Crew,
NWA, Tone Loc, and Queen Latifah have reached mainstream popularity, and each
success pushes the rap genre into new directions. Rap music is constantly testing the
boundaries of commercialism, sexism, radicalism, feminism, and realism, and a growing concern over the music's disrespect for traditional boundaries keeps it on the cutting edge.

Current literature on rap music has taken varied approaches, from content 3
analyses which analyze and critique images and messages, to trade articles which offer
promotional information on the artists and their music. One of the most important,
yet least explored, areas in this discourse is the relationship between the music and its
fans; particularly those whom it represents: black urban youths.

This [essay] will explore three controversial issues in rap music: sex, violence, 4
and racism, in relation to the social, cultural, and historical reality of urban black
American youth. My analysis will draw on both secondary and primary sources. It will
incorporate related articles and previous literature, as well as worksheet responses collected from black high school participants in the Upward Bound Program at Huston-
Tillotson College in Austin, Texas, between 1987 and 1989 and personal comments
from an October 17, 1990, discussion group with twenty-four of the Upward Bound
juniors and seniors.

In developing a conceptual framework for this examination of rap music ex- 5
perience, it is necessary to distinguish between the pop-cultural and pop-crossover
domains. The pop-cultural domain involves rap music, which, despite its popularity,
maintains a black cultural focus in its message and style. For example, rap groups like
NWA, Ice T, KRS One, Public Enemy, Ice Cube, and Queen Latifah are popular rappers with messages and styles that reflect an overt black consciousness.

In contrast, the pop-crossover domain involves rap music which follows a more 6
commercialized format. The message and style of these rap songs are more generaliz-
able and acceptable to mainstream audiences. Hammer, Salt N' Pepa, DJ Jazzy Jeff
and the Fresh Prince, Tone Loc, and Kid and Play are examples of pop-crossover rap
artists. The distinction between these two rap domains is important in recognition of

their place in the American popular culture movement. The popularity of one helps to fuel the popularity of the other, just as the acceptable nature of one limits the acceptable nature of the other.

This research evolves from a broad sociocultural ideology, focusing on the wish 7 to understand the meaning and place assigned to popular culture in the experience of a particular group in society—the young, black, urban minority. It supports the pluralist approach, which considers rap music an example of how media systems, despite their attempt to control, are basically nondominant and open to change, and can be used effectively to present alternative views. Gurevitch (1982) has examined pluralism as a component of democracy and emancipatory media. Their work advocates the idea of media as public vehicles used for enhancing and encouraging self-expression and self-consciousness by a culture. As this [essay] will highlight, cultural rap is just such a vehicle.

Black Music as Cultural Communication

In the work of Standifer (1980), the musical behaviors of black society are explained 8 as "movement with existence." From spirituals to rap, black music style is a communicative process interwoven deep within the black American experience. For example, the spiritual served as an underground form of communication and a mechanism for emotional release. Natural words and phrases had secret meanings for slave communities. According to Cone (1972), words and phrases which seemed harmless were filled with latent meanings, such as, "De promise land on the other side of Jordan," which meant: "freedom north" and later "Canada," rather than "heaven" as slave owners were led to believe.

B. B. King has told the story of how blues evolved from the unanswered 9 prayers of slaves. He explained that slaves sang to God, but remained oppressed. As a result they began to lose at least part of their faith, and started to sing what was on their minds: the blues. Walton (1972) agrees, defining the blues as a composition grounded in individual experience and one with which the audience tends to identify.

When avant-garde jazz emerged, it was in protest to mainstream-appropriated 10 music styles such as ragtime and boogie-woogie. Kofsky (1970) explains that the revolutionary jazz style used the piano as a distraction, abandoning the traditional diatonic scale, and incorporating an atonal key structure in direct opposition to Western music form. He says the harsh and abrasive music represented the dissatisfaction of Black Americans with what they had been promised, but ultimately denied: a chance to have the American dream.

Soul music in the 1960s and 1970s presented itself as a blatantly rebellious 11 black musical genre. It created for black American culture a sense of heightened black consciousness, unity and pride. Soul music, ultimately, served as a powerful catalyst for protest and social change during the civil rights and black power movements (Maultsby, 1983).

Finally, today's rap music style reflects the distinct experience of urban black 12 culture. Black slang, street attitude, and fashion are reflected in powerful spoken song. Name-brand tennis shoes, sweatsuits, and an exorbitant display of gold chains and rings create a sense of appropriated success. The heavy beat, incessant scratching, aggressive delivery, and lyrical storyline present a message of anger and frustration from urban existence.

Just as socially, culturally, and historically music has always been essential to 13 the evolution of the black American experience, an essential part of contemporary black culture is the urban environment which manifests itself within the context of rap music. Several scholars have discussed the power of rap music as a mechanism of communication involving the struggle for a recognized black cultural empowerment.

Dyson (1991) examines performance, protest, and prophecy in the culture of 14 hip hop. He suggests that t is difficult for a society that maintains social arrangements, economic conditions, and political choices so that it can create and reproduce poverty, racism, sexism, classism, and violence to appreciate a music that contests and scandalizes such problems. He fears that the pop success of rap artists often means mainstream dilution; the sanitizing of rap's expression of urban realities, resulting in sterile hip hop devoid of is original fire and offensive to no one.

The communicative power of rap music is traced back to an African tradition 15 called "nommo" by Stephens (1991). Nommo refers to the supernatural power of the spoken word. The rhyme and rhythm which are part of African-American speech, literature, music, and dance are essential elements of nommo. He says it is believed in Africa that nommo can create changes in attitude. It can evoke unity, identity, and an atmosphere where everyone can relate.

Perkins (1991) explains how the ideology of the Nation of Islam has become an 16 important element of rap music's message. Perkins feels that rap artists such as Public Enemy and KRS One are social revolutionaries and their role is to carry the black nationalist tradition forward by heightening awareness, stimulating thought, and provoking the true knowledge of self.

The messages in rap music have also been compared to the messages in blues by 17 Nelson (1991). She contrasts themes such as poverty and despair that appear in both and discusses how both musical forms are based on truth and reality. Dixon (1989) speaks about the context of rap music as truth. He feels rap music "…unites the listeners of the music into a common group with clear and readily identifiable racial, cultural, economic, and political/sexual shared concerns and emerges as the voice of its adherents."

Finally, the issue of rap as historical account is raised by Shusterman (1991). 18 He says, "Many rappers have taken their place as insightful inquirers into reality and teachers of truth, particularly those aspects of reality and truth which get neglected or distorted by establishment history books and contemporary media coverage." Shusterman attributes the audible voice of rap music in popular culture to its commercial success in the mass media, which has enabled renewed artistic investment as an undeniable source of black cultural pride.

Rap Music, Urban Reality, and Popular Culture

Popular culture is made by subordinated peoples in their own interests out of resources 19 that also, contradictorily, serve the economic interests of the dominant. Popular culture is made from within and below, not imposed from without and above as mass cultural theorists would have it. There is always an element of popular culture that lies outside of social control, that escapes or opposes hegemonic forces.

The power and promise of rap music rests in the bosom of urban America; an environment where one out of twenty-two black males will be killed by violent crimes, where the black high-school dropout rate is as high as 72 percent and where 86 percent of black children grow up in poverty. Years of degadation, welfare hand-outs, institutional racism, and discrimination have created a community where little hope, low self-esteem and frequent failure translate into drugs, teen pregnancy, and gang violence. These are the social, cultural, and economic conditions which have spurred rap's paradoxical position within American popular culture. 20

The relationship between low socioeconomic status and the negative self-evaluation of black urban youth results in problems of low self-esteem. These feelings are prominent because of limited opportunities, unsatisfied needs, instability, estrangement, racial prejudice, and discrimination (Hulbary, 1975). As these youth struggle with questions of independence and control in their environment, they embrace a sense of powerlessness. Mainstream society tends to view the lifestyles of low-income communities as deviant. The poor are believed to be perpetuating their own poverty because of their nonconforming attitudes and unconventional behavior (Gladwin, 1967). Poussaint and Atkinson (1972) suggest that the stereotypes of deviance, a lack of motivation, and limited educational achievements ultimately become a part of their identity. 21

The youth movement which is evident in popular culture has, therefore, brought about only illusions for many urban American youth. The term "youth," which came to mean a specific attitude including pleasure, excitement, hope, power, and invincibility, was not experienced by these kids. Their future was mangled by racism, prejudice, discrimination, and economic and educational stagnation. As Bernard (1991) suggests, they found themselves in a gloomy darkness without friendship, trust, or hope; backed into a corner where life is all about self. 22

As a product of the black urban community, rap music is indisputably entangled with the struggle for black identity and legitimacy within mainstream society. Although rap music is undergoing significant changes, much of it remains true to its aesthetic purpose of bringing to the forefront the problematic nature of urban American experience. 23

Cultural rap music is, therefore, often seen in a negative light. The "culture of rap music" has been characterized as a "culture of attitude" by Adler (1990), who suggests that attitude is something civilized society abhors and likes to keep under control. He concludes that the end of attitude is nihilism, which by definition leads nowhere, and that the culture of attitude is repulsive, mostly empty of political content. 24

Costello and Wallace (1990), in *Signifying Rappers*, say that vitalists have argued for forty years that postwar art's ultimate expression will be a kind of enormous psychosocial excrement and the real aesthetic (conscious or otherwise) of today's best serious rap may be nothing but the first wave of this great peristalsis. 25

Negative images of rap are dominant in the news. The 2 Live Crew controversy in Florida concerning sexually explicit lyrics made big headlines, along with the charity basketball game by rap artists in New York which resulted in nine kids being trampled to death. Violence has also been reported at movies where rap themes are 26 prominent. And, the music of defiant rap groups like NWA (Niggas with Attitude) have been considered radical and extremist. They made history as the first musical group to receive a warning from the FBI about the negative content of their song, "Fuck the Police," which encourages a lack of respect for the system.

Urban black American culture exists within a large infrastructure, segmented by 27 various negative individual and situational environments. The relationship between the rap fan and his or her music, therefore, involves the larger contextual environment of the urban street. At the same time, it is important to recognize how the mainstream success of the rap genre has made urban language, style, dance, and attitude viable components of popular cultural form.

The Issue of Sex

The 2 Live Crew appeared in the public eye in 1986 with their first album, *The 2 Live* 28 *Crew Is What We Are*. Their most successful hit, which is now considered tame, was entitled, "Hey, We Want Some Pussy." It sold a half-million copies without the backing of a major record company. The Crew's next album took sexual rap to a new level. *Move Something* sold more than a million copies and included songs like, "Head," "Booty and Cock," and "Me so Horny."

It was their third album, *As Nasty as We Wanna Be*, which made the group a 29 household name. On June 6, 1990, U.S. District Judge Jose Gonzales, Jr., said the album was "utterly without any redeeming social value." The obscenity issue created a media bonanza for 2 Live Crew and boosted the sale of their album to more than two million copies.

Luther Campbell, leader of the group, has been on a number of talk shows and 30 in many articles defending his right to produce sexually explicit rap music. In an interview in *Black Beat* magazine, he called the lyrics funny. "The stuff on our X-rated albums is meant to be funny. We sit down and laugh about our lyrics. We don't talk about raping women or committing violence against them or anything like that" (Henderson, February 1990).

An analysis by Peterson-Lewis (1991) presents a different perspective: "…their 31 lyrics lack the wit and strategic use of subtle social commentary necessary for effective satire; thus they do not so much debunk myths as create new ones, the major one being that in interacting with black women 'anything goes.' Their lyrics not only fail to satirize the myth of the hypersexual black, they also commit the moral blunder of sexualizing the victimization of women, black women in particular."

Campbell adds that the group's lyrics are a reflection of life in America's black 32 neighborhoods. Yet he admits he won't let his seven-year-old daughter listen to such music. While 2 Live Crew served as the thrust of the controversy, the negative images of women in this society have been a concern of feminists for many years, through various media forms.

Peterson-Lewis goes on to question the extent of the ethical and moral respon- 33 sibilities of artists to their audiences and the larger public. She focuses her argument on the constitutionality and racially motivated persecution and prosecution of 2 Live Crew, which she feels overshadowed the real criticism—the sexually explicit nature of their lyrics and their portrayal of women as objects for sexual assault.

Frankel (1990) agrees that the 2 Live Crew situation took away the real focus. 34 She says the attack on the 2 Live Crew group made it an issue of censorship, racism, and free speech, rather than an issue of disgust at how women are portrayed, especially since an act like Andrew Dice Clay, who also promotes women and sex from a negative perspective, has not been sanctioned by the law.

Even though the controversy about sexually explicit lyrics in rap music has be- 35 come a heated issue, out of a list of the top fifty rap groups, only about 10 percent can actually be identified as using truly obscene and violent lyrics in relation to women. An analysis of the number of more generally negative images of females as loose and whorish would probably double that percentage.

In a discussion on the subject of sex in rap with a group of Upward Bound high 36 school juniors and seniors, there was a split on the 2 Live Crew issue. Bené said their records contain too much profanity and are obscene, so maybe they should be sold in X-rated stores. Steve felt that fifteen- and sixteen-year-olds are able to drive, and if they can be trusted with their lives in a car, why not be trusted to select their own music? Tamara compared the group's lyrics to the Playboy channel or magazine, and wondered why access to 2 Live Crew's music is not limited as well. Marty said that teenagers are still going to get the album if they want it, despite warning labels. Finally, Dewan explained that the warning labels can't stop the sexual things teens think in their minds.

When asked about record censorship, most of them felt that some kind of cen- 37 sorship was acceptable for kids ages twelve and under. But they also cited television, movies, and magazines as the places where they usually receive new sexual information, rather than music.

Female rappers like Salt N' Pepa, Queen Latifah, Yo Yo, and MC Lyte have 38 stepped forward to dispel many of the negative images of women with their own lyrical rhetoric and aggressive performance style. Yo Yo, a popular nineteen-year-old female rapper, says that she got into rap to help improve women's self-esteem because a lot of black women don't believe in themselves. She has created an organization for teenage women called the Intelligent Black Women's Coalition (IBWC), which speaks on issues of social concern.

In direct opposition to positive female rappers are the controversial groups, 39 Bytches wit' Problems and Hoes wit' Attitude. According to Lyndah and Michelle of Bytches wit' Problems, "There's a little bitch in all women, and even some men... and we're just the bitches to say it" (October 1991). Lyndah and Michelle's new album, B.Y.T.C.H.E.S., reflects another side of black urban reality. They feel they can say what they want just like men do, which is evident from their songs "Two Minute Brother," "Fuck a Man," and "Is the Pussy still Good." Their definition of a bitch is "a powerful woman in control of her life, going after what she wants and saying what's on her mind" (October 1991).

The female trio, Hoes wit' Attitude, has been called the raunchiest all-girl rap 40 group. With hit songs like "Eat This," "Little Dick," and "Livin' in a Hoe House," they constantly test their motto, "If men can do it we can too." The girls, 2 Jazzy, Baby Girl, and D. Diva, argue that "hoein' is the oldest profession, whether you're sellin' your body or something else. A hoe is a business woman. We're in business, the business of selling records."

When asked about their perceptions of such aggressive female images, the dis- 41
cussion group of Upward Bound students again split. Lanietra said, "All women are
not like that and the words they use to describe themselves are not necessary." Louis
felt rappers don't actually use the lyrics they sing about as a personal thing with another person, they are using the lyrics to warn people about the females and males of
today. Tonje added concern that such rap music makes females seem like sex objects
that can only be used to satisfy a man's needs.

These youth easily identified specific popular songs which had messages that 42
were positive and negative in relation to sex. The top three songs named as "good for
moral thinking" were "Let's Wait Awhile" by Janet Jackson; "Growing Up" by Whodini;
and "I Need Love" by L L Cool J. The top three songs listed as "bad for moral thinking
about sex" were "Hey, We Want some Pussy" by the 2 Live Crew; "I Want Your Sex" by
George Michael; and "Kanday" by L L Cool J.

The Issue of Violence

Another prominent issue which seems to follow the rap music phenomenon is 43
violence. On December 28, 1991, nine youths were trampled to death at a charity basketball game with rap artists at City College in New York. On July 12, 1991,
Alejandra Phillips, a supermarket clerk, was shot outside a theater showing of *Boyz
N' the Hood.* Cultural rap is often connected with such negative images of the black
underclass. Pictures of pimps, drug dealers, and gang members riding around with
rap music blasting loudly are prevalent in the media. Scholars like Jon Spencer
have questioned the link between rap and rape made by Tipper Gore's editorial in
The Washington Post, "Hate, Rape, and Rap" and the juxtapositioning of the 2 Live
Crew's lyrics with the rape of a New York jogger in Central Park. Spencer suggests
that when people see the word "rap" they read the word "rape," and they often view
"rappists" as rapists.

One of the groups most publicized when exploring violence are NWA (Niggas 44
with Attitude). NWA consists of five L.A. rappers whose controversial lyrics include
topics like gang banging, drive-by shootings, and police confrontations. MTV refused
to air their video, "Straight Outta Compton," because they said it "glorified violence."
The ex-leader of the group, Ice Cube, says the group's lyrics deal with reality and violence is their reality. "Our goals are to show the audience the raw reality of life. When
they come out the other end they gonna say, 'damn, it's like that for real?' And, we're
gonna make money" (Hochman 1989).

Williams (1990) disagrees that rap images and music are representative of the 45
beliefs and ethics of black communities. He says when women are treated like sex
slaves and ideas like "materialism is God" are put forth, they are not true visions of
black America or black culture, but a slice of the worst of a small element of black
culture that is not emblematic of the black community at large.

The positive efforts of black rappers to eliminate violence in their music and 46
neighborhoods have not received as much publicity as the negative. For example, various popular rap stars from the West Coast such as NWA, Hammer, Young MC, and
Digital Underground came together to record a single entitled "We're All in the Same
Gang." It was a rap song that spoke out against the senseless violence of gangs.

The East Coast's "Stop the Violence" campaign raised more than $300,000   47
for youth-oriented community programs in New York. More than a dozen rappers,
like Ice T, Tone Loc, and King Tee participated in the "Self Destruction" record
and video which addressed the need to end black-on-black crime. The powerful
lyrics and images of the song brought a new positive black urban consciousness
into focus.

Kids are forced to learn from the rhythm of life around them. Rap songs often   48
include graphic images of drug dealers. The drug dealer is a very real personality in
low-income neighborhoods. When asked to write down three questions they would
include on a drug survey, Tamara asked, "Why do they (adults, authorities) allow the
pushers to sell drugs on the corner by my school?" She later told me that it was very
obvious what happens on that corner, but nobody bothers to do anything about it, so
kids come to accept it too.

There is an obvious struggle going on in these kids' lives that links them   49
to the conflict-oriented nature of cultural rap. The violent urban environment
which is a prominent theme in rap music is also a prominent reality. One example
of that reality came from a worksheet concerning a rap tune called "Wild Wild
West" by Kool Moe Dee. In the song, Kool Moe Dee raps about how he and his
buddies stop others (including gangs) from coming into their neighborhoods and
terrorizing people. He talks about taking control of his environment in a fashion
appropriate to the Old West. In response to the song, Mary said she could relate
to it because in her neighborhood, people are always getting into other people's
personal business. Tim also knew what Kool Moe Dee was talking about because
he and his homeboys (friends) were always scuffling (fighting) with somebody for
respect. Michael said the song means that kids are growing up too hard in the
streets. He added, "My school and neighborhood are a lot like that." Finally, James
said he had a friend who got shot at a party "because of the way he looked at a guy
and that's just how it is."

On a more positive side, several of the kids have come to understand and   50
change these negatives through their own raps. The Get It Girl Crew, four young
ladies who love to rap, wrote their rap as a testimony of their spirit and hope for the
future.

The Issue of Racism

The issue of race in America is not a silent one today. Separate ideologies of black   51
power and white supremacy are prominent and dividing the nation even further as
indicated by an ex-KKK leader, David Duke, running for public office, the travesty
of Rodney King's beating and trial in Los Angeles that ignited riots, and the powerful slogan of Malcolm X, "By any means necessary," as reemerging popular black
ideology.

According to Pareles (1992), rap often sounds like a young black man shouting   52
about how angry he is and how he's going to hurt people. Pareles says, "Rap's internal
troubles reflect the poverty, violence, lack of education, frustration and rage of the

ghetto.... Hating rap can be a synonym for hating and fearing young black men who are also the stars of rap."

Samuels (1991) voices concern about the acceptance of racism in this country 53 through rap. He writes, "Gangster and racist raps foster a voyeurism and tolerance of racism in which black and white are both complicit, particularly when whites treat gangster raps as a window into ghetto life."

Until recently, Public Enemy was the rap group who seemed to be in the middle 54 of the racist controversy. In response to the negative environment in the United States concerning race relations, rapper Chuck D (1990) of Public Enemy makes statements such as "a black person is better off dealing with a Klansman than a liberal." He goes on to quote Neely Fuller, Jr.'s, definition of a white liberal: "a white person who speaks and/or acts to maintain, expand and/or refine the practice of white supremacy (racism) by very skillfully pretending not to do so." Public Enemy has also called for the reorganization of the Black Panther party, a group considered radical in the 1960s that advocated violence and racism.

Public Enemy emerged into the headlines as racist when an ex-member, 55 Professor Griff, made several statements that were considered anti-Semitic in a speech. Griff's comment involved his belief that Jews financed the slave trade and are responsible for apartheid in South Africa. He went on to ask, "Is it a coincidence that Jews run the jewelry business and it's named jew-elry?" (Dougherty, 1990.)

After firing Professor Griff, Chuck D responded to his comments in *Billboard* 56 magazine. "We aren't anti-Jewish. We're pro-black," he said. "We're pro-culture, we're pro-human race. You can't talk about attacking racism and be racist" (Newman, 1989). According to Chuck D, the group is not here to offend anyone, but to fight the system which works against blacks twenty-four hours a day, 365 days a year. He adds, "We're not racists, we're nationalists, people who have pride and want to build a sense of unity amongst our own" (Newman, 1989).

Ice Cube is the second most prominent rapper to be labelled racist because 57 of several controversial songs on his hit album, *Death Certificate*. He calls Koreans "Oriental one-penny motherfuckers" and lambasts members of his old group, NWA, about their Jewish manager. He raps, "Get rid of that Devil, real simple, put a bullet in his temple, 'cause you can't be the nigger for life crew, with a white Jew telling you what to do." In response to the criticism, Ice Cube says people need to pay heed to the frustration as they [black men] demand respect.

Ideology from the Nation of Islam, which is often called racist, is a major part 58 of the controversy. Many rappers are reviving the words of black leaders like Elijah Muhammad and Louis Farrakhan, calling the white society devils and snakes, and advocating a new black solidarity. Several popular rappers are actually emerging from the Nation of Islam calling themselves "The 5 Percenters." These artists base their raps on the Islamic belief that only about 5 percent of the black nation knows that the black man *is* God and it's their duty to teach others.

Finally, racism is sometimes attributed to the Afrocentric voice; the pro-black at- 59 titude. The controversial KRS-One (Knowledge Reigns Supreme over Nearly Everyone) condemns gang violence, poor educational systems, and drug use, but his attack on the "white system" has been called racially motivated. At fourteen, KRS One was a homeless runaway sleeping on steaming New York City sidewalk grates. At twenty-four, he has become a popular, positive rap star and educator. Queen Latifah is one of the most positive and powerful black female rappers. Her albums are rich in African cultural ideology and images as she dresses in African garb and tells kids that all black men and women are kings and queens. Queen Latifah believes that the only way to fight bigotry is to teach black children their history.

Cultural rap is so direct and angry that it can be frightening to those who don't 60 understand the frustration of these storytellers. For example, the decision not to honor the birthday of Martin Luther King, Jr., as a holiday in Arizona brought forth a rap from NWA with the theme "Gonna find a way to make the state pay" and the video portrayed the violent murders of several Arizona officials. Militant rapper Paris, on his album debut, *The Devil Made Me Do It*, presents a powerful, hard-edged commentary on the murder of Yousuf Hawkins in Bensonhurst called "The Hate that Hate Made." And the logo of Public Enemy shows the black male youth as a hunted animal with the motto "Kill or Be Killed." The image of a black silhouette is chilling within the crosshairs of a gun.

When Upward Bound students were asked to respond to the work-sheet ques- 61 tion, "How has growing up black, in your opinion, made a difference in your life?" a theme ran through the responses: the need to struggle or fight. Carlos, for instance, said being black causes him to struggle more for what he wants. He said, "At school, on TV, everywhere, other people get the things they want, but not me." Titus and Karon felt they had to fight a lot because of the color of their skin. "Fighting," according to Titus, "not only with people of other races." Damon explained, "Color really doesn't matter, but just because I'm black people expect me to be able to play sports and fight." When Damon went on to list the things which he felt might hinder him in his future success, his list included skin color, money, and friends.

As a whole, the group split on the issue of whether or not they felt their skin 62 color would affect their future. About half agreed with the statement "In the past, my skin color would have hindered my success, but that is not true today," and the other half disagreed.

When asked if they see Public Enemy, NWA, and other black-conscious rappers 63 as role models and heroes, the group said yes unanimously. As William explained, "They say what's going on in their hearts and that's what needs to be said." John added, "When brothers keep the pain inside they explode and that happens a lot around here." Nichole says she owns all of Public Enemy's tapes and she feels their music is important to help white people understand how black people feel about what's happening in black communities.

Conclusion

The history of black music is a history of adaptation, rebellion, acculturation, and as- 64 similation. An essential part of black music rests inherently in black experience. As we look closely, we realize that black music has always been a communicative response to the pressures and challenges within black American society.

The cultural rap music experience exists within the realm of specific environmen- 65 tal contexts. For the black urban adolescent, the environment manifests itself through their most popular music choice: rap. As they listen, they construct both shared and personal realities. Rappers rising from this context are empowering storytellers. Their oral wit and unique street style create a purposeful presence for inner-city ideology. Rap music has become the champion of an otherwise ignored and forgotten reality. Through critical spoken song, rappers are forcing cultural realities into the public arena. Rap music, therefore, serves not only as a mirror to this problematic community, but as a catalyst for it, providing legitimacy and hope.

Within popular culture, rap music has increased the sense of awareness outside 66 urban black America and interrupted normal flow of the commercialization process with a large dose of substance. Cultural musics, such as rap, often get caught in a repetitive cycle of acculturation, and are gradually absorbed into the pop mode. But, in opposition to pop-crossover rap, cultural rap has somehow managed to maintain elements which lie outside of social control, and escape the oppressive hegemonic forces.

Fiske's (1989) observations about such resistance and popular culture can be ap- 67 plied to the rap phenomenon. "The resistances of popular culture are not just evasive or semiotic; they do have a social dimension at the micro-level. And at this micro-level, they may well act as a constant erosive force upon the macro, weakening the system from within so that it is more amenable to change at the structural level." This is the power and promise of cultural rap.

The negative climate toward rap has been challenged by various scholars as 68 inaccurate and inadequate. Spencer (1991) believes that the current emergence of rap is a by-product of the "emergency of black." He connects rap ideology to the racial concerns of scholar Manning Marable, saying, "This emergency still involves the dilemma of the racial colorline, but it is complicated by the threat of racial genocide, the obliteration of all black institutions, the political separation of the black elite from the black working class, and the benign decimation of the 'ghetto poor,' who are perceived as nonproduction and therefore dispensable."

Dyson (1991) views rap music as a form of profound musical, cultural, and 69 social creativity. He says, "It expresses the desire of young black people to reclaim their history, reactivate forms of black radicalism, and contest the powers of despair, hopelessness, and genocide that presently besiege the black community.... It should be promoted as a worthy form of artistic expression and cultural projection, and as an enabling source of community solidarity."

Finally, Stephens (1991) sees rap music as a "crossroad to a new transnational 70 culture." He believes that "by conceptualizing rap as an intercultural communication crossroads located on a racial frontier, we can conceive how rap's non-black constituents use this artform as an interracial bridge, even as many blacks by defining it as 'only black' attempt to use it as a source of power and exclusive identify formation."

In considering such a transnational culture, the source of rap's popularity for 71 white youth is then, less difficult to ascertain. It is obvious, however, that the rebellious nature of rap in many way parallels the rebellious nature of original rock and roll. Grossberg (1987), in discussing rock and roll today, says that the practice of critical encapsulation divides the cultural world into Us and Them. "While being a rock and roll fan," he goes on to explain, "sometimes does entail having a visible and self-conscious identity (such as punks, hippies, or mods), it more often does not appear visibly, on the surface of a fan's life, or even as a primary way in which most fans would define themselves."

Rap is also seen as an icon of resentment to the white status quo. According to 72 Spencer, as in any situation where an icon such as rap is attacked, there is always the potential that the attention will grant the music even further symbolic potency and, as a result, increase the population of listeners who subscribe to its newly broadened symbolism of protest.

As rock music sinks deeper into the mainstream, cultural rap music has risen 73 as a new rebellious youth movement. Self-understanding and practice are important elements in the cultural mirror of rap music style and it has fostered a liberating trans-cultural understanding. This rap experience becomes an all-encompassing one, which includes the outward projection and acceptance of rebellious identity and beliefs for all who listen.

I believe that through rap music, low-income black youth are able to develop 74 empowering values and ideologies, strengthen cultural interaction and establish posi-tive identities. Rap music acts as a distinguishing mechanism as well as an informa-tive cultural force for the mainstream system, similar to other cultural musics such as heavy metal and punk. As an integral part of the urban experience, the rap genre serves as a bridge from favorite songs and artists to personal and social realities. It is easy to see why mainstream society would feel uncomfortable with the sudden popu-larity of traditionally negative images like dope dealers, pimps, and prostitutes in rap music. Yet these are very real images and messages in the everyday world of the rapper and his original fan: the black urban youth.

Rap music offers itself up as a unique and cohesive component of urban black 75 culture and is a positive struggle for black signification within popular culture. While there remain conflicts between negative and positive, right and wrong, good and bad, the rap dynamic is an explicit means of cultural communication fostering a crucial awareness of a reawakening urban reality.

References

Adler, Jerry, "The Rap Attitude," *Newsweek*, March 19, 1990, p. 59.

Bernard, James, "Bitches and Money," *The Source*, November 1991, p. 8.

Berry, Venise, "The Complex Relationship between Pop Music and Low-Income Black Adolescents: A Qualitative Approach," Dissertation, The University of Texas at Austin, May 1989.

Chuck D, "Black II Black," *SPIN*, 6, October 1990, pp. 67–68.

Cocks, Jay, "A Nasty Jolt for the Top Pops," *Time*, July 1, 1991, p. 78.

Cone, James, *The Spirituals and the Blues*. New York: Seabury Press, 1972.

Costello, Mark, and David Foster Wallace, *Signifying Rappers: Rap and Race in the Urban Present*, New York: The Ecco Press, 1990.

Dixon, Wheeler, "Urban Black American Music in the Late 1980s: The 'Word' as Cultural Signifier," *The Midwest Quarterly*, 30, Winter 1989, pp. 229–241.

Dougherty, Steve, "Charges of Anti-Semitism Give Public Enemy a Rep That's Tough to Rap Away," *People Weekly*, 33, March 5, 1990, pp. 40–41.

Dyson, Michael, "Performance, Protest and Prophecy in the Culture of Hip Hop," *Black Sacred Music: A Journal of Theomusicology*, 5, Spring 1991, p. 24.

Fiske, John, *Reading the Popular*, Boston: Unwin Hyman, 1989.

Frankel, Martha, "2 Live Doo Doo," *SPIN*, 6, October 1990, p. 62.

Garland, Phyl, *The Sound and Soul: Story of Black Music*, New York: Simon and Schuster, 1971.

Gates, David, "Decoding Rap Music," *Newsweek*, March 19, 1990, pp. 60–63.

Gladwin, Thomas, *Poverty U.S.A.*, Boston: Little, Brown, 1967.

Green, Kim, "Sisters Stompin' in the Tradition," *Young Sisters and Brothers*, November 1991, pp. 51–53.

———, "The Naked Truth," *The Source*, November 1991, pp. 33–36.

Grossberg, Lawrence, "Rock and Roll in Search of an Audience," in *Popular Music and Communication*. Ed. James Lull, Beverly Hills: Sage Publishing, 1987, pp. 175–198.

Gurevitch, Michael, *Culture, Society and the Media*, London: Methuen, 1982.

Haring, Bruce, "Lyric Concerns Escalate," *Billboard*, 101, November 11, 1989, p. 1.

Henderson, Alex, "New Rap Pack: Public Enemy," *Black Beat*, 20, January 1989, p. 44.

———, "2 Live Crew," *Black Beat*, 21, February 1990, pp. 15–16.

———, "LA Rap All Stars: We're All in the Same Gang," *Black Beat*, 21, December 1990, p. 16.

Hochman, Steve, "NWA Cops an Attitude," *Rolling Stone*, 555, June 29, 1989, p. 24.

Hulbary, William, "Race, Deprivation and Adolescent Self-Images," *Social Science Quarterly*, 56, June 1975, pp. 105–114.

Kofsky, Frank, *Black Nationalism and the Revolution in Music.* New York: Pathfinder Press, 1970.

Kot, Greg, "Rap Offers a Soundtrack of Afro-American Experience," *Chicago Sunday Times*, February 16, 1992, Section 13, pp. 5, 24–25.

Leland, John, "Cube on Thin Ice," *Newsweek*, December 2, 1991, pp. 69.

Levine, David, "Good Business, Bad Messages," *American Health*, May 1991, p. 16.

Logan, Andy, "Around City Hall," *The New Yorker*, January 27, 1992, pp. 64–65.

Lyndah and Michelle (Bytches wit' Problems), "A Bitch Is a Badge of Honor for Us," *Rappages*, 1, October 1991, p. 46.

Maultsby, Portia, "Soul Music: Its Sociological and Political Significance in American Popular Culture," *Journal of Popular Culture*, 17, Fall 1983, pp. 51–60.

Miller, Trudy, "'91 Holiday-Week Biz 3.7% Jollier than '90," *Billboard*, February 1, 1992, p. 46.

Mills, David, "The Obscenity Case: Criminalizing Black Culture," *Washington Post*, June 17, 1990, pp. G1, G8–G9.

———, "Five Percent Revolution," *Washington Post*, January 6, 1991, pp. G-1, G-6.

Nelson, Angela, "Theology in the Hip Hop of Public Enemy and Kool Moe Dee," *Black Sacred Music: A Journal of Theomusicology*, 5, Spring 1991, pp. 51–60.

Newman, Melinda, "Public Enemy Ousts Member over Remarks," *Billboard*, 101, July 1, 1989, pp. 1, 87.

"Paralyzed Man Files Suit over Boyz N' the Hood," *Jet*, 18, April 20, 1992, p. 61.

Pareles, Jon, "Fear and Loathing Along Pop's Outlaw Trail," *New York Times*, February 2, 1992, pp. 1, 23.

Perkins, William, "Nation of Islam Ideology in the Rap of Public Enemy," *Black Sacred Music: A Journal of Theomusicology*, 5, Spring, 1991, pp. 41–51.

Peterson-Lewis, Sonja, "A Feminist Analysis of the Defenses of Obscene Rap Lyrics," *Black Sacred Music: A Journal of Theomusicology*, 5, Spring 1991, pp. 68–80.

Poussaint, Alvin, and Carolyn Atkinson, "Black Youth and Motivation," in *Black Self Concept*, Ed. James Banks and Jean Grambs, New York, McGraw-Hill, 1972, pp. 55–69.

Riley, Norman, "Footnotes of a Culture at Risk," *The Crisis*, 93, March 1986, p. 24.

Roberts-Thomas, K., "Say It Loud I'm Proud," *Eight Rock*, 1, Summer 1990, pp. 28–31.

Rogers, Charles, "New Age Rappers with a Conscience," *Black Beat*, 20, April 1989, pp. 41, 75.

Royster, Phillip, "The Rapper as Shaman for a Band of Dancers of the Spirit: 'U Can't Touch This,'" *Black Sacred Music: A Journal of Theomusicology*, 5, Spring 1991, pp. 60–68.

Samuels, David, "The Rap on Rap," *The New Republic*, 205, November 11, 1991, pp. 24–26.

Shusterman, Richard, "The Fine Art of Rap," *New Literary History*, 22, Summer 1991, pp. 613–632.

Singletary, Sharon, "Livin' in a Hoe House?" *Rappages*, 1, October 1991, p. 60.

Spencer, Jon Michael, "The Emergency of Black and the Emergence of Rap: Preface," *Black Sacred Music: A Journal of Theomusicology*, 5, Spring 1991, pp. v–vii.

Standifer, James, "Music Behavior of Blacks in American Society," *Black Music Research Journal*, 1, 1980, pp. 51–62.

Stephens, Gregory, "Rap Music's Double Voiced Discourse: A Crossroads for Interracial Communication," *Journal of Communication Inquiry*, 15, Summer 1991, p. 72.

Stephens, Ronald, "Three Waves of Contemporary Rap Music," in *Black Sacred Music: A Journal of Theomusicology*, 5, Spring 1991, pp. 25–41.

"Top 200 Albums," *Billboard*, January 18, 1992, p. 86.

Walton, Ortiz, *Music Black, White and Blue*, New York: William Morrow and Co., 1972.

Williams, Juan, "The Real Crime: Making Heroes of Hate Mongers," *Washington Post*, June 17, 1990, pp. G-1, G-8.

READING FOR CONTENT

1. Underline Berry's statement of intent. What will she explore in the essay?
2. Differentiate between pop-cultural and pop-crossover domains.
3. Explain how spirituals, the blues, jazz, soul, and rap are forms of cultural communication.
4. Why is "cultural rap" viewed negatively?
5. How did the Upward Bound students view 2 Live Crew (paragraph 36), record censorship (paragraph 37), and aggressive female images in rap (paragraph 41)?
6. Explain how black rappers have tried to eliminate violence in their music and neighborhoods.
7. Has anyone challenged the negative climate toward rap?

READING FOR GENRE, ORGANIZATION, AND STYLISTIC FEATURES

1. Comment on Berry's opening paragraphs. Are they effective? Why or why not?
2. What types of evidence (facts, statistics, references to authorities, and so forth) does Berry use to develop and support her argument?
3. Describe the features of the article that help the reader follow Berry's train of thought.

READING FOR RHETORICAL CONTEXT

1. Describe Berry's rhetorical goal. Do you think she achieves it?
2. Do you think Berry gives sufficient weight to opposing views? Why or why not?
3. Compare Berry's intended audience to Scruton's and Frith's.

WRITING ASSIGNMENTS

1. Write an essay in which you agree or disagree with Berry's views on popular culture:

   Popular culture is made by subordinated peoples in their own interests out of resources that also, contradictorily, serve the economic interests of the dominant. Popular culture is made from within and below, not imposed from without and above as mass cultural theorists would have it. There is always an element of popular culture that lies outside of social control, that escapes or opposes hegemonic forces. (paragraph 19)

2. Write a short evaluative essay about whether or not Berry's assessment of the subject of sex in rap is accurate.
3. Write a brief essay describing the cultural conditions out of which rap emerges.
4. Write a critical response to Berry's claim that rap music is not only the mirror to black urban adolescents, but also provides them with "legitimacy and hope" (paragraph 65).

■ ■ ■ ■ ■ ■ ■ ■ ■ ■ ■ ■

Digital Music: You Are What You Listen To

Lane Jennings

Lane Jennings is research director of SAI Productions in Annapolis, Maryland, a producer of future-oriented video products. A prolific writer, he has contributed many articles to The Futurist *magazine on the topic of how the reality of the present differs from what was anticipated, and how futurists and planners must confront a constantly changing social and technological horizon.*

PREREADING

Reflect for a few moments on some of the technological conveniences in daily use that would have been unimaginable ten years ago. List the new technological conveniences that mean the most to you and freewrite about them for ten minutes.

It used to be that owning a collection of "great books" was a way to show your status and sophistication: Your identity was revealed by what you read. Increasingly, however, it may be your musical library that best proclaims your identity, thanks to the ease of digital file sharing and portable devices such as the iPod.

The relationship people have with their music is so personal that some theft victims report feeling violated when their carefully constructed music collections disappear with their MP3 players.

A recent study by Georgia Tech and the Palo Alto Research Center (PARC) found that workers who shared their personal lists of music downloads tended to judge others by the selections on their lists. So playlist-sharers carefully edited their own lists before posting, so as to appear to have broader, less extreme, or simply "cooler" musical tastes.

Technologies allowing music lovers to exchange music online now also track other people's selections. Software like Apple's popular iTunes program enables users

Jennings, Lane. "Digital Music: You Are What You Listen To." *The Futurist* 39.5 (Sept./Oct. 2005): 16. *WilsonWeb.* Web. 3 June 2010. Used with permission from the World Future Society (www.wfs.org).

to select favorite performances from a huge list of commercial recordings. Instead of actually copying the music, the listener creates a playlist of selections; the music files remain stored on the host computer. This avoids violating the producers' copyrights, but also makes it easy to track who is listening to a given piece of music, and how often. It's like having your own portable jukebox, but one with a built-in statistician keeping tabs on your listening tastes.

Sharing playlists is already popular among college students, and now co-workers   5
are doing it, with some interesting implications for the workplace. For instance, in the Georgia Tech/PARC study, the 13 employees who made their personal playlists available to colleagues all did so anonymously. Yet, participants were curious enough to spend considerable time and effort guessing who had compiled which list, the researchers observed. The subjects also worried about what colleagues—particularly their managers—might think of their own selections.

The researchers conclude that music sharing served to build a community within the workplace studied. "People sharing music in our study were aware of the comings and goings of others in the office because they noticed the appearance and disappearance of others' music in the network," reports Amy Voida of Georgia Tech. "They were aware of the musical holes left when someone left the company. . . . What once was an individual jukebox became a music community."

READING FOR CONTENT

1. What consequence of sharing musical playlists does the author highlight in particular?
2. According to the author, does sharing playlists have any downsides?

READING FOR GENRE, ORGANIZATION, AND STYLISTIC FEATURES

1. How does the author try to relate personal lists of music downloads to similar activities in a less technological past?
2. Why do such lists matter to many people?
3. Describe the author's style.

READING FOR RHETORICAL CONTEXT

1. What kind of audience does the author assume?
2. What consequences result from this audience's readiness to share musical playlists?

WRITING ASSIGNMENTS

1. Write a personal response essay in which you agree or disagree with Jennings's statement: "It may be your musical library that best proclaims your identity" (paragraph 1).
2. Write a short critical evaluation of Jennings's argument about whether or not the author's assessment of shared playlists is accurate.

Of iPods and Dirty Underwear

James Rosen

James Rosen is a Fox News Washington correspondent and the author of a book on President Nixon's political downfall, The Strong Man: John Mitchell and the Secrets of Watergate *(2008).*

PREREADING

In an age of transparency and sharing private information across highly public channels such as *Facebook* and *YouTube*, what humorous consequences might follow from the unwitting exposure of your personal tastes in musical performance? Freewrite a humorous response to this question.

Behold my beloved iPod—constant companion! Battery-charged bulwark against bridge-and-tunnel boredom!   1

Engraved on its silver gleaming backside with my e-mail address and the very   2 necessary words REWARD IF RETURNED, I now find the mere act of walking without this small, once unimaginable machine..., well, small and unimaginable. And mine is just the modest 20-gigabyte model, mind you, not the unruly 60-gig beast for which I could have splurged if I were a more ostentatiously vulgar, or richer, man.

So now what the hell should I listen to? Round and round the finger goes, and   3 where it stops, only I know, or don't—and that's the whole problem in a nutshell, really. My iPod tells me I currently have 4,336 songs loaded into it, enough to provide 40 days of continuous, non-repeat play, and that I still haven't used up half its overall storage capacity.

Not that I've exhausted my underlying CD collection, on which I stage the pe-   4 riodic, furtive raids that keep my downloading habit in business. Not even close. Hell, the Beatles collection alone—some 400 neatly arranged discs that bespeak a frighteningly advanced obsessive-compulsive disorder, the (statutorily nebulous) pursuit of Every Little Thing the lads ever recorded, released and unreleased, live and in the studio—would totally overwhelm the little bugger, game as she is. And such a downloading nightmare it would be! Can you imagine weeding out the overlapping material from Ultra Rare Trax Volume 5 and Unsurpassed Masters Volume 7? Or manually typing in the track info that fails to appear (e.g., "Hey Jude [Take 7]") because iTunes, the iPod's desktop operating system, also known as "The Benevolent Mothership," gets finicky about bootlegs?

Fact is, I've collected so many bloody CDs, so much audio content—back   5 when I started, we quaintly called it "music"—that even if I spent the rest of my

Rosen, James. "Of iPods and Dirty Underwear." *The American Spectator* 39.6 (July/Aug. 2006): 60–61. *WilsonWeb*. Web. 3 June 2010. Reprinted by permission of The American Spectator, www. spectator.org.

life doing nothing but listening to it all, devotedly, without repeating a single song, I would surely die before completing the task. The same is effectively true for my iPod. Somewhere along the line, without my noticing it, the ethos that (I thought) was fueling my scrupulous transfers of material from The Collection to The Unit— This would be nice to have in there—resulted in a massive overload, not of the unit's capacity to store it all, but of my own to enjoy it: So now what the hell should I listen to?

This shocking paralysis—at what was supposed to be the precise moment of my   6 emancipation, when several thousand songs are mine to savor, and I can't choose a single freaking one—exposes the real ethos driving me, and all other iPod owners, in the downloading frenzy we keep up, beyond all rational utility: What would look cool on an iPod? So we scrupulously endeavor to ensure our fabulous portable juke-boxes, whether searched by Artist, Album, or Genre, will reflect the one trait we imagine any collection of music should boast, above all others: eclecticism. "Wow, you've sure got eclectic tastes!" we imagine others will say, admiringly, or: "What an eclectic collection!"

So let's get the Beatles' entire released canon in there, for starters and as a mat-   7 ter of Proper Respect, and a smattering of the bootlegs—both live and in-the-studio stuff—just to serve notice on my iPod's Imaginary Inspectors, those exacting little bastards, that I'm a serious collector.

And let's throw some Stones in there, so they know I can get down and dirty, too,   8 that it's not all "Lucy in the Sky" with me. In fact, we'll need the full gamut of British rock royalty—the Who, Led Zep, Pink Floyd, the Kinks, Van Morrison—and a smattering … oh, the artful smatterings! … of bootleg material for each, so they'll know I'm not some Total Tool who only buys the greatest hits packages, or even the full studio albums, including the obscure ones, but that I dig deep! And that I am well connected enough to secure unreleased material for even the most obscure artists! Need the acoustic studio demos for "Astral Weeks"? Gotcha covered, buddy! Not that I'm planning on actually listening to them anytime soon, but. …

Yes! Soon we've got Classic Rock fully represented, along with Oldies, '70s   9 Disco, Classic Funk (can't show your iFace in iPublic without some James Brown, my man, and Stevie Wonder's Talking Book and Innervisions—the greatest hits is probably permissible there), and the Acceptable '80s Music (Talking Heads, Madonna, Stevie Ray Vaughn).

And how could I have forgotten? We need some jazz! How can I consider myself   10 "eclectic" if I don't have some jazz on there? Of course, I don't actually listen to jazz, and I wouldn't know my Coltrane from my Bird, my Miles from my Mingus, but— better have some of each! Thank God my fraternity brother burned me those discs! Hooked a brother up, he did!

And some classical. Yes! But which? Doesn't matter. Throw some Bach on   11 there and call it a day. The people you care about impressing—other iPod owners, or wannabe owners—aren't going to notice if Grieg, Gorecki, or Glass aren't as Fully Represented as the Beatles and the Elvises (Presley—greatest hits and live in Hawaii— and Costello—Get Happy!! and Imperial Bedroom).

Throughout the great downloading frenzy, the same question recurs: What would   12 look cool on an iPod? In downloading a given album, should I transfer the whole thing, or just the songs I like? Wouldn't the Imaginary Inspectors see that I…skipped a song…, on Sticky Fingers? Better to enter the whole thing in there. What the hell! You've got another ten gigabytes still to play with. And if you need more space later, you can discreetly delete the Bach—Classical is always the first to go—or just swallow the extra cash and buy the 60-gig beast, which, truth be told, you should have splurged for when you had the chance.

When it's all done, you've spent a massive amount of time trying to impress 13 other people with the content entered into a device that is intended solely for your own, solitary use. You've catered to the same fears your mother used to stoke, with her exhortations for you to live clean: What if you are hit by a bus, found splayed across Fifth Avenue, a lifeless heap with a sterling resume…, and the cops find you're wearing dirty underwear? Or that your iPod, still lovingly clutched in your lifeless hand, had no Coltrane on it?

That moment may never come—but what if it does? Odds are, you'll have 14 been standing where you weren't supposed to, right in the middle of traffic, as the bus struggles, unsuccessfully, to screech to a stop, your finger going round and round, in the fruitless service of helping you to answer the question: So now what the hell should I listen to?

READING FOR CONTENT

1. From paragraph 6, paraphrase and elaborate upon the author's greatest concern in downloading music onto his iPod.
2. In paragraph 13, how does the reference to "underwear" clarify the significance of that word in the title of the article?

READING FOR GENRE, ORGANIZATION, AND STYLISTIC FEATURES

1. Describe the style conveyed in the first paragraph.
2. Describe the style conveyed in the third paragraph.
3. What is the effect of juxtaposing these two styles?

READING FOR RHETORICAL CONTEXT

1. Does the author succeed in impressing you with his knowledge of popular music and jazz?
2. How would you judge the tone of the author's references to Bach in paragraphs 11 and 12?

WRITING ASSIGNMENTS

1. Write an informal response essay in which you focus upon the social context of Rosen's commentary on high-brow versus low-brow tastes.
2. Write a short critical response to Rosen's essay in which you call attention to the author's attempts to hide or disguise his own musical preferences.

SYNTHESIS WRITING ASSIGNMENTS

1. Drawing on the selections by Frith, Scruton, and Berry, write a five-page essay in which you synthesize the three critics' ideas about the value of rock music. Address your essay to an audience of students who have read the texts.

2. Drawing on the selections by Frith and Berry, write a five-page essay in which you demonstrate how rap music serves social functions for urban African-American youth. Address your essay to an audience of students who have not read the texts.

3. Write a five-page essay explaining how Jennings might qualify Scruton's and Berry's views on rock music. Address your essay to an audience of students who have not read the texts.

4. Drawing on the selections by Scruton, Jennings, and Berry, either challenge or support Frith's argument about the social functions of music. Address your essay to an audience of students who have read the texts.

5. Draw upon the selections by Frith and Berry to write a critical response to the selection by Scruton.

6. Drawing upon the selections by Frith, Scruton, and Berry, write a five-page essay on whether their arguments apply to more recent forms such as metal, rap, and gangsta music. Are such forms of music "authentic" expression, or are they created only for the mainstream and compromised for profit?

Stories of Ethnic Difference

Within the humanities, the various disciplines of literary criticism, theater arts, history of art, and musicology attempt to assess the cultural products of human civilization. Courses in literature, drama, art, and music train students to analyze, interpret, and evaluate meaningful "texts." We use the word "text" in a broad sense to refer to any composition, whether of words, as in poetry, drama, and prose fiction or nonfiction; of color, line, and texture, as in painting, sculpture, and architecture; or of sound and movement, as in music and dance, film, and television. The questions one might ask about one sort of text resemble those one might ask about other sorts. They concern the selection and arrangement of appropriate materials; the tone, attitude, and point of view that govern their selection and arrangement; similarities to and comparisons and contrasts with other texts; and further questions about relationships between texts and the sociocultural contexts of their production and reception.

One aim of literary criticism, art history, and music theory is to make the meaning of such "texts" more accessible to us. This aim is especially visible when the text displays a social, historical, or cultural otherness whose assumptions differ from ours. Shakespeare's plays, for example, profit from a critical and historical analysis that illuminates differences between early modern attitudes and our own. Sometimes the technical jargon of an analysis may have the opposite effect: It may make the object of study appear more impenetrable than ever. For example, a musicological study of flats and sharps, harmonies and counterpoints, arpeggios and staccatos in one of Mozart's string quartets may distance us entirely from the sound of the music. If we reflect upon its purpose, however, we may find that it evokes complexity only because the process of understanding any worthwhile text is correspondingly complex. It does not seek to replace an experience of the work of art. It seeks, rather, to explore the ramifications of that experience as it connects with social, historical, moral, political, philosophical, ideological, psychological, aesthetic, and other experiences. The outcome of good criticism shows us that what we take for granted in a text may be not so simple after all.

If academic approaches to expressive forms demonstrate the otherness, difference, and complexity of those forms, many of the texts that they study deal with otherness, difference, and complexity in a primary way. Fiction, nonfiction, poetry, drama, painting, sculpture, photography, film, television, song, dance, and instrumental music all provide us with glimpses into other worlds. They can represent customs, conventions, ways of life, and human experiences that different audiences might not otherwise have. Or, if they represent a world accessible to their audience, they do so best when they afford a new perspective on that world.

The selections in this chapter deal with otherness, difference, and accessibility by focusing on a range of texts that reflect a heterogeneous world culture. The theme that draws them together is the diversity of ethnic backgrounds that compose ethnic identity in the Western hemisphere. The first selection, "A Different Mirror," is an historical meditation by Ronald Takaki on patterns of Japanese immigration to America. Takaki, a professional historian, uses techniques of personal narrative, dramatic storytelling, factual reporting, and broad historical perspective to compare distinctive qualities of immigrant groups to the United States at the end of the nineteenth century.

The remaining selections offer contemporary short stories that depict the experiences of individuals who are reminded of their ethnic identities in particularly striking ways. "Jasmine," by Bharati Mukherjee, recounts the assimilation of an illegal immigrant from the West Indies into the academic community of Ann Arbor, Michigan. Its style abounds in unexpected and good-natured humor as its title character encounters a lifestyle that she had never imagined in her native Trinidad. "Snapshots," by Helena Maria Viramontes, presents a poignant account of a middle-aged woman's struggle to adjust to a life without her husband after their divorce and without her daughter who has already left home as an adult. The woman's origins in an extended, warm, embracing Mexican family contrast with her present loneliness long after her immigration to the United States. "Between the Pool and the Gardenias," by Edwige Danticat, narrates the harrowing tragedy of a woman's life in the poverty and political factionalism of Haiti. Childless and deserted by her husband, she represents the plight of a castaway in the poorest nation in the Western hemisphere. Finally, "Bohemians," by George Saunders, presents a boy's unexpected awakening to the diversity of immigrant experience in his community as he encounters the differences between two obscure, foreign-born neighbors. Their outlandish departures from conventional behavior seem both strange and yet predictable in a nation where we all share immigrant backgrounds.

■ ■ ■ ■ ■ ■ ■ ■ ■ ■ ■

A Different Mirror

Ronald Takaki

Ronald Takaki is a professor and Chair of the Department of Ethnic Studies at the University of California, Berkeley. He is the author of Iron Cages: Race and Culture in Nineteenth-Century America *(1979),* Strangers from a Different Shore: A History of Asian Americans *(1989),* A Different Mirror *(1993),* From Different Shores: Perspectives on Race and Ethnicity in America, *and other historical studies.*

From Takaki, Ronald. *A Different Mirror: A History of Multicultural America.* Boston: Little, Brown, 1993. 1–2, 14–17, 246–51. Print. Copyright © 1993 by Ronald Takaki. Reprinted by permission of The Ward & Balkin Agency, Inc.

PREREADING

In paragraph 5 of the following essay, Takaki cites an article in *Time* magazine that reports that "white Americans will become a minority group" within the next century. How might our knowledge of past history illuminate this future? What kinds of attention should historians pay to accounts about the multicultural foundation, growth, and development of the United States? How might personal narratives contribute to this history? Freewrite some responses to these questions.

A Different Mirror

I had flown from San Francisco to Norfolk and was riding in a taxi to my hotel to attend a conference on multiculturalism. Hundreds of educators from across the country were meeting to discuss the need for greater cultural diversity in the curriculum. My driver and I chatted about the weather and the tourists. The sky was cloudy, and Virginia Beach was twenty minutes away. The rearview mirror reflected a white man in his forties. "How long have you been in this country?" he asked. "All my life," I replied, wincing. "I was born in the United States." With a strong southern drawl, he remarked: "I was wondering because your English is excellent!" Then, as I had many times before, I explained: "My grandfather came here from Japan in the 1880s. My family has been here, in America, for over a hundred years." He glanced at me in the mirror. Somehow I did not look "American" to him; my eyes and complexion looked foreign.

Suddenly, we both became uncomfortably conscious of a racial divide separating us. An awkward silence turned my gaze from the mirror to the passing landscape, the shore where the English and the Powhatan Indians first encountered each other. Our highway was on land that Sir Walter Raleigh had renamed "Virginia" in honor of Elizabeth I, the Virgin Queen. In the English cultural appropriation of America, the indigenous peoples themselves would become outsiders in their native land. Here, at the eastern edge of the continent, I mused, was the site of the beginning of multicultural America. Jamestown, the English settlement founded in 1607, was nearby: the first twenty Africans were brought here a year before the Pilgrims arrived at Plymouth Rock. Several hundred miles offshore was Bermuda, the "Bermoothes" where William Shakespeare's Prospero had landed and met the native Caliban in *The Tempest*. Earlier, another voyager had made an Atlantic crossing and unexpectedly bumped into some islands to the south. Thinking he had reached Asia, Christopher Columbus mistakenly identified one of the islands as "Cipango" (Japan). In the wake of the admiral, many peoples would come to America from different shores, not only from Europe but also Africa and Asia. One of them would be my grandfather. My mental wandering across terrain and time ended abruptly as we arrived at my destination. I said goodbye to my driver and went into the hotel, carrying a vivid reminder of why I was attending this conference.

Questions like the one my taxi driver asked me are always jarring, but I can understand why he could not see me as American. He had a narrow but widely shared sense of the past—a history that has viewed American as European in ancestry. "Race," Toni Morrison explained, has functioned as a "metaphor" necessary to the "construction of Americanness": in the creation of our national identity, "American" has been defined as "white."[1]

But America has been racially diverse since our very beginning on the Virginia   4
shore, and this reality is increasingly becoming visible and ubiquitous. Currently, one-
third of the American people do not trace their origins to Europe; in California, minorities are fast becoming a majority. They already predominate in major cities across
the country—New York, Chicago, Atlanta, Detroit, Philadelphia, San Francisco, and
Los Angeles.

This emerging demographic diversity has raised fundamental questions about   5
America's identity and culture. In 1990, *Time* published a cover story on "America's
Changing Colors." "Someday soon," the magazine announced, "white Americans will
become a minority group." How soon? By 2056, most Americans will trace their descent to "Africa, Asia, the Hispanic world, the Pacific Islands, Arabia—almost anywhere
but white Europe." This dramatic change in our nation's ethnic composition is altering
the way we think about ourselves. "The deeper significance of America's becoming a
majority nonwhite society is what it means to the national psyche, to individuals' sense
of themselves and their nation—their idea of what it is to be American."[2]

…Our diversity was tied to America's most serious crisis: the Civil War was   6
fought over a racial issue—slavery. In his "First Inaugural Address," presented on
March 4, 1861, President Abraham Lincoln declared: "One section of our country
believes slavery is *right* and ought to be extended, while the other believes it is *wrong*
and ought not to be extended." Southern secession, he argued, would be anarchy.
Lincoln sternly warned the South that he had a solemn oath to defend and preserve
the Union. Americans were one people, he explained, bound together by "the mystic
chords of memory, stretching from every battlefield and patriot grave to every living
heart and hearthstone all over this broad land." The struggle and sacrifices of the War
for Independence had enabled Americans to create a new nation out of thirteen separate colonies. But Lincoln's appeal for unity fell on deaf ears in the South. And the war
came. Two and a half years later, at Gettysburg, President Lincoln declared that "brave
men" had fought and "consecrated" the ground of this battlefield in order to preserve
the Union. Among the brave were black men. Shortly after this bloody battle, Lincoln
acknowledged the military contributions of blacks. "There will be some black men,"
he wrote in a letter to an old friend, James C. Conkling, "who can remember that with
silent tongue, and clenched teeth, and steady eye, and well-poised bayonet, they have
helped mankind on to this great consummation…." Indeed, 186,000 blacks served in
the Union Army, and one-third of them were listed as missing or dead. Black men in
blue, Frederick Douglass pointed out, were "on the battlefield mingling their blood
with that of white men in one common effort to save the country." Now the mystic
chords of memory stretched across the new battlefields of the Civil War, and black
soldiers were buried in "patriot graves." They, too, had given their lives to ensure that
the "government of the people, by the people, for the people shall not perish from the
earth."[3]

Like these black soldiers, the people in our study have been actors in history, not   7
merely victims of discrimination and exploitation. They are entitled to be viewed as
subjects—as men and women with minds, wills, and voices.

In the telling and retelling of their stories,
They create communities of memory.

They also re-vision history. "It is very natural that the history written by the victim," said a Mexican in 1874, "does not altogether chime with the story of the victor." Sometimes they are hesitant to speak, thinking they are only "little people." "I don't know why anybody wants to hear my history," an Irish maid said apologetically in 1900. "Nothing ever happened to me worth the tellin'."[4]

But their stories are worthy. Through their stories, the people who have lived America's history can help all of us, including my taxi driver, understand that Americans originated from many shores, and that all of us are entitled to dignity. "I hope this survey do a lot of good for Chinese people," an immigrant told an interviewer from Stanford University in the 1920s. "Make American people realize that Chinese people are humans. I think very few American people really know anything about Chinese." But the remembering is also for the sake of the children. "This story is dedicated to the descendants of Lazar and Goldie Glauberman," Jewish immigrant Minnie Miller wrote in her autobiography. "My history is bound up in their history and the generations that follow should know where they came from to know better who they are." Similarly, Tomo Shoji, an elderly Nisei woman, urged Asian Americans to learn more about their roots: "We got such good, fantastic stories to tell. All our stories are different." Seeking to know how they fit into America, many young people have become listeners; they are eager to learn about the hardships and humiliations experienced by their parents and grandparents. They want to hear their stories, unwilling to remain ignorant or ashamed of their identity and past.[5]

The telling of stories liberates. By writing about the people on Mango Street, Sandra Cisneros explained, "the ghost does not ache so much." The place no longer holds her with "both arms. She sets me free." Indeed, stories may not be as innocent or simple as they seem to be. Native-American novelist Leslie Marmon Silko cautioned:

> I will tell you something about stories…
> They aren't just entertainment.
> Don't be fooled.

Indeed, the accounts given by the people in this study vibrantly recreate moments, capturing the complexities of human emotions and thoughts. They also provide the authenticity of experience. After she escaped from slavery, Harriet Jacobs wrote in her autobiography: "[My purpose] is not to tell you what I have heard but what I have seen—and what I have suffered." In their sharing of memory, the people in this study offer us an opportunity to see ourselves reflected in a mirror called history.[6]

In his recent study of Spain and the New World, *The Buried Mirror*, Carlos Fuentes points out that mirrors have been found in the tombs of ancient Mexico, placed there to guide the dead through the underworld. He also tells us about the legend of Quetzalcoatl, the Plumed Serpent: when this god was given a mirror by the Toltec deity Tezcatlipoca, he saw a man's face in the mirror and realized his own humanity. For us, the "mirror" of history can guide the living and also help us recognize who we have been and hence are. In *A Distant Mirror*, Barbara W. Tuchman finds "phenomenal parallels" between the "calamitous 14th century" of European society and our own era. We can, she observes, have "greater fellow-feeling for a distraught age" as we painfully recognize the "similar disarray," "collapsing assumptions," and "unusual discomfort."[7]

But what is needed in our own perplexing times is not so much a "distant" 11 mirror, as one that is "different." While the study of the past can provide collective self-knowledge, it often reflects the scholar's particular perspective or view of the world. What happens when historians leave out many of America's peoples? What happens, to borrow the words of Adrienne Rich, "when someone with the authority of a teacher" describes our society, and "you are not in it"? Such an experience can be disorienting—"a moment of psychic disequilibrium, as if you looked into a mirror and saw nothing."[8]

Through their narratives about their lives and circumstances, the people of 12 America's diverse groups are able to see themselves and each other in our common past. They celebrate what Ishmael Reed has described as a society "unique" in the world because "the world is here"—a place "where the cultures of the world criss-cross." Much of America's past, they point out, has been riddled with racism. At the same time, these people offer hope, affirming the struggle for equality as a central theme in our country's history. At its conception, our nation was dedicated to the proposition of equality. What has given concreteness to this powerful national principle has been our coming together in the creation of a new society. "Stuck here" together, workers of different backgrounds have attempted to get along with each other

> People harvesting
> Work together unaware
> Of racial problems,

wrote a Japanese immigrant describing a lesson learned by Mexican and Asian farm laborers in California.[9]

Finally, how do we see our prospects for "working out" America's racial crisis? 13 Do we see it as through a glass darkly? Do the televised images of racial hatred and violence that riveted us in 1992 during the days of rage in Los Angeles frame a future of divisive race relations—what Arthur Schlesinger, Jr., has fearfully denounced as the "disuniting of America"? Or will Americans of diverse races and ethnicities be able to connect themselves to a larger narrative? Whatever happens, we can be certain that much of our society's future will be influenced by which "mirror" we choose to see ourselves. America does not belong to one race or one group, the people in this study remind us, and Americans have been constantly redefining their national identity from the moment of first contact on the Virginia shore. By sharing their stories, they invite us to see ourselves in a different mirror.[10]

Pacific Crossings: Seeking the Land of Money Trees

During the 1890s, American society witnessed not only the Wounded Knee massacre 14 and the end of the frontier, but also the arrival of a new group of immigrants. Unlike the Irish, the Japanese went east to America. But they, too, were pushed here by external influences. During the nineteenth century, America's expansionist thrust reached all the way across the Pacific Ocean. In 1853, Commodore Matthew C. Perry had sailed his armed naval ships into Tokyo Bay and forcefully opened Japan's doors to the West. As Japanese leaders watched Western powers colonizing China, they worried that their country would be the next victim. Thus, in 1868, they restored the Meiji emperor and established a strong centralized government. To defend Japan, they pursued a twin strategy of industrialization and militarization and levied heavy taxes to finance their program.

Bearing the burden of this taxation, farmers suffered severe economic hardships 15 during the 1880s. "The distress among the agricultural class has reached a point never before attained," the *Japan Weekly Mail* reported. "Most of the farmers have been unable to pay their taxes, and hundreds of families in one village alone have been compelled to sell their property in order to liquidate their debts." Thousands of farmers lost their lands, and hunger stalked many parts of the country. "What strikes me most is the hardships paupers are having in surviving," reported a journalist. "Their regular fare consists of rice husk or buckwheat chaff ground into powder and the dregs of bean curd mixed with leaves and grass."[11]

Searching for a way out of this terrible plight, impoverished farmers were seized 16 by an emigration *netsu*, or "fever." Fabulous stories of high wages stirred their imaginations. A plantation laborer in the Kingdom of Hawaii could earn six times more than in Japan; in three years, a worker might save four hundred yen—an amount equal to ten years of earnings in Japan. When the Japanese government first announced it would be filling six hundred emigrant slots for the first shipment of laborers to Hawaii, it received 28,000 applications. Stories about wages in the United States seemed even more fantastic—about a dollar a day, or more than two yen. This meant that in one year a worker could save about eight hundred yen—an amount almost equal to the income of a governor in Japan. No wonder a young man begged his parents: "By all means let me go to America." Between 1885 and 1924, 200,000 left for Hawaii and 180,000 for the United States mainland. In haiku, one Japanese migrant captured the feeling of expectation and excitement:

> Huge dreams of fortune
> Go with me to foreign lands,
> Across the ocean.

To prospective Japanese migrants, "money grew on trees" in America.[12]

Picture Brides in America

Initially, most of the migrants from Japan were men, but what became striking 17 about the Japanese immigration was its eventual inclusion of a significant number of women. By 1920, women represented 46 percent of the Japanese population in Hawaii and 35 percent in California. Clearly, in terms of gender, the Japanese resembled the Irish and Jews rather than the Chinese. This difference had consequences for the two Asian groups in terms of the formation of families. In 1900, fifty years after the beginning of Chinese immigration, only 5 percent were women. In this community composed mostly of "bachelors," only 4 percent were American-born. "The greatest impression I have of my childhood in those days was that there were very few families in Chinatown," a resident recalled. "Babies were looked on with a kind of wonder." On the other hand, in 1930, 52 percent of the Japanese population had been born in America. But why did proportionately more women emigrate from Japan than China?[13]

Unlike China, Japan was ruled by a strong central government that was able   18
to regulate emigration. Prospective immigrants were required to apply to the government for permission to leave for the United States and were screened by review boards
to certify that they were healthy and literate and would creditably "maintain Japan's
national honor." Japan had received reports about the Chinese in America and was
determined to monitor the quality of its emigrants. Seeking to avoid the problems of
prostitution, gambling, and drunkenness that reportedly plagued the predominantly
male Chinese community in the United States, the Japanese government promoted
female emigration. The 1882 Chinese Exclusion Act prohibited the entry of "laborers," both men and women, but militarily strong Japan was able to negotiate the 1908
Gentlemen's Agreement. While this treaty prohibited the entry of Japanese "laborers,"
it allowed Japanese women to emigrate to the United States as family members.[14]

Through this opening in immigration policy came over sixty thousand women,   19
many as "picture brides." The picture bride system was based on the established
custom of arranged marriage. In Japanese society, marriage was not an individual
matter but rather a family concern, and parents consulted go-betweens to help them
select partners for their sons and daughters. In situations involving families located
far away, the prospective bride and groom would exchange photographs before the
initial meeting. This traditional practice lent itself readily to the needs of Japanese
migrants. "When I told my parents about my desire to go to a foreign land, the story
spread throughout the town," picture bride Ai Miyasaki later recalled. "From here and
there requests for marriage came pouring in just like rain!" Similarly, Riyo Orite had
a "picture marriage." Her marriage to a Japanese man in America had been arranged
through a relative. "All agreed to our marriage, but I didn't get married immediately," she recalled. "I was engaged at the age of sixteen and didn't meet Orite until
I was almost eighteen. I had seen him only in a picture at first. . . . Being young, I was
unromantic. I just believed that girls should get married. I felt he was a little old, about
thirty, but the people around me praised the match. His brother in Tokyo sent me a
lot of beautiful pictures [taken in the United States]. . . . My name was entered in the
Orites' *koseki* [family register]. Thus we were married."[15]

The emigration of Japanese women occurred within the context of internal   20
economic developments. While women in China were restricted to farm and home,
Japanese women were increasingly entering the wage-earning work force. Thousands
of them were employed in construction work as well as in the coal mines where they
carried heavy loads on their backs out of the tunnels. Young women were leaving their
family farms for employment in textile mills where they worked sixteen-hour shifts and
lived in dormitories. By 1900, 60 percent of Japan's industrial laborers were women.
While it is not known how many of the women who emigrated had been wage-earners,
this proletarianization of women already well under way in Japan paved the way for
such laborers to consider working in America.[16]

Japanese women were also more receptive to the idea of traveling overseas than   21
Chinese women. The Meiji government required the education of female children,
stipulating that "girls should be educated . . . alongside boys." Emperor Meiji himself
promoted female education. Japanese boys as well as girls, he declared, should learn
about foreign countries and become enlightened about the world. Female education
included reading and writing skills as well as general knowledge. Japanese women,

unlike their Chinese counterparts, were more likely to be literate. "We studied English and Japanese, mathematics, literature, writing, and religion," recalled Michiko Tanaka. Under the reorganization of the school system in 1876, English was adopted as a major subject in middle school. This education exposed Japanese women to the outside world. They also heard stories describing America as "heavenly," and some of the picture brides were more eager to see the new land than to meet their husbands. "I wanted to see foreign countries and besides I had consented to marriage with Papa because I had the dream of seeing America," Michiko Tanaka revealed to her daughter years later. "I wanted to see America and Papa was a way to get there." "I was bubbling over with great expectations," said another picture bride. "My young heart, 19 years and 8 months old, burned, not so much with the prospects of reuniting with my new husband, but with the thought of the New World."[17]

The emigration of women was also influenced by Japanese views on gender. 22 A folk saying popular among farmers recommended that a family should have three children: "One to sell, one to follow, and one in reserve." The "one to sell" was the daughter. Of course, this was meant only figuratively: she was expected to marry and enter her husband's family. "Once you become someone's wife you belong to his family," explained Tsuru Yamauchi. "My parents said once I went over to be married, I should treat his parents as my own and be good to them." One day, Yamauchi was told that she would be going to Hawaii to join her future husband: "I learned about the marriage proposal when we had to exchange pictures." Emigration for her was not a choice but an obligation to her husband.[18]

Whether a Japanese woman went to America depended on which son she married—the son "to follow" or the son "in reserve." Unlike the Chinese, Japanese farmers had an inheritance system based on impartible inheritance and primogeniture. Only one of the sons in the family, usually the eldest, inherited the family's holdings: he was the son who was expected "to follow" his father. In the mountainous island nation of Japan, arable land was limited, and most of the farm holdings were small, less than two and a half acres. Division of a tiny family holding would mean disaster for the family. As the possessor of the family farm, the eldest son had the responsibility of caring for his aged parents and hence had to stay home. The second or non-inheriting son—the one held "in reserve" in case something happened to the first son—had to leave the family farm and find employment in town. This practice of relocating within Japan could easily be applied to movement abroad. Thus, although the migrants included first sons, they tended to be the younger sons. Unlike Chinese sons who had to share responsibility for their parents, these Japanese men were not as tightly bound to their parents and were allowed to take their wives and children with them to distant lands.[19]

But whether or not women migrated was also influenced by the needs in the 24 receiving countries. In Hawaii, the government initially stipulated that 40 percent of the Japanese contract labor emigrants—laborers under contract to work for three years—were to be women. During the government-sponsored contract labor period from 1885 to 1894, women constituted 20 percent of the emigrants. During the period from 1894 to 1908, thousands of additional women sailed to Hawaii as private contract laborers. Planters viewed Japanese women as workers and assigned 72 percent of them to field labor. Furthermore, they promoted the Japanese family as a mechanism of labor control. In 1886, Hawaii's inspector-general of immigration reported that Japanese men were better workers on plantations where they had their wives: "Several of the planters are desirous that each man should have his wife." After 1900, when Hawaii became a territory of the United States, planters became even more anxious to bring Japanese women to Hawaii. Since the American law prohibiting contract labor now applied to the islands, planters had to find ways to stabilize their labor force. Realizing that men with families were more likely to stay on the plantations, managers asked their business agents in Honolulu to send "men with families."[20]

Meanwhile, Japanese women were pulled to the United States mainland where 25 they were needed as workers by their husbands. Shopkeepers and farmers sent for their wives, thinking they could assist as unpaid family labor. Wives were particularly useful on farms where production was labor intensive. "Nearly all of these tenant farmers are married and have their families with them," a researcher noted in 1915. "The wives do much work in the fields."[21]

As they prepared to leave their villages for Hawaii and America, many of these 26 women felt separation anxieties. One woman remembered her husband's brother saying farewell: "Don't stay in the [United] States too long. Come back in five years and farm with us." But her father quickly remarked: "Are you kidding? They can't learn anything in five years. They'll even have a baby over there. . . . Be patient for twenty years." Her father's words shocked her so much that she could not control her tears: suddenly she realized how long the separation could be. Another woman recalled the painful moment she experienced when her parents came to see her off: "They did not join the crowd, but quietly stood in front of the wall. They didn't say 'good luck,' or 'take care,' or anything. . . . They couldn't say anything because they knew, as I did, that I would never return." As their ships sailed from the harbor many women gazed at the diminishing shore:

> With tears in my eyes
> I turn back to my homeland,
> Taking one last look.[22]

Notes

1. Toni Morrison, *Playing in the Dark: Whiteness in the Literary Imagination* (Cambridge, Mass., 1992), p. 47.
2. William A. Henry III, "Beyond the Melting Pot," in "America's Changing Colors," *Time*, vol. 135, no. 15 (April 9, 1990), pp. 28–31.
3. Abraham Lincoln, "First Inaugural Address," in *The Annals of America*, vol. 9, 1863–1865; *The Crisis of the Union* (Chicago, 1968), p. 255; Lincoln, "The Gettysburg Address," pp. 462–463; Abraham Lincoln, letter to James C. Conkling, August 26, 1863, in *Annals of America*, p. 439; Frederick Douglass, in Herbert Aptheker (ed.), *A Documentary History of the Negro People in the United States* (New York, 1951), vol. 1, p. 496.
4. Weber (ed.), *Foreigners in Their Native Land*, p. vi; Hamilton Holt (ed.), *The Life Stories of Undistinguished Americans as Told by Themselves* (New York, 1906), p. 143.
5. "Social Document of Pany Lowe, interviewed by C. H. Burnett, Seattle, July 5, 1924," p. 6, Survey of Race Relations, Stanford University, Hoover Institution Archives; Minnie Miller, "Autobiography," private manuscript, copy from Richard Balkin; Tomo Shoji, presentation, Ohana Cultural Center, Oakland, California, March 4, 1988.

6. Sandra Cisneros, *The House on Mango Street* (New York, 1991), pp. 109–110; Leslie Marmon Silko, *Ceremony* (New York, 1978), p. 2; Harriet A. Jacobs, *Incidents in the Life of a Slave Girl, written by herself* (Cambridge, Mass., 1987; originally published in 1857), p. xiii.

7. Carlos Fuentes, *The Buried Mirror: Reflections on Spain and the New World* (Boston, 1992), pp. 10, 11, 109; Barbara W. Tuchman, *A Distant Mirror: The Calamitous 14th Century* (New York, 1978), p. xiii, xiv.

8. Adrienne Rich, *Blood, Bread, and Poetry: Selected Prose, 1979–1985* (New York, 1986), p. 199.

9. Ishmael Reed, "America: The Multinational Society," in Rick Simonson and Scott Walker (Eds.), *Multi-cultural Literacy* (St. Paul, 1988), p. 160; Ito, *Issei*, p. 497.

10. Arthur M. Schlesinger, Jr., *The Disuniting of America: Reflections on a Multicultural Society* (Knoxville, Tenn., 1991); Carlos Bulosan, *America Is in the Heart: A Personal History* (Seattle, 1981), pp. 188–189.

11. *Japan Weekly Mail*, December 20, 1884, reprinted in Nippu Jiji, *Golden Jubilee of the Japanese in Hawaii, 1885–1935* (Honolulu, 1935), n.p.; Yuji Ichioka, *The Issei: The World of the First Generation Japanese Immigrants, 1885–1924* (New York, 1988), p. 45. Ichioka's is the best book on the subject.

12. Kazuo Ito, *Issei: A History of the Japanese Immigrants in North America* (Seattle, 1973), pp. 27, 38, 29. Ito's study is a massive and wonderful compilation of stories, oral histories, and poems. It is indispensable.

13. Victor and Brett de Bary Nee, *Longtime Californ': A Documentary Study of an American Chinatown* (New York, 1972), p. 148.

14. Robert Wilson and Bill Hosokawa, *East to America: A History of the Japanese in the United States* (New York, 1980), pp. 47, 113–114.

15. Eileen Sunada Sarasohn (ed.), *The Issei: Portrait of a Pioneer, An Oral History* (Palo Alto, Calif., 1983), pp. 44, 31–32.

16. Thomas C. Smith, *Nakahara: Family Farming and Population in a Japanese Village, 1717–1830* (Stanford, Calif., 1977), pp. 134, 152, 153; Sheila Matsumoto, "Women in Factories," in Joyce Lebra et al. (eds.), *Women in Changing Japan* (Boulder, Colo., 1976), pp. 51–53; Sharon L. Sievers, *Flowers in Salt: The Beginnings of Feminist Consciousness in Modern Japan* (Stanford, Calif., 1983), pp. 55, 62, 66, 84; Yukiko Hanawa, "The Several Worlds of Issei Women," unpublished M.A. thesis, California State University, Long Beach, 1982, pp. 31–34; Yasuo Wakatsuki, "Japanese Emigration to the United States, 1866–1924," *Perspectives in American History*, vol. 12 (1979), pp. 401, 404; Wilson and Hosokawa, *East to America*, p. 42.

17. Hanawa, "Several Worlds," pp. 13–16; Susan McCoin Kataoka, "Issei Women: A Study in Subordinate Status," unpublished Ph.D. thesis, University of California, Los Angeles, 1977, p. 6; Akemi Kikumura, *Through Harsh Winters: The Life of a Japanese Immigrant Woman* (Novato, Calif., 1981), pp. 18, 25; Emma Gee, "Issei: The First Women," in Emma Gee (ed.), *Asian Women* (Berkeley, Calif., 1971), p. 11.

18. Tsuru Yamauchi is quoted in Ethnic Studies Oral History Project (ed.), *Uchinanchu: A History of Okinawans in Hawaii* (Honolulu, 1981), pp. 490, 491; the folk saying can be found in Tadashi Fukutake, *Japanese Rural Society* (Ithaca, N.Y., 1967), p. 47.

19. Fukutake, *Japanese Rural Society*, pp. 6, 7, 39, 40, 42; Victor Nee and Herbert Y. Wong, "Asian American Socioeconomic Achievement: The Strength of the Family Bond," *Sociological Perspectives*, vol. 28, no. 3 (July 1985), p. 292.

20. Katherine Coman, *The History of Contract Labor in the Hawaiian Islands* (New York, 1903), p. 42; Allan Moriyama, "Causes of Emigration: The Background of Japanese Emigration to Hawaii, 1885–1894," in Edna Bonacich and Lucie Cheng (eds.), *Labor Immigration under Capitalism: Asian Workers in the United States before World War II* (Berkeley, Calif., 1984), p. 273; Republic of Hawaii, Bureau of Immigration, *Report* (Honolulu, 1886), p. 256; manager of the Hutchinson Sugar Company to W. G. Irwin and Company, February 5, 1902, and January 25, 1905, Hutchinson Plantation Records; for terms of the Gentlemen's Agreement, see Frank Chuman, *The Bamboo People: The Law and Japanese-Americans* (Del Mar, Calif., 1976), pp. 35–36.

21. H. A. Millis, *The Japanese Problem in the United States* (New York, 1915), p. 86.
22. Sarasohn (ed.), *Issei*, p. 34; Yuriko Sato, "Emigration of Issei Women" (Berkeley, 1982), in the Asian American Studies Library, University of California, Berkeley; Ito, *Issei*, p. 34.

READING FOR CONTENT

1. In paragraph 6, Takaki refers to the American Civil War as a struggle "to defend and preserve the Union." Summarize the ideas about "union" that motivate his discussion. What use does Takaki make of Lincoln's phrase "'the mystic chords of memory'"?

2. List features of Japanese history in paragraphs 14 and 15 that Takaki regards as important for understanding patterns of Japanese emigration to America.

3. Summarize Japanese views on gender that Takaki discusses in paragraphs 22 and 23 as they bear upon the history of Japanese emigration. How do Takaki's stories about "picture brides" relate to those views?

READING FOR GENRE, ORGANIZATION, AND STYLISTIC FEATURES

1. List the immigrant groups that Takaki mentions in paragraphs 6–8. Could you add other groups to this list? Why does Takaki propose that their stories are worth telling?

2. Describe the use that Takaki makes of statistics in paragraph 17. How does he interpret them to fashion an account of distinctive features of Japanese immigration?

3. Summarize the contrasts between Chinese and Japanese patterns of immigration that Takaki develops in paragraphs 18 and 20. Describe the major features of this contrast.

READING FOR RHETORICAL CONTEXT

1. Explain why Takaki begins his essay in paragraphs 1 and 2 with a personal account of his conversation with a taxicab driver. How does that account color his scholarly presentation of historical materials in the rest of the essay?

2. In paragraphs 10 and 11, Takaki cites two recent books with *Mirror* in their titles and suggests that his use of the word will differ from theirs. Explain how it differs. What role does he attribute to the idea of "mirroring" in the study of history?

3. Paraphrase Takaki's discussion of the family as a "mechanism of labor control" in paragraph 24. Describe Takaki's attitude toward that development.

WRITING ASSIGNMENTS

1. Write an argumentative essay about how American history should record patterns of racial diversity since the beginning of our nation. Reflect upon your own racial roots and comment upon how they are represented in American history.

2. Write a comparison and contrast essay drawing points of similarity and difference between Takaki's case history of Japanese picture brides and the case history of women in some other immigrant group who arrived in America with expectations of marrying and raising a family.

■ ▩ ▦ ▬ ▬ ▬ ▩ ▩ ▩ ▨

Jasmine

Bharati Mukherjee

Bharati Mukherjee was born in Calcutta and currently teaches English at the University of California, Berkeley. She has published many short stories; four novels, including The Tiger's Daughter *(1972),* Darkness *(1985),* Jasmine *(1989), and* The Holder of the World *(1993); and two works of nonfiction written with her husband, Clark Blaise,* Days and Nights in Calcutta *(1977) and* The Sorrow and Terror *(1987).*

PREREADING

Do a search on the Web for current news and information about the topics "immigration reform," "immigration policy," "Immigration and Customs Enforcement (ICE)," or similar search words. Jot down a list of issues and concerns such as overt and covert racism, economic hardship, and class tensions upon which policy has important consequences.

Jasmine came to Detroit from Port-of-Spain, Trinidad, by way of Canada. She   1
crossed the border at Windsor in the back of a gray van loaded with mattresses and box springs. The plan was for her to hide in an empty mattress box if she heard the driver say, "All bad weather seems to come down from Canada, doesn't it?" to the customs man. But she didn't have to crawl into a box and hold her breath. The customs man didn't ask to look in.

The driver let her off at a scary intersection on Woodward Avenue and gave her   2
instructions on how to get to the Plantations Motel in Southfield. The trick was to keep changing vehicles, he said. That threw off the immigration guys real quick.

Jasmine took money for cab fare out of the pocket of the great big raincoat that   3
the van driver had given her. The raincoat looked like something that nuns in Port-of-Spain sold in church bazaars. Jasmine was glad to have a coat with wool lining, though; and anyway, who would know in Detroit that she was Dr. Vassanji's daughter?

All the bills in her hand looked the same. She would have to be careful when   4
she paid the cabdriver. Money in Detroit wasn't pretty the way it was back home, or even in Canada, but she liked this money better. Why should money be pretty, like a picture? Pretty money is only good for putting on your walls maybe. The dollar bills felt businesslike, serious. Back home at work, she used to count out thousands of Trinidad dollars every day and not even think of them as real. Real money was worn and green, American dollars. Holding the bills in her fist on a street corner meant she had made it in okay. She'd outsmarted the guys at the border. Now it was up to her to use her wits to do something with her life. As her Daddy kept saying,

"Girl, is opportunity come only once." The girls she'd worked with at the bank in Port-of-Spain had gone green as bananas when she'd walked in with her ticket on Air Canada. Trinidad was too tiny. That was the trouble. Trinidad was an island stuck in the middle of nowhere. What kind of place was that for a girl with ambition?

The Plantations Motel was run by a family of Trinidad Indians who had come 5 from the tuppenny-ha'penny country town, Chaguanas. The Daboos were nobodies back home. They were lucky, that's all. They'd gotten here before the rush and bought up a motel and an ice cream parlor. Jasmine felt very superior when she saw Mr. Daboo in the motel's reception area. He was a pumpkin-shaped man with very black skin and Elvis Presley sideburns turning white. They looked like earmuffs. Mrs. Daboo was a bumpkin, too; short, fat, flapping around in house slippers. The Daboo daughters seemed very American, though. They didn't seem to know that they were nobodies, and kept looking at her and giggling.

She knew she would be short of cash for a great long while. Besides, she wasn't 6 sure she wanted to wear bright leather boots and leotards like Viola and Loretta. The smartest move she could make would be to put a down payment on a husband. Her Daddy had told her to talk to the Daboos first chance. The Daboos ran a service fixing up illegals with islanders who had made it in legally. Daddy had paid three thousand back in Trinidad, with the Daboos and the mattress man getting part of it. They should throw in a good-earning husband for that kind of money.

The Daboos asked her to keep books for them and to clean the rooms in the new 7 wing, and she could stay in 16B as long as she liked. They showed her 16B. They said she could cook her own roti; Mr. Daboo would bring in a stove, two gas rings that you could fold up in a metal box. The room was quite grand, Jasmine thought. It had a double bed, a TV, a pink sink and matching bathtub. Mrs. Daboo said Jasmine wasn't the big-city Port-of-Spain type she'd expected. Mr. Daboo said that he wanted her to stay because it was nice to have a neat, cheerful person around. It wasn't a bad deal, better than stories she'd heard about Trinidad girls in the States.

All day every day except Sundays Jasmine worked. There wasn't just the book- 8 keeping and the cleaning up. Mr. Daboo had her working on the match-up marriage service. Jasmine's job was to check up on social security cards, call clients' bosses for references, and make sure credit information wasn't false. Dermatologists and engineers living in Bloomfield Hills, store owners on Canfield and Woodward: she treated them all as potential liars. One of the first things she learned was that Ann Arbor was a magic word. A boy goes to Ann Arbor and gets an education, and all the barriers come crashing down. So Ann Arbor was the place to be.

She didn't mind the work. She was learning about Detroit, every side of it. 9 Sunday mornings she helped unload packing crates of Caribbean spices in a shop on the next block. For the first time in her life, she was working for a black man, an African. So what if the boss was black? This was a new life, and she wanted to learn everything. Her Sunday boss, Mr. Anthony, was a courtly, Christian, church-going man, and paid her the only wages she had in her pocket. Viola and Loretta, for all their fancy American ways, wouldn't go out with blacks.

One Friday afternoon she was writing up the credit info on a Guyanese Muslim 10 who worked in an assembly plant when Loretta said that enough was enough and that there was no need for Jasmine to be her father's drudge.

"Is time to have fun," Viola said. "We're going to Ann Arbor."   11

Jasmine filed the sheet on the Guyanese man who probably now would never get a   12
wife and got her raincoat. Loretta's boyfriend had a Cadillac parked out front. It was the
longest car Jasmine had ever been in and louder than a country bus. Viola's boyfriend got
out of the front seat. "Oh, oh, sweet things," he said to Jasmine. "Get in front." He was a
talker. She'd learned that much from working on the matrimonial match-ups. She didn't
believe him for a second when he said that there were dudes out there dying to ask her out.

Loretta's boyfriend said, "You have eyes I could leap into, girl."   13

Jasmine knew he was just talking. They sounded like Port-of-Spain boys of three   14
years ago. It didn't surprise her that these Trinidad country boys in Detroit were still
behind the times, even of Port-of-Spain. She sat very stiff between the two men, hands
on her purse. The Daboo girls laughed in the back seat.

On the highway the girls told her about the reggae night in Ann Arbor. Kevin   15
and the Krazee Islanders. Malcolm's Lovers. All the big reggae groups in the Midwest
were converging for the West Indian Students Association fall bash. The ticket didn't
come cheap but Jasmine wouldn't let the fellows pay. She wasn't that kind of girl.

The reggae and steel drums brought out the old Jasmine. The rum punch, the   16
dancing, the dreadlocks, the whole combination. She hadn't heard real music since
she got to Detroit, where music was supposed to be so famous. The Daboo girls kept
turning on rock stuff in the motel lobby whenever their father left the area. She hadn't
danced, really *danced*, since she'd left home. It felt so good to dance. She felt hot and
sweaty and sexy. The boys at the dance were more than sweet talkers; they moved
with assurance and spoke of their futures in America. The bartender gave her two free
drinks and said, "Is ready when you are, girl." She ignored him but she felt all hot and
good deep inside. She knew Ann Arbor was a special place.

When it was time to pile back into Loretta's boyfriend's Cadillac, she just   17
couldn't face going back to the Plantations Motel and to the Daboos with their accounting books and messy files. "I don't know what happen, girl," she said to Loretta.
"I feel all crazy inside. Maybe is time for me to pursue higher studies in this town."

"This Ann Arbor, girl, they don't just take you off the street. It *cost* like hell."   18

She spent the night on a bashed-up sofa in the Student Union. She was a well-   19
dressed, respectable girl, and she didn't expect anyone to question her right to sleep on
the furniture. Many others were doing the same thing. In the morning, a boy in an army
parka showed her the way to the Placement Office. He was a big, blond, clumsy boy, not
bad-looking except for the blond eyelashes. He didn't scare her, as did most Americans.
She let him buy her a Coke and a hotdog. That evening she had a job with the Moffitts.

Bill Moffitt taught molecular biology and Lara Hatch-Moffitt, his wife, was a per-   20
formance artist. A performance artist, said Lara, was very different from being an actress,
though Jasmine still didn't understand what the difference might be. The Moffitts had
a little girl, Muffie, whom Jasmine was to look after, though for the first few months she
might have to help out with the housework and the cooking because Lara said she was
deep into performance rehearsals. That was all right with her, Jasmine said, maybe a
little too quickly. She explained she came from a big family and was used to heavy-duty
cooking and cleaning. This wasn't the time to say anything about Ram, the family ser-
vant. Americans like the Moffitts wouldn't understand about keeping servants. Ram and
she weren't in similar situations. Here mother's helpers, which is what Lara called her—
Americans were good with words to cover their shame—seemed to be as good as anyone.

Lara showed her the room she would have all to herself in the finished base- 21
ment. There was a big, old TV, not in color like the motel's, and a portable typewriter
on a desk which Lara said she would find handy when it came time to turn in her term
papers. Jasmine didn't say anything about not being a student. She was a student of
life, wasn't she? There was a scary moment after they'd discussed what she would expect as salary, which was three times more than anything Mr. Daboo was supposed to
pay her but hadn't. She thought Bill Moffitt was going to ask her about her visa or her
green card number and social security. But all Bill did was smile and smile at her—he
had a wide, pink, baby face—and play with a button on his corduroy jacket. The button would need sewing back on, firmly.

Lara said, "I think I'm going to like you, Jasmine. You have a something about 22
you. A something real special. I'll just bet you've acted, haven't you?" The idea
amused her, but she merely smiled and accepted Lara's hug. The interview was over.

Then Bill opened a bottle of Soave and told stories about camping in northern 23
Michigan. He'd been raised there. Jasmine didn't see the point in sleeping in tents;
the woods sounded cold and wild and creepy. But she said, "Is exactly what I want to
try out come summer, man. Campin and huntin."

Lara asked about Port-of-Spain. There was nothing to tell about her hometown 24
that wouldn't shame her in front of nice white American folk like the Moffitts. The
place was shabby, the people were grasping and cheating and lying and life was full
of despair and drink and wanting. But by the time she finished, the island sounded
romantic. Lara said, "It wouldn't surprise me one bit if you were a writer, Jasmine."

Ann Arbor was a huge small town. She couldn't imagine any kind of school the 25
size of the University of Michigan. She meant to sign up for courses in the spring.
Bill brought home a catalogue bigger than the phonebook for all of Trinidad. The
university had courses in everything. It would be hard to choose; she'd have to get
help from Bill. He wasn't like a professor, not the ones back home where even high
school teachers called themselves professors and acted like little potentates. He wore
blue jeans and thick sweaters with holes in the elbows and used phrases like "in vitro"
as he watched her curry up fish. Dr. Parveen back home—he called himself "doctor"
when everybody knew he didn't have even a Master's degree—was never seen without
his cotton jacket which had gotten really ratty at the cuffs and lapel edges. She hadn't
learned anything in the two years she'd put into college. She'd learned more from
working in the bank for two months than she had at college. It was the assistant manager, Personal Loans Department, Mr. Singh, who had turned her on to the Daboos
and to smooth, bargain-priced emigration.

Jasmine liked Lara. Lara was easygoing. She didn't spend the time she had be- 26
tween rehearsals telling Jasmine how to cook and clean American-style. Mrs. Daboo
did that in 16B. Mrs. Daboo would barge in with a plate of stale samosas and snoop
around giving free advice on how mainstream Americans did things. As if she were
dumb or something! As if she couldn't keep her own eyes open and make her mind
up for herself. Sunday mornings she had to share the butcher-block workspace in the
kitchen with Bill. He made the Sunday brunch from new recipes in *Gourmet* and
Cuisine. Jasmine hadn't seen a man cook who didn't have to or wasn't getting paid to
do it. Things were topsy-turvy in the Moffitt house. Lara went on two- and three-day
road trips and Bill stayed home. But even her Daddy, who'd never poured himself a
cup of tea, wouldn't put Bill down as a woman. The mornings Bill tried out something

complicated, a Cajun shrimp, sausage, and beans dish, for instance, Jasmine skipped church services. The Moffitts didn't go to church, though they seemed to be good Christians. They just didn't talk church talk, which suited her fine.

Two months passed. Jasmine knew she was lucky to have found a small, clean, 27 friendly family like the Moffitts to build her new life around. "Man!" she'd exclaim as she vacuumed the wide-plank wood floors or ironed (Lara wore pure silk or pure cotton). "In this country Jesus givin out good luck only!" By this time they knew she wasn't a student, but they didn't care and said they wouldn't report her. They never asked if she was illegal on top of it.

To savor her new sense of being a happy, lucky person, she would put herself 28 through a series of "what ifs": what if Mr. Singh in Port-of-Spain hadn't turned her on to the Daboos and loaned her two thousand! What if she'd been ugly like the Mintoo girl and the manager hadn't even offered! What if the customs man had unlocked the door of the van! Her Daddy liked to say, "You is a helluva girl, Jasmine."

"Thank you, Jesus," Jasmine said, as she carried on. 29

Christmas Day the Moffitts treated her just like family. They gave her a red cash- 30 mere sweater with a V neck so deep it made her blush. If Lara had worn it, her bosom wouldn't hang out like melons. For the holiday weekend Bill drove her to the Daboos in Detroit. "You work too hard," Bill said to her. "Learn to be more selfish. Come on, throw your weight around." She'd rather not have spent time with the Daboos, but that first afternoon of the interview she'd told Bill and Lara that Mr. Daboo was her mother's first cousin. She had thought it shameful in those days to have no papers, no family, no roots. Now Loretta and Viola in tight, bright pants seemed trashy like girls at Two-Johnny Bissoondath's Bar back home. She was stuck with the story of the Daboos being family. Village bumpkins, ha! She would break out. Soon.

Jasmine had Bill drop her off at the RenCen. The Plantations Motel, in fact, the 31 whole Riverfront area, was too seamy. She'd managed to cut herself off mentally from anything too islandy. She loved her Daddy and Mummy, but she didn't think of them that often anymore. Mummy had expected her to be homesick and come flying right back home. "Is blowin sweat-of-brow money is what you doing, Pa," Mummy had scolded. She loved them, but she'd become her own person. That was something that Lara said: "I am my own person."

The Daboos acted thrilled to see her back. "What you drinkin, Jasmine girl?" 32 Mr. Daboo kept asking. "You drinkin sherry or what?" Pouring her little glasses of sherry instead of rum was a sure sign he thought she had become whitefolk-fancy. The Daboo sisters were very friendly, but Jasmine considered them too wild. Both Loretta and Viola had changed boyfriends. Both were seeing black men they'd danced with in Ann Arbor. Each night at bedtime, Mr. Daboo cried. "In Trinidad we stayin we side, they stayin they side. Here, everything mixed up. Is helluva confusion, no?"

On New Year's Eve the Daboo girls and their black friends went to a dance. 33 Mr. and Mrs. Daboo and Jasmine watched TV for a while. Then Mr. Daboo got out a brooch from his pocket and pinned it on Jasmine's red sweater. It was a Christmasy brooch, a miniature sleigh loaded down with snowed-on mistletoe. Before she could pull away, he kissed her on the lips. "Good luck for the New Year!" he said. She lifted her head and saw tears. "Is year for dreams comin true."

Jasmine started to cry, too. There was nothing wrong, but Mr. Daboo, Mrs. Daboo, 34 she, everybody was crying.

What for? This is where she wanted to be. She'd spent some damned uncom- 35
fortable times with the assistant manager to get approval for her loan. She thought of
Daddy. He would be playing poker and fanning himself with a magazine. Her married
sisters would be rolling out the dough for stacks and stacks of roti, and Mummy would
be steamed purple from stirring the big pot of goat curry on the stove. She missed them.
But. It felt strange to think of anyone celebrating New Year's Eve in summery clothes.

In March Lara and her performing group went on the road. Jasmine knew that 36
the group didn't work from scripts. The group didn't use a stage, either; instead, it took
over supermarkets, senior citizens' centers, and school halls, without notice. Jasmine
didn't understand the performance world. But she was glad that Lara said, "I'm not going to lay a guilt trip on myself. Muffie's in super hands," before she left.

Muffie didn't need much looking after. She played Trivial Pursuit all day, usu- 37
ally pretending to be two persons, sometimes Jasmine, whose accent she could imitate.
Since Jasmine didn't know any of the answers, she couldn't help. Muffie was a quiet,
precocious child with see-through blue eyes like her dad's, and red braids. In the early
evenings Jasmine cooked supper, something special she hadn't forgotten from her island days. After supper she and Muffie watched some TV, and Bill read. When Muffie
went to bed, Bill and she sat together for a bit with their glasses of Soave. Bill, Muffie,
and she were a family, almost.

Down in her basement room that late, dark winter, she had trouble sleeping. 38
She wanted to stay awake and think of Bill. Even when she fell asleep it didn't feel like
sleep because Bill came barging into her dreams in his funny, loose-jointed, clumsy
way. It was mad to think of him all the time, and stupid and sinful; but she couldn't
help it. Whenever she put back a book he'd taken off the shelf to read or whenever she
put his clothes through the washer and dryer, she felt sick in a giddy, wonderful way.
When Lara came back things would get back to normal. Meantime she wanted the
performance group miles away.

Lara called in at least twice a week. She said things like, "We've finally obliter- 39
ated the margin between realspace and performancespace." Jasmine filled her in on
Muffie's doings and the mail. Bill always closed with, "I love you. We miss you, hon."

One night after Lara had called—she was in Lincoln, Nebraska—Bill said to 40
Jasmine, "Let's dance."

She hadn't danced since the reggae night she'd had too many rum punches. 41
Her toes began to throb and clench. She untied her apron and the fraying, knotted-up
laces of her running shoes.

Bill went around the downstairs rooms turning down lights. "We need atmo- 42
sphere," he said. He got a small, tidy fire going in the living room grate and pulled the
Turkish scatter rug closer to it. Lara didn't like anybody walking on the Turkish rug, but
Bill meant to have his way. The hissing logs, the plants in the dimmed light, the thick
patterned rug: everything was changed. This wasn't the room she cleaned every day.

He stood close to her. She smoothed her skirt down with both hands. 43

"I want you to choose the record," he said.

"I don't know your music."

She brought her hand high to his face. His skin was baby smooth. 44

"I want *you* to pick," he said. "You are your own person now."

"You got island music?"

He laughed, "What do you think?" The stereo was in a cabinet with albums 45 packed tight alphabetically into the bottom three shelves. "Calypso has not been a force in my life."

She couldn't help laughing. "Calypso? Oh, man." She pulled dust jackets out 46 at random. Lara's records. The Flying Lizards. The Violent Femmes. There was so much still to pick up on! "This one," she said finally.

He took the record out of her hand. "God!" he laughed. "Lara must have found 47 this in a garage sale!" He laid the old record on the turntable. It was "Music for Lovers," something the nuns had taught her to fox-trot to way back in Port-of-Spain.

They danced so close that she could feel his heart heaving and crashing against 48 her head. She liked it, she liked it very much. She didn't care what happened. "Come on," Bill whispered. "If it feels right, do it." He began to take her clothes off. "Don't Bill," she pleaded.

"Come on, baby," he whispered again. "You're a blossom, a flower."

He took off his fisherman's knit pullover, the corduroy pants, the blue shorts. 49 She kept pace. She'd never had such an effect on a man. He nearly flung his socks and Adidas into the fire. "You feel so good," he said. "You smell so good. You're really something, flower of Trinidad." "Flower of Ann Arbor," she said, "not Trinidad."

She felt so good she was dizzy. She'd never felt this good on the island where 50 men did this all the time, and girls went along with it always for favors. You couldn't feel really good in a nothing place. She was thinking this as they made love on the Turkish carpet in front of the fire: she was a bright, pretty girl with no visa, no papers, and no birth certificate. No nothing other than what she wanted to invent and tell. She was a girl rushing wildly into the future.

His hand moved up her throat and forced her lips apart and it felt so good, so 51 right; that she forgot all the dreariness of her new life and gave herself up to it.

READING FOR CONTENT

1. List the business and commercial enterprises of the Daboo family in paragraphs 5, 6, and 8. What attitude does the narrator project toward those activities?
2. List the various racial and ethnic groups with which Jasmine has contact in paragraphs 5, 9, 10, 19, and 20.
3. Paraphrase and compare the story's representations of Christmastime with the Hatch-Moffitts, the Daboos, and Jasmine's parents in paragraphs 30, 33, and 35.

READING FOR GENRE, ORGANIZATION, AND STYLISTIC FEATURES

1. Summarize the features of Lara's first meeting with Jasmine in paragraphs 20, 21, 22, and 24. Why does Lara assume that Jasmine is a student, actress, and writer?
2. Explain why in paragraph 26 Jasmine thinks that the Hatch-Moffitt household is "topsy-turvy."
3. Explain the significance of Bill's "Learn to be more selfish" in paragraph 30, of Jasmine's "But" in paragraph 35, and of Lara's "guilt trip" in paragraph 36.

READING FOR RHETORICAL CONTEXT

1. Describe Jasmine's attitude toward the Daboo family in paragraph 5. Why does she feel superior to them?

2. Summarize the account of Jasmine's upbringing in Jamaica as related in paragraphs 3, 4, 6, and 20.

3. Explain the significance of Bill's "If it feels right, do it" in paragraph 48.

WRITING ASSIGNMENTS

1. Write a critical analysis of the story's action from the points of view of the Daboos, the Hatch-Moffitts, and Jasmine. Comment upon the narrator's implied attitude toward each of these points of view.

2. Write a critical evaluation of Jasmine's character. Is she an outright opportunist? Or does she acquiesce to her crises, accepting the provisional good that comes to her? To what extent does she control what's happening to her? In the final scene, who seduces whom?

■ ■ ■ ■ ■ ■ ■ ■ ■ ■ ■

Snapshots

Helena Maria Viramontes

Helena Maria Viramontes was born in East Los Angeles and now teaches at Cornell University. Her books include The Moths and Other Stories *(1985) and* Chicana Creativity and Criticism: Charting New Frontiers in American Literature *(1988).*

PREREADING

Recall the photographs that have been taken of you and your family. Is there a particular snapshot that stands out among all the rest? For ten minutes, freewrite about the memories the photo evokes in you.

It was the small things in life, I admit, that made me happy; ironing straight arrow creases on Dave's work khakis, cashing in enough coupons to actually save some money, or having my bus halt just right, so that I don't have to jump off the curb and crack my knee cap like that poor shoe salesman I read about in Utah. Now, it's no wonder that I wake mornings and try my damndest not to mimic the movements of ironing or cutting those stupid, dotted lines or slipping into my house shoes, groping for my robe, going to Marge's room to check if she's sufficiently covered, scruffling

Viramontes, Helena Maria. "Snapshots." *The Moths and Other Stories.* Houston: Arte Público Press-U of Houston, 1985. Print. Reprinted with permission from the publisher of *The Moths and Other Stories* (Houston: Arte Público Press-University of Houston, 1985).

to the kitchen, dumping out the soggy coffee grounds, refilling the pot and only later realizing that the breakfast nook has been set for three, the iron is plugged in, the bargain page is open in front of me and I don't remember, I mean I really don't remember doing any of it because I've done it for thirty years now and Marge is already married. It kills me, the small things.

Like those balls of wool on the couch. They're small and senseless and yet, every   2 time I see them, I want to scream. Since the divorce, Marge brings me balls and balls and balls of wool thread because she insists that I "take up a hobby," "keep as busy as a bee," or "make the best of things" and all that other good-natured advice she probably hears from old folks who answer in such a way when asked how they've managed to live so long. Honestly, I wouldn't be surprised if she walked in one day with bushels of straw for me to weave baskets. My only response to her endeavors is to give her the hardest stares I know how when she enters the living room, opens up her plastic shopping bag and brings out another ball of bright colored wool thread. I never move. Just sit and stare.

"Mother."   3

She pronounces the words not as a truth but as an accusation.   4

"Please, Mother. Knit. Do something." And then she places the new ball on top   5 of the others on the couch, turns toward the kitchen and leaves. I give her a minute before I look out the window to see her standing on the sidewalk. I stick out my tongue, even make a face, but all she does is stand there with that horrible yellow and black plastic bag against her fat leg, and wave good-bye.

Do something, she says. If I had a penny for all the things I have done, all the lit-   6 tle details I was responsible for but which amounted to nonsense, I would be rich. But I haven't a thing to show for it. The human spider gets on prime time television for climbing a building because it's there. Me? How can people believe that I've fought against motes of dust for years or dirt attracting floors or perfected bleached white sheets when a few hours later the motes, the dirt, the stains return to remind me of the uselessness of it all? I missed the sound of swans slicing the lake water or the fluttering wings of wild geese flying south for a warm winter or the heartbeat I could have heard if I had just held Marge a little closer.

I realize all that time is lost now, and I find myself searching for it frantically un-   7 der the bed where the balls of dust collect undisturbed and untouched, as it should be.

To be quite frank, the fact of the matter is I wish to do nothing, but allow indul-   8 gence to rush through my veins with frightening speed. I do so because I have never been able to tolerate it in anyone, including myself.

I watch television to my heart's content now, a thing I rarely did in my younger   9 days. While I was growing up, television had not been invented. Once it was and became a must for every home, Dave saved and saved until we were able to get one. But who had the time? Most of mine was spent working part time as a clerk for Grants, then returning to create a happy home for Dave. This is the way I pictured it:

> His wife in the kitchen wearing a freshly ironed apron, stirring a pot of soup, whistling a whistle-while-you-work tune, and preparing frosting for some cupcakes so that when he drove home from work, tired and sweaty, he would enter his castle to find his cherub baby in a pink day suit with newly starched ribbons crawling to him and his wife looking at him with pleasing eyes and offering him a cupcake.

It was a good image I wanted him to have and every day I almost expected him   10
to stop, put down his lunch pail and cry at the whole scene. If it wasn't for the burnt
cupcakes, my damn varicose veins, and Marge blubbering all over her day suit, it
would have made a perfect snapshot.

Snapshots are ghosts. I am told that shortly after women are married, they   11
become addicted to one thing or another. In *Reader's Digest* I read stories of closet
alcoholic wives who gambled away grocery money or broke into their children's piggy
banks in order to quench their thirst and fill their souls. Unfortunately I did not become addicted to alcohol because my only encounter with it had left me senseless and
with my face in the toilet bowl. After that, I never had the desire to repeat the performance of a senior in high school whose prom date never showed. I did consider my
addiction a lot more incurable. I had acquired a habit much more deadly: nostalgia.

I acquired the habit after Marge was born, and I had to stay in bed for months   12
because of my varicose veins. I began flipping through my family's photo albums (my
father threw them away after mom's death) to pass the time and pain away. However
I soon became haunted by the frozen moments and the meaning of memories.
Looking at the old photos, I'd get real depressed over my second grade teacher's smile
or my father's can of beer or the butt naked smile of me as a young teen, because every
detail, as minute as it may seem, made me feel that so much had passed unnoticed. As
a result, I began to convince myself that my best years were up and that I had nothing
to look forward to in the future. I was too young and too ignorant to realize that that
section of my life relied wholly on those crumbling photographs and my memory and
I probably wasted more time longing for a past that never really existed. Dave eventually packed them up in a wooden crate to keep me from hurting myself. He was good
in that way. Like when he clipped roses for me. He made sure the thorns were cut off
so I didn't have to prick myself while putting them in a vase. And it was the same thing
with the albums. They stood in the attic for years until I brought them down a day
after he remarried.

The photo albums are unraveling and stained with spills and fingerprints and   13
filled with crinkled faded gray snapshots of people I can't remember anymore, and
I turn the pages over and over again to see if somehow, some old dream will come
into my blank mind. Like the black and white television box does when I turn it on. It
warms up then flashes instant pictures, instant lives, instant people.

Parents. That I know for sure. The woman is tall and long, her plain, black dress   14
is over her knees, and she wears thick spongelike shoes. She's over to the right of the
photo, looks straight ahead at the camera. The man wears white, baggy pants that go
past his waist, thick suspenders. He smiles while holding a dull-faced baby. He points
to the camera. His sleeves pulled up, his tie undone, his hair is messy, as if some wild
woman has driven his head between her breasts and run her fingers into his perfect
greased ducktail.

My mother always smelled of smoke and vanilla and that is why I stayed away   15
from her. I suppose that is why my father stayed away from her as well. I don't even remember a time when I saw them show any sign of affection. Not like today. No sooner
do I turn off the soaps when I turn around and catch two youngsters on a porch swing,
their mouths open, their lips chewing and chewing as if they were sharing a piece of
three day old liver. My mom was always one to believe that such passion be restricted

to the privacy of one's house and then, there too, be demonstrated with efficiency and not this urgency I witness almost every day. Dave and I were good about that.

Whenever I saw the vaseline jar on top of Dave's bedstand, I made sure the door 16 was locked and the blinds down. This anticipation was more exciting to me than him lifting up my flannel gown over my head, pressing against me, slipping off my underwear then slipping in me. The vaseline came next, then he came right afterwards. In the morning, Dave looked into my eyes and I could never figure out what he expected to find. Eventually, there came a point in our relationship when passion passed to Marge's generation, and I was somewhat relieved. And yet, I could never imagine Marge doing those types of things that these youngsters do today, though I'm sure she did them on those Sunday afternoons when she carried a blanket and a book, and told me she was going to the park to do some reading and returned hours later with the bookmark in the same place. She must have done them, or else how could she have gotten engaged, married, had three children all under my nose, and me still going to check if she's sufficiently covered?

"Mother?" Marge's voice from the kitchen. It must be evening. Every morning 17 it's the ball of wool, every evening it's dinner. Honestly, she treats me as if I have an incurable heart ailment. She stands under the doorway.

"Mother?" Picture it: She stands under the doorway looking befuddled, as if a 18 movie director instructs her to stand there and look confused and upset; stand there as if you have seen you mother sitting in the same position for the last nine hours.

"What are you doing to yourself?" Marge is definitely not one for originality and 19 she repeats the same lines every day. I'm beginning to think our conversation is coming from discarded scripts. I know the lines by heart, too. She'll say: "Why do you continue to do this to us?" and I'll answer: "Do what?" and she'll say: "This"—waving her plump, coarse hands over the albums scattered at my feet—and I'll say: "Why don't you go home and leave me alone?" This is the extent of our conversation and usually there is an optional line like: "I brought you something to eat," or "Let's have dinner," or "Come look what I have for you," or even "I brought you your favorite dish."

I think of the times, so many times, so many Mother's Days that passed without 20 so much as a thank you or how sweet you are for giving us thirty years of your life. I know I am to blame. When Marge first started school, she had made a ceramic handprint for me to hang in the kitchen. My hands were so greasy from cutting the fat off some pork-chops, I dropped it before I could even unwrap my first Mother's Day gift. I tried gluing it back together again with flour and water paste, but she never forgave me and I never received another gift until after the divorce. I wonder what happened to the ceramic handprint I gave to my mother?

In the kitchen I see that today my favorite dish is Chinese food getting cold in 21 those little coffin-like containers. Yesterday my favorite dish was a salami sandwich, and before that a half eaten rib, no doubt left over from Marge's half hour lunch. Last week she brought me some Sunday soup that had fish heads floating around in some greenish broth. When I threw it down the sink, all she could think of to say was: "Oh, Mother."

We eat in silence. Or rather, she eats. I don't understand how she can take my 22 indifference. I wish that she would break out of her frozen look, jump out of any snapshot and slap me in the face. Do something. Do something. I began to cry.

"Oh, Mother," she says, picking up the plates and putting them in the sink.   23

"Mother, please."   24

There's fingerprints all over this one, my favorite. Both woman and child are   25
clones: same bathing suit, same ponytails, same ribbons. The woman is looking directly at the camera, but the man is busy making a sand castle for his daughter. He doesn't see the camera or the woman. On the back of this one, in vague pencil scratching, it says: San Juan Capistrano.

This is a bad night. On good nights I avoid familiar spots. On bad nights I am   26
pulled towards them so much so that if I sit on the chair next to Dave's I begin to cry. On bad nights I can't sleep and on bad nights I don't know who the couples in the snapshots are. My mother and me? Me and Marge? I don't remember San Juan Capistrano and I don't remember the woman. She faded into thirty years of trivia. I don't even remember what I had for dinner, or rather, what Marge had for dinner, just a few hours before. I wrap a blanket around myself and go into the kitchen to search for some evidence, but except for a few crumbs on the table, there is no indication that Marge was here. Suddenly, I am relieved when I see the box containers in the trash under the sink. I can't sleep the rest of the night wondering what happened to my ceramic handprint, or what was in the boxes. Why can't I remember? My mind thinks of nothing but those boxes in all shapes and sizes. I wash my face with warm water, put cold cream on, go back to bed, get up and wash my face again. Finally, I decide to call Marge at 3:30 in the morning. The voice is faint and there is static in the distance.

"Yes?" Marge asks automatically.

"Hello," Marge says. I almost expected her to answer her usual "Dave's Hardware."

"Who is this?" Marge is fully awake now.

"What did we…" I ask, wondering why it was suddenly so important for me to   27
know what we had for dinner. "What did you have for dinner?" I am confident that she'll remember every movement I made or how much salt I put on whatever we ate, or rather, she ate. Marge is good about details.

"Mother?"

"Are you angry that I woke you up?"

"Mother. No. Of course not."

I could hear some muffled sounds, vague voices, static. I can tell she is covering   28
the mouthpiece with her hand. Finally George's voice.

"Mrs. Ruiz," he says, restraining his words so that they almost come out slurred,   29
"Mrs. Ruiz, why don't you leave us alone?" and then there is a long, buzzing sound. Right next to the vaseline jar are Dave's cigarettes. I light one though I don't smoke. I unscrew the jar and use the lid for an ashtray. I wait, staring at the phone until it rings.

"Dave's Hardware," I answer. "Don't you know what time it is?"

"Yes." It isn't Marge's voice. "Why don't you leave the kids alone?" Dave's voice is not angry. Groggy, but not angry. After a pause I say:

"I don't know if I should be hungry or not."

"You're a sad case." Dave says it as coolly as a doctor would say, you have terminal cancer. He says it to convince me that it is totally out of his hands. I panic. I picture him sitting on his side of the bed in his shorts, smoking under a dull circle of light. I know his bifocals are down to the tip of his nose.   30

"Oh, Dave," I say. "Oh, Dave." The static gets worse.

"Let me call you tomorrow."

"No. It's just a bad night."

"Olga," Dave says so softly that I can almost feel his warm breath on my face.

"Olga, why don't you get some sleep?"

The first camera I ever saw belonged to my grandfather. He won it in a cock 31 fight. Unfortunately he didn't know two bits about it, but he somehow managed to load the film. Then he brought it over to our house. He sat me on the lawn. I was only five or six years old, but I remember the excitement of everybody coming around to get into the picture. I can see my grandfather clearly now. I can picture him handling the camera slowly, touching the knobs and buttons to find out how the camera worked while the men began milling around him expressing their limited knowledge of the invention. I remember it all so clearly. Finally he was able to manage the camera, and he took pictures of me standing near my mother with the wives behind us.

My grandmother was very upset. She kept pulling me out of the picture, yell- 32 ing to my grandfather that he should know better, that snapshots steal the souls of the people and that she would not allow my soul to be taken. He pushed her aside and clicked the picture.

The picture, of course, never came out. My grandfather, not knowing better, 33 thought that all he had to do to develop the film was unroll it and expose it to the sun. After we all waited for an hour, we realized it didn't work. My grandmother was very upset and cut a piece of my hair, probably to save me from a bad omen.

It scares me to think that my grandmother may have been right. It scares me 34 even more to think I don't have a snapshot of her. If I find one, I'll tear it up for sure.

READING FOR CONTENT

1. What clues does the opening paragraph give you about the type of family life Mrs. Ruiz has led?

2. Even though Marge is intent on getting her mother interested in a hobby, Mrs. Ruiz wishes to do nothing. Explain why she feels that way.

3. Explain what Mrs. Ruiz means when she says that after her daughter was born, she became addicted to nostalgia.

4. How do you think Mrs. Ruiz views Marge's daily visits? What does she mean when she says, "I wish that she would break out of her frozen look, jump out of any snapshot and slap me in the face" (paragraph 22)?

5. Why does Mrs. Ruiz think that her grandmother's remark that "snapshots steal the souls of the people" (paragraph 32) may be correct?

READING FOR GENRE, ORGANIZATION, AND STYLISTIC FEATURES

1. How does Viramontes establish the conflict between Mrs. Ruiz and her daughter? Point out specific details.

2. Explain what the references to snapshots, photo albums, television, movie scripts, and cameras contribute to the story.

3. How do you react to Mrs. Ruiz's image of the "happy home"? How did that image control her life?

4. Underline passages that contain humor. How would the story's impact be different if the humor were left out?

5. What is the function of Mrs. Ruiz's recollection of her grandfather's camera? What does this scene add to the story?

READING FOR RHETORICAL CONTEXT

1. How do you think Viramontes wants you to view Mrs. Ruiz?

2. What point do you think Viramontes is making about living in the past rather than dealing with present realities?

3. How would the story have been different if it had been narrated by Marge instead of by her mother?

WRITING ASSIGNMENTS

1. Write a short critical analysis of the story's point of view.

2. Write an essay discussing Mrs. Ruiz's image of the perfect family in paragraph 9. Is that image borne out in reality? In Mrs. Ruiz's life? In your own family experience?

■ ■ ▓ ▓ ■ ■ ▓ ■ ▓ ▓

Between the Pool and the Gardenias

Edwidge Danticat

Edwidge Danticat (b. 1969) emigrated at the age of twelve from Haiti to the United States and received a B.A. from Barnard College and an M.F.A. from Brown University. Her novels about Haitians and Haitian immigrants include Breath, Eyes, Memory *(1994),* The Farming of Bones *(1999), and* The Dew Breaker *(2004). Her early short stories are collected in* Krik? Krak! *(1996). She lives and writes in Brooklyn, New York.*

PREREADING

As the poorest nation in the Western hemisphere, the Republic of Haiti has suffered a tumultuous political history for more than fifty years, first under the dictatorial Duvalier father-and-son rulers, and then since 1991 under a series of military and rebel terrorist coups that twice ousted the democratically elected president, Jean-Bertrand Aristide, and paralyzed the government of his successor, René Préval. With a dismal record of human rights violations, violence against women, drug and arms smuggling, and deplorable health issues, Haiti has lost great numbers of its population to disease, torture, death, and stealth emigration, culminating in a disastrous earthquake in 2010. Browse the Internet for sites about the nation's social, political, economic, and health problems, and compile a list of issues that recur on various Web sites.

She was very pretty. Bright shiny hair and dark brown skin like mahogany cocoa. 1 Her lips were wide and purple, like those African dolls you see in tourist store windows but could never afford to buy.

I thought she was a gift from Heaven when I saw her on the dusty curb, wrapped 2 in a small pink blanket, a few inches away from a sewer as open as a hungry child's yawn. She was like Baby Moses in the Bible stories they read to us at the Baptist Literary Class. Or Baby Jesus, who was born in a barn and died on a cross, with nobody's lips to kiss before he went. She was just like that. Her still round face. Her eyes closed as though she was dreaming of a far other place.

Her hands were bony, and there were veins so close to the surface that it looked 3 like you could rupture her skin if you touched her too hard. She probably belonged to someone, but the street had no one in it. There was no one there to claim her.

At first I was afraid to touch her. Lest I might disturb the early-morning sun rays 4 streaming across her forehead. She might have been some kind of *wanga*, a charm sent to trap me. My enemies were many and crafty. The girls who slept with my husband while I was still grieving over my miscarriages. They might have sent that vision of loveliness to blind me so that I would never find my way back to the place that I yanked out my head when I got on that broken down minibus and left my village months ago.

The child was wearing an embroidered little blue dress with the letters *R-O-S-E* 5 on a butterfly collar. She looked the way that I had imagined all my little girls would look. The ones my body could never hold. The ones that somehow got suffocated inside me and made my husband wonder if I was killing them on purpose.

I called out all the names I wanted to give them: Eveline, Josephine, Jacqueline, 6 Hermine, Marie Magdalène, Célianne. I could give her all the clothes that I had sewn for them. All these little dresses that went unused.

At night, I could rock her alone in the hush of my room, rest her on my belly, 7 and wish she were inside.

When I had just come to the city, I saw on Madame's television that a lot of poor 8 city women throw out their babies because they can't afford to feed them. Back in Ville Rose you cannot even throw out the bloody clumps that shoot out of your body after your child is born. It is a crime, they say, and your whole family would consider you wicked if you did it. You have to save every piece of flesh and give it a name and bury it near the roots of a tree so that the world won't fall apart around you.

In the city, I hear they throw out whole entire children. They throw them out 9 anywhere: on doorsteps, in garbage cans, at gas pumps, sidewalks. In the time that I had been in Port-au-Prince, I had never seen such a child until now.

But Rose. My, she was so clean and warm. Like a tiny angel, a little cherub, 10 sleeping after the wind had blown a lullaby into her little ears.

I picked her up and pressed her cheek against mine. 11

I whispered to her, "Little Rose, my child," as though that name was a secret. 12

She was like the palatable little dolls we played with as children—mango seeds 13
that we drew faces on and then called by our nicknames. We christened them with
prayers and invited all our little boy and girl friends for colas and cassavas and—when
we could get them—some nice butter cookies.

Rose didn't stir or cry. She was like something that was thrown aside after she be- 14
came useless to someone cruel. When I pressed her face against my heart, she smelled
like the scented powders in Madame's cabinet, the mixed scent of gardenias and fish
that Madame always had on her when she stepped out of her pool.

I have always said my mother's prayers at dawn. I welcomed the years that were 15
slowing bringing me closer to her. For no matter how much distance death tried to put
between us, my mother would often come to visit me. Sometimes in the short sighs
and whispers of somebody else's voice. Sometimes in somebody else's face. Other
times in brief moments in my dreams.

There were many nights when I saw some old women leaning over my bed.   16

"That there is Marie," my mother would say. "She is now the last one of us left." 17

Mama had to introduce me to them, because they had all died before I was 18
born. There was my great grandmother Eveline who was killed by Dominican soldiers
at the Massacre River. My grandmother Défilé who died with a bald head in a prison,
because God had given her wings. My godmother Lili who killed herself in old age
because her husband had jumped out of a flying balloon and her grown son left her to
go to Miami.

We all salute you Mary, Mother of God. Pray for us poor sinners, from now until 19
the hour of our death. Amen.

I always knew they would come back and claim me to do some good for some- 20
body. Maybe I was to do some good for this child.

I carried Rose with me to the outdoor market in Croix-Bossale. I swayed her in 21
my arms like she was and had always been mine.

In the city, even people who come from your own village don't know you or care 22
about you. They didn't notice that I had come the day before with no child. Suddenly,
I had one, and nobody asked a thing.

In the maid's room, at the house in Pétion-Ville, I laid Rose on my mat and 23
rushed to prepare lunch. Monsieur and Madame sat on their terrace and welcomed
the coming afternoon by sipping the sweet out of my sour-sop juice.

They liked that I went all the way to the market every day before dawn to get 24
them a taste of the outside country, away from their protected bourgeois life.

"She is probably one of those *manbos*," they say when my back is turned. 25
"She's probably one of those stupid people who think that they have a spell to
make themselves invisible and hurt other people. Why can't none of them get a
spell to make themselves rich? It's that voodoo nonsense that's holding us Haitians
back."

I lay Rose down on the kitchen table as I dried the dishes. I had a sudden desire 26
to explain to her my life.

"You see, young one, I loved that man at one point. He was very nice to me. He 27
made me feel proper. The next thing I know, it's ten years with him. I'm old like a
piece of dirty paper people used to wipe their behinds, and he's got ten different babies
with ten different women. I just had to run."

I pretended that it was all mine. The terrace with that sight of the private pool 28
and the holiday ships cruising in the distance. The large television system and all those
French love songs and *rara* records, with the talking drums and conch shell sounds
in them. The bright paintings with white winged horses and snakes as long and wide
as lakes. The pool that the sweaty Dominican man cleaned three times a week. I pretended that it belonged to us: him, Rose, and me.

The Dominican and I made love on the grass once, but he never spoke to me 29
again. Rose listened with her eyes closed even though I was telling her things that were
much too strong for a child's ears.

I wrapped her around me with my apron as I fried some plantains for the eve- 30
ning meal. It's so easy to love somebody, I tell you, when there's nothing else around.

Her head fell back like any other infant's. I held out my hand and let her three 31
matted braids tickle the lifelines in my hand.

"I am glad you are not one of those babies that cry all day long," I told her. "All 32
little children should be like you. I am glad that you don't cry and make a lot of noise.
You're just a perfect child, aren't you?"

I put her back in my room when Monsieur and Madame came home for their 33
supper. As soon as they went to sleep, I took her out by the pool so we could talk some
more.

You don't just join a family not knowing what you're getting into. You have to 34
know some of the history. You have to know that they pray to Erzulie, who loves men
like men love her, because she's mulatto and some Haitian men seem to love her kind.
You have to look into your looking glass on the day of the dead because you might see
faces there that knew you even before you ever came into this world.

I fell asleep rocking her in a chair that wasn't mine. I knew she was real when 35
I woke up the next day and she was still in my arms. She looked the same as she did
when I found her. She continued to look like that for three days. After that, I had to
bathe her constantly to keep down the smell.

I once had an uncle who bought pigs' intestines in Ville Rose to sell at the 36
market in the city. Rose began to smell like the intestines after they hadn't sold for a
few days.

I bathed her more and more often, sometimes three or four times a day in the 37
pool. I used some of Madame's perfume, but it was not helping. I wanted to take her
back to the street where I had found her, but I'd already disturbed her rest and had
taken on her soul as my own personal responsibility.

I left her in a shack behind the house, where the Dominican kept his tools. 38
Three times a day, I visited her with my hand over my nose. I watched her skin grow
moist, cracked, and sunken in some places, then ashy and dry in others. It seemed like
she had aged in four days as many years as there were between me and my dead aunts
and grandmothers.

I knew I had to act with her because she was attracting flies and I was keeping 39
her spirit from moving on.

I gave her one last bath and slipped on a little yellow dress that I had sewn while 40
praying that one of my little girls would come along further than three months.

I took Rose down to a spot in the sun behind the big house. I dug a hole in the 41
garden among all the gardenias. I wrapped her in the little pink blanket that I had

found her in, covering everything but her face. She smelled so bad that I couldn't even bring myself to kiss her without choking on my breath.

I felt a grip on my shoulder as I lowered her into the small hole in the 42 ground. At first I thought it was Monsieur or Madame, and I was real afraid that Madame would be angry with me for having used a whole bottle of her perfume without asking.

Rose slipped and fell out of my hands as my body was forced to turn around. 43

"What are you doing?" the Dominican asked. 44

His face was a deep Indian brown but his hands were bleached and wrinkled 45 from the chemicals in the pool. He looked down at the baby lying in the dust. She was already sprinkled with some of the soil that I had dug up.

"You see, I saw these faces standing over me in my dreams—" 46

I could have started my explanation in a million of ways. 47

"Where did you take this child from?" he asked me in his Spanish Creole. 48

He did not give me a chance to give an answer. 49

"I go already." I thought I heard a little *méringue* in the sway of his voice. "I call 50 the gendarmes. They are coming. I smell that rotten flesh. I know you kill the child and keep it with you for evil."

"You acted too soon," I said. 51

"You kill the child and keep it in your room." 52

"You know me," I said. "We've been together." 53

"I don't know you from the fly on a pile of cow manure," he said. "You eat little 54 children who haven't even had time to earn their souls."

He only kept his hands on me because he was afraid that I would run away and 55 escape.

I looked down at Rose. In my mind I saw what I had seen for all my other 56 girls. I imagined her teething, crawling, crying, fussing, and just misbehaving herself.

Over her little corpse, we stood, a country maid and a Spaniard grounds man. 57 I should have asked his name before I offered him my body.

We made a pretty picture standing there. Rose, me, and him. Between the pool 58 and the gardenias, waiting for the law.

READING FOR CONTENT

1. Describe in your own words the dramatic situation implied in paragraph 2. What kind of relationship does the narrator appear to have with her mother and other female members of her family in paragraphs 15 and 18?

2. Describe in your own words the narrator's relationship with her husband in paragraph 27. What impact does her inability to bear a child have on the situation implied in paragraph 2?

3. How clear is the story about the death of baby Rose? Does she die in paragraph 35? Or was she already dead in paragraph 14? What is her probable history? Why does the Dominican man conclude in paragraph 50 that the narrator killed her? Did she? How do the ambiguities allow the narrator to stand in for many different women who share her plight?

READING FOR GENRE, ORGANIZATION, AND STYLISTIC FEATURES

1. The genre of the short story often draws great power from deliberate vagueness and crushing irony. List important features that you find vague about this story and speculate on the irony of the childless woman being accused of the child's death in its final paragraphs.

2. How do the interruptions in the story before paragraphs 15 and 20 help to organize the narrative? What do paragraphs 14 and 21 contribute to the characterization of the narrator and the atmosphere of the setting?

3. What stylistic effects heighten the attention called to the differences between country and city in paragraph 22? What stylistic effects heighten the attention called to casual sexual practices in paragraphs 29 and 34?

READING FOR RHETORICAL CONTEXT

1. What cultural practices do the comparisons in paragraphs 13–14 evoke?

2. What cultural differences between the narrator and the rich people who have hired her as a maid do paragraphs 23–25 suggest?

WRITING ASSIGNMENTS

1. Write a literary analysis of 1,000 words on the character of the narrator. What is her background? What has brought her into contact with baby Rose? What is she doing with the baby? What psychological factors might explain her actions?

2. Write a literary analysis of 1,000 words on the relationship between the story and its social context. What is the setting? What social classes do the narrator and the other characters come from? What factors cause the events and their likely outcome?

Bohemians

George Saunders

George Saunders (b. 1958) grew up in Chicago, Illinois, received a B.S. from the Colorado School of Mines, and pursued a career as (among other things) a geophysical engineer before turning to writing. He has published three collections of short stories, Civilwarland in Bad Decline *(1996),* Pastoralia *(1999), and* In Persuasion Nation *(2006); a novella,* The Brief and Frightening Reign of Phil *(2005); an all-ages book,* The Very Persistent Gappers of Frip *(2006); and nonfiction articles in* The New Yorker *and* Gentleman's Quarterly. *He is a professor of English at Syracuse University.*

From *In Persuasion Nation: Stories by George Saunders.* Copyright 2006 by George Saunders. Used by permission of Riverhead Books, an imprint of Penguin Group (USA), Inc.

PREREADING

Scan through paragraphs 1–3 to find the profiles of important characters in the story. What do these profiles tell you (or not tell you) about them? What does Dad's greeting them so incongruously with the Czech word for "door" tell you about him? about them? about the narrator's family? about the humor of the story that will follow? Speculate about possible situations that might bring together the narrator and the two "Bohemians." As you read the complete story, check your speculations against unforeseen ways in which the story managed to surprise you.

In a lovely urban coincidence, the last two houses on our block were both occu-   1
pied by widows who had lost their husbands in Eastern European pogroms. Dad called
them the Bohemians. He called anyone white with an accent a Bohemian. Whenever
he saw one of the Bohemians, he greeted her by mispronouncing the Czech word for
"door." Neither Bohemian was Czech, but both were polite, so when Dad said "door"
to them they answered cordially, as if he weren't perennially schlockered.

Mrs. Poltoi, the stouter Bohemian, had spent the war in a crawl space, splitting   2
a daily potato with six cousins. Consequently she was bitter and claustrophobic and
loved food. If you ate something while standing near her, she stared at it going into
your mouth. She wore only black. She said the Catholic Church was a jeweled harlot
drinking the blood of the poor. She said America was a spoiled child ignorant of grief.
When our ball rolled onto her property, she seized it and waddled into her backyard
and pitched it into the quarry.

Mrs. Hopanlitski, on the other hand, was thin, and joyfully made pipecleaner   3
animals. When I brought home one of her crude dogs in tophats, Mom said, "Take
over your Mold-A-Hero. To her, it will seem like the toy of a king." To Mom, the
camps, massacres, and railroad sidings of twenty years before were as unreal as covered
wagons. When Mrs. H. claimed her family had once owned serfs, Mom's attention
wandered. She had a tract house in mind. No way was she getting one. We were rent-
ing a remodeled garage behind the Giancarlos. Dad was basically drinking up the
sporting-goods store. His NFL helmets were years out of date. I'd stop by after school
and find the store closed and Dad getting sloshed among the fake legs with Bennie
Delmonico at Prosthetics World.

Using the Mold-A-Hero, I cast Mrs. H. a plastic Lafayette, and she said she'd   4
keep it forever on her sill. Within a week, she'd given it to Elizabeth the Raccoon.
I didn't mind. Raccoon, an only child like me, had nothing. The Kletz brothers called
her Raccoon for the bags she had under her eyes from never sleeping. Her parents
fought nonstop. They fought over breakfast. They fought in the yard in their underwear. At dusk they stood on their porch whacking each other with lengths of weather
stripping. Raccoon practically had spinal curvature from spending so much time
slumped over with misery. When the Kletz brothers called her Raccoon, she indulged
them by rubbing her hands together ferally. The nickname was the most attention
she'd ever had. Sometimes she'd wish to be hit by a car so she could come back as a
true Raccoon and track down the Kletzes and give them rabies.

"Never wish harm on yourself or others," Mrs. H. said. "You are a lovely child."   5
Her English was flat and clear, almost like ours.

"Raccoon, you mean," Raccoon said. "A lovely Raccoon."

"A lovely child of God," Mrs. H. said.

"Yeah right," Raccoon said. "Tell again about the prince."

So Mrs. H. told again how she'd stood rapt in her yard watching an actual prince 6 powder his birthmark to invisibility. She remembered the smell of burning compost from the fields, and men in colorful leggings dragging a gutted boar across a wooden bridge. This was before she was forced to become a human pack animal in the Carpathians, carrying the personal belongings of cruel officers. At night, they chained her to a tree. Sometimes they burned her calves with a machine-gun barrel for fun. Which was why she always wore kneesocks. After three years, she'd come home to find her babies in tiny graves. They were, she would say, short-lived but wonderful gifts. She did not now begrudge God for taking them. A falling star is brief, but isn't one nonetheless glad to have seen it? Her grace made us hate Mrs. Poltoi all the more. What was eating a sixth of a potato every day compared to being chained to a tree? What was being crammed in with a bunch of your cousins compared to having your kids killed?

The summer I was ten, Raccoon and I, already borderline rejects due to our 7 mutually unraveling households, were joined by Art Siminiak, who had recently made the mistake of inviting the Kletzes in for lemonade. There was no lemonade. Instead, there was Art's mom and a sailor from Great Lakes, passed out naked across the paper-drive stacks on the Siminiaks' sunporch.

This new, three-way friendship consisted of slumping in gangways, glovelessly 8 playing catch with a Wiffle, trailing hopefully behind kids whose homes could be entered without fear of fiasco.

Over on Mozart lived Eddie the Vacant. Eddie was seventeen, huge and simple. 9 He could crush a walnut in his bare hand, but first you had to put it there and tell him to do it. Once he'd pinned a "Vacant" sign to his shirt and walked around the neighborhood that way, and the name had stuck. Eddie claimed to see birds. Different birds appeared on different days of the week. Also, there was a Halloween bird and a Christmas bird.

One day, as Eddie hobbled by, we asked what kind of birds he was seeing. 10

"Party birds," he said. "They got big streamers coming out they butts."

"You having a party?" said Art. "You having a homo party?"

"I gone have a birthday party," said Eddie, blinking shyly.

"Your dad know?" Raccoon said.

"No, he don't yet," said Eddie.

His plans for the party were private and illogical. We peppered him with ques- 11 tions, hoping to get him to further embarrass himself. The party would be held in his garage. As far as the junk car in there, he would push it out by hand. As far as the oil on the floor, he would soak it up using Handi Wipes. As far as music, he would play a trumpet.

"What are you going to play the trumpet with?" said Art. "Your asshole?"

"No, I not gone play it with that," Eddie said. "I just gone use my lips, okay?"

As far as girls, there would be girls; he knew many girls, from his job man- 12 aging the Drake Hotel. As far as food, there would be food, including pudding dumplings.

"You're the manager of the Drake Hotel," Raccoon said.

"Hey, I know how to get the money for pudding dumplings!" Eddie said.

Then he rang Poltoi's bell and asked for a contribution. She said for what. He said   13
for him. She said to what end. He looked at her blankly and asked for a contribution.
She asked him to leave the porch. He asked for a contribution. Somewhere he'd got the
idea that, when asking for a contribution, one angled to sit on the couch. He started in,
and she pushed him back with a thick forearm. Down the front steps he went, ringing
the iron banister with his massive head.

He got up and staggered away, a little blood on his scalp.

"Learn to leave people be!" Poltoi shouted after him.

Ten minutes later, Eddie Sr. stood on Poltoi's porch, a hulking effeminate tailor   14
too cowed to use his bulk for anything but butting open the jamming door at his shop.

"Since when has it become the sport to knock unfortunates down stairs?" he asked.

"He was not listen," she said. "I tell him no. He try to come inside."

"With all respect," he said, "it is in my son's nature to perhaps be not so responsive."

"Someone so unresponse, keep him indoors," she said. "He is big as a man. And
I am old lady."

"Never has Eddie presented a danger to anyone," Eddie Sr. said.

"I know my rights," she said. "Next time, I call police."

But, having been pushed down the stairs, Eddie the Vacant couldn't seem to   15
stay away.

"Off this porch," Poltoi said through the screen when he showed up the next day,
offering her an empty cold-cream jar for three dollars.

"We gone have so many snacks," he said. "And if I drink a alcohol drink, then
watch out. Because I ain't allowed. I dance too fast."

He was trying the doorknob now, showing how fast he would dance if alcohol   16
was served.

"Please, off this porch!" she shouted.

"Please, off this porch!" he shouted back, doubling at the waist in wacky laughter.

Poltoi called the cops. Normally, Lieutenant Brusci would have asked Eddie   17
what bird was in effect that day and given him a ride home in his squad. But this was
during the OneCity fiasco. To cut graft, cops were being yanked off their regular beats
and replaced by cops from other parts of town. A couple Armenians from South Shore
showed up and dragged Eddie off the porch in a club-lock so tight he claimed the
birds he was seeing were beakless.

"I'll give you a beak, Frankenstein," said one of the Armenians, tightening the   18
choke hold.

Eddie entered the squad with all the fluidity of a hat rack. Art and Raccoon and   19
I ran over to Eddie Sr.'s tailor shop above the Marquee, which had sunk to porn. When
Eddie Sr. saw us, he stopped his Singer by kicking out the plug. From downstairs came
a series of erotic moans.

Eddie Sr. rushed to the hospital with his Purple Heart and some photos of Eddie   20
as a grinning wet-chinned kid on a pony. He found Eddie handcuffed to a bed, with
an IV drip and a smashed face. Apparently, he'd bitten one of the Armenians. Bail was
set at three hundred. The tailor shop made zilch. Eddie Sr.'s fabrics were a lexicon of
yesteryear. Dust coated a bright-yellow sign that read "Zippers Repaired in Jiffy."

"Jail for that kid, I admit, don't make total sense," the judge said. "Three months 21
in the Anston. Best I can do."

The Anston Center for Youth was a red-brick former forge now yarded in 22
barbed wire. After their shifts, the guards held loud hooting orgies kitty-corner at
Zem's Lamplighter. Skinny immigrant women arrived at Zem's in station wagons and
emerged hours later adjusting their stockings. From all over Chicago kids were sent to
the Anston, kids who'd only ever been praised for the level of beatings they gave and
received and their willingness to carve themselves up. One Anston kid had famously
hired another kid to run over his foot. Another had killed his mother's lover with a can
opener. A third had sliced open his own eyelid with a poptop on a dare.

Eddie the Vacant disappeared into the Anston in January and came out in 23
March.

To welcome him home, Eddie Sr. had the neighborhood kids over. Eddie the 24
Vacant looked so bad even the Kletzes didn't joke about how bad he looked. His nose
was off center and a scald mark ran from ear to chin. When you got too close, his
hands shot up. When the cake was served, he dropped his plate, shouting, "Leave a
guy alone!"

Our natural meanness now found a purpose. Led by the Kletzes, we cut through 25
Poltoi's hose, bashed out her basement windows with ball-peens, pushed her little
shopping cart over the edge of the quarry and watched it end-over-end into the former
Slag Ravine.

Then it was spring and the quarry got busy. When the noon blast went off, our 26
windows rattled. The three-o'clock blast was even bigger. Raccoon and Art and I made
a fort from the cardboard shipping containers the Cline frames came in. One day,
while pretending the three-o'clock blast was atomic, we saw Eddie the Vacant bound-
ing toward our fort through the weeds, like some lover in a commercial, only fatter
and falling occasionally.

His trauma had made us kinder toward him. 27

"Eddie," Art said. "You tell your dad where you're at?"

"It no big problem," Eddie said. "I was gone leave my dad a note."

"But did you?" said Art.

"I'll leave him a note when I get back," said Eddie. "I gone come in with you now."

"No room," said Raccoon. "You're too huge."

"That a good one!" said Eddie, crowding in.

Down in the quarry were the sad Cats, the slumping watchman's shack, the piles 28
of reddish discarded dynamite wrappings that occasionally rose erratically up the hill-
side like startled birds.

Along the quarryside trail came Mrs. Poltoi, dragging a new shopping cart. 29

"Look at that pig," said Raccoon. "Eddie, that's the pig that put you away."

"What did they do to you in there, Ed?" said Art. "Did they mess with you?"

"No, they didn't," said Eddie. "I just a say to them, 'Leave a guy alone!' I mean,
sometime they did, okay? Sometime that one guy say, 'Hey Eddie, pull your thing! We
gone watch you.'"

"Okay, okay," said Art.

At dusk, the three of us would go to Mrs. H.'s porch. She'd bring out cookies and 30
urge forgiveness. It wasn't Poltoi's fault her heart was small, she told us. She, Mrs. H.,

had seen a great number of things, and seeing so many things had enlarged her heart. Once, she had seen Göring. Once, she had seen Einstein. Once, during the war, she had seen a whole city block, formerly thick with furriers, bombed black overnight. In the morning, charred bodies had crawled along the street, begging for mercy. One such body had grabbed her by the ankle, and she recognized it as Bergen, a friend of her father's.

"What did you do?" said Raccoon.

"Not important now," said Mrs. H., gulping back tears, looking off into the quarry.

Then disaster. Dad got a check for shoulder pads for all six district football 31 teams and, trying to work things out with Mom, decided to take her on a cruise to Jamaica. Nobody in our neighborhood had ever been on a cruise. Nobody had even been to Wisconsin. The disaster was, I was staying with Poltoi. Ours was a liquor household, where you could ask a question over and over in utter sincerity and never get a straight answer. I asked and asked, "Why her?" And was told and told, "It will be a adventure."

I asked, "Why not Grammy?"

I was told, "Grammy don't feel well."

I asked, "Why not Hopanlitski?"

Dad did this like snort.   32

"Like that's gonna happen," said Mom.

"Why not, why not?" I kept asking.

"Because shut up," they kept answering.

Just after Easter, over I went, with my little green suitcase.   33

I was a night panicker and occasional bed-wetter. I'd wake drenched and pant- 34 ing. Had they told her? I doubted it. Then I knew they hadn't, from the look on her face the first night, when I peed myself and woke up screaming.

"What's this?" she said.

"Pee," I said, humiliated beyond any ability to lie.

"Ach, well," she said. "Who don't? This also used to be me. Pee pee pee. I used to dream of a fish who cursed me."

She changed the sheets gently, with no petulance—a new one on me. Often 35 Ma, still half asleep, popped me with the wet sheet, saying when at last I had a wife, she herself could finally get some freaking sleep.

Then the bed was ready, and Poltoi made a sweeping gesture, like, Please.   36

I got in.   37

She stayed standing there.   38

"You know," she said, "I know they say things. About me, what I done to that 39 boy. But I had a bad time in the past with a big stupid boy. You don't gotta know. But I did like I did that day for good reason. I was scared at him, due to something what happened for real to me."

She stood in the half-light, looking down at her feet.   40

"Do you get?" she said. "Do you? Can you get it, what I am saying?"

"I think so," I said.

"Tell to him," she said. "Tell to him sorry, explain about it, tell your friends also. If you please. You have a good brain. That is why I am saying to you."

Something in me rose to this. I'd never heard it before but I believed it: I had a 41 good brain. I could be trusted to effect a change.

Next day was Saturday. She made soup. We played a game using three slivers of 42 soap. We made placemats out of colored strips of paper, and she let me teach her my spelling words.

Around noon the doorbell rang. At the door stood Mrs. H. 43

"Everything okay?" she said, poking her head in.

"Yes, fine," said Poltoi. "I did not eat him yet."

"Is everything really fine?" Mrs. H. said to me. "You can say."

"It's fine," I said.

"You can say," she said fiercely.

Then she gave Poltoi a look that seemed to say, Hurt him and you will deal 44 with me.

"You silly woman," said Poltoi. "You are going now." 45

Mrs. H. went. 46

We resumed our spelling. It was tense in a quiet-house way. Things ticked. 47 When Poltoi missed a word, she pinched her own hand, but not hard. It was like symbolic pinching. Once when she pinched, she looked at me looking at her, and we laughed.

Then we were quiet again. 48

"That lady?" she finally said. "She like to lie. Maybe you don't know. She say she is come from where I come from?"

"Yes," I said.

"She is lie," she said. "She act so sweet and everything but she lie. She been born in Skokie. Live here all her life, in America. Why you think she talk so good?"

All week Poltoi made sausage, noodles, potato pancakes; we ate like pigs. She had 49 tea and cakes ready when I came home from school. At night, if necessary, she dried me off, moved me to her bed, changed the sheets, put me back, with never an unkind word.

"Will pass, will pass," she'd hum. 50

Mom and Dad came home tanned, with a sailor cap for me, and in a burst of 51 post-vacation honesty, confirmed it: Mrs. H. was a liar. A liar and a kook. Nothing she said was true. She'd been a cashier at Goldblatt's but had been caught stealing. When caught stealing, she'd claimed to be with the Main Office. When a guy from the Main Office came down, she claimed to be with the FBI. Then she'd produced a letter from Lady Bird Johnson, but in her own handwriting, with "Johnson" spelled "Jonsen."

I told the other kids what I knew, and in time they came to believe it, even the 52 Kletzes.

And, once we believed it, we couldn't imagine we hadn't seen it all along. 53

Another spring came, once again birds nested in bushes on the sides of the 54 quarry. A thrown rock excited a thrilling upwards explosion. Thin rivers originated in our swampy backyards, and we sailed boats made of flattened shoeboxes, Twinkie wrappers, crimped tinfoil. Raccoon glued together three balsawood planes and placed on this boat a turd from her dog Svengooli, and, as Svengooli's turd went over a little waterfall and disappeared into the quarry, we cheered.

READING FOR CONTENT

1. In paragraphs 4, 7, and 9, how does the narrator introduce his friends Racoon, Art, and Eddie as characters in many ways similar to him, yet also different from him?

2. In paragraphs 13 and 30, how does the narrator depict Mrs. Poltoi and Mrs. Hopanlitski as characters so different from each other, yet also similar in some ways?

3. How do paragraphs 34 and 35 prepare for the story's reversal?

READING FOR GENRE, ORGANIZATION, AND STYLISTIC FEATURES

1. How does the phrase "Then disaster" in paragraph 31 divide the story into two distinct parts? What occupies the focus of the first part? What occupies the focus of the second part? How do these parts contrast with and yet relate to each other?

2. How does the dialogue indicate contrasts between and among characters in paragraphs 10, 14, 15, 27, 29, 30, 31, 39, 40, 43, and 48?

3. As we have seen with Bharati Mukherjee's "Jasmine," the genre of the short story frequently draws great power from a sudden ironic reversal. In "Bohemians," how does paragraph 51 amount to such a reversal? Is it funny, sad, surprising, bizarre, or some combination of each?

READING FOR RHETORICAL CONTEXT

1. What social commentary does the story imply about a mixed ethnic neighborhood such as the one it depicts? Do its inhabitants cohere? fall apart? harbor impenetrable secrets? perform acts of redeeming grace?

2. What does the narrator mean by "our natural meanness" in paragraph 25? How does the story prove or disprove the implications of this phrase?

WRITING ASSIGNMENTS

1. Write a literary analysis of 1,000 words on the predicament of the narrator. In his relationships with his neighborhood peers, is he a typical young person or is he a misfit? Does his relationship with his mom and dad suggest that theirs is a functional family? a dysfunctional one? Does he fully comprehend the behavior of the adults in the story?

2. Write a literary analysis of 1,000 words on the relationship between the narrator and his social context. What may be his implied ethnic background? How funny, sad, uplifting, or puzzling are the overlapping features of his contact with people of the same age? of an older generation? of other ethnic backgrounds?

SYNTHESIS WRITING ASSIGNMENTS

1. Drawing on selections by Takaki, Mukherjee, and Viramontes, write a five-page essay in which you synthesize their representations of the immigrant experience in America. Address your essay to an audience of classmates from high school with whom you have not been in contact since starting college.

2. Drawing on selections by Takaki and Danticat, write a five-page essay in which you compare and contrast the experiences of different ethnic groups as conditions in their

countries of origin give them cause to contemplate emigration to a less stressful environment. Comment on the blurred lines between fictional and nonfictional situations that these authors sustain. Address your essay to students who have already read these texts.

3. Drawing on the stories of Mukherjee and Saunders, write a five-page essay in which you respond to their characters' various efforts, both successful and unsuccessful, to preserve their ethnic identities. Address your essay to members of the academic community at large as a critical review in your college newspaper.

4. Drawing on the stories of Viramontes and Mukherjee, write a five-page essay in which you evaluate their narrative representations of outsiders' efforts to succeed as insiders in multicultural societies. Address your essay to members of the academic community at large as a critical review in your college newspaper.

5. Drawing on the stories of Mukherjee and Saunders, write a five-page essay in which you evaluate the authors' use of humor and irony to record the complexities of interacting with people of different ethnic origins in multicultural neighborhoods and workplaces. Address your essay to classmates with whom you have discussed the texts.

Sixteen

Three Visual Portfolios

In this chapter we present three portfolios of photographs on topics related to other chapters in our anthology. The first consists of seven photographs depicting various images of family life in modern America, some of them alluding to issues discussed in the essays of Chapter 12 on the changing American family. The second consists of seven photographs depicting various images of wealth, poverty, and the social markers that distinguish between them, some of them alluding to issues discussed in the essays of Chapter 13 on social class and inequality. The third consists of seven photographs depicting various images of immigrant experience in the United States, some of them alluding to issues represented in the selections of Chapter 15 on stories of ethnic difference.

These portfolios combine studio-posed pictures with newsworthy action shots, pictures taken by amateurs and by professionals, photos capturing the pulse of the present, and photos capturing scenes from the past. The first portfolio, Images of Families, opens with two idealized portraits, the first of a three-generational family, the second of young parents with identical twins. Juxtaposed against them is the enigmatic "Vengeful Sister, Chicago," taken in 1956 by the prominent social landscape photographer David Heath (1931–), and a newspaper photo from 2004 showing a lesbian couple and their adopted children being heckled by antigay demonstrators. The ideal and the real confront each other in these two pairs of images, as the composure of the initial pair gives way to the turmoil of its successor.

Two socially-conscious images follow. Beneath the surface tranquility of their compositions lies an unspoken agitation. The first of them, taken in 1912 by the renowned photographer Lewis Wickes Hine (1874–1940), depicts a mother and her adolescent children sitting at a dining room table. On closer inspection, it appears that the family is working at menial tasks for inevitably small wages. This picture belongs to the photographer's classic collection "Let Children Be Children: Lewis Wickes Hine's Crusade Against Child Labor."

The second, undated, though likely from the early twentieth-century and anonymously attributed, repeats this topic. It comes to us from the American photographic archives of the Library of Congress with an attached caption: "This mother and her two children…were living in a tiny one room and were finishing garments…. Said they make from $1 to $2 a week and the boy makes some selling newspapers." Despite its anonymity, it packs a powerful punch.

The first portfolio concludes with "Portrait of a Boy Overlooking Ocean" by the Cuban-American photographer Antonio Fernandez (1941–). Taken in Miami in 1968, it is part of a series entitled "Vision and Expression" that captures ordinary events from startling perspectives, investing them with a sense of mystery that defies the apparent subject matter. The minimal amount of visual information seems to cut the boy off from his family and erase any links he might have to a broader social environment.

The second portfolio presents Images of Inequality, and it too juxtaposes two pairs of contrasting images against a trio of related photographs. It opens with the portrait of an elegant table set for an elegant gourmet dessert in an upscale environment, and it then shifts to the picture of volunteer servers and their guests at a soup kitchen for the homeless in Sacramento, California. Next, it offers the image of a homeless man pulling a cart containing his belongings against a backdrop of San Diego's downtown prosperity. The disparity in this image leads to the following one in which a homeless person amid a sea of other homeless people views a television monitor of George W. Bush during a presidential debate in 2000. This image of a picture-within-a-picture conveys a striking difference between political rhetoric and social reality.

Images of Inequality concludes with a trio of photographs that weigh contemporary representations of civil rights action against their counterparts more than four decades ago. First, a lifelike modern sculpture of Rosa Parks sits in the replica of a Montgomery, Alabama, city bus where Ms. Parks defied segregation policies in the 1950s. Located at the National Civil Rights Museum in Memphis, the sculpture attracts the attention of a middle-aged couple visiting the museum upon its opening in 1998. Next, a famous photograph of Martin Luther King, Jr. at his "I Have a Dream" speech captures the galvanizing energy of the historic March on Washington, DC, in 1963. Finally, a newspaper photograph of a rally to reverse a 2001 ban on affirmative action depicts students supporting affirmative action against those who oppose it. People who were alive during the earlier period would find it hard to believe that the gains of their political conscience could come under such attack less than forty years later.

The third portfolio serves up Images of Ethnic Difference with an accent on conflicting experiences of immigrant groups arriving in the United States over the past century. The initial image, identified as "Arriving at Ellis Island, 1907," affirms the aspirations and the promise that coincided with an immigrant's arrival in America at the time. Balancing it is a fairly cynical snapshot of a recent sign warning motorists of illegal border crossings in the Southwest. Aspirations and promise are radically dashed in the next two photos, which depict the potentially tragic consequences of illegal immigration. The first shows a U.S. Border Patrol Officer searching illegal aliens on the Texas border, and the second illustrates a newspaper account of the deaths and injuries to several Chinese illegal aliens who attempted to reach shore from a grounded vessel off New York harbor in 1993.

The final three photographs represent diverse aspects of coping with life in America after immigration. In the first one, survivors of the Haitian earthquake in January 2010, await medical treatment that would require the amputation of a leg for both the mother and her daughter in the foreground. In another, three Arab-Americans assemble at their office for an antidiscrimination group that they have just formed. In the wake of the September 11 terrorist attacks, many Americans of Muslim descent have experienced prejudice, discrimination, and curtailment of their civil liberties, a condition that this picture directly addresses. In the third, demonstrators march in a rally against draconian immigration reforms slated for legislation in Spring 2006. Proclaiming their valuable contributions to America, hundreds of thousands of illegal aliens and their supporters took to the streets to petition for citizenship for immigrants and to protest measures against citizenship proposed by a Republican Congress.

The images in these portfolios fold into one another even as they refer back to earlier chapters in this anthology. The struggle for immigrants' rights in the last three pictures of Portfolio 3, for example, joins the conversation about civil rights in the last three pictures of Portfolio 2, and both sets of pictures echo the conversations about social class and inequality and the stories of ethnic difference conducted in Chapters 13 and 15 above. The pictures that depict various families in Portfolio 1 display markers of social class and inequality as well as ethnic difference, and they sustain as many possible links to the previously mentioned anthology chapters as they do to Chapter 12 on the changing American family. Pictures may constitute an international language, and they serve an important purpose as they stimulate each of us to formulate our own arguments about the topics they represent, to articulate them in the language of written discourse, and to enter the conversation about issues of our time as it is conducted in academic disciplines across the college curriculum.

PREVIEWING

Survey the pictures offered in each of the three following portfolios. Jot down relationships that might link them to one another, both within a single portfolio and across different portfolios. Do you think that these pictures offer plausible representations of the world as you know it? Or do they instead project biased, limited, or idealized representations? Freewrite your response to this question. Do you know or can you imagine other photos that would better represent these topics? Search an online photographic archive such as corbis.com, accuweather.ap.org, or photosearch.com for different possibilities and download your most important findings for future reference and comparison.

PORTFOLIO I

IMAGES OF FAMILIES

Photo 16–1   Aging, generation gap, summer. Courtesy of George Doyle/
Stockbyte/Getty Images.

Photo 16–2   Parents sitting on a sofa with twin babies. Courtesy of FOTOSEARCH.com.

Photo 16–3 David Heath, "Vengeful Sister, Chicago" (1956). © Dave Heath. Courtesy Howard Greenberg Gallery, NYC and Stephen Bulger Gallery.

Photo 16–4 Stacey and Jessie Harris, of New Jersey, walk with their children, Zion, 4, and Torin, 15 months, through Rawson Square in downtown Nassau past a demonstration held to oppose the gay cruise on which the Harris family traveled Friday, July 16, 2004, to the Bahamas. Photo by Tim Aylen, courtesy of Associated Press/World Wide Photos.

Photo 16–5   Lewis Wickes Hine, "Child Labor," from "Let Children Be Children: Lewis Wickes Hine's Crusade Against Child Labor" (1912). Courtesy of Lewis Wickes Hine/Library of Congress.

Photo 16–6   High up on the top floor of a rickety tenement, 214 Elizabeth Street, New York City. Courtesy of Library of Congress.

Photo 16–7   Antonio Fernandez, "Portrait of a Boy Overlooking Ocean" (1968). Courtesy of the George Eastman House, Rochester, N.Y.

PORTFOLIO 2

IMAGES OF INEQUALITY

Photo 16–8   Fresh fruits baked en papillote with vanilla ice cream. Photo by Philippe Desnerck, courtesy of Fresh Food Images/Photolibrary.

Photo 16–9   People enjoy a free meal at Loaves and Fishes, a non-profit that helps local homeless people in Sacramento, California. Photo by Melissa Barnes, courtesy of Aurora Photos/Alamy.

Photo 16–10   Homeless man dragging a cart in San Diego.
Courtesy of James Steidl/Shutterstock.

Photo 16–11   A homeless registered voter joins a former homeless person and an estimated 200 other homeless persons to watch George W. Bush on one of the television monitors set up for the second presidential debate in New York's Union Square Park, Wednesday, October 11, 2004. Photo by Tina Fineberg, courtesy of Associated Press/World Wide Photos.

Photo 16–12   Visitors at the National Civil Rights Museum in Memphis listen as a recording of the bus driver "threatens" the figure of Rosa Parks seated in the front of the bus. The bus, a real Montgomery, Alabama, city bus of the 1950s is one of the displays at the museum. Courtesy of Martin Thomas Photography/Alamy.

Photo 16–13   The Rev. Martin Luther King Jr. acknowledges the crowd at the Lincoln Memorial for his "I Have a Dream" speech during the March on Washington, DC, on August 28, 1963. Courtesy of UPI Photo Service/Newscom.

Photo 16–14   Students for affirmative action during the Day of Action to Reverse the Ban on Affirmative Action rally held on the University of California-Berkeley campus Thursday, March 8, 2001. Photo by Lonny Shavelson, courtesy of Newscom.

PORTFOLIO 3

IMAGES OF ETHNIC DIVERSITY

Photo 16–15   Arriving at Ellis Island, 1907. Courtesy of Library of Congress.

Photo 16–16   Sign Warning Drivers of Illegal Border Crossings. Courtesy of Chase Swift/Corbis.

Photo 16–17   A U.S. Border Patrol Officer Searching Illegal Aliens in Del Rio, Texas. Photo by John Boykin, courtesy of Stock Connection Distribution/Alamy.

Photo 16–18   A rescuer holds a Chinese illegal immigrant by the pants as he tries to transfer to a small boat from the grounded freighter Golden Vent off New York City, June 6, 1993. The vessel was carrying at least 200 Chinese illegals trying to enter the United States. Six were reported dead and at least sixteen were injured while trying to reach the shore. Photo by Michael Alexander, courtesy of Associated Press/World Wide Photos.

Photo 16–19   Immigrant Mother from Haiti with daughter. Photo by Eduardo Munoz, courtesy of REUTERS/ Landov Media.

Photo 16–20   Three members of the American-Arab Anti-Discrimination Committee pose at their new office in Clifton, N.J., Sunday, January 8, 2006. With bias incidents against Arab-Americans and Muslims running high in New Jersey, this antidiscrimination group is strengthening its presence here, hoping to become a larger part of the fight to defend civil rights and project a positive image of the state's Muslim community. Photo by Mike Derer, courtesy of Associated Press/World Wide Photos.

Photo 16–21   Immigrants and other supporters march down Broadway to call attention to the valuable position of immigrants in American society, Monday, April 10, 2006, in New York City. Hundreds of thousands of people demanding U.S. citizenship for illegal immigrants took to the streets in dozens of cities across the nation in peaceful protests against impending Republican legislation to limit immigrants' rights. Photo by D on Emmert, courtesy of AFP/Getty Images/Newscom.

VIEWING FOR CONTENT

1. What stories or dramas do individual pictures represent? What preceded the action in each picture? What will follow it? How probable is the scenario we might imagine?

2. What stories or drama do groups of pictures represent? What "conversations" do these pictures conduct among themselves?

3. Who or what are the participants in each picture, and how do they relate to one another? Which ones are visible in the picture? Which ones are omitted?

4. Why does some of the action seem familiar and understandable? Why does some of it seem strange or unusual? What elements are mirrored or repeated within the frame?

5. When and where does the action occur? Is the setting likely or unlikely? Is it near or far? Is it contemporary or remote in time?

VIEWING FOR GENRE, ORGANIZATION, AND STYLISTIC FEATURES

1. What kinds of content dominate the picture? What purposes does the picture serve: to document what happened? to teach a lesson? to aid in instruction or installation? to inform, advise, or warn? to advertise? to entertain? to preserve personal or group memories?

2. Which sorts of images dominate the picture? Which details are emphasized? Which ones are intensified? Which ones are exaggerated?

3. Which cultural values heighten the composition? Which historical values determine it? Which positive and negative emotions emanate from the picture?

4. What evidence of manipulation through selection, arrangement, cropping, and editing does the picture display?

5. Which images appear in focus? Which ones appear out of focus?

6. Which images dominate the background? Which ones dominate the foreground? Which appear on top? Which on bottom?

7. Which parallelisms, duplications, or analogues appear in the picture? Which contrasts, oppositions, or inversions appear in it? What hierarchical relationships do they suggest?

8. Is the picture posed or spontaneous?

9. What is the distance of the camera from the object photographed? Is it placed above or below the object? Is it natural or is it instead achieved by using a special lens?

10. What is the source of the lighting? Is it natural or artificial? Is it placed in front, in back, or to the side? How do shadows heighten or diminish the shape of the object?

11. Were the stylistic effects planned before the picture was taken, or did they result from studio manipulation afterward?

12. What emotional effects do such stylistic features summon?

VIEWING FOR RHETORICAL CONTEXT

1. Who photographed, sponsored, or otherwise produced the image? Who are the intended viewers? Does the picture seek to gratify them? to challenge their assumptions? to motivate them to some specific action? What might be controversial about its content?

2. What normalizing effects does the picture project? Do its images invite acceptance and imitation? Do they invite repulsion or attack?

3. What alienating effects does the picture project? Do its images invite consideration and appraisal? Do they invite resistance and criticism?

4. What advertising or promotional effects does the picture evoke? Do its images move us to buy a product or buy into a movement represented by them? Do they convey options or alternatives to the outcomes suggested by them?

WRITING ASSIGNMENTS

1. In an essay of 1,000 words, analyze the form and content of the photographs in one of the visual portfolios. Discuss the relationships to one another of the persons or objects pictured and offer a plausible argument about the rhetorical context of the picture or pictures you've selected.

2. In an essay of 1,000 words, analyze the form and content of photographs that link up with one another across two or more of the visual portfolios. Discuss the relationships and present a plausible argument about their rhetorical contexts.

3. Search an online photographic archive for images that complement or supplement those in one of the portfolios. Download them into your own portfolio and write an essay of 1,000 words explaining how they relate to the selection offered in this anthology.

4. Search an online photographic archive such as CorbisImages <http://www.corbisimages.com/>; Flickr Creative Commons <http://www.flickr.com/creativecommons/>; or Google Images for images that update, revise, or contrast with those in one of the portfolios. Download them into your own portfolio and write an essay of 1,000 words explaining how they represent the theme or topic better than the selection offered in this anthology.

5. Search an online photographic archive for images on any topic of your choice, such as sports events, historical events, cultural fashions, human-interest stories, and the like. Download them into you own portfolio and write an essay of 1,000 words explaining the significance of what they represent and the principles by which they cohere and relate to one another.

Appendix

Documenting Sources

■▰ MLA DOCUMENTATION STYLE

With the exception of the sample research paper in Chapter 7, all the sample student essays in this book are written according to the MLA (Modern Language Association) rules for page format (margins, page numbering, titles, and so forth) and source documentation. In addition to providing many sample pages that illustrate MLA style, we describe how to type papers in MLA format (pp. 114–17); follow MLA guidelines for using parenthetical documentation to cite sources that you summarize (p. 53), paraphrase (p. 47), or quote (pp. 62–64); and construct a Works Cited list (p. 100).

The first section of this appendix is an MLA "Quick Guide" that includes examples of how to document the types of sources that students use most often in academic papers. The next section explains the principles and rules for MLA documentation. The third section is a list of MLA documentation examples that covers a wider range of situations than does the Quick Guide. For an exhaustive discussion of MLA documentation style, see the *MLA Handbook for Writers of Research Papers*, seventh edition.

■▰ MLA QUICK GUIDE

Parenthetical References in the Text

Texts by a single author

> Satel corrects critics' misconception that legalized markets "will inevitably replicate the sins of unauthorized markets" (11).
>
> Critics of legalized sales of organs claim that a legal market "will inevitably replicate the sins of unauthorized markets" (Satel 11).

Texts by multiple authors

> This theory (Sarver and Stearns 9) is supported by major work in the field (Lessig, Knight, and Washburn 16).

Texts without an author

> The principles were developed by the officers of the Renaissance Society (*Report* 5).

Works Cited List

Arrange entries in alphabetical order according to the author's last name or by the title if the author's name is not available. If you are citing two or more works by the same author, write the name for the initial entry. For subsequent entries, type three hyphens followed by a period in place of the name.

The following examples illustrate how to document in MLA style. We begin with the most commonly cited source types. If the Quick Guide does not provide a model appropriate for the source you are citing, look through the more extensive list of examples on pages 602–08.

■ Print Sources

Book

Hower, Edward. *Shadows and Elephants*. Wellfleet: Leapfrog, 2002. Print.

Article, essay, poem, or short story in a scholarly journal

Mirskin, Jerald. "Writing as a Process of Valuing." *College Composition and Communication* 46 (1995): 387–410. Print.

Article, essay, poem, or short story in a magazine

Dickinson, Amy. "Video Playgrounds: New Studies Link Violent Video Games to Violent Behavior. So Check Out These Cool Alternatives." *Time* 8 May 2000: 100. Print.

Article in a newspaper

Becker, Elizabeth. "A New Villain in Free Trade: The Farmer on the Dole." *New York Times* 25 Aug. 2002, sec. 4: 10. Print.

Article, essay, poem, or short story that appears in print for the first time in an anthology

McPherson, Diane. "Adrienne Rich." *Contemporary Lesbian Writers of the United States: A Bio-Bibliographical Critical Sourcebook*. Ed. Sandra Pollack and Denise D. Knight. Westport: Greenwood, 1993. 433–45. Print.

Article, essay, poem, or short story that is reprinted in a textbook anthology

Vogel, Steven. "Grades and Money." *Dissent* 4.4 (1997): 102–04. Rpt. in *Reading and Writing in the Academic Community*. 2nd ed. Ed. Mary Lynch Kennedy and Hadley M. Smith. Upper Saddle River: Prentice Hall, 2001. 337–40. Print.

Section, chapter, article, essay, poem, short story, or play in a book with one author

Brown, Cory. "Drought." *A Warm Trend*. Wesley Chapel: Swallow's Tale Press, 1989. 29. Print.

■ Online Sources

A word about URLs: Include the URL for online material only if you think your readers will be unable to locate the material without it or if your professor requires it.

"Citation Management." *Cornell University Library.* Cornell University, 2009. Web. 5 Oct. 2010. <http://www.library.cornell.edu.proxy.library.cornell.edu/resrch/citmanage>.

Book

Pease, Verne Seth. *In the Wake of War, a Tale of the South under Carpet-Bagger Administration.* 1900. *Google Book Search.* Web. 5 Oct. 2010.

Article, essay, poem, or short story in a scholarly journal

Brown, Carol A. "Two Views of Motherhood." *Qualitative Sociology* 23.3 (2000): 355–58. *Academic Search Premier.* Web. 29 Sept. 2010.

Article, essay, poem, or short story in a magazine

Lethem, Jonathan. "The Ecstasy of Influence, A Plagiarism." *Harper's.* Harper's Magazine, Feb. 2007. Web. 8 Oct. 2010.

Article in a newspaper

Gay, Malcolm. "More States Allowing Guns in Bars." *New York Times.* New York Times, 3 Oct. 2010. Web. 5 Oct. 2010.

▪ PRINCIPLES AND RULES FOR MLA DOCUMENTATION

▪ Printed Books

When documenting books, arrange the documentary information in the following order, including as many of the following items as are available:

1. Name of author(s)
2. Title of the part of the book (if you are referring to a section or chapter) in quotation marks
3. Title of the book (italicized)
4. Name of the editor or translator, if other than author(s)
5. Edition
6. Number of volumes
7. Name of the series if the book is part of a series
8. City of publication
9. Abbreviated name of the publisher
10. Date of publication
11. Page numbers (if you are referring to a section or chapter)
12. Medium of publication (Print)

Kennedy, Mary Lynch, William J. Kennedy, and Hadley M. Smith, eds. *Writing in the Disciplines.* 4th ed. Upper Saddle River: Prentice Hall, 2000. Print.

■ Online Books

Record the information in items 1–11 above and then add the following information:

1. Title of the database or Web site (italicized)
2. Medium of publication (Web)
3. Date of access (day, month, year)

Pease, Verne Seth. *In the Wake of War, a Tale of the South under Carpet-Bagger Administration.* 1900. *Google Book Search.* Web. 5 Oct. 2010.

■ Books Without Complete Publication Information or Pagination

Supply as much information as you can, enclosing the information you supply in square brackets to show your reader that the source did not contain this information—for example, Metropolis: U of Bigcity P, [1971]. Enclosing the date in brackets shows your reader that you found the date elsewhere: another source that quotes your source, the card catalog, your professor's lecture, and so on. If you are not certain of the date, add a question mark—for example, [1971?]. When you cannot find the necessary information, use one of the following abbreviation models to show this to your reader: n.d. (no date); n. pag. (no pagination); n.p. (no place of publication); n.p. (no publisher). For example, the following Works Cited entry would be used if you knew only the title of the book that served as your source:

Photographic View Album of Cambridge. [England]: N.p., n.d. N. pag.

■ Book Cross-References

If you cite two or more articles from the same anthology, list the anthology with complete publication information, and then cross-reference the individual articles. In the cross-reference, the anthology editor's last name and the page numbers follow the article author's name and the title of the article. In the example below, the first and third entries are for articles appearing in the second entry, the anthology edited by Kennedy, Kennedy, and Smith.

Frude, Neil. "The Intimate Machine." Kennedy, Kennedy, and Smith 268–73.
Kennedy, Mary Lynch, William J. Kennedy, and Hadley M. Smith, eds. *Writing in the Disciplines.* 4th ed. Upper Saddle River: Prentice Hall, 2000. Print.
Rifkin, Jeremy. "The Age of Simulation." Kennedy, Kennedy, and Smith 284–93.

■ Print Periodicals

When documenting articles in a journal, magazine, or newspaper, arrange the documentary information in the following order, including as many of the following items as are available:

1. Name of author(s)
2. Title of the article (in quotation marks)
3. Name of the periodical (italicized)

4. Series number or name
5. Volume number (followed by a period and the issue number, if available)
6. Date of publication
7. Inclusive page numbers
8. Medium of publication (Print)

McKee, Heidi, and James E. Porter. "The Ethics of Digital Writing Research: A Rhetorical Approach." *College Composition and Communication* 59.4 (2008): 711–49. Print.

▨ Online Periodical

For articles in online journals, magazines, and newspapers, record as much of the information in items 1–7 that is available. Then add the following information:

1. Title of the database (italicized)
2. Medium of publication (Web)
3. Date of access (day, month, year)

Gosling, Sam. "Mixed Signals." *Psychology Today* 42.5 (2009): 62–71. *Academic Search Premier.* Web. 10 Oct. 2010.

▨ Content Endnotes

In addition to a Works Cited list, MLA style allows a list of comments, explanations, or facts that relate to the ideas discussed in the essay but do not fit into the actual text. You may occasionally need these content endnotes to provide information that is useful but must, for some reason, be separated from the rest of the essay. The most common uses of endnotes are listed below.

1. Providing references that go beyond the scope of the essay but that could help the reader understand the issues in more depth
2. Discussing a source of information in more detail than is possible in a Works Cited list
3. Acknowledging help in preparing the essay
4. Giving an opinion that does not fit into the text smoothly
5. Explaining ideas more fully than is possible in the text
6. Mentioning concerns not directly related to the content of the essay
7. Providing additional, necessary details that would clutter the text
8. Mentioning information that goes against the general point of view presented in the essay
9. Evaluating ideas explained in the essay

In MLA style, endnotes are listed on separate pages just before the Works Cited list. The endnote list is titled "Notes." Notes are numbered sequentially (1, 2, 3,...), and a corresponding number is included in the text of the essay, typed halfway between the lines (in superscript), to show the material to which the endnote refers. Notice in the example below that the reference numeral (that is, the endnote number) is placed in the text of the essay immediately after the material to which it refers. Usually, the reference numeral will appear at the end of a sentence. No space is left between the reference numeral and the word or punctuation mark that it follows. However, in the notes list, one space separates the numeral and the first letter of the note. Notes are numbered according to the order in which they occur in the essay.

Any source that you mention in an endnote must be fully documented in the Works Cited list. Do not include this complete documentation in the endnote itself. Never use endnotes as a substitute for the Works Cited list, and do not overuse endnotes. If possible, include all information in the text of your essay. For most essays you write, no endnotes will be necessary.

The following excerpts from the text of an essay and its list of endnotes illustrate MLA endnote format. For example, in your text you would type

> For hundreds of years, scientists thought that the sun's energy came from the combustion of a solid fuel such as coal.[1] However, work in the early twentieth century convinced researchers that the sun sustains a continuous nuclear fusion reaction.[2] The sun's nuclear furnace maintains a temperature....

The notes on the notes page would be formatted with the first line of each note indented five spaces.

> [1] Detailed accounts of pre-twentieth-century views of solar energy can be found in Banks and Rosen (141–55) and Burger (15–21).
> [2] In very recent years, some scientists have questioned whether or not the sun sustains a fusion reaction at all times. Experiments described by Salen (68–93) have failed to detect the neutrinos that should be the by-products of the sun's fusion. This raises the possibility that the sun's fusion reaction turns off and on periodically.

■ MLA DOCUMENTATION MODELS

■ Books

Book with one author

Kennedy, William J. *Rhetorical Norms in Renaissance Literature.* New Haven: Yale UP, 1978. Print.

Two or more books by the same author (alphabetize by title)

Kennedy, William J. *Jacopo Sannazaro and the Uses of the Pastoral.* Hanover: UP of New England, 1983. Print.

———. *Rhetorical Norms in Renaissance Literature.* New Haven: Yale UP, 1978. Print.

Book with two authors

Kramnick, Isaac, and R. Laurence Moore. *The Godless Constitution: The Case against Religious Correctness.* New York: Norton, 1996. Print.

Book with three authors

Bulkin, Elly, Minnie Bruce Pratt, and Barbara Smith. *Yours in Struggle: Three Feminist Perspectives on Anti-Semitism and Racism.* Ithaca: Firebrand, 1988. Print.

Book with more than three authors

Glock, Marvin D., et al. *Probe: College Developmental Reading.* 2nd ed. Columbus: Merrill, 1980. Print.

Book with a corporate author

Boston Women's Health Collective Staff. *Our Bodies, Ourselves.* Magnolia: Peter Smith, 1998. Print.

Book with an anonymous author

Writers' and Artists' Yearbook, 1980. London: Adam and Charles Black, 1980. Print.

Book with an editor instead of an author

Kennedy, Mary Lynch, ed. *Theorizing Composition: A Critical Sourcebook of Theory and Scholarship in Contemporary Composition Studies.* Santa Barbara: Greenwood, 1998. Print.

Book with two or three editors

Anderson, Charles M., and Marian M. MacCurdy, eds. *Writing and Healing: Toward an Informed Practice.* Urbana: NCTE, 1999. Print.

Book with more than three editors

Kermode, Frank, et al., eds. *The Oxford Anthology of English Literature.* 2 vols. New York: Oxford, 1973. Print.

Book with a translator

Allende, Isabel. *The Stories of Eva Luna.* Trans. Margaret Sayers Peden. New York: Macmillan, 1991. Print.

Book in edition after the first

Kennedy, Mary Lynch, William J. Kennedy, and Hadley M. Smith. *Writing in the Disciplines.* 5th ed. Upper Saddle River: Prentice Hall, 2004. Print.

Book that has been republished

Conroy, Frank. *Stop-time.* 1967. New York: Penguin, 1977. Print.

▦ Parts of Books

Section, chapter, article, essay, poem, short story, or play in a book with one author

Chomsky, Noam. "Psychology and Ideology." *For Reasons of State*. New York: Vintage, 1973. 318–69. Print.

Walker, Alice. "Everyday Use." *In Love and Trouble: Stories of Black Women*. San Diego: Harcourt, 1973. 47–59. Print.

Introduction, preface, or foreword written by someone other than the book's author

Piccone, Paul. General Introduction. *The Essential Frankfurt Reader*. Ed. Andrew Arato and Eike Gebhardt. New York: Urizen, 1978. xi–xxiii. Print.

Article or essay reprinted in an anthology

Au, Kathryn H. "Literacy for All Students: Ten Steps Toward Making a Difference." *The Reading Teacher* 51.3 (1997): 186–94. Rpt. in, *Perspectives: Literacy*. Ed. C. Denise Johnson. Madison: Coursewise, 1999. 3–9. Print.

1st + last pages

Article, essay, poem, or short story that appears in print for the first time in an anthology

Horn, Wade F. "Promoting Marriage as a Means for Promoting Fatherhood." *Revitalizing the Institution of Marriage for the Twenty-First Century: An Agenda for Strengthening Marriage*. Ed. Alan J. Hawkins, Lynn D. Wardle, and David Orgon Coolidge. Westport: Praeger, 2002. 101–09. Print.

Novel or play in an anthology

Gay, John. *The Beggar's Opera. Twelve Famous Plays of the Restoration and Eighteenth Century*. Ed. Cecil A. Moore. New York: Random, 1960. 573–650. Print.

Signed article in a reference work

Tilling, Robert I. "Vocanology." *McGraw Hill Encyclopedia of Science and Technology*. 8th ed. 1997. Print.

Unsigned article in a reference work

"Tenancy by the Entirety." *West's Encyclopedia of American Law*. 1998. Print.

▦ Periodicals

Article in a scholarly/professional journal; each issue numbers its pages separately

McCarty, Roxanne. "Reading Therapy Project." *Research and Teaching in Developmental Education* 18.2 (2002): 51–56. Print.

Article in a scholarly/professional journal; entire volume has continuous page numbering

Trainor, Jennifer Seibel, and Amanda Godley. "After Wyoming: Labor Practices in Two University Writing Programs." *College Composition and Communication* 50 (1998): 153–81. Print.

Signed article in a weekly or monthly magazine

Jenkins, Henry. "Cyberspace and Race." *Technology Review* Apr. 2002: 89. Print.

Unsigned article in a weekly or monthly magazine

"Dip into the Future, Far as Cyborg Eye Can See: And Wince." *The Economist* 3 Jan. 1998: 81–83. Print.

Poem or short story in a magazine

Flanagan, David. "Pilgrimage." *Creations Magazine* June/July 2001: 8. Print.

Signed article in a newspaper (in an edition with lettered sections)

Miller, Marjorie. "Britain Urged to Legalize Cloning of Human Tissue." *Los Angeles Times* 9 Dec. 1998: A1. Print.

Unsigned article in a newspaper (in a daily without labeled sections)

"Justice Proposes Immigration Laws." *Ithaca Journal* 28 Aug. 2002: 2. Print.

Editorial or special feature (in identified edition with numbered sections)

"The Limits of Technology." Editorial. *New York Times* 3 Jan. 1999, early ed., sec. 4: 8. Print.

Published letter to the editor of a newspaper

Plotnick, Mermine. Letter. *New York Times* 25 Aug. 2002, sec. 4: 8. Print.

Review

Hoberman, J. "The Informer: Elia Kazan Spills His Guts." Rev. of *Elia Kazan: A Life*, by Elia Kazan. *Village Voice* 17 May 1988: 58–60. Print.

Article whose title contains a quotation

Nitzsche, Jane Chance. "'As swete as is the roote of lycorys, or any cetewale': Herbal Imagery in Chaucer's Miller's Tale." *Chaucerian Newsletter* 2.1 (1980): 6–8. Print.

■ Other Written Sources

Government publication

United States Dept. of Energy. *Winter Survival: A Consumer's Guide to Winter Preparedness.* Washington: GPO, 1980. Print.

Congressional Record

Cong. Rec. 13 Apr. 1967: S5054–57. Print.

Pamphlet

Bias-Related Incidents. Ithaca: Ithaca College Bias-Related Incidents Committee, 2001. Print.

Dissertation

Boredin, Henry Morton. "The Ripple Effect in Classroom Management." Diss. U of Michigan, 1970. Print.

Personal letter

Siegele, Nancy. Letter to the author. 13 Jan. 2002. Print.

Public document

United States Dep. of Agriculture. "Shipments and Unloads of Certain Fruits and Vegetables. 1918–1923." Statistical Bulletin 7 Apr. 1925: 10–13. Print.

CD-ROM

Stucky, Nathan. "Performing Oral History: Storytelling and Pedagogy." Communication Education 44.1 (1995): 1–14. CD-ROM. CommSearch. 2nd ed. Electronic Book Technologies. 1995.

■ Online Sources

Book originally available in print that was located online

Bronte, Charlotte. Jane Eyre. London, 1895. Google Books. Web. 12 Oct. 2010.

Poem originally available in print that was located online

Dickinson, Emily. "Because I Could Not Stop for Death—." The Poems of Emily Dickinson. Ed. R. W. Franklin, 1999. Poetry Foundation. Web. 13 Oct. 2010.

Magazine article originally available in print that was located online

Gregory, Sean. "The Price of Free Speech." Time 176.14 (2010): 30–34. Academic Search Premier. Web. 11 Oct. 2010.

Journal article originally available in print that was located through a library-based subscription service

Dyson, Anne Haas. "Literacy in a Child's World of Voices, or, the Fine Print of Murder and Mayhem." Research in the Teaching of English 41.2 (2006): 147–51. JSTOR. Web. 8 Oct. 2010.

Online book

Bazerman, Charles, and David R. Russell, eds. Writing Selves/Writing Societies: Research from Activity Perspectives. Fort Collins: The WAC Clearinghouse and Mind, Culture, and Activity. 1 Feb. 2003. Web. 9 Feb. 2007.

Online article

Purdy, James P., and Joyce R. Walker. "Digital Breadcrumbs: Case Studies of Online Research." *Kairo, A Journal of Rhetoric, Technology, and Pedagogy* 11.2 (2007). Web. 9 Feb. 2007.

Online photo

Mother Holding Her Daughter and Using Her Computer. 2010. *Fotosearch.* Web. 30 Sept. 2010.

Discussion list, listserv, or blog

Nelms, Gerald. "Re: Commas and Quotation Marks." *WPA-L Digest.* 2010–329. Council of Writing Program Administrators. Web. 4 Oct. 2010.

Web sites

Harbin, Andrea. *NetSerf, The Internet Connection for Medieval Resources.* Web. 15 Oct. 2010. *Nobelprize.org.* The Nobel Foundation. 18 June 2010.

A page on a Web site

Kennedy, Mary Lynch. "Academic Integrity." *Writing Resource Center.* SUNY, Cortland, n.d. Web. 20 Sept. 2010. <http://www2.cortland.edu/departments/english/wrc/students/integrity.dot>.

E-mail

Stone, Stephen. "Re: Research on the Mommy Wars." Message to the author. 9 Feb. 2007. E-mail.

Blog

Brooklynbadboy. "No Country for Zuckerbergs." *Daily Kos* 3 Oct. 2010. Web. 4 Oct. 2010.

▧ Additional Sources

Films, Videos, DVDs

Rebel without a Cause. Dir. Nicholas Ray. Perf. James Dean, Sal Mineo, and Natalie Wood. Warner Brothers, 1955. Film.

Flying Deuces. Dir. A. Edgar Sutherland. Perf. Stan Laurel and Oliver Hardy. 1939. Delta, 1998. Videocassette.

Some Like It Hot. Dir. Billy Wilder. Perf. Marilyn Monroe, Tony Curtis, Jack Lemmon, George Raft, and Pat O'Brien. 1959. MGM, 2001. DVD.

"How to Format Your Paper in MLA Style." Online posting. *YouTube.* 27 Oct. 2008. Web. 4 Oct. 2010.

Television or Radio Broadcast

Comet Halley. Prod. John L. Wilhelm. PBS. WNET, New York, 26 Nov. 1986. Radio.

Sound Recording: Audiocassette, Audiotape, CD, or LP

Cohen, Leonard. *Ten New Songs.* Sony, 2001. CD.

Tchaikovsky, Piotr Ilich. *Violin Concerto in D,* op. 35. Perf. Itzhak Perlman. RCA, 1975. Audiocassette.

Taylor, James. "You've Got a Friend." *Mud Slide Slim and the Blue Horizon.* Warner, 1971. LP.

Performance of music, dance, or drama

Corea, Chick, dir. *Chick Corea Electrik Band.* Cornell U., Ithaca. 15 Oct. 1985. Performance.

Work of visual art: Painting, sculpture, photograph, etc.

da Vinci, Leonardo. *The Virgin, the Child and Saint Anne.* 1499–1500? Drawing. Louvre, Paris.

Ray, Man. *Joseph Stella and Marcel Duchamp.* 1920. Photographic print. J. Paul Getty Museum, Los Angeles.

Interviews: Published, broadcast, personal, and telephone

Hall, Donald. Personal interview. 19 Apr. 2001.

Grahn, Judy. Telephone interview. 23 Mar. 2000.

Lecture, speech, address, reading

Gebhard, Ann O. "New Developments in Young Adult Literature." New York State English Council, Buffalo. 15 Nov. 1984. Lecture.

Cartoon

Noth, Paul. Cartoon. *New Yorker* 20 Sept. 2010: 85. Print.

Advertisement

Cadillac. Advertisement. *New Yorker* 20 Sept. 2010: 55. Print.

Map or chart

Ireland. Map. Chicago: Rand, 1984. Print.

Adolescents and AIDS. Chart. New York: Earth Science Graphics, 1988. Print.

For more detailed information, see the *MLA Handbook for Writers of Research Papers.* 7th ed. New York: Modern Language Association of America, 2009. Print.

■ APA DOCUMENTATION STYLE

While MLA documentation style is an important standard in the humanities, APA (American Psychological Association) style is used widely in the social sciences. APA style differs from MLA style in many details, but they share the basic principles of including source names and page numbers (APA also adds the publication date) in parentheses within the text of the paper and of including complete publication information for each source in an alphabetized list. Below are a Quick Guide to APA style and a point-by-point comparison of APA and MLA styles. For a complete explanation of APA style, consult the *Publication Manual of the American Psychological Association*, sixth edition. Pages 274–81 of this book contain a sample student paper written in APA style.

■ APA QUICK GUIDE

The following examples illustrate how to use APA style to document the types of sources that most often appear in college students' essays. The examples are arranged beginning with the most commonly cited source types. It may be helpful to contrast them with the entries in the MLA Quick Guide on pages 597–99, since the same examples are used in both Quick Guides.

Parenthetical References in the Text

Texts by a single author

> As Herman (1992) points out, trauma research was halted for decades.
> As a result, trauma research was halted for decades (Herman, 1992).

Texts by multiple authors

> Smyth and Helm (2003) point out that therapists have been using writing, especially journal writing, as a means of disclosure during the therapeutic process for decades.
>
> Therapists have been using writing, especially journal writing, as a means of disclosure during the therapeutic process for decades (Smyth & Helm, 2003).

Texts without an author

Cite the first two or three words of the title.

> The district used a "system-wide education reform strategy built on a foundation of providing high-quality pre-kindergarten" ("pre[K]now," 2010).

Specific parts of texts

Include the page number.

> As Pennebaker (2000) puts it, "The act of converting emotions and images into words changes the way the person organizes and thinks about the trauma" (p. 8).

References List

List references in alphabetical order according to the author's last name or according to the title if no author is given.

Write the last name, a comma, and initials of the first and middle names. Separate two or more authors with an ampersand (&).

Capitalize only the first word of book and article titles. Put books and journal titles in italics. Put article titles, chapter titles, and titles of other short works in quotation marks.

■ Examples

Book

Herman, J. L. (1992). *Trauma and recovery.* New York, NY: HarperCollins.

Edited book

Anderson, C., & MacCurdy, M. (Eds.). (1999). *Writing and healing: Toward an informed practice.* Urbana, IL: National Council of Teachers of English.

Scholarly journal article obtained from an online database

List author(s), date of publication, article title, journal title (italicized), volume number, issue number (if needed), and page numbers. Give the DOI, digital object identifier, if it is available.

LeDoux, J. E., Romanski, L., & Xagoraris, A. (1989). Indelibility of subcortical emotional memories. *Journal of Cognitive Neuroscience, 1*(3), 238–243. doi:10.1162/jocn.1989.1.3.238

Article obtained from an online journal

Baulch, J., Chester, A., & Brennan, L. (2010). Adolescent and parent content preferences and predictors of intention to use an online healthy weight website for adolescents. *E-Journal of Applied Psychology, 6*(1), 19–27. Retrieved from http://ojs.lib.swin.edu.au/index.php/ejap/issue/current

Article, essay, poem, or short story that is reprinted in a textbook anthology

Vogel, S. (2001). Grades and money. In M. L. Kennedy & H. M. Smith (Eds.), *Reading and writing in the academic community* (pp. 337–340). Upper Saddle River, NJ: Prentice Hall.

Document or report accessed online

Lundberg, S., & Pollack, R. (2007). *The American family and family economics* (NBER Working Paper 12908). Cambridge, MA: National Bureau of Economic Research. Retrieved from http://www.nber.org/papers/w12908

PEW Charitable Trusts. (2008). *Survey: Americans want to know about physicians' payments.* Retrieved from http://www.pewtrusts.org/our_work_report_detail.aspx?id=40752&category=206

Article, essay, poem, or short story in a magazine

Dickinson, A. (2000, May 8). Video playgrounds: New studies link violent video games to violent behavior. So check out these cool alternatives. *Time, 155,* 100.

Signed article in a newspaper

Becker, E. (2002, August 25). A new villain in free trade: The farmer on the dole. *The New York Times,* p. 4.

For more detailed information, see the *Publication Manual of the American Psychological Association* (6th ed.). (2010). Washington, DC: American Psychological Association.

◼ COMPARISON OF MLA AND APA DOCUMENTATION STYLES

◼ Parenthetical Documentation

MLA

Give the last name of the author and the page number if you are quoting a specific part of the source.

> The question has been answered before (O'Connor 140–43).
> O'Connor has already answered the question (140–43).

APA

Give the last name of the author, the publication date, and the page number if you are quoting a specific part of the source.

> The question has been answered before (O'Connor, 2002, pp. 140–143).
> O'Connor (2002) has already answered the question (pp. 140–143).

MLA

Omit the abbreviation for "page." Drop redundant hundreds digit in the final page number.

> Walsh discusses this "game theory" (212–47).

APA

Use the abbreviation "p." for "page" or "pp." for "pages" for the page citation. Retain redundant hundreds digit in the final page number.

> Walsh (1979) discusses this "game theory" (pp. 212–247).

MLA

Omit commas in parenthetical references.

> The question has been answered before (O'Connor 140–43).

APA

Use commas within parentheses.

> The question has been answered before (O'Connor, 2002, pp. 140–143).

MLA

Use a shortened form of the title, and a page number if relevant, to distinguish between different works by the same author.

> Jones originally supported the single-factor explanation (*Investigations* 93) but later realized that the phenomenon was more complex (*Theory* 209).

APA

Use publication dates to distinguish between different works by the same author.

> Jones originally supported the single-factor explanation (1996) but later realized that the phenomenon was more complex (2001).

▪ List of Sources

MLA

The title of the page listing the sources is "Works Cited."

APA

The title of the page listing the sources is "References."

MLA

Use the author's full name.

> O'Connor, Mary Beth.

APA

Use the author's last name, but only the initials of the author's first and middle names.

> O'Connor, M. B.

MLA

When there are two or more authors, invert the first author's name, insert a comma and the word "and," and give the second author's first name and surname in the common order.

> Kennedy, Mary Lynch, and Hadley M. Smith.

APA

When there are two or more authors, invert all the names. After the first author's name, insert a comma and an ampersand (&).

> Kennedy, M. L., & Smith, H. M.

MLA

Capitalize major words in the titles of books and periodicals, and italicize all words in those titles.

> *Silicon Snake Oil: Second Thoughts about the Information Highway*
> *Reading Research Quarterly*

APA

Capitalize only the first word and all proper nouns of the titles (and subtitles) of books, and italicize all words in those titles. Capitalize all major words in the titles of periodicals.

> *Silicon snake oil: Second thoughts about the information highway*
> *Reading Research Quarterly*

MLA

List book data in the following sequence: author, title of book, city of publication, shortened form of the publisher's name, date of publication.

Ozeki, Ruth L. *My Year of Meats.* New York: Penguin, 1998.

APA

List book data in the following sequence: author, date of publication, title of the book, place of publication, publisher.

Ozeki, R. L. (1998). *My year of meats.* New York: Penguin.

MLA

List journal article data in the following sequence: author, title of the article, title of the journal, volume number, date of publication, inclusive pages.

Yagelski, Robert P. "The Ambivalence of Reflection." *College Composition and Communication* 51 (1999): 32–50.

APA

List journal article data in the following sequence: author, date of publication, title of the article, title of the journal, volume number, inclusive pages.

Yagelski, R. P. (1999). The ambivalence of reflection. *College Composition and Communication, 51*, 32–50.

MLA

List the data for an article in an edited book in the following sequence: author of the article, title of the article, title of the book, editor of the book, place of publication, publisher, date of publication, inclusive pages.

Donaldson, E. Talbot. "Briseis, Briseida, Criseyde, Cresseid, Cressid: Progress of a Heroine." *Chaucerian Problems and Perspectives: Essays Presented to Paul E. Beichner, C.S.C.* Ed. Edward Vasta and Zacharias P. Thundy. Notre Dame: Notre Dame UP, 1979. 3–12.

APA

List the data for an article in an edited book in the following sequence: author of the article, date, title of the article, name of the editor, title of the book, inclusive pages, place of publication, and publisher.

Donaldson, E. T. (1979). Briseis, Briseida, Criseyde, Cresseid, Cressid: Progress of a heroine. In E. Vasta & Z. P. Thundy (Eds.), *Chaucerian problems and perspectives: Essays presented to Paul E. Beichner, C.S.C.* (pp. 3–12). Notre Dame, IN: Notre Dame University Press.

Note: The proper names in the article title are capitalized, as is the word following the colon.

■ Content Endnotes

MLA

Title of the list of endnotes: "Notes."

APA

Title of the list of endnotes: "Content Notes."

MLA

Place the endnote list immediately before the Works Cited page.

APA

Place the endnote list immediately after the References page.

MLA

Leave a space between the reference numeral and the endnote.

[1] For more information, see Jones and Brown.

APA

Do not leave any space between the reference numeral and the endnote.

[1]For more information, see Jones (1983) and Brown (1981).

Index